ILLINOIS REAL ESTATE

Principles and Practices

SECOND EDITION

RALPH A. PALMER
JOAN JOSEPH
TIM RICE

GSP

GORSUCH SCARISBRICK, PUBLISHERS
A imprint of PRENTICE HALL
Upper Saddle River, New Jersey 07458

The publisher makes every reasonable best effort to ensure the accuracy and completeness of the information and answers contained in this book. Due to the ever-changing nature of applicable laws and practices, the reader is cautioned and advised to always consult with the instructor when questions arise. Test answers have been checked for correct correlation with the question answered. If the reader encounters a questionable answer, the reader should always consult the text or the instructor for a more complete answer and analysis of the answer. Should the reader believe that an alternative interpretation of the information contained in this book is possible, he or she is encouraged to consult with the instructor.

Library of Congress Cataloging-in-Publication Data

Palmer, Ralph A.
    Illinois real estate : principles & practices / by Ralph A. Palmer,
Joan Joseph, Tim Rice. — 2nd ed.
    p. cm.
    Includes index.
    ISBN 0-13-777210-6 (alk. paper)
    1. Real estate business—Illinois. 2. Real property—Illinois.
I. Joseph, Joan. II. Rice, Tim. III. Title.
HD266.I3P35   1996
333.33'0973—dc20   96–32893
                                                                                                    CIP

Publisher:	Gay L. Pauley
Editor:	Shari Jo Hehr
Developmental Editor:	Katie E. Bradford
Production Editor:	Ann Waggoner Aken
Typesetting:	Ash Street Typecrafters, Inc.

Copyright © 1997 by Gorsuch Scarisbrick, Publishers
Published by Prentice-Hall, Inc.
Simon & Schuster / A Viacom Company
Upper Saddle River, New Jersey 07458

All rights reserved. No part of this book may be reproduced, in any form or by any means, without written permission from the publisher.

Printed in the United States of America

10 9 8 7 6 5 4 3

ISBN: 0-13-777210-6

Prentice-Hall International (UK) Limited, *London*
Prentice-Hall of Australia Pty. Limited, *Sydney*
Prentice-Hall Canada Inc., *Toronto*
Prentice-Hall Hispanoamericana, S.A., *Mexico*
Prentice-Hall of India Private Limited, *New Delhi*
Prentice-Hall of Japan, Inc., *Tokyo*
Simon & Schuster Asia Pte. Ltd., *Singapore*
Editora Prentice-Hall do Brasil, Ltda., *Rio de Janeiro*

Contents

Preface   *xvi*

CHAPTER 1   BASIC REAL ESTATE CONCEPTS   2

GENERAL CHARACTERISTICS OF REAL ESTATE   3
    Terminology and Classes of Property   3
    Physical Characteristics   4
        Permanence (Indestructibility) • Immobility • Nonhomogeneity (Uniqueness)
    Economic Characteristics   4
        Scarcity/Limited Availability • Permanence of Investment • Location (Situs) • Modification by Improvement

GENERAL CONCEPTS OF LAND USE AND INVESTMENT   6
    Physical Factors Affecting Land Use   6
    Economic Factors Affecting Land Use   6
    Highest and Best Use   6
    Land Use Restrictions   7
    Investment Objectives   7

THE REAL ESTATE BUSINESS   8
    National Association of REALTORS®   8
    National Association of Real Estate Brokers   9
    Association of Real Estate License Law Officials   9
    Real Estate Licensees   10
    The Fundamentals of a Real Estate Transaction   10
        Listing • Marketing the Property • Offer and Acceptance • Financing • Title Examination • Settlement

THE REAL ESTATE MARKET   11
IMPORTANT POINTS   12
REVIEW QUESTIONS   12

CHAPTER 2   PROPERTY OWNERSHIP AND INTERESTS   16

THE CONCEPT OF PROPERTY   17
    Bundle of Rights   17
    Real Property   18
        Air and Subsurface Rights • Water Rights • Accession Rights
    Personal Property   20
    Land, Minerals, Fruits of the Soil   20
    Fixtures   21
    Trade Fixtures   21
    Uniform Commercial Code (UCC)   22
    Land, Tenements, and Hereditaments   22

ESTATES IN REAL PROPERTY 23
   Definition of Estate 23
   Groups of Estates in Land 23
FREEHOLD ESTATES 23
   Fee Simple Estates 23
      Fee Simple Absolute • Fee Simple Defeasible
   Life Estates 25
      Rights and Responsibilities of Life Tenants • Legal or Statutory Life Estates • Homestead
NONFREEHOLD ESTATES (LEASEHOLD ESTATES) 28
OWNERSHIP OF REAL PROPERTY 28
   Ownership in Severalty 29
   Concurrent Ownership 29
      Tenancy in Common • Joint Tenancy • Tenancy by the Entirety • Community Property
COMBINATION FORMS OF OWNERSHIP 33
   Condominiums 33
   Cooperatives 34
   Timesharing 36
REAL PROPERTY OWNERSHIP BY BUSINESS ORGANIZATIONS 36
   Sole Proprietorship 37
   Partnership 37
   Corporation 38
   Limited Liability Company 39
   Syndication 39
   Joint Venture 40
   Trust 40
      Land Trust • Real Estate Investment Trust (REIT)
IMPORTANT POINTS 41
REVIEW QUESTIONS 43

CHAPTER 3

Encumbrances and Government Restrictions 46

EASEMENTS 47
   Easements in Gross 47
   Easements Appurtenant 48
      Negative and Affirmative Easements Appurtenant • Creation of Easements Appurtenant • Termination of Easements Appurtenant
LICENSE 51
LIENS 51
   Priority of Liens 51
   Specific Liens 51
      Mortgage Liens • Mechanics' and Materialmen's Liens • Bail Bond Liens • Vendors' and Vendees' Liens • Real Property Tax Liens • Special Assessments
   General Liens 57
      Judgment Liens • Lis Pendens • Writs of Attachment • Income Tax Liens • Estate and Inheritance Tax Liens
RESTRICTIVE COVENANTS 58

ENCROACHMENTS 59
GOVERNMENT RESTRICTIONS ON REAL PROPERTY 59
   Power of Eminent Domain 59
   Police Power 60
   Power of Taxation 60
   Power of Escheat 60
IMPORTANT POINTS 60
REVIEW QUESTIONS 62

CHAPTER 4 — BROKERAGE AND AGENCY 67

CLASSIFICATION OF AGENCY RELATIONSHIPS 67
   Universal Agent • General Agent • Special Agent
COMMON LAW AGENCY 68
   Creation of Agency 68
   Fiduciary Relationship 68
      Care, Skill, and Diligence • Obedience • Loyalty • Accountability • Notice (Disclosure)
   Seller–Broker Relationship Under Common Law 70
   Buyer–Broker Relationship Under Common Law 70
   Buyer Agency Under Common Law 70
   Dual Agency Under Common Law 71
      Undisclosed Dual Agency
   Accidental Agency Under Common Law 71
   Termination of Agency 71
AGENCY IN ILLINOIS—DESIGNATED AGENCY 72
   Brokerage Relationships—Article 4 72
      Duties of Licensee to Client • Duties of Licensee to Customer • Agency Disclosure • Confidential Information • Ministerial Acts • Dual Agency • Subagency • Vicarious Liability • Termination of Brokerage Agreement
   Escrow Accounts 76
   Brokerage 76
      Brokerage Firms • Multiple Listing Services (MLS) • Types of Commission Arrangements • Commercial Real Estate Broker Lien Act
ANTITRUST VIOLATIONS 78
IMPORTANT POINTS 79
REVIEW QUESTIONS 79

CHAPTER 5 — REAL ESTATE CONTRACTS 84

BASIC CONTRACT LAW 85
   Terms and Classifications 85
      Express Contracts • Implied Contracts • Bilateral Contracts • Unilateral Contracts • Executory Contracts • Executed Contracts • Valid Contracts • Unenforceable Contracts • Void Contracts • Voidable Contracts
ESSENTIAL ELEMENTS OF CONTRACTS 89
   Offer and Acceptance 89
   Consideration 90

Legal Capacity of the Parties   91
Reality of Consent   91
   Fraud (Actual Fraud) • Misrepresentation (Negative Fraud) • Mutual Mistake • Undue Influence • Menace and Duress
Legality of Object   92
Possibility to Complete   93
STATUTE OF FRAUDS   93
ILLINOIS RESIDENTIAL REAL PROPERTY DISCLOSURE ACT   93
FEDERAL LEAD-BASED PAINT DISCLOSURE REGULATIONS   94
DISCHARGE OF CONTRACTS   95
Agreement of the Parties   95
Complete Performance   95
Impossibility of Performance   95
Operation of Law   96
Illinois Uniform Vendor and Purchaser Risk Act   96
ASSIGNMENT OF CONTRACT RIGHTS   96
INTERPRETATION OF CONTRACTS   97
CONTRACT REMEDIES   98
Specific Performance   98
Rescission   98
Compensatory Damages   98
Liquidated Damages   99
AUCTION SALES   99
LISTING CONTRACTS AND PRACTICES   100
Definition and Purpose   100
Commission Entitlement   100
Types of Listings   101
   Open Listing • Exclusive Agency Listing • Exclusive Right-to-Sell Listing
Listing Contract Provisions   102
Data Sheet   104
Termination   105
Competitive Market Analysis   105
SALES CONTRACTS AND PRACTICES   106
Real Estate Sales Contract   106
Installment Agreement/Contract for Deed   110
UNILATERAL CONTRACTS AND PRACTICES   112
Options   112
Right of First Refusal   114
IMPORTANT POINTS   114
REVIEW QUESTIONS   116

CHAPTER 6 — TRANSFER OF TITLE TO REAL PROPERTY   120

METHODS OF TRANSFERRING TITLE   121
Intestate Descent   121
Testate Descent   121
Voluntary Alienation   122

Involuntary Alienation   123
Lien Foreclosure Sale and Sheriff's Sale • Adverse Possession • Filing of Bankruptcy • Condemnation Under Eminent Domain

DEEDS   124
Essential Elements of a Valid Deed   124
In Writing • Grantor • Grantee • Property Description • Consideration • Words of Conveyance • Execution • Witnessing • Acknowledgment • Delivery and Acceptance

Types of Deeds   126
General Warranty Deed • Special Warranty Deed • Quitclaim Deed • Grant, Bargain, and Sale Deed • Grant Deed • Deed of Confirmation • Deed of Release • Deed of Surrender • Deed of Gift • Judicial Deed

TRANSFER TAXES   132
Illinois Real Estate Transfer Tax Act   132
Illinois Affordable Housing Act of 1989   132
Land Trust Recordation and Transfer Tax Act   133
Inspection Ordinances   133

TITLE ASSURANCE   133
Title Examination   133
Abstract of Title with Attorney Opinion   134
Policy of Title Insurance   134
Owner's Policy • Mortgagee's Policy • Leasehold Policy • Contract Buyer's Policy

Recordation   135
Title Registration/Torrens System   136

PROPERTY DESCRIPTION   136
Monuments and Markings   136
Metes and Bounds   137
Government Rectangular Survey System   137
Subdivision, Lot, Block, and Tract   141
Assessor's Parcel Numbers • Types of Lots • Contour Maps

Vertical Land Description   142
IMPORTANT POINTS   143
REVIEW QUESTIONS   144

CHAPTER 7 REAL ESTATE FINANCE PRINCIPLES   146

NOTES   147
PRINCIPAL, INTEREST, AND PAYMENT PLANS   147
MORTGAGE AND DEED OF TRUST   148
Requirements for Validity of a Mortgage or Deed of Trust   149
Mortgage Clauses and Covenants   150
Recordation   151
Priority and Subordination   151
Releases   151
RIGHTS OF BORROWER   151

Contents

RIGHTS OF LENDER 152
   Foreclosure 152
      Judicial Foreclosure • Equity of Redemption • Statutory Foreclosure • Strict Foreclosure • Deed in Lieu of Foreclosure • Distribution of Sale Proceeds • Deficiency Judgment • Nonrecourse Note
TYPES OF SALES TRANSACTIONS 154
   Cash Sales 154
   New Financing 154
   Mortgage Assumption 154
   Taking "Subject to" a Mortgage 154
PRIMARY SOURCES OF REAL ESTATE FINANCE 155
   Savings and Loan Associations 155
   Mutual Savings Banks 155
   Commercial Banks 156
   Mortgage Bankers 156
   Rural Economic and Community Development 156
   Life Insurance Companies 156
   Credit Unions 156
   Real Estate Investment Trusts (REITs) 157
   Individual Investors 157
SECONDARY MORTGAGE MARKET 157
   Secondary Market Activities 158
      Activities Between Lending Institutions • Sale to Organizations
   Other Aspects of the Market 159
IMPORTANT POINTS 160
REVIEW QUESTIONS 161

CHAPTER 8 REAL ESTATE FINANCE PRACTICES 164

CONVENTIONAL MORTGAGE LOANS 165
   Types of Conventional Mortgage Loans 166
      Junior Mortgage • Term Mortgage • Amortizing Mortgage • Fifteen-Year Mortgage • Balloon Mortgage • Open-End Mortgage • Graduated Payment Mortgage (GPM) • Adjustable Rate Mortgage (ARM) • Graduated Payment Adjustable Mortgage • Shared Appreciation Mortgage (SAM) • Growing Equity Mortgage (GEM) • Participation Mortgage • Wraparound Mortgage • Package Mortgage • Blanket Mortgage • Construction Mortgage • Purchase Money Mortgage • Installment Agreement • Leasehold Mortgage
FHA-INSURED MORTGAGE LOANS 174
   Types of FHA Mortgage Loans 175
      FHA 203(b) Regular Loan Program • FHA 245 Graduated Payment Loan • FHA 203(b)(2) FHA-VA Loan • FHA 234(c) Condominium Loan
   FHA Mortgage Insurance Premium (MIP) 176
   FHA Loan Qualification 176
   FHA Maximum Loan Amount 176
   FHA Loan Assumption Policies 177
   FHA Changes 179
   Contract Requirement 179

DEPARTMENT OF VETERAN AFFAIRS GUARANTEED LOAN PROGRAM   180
  Eligibility   180
    Group I • Group II • Group III
  Qualifying for VA Loans   181
  Restoration of Eligibility   182
  Unused Eligibility   183
  History of Loan Guarantees   183
OTHER ASPECTS OF FHA AND VA LOANS   184
  Escrow Account   184
  Down Payment   184
  Miscellaneous   185
RESIDENTIAL LENDING PRACTICES AND PROCEDURES   185
  Loan Origination   185
    Application • Authorizations
  Loan Processing   190
    Appraisal • Credit Report • Application Review
  Loan Underwriting   191
    Buyer Ability to Pay • Buyer Willingness to Pay • Property Evaluation
  Discount Points   194
CLOSING OR SETTLEMENT COSTS   195
FINANCING LEGISLATION   195
  Truth-in-Lending Simplification and Reform Act (TILSRA)   195
    Disclosure • Cooling-Off Period • Advertising • Penalties
  Real Estate Settlement Procedures Act (RESPA)   197
    Purpose of RESPA • RESPA Requirements
  HUD's New Escrow Rules   199
  Illinois Mortgage Escrow Account Act   199
  Equal Credit Opportunity Act (ECOA)   202
IMPORTANT POINTS   202
REVIEW QUESTIONS   203

CHAPTER 9   CLOSING REAL ESTATE TRANSACTIONS   206

METHODS OF CLOSING   207
  Face-to-Face Closing   207
  Escrow Closing   207
    Title and Escrow Companies
PRELIMINARIES TO CLOSING   208
  Parties   209
  Survey   209
  Pest Inspection   209
  Title Examination, Insurance, and Defects   209
  Property Inspection   209
  Insurance   210
  Perc and Soil Tests   210
  Additional Documents   210
PRORATIONS AT CLOSING   211
  Items Prorated   211

Proration Rules and Methods   211
PREPARATION OF CLOSING STATEMENTS   213
    Format and Entries   213
    Handling Closing Funds   213
CASH SALE STATEMENT   213
    Analysis of the Cash Sale Statement   215
        Settlement Date • Purchase Price • Earnest Money • Hazard Insurance Premium • Real Property Taxes • Title Insurance and Deed Preparation • Deed Recording • Transfer Taxes • Broker's Fee (Commission Due) • Balance Due from Buyer • Balance Due Seller • Other Comments
PURCHASE MONEY MORTGAGE STATEMENT   217
    Analysis of Purchase Money Mortgage Statement   218
        Prorated Insurance Premium • Purchase Money Mortgage • Seller's Existing Mortgage • Cost of Preparing Mortgage • Other Comments
    Reconciliation   219
MORTGAGE ASSUMPTION STATEMENT   220
    Analysis of Mortgage Assumption Statement   220
        Prorated Real Property Taxes • Mortgage Interest Through November 13 • Mortgage Assumption Fees • Other Comments
NEW FIRST MORTGAGE STATEMENT   222
    Analysis of New First Mortgage Statement   222
IMPORTANT POINTS   223
PRACTICE PROBLEM 1: MORTGAGE ASSUMPTION   224
PRACTICE PROBLEM 2: NEW FIRST MORTGAGE   225
SOLUTIONS TO PRACTICE PROBLEMS   226
REVIEW QUESTIONS   228

CHAPTER 10   PROPERTY VALUATION   230

DEFINING APPRAISAL AND VALUATION   231
    Valuation Versus Evaluation   232
    Types of Value   232
        Assessed Value • Investment Value • Liquidation Value • Value in Use • Insurance Value • Condemnation Value • Book Value
APPRAISAL VERSUS COMPETITIVE MARKET ANALYSIS   234
BASIC REAL ESTATE APPRAISAL CONCEPTS   234
    Characteristics of Real Property   234
        Utility • Scarcity • Transferability • Effective Demand
    Factors Affecting Value   235
        Physical Factors • Economic Factors • Social Factors • Governmental Factors
BASIC ECONOMIC VALUATION PRINCIPLES   236
    Highest and Best Use   236
    Substitution   237
    Supply and Demand   237
    Conformity   238
    Progression and Regression   238
    Anticipation   238
    Contribution   238
    Increasing and Decreasing (Diminishing)   239

Competition   239
Balance   239
Change   240
Growth, Equilibrium, and Decline   240
Age   240
APPRAISAL METHODOLOGY   240
APPROACHES TO VALUE: MARKET, COST, INCOME   241
Market Data or Comparison Approach   241
Income Approach   246
Analysis of Operating Statement • Gross Rent Multiplier
Cost Approach or Approach by Summation   249
Depreciation   250
Physical Deterioration • Functional Obsolescence • Economic Obsolescence (External, Environmental, or Locational)
CORRELATION AND RECONCILIATION   252
IMPORTANT POINTS   253
REVIEW QUESTIONS   254

CHAPTER 11 LAND USE CONTROLS   256

HISTORICAL DEVELOPMENT OF LAND USE CONTROLS   257
PUBLIC LAND USE CONTROLS   258
Local Controls   258
Home Rule • Zoning • Urban and Regional Planning • Building Codes • Subdivision Regulations
State Controls   261
Illinois Plat Act • Illinois Land Sales Registration Act • Illinois Environmental Protection Act • Illinois Responsible Property Transfer Act
Federal Controls   263
Interstate Land Sales Full Disclosure Act • FEMA Flood Hazard Areas • Environmental Protection Legislation
PRIVATE LAND USE CONTROLS   265
Typical Restrictive Covenants   266
Enforcement of Covenants   266
Termination of Covenants   267
IMPORTANT POINTS   267
REVIEW QUESTIONS   268

CHAPTER 12 FAIR HOUSING   272

CIVIL RIGHTS ACT OF 1866   273
Enforcement   273
FEDERAL FAIR HOUSING ACT OF 1968   273
1988 Amendments to Fair Housing Act   274
Prohibited Acts   275
Blockbusting • Steering • Discriminatory Advertising • Redlining • Discrimination in Providing Brokerage Services
Exemptions   278

xii Contents

       Enforcement and Penalties   278
   COMMUNITY REINVESTMENT ACT   279
   ILLINOIS HUMAN RIGHTS ACT   279
      Exemptions   280
      Enforcement and Penalties   280
   EQUAL HOUSING OPPORTUNITY TODAY   280
   ILLINOIS REAL ESTATE SOLICITATION STATUTE   281
   AMERICANS WITH DISABILITIES ACT   281
   IMPORTANT POINTS   282
   REVIEW QUESTIONS   283

CHAPTER 13   LANDLORD AND TENANT (LEASEHOLD ESTATES)   286

   DEFINITIONS CONCERNING THE LANDLORD/TENANT RELATIONSHIP   287
   ESSENTIAL ELEMENTS OF A LEASE   287
      Property Description   288
      Term   288
      Rent   288
      Other Lease Provisions   288
      Written or Oral Provisions   288
      Recordation   290
   OBLIGATIONS OF LANDLORD AND TENANT   290
      Mutual Obligations   290
      Landlord's Duties   290
      Tenant's Duties   291
      Law of Negligence   291
      Lead Paint Disclosures   292
      Withholding Rent   292
      Security Deposits   292
      Other Laws Affecting the Rental of Property   293
      Termination and Eviction Remedies   293
   LEASEHOLD (NONFREEHOLD) ESTATES   294
      Estate for Years   294
      Periodic Estate (Estate from Year-to-Year)   295
      Estate (Tenancy) at Will   295
      Estate (Tenancy) at Sufferance   296
   TYPES OF LEASES   296
      Gross and Net Leases   296
      Graduated Lease   296
      Escalated Lease   297
      Index Lease   297
      Fixed Lease   297
      Reappraisal Lease   297
      Percentage Lease   297
      Ground Lease   297
      Oil and Gas Leases   297
      Sale and Leaseback   298
   IMPORTANT POINTS   298
   REVIEW QUESTIONS   299

CHAPTER 14 — PROPERTY MANAGEMENT AND INSURANCE   302

- THE BASICS OF PROPERTY MANAGEMENT   303
  - Types of Properties and Management   304
    - *Residential Property Management • Retail Property Management • Industrial Property Management • Farm Property Management • Management by Homeowners' Associations*
- THE OWNER–MANAGER RELATIONSHIP   305
  - Authority   305
  - Duties   305
  - Fees   306
- PRINCIPAL FUNCTIONS OF PROPERTY MANAGERS   306
  - Rental Schedule   306
  - Budget   306
  - Marketing   307
  - Handling Funds   307
  - Legal Actions   307
  - Maintenance   308
  - Records   308
- BASIC INSURANCE CONCEPTS AND TERMINOLOGY   308
  - Property Insurance   308
  - Liability Insurance   309
  - Package Policy (Homeowner's Policy)   309
- STANDARDIZED HOMEOWNER'S INSURANCE POLICIES   309
- SELECTED LEGAL ISSUES   309
  - Insurable Interest   309
  - Coinsurance   310
  - Unoccupied Building Exclusion   310
  - Policy Interpretation   311
  - Homeowner's Warranty (HOW) Policies   311
- *IMPORTANT POINTS*   312
- *REVIEW QUESTIONS*   313

CHAPTER 15 — FEDERAL INCOME TAXATION OF REAL ESTATE   314

- REVENUE RECONCILIATION ACT OF 1993   315
  - Capital Gain   315
  - Depreciation   316
  - Passive Income   316
- TAX IMPLICATIONS OF HOME OWNERSHIP   317
  - Rollover Rule or Deferred Reporting   317
  - Effect of Purchase and Sale   318
  - The Age-55-and-Over Exclusion   320
  - Computation of Gain   320
  - Inheritance Basis   322
  - Mortgage Interest Deduction   322
  - Points   322
  - Vacation Homes   323

INSTALLMENT SALES 323
INVESTMENT PROPERTY 323
  Depreciation 323
  Income Shelter 324
  Deductible Expenses 325
  Tax-Deferred Exchanges 325
    Like-Kind Property • Business or Investment Property • Property Not Held for Sale • Boot • Basis • Multiple Exchange • Starker Exchange (Starker Trust)
INVESTMENT SYNDICATES 327
IMPORTANT POINTS 328
REVIEW QUESTIONS 329

CHAPTER 16 — ILLINOIS REAL ESTATE LICENSE LAW 332

ILLINOIS REAL ESTATE LICENSE ACT 333
  Article I: Real Estate Licensing 333
    Governing Bodies • Activities Requiring a License • Fines and Disciplinary Action • Classification of Licenses • Application for Licensure • Reciprocity • Brokerage Office • License Renewal • Distribution of Fees
  Article II: Real Estate Appraiser Certification 341
    Nonresident Certification and Reciprocity • Appraisal Administrator • Appraisal Violations • Real Estate Appraisal Committee
  Article III: Salesperson and Broker Continuing Education 344
REAL ESTATE LICENSING INFORMATION 344
REVIEW QUESTIONS 346

CHAPTER 17 — REAL ESTATE MATH 350

APPLICATIONS OF REAL ESTATE MATH 351
  Finance 351
  Appraisal 352
  Closing 352
  Miscellaneous Calculations 352
GENERAL PRACTICE IN REAL ESTATE MATHEMATICS 353
  Percentages 353
  Formulas 353
  Commission Problems 354
    Sales • Rentals • Splits • Estimating Net to Seller
  Estimating Partial Sales of Land 355
  Profit/Loss on Sale of Real Estate 356
AREA CALCULATIONS 356
  Acreage 357
  Square Footage 357
  Cost/Size 358
AD VALOREM PROPERTY TAXES 359
TRANSFER TAX CALCULATIONS 360
PRORATIONS AT CLOSING 361

FINANCIAL CALCULATIONS   362
  Simple Interest   362
    Principal and Interest   363
    Debt Service   363
    Fees and Points   363
    Loan-to-Value Ratios   364
    Yields   365
    Qualifying for Loan   365
APPRAISAL CALCULATIONS   365
  Capitalization   366
  Depreciation   366
INCOME TAX CALCULATIONS   367
  Deductions   367
  Basis   367
MISCELLANEOUS CALCULATIONS   368
REVIEW PROBLEMS   369
SOLUTIONS TO REVIEW PROBLEMS   374

APPENDIX A: BASIC HOUSE CONSTRUCTION   379
APPENDIX B: A GUIDE TO COMMON REAL ESTATE ENVIRONMENTAL HAZARDS   387
APPENDIX C: PREPARING FOR THE ILLINOIS REAL ESTATE EXAM   397
APPENDIX D: PRACTICE EXAM 1   407
APPENDIX E: PRACTICE EXAM 2   417

Answer Key   429
Glossary   433
Index   457

Preface

Illinois Real Estate: Principles and Practices provides beginning students with the fundamentals for a career in real estate. The subject matter and study materials are presented with the assumption that readers have no previous background in this subject. The overall goal of this book is to prepare each student with the appropriate material, guidance, and practice to enable him or her to pass the state licensing examination on the first attempt and in turn to become a successful practitioner.

In covering the material, we have made every effort to present step-by-step explanations and give guidance regarding the most effective use of this material. Each chapter begins with *Important Terminology*. The *Putting It to Work* feature lends practical application to topics particularly relevant to today's practitioners. Chapters conclude with *Important Points* that summarize the chapter's key ideas in a succinct list format, facilitating student review. In addition, chapter-end *Review Questions* allow students to self-test and apply what they have learned. Appendices A and B cover the basics of residential construction and answer questions about environmental hazards related to real estate. Appendix C provides a content breakdown of the exam, test-taking tips, and practice questions related to Illinois. To help ensure students' successful preparation for the licensing examination, two 100-question *Practice Exams* are included. An *Answer Key* for the chapter-end questions and practice exams, and a *Glossary* complete the text.

The book's clear, concise writing style and practical study features will aid students in understanding and retaining relevant information. Even more importantly, the text will prepare them for a successful career in real estate.

ACKNOWLEDGMENTS

I owe my thanks to the many people involved in the production of this text. I especially want to thank my partner, Joan Delaurenti. Without Joan as my partner, I never would have been able to spend time away from our companies to work on this text. Sincere thanks go to Bill Reilly and Bill DeCicco of Valuation Professionals, Inc. Bill Reilly was the source of information and verification of many of the legal details in this book. Bill DeCicco corrected and edited much of the grammar and word usage in the text. My thanks and appreciation to Maureen Cain, Attorney at Law, Chicago. As a fellow real estate educator for the past 13 years, she has provided me with a wealth of real estate and legal knowledge, as well as her friendship.

I am grateful to those that pushed me along in my career as a real estate appraiser and educator. Special thanks are owed to my good friends Bob Gorman, MAI, Gorman Group, Ltd.; Kevin Reynolds, Reynolds Realty Better Homes and Gardens; and Joel Rich, Chicago Association of REALTORS® (CAR). Additional thanks to Tom Hughes and Darci and Bob Dougherty of the Chicago Association of REALTORS® for letting me teach and develop programs for CAR over the past 13 years. Together, these people have given me confidence and encouragement and have provided me with career opportunities.

Finally, I thank John Gorsuch for inviting me to work on this text. John's staff of Shari Jo Hehr, Ann Waggoner Aken, and Gay Pauley kept this project together. Having now gone through the writing and publishing process with these professionals, I have a much greater appreciation for them and their jobs. The many conversations with Shari Jo convinced me of their collective desire to publish the best available Illinois-specific real estate text. I think we've succeeded.

Tim Rice

Learning Tools: The Complete Program

The Text

This easy-to-read text offers you all of the information you need to prepare for your licensing exam and a successful career in real estate. **Including two 100-question *Practice Exams!***

The Interactive Software Tutorial

Preparing for the Real Estate Salesperson Examination
600-plus questions cross-referenced specifically to your Illinois text by chapter and page number; you'll know exactly where to check to restudy an incorrect answer. Includes explanations of both correct and incorrect responses for each question. Take chapter quizzes and practice for your Illinois licensing test with a timed, comprehensive exam.

New! Audio Tapes (national coverage)

Important Point Review for Real Estate Principles and Practices
Make the most of your study time with this 2½ hour review of the most important national material. Great for use on the road!

For more information about the software tutorial and audio tapes, see your instructor. If these items are unavailable to you through your school, call (602) 991-7881.

CHAPTER 1

Important Terminology

- allodial system
- Code of Ethics and Standards of Practice
- feudal system
- free market
- highest and best use
- immobility
- investment
- land use controls
- listing contract
- National Association of Real Estate Brokers (NAREB)
- National Association of REALTORS® (NAR)
- nonhomogeneity
- permanence
- personal property
- real estate
- real property
- Realtist®
- REALTOR®
- realty
- scarcity
- situs
- supply and demand

Basic Real Estate Concepts

IN THIS CHAPTER This chapter presents a brief introduction to real estate and the real estate business. It provides definitions of real property, personal property, and related terms and discusses the factors affecting real estate and the real estate business. Many of the topics introduced here are discussed in more detail in subsequent chapters.

GENERAL CHARACTERISTICS OF REAL ESTATE

Terminology and Classes of Property

Real estate, real property, or **realty** consists of *land and everything that is permanently attached to the land.* Ownership of land encompasses not only the surface of the earth but also the area below the surface and the area above the surface, theoretically into outer space. These three components of land ownership are separable. The owner of the land may retain ownership of the surface but may sell the air space above and the mineral rights below.

All structures on the lands including improvements such as fences, swimming pools, flagpoles, and things growing in the soil naturally without cultivation are included in the definition of real estate. When conveying the title to their property, property owners convey all aspects of real estate unless a prior agreement excludes some portion of the real estate from the conveyance.

The only category of property other than real property, as defined in law, is personal property. Therefore, by the definition of real property, we are able to classify **personal property** as *everything that is not real property*. Tangible personal property is everything that is readily movable. Personal property is an entirely different commodity than real property and does not have the special characteristics of real property. Personal property is more fully discussed in Chapter 2.

Real property has specific characteristics that set it apart from other marketable and valuable commodities. These characteristics are both physical and economic. The physical characteristics of real property, which can easily be remembered by using the acronym PIN, are:

1. Permanence (indestructibility)
2. Immobility
3. Nonhomogeneity (uniqueness)

The economic characteristics of real property are:

1. Scarcity/limited availability
2. Permanence of investment

3. Location (situs)
4. Modification by improvement

Physical Characteristics

Permanence (Indestructibility)

Land is a permanent commodity. Land cannot be destroyed. It may be altered substantially in its topography or other aspects of its appearance, but it remains. The **permanence,** or *indestructibility,* of land makes it attractive as a long-term investment. This is substantially different from most personal property, which often devalues, resulting in little or no salvage value. Land values, however, can change as a result of changing conditions in the area surrounding the land. Land values may suffer economic obsolescence, which results from changes in surrounding areas that adversely affect its value. For example, the construction of an interstate highway can radically affect land values of property located several miles away on a minor highway that loses a tremendous volume of traffic to the newly constructed nearby interstate.

Immobility

A physical characteristic of major importance in real estate is the **immobility** of land. This is the primary difference between land and tangible personal property, which is highly mobile. Land *cannot be relocated.*

The physical characteristic of immobility is a major reason why the location of real estate is so important and is a major factor affecting land value. Those who have specific knowledge of the local market in real estate have to be available to serve the buyers and sellers in each community.

Nonhomogeneity (Uniqueness)

Nonhomogeneity means that *no two parcels of land are identical.* In agricultural land, fertility varies from location to location. In urban real estate, accessibility and zoning differ. Each parcel of real estate has its own topography, soil type, zoning, size, shape, and so on. These differences, whether minor or major, bestow on each parcel of realty its own unique functionality and appeal.

The uniqueness of each parcel of land gives rise to the legal concept of *specific performance,* a legal remedy provided by the U.S. court system for breach of contract. If a seller contracts to sell her real property, the law does not consider money to be a substitute for her duty to convey that title. Therefore, if the seller intends to breach her contract and pay financial damages instead, the buyer may refuse to accept the money and insist on taking title to the agreed-upon land as the only acceptable contract performance.

Economic Characteristics

Scarcity/Limited Availability

An important economic characteristic of real property is its **scarcity,** *its availability or lack of availability.* It follows the principle of **supply and demand,** which states that

FIGURE 1.1
The physical characteristics of real estate.

1. Permanence (indestructibility)
2. Immobility
3. Nonhomogeneity (uniqueness)

the greater the supply of any commodity in comparison to demand, the lower the value will be. Land is a commodity that is in *fixed supply*; no additional supply of land is being produced to keep pace with the ever-increasing population. Moreover, not all land is suitable for human use. The problems created by an ever-increasing demand for the limited supply of desirable land, however, have been eased substantially by the increase in economic supply of land.

An increase in economic supply comes from the increased utilization of land. For example, in agricultural land, fewer and fewer acres are needed to produce the world's supply of food. As a result of advances in technology, people are able to create high-rise office buildings, apartments, and multilevel shopping centers. Consequently, one acre of land now may serve many more people than could have utilized that land in the past.

Another factor that has increased the economic supply of land is the improvement and expansion of our public air, water, sewer, and land transportation systems through construction of highways, bridges, water reservoirs, purification plants, and public utilities. Accomplishments in construction and transportation have converted land that was previously useless into land that now can be utilized.

PUTTING IT TO WORK

Television real estate "gurus" often say, "Buy land because they ain't makin' no more of it," implying that any land purchase is wise. The concept of scarcity, however, is inseparable from the concepts of quality, desirability, and utility. The statement should be, "Buy *good* land, because everybody wants it and there's only so much of it."

Permanence of Investment

Ownership of land is considered an investment because land is permanent. Because land is indestructible and immobile, owners of land are willing to invest large sums of money to improve the land itself or to place improvements on the land. Examples of this are found in the building of homes, office buildings, apartment buildings, golf courses, and so on. The permanence of land means that ownership of land is economically desirable.

Location (Situs)

Of all the characteristics of land, location has the greatest effect on property value. The physical characteristic of immobility dictates that the **situs,** or *location of a parcel of land,* is both unique and permanent. Therefore, if the land is located in an area where available land has a high demand, the land has a substantially higher value. Conversely, if the land is inaccessible from a practical standpoint or is located in an area with little or no demand, the economic value is depressed.

In addition, the value of the location can change as people's preferences change. During the 1950s people took flight from urban centers to the suburbs, which resulted in substantial property value reductions in many urban areas. Recently this trend has begun to reverse itself. People are rediscovering inner cities and rehabilitating older properties and restoring lost value.

Modification by Improvement

Improvements to the land or on the land can greatly affect the land's value. As a parcel of real estate is transformed from a plot of vacant land to a completed dwelling, the appeal of the land increases, resulting in increased value. Improvements to or on the

6 Chapter 1

FIGURE 1.2
The economic characteristics of real estate.

1. Scarcity/limited availability
2. Permanence of investment
3. Situs (location)
4. Modification by improvement

land are not limited to buildings. They include, as examples, landscaping, grading, clearing, connection of public utilities, improved road access, better drainage, and even the building of golf greens and fairways for a new golf course.

PUTTING IT TO WORK

Real estate is a huge factor in national and local economies; the price for real estate is greater than that of virtually all other "ownable" assets. The improvability of real estate provides jobs and even more value, and the permanence of real estate makes it desirable to own for the future. Think about which asset will hold its value or appreciate most to a buyer ten years after purchase: a $20,000 vacant lot, a $20,000 car, or $20,000 of clothing and furniture.

GENERAL CONCEPTS OF LAND USE AND INVESTMENT

Physical Factors Affecting Land Use

Physical factors affecting land utilization can be either natural or artificial. Natural factors include location, topography, soil conditions, size, shape, subjection to flooding, action of the sun, and the presence or absence of minerals. Artificial factors include streets, highways, adjacent land use patterns, and availability of public utilities. Natural and artificial physical factors always must be considered in analyzing the utility of land.

Economic Factors Affecting Land Use

Local property tax assessments, tax rates, wage and employment levels, availability of financing, interest rates, growth in the community, zoning, fire regulations, building codes, and extent of community planning are all examples of economic factors that affect land use. All of these economic factors have a definite effect on the uses to which real estate can or should be put.

Highest and Best Use

The concept of **highest and best use** is of extreme importance in real estate. It is the *use of land that will preserve the land utility, provide the greatest income, and result in the greatest present value of the land.* To achieve the highest and best use, land is improved by the use of capital and labor to make the land productive.

All of the physical and economic factors set out above are taken into consideration to determine the highest and best use of land. A given parcel of land has only one highest and best use at any particular time. Loss of income to the land resulting from failure to use the land to its highest and best use will cause the value of the property to be less than fully realized.

PUTTING IT TO WORK

The highest and best use for most improved land is its current use, assuming that the use conforms to the expectations of the local marketplace. Highest and best use analysis and decisions become highly relevant in developing unimproved land and considering urban renewal and renovations in blighted areas.

Land Use Restrictions

An owner's use of land is affected by government and private **land use controls,** or *restrictions on land use.* In the past, under a **feudal** type of ownership, land was *owned or controlled by the king. Individual, private ownership of land,* called **allodial** ownership, did not come about in the United States until 1785. Even with the advent of private ownership of land, the general public had a vested interest in the use of all land, because of the effect on surrounding land. The use of land requires some regulations for the benefit of all. This is especially true in areas of high population density, where land uses are more extreme and affect a greater number of people.

Government or public land use controls exist in the form of city planning and zoning, state and regional planning, building codes, suitability-for-occupancy requirements, and environmental control. In addition, direct public ownership exerts substantial public control of land uses. Direct public ownership exists in the ownership of public buildings, parks, watersheds, streets, and highways. Private restrictions on land use exist in the form of restrictive covenants established by developers, restrictions in individual deeds requiring the continuation of a specified land use or prohibiting a specified land use, and use restrictions imposed on the tenant in lease contracts.

In both public and private land use regulation, the restriction must be reasonable, necessary, and legal. Certain types of zoning can be discriminatory and thus illegal. Certain private restrictions, especially those pertaining to race or gender, are illegal. Land use restrictions are presented in detail in Chapter 11.

Investment Objectives

Investment refers to either *the outlay of money or the acquisition of property with the expectation of income or profit.* Therefore, the objective of a person who purchases a parcel of land for investment is to make an income or a profit. Different landowners may achieve this objective in different ways. Some owners desire to generate income from the land. Other owners are satisfied if the ownership of land indirectly provides income through tax savings. Some owners may be willing to wait many years for income or profit—buying vacant land, for example, in anticipation of extensive growth in ten years, with the profit to be realized only upon final sale of the land.

The investment objective may be varied. Some common objectives of owning land are:

- as a hedge against an inflationary economic trend
- for the tax savings generated by passive losses or depreciation deductions
- as a means of providing regular income
- to build a strong portfolio of properties for resale at retirement or other future needs

In analyzing a property for investment purposes, in addition to their personal investment objectives, investors must consider the physical and economic characteristics of land, the highest and best use of the land, and any public or private restrictions that may affect the investment goal.

THE REAL ESTATE BUSINESS

The business of real estate is *big business*—big in the number of people it touches and big in the money it generates. For most people, buying and selling real estate represent the most significant monetary transactions of their lives. The sale of real estate, known as *real estate brokerage,* is organized at local, state, and national levels. Real estate organizations promote and police the real estate business. They also promote professionalism and specialization in the real estate business.

In addition to real estate sales, many other types of businesses are based on real estate. These include appraising, abstracting, lending, property management, development, construction, insuring, renovating, and remodeling. Various professional organizations exist to regulate and promote professional conduct and standards.

National Association of REALTORS®

The largest association is the **National Association of REALTORS® (NAR),** first organized in 1908. To be a full member of this association, a person must be licensed in an individual state to sell real estate and must join the local board of the NAR. In most areas this board is called the Board or Association of REALTORS®. To be an affiliate member of the NAR, a person must be closely affiliated with the real estate business, such as an attorney, a lender, or an abstractor. Only members of the NAR are REALTORS®. The term REALTOR® is a registered trademark owned and controlled by the NAR, indicated by the symbol "®" accompanying every use of the term.

A **REALTOR®** is *a professional in real estate who subscribes to a strict code of ethics* known as the **Code of Ethics and Standards of Practice,** which is available through NAR.

The NAR at the local level promotes local real estate business. The local board or association may sponsor seminars on home ownership, civil rights, recycling, or other issues of public concern. The local board is also instrumental in policing the local real estate business. The goal of local NAR boards is to promote the highest ethical standards in the brokerage business. Also, cooperative agreements between brokers to share information, such as the Multiple Listing Service (MLS), usually are established at the local level. At the state and national levels, the NAR lobbies in the state legislatures and Congress on matters specific to the real estate business. Joining a local board of REALTORS® automatically incurs membership in the Illinois Association of REALTORS® as well as the NAR.

The NAR has developed special institutes that provide designations and certifications in specialized areas of real estate. This function of the NAR has added to the professional image of the real estate business. Some of the institutes and designations are listed in Figure 1.3.

PUTTING IT TO WORK

Holding a real estate license does not make one a REALTOR®. A licensee must apply to and join a board of REALTORS® to become a member and be allowed to use the designation and logo. This involves membership fees, orientation classes, and induction into the board.

National Association of Real Estate Brokers

The **National Association of Real Estate Brokers** (NAREB) is *an organization consisting predominantly of African American real estate brokers.* The Association was chartered in 1947 and remains the largest minority real estate organization. *One must be a member of the NAREB to use the trade name* **Realtist®**.

Association of Real Estate License Law Officials

Another organization that impacts on the real estate business is the Association of Real Estate License Law Officials (ARELLO). This organization was established in 1929 by license law officials on the state commissions to assist each other in creating, administering, and enforcing license laws. The first licensing laws were passed in 1917 in California. Through the efforts of ARELLO, each state now has licensing laws. Also through the effort of ARELLO, uniform legislation has been developed and put into effect to protect the consuming public against misrepresentation and fraud in the real estate business. Some of such legislation relates to timesharing, real estate scams, and consumer fraud.

NATIONAL ASSOCIATION OF REALTORS®
REALTOR® Institute
    —Graduate, REALTOR® Institute (GRI)
    —Certified International Property Specialist (CIPS)
American Society of Real Estate Counselors (ASREC)
    —Counselor of Real Estate (CRE®)
Commercial-Investment Real Estate Institute (CIREI)
    —Certified Commercial-Investment Member (CCIM)
Institute of Real Estate Management (IREM)
    —Accredited Management Organization® (AMO®)
    —Accredited Residential Manager® (ARM®)
    —Certified Property Manager® (CPM®)
REALTORS® Land Institute (RLI)
    —Accredited Land Consultant (ALC®)
REALTORS® NATIONAL MARKETING INSTITUTE (RNMI®)
    —Real Estate Brokerage Council: Certified Real Estate Brokerage Manager (CRB®)
    —Residential Sales Council: Certified Residential Specialist (CRS®)
Society of Industrial and Office REALTORS® (SIOR®)
    —Professional Real Estate Executive (P.R.E.)
Women's Council of REALTORS® (WCR)
    —Leadership Training Graduate (LTG)
Illinois Association of REALTORS®

NATIONAL ASSOCIATION OF RESIDENTIAL PROPERTY MANAGERS
Residential Property Managers (RPM)
Master Property Managers (MPM)
Certified Residential Management Company (CRMC)

APPRAISAL INSTITUTE
MAI   —Appraisers experienced in commercial and industrial properties
SRA   —Appraisers experienced in residential properties
RM   —Appraisers experienced in single-family dwellings and two-, three-, and four-unit residential properties
SREA —Appraisers experienced in real estate valuation and analysis
SRPA —Appraisers experienced in valuation of commercial, industrial, residential, and other property

FIGURE 1.3
Some of the many real estate institutes, societies, and councils, together with their related designations.

Real Estate Licensees

An individual licensed and engaged in the real estate business is not limited to selling residential real estate. A person licensed to sell real estate may specialize in one or more of many fields, such as farmland, multi-family dwellings, commercial, retail, or industrial sales. Some other areas in real estate aside from sales are appraising, building and development, property management, financing, real estate consulting, and education.

Effective real estate salespeople and brokers must have a clear picture of their role in the real estate transaction. Successful real estate licensees do not use "hard sell" techniques. Rather, they are advisors working diligently to assist buyers and sellers of real estate.

The real estate licensee's ability to serve the parties in a real estate transaction will determine his success. A career in real estate can provide a real estate licensee with satisfaction from serving the needs of others, as well as with financial rewards. Success in the real estate business is built upon knowledge, ethical conduct in all dealings, and, above all, service to others.

The Fundamentals of a Real Estate Transaction

The basic stages of a real estate transaction are listing, marketing the property, offer and acceptance, real estate sales contract, financing, and settlement. These aspects are highlighted briefly below, and each is presented in more detail in later chapters.

Listing

The real estate transaction begins when an owner decides to sell a property. The owner often will enlist the aid of a real estate professional through a **listing,** which is *a contract wherein a property owner employs a real estate firm to market a property for a prescribed period of time at a prescribed price and terms.* Under this contract the real estate firm becomes the agent of the seller. Real estate professionals are trained to prepare competitive market analyses (CMA) and to analyze the prices of recent sales, current listings, and properties that have been pulled off the market without being sold. This information is used to help the seller set an asking price for the property.

Real estate professionals play an integral part in real estate transactions. The National Association of REALTORS® reported in *Homebuying and Selling Process: 1993* that 81 percent of buyers purchasing property used the services of a real estate professional.

Marketing the Property

The broker's expertise essentially lies in the marketing of the property. The broker will develop a marketing plan, which may call for the listing agent to enter the property into an MLS, hold open houses, and advertise the property in various media. While the listing agent implements the marketing plan, other brokers assist buyers in locating properties that meet their requirements. Today, whether a broker is the designated agent of the seller or of the buyer is defined both in common law and in the real estate license law of many states. Agency is discussed in detail in Chapter 4.

Offer and Acceptance

Prospective buyers inspect the seller's property, and if the seller is fortunate, one of these prospective buyers will make an offer. The buyer's agent or attorney will prepare an offer to purchase. The offer to purchase will state the buyer's offer for the property and the contingencies or conditions upon which the buyer is making the offer.

Financing

After the acceptance of the offer, the buyer applies for financing. The lender underwrites the loan (risk evaluation). The lender verifies the borrower's employment and other assets and completes a credit check to determine the creditworthiness of the borrower. The lender is also concerned with the property to be used as collateral and whether it will warrant the amount of loan the borrowers are seeking. An appraiser will provide the lender with information about the property's features, condition, and value. Chapters 7 and 8 discuss finance.

Title Examination

How can the buyer be sure the seller really owns the property being sold? While the lender is underwriting the loan, the attorneys in the transaction will hire a professional called an abstractor or a title insurance company to search the public record. This search of documents recorded in the public record will reveal how the seller came to be vested in the property. Chapter 6 discusses title assurance.

Settlement

After the lender has underwritten the loan and the attorneys have reviewed the title search, the parties are ready for a closing. At the closing, the closing agent will make sure the moneys for taxes and other costs have been properly prorated between the buyer and seller and the proper escrows set up for the payment of future real estate taxes. The seller's attorney will have the seller execute the deed and deliver it to the buyer. The buyer's attorney will make sure the deed is recorded. Many legal documents are exchanged among the seller, buyer, and lender. Chapter 9 deals with the closing or settlement of a real estate transaction.

The degree to which an agent can become legally involved in the closing of a real estate transaction varies from state to state. While in some states the broker will become quite involved in many of the functions in a transaction, in Illinois, the Illinois Real Estate License Act restricts the functions Illinois licensees can perform. Chapter 16 discusses the Illinois Real Estate License Act.

THE REAL ESTATE MARKET

The real estate market is an excellent example of the free-market concept. A **free market** *provides ample time for buyer and seller to effect a mutually beneficial purchase and sale without undue pressure or urgency.* In the real estate market, properties are given substantial exposure, particularly at the local level. Properties are available for inspection by prospective buyers, and these buyers have the opportunity to inspect several properties before making a final selection.

The physical characteristics of land create special conditions in the real estate market that do not exist in other markets. The immobility of real estate causes the market to be local in nature, requiring local specialists who are familiar with local market conditions, property values, and availability.

The real estate industry traditionally has been subject to cyclical periods of recession and prosperity. It is often the first industry to feel the adverse effects of depressed conditions in the national and local economies. When supply substantially exceeds demand, existing properties cannot be withdrawn from the local market and relocated to an area with higher demand. Conversely, when the demand exceeds supply, new supplies of housing and business properties cannot be constructed quickly. Thus, the real estate industry takes longer than the economy as a whole to climb out of a recession, because of the inability to react quickly to radical changes in supply and demand.

The goal of an effective real estate salesperson is to read the market and act. Effective real estate salespeople are aware of new industries coming to the community. They keep abreast of new legislation and local ordinances affecting real estate. They recognize trends in interest rates and closing costs. Effective real estate salespeople must learn to adapt to the ever-changing real estate market.

Supply and demand in the real estate market is affected by many factors: money supply, interest rates, population migrations, zoning, planning and environmental concerns, and local and federal taxing laws. Informed real estate licensees strive to stay abreast of these factors.

IMPORTANT POINTS

1. Real property includes the surface of the land, improvements attached to the land, minerals beneath the surface, and air space above the land.
2. Everything that is not real property is personal property. Generally, personal property is readily movable.
3. Real property has the physical characteristics of permanence, immobility, and nonhomogeneity.
4. Real property has unique economic characteristics based on scarcity, permanence of investment, location, and improvements.
5. Land use controls are found both in private deed restrictions and in public laws.
6. The real estate business involves many specialties besides residential sales and requires knowledge of such fields as financing, housing codes, and other related fields.
7. The real estate business is organized at local, state, and national levels primarily through the National Association of REALTORS®.
8. A real estate market is local in nature and is a good example of the free-market concept.
9. The National Association of Real Estate Brokers is a real estate organization consisting of African Americans. Members of the NAREB use the trade name Realtist®.
10. Real estate licensees act as advisors and agents for the benefit of their clients. Because a home's sale and purchase often involve the seller's most important financial asset and create long-term financial obligations for the buyer, licensees have to be thoroughly knowledgeable and competent in their duties.

REVIEW QUESTIONS

Answers to these questions are found in the Answer Key section at the back of the book.

1. All of the following are separable ownerships in land EXCEPT:
   a. surface of the land
   b. area below the surface
   c. nonhomogeneity
   d. air space above the land

2. The characteristic of land that causes the real estate market to be essentially a local market is the physical characteristic of:
   a. permanence
   b. immobility
   c. availability
   d. natural features

3. The basis for the legal remedy of specific performance when dealing with land is its:
   a. nonhomogeneity
   b. immobility
   c. permanence
   d. availability

4. All of the following have contributed to the increase in the economic supply of land EXCEPT:
   a. increased utilization of the physical supply of land
   b. modifications by improvements to the land
   c. construction of condominiums
   d. lack of demand for land

5. The quality of the location of land, and consequently the value of the land, can be changed by:
   a. the principle of nonhomogeneity
   b. relocation of the land
   c. changes in the local trend of real estate business
   d. improvements to the land resulting in accessibility

6. The concept of highest and best use does NOT:
   a. include consideration of the physical and economic factors affecting land use
   b. result in the greatest present value of the land
   c. result in use in violation of present zoning
   d. include consideration for the improvements or modifications to the land

7. Public land use controls exist in the form of:
   a. restrictive covenants
   b. zoning laws
   c. deed restrictions
   d. conditions in a platted subdivision

8. Specializations within the real estate business include:
   a. transportation
   b. farming
   c. accounting
   d. property management

9. The type of land ownership that existed in colonial times was feudal. The private ownership of land is called:
   a. alliance
   b. allodial
   c. conservation
   d. fundamental

10. The real estate market may be described by all of the following EXCEPT:
    a. free market
    b. local market
    c. movable market
    d. slow to react to changes in supply and demand

11. The function of a real estate licensee in dealings with buyers and sellers in the real estate market may best be described as:
    a. financier
    b. counselor
    c. contractor
    d. adversary

12. Improvements or modifications to real estate alter a(n) _____ characteristic of that real estate.
    a. physical
    b. economic
    c. natural
    d. financial

13. The typical real estate licensee must have specialized knowledge in a variety of subjects that include all of the following EXCEPT:
    a. financing
    b. contracts
    c. excavation
    d. valuation

14. All of the following are real property EXCEPT:
    a. surface of the earth
    b. area below the surface
    c. readily movable items
    d. air space above the earth

15. Economic characteristics of real property include which one of the following?

    a. situs

    b. immobility

    c. permanence

    d. nonhomogeneity

16. Which of the following is an example of the private control of land use?

    a. zoning

    b. restrictive covenants

    c. building codes

    d. environmental controls

17. The term REALTOR® is a registered trademark of:

    a. National Association of REALTORS®

    b. Association of Real Estate License Law Officials

    c. REALTORS® International

    d. National Association of Real Estate Brokers

18. Which of the following is a contract wherein a property owner employs a real estate broker to market the property?

    a. assumption

    b. contract for sale

    c. consummation

    d. listing

19. The Code of Ethics and Standards of Practice of real estate was established by:

    a. NAR

    b. ARELLO

    c. NAREB

    d. MAI

20. The predominantly African American real estate organization that uses the trade name Realtists® is the:

    a. National Association of Real Estate Brokers

    b. Association of African American Real Estate Specialists

    c. Association of Real Estate License Law Officials

    d. National Association of Home Builders

CHAPTER 2

Important Terminology

- accretion
- air rights
- alienation
- alluvion
- avulsion
- bill of sale
- blue sky laws
- bundle of rights
- chattel
- community property
- condominium
- convey
- cooperative
- co-ownership
- corporeal
- declaration of condominium
- deed
- defeasible
- emblements
- estovers
- fee simple absolute
- fixture
- freehold estates
- fruits of industry
- fruits of nature
- hereditaments
- homestead
- incorporeal
- interval ownership
- intestate succession
- joint tenancy
- land trust
- leasehold estate
- life estate
- life tenant
- limited common elements
- limited liability company
- littoral rights
- master deed
- mineral rights
- National Association of Securities Dealers Regulatory (NASDR)
- nonfreehold estate
- partnership
- public offering statement
- pur autre vie
- remainder
- reversion
- right of first refusal
- right of inheritance
- right of survivorship
- Securities and Exchange Commission (SEC)
- security
- separate property
- severalty
- sole proprietorship
- subsurface rights
- tenancy in common
- tenants by the entirety
- tenements
- timesharing
- trade fixture
- trust
- unities

Property Ownership and Interests

IN THIS CHAPTER We begin the discussion of the various types of ownership of real property. Real estate terminology is like a new language, so real estate students should memorize the vocabulary of real estate and then search for understanding. Real estate students must avoid the temptation to give legal advice; attorneys are the only ones authorized to practice law. Nevertheless, real estate licensees have to recognize basic concepts of law as they may affect clients and prospects, and encourage them to become properly informed of their rights and obligations through appropriate legal counsel.

THE CONCEPT OF PROPERTY

Bundle of Rights

Real estate and *real property* are terms that are often used interchangeably, but they have a slight difference in meaning. Real estate is the land and all improvements made both on and to the land, whether found in nature or placed there by humans. Real property is broader in meaning. It is real estate plus all legal rights, powers, and privileges inherent in ownership of real estate. The legal rights, powers, and privileges are many in number and varied in nature. These legal rights, powers, and privileges have value, are usually salable, and affect the value of the underlying real estate (dirt). The concept encompasses things such as leases, easements, mortgages, options, water rights, and so on.

To understand the subtle difference between real estate and real property, visualize real property as a bundle of sticks (Figure 2.1). The sticks in the bundle include the major sticks of land, fixtures, and fruits of soil, all of which are *tangible* (movable). The bundle also includes *intangible* rights such as air rights, water rights, mineral rights, easements, leases, mortgages, licenses, profits, and so on. This visual concept, referred to as a **bundle of rights,** illustrates that real estate licensees sell more than dirt and houses. They also can sell *any rights to, interests in, and title to real property that affect the value of the real property.* Every bundle of sticks (piece of real property) can be divided in many ways. The division referred to here is not that of acres or lots. Instead, it refers to the various rights that can be held in real property, often classified as the rights of possession, disposition, quiet enjoyment, and control. An owner of the entire bundle has the right to possess the property, dispose of the property (sell, lease, give it away, will it, etc.), the right of enjoyment (use the property subject to valid private and governmental restrictions), and the right to control the property. The bundle of rights is simply and descriptively defined in modern usage as the right to sell, lease, use, give away, and enter, or the right to refuse to do any of these things.

FIGURE 2.1 Real estate ownership as a bundle of rights.

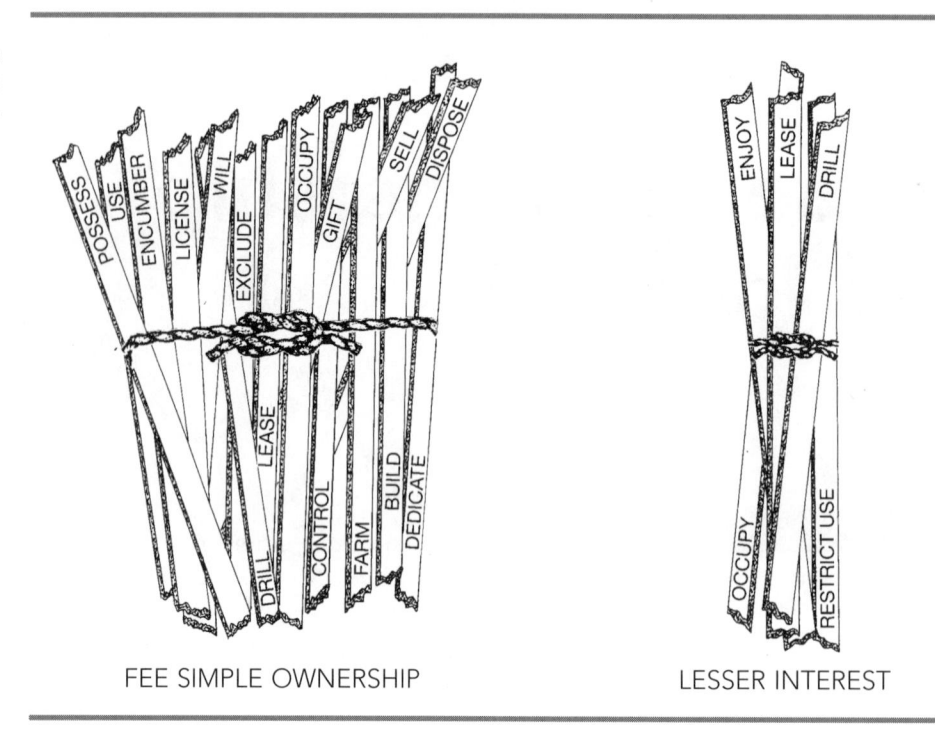

FEE SIMPLE OWNERSHIP

LESSER INTEREST

Real Property

We have learned that real property consists of land and everything permanently attached to land, as well as the rights of ownership. Ownership in land includes not only the face of the earth but also the area below the surface to the center of the earth and the area above the surface theoretically to outer space. Real property also includes everything that is permanently attached to the land. Therefore, the land owner owns all structures on the land as well as other improvements to the land. Improvements on the land include things such as buildings, swimming pools, flagpoles, fences, and other structures. Improvements to the land refer to clearing the land, building roads, placing utilities, and the like.

Ownership of real property is transferred and evidenced by a document called a **deed,** which *conveys real property only and cannot convey personal property.*

Air and Subsurface Rights

Ownership of real property inherently includes ownership of the rights to the area above and below the earth's surface. *Rights to the area above the earth* are called **air rights.** The right of ownership of air space enables the land owner to use that space to construct improvements and to lease or sell the air space to others. Sale or lease of air space is becoming more common in high-density urban areas. In purchasing air rights, the purchaser must obtain an easement appurtenant over the ground if someone else controls the ground. For example, if owner A has a two-story building and sells the air rights above the two stories to owner B, A must include in the purchase and transfer an appurtenant easement allowing access over the first and second stories to the property above.

The right of ownership and control of air space, however, is limited by zoning ordinances and federal laws providing for use of the air space by aircraft. Zoning ordinances also can restrict the height of improvements constructed on the land so as not to overburden municipal support systems such as police, water, sewer, traffic, and so on.

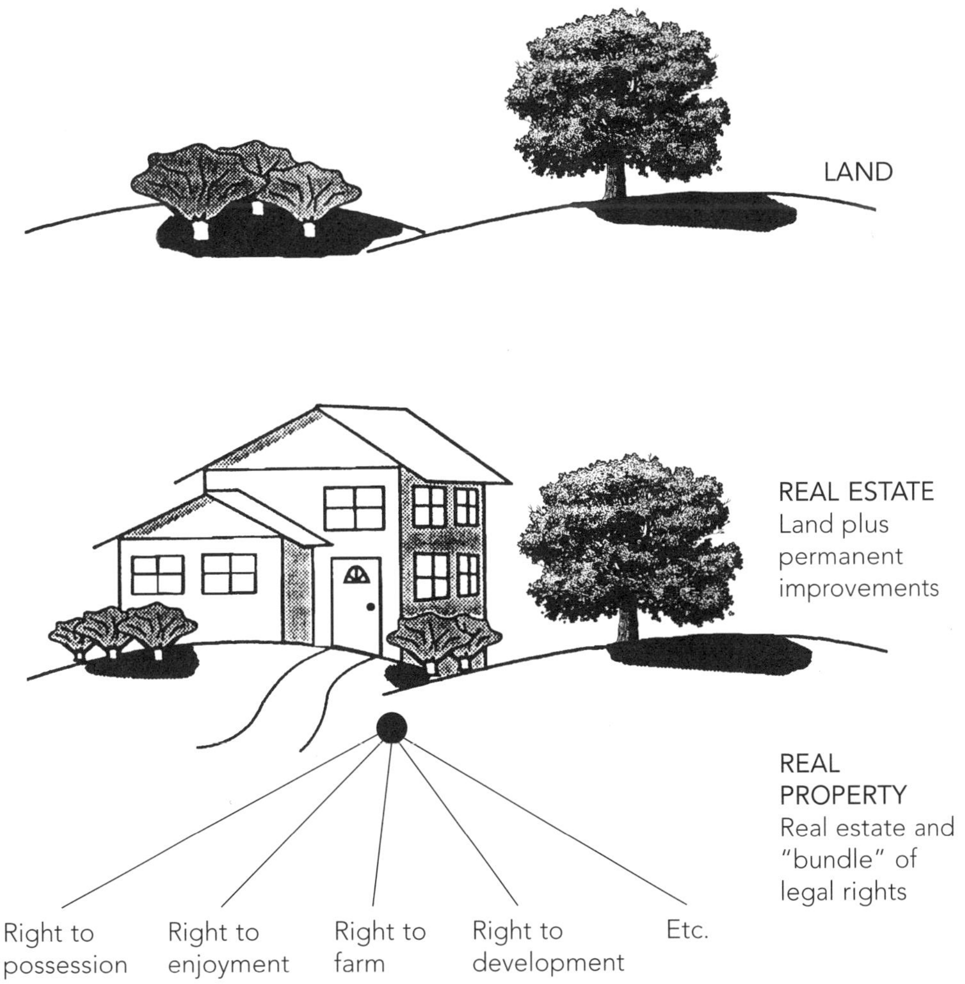

FIGURE 2.2 Land, real estate, and real property.

LAND

REAL ESTATE
Land plus permanent improvements

REAL PROPERTY
Real estate and "bundle" of legal rights

Right to possession | Right to enjoyment | Right to farm | Right to development | Etc.

Rights to the area below the earth's surface are called **subsurface rights,** often referred to as **mineral rights.** These rights also are subject to restriction by local, state, and federal laws. The owner of mineral rights may conduct mining operations or drilling operations personally or may sell or lease these rights to others on a royalty basis. A mineral lease permits use of the land for mineral exploration and mining operations. The lease may be for a definite period of time or for as long as the land is productive.

Water Rights

Water rights in real property include percolating water rights, riparian water rights, and surface water rights. Percolating water is the water underground drawn by wells. Land owners have the inherent right in that land to draw out the percolating water for their own reasonable use. Local health codes may restrict that use.

The right of natural drainage is at the heart of surface water rights. No land owner can substantially change the natural drainage of surface water (runoff) in such a manner as to damage neighboring land owners. The issue of surface water and drainage is an important consideration in building commercial developments with extensive paving, which reduces the absorption of water by the soil and intensifies runoff, possibly causing flooding.

Riparian rights *belong to the owner of property bordering a flowing body of water.* **Littoral rights** *apply to property bordering a body of water that is nonflowing,* such as a lake or a sea. Generally, property adjacent to a river or a watercourse affords the land owner the right of access to and use of the water. Actual ownership of the water in a flowing watercourse, however, is complex and depends on numerous factors. With a navigable watercourse, adjacent owners are limited to banks of the watercourse, and the state or the public owns the actual body of water. With a non-navigable watercourse, ownership lines extend to the center of the watercourse. With littoral bodies of water, the boundary is at the average high-water mark.

Accession Rights

Owners of real property have the *right to all that their land produces or all that is added to the land, either intentionally or by mistake*—the ownership right of *accession*. This right becomes an issue when a watercourse changes gradually or rapidly. The *gradual building up of land in a watercourse over time by deposits of silt, sand, and gravel* is called **accretion.** The *land mass added to property over time* by accretion, called **alluvion,** is owned by the owner of the land to which it has been added. **Avulsion** is the *loss of land when a sudden or violent change in a watercourse results in its washing away.* Avulsion does not change boundaries or ownership as does the slow, gradual change of accretion.

Personal Property

Other than real property, the only category of property defined in law is personal property. *Everything that is not real property is personal property,* or **chattel**. Generally, personal property is everything that is readily movable. Personal property is "your stuff," consisting of household furniture, cars, tractors, mobile homes, jewelry, and so on. Personal property also includes growing crops that are harvested annually. *Ownership of personal property is transferred and evidenced by a document called a* **bill of sale.**

Land, Minerals, Fruits of the Soil

Land is defined as the earth's surface extending downward to the center of the earth and upward to infinity, including things permanently attached by nature. Land includes the dirt and soil, as well as boulders and growing things such as trees and bushes. Land also includes minerals located below the surface, such as oil, gold, silver, bauxite, and so on. The right to mine minerals in land is evidenced by ownership of subsurface rights.

Growing things that do not require regular planting or cultivation but continue to grow naturally (perennials) are called *fructus naturales,* **fruits of nature,** and are designated by law as real estate. These include forest trees, native shrubs, and wild berries. Fruits of nature pass to a buyer of real estate by execution and delivery of the deed from the seller unless specifically reserved by the grantor.

Growing things that require planting each season and cultivation are called *fructus industriales,* **fruits of industry,** and are designated by law as personal property. Examples include crops such as corn, wheat, melons, and soybeans. These *fruits of industry* are called **emblements.** Emblements also denote the tenant's right to reenter the property and harvest the emblements after termination of the tenancy. Fructus industriales, or emblements, do not pass to a buyer of real estate by deed; instead, they pass via a bill of sale because they are personal property.

Fixtures

The real estate term for *improvements both on and to the land* is **fixture.** The object that becomes a fixture, and thus part of the real estate, was at one time a piece of personal property. Lumber to build a structure is personal property or chattel when it is delivered to the building site. By attachment and intent of the builder, however, the lumber becomes a building on the land and thus real estate. The same is said for light fixtures, showers, bathtubs, toilets, windows, bricks, clotheslines, woodstoves, window shades, and so on.

Determining what a fixture is can be a problem during real estate transactions because the buyer and seller may have different perceptions. For example, an owner may have installed a chandelier in the dining room and then want to remove it upon sale of the home, contending that it is his personal property. If the buyer wishes to establish that the chandelier is a fixture and should remain with the home, the courts may apply several tests to resolve this issue. The typical tests are:

1. *Agreement between the parties.* Because different people may view determination of fixture status differently, the real estate salesperson is responsible for ensuring that all parties to the contract clearly understand who owns the fixtures. This can be achieved through a carefully written, explicit listing contract between real estate agent and seller and the purchase contract between buyer and seller. The real estate sales contract is the final contract between buyer and seller. In the case of the chandelier, the buyer is not bound by the listing because she is not a party to it. The real estate sales contract dictates ownership of the fixture. It should list any items that could cause confusion among the parties as included or excluded from the contract. If an item is not dealt with in the contract and the parties to the transaction fail to agree to the status of the item, the parties will probably seek reparation in court, where the court will apply the other four tests to the disputed item.

2. *Intention of the parties.* Whether an item is real or personal depends on whether the installer intended for the item to be temporary or permanent. In the absence of an agreement between the parties, the court will look at the remaining tests to determine the intent of the parties.

3. *Adaptability of the item.* The court will consider whether the item is customized or can be interchanged with other items. For instance, storm windows, though movable, only fit one window. Another example would be a key, which only fits one lock. Draperies or an area rug, however, are interchangeable and can be used without modification in another home or apartment dwelling.

4. *Method of attachment.* The court will look at how the item is attached. Generally things screwed or nailed into the wall are considered permanently attached and therefore, real property. Drapery rods are considered real property (permanently attached). The draperies themselves are personal property, as they are simply hung on the rod. Items that are built in, such as a dishwasher or a range/oven are considered real property. An in-ground pool is considered real property; an above-ground pool is considered personal property.

5. *Relationship of the parties.* The court will also look at the relationship of the parties. Generally, when an owner makes an improvement to property, the improvement is intended to be a permanent improvement, whereas when a tenant makes an improvement, the improvement is generally considered a temporary improvement for the tenant's enjoyment during the term of the lease. Using these criteria, courts generally rule for the purchaser over the seller and for the tenant over the landlord.

Trade Fixtures

The law of real estate recognizes an exception to the fixture rule. Items of personal property that a business operator installs in rented building space are presumed to remain personal property. These are called **trade fixtures.** An example would be built-in shelves for displaying merchandise. Although they are attached to the property, these fixtures remain the personal property of the rental tenant and may be removed at the end of the lease period. Of course, the lease contract should be clear on the point of trade fixtures. The rental agreement may allow the landlord to retain these items. If the rental agreement does not have this provision, trade fixtures remain the property of the installing tenant.

Upon removal of a trade fixture, the tenant does have the responsibility to restore the property to its original condition. This may involve capping plumbing, repairing walls, filling holes, and so on.

Physically similar to trade fixtures, but legally different, are *leasehold improvements.* Even though a leasehold improvement may be physically identical to a trade fixture, the difference lies in who installed the item. If the landlord installed it, it remains with the building and is a leasehold improvement. If the tenant installed it, it is a trade fixture and removable.

Technically, if the tenant does not remove trade fixtures before the lease expires, the fixtures become the property of the landlord by abandonment.

Uniform Commercial Code (UCC)

A special situation occurs when a property owner has financed the purchase of a piece of personal property. The Uniform Commercial Code (UCC), adopted in Illinois and most states, provides for the lender to retain a security interest in the personal property or chattel until the lender is paid in full. The security interest is available to the lender even though the chattel is installed in real property. The security interest is created by an instrument called a *security agreement.* An example of this type of financing and security agreement is a farmer financing the building of grain storage bins. The lender does not take a mortgage on the land on which the bins are built but instead takes a security interest in the bins themselves.

This type of agreement is evidenced on the public record by filing a notice, called a *financing statement,* in the office of the County Recorder. This filing provides constructive notice to all the world that a security interest exists in the personal property that is the subject of the security agreement. As a result, the attached item does not become a fixture or a part of the real estate. Consequently, if the buyer/borrower defaults in payment, the lender can remove the article of personal property even though it has been attached to real property.

Land, Tenements, and Hereditaments

Real property consists of land, tenements, and hereditaments. Land was described earlier as the earth's surface extending downward to the center of the earth and upward to infinity, including things permanently attached by nature. Land includes the dirt and soil, plus boulders and growing things such as trees and bushes. Land also includes minerals located below the surface.

Tenements include *all of the things in the definition of land plus the corporeal and incorporeal rights in land.* **Corporeal** rights are *rights to things that are tangible,* that can be touched and seen, such as buildings, trees, and fences. **Incorporeal** rights are *rights to things that are intangible,* that cannot be touched or seen, including easements, encroachments, licenses, and so on.

Hereditament, a larger and more comprehensive term than land or tenement, consists of *everything included in the definitions of land and tenement plus every interest in real property that is capable of being inherited.* This includes corporeal rights and incorporeal rights.

ESTATES IN REAL PROPERTY

Definition of Estate

An estate in real property is *an interest in the property sufficient to give the holder of the estate the right to possession of the property.* (This does not necessarily imply ownership of the property, only possession.) Here, we must further distinguish between the right of possession and right of use. As in the earlier analogy of rights in real estate being like a bundle of sticks, the owner of an estate in land has the right of possession, a bigger stick than a mere right to use or have access to the land, as in the case of an easement.

The Latin word for "estate" is *status,* indicating the relationship in which the estate owner stands with reference to rights in the property. It establishes the degree, quantity, nature, and extent of interest a person has in real property.

The word "estate" is generally interchangeable with the word "tenancy." Both of these words imply a right to possession.

Under the feudal system of land ownership common in Europe almost a thousand years ago, only the king could hold title to real property. The king granted *feuds* to loyal subjects. These feuds did not provide ownership in land but simply a right to use and possess the land as long as the holder of the feud provided certain services to the king. The feuds approximated the modern concept of leasing. Under the feudal system, outright ownership would never be obtained.

The feudal system of ownership was transplanted to America when people from England settled and founded the colonies. The King of England or his ambassadors owned and controlled all the land.

One of the basic reasons for the American Revolution was the colonists' insistence on outright and absolute ownership of land, called allodial ownership. Allodial, or private, ownership of land did not begin until 1785. The conveyance of lands from the government to individuals allowed after passage of the Ordinance of 1785 was by patent or land grant. With the transfer of land came the need for an accurate method of measurement or survey. The Ordinance of 1785 also provided the first official survey system, called *governmental* or *rectangular survey.* As a result, the present system of land ownership in the United States is the allodial system, not the feudal system. Individuals can hold title to real property outright.

Groups of Estates in Land

Estates in land are divided into two groups: (a) estates of freehold and (b) nonfreehold estates. **Freehold estate** is *ownership for an undetermined length of time.* A **nonfreehold,** or leasehold, estate signifies *possession with a determinable end.* Each of these two major divisions has various groupings or subheadings, which will be discussed next. Figure 2.3 shows the estates in land.

FREEHOLD ESTATES

Freehold estates are (a) the various fee simple estates and (b) life estates. Fee simple estates are inheritable; life estates are not.

Fee Simple Estates

Fee Simple Absolute

The estate of **fee simple absolute** provides the most complete form of ownership and bundle of rights available in real property. This estate is also called fee simple or

FIGURE 2.3 Estates and rights in real property.

FREEHOLD ESTATES

I. Fee simple (all inheritable)
   a. Absolute
   b. Defeasible
      1. Condition subsequent
      2. Determinable

II. Life estates (not inheritable)
   a. Conventional
   b. Legal/statutory
      1. Dower
      2. Curtesy
      3. Homestead

Note: Freehold estates provide title (ownership).

NONFREEHOLD ESTATES
(Leasehold Estates)

I. Estate for years
II. Estate from year-to-year (periodic estate)
III. Estate at will
IV. Estate at sufferance

Note: Nonfreehold estates provide possession and control but not ownership.

---

ownership in fee. Ownership in fee simple absolute *provides certain legal rights usually described as a bundle of legal rights.* This bundle includes the right to possession of the property; the right of quiet enjoyment of the property; the right to dispose of the property by gift, sale by deed, or by will; the right of exclusion; and the right to control use of the property within limits of the law.

The owner in fee simple absolute may **convey,** or *pass to another,* a life estate in reversion or in remainder (defined and discussed later in the text); pledge the property as security for a mortgage debt; convey a leasehold estate to another; grant an easement in the land to another; or give to another a license to conduct some activity on the property. Certain of these rights may be removed from the bundle while leaving the other rights intact. For example, if the owner pledges the title as security for a mortgage debt, the balance remaining is a fee simple title subject to the mortgage debt. Also, if the owner conveys an estate for years or conveys an easement in the property to another, the remaining rights are fee simple subject to a lease or subject to the existence of an easement.

Most real estate transfers convey a fee simple absolute. No special words are required on a deed to create this freehold estate. It is the assumed estate.

Fee Simple Defeasible

Although a fee simple absolute is the most complete form of ownership, showing the greatest title, possession, and control, some conveyances create what begins as a *fee simple absolute but with a condition or limitation attached.* These are termed **defeasible** estates. Defeasible means destructible or defeatable. A frequent use of defeasible freeholds occurs when someone wishes to donate land to a church, school, or community for a specific purpose. The two types of defeasible fees are (a) fee simple subject to a condition subsequent and (b) fee simple determinable.

Fee simple subject to a condition subsequent. The fee simple subject to a condition subsequent can continue for a potentially infinite time, as is the case with the fee simple absolute. The fee simple subject to a condition subsequent, however, can be defeated and is, therefore, a defeasible title. A fee simple subject to a condition is easily recognized by the words "but if" in the transfer. For example, grantor conveys 40 acres to his son, but if alcoholic beverages are ever sold on the premises, his son's ownership terminates.

Fee simple subject to a condition subsequent is created by the grantor (the one conveying title) specifying in the conveyance of title a use of the property that is prohibited. The deed must specifically state the condition. In the example above, the grantor conveyed property to his son with the condition that it never can be used for the sale of alcoholic beverages. As long as the property is not used for this purpose, the title will continue indefinitely with the initial grantee, his son, or any subsequent grantee. At any time in the future if the property is used for the sale of alcoholic beverages, however, the original grantor or his heirs may reenter the property and take possession or go to court and sue to regain possession. By doing this, the titleholder's estate is terminated. Breach of the condition causes the termination.

Fee simple determinable. Fee simple determinable is another inheritable freehold estate in the form of a fee simple estate. It is also a defeasible fee, however, and, therefore, the grantor can terminate the title. This type of estate is easily recognized by use of the words "as long as" in the deed of transfer. For example, grantor transfers 10 acres to her daughter, as long as the property is used for educational purposes. Title received by her daughter can be for an infinite time. If the property is not used for the purpose specified in the conveyance, however, the title will terminate automatically and revert to the original grantor or her heirs.

In the case of a fee simple determinable, the estate in the grantee terminates automatically in the event the designated use of the property is not continued. This is called the *possibility of reverter.* It is contrasted with the fee simple subject to a condition subsequent, in which the termination is not automatic. In the fee subject to the condition subsequent, the grantor or heirs must either reenter the property or go to court to obtain possession of the property and to terminate the estate in the grantee. This is called *the right of reentry.* A major difference between reverter and reentry is where the burden of proof lies. With reverter, the burden of proof rests with the party trying to keep ownership. In reentry, the burden rests with the party trying to reclaim ownership.

In the case of very old conditions, the grantor or heirs may no longer remember the condition. Therefore, a condition may be broken with no consequences. If no one seeks termination of the defeasible fees, the title will not terminate. Also, some old conditions are no longer enforceable because they violate present laws. For instance, conditions that the property not transfer to other than white males are now discriminatory and unenforceable.

PUTTING IT TO WORK

Defeasible fee estates are relatively rare. Most ownership positions are fee simple absolute. This latter form of ownership does not imply that all of these properties are free and clear of liens or other encumbrances but only that there are no involuntary conditions of ownership.

Life Estates

The **life estate** is a freehold estate that defines itself. It is *ownership, possession, and control for the life of someone.* Ownership, possession, and control are contingent upon living; therefore, the ownership, possession, and control are lost at death. If ownership terminates as soon as a person stops breathing, the heirs of the deceased owner will inherit nothing. Under a life estate, ownership lies only with the living.

The life estate is a freehold estate that is *not* inheritable. It may be created for the life of the named life tenant or for the life of some other named person. A life estate created for the duration of the life tenant's own life is called an *estate for life* or *ordinary life estate.* For example: B conveys 40 acres to C for C's life. When the life estate is for the life of a person other than the life tenant, it is called an estate **pur autre vie,** meaning *for the life of another.* For example: D conveys 40 acres to E until the death of F.

Two outcomes are possible upon death: (a) an estate in remainder and (b) an estate in reversion. If the *conveyance is from grantor to G for life and then to a named person or persons upon the death of G,* it is an estate in **remainder.** The *person or persons receiving the title upon the death of G,* the **life tenant,** are called *remaindermen,* and the conveyance is a *conveyance in remainder.* The remaindermen receive a fee simple title. The life tenant has only an estate or ownership for his or her life. Immediately upon his or her death or upon the death of some other person named in the conveyance, the title automatically vests in the remaindermen.

If the *conveyance does not specify a person or persons to receive the title upon the death of the life tenant or other specified person,* a life estate in **reversion** is created. Upon the death of life tenant, the title will revert to the grantor or the grantor's heirs. The grantor has a reversionary interest in the estate. Let's use the following examples:

Example 1: Grantor A conveys title by deed to his son for life.

Example 2: Grantor A conveys title by deed to his son for life, and after the death of his son to the Red Cross.

In both examples Grantor A has intentionally created a life estate in his son. Grantor A has given his son a "stick" from the bundle of rights. As long as his son is alive, the son has control, title, and possession. In both examples, the son can sell his ownership interest, but he can sell only what he owns. His ownership ends at his death. Therefore, anyone who buys from the son will lose ownership when the son dies. This outcome makes the sale or mortgage of a life estate unlikely, although not impossible.

FIGURE 2.4 Life estate in reversion.

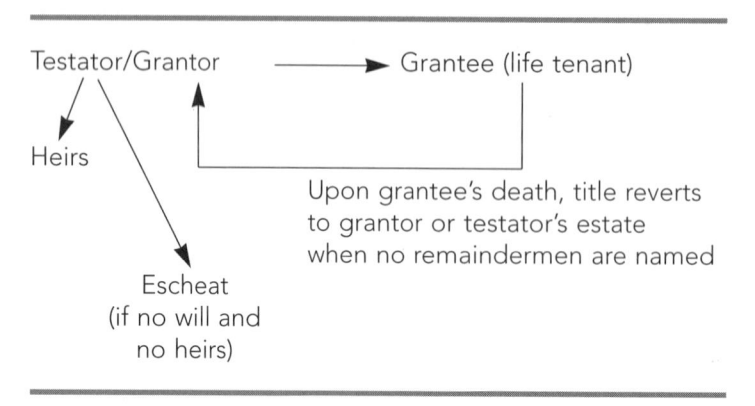

Testator/Grantor ⟶ Grantee (life tenant)
↓
Heirs
↓
Escheat (if no will and no heirs)

Upon grantee's death, title reverts to grantor or testator's estate when no remaindermen are named

FIGURE 2.5 Life estate in remainder.

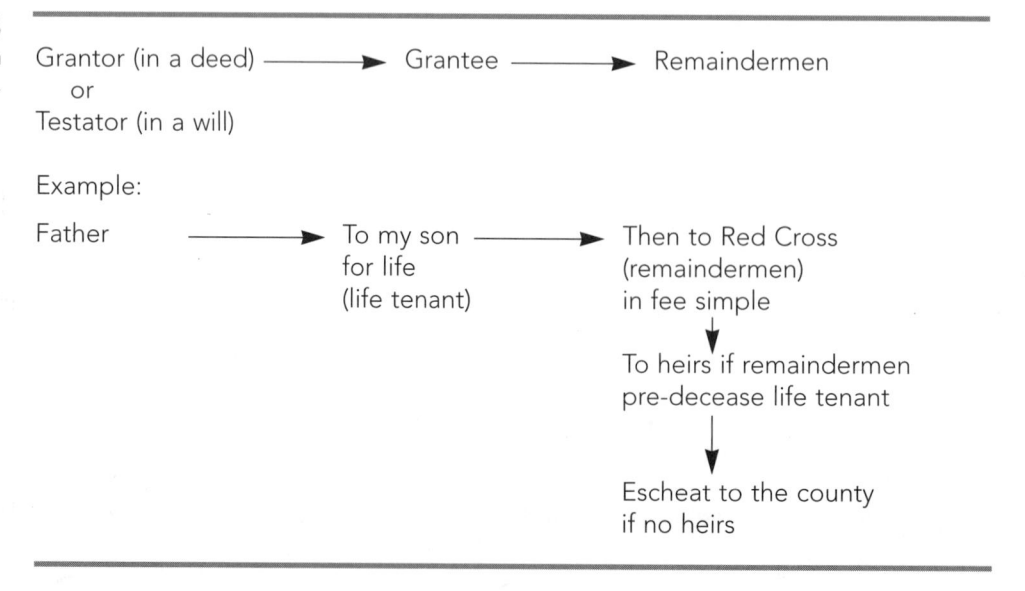

Grantor (in a deed) or Testator (in a will) ⟶ Grantee ⟶ Remaindermen

Example:

Father ⟶ To my son for life (life tenant) ⟶ Then to Red Cross (remaindermen) in fee simple
↓
To heirs if remaindermen pre-decease life tenant
↓
Escheat to the county if no heirs

The real difference in the two examples exists in what occurs at the death of the son. In Example 1, because Grantor A has not designated who or what gets the bundle of sticks at his son's death, the bundle reverts to Grantor A or his heirs if he is deceased. This is the reversionary interest. In Example 2, Grantor A designated that the Red Cross is to receive the bundle of sticks at his son's death. What the Red Cross has is called a *remainder interest.* The Red Cross is a remainderman. Each example displays a conventional life estate. A conventional life estate is one created voluntarily by the parties. This may be accomplished during one's life with a deed or upon death in one's will. Someone or some entity is going to become the owner at some time in the future at the death of the life tenant.

Life estates are by no means worthless. Any ownership right that gives title, possession, and control has value. Nevertheless, life estates are clearly temporary.

Rights and Responsibilities of Life Tenants

The life tenant under any type of life estate has the right of **alienation,** whereby the life tenant *may transfer title to another person or pledge the title as security for debt, but no more than the title.* Of course, the individual cannot give title for a duration longer than the life of the person named in the creation of a life estate to establish its duration, usually himself or herself. The life tenant also has the right to the net income produced by the property, if any.

The life tenant also may legally mortgage the life estate. A lending institution would not likely accept a life estate as security for a mortgage, however, because the estate terminates on the death of the life tenant or some other named person. This is possible, though, if a life insurance policy is obtained to protect the lender against the life tenant's premature death.

A life tenant has certain responsibilities. Basically, the individual must preserve and protect the estate for the benefit of the remainderman or reversionary interest. The life tenant, however, has a legal right called the right to **estovers.** This right provides that the *life tenant may cut and use reasonable amounts of timber from the land to repair buildings or to use for fuel on the property, but not for profit.* A violation of the right of estovers is called an *act of waste.*

A life tenant has an obligation to pay the real property taxes on the property in which he or she has a life estate. The life tenant also has the duty to pay any assessments levied against the property by a county or a municipality for improvements to the property. Assessments are levied against land for improvements made to the land, such as paving streets and laying water lines and sewer lines.

The life tenant has a duty to make repairs to improvements on the land. He or she cannot permit the property to deteriorate because of lack of repairs and thus cause depreciation to existing improvements. This is called the duty of preservation.

If a life tenant violates these responsibilities, those persons having the remainder or reversionary interest may bring suit to protect the real estate subject to the life estate.

Legal or Statutory Life Estates

In addition to being created by an intentional conveyance (conventional), life estates also can be created by law. As differentiated from life estates created by act of the parties, either by deed or in a will (conventional life estates), *life estates created by operation of law* are called *legal life estates* or *statutory life estates.*

Prior to adoption of the Uniform Probate Code, the most common life estates created by law or statute were dower and curtesy. Both *dower* and *curtesy* refer to an automatic life estate owned by a surviving spouse in inheritable property owned by the deceased spouse alone during the marriage. If the owner of the land was the husband, the wife has a life estate called *dower.* If the owner of the land was the wife, the husband has a life estate called *curtesy.* Illinois is one of several states that do not recognize these statutory or legal life estates. Dower and curtesy should not be confused with community property laws.

Illinois and some other states recognize a homestead life estate for a surviving spouse. A homestead life estate (discussed later in this chapter) is available only on the family home, not on all the inheritable property, as with dower and curtesy.

In states where dower and curtesy have been abolished, such as in Illinois, a substitute usually is provided by intestate succession as set out in the Uniform Probate Code. **Intestate succession** statutes set forth *the manner in which the property of an intestate* (one who has died without leaving a valid will) *is distributed to heirs.*

Illinois provides that the estate of a person who dies without a will (intestate) will be probated to ascertain who will inherit the estate. The estate then is distributed according to the Illinois Law of Descent and Distribution (see Figure 6.1 in Chapter 6). From these requirements, one can readily see the importance for both husband and wife to join the conveyance of any property either of them owns while they are married. Title to property owned in severalty requires the signature of the spouse only if the title being conveyed is the family homestead property.

Homestead

Another form of legal life estate that provides protection for a limited amount of equity in a home is called the **homestead** exemption. This exemption *allows every Illinois resident an estate of homestead in the principal place of residence.* An amount of up to $7,500 per individual but a maximum of $15,000 is protected from unsecured creditors. The protection continues to exist for a surviving spouse and any children up to age 18 as long as they live in the homestead residence. This exemption exists without having to provide notice. Homestead rights are released or waived only in writing and with the signature of the individual or, if married, both spouses.

Putting It to Work

Those holding title to real estate in severalty in Illinois, if married, may be required to have the spouse's signature to release possible homestead estate rights.

Nonfreehold Estates (Leasehold Estates)

A **nonfreehold estate,** also called a **leasehold estate,** is a *less than freehold estate* (less than a lifetime) and therefore is of *limited duration.* Leasehold, or *rental* estates, are *created by a contract called a lease or rental agreement,* which provides contractual rights and duties to both parties. Leasehold estates *grant possession, but not title, to the tenant.* Title stays with the owner. Leasehold estates create the relationship of lessor (landlord) and lessee (tenant) between the parties. These estates may be called estates, tenancies, or leaseholds. This chapter deals with freehold estates. Leaseholds will be discussed in Chapter 13.

Ownership of Real Property

Ownership of real property may be by one person alone or by many persons or even by non-natural entities such as partnerships and corporations. Co-ownership of property may be used to control transfer of the property at death or to allow pooling monies to purchase an investment, which then will be owned by several people. Co-ownership can happen accidentally or may require intentional action and words.

When acquiring property, buyers have many options in how to acquire the property. The various choices are referred to as *vesting options.* The vesting is shown in a deed (or will) immediately following the names of the grantee(s) (or devisees).

Vesting options may range from a basic tenancy in common to a complicated tenancy in partnership or trust agreement. The various options create stronger or weaker responsibilities and rights between co-owners with respect to one another. A co-owner's conduct may be very different under different vesting with different rights.

PUTTING IT TO WORK

The decision regarding vesting is vastly important to buyers, although they probably do not realize this. Real estate licensees should know the vesting alternatives and inform the buyer of the importance of the decision, as well as the various alternatives available, but they should be careful not to practice law or give legal advice. A statement such as "joint tenancy is always best for a married couple" exposes the licensee to liability, and deservedly so.

Ownership in Severalty

When *title to real property is held in the name of only one person or entity,* it is called ownership in **severalty,** because the interest is "severed" from all others. The person or entity holding title is the sole or only owner. If *the titleholder marries,* the property is called **separate property.** The owning spouse holds title separately from the other spouse. Again, those holding title to real estate in severalty, if married, may be required to have the spouse's signature to release possible homestead estate rights.

Concurrent Ownership

Simultaneous ownership of real property by two or more people is called **co-ownership.** That term is used rather than joint ownership because the word "joint" describes a specific type of ownership. There are various types of co-ownership. The rights of the owners depend upon the type of ownership they have. The types of co-ownership are: tenancy in common, joint tenancy, tenancy by the entirety, and community property. To adequately understand the distinctions among the co-ownerships, the difference between right of survivorship and right of inheritance must be understood. **Right of survivorship** means that *if one (or more) of the co-owners dies, the surviving co-owners automatically receive the interest of the deceased co-owner.* Right of survivorship defeats passing of title by will. The last survivor of all of the co-owners owns the entire property in severalty. **Right of inheritance,** by contrast, means that *a co-owner's share of the real estate will pass at his death to his heirs or in accordance with his last will and testament.*

Concurrent ownerships such as tenancy in common, joint tenancy, and tenancy by the entirety require certain unities of ownership: *time, title, interest, and possession.* For the co-ownership to be recognized, the different concurrent ownerships require one or more of the unities between the co-owners. The unity of time exists when co-owners receive their title at the same time in the same document or conveyance. The unity of title exists if the co-owners have the same type of ownership, such as a life estate, fee simple, or conditional fee. The unity of interest exists if the co-owners all have the same percentage of ownership. The unity of possession exists if all co-owners have the right to possess or access any and all portions of the property owned without physical division. This type of possession is called *possession of an undivided interest.*

Tenancy in Common

Tenancy in common is characterized by *two or more persons holding title to a property at the same time.* The only required unity is that of possession. Any two or more parties can hold title as tenants in common. Each tenant in common holds an undivided possession of the entire property, rather than any specific portion of it. There is no right of survivorship; upon the death of a tenant in common, the deceased's share will go to the person's heir or as designated in the last will and testament.

Tenancies in common may occur when property is inherited by more than one person. If the will does not designate the type of co-ownership, or in the event of no will, the inheriting parties receive title as tenants in common.

In the event the deed does not name the type of tenancy being conveyed, Illinois presumes that all grantees will hold title as tenants in common. If the deed does not specify each tenant's proportional share, all are presumed to own equal, undivided shares.

A tenant in common may sell his or her share to anybody without destroying the tenancy relationship. Each tenant in common also may individually pledge only his or her share of the property as security for a loan that creates a lien or encumbrance against that share only, not the entire property. If the loan is not repaid and the lien of one co-owner is foreclosed, the property foreclosed upon is only that share belonging to the defaulting co-owner. Tenants in common do not have to have equal interest in the property. For example, one co-tenant may hold one-half interest and two other co-tenants may hold one-quarter each.

A tenant in common may bring legal action to have the property *partitioned* so each tenant may have a specific and divided portion of the property exclusively. If this can be done equitably with a piece of land, each would receive title to a separate tract according to his or her share of interest. If this cannot physically be done to the land, the court may order the sale of the property with appropriate shares of the proceeds distributed to the tenants in common.

Joint Tenancy

The **joint tenancy** form of co-ownership normally *requires all four unities of time, title, interest, and possession,* although Illinois provides for one exception to the requirement of the four unities. A deed may be granted by a sole owner to himself and "others as joint tenants and not as tenants in common" and thereby create a joint tenancy. Otherwise, joint tenants must have the same interest in the property, must receive their title at the same time from the same source, must have the same percentage of ownership, and must have the right to undivided possession in the property. For example, if there are three joint tenants, each must own one-third interest in the property, they must all receive their title from the same conveying document (will or deed), each must own the same type of freehold (fee simple, life estate, or conditional fee), and each must have the right to possession and use of any and all portions of the property.

A special characteristic of joint tenancy is the *right of survivorship.* When one joint tenant dies, his or her share goes automatically to other surviving joint tenants equally, instead of passing to the heirs of the deceased. A joint tenant therefore cannot convey ownership by will. By acquiring as a joint tenancy, each joint tenant gives up the right of inheritance (control over passage of the property).

If a joint tenant, prior to his death, sells his share of ownership, the person purchasing this share will not become a joint tenant with the others. The necessary four unities will not exist. The document that gives title to the new purchaser is not at the same time as the document giving title to the original joint tenants. The unity of time has been destroyed. The new co-owner thus will enter the relationship as a tenant in common. The remaining original joint tenants continue as joint tenants, with the right of survivorship among themselves. The new purchaser, as a tenant in common with the original joint tenants, will be able to pass his share at his death to his heirs or by will.

PUTTING IT TO WORK

> Many investment partners will acquire title as joint tenants thinking that the stronger link between co-owners will create a more desirable, stronger partnership. This usually is not what unrelated investors want. The partners will not likely want to waive their rights of inheritance and thereby "shut out" their heirs. What they probably want is a tenancy in common or a more formal tenancy in partnership outlining their rights and duties to each other. As indicated earlier, however, the real estate licensee should not offer advice on these matters but, instead, refer buyers to legal counsel.

In Illinois a court will not recognize a joint tenancy unless the deed of conveyance makes it absolutely clear that the parties intend the right of survivorship.

A joint tenancy also is subject to partition through legal action, just as a tenancy in common.

Tenancy by the Entirety

Ownership as **tenants by the entirety** is *limited to husband and wife.* To receive title as tenants by the entirety, husband and wife must have a legal marriage at the time they receive title to the property. In Illinois, however, it *is* necessary for the deed to read "to husband and wife as tenants by the entirety" to create a tenancy by the entirety. (A tenancy by the entirety is not automatically created.)

Like a joint tenancy, tenancy by the entirety contains the right of survivorship. Upon the death of one spouse, the surviving spouse automatically receives title to the property by operation of law. Creation of a tenancy by the entirety *requires unity of time, title, interest, possession, and marriage.* In Illinois, only the homestead property may be held as tenants by the entirety.

A husband or wife owning land as tenants by the entirety may not legally convey or pledge property as security to a third party without the other spouse joining in the deed or pledge instrument. A spouse who is a tenant by the entirety may convey her interest to the other spouse with only the signature of the conveying spouse on the deed. There can be no action for partition of real estate held as tenants by the entirety.

Tenancy by the entirety exists only as long as the tenants hold title to the property and are legally married. Tenancy by the entirety is abolished automatically by decree of divorce. A mere legal separation is not sufficient. When a final decree of absolute divorce is obtained, the ownership is automatically changed to tenancy in common by operation of law, eliminating the right of survivorship.

If they elect to do so, married people may own property as tenants in common. They do not have to take title as tenants by the entirety. A husband or wife also may own separate property in severalty. In Illinois, the other spouse has to join in the deed if the title is to be conveyed, to be certain that no spousal claim is remaining after the conveyance.

FIGURE 2.6 Comparison of the forms of co-ownership.

JOINT TENANCY WITH RIGHT OF SURVIVORSHIP	TENANCY IN COMMON	TENANCY BY THE ENTIRETY
Always equal interests —each has right to possession of the whole —at death, interest of decedent passes to surviving tenants automatically (right of survivorship)	Not necessarily equal interests —each entitled to possession of the whole —each interest inheritable (no right of survivorship)	Equal interests of husband and wife —each spouse entitled to possession of the whole —divorce converts to a tenancy in common —on death, interest of decedent passes automatically to surviving tenant (right of survivorship)
Must be created on purpose —one deed —equal interests —survivorship must be specified —four unities—time, title, possession, and interest—must exist	May happen accidentally —through inheritance by more than one heir —through purchase in which shares may or may not be equal —through failure to specify joint tenancy with right of survivorship	Created by a deed to a husband and wife
Each tenant has an undivided share in the whole property; is equally responsible for expenses and equally entitled to rents and profits	Each tenant has an undivided share in the whole property; is equally responsible for expenses and equally entitled to rents and profits	Requires the four unities plus the unity of marriage; each is equally responsible for expenses. Only the principal residence can be held in the entirety.
Terminated by sale of one co-tenant or more than one tenant —unities destroyed —new owner is tenant in common	Sale by one co-tenant does not terminate —buyer succeeds to interest; substitution occurs	One member cannot sell his or her interest —right of survivorship is not defeated by attempted sale —divorce converts ownership to tenancy in common

Community Property

Nine states (Arizona, California, Idaho, Louisiana, Nevada, New Mexico, Texas, Washington, and Wisconsin) are **community property** states. By law, in these states, *husband and wife must acquire title to real estate as community property.* A husband and wife may hold title to both real and personal property as community property. They also may hold title separately in severalty, as explained in the following paragraphs.

The theory of community property is that husband and wife share equally in the ownership of property acquired by their joint efforts during the community of marriage. The title to this property will vest in husband and wife as community property whether the deed is made only to the husband, only to the wife, or to both husband and wife.

Although Illinois is not a community property state, the Illinois Marriage and Dissolution of Marriage Act allows the courts to determine the division of marital property. Property acquired during the marriage is considered marital property in which both the husband and wife have joint rights.

Contrary to widely held opinion, there is no right of survivorship in community property, and therefore the one-half interest of a deceased spouse will descend to heirs and will not automatically go to the surviving spouse. To pledge or convey title to community property during life, both husband and wife must sign the pledge or deed.

In community property states, separate property is any property acquired by one spouse during marriage by gift or inheritance. Also, any property purchased with the separate funds of the husband or wife becomes separate property of the purchasing spouse. Property acquired prior to marriage by either husband or wife is also separate property. Because community property states do not recognize dower or curtesy, a spouse may mortgage or convey title to separate property without participation of the other spouse. In these states, separate property is completely under the ownership and control of the spouse holding title in severalty. In most of the community property states, however, both husband and wife must execute deeds and mortgages involving the separate property of either spouse if the property is being used as their home.

COMBINATION FORMS OF OWNERSHIP

Condominiums

The term **condominium** comes from the Latin words meaning "to exercise dominion over" and "together." Thus, condominium developments are *jointly controlled*. Formerly, condominium ownership was not recognized under common law; special statutes were required to create this form of ownership. The first condominium statute enacted in the United States was the California Horizontal Property Act, in 1961. In July 1963 the Illinois Condominium Property Act took effect; it essentially conforms to all fundamental principles cited above. Condominium ownership is now recognized in all states.

PUTTING IT TO WORK

Condominium statutes are called "horizontal property acts" because they authorize a three-dimensional property description, with a property line above and below the condominium. These horizontal property lines create a cube of air space or a volume that is the privately owned condominium. Air rights and area below the land surface are owned as tenants in common.

Though laws creating condominium ownership vary from state to state, the fundamental principles are reasonably uniform. Condominium statutes set forth the manner in which a condominium is to be created and managed. These include a declaration of condominium (master deed), articles of association, and the bylaws. The declaration, articles of association, and bylaws must be recorded in the public record in the county where the property is located. If all the owners agree, along with the lienholders of record, the property can be removed from the Condominium Property Act. Title then would be held by all owners as tenants in common.

Condominium ownership is a way of life as well as a type of concurrent ownership. Condominiums come in all shapes and sizes. They may be one story or many stories. They may be residential, industrial, or commercial. They may be new construction or conversion of a present structure. Condominium ownership is a combination of ownerships—individual unit plus co-ownership of the *common areas* available to all owners in the condominium project. The individual unit may be held as a fee in severalty, fee in joint tenancy, fee in common, or fee as tenants by the entireties. Common areas, such as the yard, roof, hallways, elevators, pool, tennis courts, and parking lots, are owned as tenants in common. Some common elements are considered **limited common elements**, or *part of the common elements that only a particular unit owner has the right to use.* Assigned parking spaces, balconies, and storage lockers are limited common elements. Someone who purchases a unit does not get a deed for these areas, which are not part of the owner's defined air space; however, only the owner has the right to use them.

The *legal description of the condominium facility* is found in the **declaration,** or **master deed.** The declaration contains a plat of the property showing the location of buildings, plans and specifications for the buildings and the various units, a description of the common areas, and the degree of ownership in the common areas available to each individual unit owner. The declaration also sets forth the specific purpose of the condominium facility. It also may include a *right of first refusal* clause, giving the association the first opportunity to purchase an individual owner's unit if the owner wishes to sell, though this is fairly rare.

Title to the individual unit may be transferred by deed or by leaving it to an heir by will. Title to the individual unit may be encumbered by a mortgage or a mechanic's lien (discussed in Chapter 3).

Real property taxes are levied against the title to an individual unit. Marketable title to the individual unit is evidenced by an abstract of title or title insurance policy. The individual unit basically is treated like any other single-family dwelling. Condominium units may be purchased with cash or financed.

Certain condominiums can be financed with FHA or VA mortgages. Condominiums qualifying for these mortgages must be in projects that HUD or the VA has approved. This approval would have to have been sought for the entire project by the developer during construction or by a converter during the conversion. The VA and the FHA do not give approvals on individual condominium units. An FHA- or VA-approved lender can provide the list of approved projects.

Units also can be sold on contract for deed. If the individual unit's taxes or mortgage is not paid, only the individual unit will be placed in a tax sale or a foreclosure action. The other units in the condominium facility will not be affected.

Title to the common areas is held as a tenant in common with all other unit owners. The common areas are the responsibility of all unit owners. The *articles of association* establish an association to provide for maintenance and management of the common areas. The articles of association also establish the method and procedure for assessing the individual unit owners for each unit's share of the common maintenance items such as mowing, painting, and landscaping. If an individual unit owner fails or refuses to pay this assessment, the association may bring legal action against the unit owner to collect the unpaid assessment. If the individual unit owner files bankruptcy and thus cannot be forced to pay the assessment, the other unit owners will be required to pay an additional prorated assessment for the defaulting unit owner.

The *bylaws* are the operative rules for the condominium facility and individual unit owners. The bylaws set forth the officers of the association, who are usually owners of the individual units in the facility. They are elected by the individual unit owners and serve for the benefit of the whole. The bylaws also set out the method and procedure for amending the bylaws, declaration, and articles of association.

By the same token, many local governments have enacted conversion ordinances to protect tenants whose buildings may be submitted to the Condominium Property Act. Tenant rights may include first-purchase rights, extension of lease, and disclosure of material facts concerning the property.

In Illinois, buildings on leased land cannot be considered for condominium ownership.

PUTTING IT TO WORK

It should be noted that Illinois law requires the board of managers of a condominium association, in addition to its other responsibilities, to maintain fire and extended coverage insurance on the property for full replacement cost.

Cooperatives

The same types of structures that house condominiums can also house cooperative ownership. Cooperatives can be new construction or conversion of a present structure.

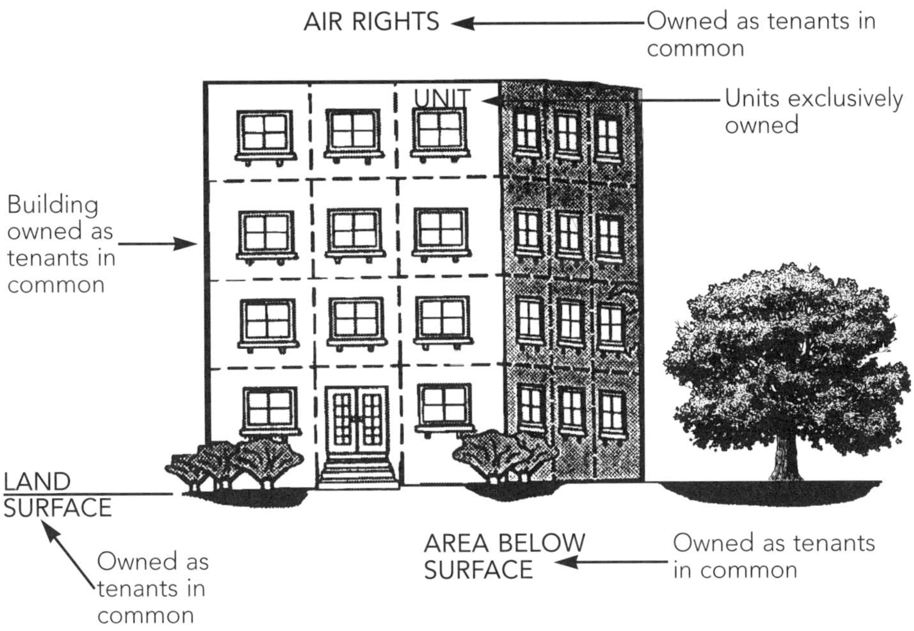

FIGURE 2.7 Condominium ownership.

They can be residential or commercial. Cooperatives can be single story or multi-story. The type and form of ownership in a cooperative, however, are vastly different from ownership in a condominium facility.

In a **cooperative,** the *buildings, land, all real property rights, and interests are owned by a corporation in severalty.* Cooperatives, like any corporation, are set up under state corporation laws. The title to the property, as shown on the deed, is in the name of the corporation. The shareholders of the corporation are tenants in the building. The tenants have the right of occupancy as evidenced by a *proprietary lease,* which is usually an estate for years and for a long period of time. Thus, ownership in a cooperative is really ownership of shares of stock in a corporation plus a long-term lease for the apartments. There is no tenancy in common ownership in the common areas, even though all tenants can use the common areas. The common areas, as all of the building, are owned in fee by the corporation.

An owner in a cooperative does not receive a deed, an abstract of title, or title insurance. An owner in a cooperative does not own real estate in the typical sense, although the Internal Revenue Service considers this as ownership by recognizing the traditional benefits of home ownership such as mortgage interest and property tax deductions (on a pro rata basis). The only real property interest the shareholders hold is a leasehold estate providing the right to possession of an apartment and use of the common areas. As lessees, the shareholders pay no rent but do pay an assessment to cover the cost of maintaining and operating the building, real property taxes, and debt service if the corporation has placed a mortgage against the real estate. The shareholder's rights and obligations are specified in the lease and the corporation's bylaws.

A **right of first refusal** often exists in favor of the corporation. It *requires a selling shareholder to first offer the share of stock to the corporation before sale to an outside buyer is allowed.* If a right of first refusal does not exist, there is usually a right of approval before cooperative stock may be sold. Either of these features has a tendency to restrict or inhibit the resale potential for cooperatives. In addition, if there is high vacancy or economic recession among the owners, causing some people not to pay assessments, the corporation may be forced to increase assessments among remaining owners to keep the bills paid.

Timesharing

Timesharing, another relatively new form of ownership, stretches the common law meaning of real estate ownership. Timesharing *combines the ownership or use of a condominium (or other separate unit) in fee with the sharing of use of the unit by many owners.* In Illinois, timeshare units can be either a timeshare estate with a deed granting fee ownership including the right to use of the space for a specified period of less than one year on a recurring basis of more than three years, or a timeshare *use,* not ownership, of the space for a specified period of time less than one year on a recurring basis of more than three years. *Co-ownership based upon intervals of time* is called **interval ownership.** Several different people purchase the condominium unit in fee and then divide the use of the unit by weeks or months. Each owner of the unit purchases the exclusive right to use of the unit for the specified period of time.

Timesharing is especially attractive to people wishing to purchase a condominium for vacationing purposes. Many people vacation two to four weeks a year. Purchasing a timeshare allows them to enjoy a vacation home without year-round expense. Maintenance and repair costs, taxes, insurance, and general care of the timeshared property are prorated among the interval owners. The percentage of the expense equals the percentage of the year purchased. Owners of a timeshare interest also hope that the property will increase in value, building up equity and at the same time providing them housing while they vacation.

Timeshare ownership has become so popular that programs for exchanging timeshare units are now available. The exchange programs allow the owner of specified time at a property to trade that time with the owner of a specified time at a totally different property. For example, the owner of a timeshare in Illinois could trade for use of a timeshare of equal time in Maine.

The Illinois Real Estate Time-Share Act became effective in 1985 and today covers the sale of timeshares sold or marketed to Illinois residents, whether these timeshares are located in or out of Illinois. Under the Real Estate License Act, timeshares are considered real estate, and therefore those selling timeshares in Illinois (regardless of the location of the timeshares) are required to have an Illinois sales or broker's license. The Time-Share Act is administered by the Office of Banks and Real Estate (OBRE). Registration of timeshares with the office is required, along with the payment of certificate fees and the posting of surety bonds. Certificates and licenses of persons issued under this act can be suspended or revoked for violation of the act.

Complete disclosure concerning the developer and the project in the form of a **public offering statement** must be given to the prospect. The purchaser has three business days from the signing of the contract or the receipt of the public offering statement, whichever is later, to cancel the contract. Any down payment or earnest money received must be refunded within 14 days after the receipt of the notice of cancellation.

Timeshares used as a part of a promotion are subject to this act. All of the contest rules, quantity, value, and method of awarding the prizes are to be completely disclosed to the purchaser.

REAL PROPERTY OWNERSHIP BY BUSINESS ORGANIZATIONS

Business organizations can take several different forms including sole proprietorship, partnership, corporation, limited liability companies, syndicate, joint venture, and real estate investment trust. All of these business organizations can receive, hold, and convey title in the same ways individuals do.

Sole Proprietorship

A **sole proprietorship** is simply *a business owned by one individual.* An individual may use his or her own name as the name of the business or may assume a name for business purposes. Under the assumed name, the owner is sometimes referred to as DBA (doing business as) or AKA (also known as) a fictitious name. The sole proprietor can receive, hold, and convey title to real estate either in his or her name or in the assumed name of the business.

If the business name does not contain the owner's surname, the business must be registered with the proper authority in the county in which the business is located. The owner of a sole proprietorship is fully liable for all business debts. If business debts exceed business assets, the owner's personal assets may be attached by creditors to satisfy defaulted debts. Filing bankruptcy by the business alone will not alleviate possible attachment of the owner's personal assets to satisfy business debts. In a sole proprietorship, the business and the owner are one and the same.

Partnership

A **partnership** is *a form of business organization in which the business is owned by two or more persons, called partners.* A partnership is created by contract between the partners. This contract or agreement should establish the partners' ownership and management rights and obligations. The partners do not have to have the same degree of interest in the partnership or the same extent of management authority or be the same type of partners, limited or general (see below). The contract or agreement also should contain the method and procedure for dividing ownership interest upon the withdrawal, death, or removal of a partner. The purpose of this portion of the agreement, usually called the buy–sell agreement, is to control the change in partners without significantly disrupting business operations. At the death or withdrawal of a partner, the other partners may not want to have the estate as a partner or a stranger to the organization as a partner.

Under the Uniform Partnership Act, which has been adopted by most states and was enacted in Illinois in 1917, a partnership may hold title to real property in the name of the partnership as a tenancy in partnership. In addition, under the common law, partnerships may hold title to real property in the names of the individual partners.

The partners may be of two categories: general or limited. In *general partnerships,* the partners are personally liable for partnership debts exceeding partnership assets. Partners are jointly (together) and severally (separately) liable for these debts. Joint and several liability means that the creditors can attach the assets of all of the partners or any one of the partners to satisfy the debt. If one of the partners files bankruptcy, this does not relieve the other partners of the debt.

A *limited partnership* consists of one or more general partners who are jointly and severally liable and one or more special, silent, or limited partners who contribute money or other assets of value to the extent of their ownership interest. Limited partners are not liable for the debts of the partnership beyond the amount of money they have contributed or have agreed to contribute to the partnership. To retain the protected status from partnership debts, a limited partner may not participate in managing the partnership. If limited partners exert any management authority, they lose the protection beyond limited liability. Limited partners thus may become general partners by their mere actions.

The limited partnership organization is used frequently in real estate investments. Typically, a general partner conceives of the investment opportunity and then solicits monies from limited partners to purchase, construct, or improve a property. The general partners do all of the work and management necessary to create the investment. The limited partners provide the funds to purchase the investment. The return on the investment is divided among the partners—both general and limited—on a predetermined basis as set out in the partnership agreement. The purpose of the investment may be to provide an income stream or to improve a property and sell the improved property at a higher price.

The Illinois Real Estate License Act requires persons who practice real estate in the form of a partnership to file an application with the Office of Banks and Real Estate, pay the proper fees, and provide other documentation as required by the rules. Every general partner must hold a license as a real estate broker. All employees who act as salespersons must hold either a real estate salesperson or broker license. All licensed salespersons who have ownership must be limited partners. The Illinois Real Estate License Act prohibits any salesperson or group of salespersons from owning or controlling more than a 49 percent interest in the partnership.

Corporation

A corporation is an artificial being, invisible, intangible, and existing only pursuant to law. A corporation is a thing, a taxable legal entity recognized by law with tax rates separate from individual income tax rates. Corporations did not exist at common law. A corporation is created by a charter granted by the state of incorporation. Evidence of incorporation is called a certificate of incorporation.

The corporation's activities are essentially limited to the state within which it is incorporated, and it may not "do business" in another state without permission. Thus, a corporation is initially geographically bound. Permission to conduct business in another state is granted by the Secretary of State in the state where business is desired to be conducted. A corporation is called a *domestic corporation* within the state in which it is incorporated. A corporation doing business in another state is called a *foreign corporation* in that state.

Corporations are divided into two basic classes according to their objectives and purposes. *Public corporations* are the various governmental corporations such as cities, towns, counties, school districts, and special bodies for public improvements. *Private corporations* are not organized to perform governmental functions. Private corporations can be further divided into "for profit" and "not for profit" corporations.

Not for profit corporations are churches, fraternal organizations, foundations, charitable organizations, and other groups that perform services for the public other than in a governmental capacity. For profit corporations are all other private corporations. Not for profit corporations may be exempt from the real property tax assessments and income tax assessments imposed upon for profit corporations.

Because a corporation exists only upon compliance with the laws of the state of incorporation, if the corporation ever fails to comply with the law, the corporation vanishes. The term for vanishing a corporation is *dissolution*. Dissolution of a corporation is by operation of law (automatic) if compliance with the law ceases. Dissolution of a corporation also may occur upon the vote of shareholders in the corporation. Just as creation of a corporation requires compliance with the state laws, voluntary dissolution by the shareholders requires compliance with any state laws.

A corporation has the power to receive, hold, and convey title to real property for all purposes for which the corporation was created. A corporation is empowered to give a mortgage on real estate to secure a financial debt of the corporation. A corporation also is empowered to hold a mortgage on real estate to secure a debt owed to the corporation. The power to hold, receive, and convey title to real property normally is given expressly in the corporate charter or creating documents. The proper method for conveying property is set out in the corporation's bylaws. The bylaws expressly state which officers, directors, or other persons must sign conveying documents and whether a special corporate resolution or meeting is required to authorize the conveyance.

The Illinois Real Estate License Act requires persons who organize their real estate business as a corporation to file an application and other supporting documents with the OBRE. In a real estate business organized as a corporation, only those officers actively engaged in the real estate part of the business must have real estate broker's licenses. Officers or shareholders not engaging in real estate activities need not be licensed. The corporation may hire a licensed broker to manage the day-to-day operations. All employees who act as salespersons must hold either a broker's or salesperson license. An individual salesperson or group of salespersons cannot directly or indirectly control or own more than 49 percent of the shares of stock in the corporation.

Limited Liability Company

In January 1994 the Illinois Legislature passed the Illinois Limited Liability Company Act (LLC). Limited liability companies have become more popular in recent years, and Illinois joins the majority of states that have passed LLC legislation. The **limited liability company** *provides the liability protection of a corporation, but is taxed as a partnership.* There is a manager rather than a president, and the investors are called members rather than partners or shareholders. An LLC has membership interests rather than stock. The members in the LLC are liable only for the amount of capital invested and are not liable for the company's debts.

In January 1995 Illinois amended the Illinois Real Estate License Act to allow the licensing of real estate businesses as LLCs. In a real estate LLC, all of the members must be licensed as Illinois real estate brokers.

Syndication

Syndication denotes multiple joint participation in a real estate investment. The syndication may involve joining of assets and talents of individuals, general partnerships, limited partnerships, or corporations in some combination. Although the people and entities invest in real estate, some investors are hoping to make money based solely on the efforts of another without liability, so the organization may be considered to be dealing in securities. An investment is a **security,** as defined by the Federal Securities Act of 1933, if it is:

- *an investment of money*
- *a common or joint enterprise*
- *undertaken for the purpose of making a profit*
- *one in which profit will be derived solely or substantially from the management efforts of others*

Because most syndications intend to make a profit for many from the efforts of a few, they must comply with the rules and regulations of the **Securities and Exchange Commission (SEC),** which *regulates the sale and issuing of securities.* Syndications typically are used in cases of multiple, continuing projects that require the investment of substantial amounts of money from many different sources.

Licensing for the sales of securities on the federal level requires an applicant to pass a test given by the **National Association of Securities Dealers Regulatory (NASDR).**

In some cases, the registration of securities on the federal level with the SEC is exempt. Individual states have their own security laws, collectively known as **blue sky laws,** that *regulates securities issued within their borders.* The security issued may have to be registered and approved by the state's chief security office. In Illinois, securities are registered with the Secretary of State. In 1911, Kansas became the first state to pass its own security laws. The Kansas legislature was reacting to land sale schemes that had defrauded investors. It was said that the defrauded investors might just as well have purchased a chunk of the "blue sky."

Joint Venture

A joint venture is an organization formed by two or more parties for the purpose of investing in real estate or any other type of investment. The joint venture may be in the form of a corporation or a partnership, or the parties may hold title as joint tenants or as tenants in common. Joint ventures usually are devised for only one project.

Trust

A **trust** is a *legal relationship under which title to property is transferred to a person known as a trustee.* The beneficiary of the trust has all the benefits of ownership but not legal title. There is a fiduciary relationship between the trustee and the beneficiary. Any assets, real or personal, may be held in trust. Anyone can create a trust, naming anyone, including oneself, as beneficiary, trustee, or both.

Land Trust

Illinois allows title to real property to be held in a **land trust.** A land trust is *created by transferring the title of the land to a trustee, who holds the title for the benefit of the beneficiaries.* The trustee's power and duties are expressly set out in the document establishing the trust. Persons wishing to place their real property in a trust would use a *deed in trust.* The owner(s) of the property or the trustor names a trustee who will hold legal title to the property. The trustee is required to manage and control the property in accordance with the trust agreement as established by the trustor. The named beneficiary is usually the trustor. The trust is operated for the benefit of the beneficiary, who has the right of possession and to the income generated from the property or the income from sale of the property.

Many advantages can be derived from having title to real property held in a land trust, the foremost of which is that the name of the beneficiary can be concealed. This form of ownership also protects the beneficiary against such things as liens and other laws regarding real estate, as the beneficial interest is considered personal property, not real property. The identity of the beneficiary may be revealed under certain circumstances, such as pursuant to an IRS or court order, when in violation of a building ordinance or law, when seeking a license or permit affecting the property in the trust, and when leasing the property to a government agency.

Land trust agreements usually are established for 20 years. This time limit can be lengthened by an extension agreement executed by the beneficiary.

Real Estate Investment Trust (REIT)

Real estate investment trusts (REITs) were created in 1967, stemming from changes in the Internal Revenue Code that became effective in September of 1967. As a result, the beneficiaries were not taxed doubly on trust income. The trust can now earn income from real estate investments without paying trust income tax. To avoid the trust income tax, however, the trust must distribute 95 percent of the ordinarily taxable income to the trust beneficiaries. The beneficiaries then report the income for tax purposes. Congress' stated purpose for this trust tax advantage was to allow and encourage small investors to pool their money to participate in larger real estate transactions and help make financing available for large real estate developments.

The two major investment choices for REITs are (a) to lend or (b) to buy, rent, or sell property. If the REIT primarily lends money for the interest return, it is called a *mortgage REIT.* If the REIT primarily owns, manages, rents, and sells property, it is called an *equity REIT.*

Important Points

1. Real property consists of land and everything attached to the land, including things that grow naturally without requiring planting and cultivation.
2. Annual crops that require planting and cultivation are personal property and are called emblements. (fruids of Industry)
3. Ownership in land includes the surface of the earth and the area above and below the surface, although these rights may be assigned.
4. Inherent ownership rights include air rights, subsurface rights, riparian rights, and littoral rights.
5. Ownership of property may be transferred by accretion, alluvion, and avulsion. Collectively, these terms are called accession rights.
6. A fixture is formerly personal property that has become attached to real property and thus is now a part of the real property.
7. Trade fixtures are items of personal property used in business that even if attached do not become real estate.
8. The status of a fixture can be created by agreement. If not settled by agreement, the court will apply the other four tests: intention of the parties, method of attachment, relationship of the parties, and adaptability of the item.
9. The allodial system of real property ownership used in the United States provides for private ownership of real estate.
10. Estates in land are divided into two groups: freehold estates and estates of less than freehold (nonfreeholds or leaseholds).
11. Freehold estates are the fee simple estates, which are inheritable, and life estates, which are not inheritable.
12. The greatest form of ownership in real property is fee simple absolute.
13. Life estates may be in reversion or in remainder.
14. The duration of a life estate may be measured by the life tenant or by the life of another (pur autre vie).
15. Conventional life estates are those created by someone's intentional act. Legal or statutory life estates are created by operation of law.
16. Property of owners who die without a will is distributed according to the Illinois Law of Descent and Distribution.
17. Illinois residents are allowed a homestead exemption in their principal place of residence. An amount of up to $7,500 per individual (maximum of $15,000) is protected from unsecured creditors.
18. Title to property owned in severalty requires the spouse's signature if the title being conveyed is the family homestead.
19. A life tenant has the right of alienation, the right of encumbrance, the right of possession and enjoyment of the property, and the right to derive certain income from it.
20. A life tenant is obligated to preserve and maintain the property for the benefit of the future owners.
21. The less than freehold estates (also called leasehold estates or nonfreeholds) are estates of limited duration, providing possession and control but not title as in the case of freehold estates.
22. Title held in the name of one person only is called ownership in severalty, and is also called separate property if the owner is married.
23. When two or more persons or organizations hold title concurrently, it is called co-ownership or concurrent ownership. The forms of co-ownership are tenancy in common, joint tenancy, tenancy by the entirety, community property, and certain aspects of condominiums, cooperatives, and timeshares.

24. Illinois considers property to be held as tenants in common if the deed does not specify the way title is to be held.
25. Joint tenancy and tenancy by the entirety include the right of survivorship and require the unities of time, title, interest, and possession. Tenancy by the entirety is restricted to husband and wife and adds the fifth unity of marriage (unity of person).
26. Illinois provides for an exception to the four unities of time, title, interest, and possession in order to create a joint tenancy. An owner in severalty may execute a deed conveying title to himself and others as joint tenants.
27. Only homestead property may be held in tenancy by the entirety in Illinois. For this type of tenancy to be created, the deed must state "to husband and wife as tenants by the entirety."
28. The owner of a condominium unit holds title to the unit either in severalty or as co-owner with another, as well as title to the common areas as tenants in common with the other unit owners.
29. Limited common areas are part of the common areas that only a certain unit holder has the right of use. Examples of limited common elements are storage lockers, balconies, and assigned parking spaces.
30. Creating a condominium requires recording a declaration (also called master deed), articles of association, and bylaws.
31. A cooperative requires stock ownership in a corporation that owns a building containing cooperative apartments. Stockholders occupy apartments under a proprietary lease.
32. Interval ownership of land is called timesharing.
33. Anyone selling in-state or out-of-state timeshares must have an Illinois real estate sales or broker's license. All offerings must be registered with the Office of Banks and Real Estate. Timeshares can be either an estate with fee ownership or use of space without ownership.
34. Illinois allows the purchaser of a timeshare unit three business days from the signing of the contract or the receipt of the public offering statement, whichever is later, to cancel the contract.
35. Business organizations may receive, hold, and convey title to real property.
36. Partnerships are people (two or more) investing in a business or an investment together without setting up a separate legal owner in the form of a corporation.
37. General partnerships have one class of partner only; all partners are fully liable.
38. Limited partnerships have two classes of partner; limited partners are liable only to their extent of investment.
39. A corporation is a separate legal entity created by the investors. A corporation may be subject to greater taxation if certain elections are not timely filed with the IRS.
40. Illinois allows a business entity to be structured as a limited liability company (LLC).
41. Illinois does not allow a salesperson or group of salespersons to own or control more than 49 percent of a real estate business arranged as a corporation, limited liability company, or partnership.
42. Other business or investment structures include syndications, joint ventures, sole proprietorships, and real estate investment trusts (REITs).
43. Property may be placed in a land trust via a deed in trust. The trustor (owner) names a trustee (holder of legal title), who manages the property for the named beneficiary (usually the owner). The beneficial interest is personal property. The identity of the owner of the real property in a land trust can be concealed.

Review Questions

Answers to these questions are found in the Answer Key section at the back of the book.

1. Personal property attached to real property is prevented from becoming real property by which of the following?
   a. ownership in severalty
   b. ownership as tenants in common
   c. security interest and financing statement (UCC)
   d. right of survivorship

2. An estate in fee simple determinable is an example of a:
   a. freehold estate
   b. nondefeasible fee
   c. nonfreehold estate
   d. leasehold estate

3. If a widow inherits an estate by will, which grants her the right of use and possession of a parcel of land for the rest of her life with the provision that the estate will go to her children in fee simple upon her death, she has received:
   a. an inheritable freehold estate
   b. a life estate in remainder
   c. a life estate in reversion
   d. a fee simple absolute

4. The highest and best form of estate in real property is a:
   a. leasehold for years
   b. defeasible fee
   c. life estate in reversion
   d. fee simple absolute

5. All of the following are concurrent forms of ownership EXCEPT:
   a. tenants in common
   b. joint tenancy
   c. tenancy by the entirety
   d. severalty

6. Which of the following statements regarding the homestead exemption in Illinois is NOT true:
   a. every resident in Illinois is allowed a homestead exemption in the principal place of residence.
   b. the protection exists for the surviving spouse and all of the children of any age
   c. each individual is protected from unsecured creditors in an amount of up to $7,500
   d. notice is not required to create the exemption

7. All of the following are rights or responsibilities of a life tenant EXCEPT:
   a. estovers
   b. inchoate dower
   c. alienation
   d. preservation

8. A, B, and C own property as joint tenants. If A dies, what happens to A's shares?
   a. A's shares pass to B and C
   b. A's shares pass to A's heirs
   c. A's shares must be sold to either B or C
   d. A's shares pass to A's spouse

9. Which of the following forms of ownership cannot be partitioned:
   a. tenancy by the entirety
   b. tenancy in common
   c. joint tenancy
   d. community property

10. Of the following, which is not a limited common element:
    a. balconies
    b. storage lockers
    c. assigned parking spaces
    d. swimming pool

11. Which best describes the first condominium statute enacted in the U.S.:
    a. Master Deed
    b. Horizontal Property Act
    c. Declaration of Condominium
    d. Law of Cooperative Exclusions

12. Illinois recognizes all of the following ways to hold title to real property EXCEPT:
    a. tenancy in common
    b. dower and curtesy
    c. joint tenancy
    d. tenancy by the entirety

13. Title to real property held in the name of one person only is owned:
    a. in severalty
    b. as tenancy in common
    c. as tenancy by the entirety
    d. as joint tenancy

14. Which of the following type of ownership requires unity of interest, title, time, and possession:
    a. cooperative
    b. tenancy in common
    c. joint tenancy
    d. community property

15. In Illinois, ownership as tenants by the entirety is NOT:
    a. limited to husband and wife
    b. limited to the homestead estate
    c. granted automatically in a deed
    d. abolished automatically by a decree of divorce

16. Which of the following includes the right of survivorship:
    a. cooperative
    b. tenancy in common
    c. joint tenancy
    d. community property

17. The purchaser of a condominium unit receives title to the land and common areas whereon the condominium is situated as a:
    a. tenant by the entirety
    b. tenant in common
    c. joint tenant
    d. tenant in severalty

18. All of the following are true of the purchaser of a condominium timeshare EXCEPT:
    a. she receives a title for the same time period(s) each calendar year
    b. she may convey this title to anyone else
    c. she owns a share of stock in the land and a proprietary lease in the unit
    d. she will pay a prorated share of the maintenance

19. In the cooperative form of ownership:
    a. ownership is evidenced by shares of stock in a corporation holding title to the building
    b. each owner owns a fee simple interest in the land on which the building is located
    c. all owners pay real property taxes on their individual units
    d. each owner holds a freehold interest in the land

20. In Illinois a joint tenant may do all of the following with his interest EXCEPT:
    a. sell his interest in the property
    b. pledge his interest as security for a mortgaged loan
    c. pass his interest by will
    d. gift his interest prior to death

21. Ownership as tenants by the entirety includes:
    a. the right of one owner to convey title to her share of ownership without the participation of the other owner
    b. the right of survivorship
    c. ownership of an unequal interest in the property with another
    d. conversion to ownership as joint tenants if the owners are divorced

22. Condominium owners may own:
    a. a unit as joint tenants in fee simple and the common elements in determinable fee
    b. a unit as tenants in common and the common areas as joint tenants
    c. a unit as joint tenants and the common elements as tenants in common
    d. a unit as joint tenants while the common elements are owned by the condominium association

23. All of the following statements regarding timeshares in Illinois are true EXCEPT:

    a. persons selling timeshares must hold an Illinois real estate broker's license
    b. persons selling timeshares must register with the Office of Banks and Real Estate
    c. timeshare units must be sold with a deed granting fee ownership
    d. timeshare units can be sold granting ownership or use of the space

24. Which of the following statements is TRUE concerning a land trust in Illinois?

    a. the owner of property in a land trust cannot be concealed
    b. the owner of property in a land trust cannot be named the beneficiary
    c. a trust deed is used to place property in a land trust
    d. a land trust agreement usually is established for 20 years

25. Cooperatives are organized under:

    a. federal housing laws
    b. federal corporation laws
    c. state corporation laws
    d. state civil code

26. Under the Illinois Real Estate Time–Share Act, the recission period allowing the buyer to cancel a contract is:

    a. 48 hours
    b. 2 business days
    c. 3 days
    d. 7 business days

27. In an Illinois land trust, the two parties that are most often the same individual are:

    a. trustor and beneficiary
    b. trustee and beneficiary
    c. trustor and trustee
    d. lender and trustee

28. All of the following are considered part of real property EXCEPT:

    a. trees
    b. fences
    c. growing crops
    d. garage

29. Which of the following is NOT true regarding Illinois limited liability companies:

    a. LLCs provide the liability protection of a corporation
    b. LLCs are taxed as a partnership
    c. LLCs are managed by a president and a board of directors
    d. investors in an LLC are called members rather than shareholders

30. Q, R, and S own a piece of commercial property as joint tenants. Q sells her interest to R. R, a single person, later dies leaving a will stating that his share in the property should go to his girlfriend, Ms. X. Which of the following is TRUE?

    a. R is a joint tenant and cannot will his share to Ms. X
    b. R is a joint tenant and Q and R will receive R's share equally
    c. R must will the property first to family before leaving it to nonrelatives
    d. R is a tenant in common and can will his share in the property to Ms. X

CHAPTER 3

Important Terminology

- annual tax sale
- appurtenance
- assessment
- condemnation
- dedication
- dominant tenement
- easement
- easement appurtenant
- easement by condemnation
- easement by grant
- easement by implication
- easement by necessity
- easement by prescription
- easement in gross
- eminent domain
- encroachment
- encumbrance
- equalization factor
- escheat
- execution of judgment
- fair market value
- general lien
- intestate
- judgment
- judgment lien
- license
- lien
- lis pendens
- materialman's lien
- mechanic's lien
- merger
- police power
- priority liens
- restrictive covenants
- running with the land
- scavenger sale
- servient tenement
- special assessment
- specific lien
- statutory redemption period
- testate
- trespasser
- vendee
- vendor
- writ of attachment

Encumbrances and Government Restrictions

IN THIS CHAPTER An **encumbrance** is *anything that lessens the bundle of rights in real property.* It is a stick that has been given away, and thus the remaining bundle is of less value. Most encumbrances are interests in the property that create debt or give use or control, or both, to another. In this chapter we discuss easements, licenses, liens, restrictive covenants, encroachments, and government restrictions. We also discuss the inherent or automatic rights that arise from the ownership of real property. Chapter 11 focuses on other land use controls, private and governmental.

EASEMENTS

An **easement** is *a nonpossessory interest in land owned by another.* Someone who owns an easement right does not own or possess the land where the easement lies. The easement owner merely owns the right to use or have access to the land. The right of ingress and egress (entry and exit) to and from real estate is one primary basis for easements. Other standard needs for easements are for a common wall in a duplex or condominium, the right to take water from the land of another, and the rights to receive light and air. The common terminology for easement is *right-of-way.* The real estate industry recognizes easements in gross and easements appurtenant. These easements can be negative or affirmative. Easements can be created by humans, by law, or by use.

Easements in Gross

An **easement in gross,** also called a commercial easement in gross, provides *a right of use in the land of another without the requirement that the holder of the easement own adjacent land.* This category of easements is usually owned by the government, an agency of the government, or a public utility. Examples are the water lines and electric lines that run underground in most lots in subdivisions. For example, as the owner of an easement in gross, the utility company has the right to place utility lines on the land and to go onto the land to maintain and repair the utilities. Commercial easements in gross are assignable by the owner. The governmental agency or utility that owns the easement right can allow other utilities to use the same easement. The owner of a commercial easement in gross also can sell or assign the right to use the easement to others. For instance, a telephone company can sell to a cable television company the right to place cable lines in the telephone easement.

The easement in gross is the most common form of easement, as virtually all urban and suburban property is subject to several government easements for things such as utilities, roadway widening, and alleyways. Easements in gross also may be held by the private sector. Examples are the right of access allowed to a planned unit development association onto the land of private owners to repair walls or fences or gain access to other common areas.

Much controversy has arisen concerning abandoned railroad easements throughout the United States. The question is: Who owns the land where the railroad tracks used to lie? The answer depends on what kind of "stick" the railroad received when the tracks were laid. If the railroad received a deed for the land, the railroad holds ownership in fee. If, however, the railroad received only an easement in gross, the adjoining landowners own the land, subject to the easement rights of the railroad or the successors in interest of the railroad. The question of railroad rights-of-way has generated so much controversy and litigation that some states have passed laws designating ownership of the railroad easements by statute.

Easements Appurtenant

An **appurtenance** is *a right or privilege that passes with and belongs to the land, but is not necessarily part of the land,* and includes such tangible and intangible items as condominium parking stalls, storage lockers, water rights, and certain easements. The **easement appurtenant** category includes *all easements that are not easements in gross.* For an easement appurtenant to exist, two landowners must be involved; one must receive a benefit and the other must accept a burden. The *land that benefits from an easement appurtenant* is called the **dominant tenement** or estate. The *land that must suffer and allow the use* is called the **servient tenement** or estate.

An example of an easement appurtenant is shown in Figure 3.1. In the illustration, if landowner B sells her property to X, the easement appurtenant follows the transfer of title to the land now owned by X. When *an easement appurtenant follows the transfer of title to land from one owner to another and attaches to the land,* this is called **running with the land.** For an easement to run with the land, the owner of the easement must own land to which the easement attaches (dominant tenement). Just as the dominant nature of the easement appurtenant runs with the land, so does the servient nature run with the land. If A should sell his land to Z, Z must allow B use of the easement.

PUTTING IT TO WORK

The typical purpose of an easement appurtenant is to allow access to some desirable feature, such as water, an access road, or perhaps other land owned by the dominant owner on the other side of the servient owner.

Negative and Affirmative Easements Appurtenant

Easements appurtenant can be divided into two categories: negative and affirmative. The easement appurtenant illustrated in Figure 3.1 is an *affirmative easement.* The dominant tenement or estate is given the right to physically cross the servient tenement. When a *negative easement* appurtenant exists, the dominant tenement does not have the right to physically enter the land of the servient tenement. Instead, the dominant tenement has the right to restrict some activity or use of the servient tenement.

An example of a negative easement is illustrated in Figure 3.2. It shows landowner C bordering the lake and landowner D bordering landowner C. In this case, C is prohibited from erecting a fence or landscaping that would block the view of the lake to D. D does not get to cross C to get to the lake. (If D did have the right to cross

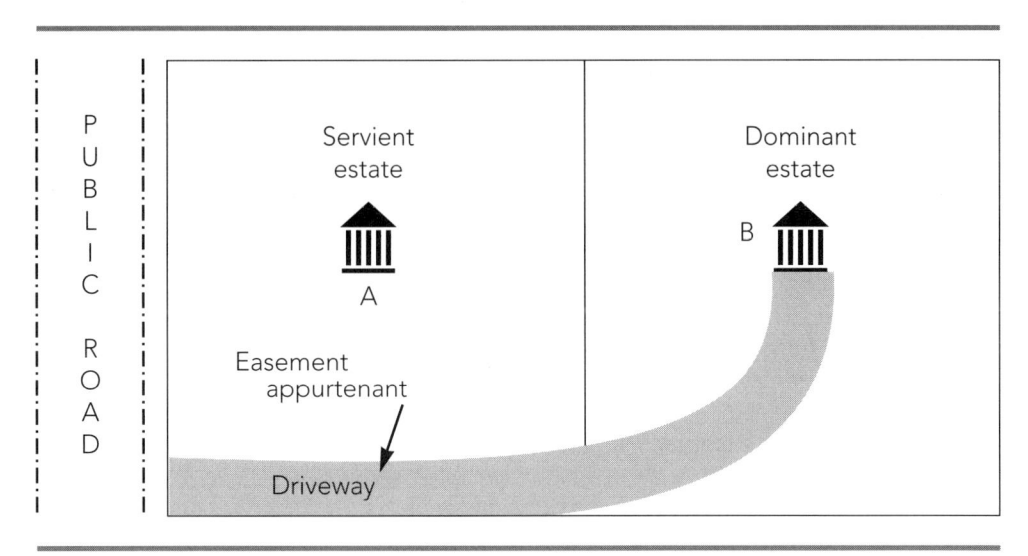

FIGURE 3.1 An example of an easement appurtenant.

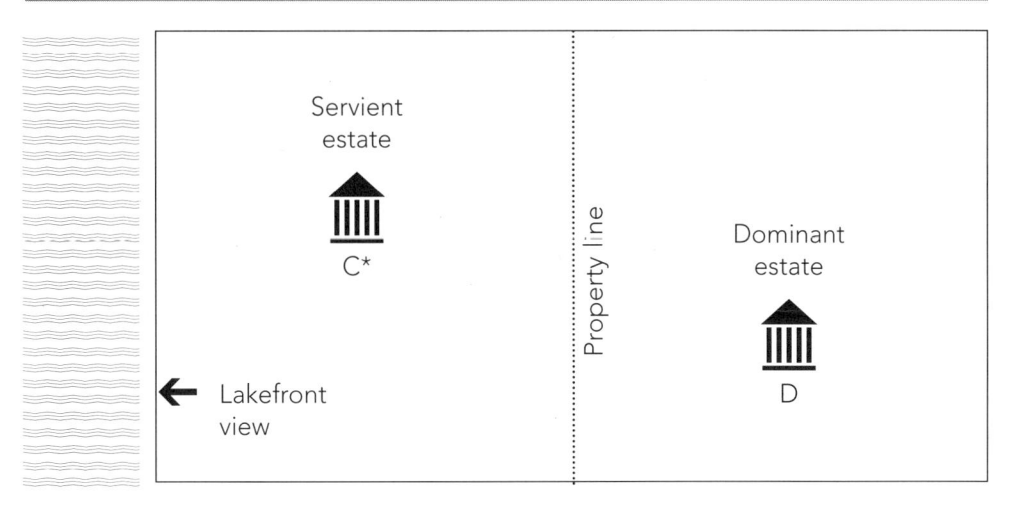

FIGURE 3.2 An example of a negative easement appurtenant.

*Servient tenement C is not allowed to erect fence or landscape in such a way that tenement D's view of the lake will be blocked.

the land to get to the lake, this would be an affirmative easement.) Instead, D merely gets to restrain C in developing her land so as to block the view. This type of negative easement often is called an "easement of light and air," or view easement. Negative and affirmative easements both run with the land.

Typical negative easements appurtenant include view easements, aviation easements, and solar easements. Figure 3.2 illustrates a view easement, by virtue of which the servient tenement cannot block the view of the dominant tenement. An aviation easement exists near airports and dictates that landowners are prohibited from obstructing aircraft flight patterns. A solar easement, similar to a view easement, specifically prohibits blocking the sun.

Creation of Easements Appurtenant

Easements appurtenant are created by:

1. grant or reservation (deed)
2. necessity and intent
3. prescription

4. implication
5. condemnation

Easements by grant or reservation are those *created by the express written agreement of the landowners,* usually in a deed. The written agreement sets out the location and extent of the easement. An owner may convey land and reserve to himself an easement. This is the retention of an easement (retaining a stick in the bundle) on land conveyed to another. A common example of an easement by grant or deed is found when a developer, in the plat, *sets aside a portion of the land for common area, parks, sidewalks, and so on.* This practice also is called **dedication** of the land.

Easements by necessity *exist when a landowner has no access to roads and is landlocked.* Access, also known as ingress and egress (entry and exit), is required by law. The servient tenement may be entitled to some compensation for the interest taken. Landowner B is landlocked. To have access (ingress and egress) to the public road, B must cross the property of landowner A. B receives the benefit of the easement. A must suffer and allow the use of access by B.

Easements by prescription are *obtained by use of the land of another for the legally prescribed length of time.* The use must be open and well-known to others, hostile to the owners of the land, and continued and uninterrupted for the period of time required by the laws of the state; in Illinois, this is 20 years. The user must prove in court action that he or she has satisfied all the requirements for the intended use. The easement by prescription gives only the right of continued use, not ownership of the land. A common example of an easement by prescription is the driveway established by owner B at or near her boundary line without the benefit of a survey. After B has used the driveway for many years a survey shows the driveway to be partially or completely on the land of owner C. Owner B will have an easement by prescription to use the driveway. Landowner B is the dominant tenement, and C is the servient tenement. Illinois law allows for the prevention of prescriptive easements by posting signs granting permission to cross along the boundary of the property.

PUTTING IT TO WORK

Easements and boundary disputes often can be discovered only by a survey. If boundary problems are suspected, or if nearby construction is anticipated, real estate salespersons should suggest a survey.

Easements by implication *arise out of the conduct of the parties.* For example, when landowner X sells mineral rights to Company Y, Company Y has an easement by implication to go on the property of X to mine the minerals. Use of the easement by Company Y must be reasonable and only for the purpose of obtaining minerals.

Easements by condemnation are *created by the exercise of the government's right of eminent domain* (this government power is discussed later in this chapter). Through eminent domain the *government can take title to land and take the right to use land for some purpose in the future.* Most road widening, sidewalk, alley, and utility easements are created through eminent domain.

Termination of Easements Appurtenant

Easements may be terminated by:

1. release of the easement by the dominant tenement
2. *combining the dominant and servient lands into one tract,* called **merger**
3. abandonment of the easement by the dominant tenement

4. the purpose for the easement ceasing to exist; an example is when land is no longer landlocked because a new road has been built
5. expiration of a specified time period for which the easement was created

LICENSE

Unlike easements, which are rights, a **license** is a *temporary privilege granting permission to do a particular act or series of acts on land of another without possessing any estate or interest in the land.* A license is a personal privilege that the licensor may revoke at any time unless the licensee has paid for the license. An example of a license that has been paid for is a right to fish or hunt in a specified lake or forest. The licensee has the right to be at the lake or forest for the purpose of fishing or hunting. The licensor may not revoke the license unless the licensee has gone outside the authority of the license. A license is not assignable and is not inheritable.

LIENS

A **lien** is a *claim or charge against the property of another.* This stick in the bundle is usually security for a debt. In most cases, if the claim or lien is not satisfied in the prescribed time, the lienholder may execute on the lien—to force payment of the claim or charge. In real estate terminology this is known as the process of foreclosure. Proceeds of the foreclosure sale are applied to the claims, charges, or liens in the order of priority.

Priority of Liens

At the execution and foreclosure of the liens, priority for payment is based upon the time (day and hour) they were recorded in the proper public office. Certain liens, however, have special priority or *receive preferential treatment.* Examples of special **priority liens** are mechanics' liens, or materialmen's liens in Illinois. The theory given for giving the priority treatment lies in the nature of the services and materials provided that increased the value of the real estate. Other lienholders benefit from the work and materials of the contractors and suppliers. Thus, the contractors and suppliers should be paid first. As explained below, in most states the highest priority of all liens is given to liens for real property taxes and special assessments.

Liens fall into two groups:

1. **specific liens:** *claims against a specific and readily identifiable property,* such as a mortgage
2. **general liens:** *claims against a person and all of his or her property,* such as the disposition of a lawsuit

A chart of the various liens is shown in Figure 3.3.

Specific Liens

Mortgage Liens

Mortgages are discussed in detail in Chapters 7 and 8. The discussion here is limited to the type of lien created by a mortgage. A mortgage is a document pledging a specific property as collateral for payment of a debt. In most cases, the debt was incurred to purchase the property specified in the mortgage. The property is pledged

FIGURE 3.3
Classification of liens.

1. *Specific liens:* claims against a particular property
   a. Mortgage
   b. Mechanic's and materialman's
   c. Bail bond
   d. Vendor's and vendee's
   e. Real property tax
2. *General liens:* claims against all assets of a person
   a. Judgment
   b. Writ of attachment
   c. Income tax
   d. Estate and inheritance tax

as security. If the borrower does not pay the debt as promised, the lender can foreclose the mortgage by having the property sold at public auction. Proceeds from the sale are utilized to satisfy the liens in order of priority.

Mechanics' and Materialmen's Liens

In real estate terminology, the term "mechanic" refers not to someone who works on vehicles but, instead, to a person who provides labor to a specific property, such as a carpenter or plumber. A materialman is a supplier, such as a lumber company providing the wood materials that go into construction of a home. Therefore, a **mechanic's lien** is a *specific lien filed by a person who provides labor to a property;* a **materialman's lien** is a *specific lien filed by a supplier of products required in construction or improvement of a building.* In Illinois the term mechanic's lien is used to include both mechanic and materialman's liens.

In Illinois, those who can provide proof of having supplied materials or labor for the improvement of real property have a legal right of lien. Even if general contractors may have been paid in full, unpaid subcontractors still have the right to file a lien. A lien notice must be filed within four months after the work is completed. This time period allows title companies and buyers of property to obtain assurance that no unrecorded liens are lurking in the shadows upon the purchase of a newly constructed or remodeled home. The lien attaches as of the date the contract is signed or the work is begun. This attachment date establishes the lien's priority. To collect funds owed, a suit for foreclosure must be filed within two years of completion of the work.

PUTTING IT TO WORK

Property owners should have a list, in a sworn statement, of the names of all subcontractors the contractor is using. All subcontractors or persons who supply materials should provide the owner with a waiver of lien as each subcontractor is paid for work or materials.

Mechanic's and materialman's lien laws typically attach only to the interest of the person ordering the work and materials. In most cases this person is the owner. In some cases, however, a tenant under a lease orders work done to a leased house. If the landlord did not give the authority for the tenant's actions, the lien attaches only to the leasehold interest of the tenant. If the tenant is evicted or the lease terminates naturally, the lien is null and void.

Bail Bond Liens

A bail bond is executed by a defendant under criminal charges to obtain temporary release from custody. The release is conditioned upon a later appearance in court to answer to the criminal charges. If real property is pledged as security for the bail bond, the bond creates a specific lien against the property pledged. If the defendant does not appear in court as scheduled, the bond is forfeited (lost) and the lien is executed. The result is a lien foreclosure sale of the property, and the proceeds are applied to satisfy the financial obligations the bond created.

Vendors' and Vendees' Liens

A **vendor** is a *seller*. A **vendee** is a *buyer*. Vendors' liens come into existence upon the sale of real property and conveyance of title to the buyer without full payment of the purchase price. The vendor is given a specific lien against the property for the amount of the balance of the purchase price. If the buyer does not satisfy the lien, the vendor can foreclose to obtain the money to satisfy the lien.

Vendees' liens are created in the case of a contract for deed sale when the vendor defaults. In this case, the vendee has a lien against the property in the amount of money the vendee has paid toward the purchase price. A vendee's lien also can be enforced by foreclosure.

Real Property Tax Liens

Taxes levied by a local government constitute a specific lien against the real estate. State laws provide that real property tax liens have priority over all other liens. If the assessed real estate property taxes are not paid when due, the local official responsible for collecting the tax can bring legal action to collect the taxes. The typical action for collection is the forced sale of the property at a tax sale. (Actual calculation of property taxes is detailed in Chapter 17.) Tax sales are discussed in more detail later in this chapter.

Valuation of property for tax purposes. Property is taxed on an *ad valorem* basis—that is, according to value. Illinois uses market value, which is discussed further in the following paragraphs. The assessed value is multiplied by the tax rate for the jurisdiction. The tax rate stated in dollars or mills (1/1000th of a dollar) is applied to the assessed value to determine the amount of tax. The rate must be sufficient to provide the amount of revenue required to accomplish the budgetary necessities of the local governmental unit. Real property taxes are by far the biggest source of revenue for local governments.

Assessment of property for tax purposes involves first establishing the value of each parcel of land to be taxed within the taxing unit, such as a city, town, or county. The tax assessor is responsible for the *valuation of property for tax purposes*. Property values must be reasonably uniform to provide equal taxation of property owners. Reassessment of property for tax purposes is established by statutes and occurs triannually, as well as when improvements are made to the real estate.

Property values are determined by reviewing the sales price of similar homes in the same neighborhood although the assessor adjusts these sales prices for inflation. The result is an accurate estimate of what each home would be worth if it were to be sold during the assessment year. The assessor then uses this estimate to establish a market value for each home. The **fair market value** of a home is determined by *dividing the assessed value on one's tax bill by the percentage used to determine the* *assessed value.* With the exception of Cook County, Illinois counties assess real property at 33⅓ percent of fair market value. Cook County assesses residential property at 16 percent of fair market value.

Market value × .16 (16%) = assessed valuation for single family homes

For example, a single family home in Cook County with an assessed value of $16,000 indicates a market value estimate of $100,000. Nonresidential real property in Cook County may be assessed at varying percentages of fair market value depending on the classification. Illinois makes an adjustment to the assessed value by applying an equalization factor to compensate for the differences in county assessments of fair market value. The Illinois Department of Revenue requires that all assessed valuations be multiplied by the equalization factor. This department examines the assessment procedure in each county and makes *adjustments by assigning a multiplier,* or **equalization factor,** to each county. The equalization factor should provide that all Illinois real estate is taxed at the same rate.

Assessed value × equalization factor = equalized assessed valuation

The tax rate is applied to the *equalized assessed value.* A taxpayer may contest the assessed valuation placed on the property by filing a complaint with the county assessment official or going directly to the board of review. If this brings no satisfaction, the taxpayer can appeal to the Property Tax Appeal Board in Springfield.

The total equalized assessed value of all the properties in one taxing district (e.g., school district, park district) constitutes its tax base. Each taxing district has a separate budget that determines the total revenues needed to provide services throughout the year. The sum of the monies needed each year by all of the taxing districts in which a property is located determines the tax rate for the property. The tax rate, when applied to each $100 value of a property's equalized assessed valuation, yields the total tax bill.

Government properties, as well as schools, religious institutions, cemeteries, and charitable institutions, are exempt from taxes. Mobile homes are not taxed as real estate in Illinois unless the mobile home is permanently attached to the land. Mobile homes usually are considered personal property.

Taxes in Illinois are due and payable in two installments in the year after they are levied. If the taxes are not paid on these "penalty dates," a 1½ percent per-month penalty is added to the unpaid amount.

Tax relief. The real estate tax system in Illinois provides for tax relief on owner-occupied residences. These exemptions include the General Homestead Exemption (homeowner's exemption), the Senior Citizen Homestead Exemption, the Home Improvement Exemption, the Senior Citizen Assessment Cap, the Circuit Breaker, The Senior Citizen Tax Deferral, property tax credits, and property tax caps.

- *General Homestead Exemption* (Homeowner's Exemption): The Homeowner's Exemption exempts from taxation the first $3,500 increase in equalized assessed valuation (EAV) over the 1977 EAV. In Cook County this amount is $4,500. For example, if the EAV were to increase by $4,000 between the 1977 EAV and the current assessment, only $500 would be used to compute additional taxes. Application for this exemption must be made each year; it is not automatically applied to a tax bill.

- *Senior Citizen Homestead Exemption:* The Senior Citizen Homestead Exemption allows the assessor to reduce by $2,000 the equalized assessed valuation of the home of persons 65 years of age or older. In Cook County this amount is $2,500. To apply for this exemption, a senior citizen must present a birth certificate, a warranty deed, and his latest tax bill. The application must be renewed every year.

- *Home Improvement Exemption:* Under the Home Improvement Exemption Act of 1976, owners of single-family residences are allowed to make up to $35,000 worth of improvements to their property without having the value of the

PROPERTY CLASS	TYPE	ASSESSMENT LEVEL
Class 1	Vacant land	22%
Class 2	Single family homes, residential condominiums, residential cooperatives, apartment buildings less than 6 units	16%
Class 3	All improved real estate used for residential purposes not included in Class 2	33%
Class 4	Real estate owned and used by a not-for-profit corporation in furtherance of the purposes set forth in its charter (if such property is used for residential purposes, it should be classified in the appropriate residential class)	30%
Class 5a	Commercial structures	38%
Class 5b	Industrial properties	36%

FIGURE 3.4
Assessment levels in Cook County.

improvements added to the value of the property for at least four years. This exemption is automatically applied after application for a building permit and inspection by an assessor who has given notification of compliance. Disabled veterans or surviving spouses may apply for an exemption of up to $47,500 on residences specially adapted to suit their disability.

- *Senior Citizen Assessment Cap:* The Senior Citizen Assessment Cap was passed in 1994. This tax relief for qualified seniors caps the equalized assessed value of their homes at the EAV level of the year in which they qualify and apply for the exemption. It affects seniors age 65 or older who earn $35,000 or less a year. Seniors must re-apply each year for the exemption.

- *Circuit Breaker:* Illinois also provides property tax relief. Though real estate taxes are local taxes, the state has several programs providing tax relief. The Circuit Breaker was enacted in 1970 to help senior citizens, many of whom are on fixed incomes, pay the increasing property taxes attributable to increases in the value of their homes. The Circuit Breaker program provides seniors with a grant from the state that helps offset increases in property taxes. To be eligible for the program, a senior must have an income of less than $14,000 and must be at least 65 years of age or be a widow or widower at least 63 years of age before the spouse's death.

- *Senior citizen tax deferral:* This state program is administered by county treasurers but directly funded by the state. Those qualifying for the Circuit Breaker program are allowed to defer property tax payments on their home up to an amount equal to 80 percent of their equity. The state pays the deferred taxes to the county treasurer and is repaid upon the sale of the property or the death of the taxpayer. The state charges 6 percent annual interest on the deferred payments.

- *Property tax credit:* Illinois allows taxpayers to apply a credit of 5 percent of their property taxes toward their state income tax. This 5 percent credit is subtracted directly from the taxpayer's income tax liability.

- *Property tax caps:* In 1991, the state passed a law that capped the increase in real estate taxes at 5 percent or the rate of inflation, whichever is less, for DuPage, Kane, Lake, McHenry, and Will counties. In 1995, Cook County was added to this list. This law was designed to slow the growth of property taxes in these counties.

The law affects total extension of non-homerule taxing bodies and school districts in these areas. The cap does not apply to individual tax bills, so tax bills on individual properties may rise more than 5 percent. The cap was lowered to 2.7 percent in 1996.

Special Assessments

At times, taxing units levy special assessments in addition to real property taxes to collect payment for a share of the cost of improvements made to areas nearby or adjoining the property. These assessments can be levied against property only if the property is benefited by the improvement. Examples are assessments for streets, sidewalks, sewers, rural drainage ditches, and other public improvements. The **special assessment** is a *specific lien against the property until paid.* If the lien is not paid, the taxing unit may execute on the lien, forcing a sale of the property for payment of the assessments. These assessments may be calculated on an ad valorem basis or alternative method, such as length of road frontage or percentage of cost. Illinois requires that special assessments must be paid annually on January 2.

PUTTING IT TO WORK

Though special assessments resemble property taxes in that they are collected in the same way, they are not the same. Special assessments can be a major drawback for a property owner because the IRS will not allow assessments to be deducted as is currently allowed with property taxes.

Tax lien enforcement. The state has two types of sales for properties with unpaid taxes: annual tax sales and scavenger sales. Prospective purchasers should have a thorough knowledge of the complicated procedures involved in these sales.

Properties with unpaid taxes are sold at **annual tax sales** for the amount of the unpaid taxes and penalties. A prospective buyer pays the delinquent taxes and bids on the interest rate she will accept on repayment of the taxes if the owner redeems the property within the statutory redemption period. The lowest interest rate wins the bid. The highest bid permitted is 18 percent for six months.

Within five months of the sale, the tax buyer must deliver a notice of the sale to the county clerk. The clerk forwards the notice of the sale to the delinquent owner and urges him to redeem. During the **statutory redemption period,** *the delinquent taxpayer may redeem the property from the buyer by paying the delinquent taxes and penalties plus interest due at the bid-upon rate.* Owner-occupied homes have a redemption period of two and a half years from date of sale, while nonowner-occupied properties have a two-year period. Commercial and industrial properties have a redemption period of only six months. The delinquent taxpayer makes the redemption payment to the county clerk, who forwards it to the tax buyer.

If the owner does not redeem the property and the subsequent taxes on the property are not paid, the tax buyer may buy (pay) these subsequent taxes before the next tax sale. The tax buyer will automatically be entitled to a statutory penalty of 18 percent per year or portion of a year on these subsequent taxes. This automatic provision avoids competition with other bidders that might drive the penalty down. Before the redemption period comes to an end, the tax buyer must provide the delinquent taxpayer with specific notices stressing that the redemption period is coming to an end. Within five months prior to the expiration of the period, the tax buyer must file a petition in court seeking a tax deed. If the property has not been redeemed, the court will order the county clerk to issue a tax deed to the buyer, which must be recorded within one year after the redemption period expires.

Properties with taxes that have been delinquent for more than two years and that are not purchased at a tax sale are sold at **scavenger sales.** Here prospective buyers bid an actual dollar amount for a property rather than an interest rate. The starting bid is half of the taxes due or $250, whichever is less. Redemption periods and procedures for scavenger sales are the same as for tax sales.

PUTTING IT TO WORK

Holders of a certificate of purchase stand to gain either title to the unredeemed property or reimbursement of the taxes paid, penalties, and other costs plus interest.

General Liens

Judgment Liens

A **judgment** is a *court decree resulting from a lawsuit.* The court decree establishes that one person is indebted to another and the amount of the debt. The person who owes the judgment is called the judgment debtor. The person who is owed the judgment is called the judgment creditor. A **judgment lien** is *against all of the real and personal property the judgment debtor owns in the county* in which the judgment is recorded. A judgment lien does not apply to real property owned by husband and wife by the entireties if the judgment is against only the husband or only the wife. For the judgment lien to attach to property of a husband and wife, the judgment obtained must be against both husband and wife on a debt they both incurred. A judgment creditor may record the judgment in any other county in the state (and possibly in other states), and it will become a general lien against all the property of the judgment debtor in that county. This is called *notice of lien.*

The lien takes effect at the time the judgment is entered in the court records. The lien attaches to all of the property of the judgment debtor at the time of the judgment. It also attaches as a lien to any property the judgment debtor acquires after the judgment and prior to satisfaction of the judgment. The judgment lien is enforced by an **execution of judgment,** *an order signed by the judge or clerk of the court instructing the sheriff to attach and seize the property of the judgment debtor.* The sheriff then is to sell the property, real and personal, of the judgment debtor. Proceeds from the sale are applied to satisfy the judgment.

In Illinois, judgment liens remain in effect for a period of seven years and may be renewed for another seven years unless the judgment is paid or discharged by filing a petition in bankruptcy. A judgment may be renewed and kept in force for additional periods if the judgment creditor brings another action on the original judgment. Illinois also allows for interest to be paid on the judgment.

Judgment liens have a priority relationship based upon the time of recording in the court records. The judgment creditor who obtains a judgment in the court records before another creditor will have the priority claim. The judgment debtor's obligation to the creditors is paid in order of highest priority to lowest priority.

Lis Pendens

The term **lis pendens** is Latin and literally means *pending litigation.* This is *a notice to the world that a lawsuit has been filed and is awaiting trial concerning the specific property.* The notice is filed in the office of the county or local official responsible for the record keeping of pending litigation. The notice is a warning to a prospective purchaser of the property that the lawsuit could result in a judgment that in turn would create a lien against the property of the defendant in the suit. A lien resulting from the lawsuit will attach to the property even though the title was transferred to someone else prior to the final judgment in the suit, if the transfer occurred after the notice was placed on the public record in the county in which the property is located.

Writs of Attachment

Though similar to a lis pendens, a **writ of attachment** is stronger. It is an actual *court order preventing any transfer of the attached property during the litigation.* Violation of the order can result in a contempt of court citation.

Income Tax Liens

The Internal Revenue Service of the United States and the Illinois Department of Revenue may create a general lien against all of the taxpayer's property for taxes due and unpaid. The lien may be for a variety of types of taxes owed. The taxes due might be personal income tax, employee withholding tax, federal unemployment tax, FICA for employees, self-employment taxes, sales tax, use tax, or any other tax relating to income. The period of time for validity of these liens varies with the type of tax due and unpaid.

This lien is created by filing a certificate of lien against the landowner in the county in which the taxpayer's land is located. Liens held by the Internal Revenue Service or the state do not automatically receive priority status or preferential treatment for payment purposes. Priority of the tax lien is determined by the date the lien was placed on the real estate or against the individual, just as with a judgment lien.

Estate and Inheritance Tax Liens

Federal estate and state inheritance taxes are calculated and incurred at the time of death of an individual owning property. A general lien on the property in the estate passes through the estate to assure payment of the taxes due at death.

Most states impose some type of tax upon the inheritance of real and personal property.

The federal government imposes a tax on the estate of deceased persons. Called the federal estate tax, this tax creates a lien that attaches to all of the property in the estate.

The federal tax laws allow property to pass to surviving spouses without taxation or with favorable tax treatment.

RESTRICTIVE COVENANTS

Restrictions placed on a private owner's use of land by a nongovernmental entity or individual are **restrictive covenants.** These are not to be confused with the restrictions on use of land by the government or the government's agencies (discussed in Chapter 11). The purpose of covenants by private owners is to preserve and protect the quality of land in subdivisions and to maximize land values by requiring the homogeneous use of land by purchasers of land in the subdivision. Covenants are promises by purchasers to limit their use of the property by complying with requirements of the restrictive covenants.

Typically, restrictive covenants are found in residential subdivisions. These may include minimum square feet in the homes to be constructed, prohibition against detached garages, prohibitions on exterior antennas, or other concerns of the owner/developer. Because these are private restrictions, they are enforced not by local zoning officials and building departments but, rather, by some agent of the subdivision or owner/developer.

If a landowner subject to a restrictive covenant violates the covenant, any other landowner in the subdivision can bring an action to end the violation. An injunction, a cease-and-desist order, or a restraining order is sought from a local court to enforce the restrictive covenant.

ENCROACHMENTS

An **encroachment,** a *trespass on the land of another,* is created by the intrusion of some structure or object across a boundary line. Typical encroachments in real estate include tree limbs, bushes, fences, antennas, roof lines, driveways, and overhangs.

The encroaching owner is a **trespasser.** In most encroachment situations the encroachment is accidental and unintentional. The only method to accurately determine the existence of an encroachment is by a survey of the boundary line.

Almost every subdivision in the United States has classic examples of encroachments. At the time a new home is built, small trees and shrubs are planted on or near boundary lines to commemorate the boundaries. As the bushes and trees grow, the branches extend beyond the boundaries. The small apple tree planted many years ago is now dropping rotten apples in the neighbor's back yard. The lilac bush planted at the corner of the house has now grown to such a breadth that the branches rub the side of the neighboring house. The garage that was built within six inches of the boundary line has a roof line and eaves extending over the boundary line and draining on the neighbor's yard. These are all examples of accidental and unintentional encroachments.

Although accidental and unintentional, they are still an encroachment on the real property. In Illinois a trespass or encroachment that continues for 20 years may become an easement by prescription or even ownership in fee. Until that time, the landowner being encroached upon has the right to bring legal action for removal of the encroachment or a suit for damages (judgment by that court requiring the encroacher to compensate the landowner for the encroachment). Illinois law allows for the prevention of prescriptive easements by posting signs along the boundary of the property.

An order to remove the encroachment of a branch over the boundary line does not mean that the tree will be cut down. The only part of the tree that must be removed is the portion encroaching.

GOVERNMENT RESTRICTIONS ON REAL PROPERTY

Since the Ordinance of 1785, land ownership by private individuals has been allowed in the United States. Even the allodial system of property ownership, however, is subject to four important powers of federal and local governments: (a) the power of eminent domain, (b) police power, (c) power of taxation, and (d) the power of escheat.

Power of Eminent Domain

The right or power of **eminent domain** is the *power of the government or its agencies to take private property for public use.* Governments exercise this power themselves and also delegate it to public utility companies. Actual *taking of property under the power of eminent domain* is called **condemnation.**

The power of eminent domain has two limitations. The right of eminent domain can be used only if (a) the property condemned is for the use and benefit of the general public and (b) the property owner is paid the fair market value of the property lost through condemnation. Property owners have the right to appeal to the courts if they are not satisfied with the compensation the condemning authority offers.

The bundle of rights concept as it relates to eminent domain prompts the question of who receives the money from the condemnation action. The answer is that the money is divided among any parties having an interest in the property, based upon the value of the interest owned by those individuals.

Police Power

Police power *enables government to fulfill its responsibility to provide for public health, safety, and welfare.* The government may exercise this power even if it restricts some of the fundamental freedoms of the people. Exercise of the power, however, always must be in the best interest of the public.

Examples of the exercise of police power affecting property use are zoning ordinances, subdivision ordinances, building codes, and environmental protection laws. (Detailed discussion of the specifics of zoning, subdivision control, and the like are found in Chapter 11.) Property owners affected by the exercise of police power are not compensated for the restrictions and loss of use of their property resulting from the exercise of this power. Its underlying premises are that any restrictions imposed must reasonably provide for the health, safety, and welfare of the public.

Power of Taxation

Real property taxation was discussed earlier as a specific lien on real property. Exercise of the *power of taxation is one of the inherent burdens on private ownership of land.* Land owned by the government, a governmental agency, or a nonprofit organization is exempt from real property taxation.

Power of Escheat

If a property owner dies **testate**—*leaves a valid will*—the individual's property is distributed to persons as specified in the will. If an owner dies **intestate**—*without having a valid will*—the decedent's property is distributed to heirs in accordance with state statutory provisions. These statutes are called the Illinois Law of Descent and Distribution (as discussed in Chapter 2) and specify how property will be distributed based on the relationship of the deceased's heirs who come forth (or can be located).

In most states, *if no one is qualified to receive title* to property the deceased leaves, the state uses its power of **escheat** and *the property goes to the state.* In Illinois, real property escheats to the county in which it is located and personal property escheats to the state.

IMPORTANT POINTS

1. An encumbrance is a claim, lien, charge, or liability attached to and binding upon real property. Examples are encroachments, easements, liens, assessments, and restrictive covenants.
2. A license in real property is not transferable or inheritable. License is considered a temporary privilege.
3. Easements are nonpossessory interests in land owned by another. Easements can be in gross or appurtenant in nature. Easements are created by grant, necessity, prescription, implication, reservation, and condemnation.

4. Easements appurtenant can be negative or affirmative.
5. Easements are terminated by grant, merger, abandonment, end of necessity, or expiration of the prescribed time period.
6. In Illinois, an easement by prescription or adverse possession may be gained after 20 years of open, continuous, uninterrupted use of the property, hostile to the true owners. Posting signs on the property may prevent gaining of an easement by prescription.
7. Specific liens are claims against a specific and readily identifiable property, such as a mortgage lien and a mechanic's or materialman's lien.
8. General liens are claims against a person and all of his or her property, such as a judgment resulting from a lawsuit.
9. The lien for real property taxes is a specific lien and in most states is given the highest priority for payment.
10. Real property taxation is on an ad valorem basis.
11. Market value × assessed rate = assessed value. Assessed value × equalization factor = equalized assessed value.
12. Illinois provides for a homeowner's exemption, which exempts from taxation the first $3,500 increase ($4,500 in Cook County) in equalized assessed value. This exemption must be applied for annually.
13. The Senior Citizen Homestead exemption reduces the equalized assessed value of a home by $2,000 ($2,500 in Cook County). This exemption must be applied for annually.
14. The Home Improvement Exemption allows up to $35,000 of improvements to be made to a principal residence without taxing the added value for at least four years.
15. Mechanics' liens and materialmen's liens are specific liens that may receive preferential treatment for priority of liens.
16. Mechanics' liens in Illinois attach to the property on the date the contract was signed or the work was ordered. The lien must be filed within four months of the date of completion of the work.
17. The property of a judgment debtor is subject to execution and forced sale to satisfy an unpaid judgment.
18. Property sold at a tax sale may be redeemed within 2 to 2½ years after the sale. To redeem the property, all delinquent taxes, interest, and penalties must be paid.
19. Lis pendens notice provides specific and constructive notice to the public that a lawsuit concerning certain real estate is pending.
20. Restrictive covenants are used to preserve the quality of land and maximize land values.
21. An encroachment is a trespass on land—an intrusion or breaking over the boundary of land.
22. Proof of the existence or lack of existence of an encroachment is evidenced by a survey of the boundary.
23. Private ownership of property is subject to the four powers of government: eminent domain, police power (such as zoning, health codes, and building codes), taxation, and escheat.
24. In Illinois, real property escheats to the county in which the property is located. Personal property escheats to the state.

Review Questions

Answers to these questions are found in the Answer Key section at the back of the book.

1. Which of the following is a right that results from ownership in a particular parcel of real estate?
   a. easement in gross
   b. police power
   c. license
   d. condemnation

2. All of the following statements about easements are true EXCEPT:
   a. an easement provides a nonpossessory interest in land
   b. a servient tenement is the land burdened by an easement
   c. a dominant tenement is the land benefited by an easement
   d. an easement appurtenant is terminated by transfer of the benefited tenement

3. Property owner A held an enforceable right to prevent property owner B from erecting a structure that would interfere with the passage of light and air to A's property. This right is a(n):
   a. implied easement
   b. easement by necessity
   c. easement by prescription
   d. negative easement

4. Easements may be created in all of the following ways EXCEPT:
   a. condemnation
   b. dedication
   c. prescription
   d. assessment

5. An appurtenant easement may be terminated by all of the following EXCEPT:
   a. merger
   b. death
   c. grant or deed of release
   d. abandonment

6. A property owner gives another person permission to fish in a lake on the property. The permission is a temporary privilege and exists in the form a(n):
   a. license
   b. easement
   c. lease
   d. appurtenance

7. The creation of an easement by condemnation results from the exercise of:
   a. prescription
   b. eminent domain
   c. dedication
   d. implication

8. Liens, easements, encroachments, and restrictive covenants are all examples of:
   a. emblements
   b. estovers
   c. estates
   d. encumbrances

9. All of the following are examples of specific liens EXCEPT:
   a. mortgage
   b. mechanic's lien
   c. income tax lien
   d. vendor's lien

10. Creditor A, whose lien is secured by Smith's property, obtained a judgment against Smith on July 10; Banker B lent money to Smith and took back a mortgage on August 1; Creditor C obtained a judgment for failure to pay child support on August 20. Which of the above-listed liens will be paid first at foreclosure?
    a. Creditor A
    b. Banker B
    c. Creditor C
    d. they will all be paid on a pro rata basis

11. Which of the following liens will receive priority in payment:
    a. inheritance tax
    b. income tax
    c. estate tax
    d. property tax

12. All of the following statements are true regarding real estate property taxes in Illinois EXCEPT:

    a. market value × the assessed rate = assessed value

    b. assessed value × the equalization factor = the equalized assessed value

    c. real property sold at a tax sale may be redeemed by the owner within a specified period of time

    d. all Illinois counties assess all classifications of real property at 33⅓ percent of its fair market value

13. To enforce restrictive covenants in a subdivision, a landowner will bring legal action for:

    a. trespass
    b. nuisance
    c. injunction
    d. eviction

14. The doctrine of merger in easements means:

    a. the dominant tenement is larger and more valuable than the servient tenement

    b. the servient tenement must allow the dominant tenement complete access

    c. the easement will be terminated when the dominant tenement and the servient tenement are owned by the same person

    d. the easement is an easement in gross and is utilized by all of the government agencies in the jurisdiction for delivering utility services

15. The court order directing the sheriff to seize the property of a judgment debtor to satisfy a judgment is called:

    a. satisfaction of judgment
    b. writ of execution
    c. release of judgment
    d. surrender of judgment

16. An easement can be extinguished by all of the following EXCEPT:

    a. the servient tenement
    b. the dominant tenement
    c. the merger of the tenements
    d. abandonment

17. Permission to go onto the land of another for a specific purpose is called a(n):

    a. lien
    b. license
    c. profit
    d. easement

18. Which of the following liens has priority over the others?

    a. general real estate taxes
    b. federal income taxes
    c. first mortgage or first trust deed liens
    d. judgments

19. An act of taking land by the government is called:

    a. condemnation
    b. eminent domain
    c. escheat
    d. taxation

20. Escheat occurs when a person dies:

    a. testate with no living heirs
    b. intestate with no living heirs
    c. in an accident with no living heirs
    d. intestate and has never been married

21. Jones, an Illinois property owner, died intestate and did not leave any traceable heirs. Jones's real property will:

    a. be disposed of according to U.S. Laws of Descent and Distribution
    b. escheat to the state
    c. escheat to the county in which the property is located
    d. be claimed by adverse possession

22. The government's right to protect the health and welfare of the public is called:

    a. public policy
    b. police power
    c. public domain
    d. police justice

23. When zoning laws create problems for a landowner:

   a. the land owner will receive just compensation with the passage of the laws
   b. payment will be made to the land owner under the rule of eminent domain
   c. no compensation is dictated by law
   d. a variance will be granted in lieu of compensation

24. Mechanics' liens in Illinois:

   a. attach as of the date of the contract or the date the work was begun
   b. are illegal
   c. can be filed any time after the work is completed
   d. can be filed only by the general contractor

25. A carpenter who does NOT expect to be paid for his work can file a:

   a. carpenter's equity lien
   b. specific lien
   c. mechanic's lien
   d. materialman's lien

CHAPTER 4

Important Terminology

- accidental agency
- agent
- brokerage agreement
- Brokerage Relationships in Real Estate Transaction Law (Article 4)
- buyer brokerage
- client
- Commercial Real Estate Broker Lien Act
- common law agency
- confidential information
- consumer
- customer
- designated agent
- dual agency
- estoppel
- expressed agency
- fiduciary relationship
- general agent
- implied agency
- ministerial acts
- multiple listing service (MLS)
- ostensible agency
- principal
- special agent
- subagent
- unintended agency
- universal agent
- vicarious liability

Brokerage and Agency

IN THIS CHAPTER There are two main categories of agency: common law agency and statutory agency. Illinois no longer follows common law agency but instead a form of statutory agency called designated agency. *The law creating designated agency,* the **Brokerage Relationship in Real Estate Transaction Law,** was added to the Illinois Real Estate License Act as Article 4 and became effective January 1, 1995. Article 4 stipulates that a real estate licensee represents the consumer the licensee is working with, in effect wiping out common law agency and subagency in Illinois. Since Illinois licensees may take advantage of Illinois' license reciprocity with many states, licensees must not only have a thorough understanding of Illinois' designated agency, but also of common law agency. Some of the states with which Illinois has reciprocity still follow common law in regard to agency, and licensees must follow the law of the state in which the property is located.

CLASSIFICATION OF AGENCY RELATIONSHIPS

Most states, including Illinois, recognize three classifications of agents: universal agents, general agents, and special agents. The differences between each type of agency revolve around the authority given to the agent by the principal and the services to be provided.

Universal Agent

A **universal agent** is *someone authorized to handle all affairs of the principal.* An example of a universal agent is a guardian. The guardian has complete authority in acting on behalf of his ward.

General Agent

A **general agent** is *someone authorized to handle all affairs of the principal concerning a certain matter or property, usually with some limited power to enter into contracts.* An example is a person who has been appointed property manager of an apartment complex. The property manager may collect rent, evict, enter into leases, repair the premises, advertise for tenants, and perform a range of activities on behalf of the principal. Also, the agency relationship between the salesperson (agent) and her principal (broker) is a general agency. The salesperson will be negotiating commission and management fees on behalf of the broker.

Special Agent

A **special agent** *has very narrow authorization to act on behalf of the principal.* The agency relationship between the seller and a broker under a listing agreement is a special agency. The broker can market the property for sale but cannot make decisions as to price, repairs, financing, and the like. A special agent cannot bind a principal to a contract. The range of authority is limited and the services provided are specialized.

Common Law Agency

Under **common law agency,** *an agency relationship is created when one person is hired to act on behalf of another person. The person hired on another's behalf* is the **agent.** *The person who selects the agent to act on his behalf* is the **principal.** Upon creation of the agency relationship, the agent is placed in a position of trust and loyalty to the principal. The principal may authorize the agent to use *other people to assist in accomplishing the purpose of the agency.* These people are called **subagents** and owe the same relationship of trust and loyalty to the principal.

Creation of Agency

An agency relationship created by an oral or a written agreement between the principal and the agent is called an **expressed agency.** Typical examples are the written listings, or brokerage agreements, between a broker and a seller of real estate or between a broker and a prospective buyer of real estate.

An agency relationship also may be created by the actions of the principals and agent indicating that they have an agreement. This is called an **implied agency** or **ostensible agency.** When a person claims to be an agent but has no express agreement, the principal can establish agency by ratifying the actions of the agent. For example, a broker introduces a prospective buyer to a piece of property for which the broker does not have a listing. If the seller does not disapprove of the broker's actions, the broker will be considered the seller's agent.

An agency relationship also can be created by **estoppel** *if an individual claims incorrectly that a person is her agent and a third party relies on the incorrect representation.* In these cases, the person making the incorrect statement is estopped (prohibited) from later claiming that the agency relationship does not exist. For example, if Broker Alfred states to Mr. and Mrs. Reynaldo that Betty is a sales agent in his office when he knows that she is not, and the Reynaldos rely on this incorrect information, Alfred cannot later claim that Betty is not his agent, and he is liable for her actions.

It is important to note that the creation of an agency relationship has nothing to do with who is paying whom. Agency relationships are created by express agreement, by a licensee's actions or inactions, and even by implication. The source or amount of compensation does not create an agency relationship.

Fiduciary Relationship

Under common law agency, a **fiduciary relationship** is created between principal and agent, or fiduciary. The term "fiduciary" means *one who holds a position of trust.* The agent has certain obligations to the principal that are required by law. The agent's duties and responsibilities include *c*are, skill, and diligence; *o*bedience; *l*oyalty; *a*ccountability; and *n*otice, or disclosure. These duties can be remembered using the acronym "COLAN."

Care, Skill, and Diligence

In offering services to the principal, the agent asserts that she possesses the necessary skill and training to perform the services. In performing her duties, the agent must exercise the skill, care, and diligence the public is entitled to expect of the agents in that field. The agent is liable for any financial loss the principal incurs as a result of his agent's negligence or failure to meet the standards of skill, diligence, and reasonable care, and the principal is not required to pay any compensation to the agent.

Obedience

The agent must obey reasonable and legal instructions from the principal. For example, the seller, as principal, may specify that the property be shown only during certain times of the day or not on days of her religious observance. The buyer being represented might instruct the broker not to disclose the buyer's identity to the parties without the buyer's consent. Of course, the principal cannot require the agent to do any illegal acts, such as violating fair housing laws. If the principal does insist on an illegal act, the broker can disobey.

Loyalty

Under the terms of the employment agreement creating the agency, an agent must be loyal to the principal and must work diligently to serve the principal's best interests. The agent may not work for his own personal interest or the interest of others adverse to the principal's interest. The agent cannot legally represent any other person who directly affects the principal's interest without disclosing this fact to the principal and obtaining the principal's consent. A real estate agent cannot represent both the buyer and seller in the same transaction and cannot receive a commission from both without the knowledge and written consent of both the buyer and seller.

Accountability

An agent must account for and promptly remit as required all money or property entrusted to her for the benefit of others. The agent is required to keep adequate and accurate records of all receipts and expenditures of other people's money in order to provide a complete accounting. For example, a real estate broker must maintain a special account for depositing other people's money. This account should be labeled either "trust account" or "escrow account."

Notice (Disclosure)

An agent is required to keep the principal fully informed of all important matters through notice, or disclosure, of information by promptly and totally communicating to the principal any information that is material to the transaction for which the agency is created. As an example, the requirement for disclosure of information requires that a broker present every offer to the seller. The seller has the prerogative to decide whether to reject or to accept any offer for purchase of the property. In presenting the offer, the broker should provide the seller with any knowledge of all circumstances surrounding the offer. In the case of a buyer's broker, the broker should indicate to the buyer what the market value of the property is and use all negotiating techniques possible to obtain the most favorable terms for the buyer. In addition, agents must disclose any interest they have in a subject property (such as ownership or financing).

Seller–Broker Relationship Under Common Law

Under common law the seller is considered the principal. The relationship of the seller and the broker typically is stated in the listing agreement. In the listing agreement, the broker is appointed as the agent of the seller. The broker, as agent, owes the seller a fiduciary duty. The broker must act in the best interest of the seller and, in doing so, may seek the assistance of other brokers to sell the property. These brokers, called cooperating brokers, are subagents of the listing broker. These cooperating brokers also have a fiduciary relationship with the seller (considered the client), even though they make be working with the buyer (considered the customer). Subagency requires the cooperating broker to act in the best interest of the seller, even at the expense of the buyer that he is working with. Under common law, the agent and subagent have no fiduciary relationship with the buyer. Therefore, information revealed by the buyer to the broker should be revealed to the seller to use to the seller's advantage.

Buyer–Broker Relationship Under Common Law

Since the fiduciary relationship exists with the seller, the buyer must be careful what he reveals to the broker. The broker does have certain duties toward the buyer. The buyer must be treated fairly and honestly. The broker cannot engage in any misrepresentations or commission of fraudulent acts. Brokers also must disclose to the buyer any material facts of which they have knowledge or should have knowledge regarding the condition of the property. For example, a broker must reveal a defective septic system, wet basement, and so on. Liability may be imposed upon the agent for concealing defects in the property or for failing to disclose the defects or even failing to take reasonable steps to discover the defects.

Buyer Agency Under Common Law

In **buyer brokerage,** a buyer can hire a broker to look out for the buyer's best interest in purchasing a home, and the broker accepting this arrangement will have a fiduciary relationship with the buyer. In such cases, *the agency relationship exists between the buyer and the broker: the buyer is the principal and the broker is the agent.* In these cases, since the broker will be in the nontraditional role of representing the buyer, the broker will be required to serve notice on the seller or the seller's agent that he is representing the buyer and not the seller as a client. Many states require this disclosure to be made in writing and given to the seller or the seller's agent prior to the showing of the property.

The advantages to the buyer in establishing this type of relationship include gaining both the technical expertise to negotiate a better price and the broker's fiduciary confidentiality and trust. A buyer wants assurance that she is paying a reasonable price for a property. A buyer's broker can perform a market analysis and advise her on her offer. A buyer's broker also may suggest creative financing that is in the buyer's interest. A written buyer's broker agreement signed by both buyer and broker is essential to prevent any disputes.

Buyer's brokers have been common in commercial real estate transactions for many years. In commercial transactions, a buyer employs a broker to locate a certain type of property for purchase. Today, this approach is becoming more common in residential real estate as well.

Dual Agency Under Common Law

When *an agent represents both buyer and seller in the same transaction,* this situation is called **dual agency.** Dual agency can create difficulties in abiding by the fiduciary relationship inherent in an agency agreement. Since common law agency stresses the fiduciary relationship between agent and seller, a problem arises when a salesperson wants to act as a buyer's agent for a property that is listed with the salesperson's broker. A fiduciary relationship already exists between the seller and the broker and the broker's agents (subagents). Another conflict arises when a cooperating broker, usually considered a subagent of the listing broker, tries to act as a buyer broker.

Undisclosed Dual Agency

Consensual dual agency requires disclosure to both buyer and seller of the dual agency and a written consent from both. If dual agency relationships are not disclosed in writing and agreed to by both parties, either party could claim an undisclosed dual agency and could resort to a number of available remedies through the courts. For instance, if a seller feels that a buyer would have made a higher offer for a property if the agent had not told the buyer of the seller's pending foreclosure, the buyer may take court actions asking for damages from the agent or seek to have the sale rescinded. An agent involved in an undisclosed dual agency may find his license revoked or suspended.

Accidental Agency Under Common Law

Unintended or **accidental agency** *can occur if the buyer is led to believe by the broker's actions and representations that the buyer is being represented by that broker.* This implication can arise, for example, when a broker gives a buyer advice on negotiations or suggestions on what price to offer when in fact the broker is representing the seller. There may also be confusion when a seller uses a broker to sell a property and then enters the market as a buyer. The former seller may go to the same broker looking for property to purchase and assume that the broker is automatically representing him in the new transaction. Unless he establishes a new agency relationship with the broker in his new role as buyer, however, the broker represents the owner, not the buyer, of the property he is trying to buy. Actually, the former seller may argue successfully that an ostensible agency exists because of the broker's knowledge of his needs, desires, and abilities pursuant to their prior agency relationship.

Termination of Agency

There are several ways in which agency relationships in real estate may terminate:

- An agency relationship ends in accordance with the terms of the agency contract. For example, when a listing contract for the sale of real estate terminates, so does any authority for the broker to act on behalf of the principal.
- Another means of terminating an agency relationship is by completing the terms of the agency. For instance, when listed real estate sells and the seller pays a commission, the terms in the contract have been met and agency ends.
- In some cases, agency relationship may be terminated by operation of law. For instance, a real estate listing or brokerage agreement terminates automatically at the death of either the principal or agent. Another example is the termination of a listing contract held by a broker whose license is revoked.
- The destruction of the listed property will also terminate a listing.

Unless there is a written agreement providing for additional duties after the termination of agency, only two remaining duties are owed to the principal after termination: (a) accounting for all moneys and property relating to the transactions and (b) keeping confidential all confidential information received during the course of the agency.

AGENCY IN ILLINOIS— DESIGNATED AGENCY

A Federal Trade Commission (FTC) study completed years ago verified the confusion consumers experience in real estate transactions. The study polled hundreds of consumers that had either sold or purchased a home in the six months prior to the study. Of the buyers surveyed, 72 percent thought that the selling brokers were representing them, when under common law the selling brokers were subagents of the listing broker and represented the sellers. Of the sellers surveyed, 77 percent thought that the selling brokers were representing the buyer. Clearly, common law agency and subagency are misunderstood by the consumer. Today, more than 30 states have some kind of mandatory agency disclosure laws. Agency law continues to evolve, seeking to adapt to the realities of today's real estate marketplace.

Brokerage Relationships—Article 4

The Brokerage Relationships in Real Estate Transactions Law, or Article 4 of the Illinois Real Estate License Act, became effective January 1, 1995. This law is not intended to affect contractual relationships that exist between brokers and their licensees but is intended to prevent the detrimental misunderstandings and misinterpretations of relationships among consumers, real estate brokers, and salespersons found in the FTC study.

Article 4 excludes the common law concepts of principal and agent and their fiduciary relationship and duties: Common law agency and subagency can be considered dead in Illinois. The duties required of an Illinois real estate professional are statutorily defined by Article 4. Article 4 also may serve as a basis for private rights of action and defenses by sellers, buyers, landlords, tenants, and real estate brokers and salespersons. This private right of action is only in Article 4 and is not extended in other parts of the Illinois Real Estate License Act. In addition, licensees are still subject to liability under the Illinois Fraud and Deceptive Practices Act, and there is nothing in Article 4 that should be construed as changing a licensee's duty under common law regarding the negligent or fraudulent misrepresentation of material information.

Article 4 defines several terms. A **brokerage agreement** is *an agreement that could be either a listing contract* or *buyer brokerage agreement*. A **client** is *a person represented by a licensee*. A **consumer** is *a person* or *entity seeking* or *receiving real estate brokerage services*. A **customer** is *a consumer who is not being represented by a licensee, but for whom the licensee is performing ministerial acts*.

In its most basic definition, the one that most separates it from common law, Article 4 states that licensees are **designated agents** *considered to be representing the consumer with whom they are working*, unless there is a written agreement between the broker and the consumer providing a different relationship. An exception to this is a licensee who is performing only ministerial acts on behalf of the consumer. (Ministerial acts are discussed later in the chapter.) Payment or the promise of payment has nothing to do with whether an agency relationship has been created.

If a client is interested in a property and her designated agent shows that property to other prospective buyers, it might seem to be a breach of duty to the client. Article 4 specifically states, however, that a licensee does not breach a duty or obligation as a designated agent by showing alternative properties to prospective buyers or tenants or by showing properties in which the client is interested to other prospective buyers or tenants. A licensee who receives a higher fee or compensation based on a higher selling price or lease cost also does not violate a duty or obligation.

Duties of Licensee to Client

Under Article 4, the licensee must perform to the terms of the brokerage agreement and promote the best interests of the client. The licensee should seek a transaction at a price and terms stated in the brokerage agreement, presenting all offers to and from the client and disclosing any material facts of which the licensee has actual knowledge that concerns the transaction. If this information is confidential, however, the licensee is prohibited from revealing it. The licensee must also provide for a timely accounting of all moneys and property received and must obey the specific instructions of the client that are not contrary to law. The licensee should exercise reasonable skill and care in the performance of brokerage services and promote the client's best interests as opposed to the licensee's or any other person's self-interest. A licensee will not be held liable to a client for providing false information to the client (a) if the false information was provided to the licensee by the customer or (b) unless the licensee knew or should have known the information was incorrect.

Duties of Licensee to Customer

Under Article 4, the licensee must treat all customers honestly and cannot negligently or knowingly give them false information. The licensee also must provide timely disclosure of all material adverse defects actually known to the licensee concerning the physical condition of the property that could not be discovered by the customer completing a reasonably diligent inspection of the property. This is the only instance in which a licensee owes a duty to disclose information to someone other than the client. A licensee is not liable to a customer for providing false information to the customer (a) if the false information was provided to the licensee by the client or (b) unless the licensee knew or should have known the information was incorrect.

Agency Disclosure

Article 4 requires the broker to advise the consumer of the designated agency relationship that will exist unless there is a written agreement between them providing for a different brokerage relationship. This must be done no later than the time at which the broker enters into a brokerage agreement with the consumer. Additionally, the broker must advise the consumer of any other agency relationships available through the broker and provide the name or names of the consumer's designated agents in writing. Although the broker need not state the amount of the commission to be received, the broker must advise the consumer as to whether the broker will share the compensation with brokers who represent others in a transaction.

The licensee must disclose in writing to the customer that the licensee is not acting as the agent of the customer at a time that will prevent the disclosure of confidential information from the customer to a licensee. This disclosure may take place no later than at the preparation of an offer to purchase or lease real property. This disclosure does not apply to residential leases, unless the lease includes an option to purchase.

Confidential Information

Article 4 defines **confidential information** as *information obtained by a licensee from a client during the term of a brokerage agreement or information that was made confidential by the written request or written instruction of the client. Any information* *dealing with the negotiating position of the client or information the disclosure of which could materially harm the position of the client is considered confidential.* The designated agent of a buyer could not reveal to the seller or the seller's designated agent that the buyer had to be out of his present home in a week or would make a higher offer for the property if his first offer was rejected.

Confidential information can be disclosed only if (a) the client permits disclosure, (b) the disclosure is required by law, (c) the information becomes public from another source, or (d) the information concerns the physical condition of the property.

Ministerial Acts

A licensee representing a client in a real estate transaction may provide assistance to a customer by performing ministerial acts. Ministerial acts should not be performed in a manner that would violate the brokerage agreement with the client or would form a brokerage agreement with the customer. **Ministerial acts** include, but are not limited to *those acts that are informative in nature but that do not rise to an active level of representation on behalf of the customer.* Some examples of ministerial acts are:

- responding to phone inquiries by consumers as to the availability and pricing of brokerage services
- responding to phone inquiries from consumers concerning the price or location of property
- attending an open house and responding to questions about the property from a consumer
- setting an appointment to view property with a consumer
- responding to questions of walk-in consumers concerning brokerage services or particular properties
- accompanying an appraiser, inspector, contractor, or similar third party on a visit to a property
- describing a property or a property's condition in response to a consumer's inquiry
- completing business or factual information for a consumer on an offer to purchase on behalf of the client
- showing a client through a property being sold by an owner
- referring a consumer to another broker or service provider

Dual Agency

Dual agency situations arise *when a licensee is representing both the buyer and the seller in the same transaction.* This usually takes place on the licensee's personal listings rather than the office's listings, as the licensee would probably not have been named the designated agent on an office listing if there were any question of dual agency.

A licensee answering a phone call in response to an ad on a personal listing or talking to a consumer at an open house on a personal listing would not be considered the agent of that consumer, as these situations are ministerial acts. However, the licensee must be careful not to go beyond ministerial acts and act as an agent for such consumers. The licensee should keep in mind the written disclosure requirements previously mentioned.

Article 4 allows for consensual dual agency, provided certain requirements are met. Consent to a dual agency requires that the licensee who is to act as a dual agent must present the clients with a dual agency disclosure form that includes required statutory language. This form should be presented to the clients at the time the brokerage agreement is entered into and must be signed by the clients before the licensee may act as a dual agent. Consent to act as a dual agent is presumed to have been given when the clients sign this form.

In addition to this initial disclosure, when the clients are executing an offer to purchase or lease in a transaction in which the licensee acted as a dual agent, the licensee must obtain a written confirmation from the clients giving their consent for the licensee to act as a dual agent. This confirmation may be included in another document such as a contract to purchase, in which case the clients may initial the confirmation of dual agency.

If a client declines to enter into or wishes to withdraw from a dual agency agreement, the withdrawing client may be referred to another designated agent. To receive a referral fee in this situation, written disclosure of the fee must be given to the withdrawing client and the client that continues to be represented. Note that only disclosure is required, not permission.

In a dual agency relationship, the client and the licensee are considered to possess only actual knowledge and information. There is no imputation of knowledge or information among or between the clients, brokers, or their affiliated licensees.

Subagency

Article 4 states that a broker is not considered a subagent of another broker solely by reason of membership in or other affiliation with the brokers in a multiple listing service or other similar information source. It also prohibits offering subagency through

---

1. Article 4 effectively kills subagency in real estate transactions within Illinois and replaces it with designated agency.
2. Having preempted common law and common law actions, Article 4 allows for a private right of action for a violation of Article 4.
3. In the absence of another agreement between them, the licensee is considered a designated agent of the consumer with whom the licensee is working.
4. No later than the time at which the licensee enters into a brokerage agreement (with seller or buyer), the licensee must advise the consumer of the agency relationship (designated agency) that will exist unless there is written agreement between them providing for a different relationship. At this time the licensee must advise the consumer of any other agency relationships available through the broker and must give the names of the consumer's designated agents in writing. The licensee must also advise the consumer if the licensee will be sharing the compensation with brokers representing other parties in the transaction.
5. No disclosure of agency or nonagency is required when a licensee is performing ministerial acts. Written disclosure that the licensee is not acting as the agent of the customer must be made to a customer at a time that will prevent disclosure of confidential information from the customer to the licensee.
6. Confidential information and ministerial acts are specifically defined in Article 4.
7. Consensual dual agency is permitted. The agency relationship exists with individuals and not with an office. Therefore, a broker showing his own listing could be in a dual agency situation, while a broker showing an office listing would not. The parties must consent to dual agency in writing, and when executing a contract, they must confirm either in the sales contract or another document that they previously agreed to dual agency. If a consumer denies or withdraws from a dual agency, the licensee may refer the party withdrawing to another licensee to act as their agent. Written disclosure (not permission) to the parties is required to obtain a referral fee.
8. Article 4 eliminates the vicarious liability of a principal for the acts of a broker.
9. After the expiration of a brokerage agreement, the broker's only duties to the client are to keep confidential information confidential and to return any moneys or property to the client, as well as any other duties previously provided for by written agreement.

FIGURE 4.1 A summary of the Brokerage Relationships in Real Estate Transactions Law.

a multiple listing service or other similar information source. The only way a subagency can be created in Illinois is through a written brokerage agreement. The Illinois Association of REALTORS® recommends that its members not offer subagency.

Vicarious Liability

Common law agency calls for **vicarious liability,** stating that *a principal is responsible for his agent's actions whether or not he is aware of the actions committed by the agent.* In contrast, Article 4 states that the consumer shall not be vicariously liable for the acts of omissions of a licensee for or on behalf of the consumer.

Termination of Brokerage Agreement

After the termination, expiration, or completion of a brokerage agreement, the broker does not owe any further duties except to account for all moneys and property relating to the transaction, to keep confidential information confidential, or as provided by written agreement.

Escrow Accounts

In Illinois, escrow accounts, often referred to as trust or earnest money accounts, must be maintained in a federally insured depository. Escrow moneys in Illinois include earnest moneys and rental security deposits. Illinois requires all escrow accounts to be non-interest-bearing, unless the principals have a written agreement stating that escrow funds be placed in an interest-bearing account. This agreement also must specify the recipients of the interest earned in the account. A broker may maintain more than one special account. It is a violation of the laws of agency for brokers to commingle the funds or property held in trust for others with personal accounts or with the operating account of the real estate firm. Misappropriation of a client's money is called conversion. Additional information on escrow accounts is provided in Chapter 16.

Brokerage

Brokerage Firms

A brokerage firm, or company, may be owned by a single licensed broker (a sole proprietor) or by more than one licensed person, such as a partnership or a corporation. If a broker who was a sole proprietor dies, the listings are terminated.

A brokerage firm is thought of as an independent broker if the brokerage is not associated with a real estate franchise organization. Association with a national or local real estate franchise licenses the brokerage firm to use the franchise's trade name, operating procedures, reputation, and referral services. The franchisee still owns and operates the brokerage firm.

Brokerage firms usually have more than one licensed broker or salesperson working with the firm. Sales associates affiliated with a brokerage firm are agents of the broker and may be named by the broker as designated agents for the firm's principals (clients). The fiduciary duty of the sales associates thus extends to both their employing firm and the firm's principals. Brokerage contracts are between the clients and the firm and are owned by the firm; if an associate quits the firm, her listings remain the broker's.

The broker is in two separate agency relationships: (a) the agent for the principal under the brokerage agreement and (b) the principal of the sales associates under an employment agreement in the brokerage firm. Therefore, the broker is responsible for the actions of the sales associates even though in almost all cases the sales associate is an independent contractor. As an agent of the broker, the sales associate is required to comply with the terms of the brokerage agreement and all rules of the brokerage firm.

Illinois licensees are either independent contractors or employees and are required to have a written employment contract defining the relationship with their employing broker. The contract states the terms regarding supervision, duties, compensation, and termination, as well as other aspects of their relationship. Independent contractors do not receive any compensation or benefits directly from an employer and must file and pay their own social security tax.

Salespersons may have only one employing broker at a time. All commissions earned are paid to the sales associate by the employing broker. Gifts or extra bonuses from appreciative clients must be conveyed through the employing broker.

Multiple Listing Services (MLS)

A **multiple listing service (MLS)** is *a system that pools the listings of all member companies, and all members are authorized to show any of the properties in the pool.* This arrangement greatly expands the offerings real estate salespersons may show to prospective buyers and increases the exposure of their own listings. The pooling of listings is an offer of cooperation and compensation to all members of the MLS. It is not an offer of subagency—Article 4 specifically prohibits an offer of subagency through an MLS or similar information source. A listing cannot be placed in an MLS without the written consent of the owner(s). Per the brokerage agreement, the seller is responsible for the payment of commission to only one broker, who may split the commission with other brokerages per previous agreement between them.

Types of Commission Arrangements

The amount or rate of commission to be charged by or paid to a real estate broker is negotiable and is strictly between the broker and the seller or buyer. Federal law is violated if any person or organization even recommends a commission schedule to a broker or group of brokers. It is also illegal for two or more brokers to agree to charge certain rates of commission to listing sellers. This is price fixing and is an act in restraint of trade, violating the Sherman Antitrust Act.

Percentage of final sales price. The most usual type of commission arrangement in listing contracts is for a specified percentage of the final sales price of the property. For example, the contract may call for the broker to be paid six or seven percent of the home's sales price.

Net listings. Another type of commission arrangement is the net listing, in which the seller specifies a net amount of money that he must receive upon the sale of the property. Anything above the net amount is designated as the broker's commission.

This type of commission arrangement is legal in Illinois, although it is not recommended. It can lead to the dissatisfaction of the seller if the property sells for substantially more than the listed price, as one of the broker's responsibilities is to establish a fair market price for the property. For these reasons, net listings are against the Code of Ethics of the National Association of REALTORS®. Thus, recommending a fair market price, including a reasonable commission established as a percentage of final sales price, is much more professional.

Flat fee. Under the flat fee listing arrangement, the broker takes the listing based on a specified payment at the time of the listing. This is called an upfront fee. The broker is entitled to retain this fee for efforts in attempting to market the property. Compensation under this listing does not depend on the sale of the property; thus, a flat fee typically is substantially less than a percentage of final sales price. Under this arrangement, the broker typically advertises the property but is not involved in showing the property or negotiating the terms of the sale between seller and buyer.

Commission to sales associates. Commission splits paid to sales associates in a real estate brokerage firm are established by the owner of the firm and the sales associate.

Under the usual commission split agreement, a share of the commission is paid directly to the cooperating broker by the listing broker. The listing broker will pay the sales associate that listed the property, and the cooperating broker will pay the sales associate that sold the property. If a sales associate both lists and sells a property, the associate will receive both the listing and selling share of the commission.

Referral fees. Brokerage firms often pay a referral fee to licensees from other localities when the licensee refers prospective buyers or sellers. In Illinois, the referral fee is paid directly to the referring broker. The referring broker pays the referring agent according to the terms of their employment agreement.

Commercial Real Estate Broker Lien Act

Illinois' **Commercial Real Estate Broker Lien Act** *allows lien rights to a real estate broker who is entitled to a commission in regard to a sale or lease of commercial property.* The act defines commercial real estate as (a) any real estate containing seven or more residential units, (b) vacant land, and (c) real estate classified as farmland for tax assessment purposes.

In order to claim a lien under the act, there must be a written brokerage agreement between the brokerage agency claiming the lien and the party whom the broker is representing. The lien can be claimed when the broker becomes entitled to the commission as evidenced by a written agreement. The notice of lien must be filed in the recorder's office prior to the actual conveyance of the property and takes effect the day of the recording. Exceptions to the recording of the lien before the conveyance include (a) situations when the commission due the broker is payable in installments, in the case of a lease, and (b) when the broker claiming the lien actually has a written agreement with a prospective buyer for the payment of the commission to the broker. Each of these exceptions has specific stipulations that must be followed.

The act includes an escrow provision. When there is a notice of lien that would prevent a property from closing, an amount sufficient to satisfy the lien can be paid into escrow. Upon payment of the moneys into escrow, the broker must release the lien so that the transaction can close. After the closing, the broker must pursue the case through litigation. The prevailing party is entitled to have attorney and court costs paid by the other party, in order to discourage frivolous claims.

ANTITRUST VIOLATIONS

When two or more brokers agree or conspire on the setting of commission rates, employee commission splits, etc., the brokers are price fixing and in violation of the Sherman Antitrust Act. A broker acting individually can set her own commission rates. No group or association of brokers can set, encourage, or even suggest a certain commission rate. Commission rates are strictly negotiable between the seller and the broker or the buyer and broker in the case of buyer brokerage. The MLS, therefore, cannot restrict listings with low or non-traditional commissions or commission splits, and it cannot restrict the type of listing (open, exclusive, etc.) submitted.

Brokers that conspire to refuse to cooperate with flat fee brokers or other brokers with less traditional commission splits are guilty of boycotting, another violation of the Sherman Antitrust Act.

Territorial allocation and tying arrangements are two more examples of antitrust violations. When brokers reduce competition between themselves by setting up territories in which each would have exclusive marketing rights, they are violating antitrust laws. Also illegal are agreements such as a broker/developer selling a lot or home to a buyer requiring, as a condition of the sale, the buyer to list the buyer's home with the broker/developer.

Important Points

1. Under common law, agency is usually created with an agreement but also can be implied by the agent's conduct. Compensation or the promise of compensation does not determine agency.
2. A person hired to represent another person is an agent. The agent may seek the assistance of other agents called subagents. The person being represented by the agent is called the principal. Subagency requires the subagent to work on behalf of the principal.
3. The type of agents are universal, general, and special. The type of agency depends on the scope of authority given by the principal.
4. A fiduciary relationship exists between the principal and the agent. Fiduciary duties consist of care, skill, and diligence; obedience; loyalty; accountability; and notice (disclosure).
5. Brokers must disclose all material facts to the buyer.
6. Under common law, a broker works for the seller. A broker specifically hired by a buyer to act as the agent of the buyer is called a buyer broker.
7. Representing both principals in a transaction is called dual agency. The permission of both the buyer and the seller is required for a dual agency.
8. Illinois law requires that all escrow moneys be placed in a non-interest-bearing account, unless otherwise specified by the principals to the transaction.
9. A broker is in two separate agency relationships. The broker is the agent for the principal under a brokerage agreement and is a principal under an employment agreement in the brokerage firm.
10. A multiple listing service (MLS) offers cooperation and compensation to participating members. It pools members' listings in a centralized system.
11. Net listings are legal in Illinois. They are, however, against the Code of Ethics of the National Association of REALTORS®.
12. The Commercial Broker Lien Act allows a real estate broker to create a lien against a property for nonpayment of a commission. The act defines commercial properties as (a) having seven or more residential units, (b) vacant land, and (c) farmland.

Review Questions

Answers to these questions are found in the Answer Key section at the back of the book.

1. An agent's duties to the principal include all of the following EXCEPT:
   a. loyalty
   b. accounting
   c. obedience
   d. legal advice

2. All of the following represent an agency relationship EXCEPT:
   a. the relationship between an owner of rental property and the tenant
   b. the relationship between an owner of rental property and the property manager
   c. the relationship between a designated agent and a buyer under a brokerage agreement
   d. the relationship between seller of property and the broker under a listing

3. All of the following statements are true regarding real estate salespersons in Illinois EXCEPT:

   a. they must have a written employment contract with their employing broker
   b. they are prohibited from advertising without including the name of the broker
   c. they may accept a commission only from their employing broker
   d. they may accept gifts or a bonus directly from an appreciative seller

4. A real estate sales agent presents an offer to the property owner during the listing term for the listed price payable in cash with no contingencies and the specified earnest money deposit. In this situation, which of the following statements is correct?

   a. the property owner is required to accept the offer
   b. the listing brokerage company is legally entitled to the commission agreed upon in the listing contract
   c. the sales agent will get the earnest money deposit if the offer is refused
   d. the property owner will forfeit the earnest money deposit if she refuses to accept the offer

5. A real estate agent advises a buyer that a property is zoned for commercial use of the type the buyer intends to make of the property. Relying upon the agent's advice, the buyer contracts to purchase the property. In making the statement regarding the zoning, the agent did not know what zoning applied to the property. The buyer subsequently learns that the zoning is such that he cannot use the property as he intended. Which of the following is correct?

   a. the agent committed an act of misrepresentation and is liable to the buyer for any loss the buyer suffered as a consequence
   b. because the agent did not know the true facts regarding the zoning, no misrepresentation of the property to the buyer took place, and therefore the agent is not liable
   c. the agent is not liable because the buyer was responsible to find out the facts on his own
   d. the agent is not liable because the property was for commercial use instead of residential

6. When a licensed real estate salesperson desires to buy property listed with her broker's office, she may:

   a. buy the property at any time and on any terms
   b. not buy the property because of the subagency relationship with the seller through her office
   c. buy the property, provided her interest is made known to all parties
   d. buy the property if she informs her broker; she doesn't have to notify the principal

7. All of the following terminate an agency agreement EXCEPT:

   a. expiration of time period set out in the agreement
   b. death of the principal
   c. bankruptcy of the salesperson
   d. completion of the sale of the property subject to the agency agreement

8. A licensee can accept compensation from both buyer and seller:

   a. only if there is a written listing from both
   b. only if the total amount is equal to the total commission
   c. under no circumstances
   d. only after full disclosure and agreement of both parties

9. Buyer Tsang wishes to make an offer on one of his designated agent's listings. The designated agent must:

   a. withdraw from the transaction
   b. inform Tsang that brokerage law will not allow her to represent him in a dual agency relationship
   c. obtain written confirmation from both clients for her to act as a dual agent in this transaction
   d. show Tsang all of her listed properties

10. Which of the following statements is true regarding dual agency in Illinois?

    a. a licensee acting as a dual agent may not disclose material facts
    b. dual agency is prohibited under any circumstances
    c. confirmation of the clients' consent to dual agency is required after the offer to purchase has been presented and accepted
    d. clients must act without the benefit of the dual agent in negotiating final contract price and other terms of the sale

11. Which of the following is correct regarding Article 4?

    a. the requirement to keep confidential information confidential ends when the listing expires or the property is sold
    b. confidential information consists of only information that the client expressly states that she wishes to keep confidential
    c. in certain instances, confidential information may be revealed to the employing or managing broker
    d. a broker acting as a dual agent can reveal confidential information to both the parties

12. Someone who has an unlimited power of attorney is typically a:

    a. special agent
    b. general agent
    c. universal agent
    d. trust agent

13. MLS is best defined as:

    a. listings of multiple-unit properties in one area
    b. listings of properties that have multiple owners
    c. a means of sharing listings between member brokers and their agents, allowing for cooperation and shared compensation
    d. sharing lists of buyers with builders in an effort to multiply the magnitude and construction of home sales

14. A property manager is typically a:

    a. special agent
    b. general agent
    c. universal agent
    d. trust agent

15. A principal is one who:

    a. empowers another to act for him
    b. buys direct from the owner, without a broker's representation
    c. expects care, obedience, accounting, and loyalty from the buyer of his property
    d. owns a brokerage firm

16. When taking a listing, the agent is told by the property owner that the septic system has not been working properly. This fact is disclosed on the listing sheet or on the MLS sheet. At a showing of the property, the agent:

    a. does not have to disclose this information unless the prospective buyer asks about the septic system
    b. does not have to disclose this information because it was disclosed on the listing sheet and MLS sheet
    c. must disclose this information whether asked or not, as the agent is to be fair, open, and honest in all dealings
    d. does not have to disclose this information unless in a dual agency situation representing both buyer and seller

17. Which of the following statements is true regarding escrow accounts in Illinois?

    a. escrow moneys must be placed in an interest-bearing account
    b. a written agreement by the principals must state how the interest from moneys placed in escrow is to be distributed
    c. security deposits are not considered escrow moneys
    d. brokers may not have more than one escrow account

18. A buyer walks into Broker Lyons' office located in Illinois. Broker Lyons, unless other arrangements are made:

    a. will automatically be the designated agent of the buyer
    b. will automatically be the general agent of the buyer
    c. they must have a written agreement between them
    d. Lyons cannot show the buyer his own listings

19. Salesperson Torres represents Buyer Andrews. If Torres shows Andrews a property listed with Torres' office, which of the following is TRUE under Article 4?

    a. Torres is acting as a dual agent only if it is Torres' own listing
    b. Torres is acting as a dual agent if the office has the property listed
    c. Torres cannot represent Andrews under these circumstances and must refer Andrews to another office
    d. Torres can represent Andrews, but can only receive a commission from the seller

20. To create a dual agency in Illinois all of the following must be adhered to EXCEPT:
    a. buyer and seller must agree in writing to the dual agency
    b. at time of execution of any contract to purchase, buyer and seller must confirm in writing their previous agreement to allow dual agency
    c. the broker cannot receive a fee or commission from both the buyer and the seller
    d. written disclosure of receiving a fee from both the buyer and the seller, and not permission to receive a fee, is all that is required

CHAPTER 5

Important Terminology

acceptance
accord and satisfaction
assignee
assignment
assignor
bilateral contract
breach of contract
compensatory damages
competence
complete performance
consideration
contract
contract for deed
counteroffer
duress
earnest money
equitable title
exclusive agency listing
exclusive right-to-sell listing
executed contract
executory contract
express contract
fraud
implied contract
installment agreement
installment land contract
laches
liquidated damages
listing contract

menace
misrepresentation
mutual assent
mutual mistake
novation
offer and acceptance
open listing
operation of law
option
parol evidence rule
punitive damages
ready, willing, and able
reality of consent
rescission
Residential Real Property Disclosure Act
right of first refusal
specific performance
Statute of Frauds
undue influence
unenforceable contract
Uniform Vendor and Purchaser Risk Act
unilateral contract
valid contract
voidable contract
void contract
with reserve

Real Estate Contracts

IN THIS CHAPTER Contracts are involved in every aspect of real estate. Some of the most common real estate contracts are listings, sales contracts, leases, options, mortgages, and installment agreements/contracts for deed. Before learning the specifics of the various contracts normally encountered in the real estate business, we must understand the basics of contract law, which apply to real estate contracts as well as all other contracts. Nearly every controversy or question arising in the real estate business involves the contracts between parties and can be answered by applying basic contract law.

BASIC CONTRACT LAW

Terms and Classifications

A **contract** is *an agreement between competent legal parties to do some legal act or to refrain from doing some legal act in exchange for consideration.* A contract establishes both the rights and the duties or responsibilities of the parties to the contract. Because the rights and responsibilities can differ from contract to contract, various classifications or types of contracts have evolved. Contracts can be classified as:

1. express versus implied
2. unilateral versus bilateral
3. executory versus executed
4. valid (enforceable) versus unenforceable, void, or voidable

Express Contracts

Under an **express contract,** *the parties to the contract have definitely agreed on all the terms and conditions in the contract.* An express contract can be written or spoken (oral). Among real estate contracts, which include listings, real estate sales contracts, mortgages, land contracts, options, and leases, the majority are in writing and thus are express contracts. In some cases, parties have oral leases. Oral contracts are also express contracts.

Putting It to Work

People often question the validity of an oral contract because of the difficulty in proving it when parties dispute the contract terms. Though proof may be a problem, this does not affect the validity of oral contracts when there is proof.

Implied Contracts

An **implied contract** (or ostensible contract) is one *inferred from the conduct and actions of another without express agreement.* Implied contracts arise when the conduct of the parties clearly illustrates the intention to contract. A court implies the existence of a contract if one party has received the benefit at the expense of the other party. The court requires the recipient of the benefit to pay a reasonable compensation to the party rendering the benefit. An exception is if the benefit received is truly a gift. An implied contract is created, for example, if C hires D to cut his hair without stipulating the price to be paid for the haircut. An implied contract to pay the reasonable value of the service delivered is created by C's allowing the haircut.

The law does not favor implied contracts because of the uncertainty of terms of the agreement of the parties and because the parties are placed in a contract relationship without actual express consent to contract. Implied contracts should be avoided in real estate. They arise most often in the agency relationship created by a listing. Under the listing, the seller and the real estate agent have an express contract setting out the agreement and terms of the parties. Because the real estate agent also may spend much time with the prospective buyer, the buyer may infer that a contract for services exists between the buyer and the real estate agent. This may occur when the agent is involved in negotiating the terms of the offer to purchase between the seller and the buyer. Both parties believe the agent is working in their own best interests. This is a classic example of an implied contract in real estate that may result in an unintended or undisclosed dual agency.

Bilateral Contracts

"Bi" means two. In its meaning here, two does not refer to two parties to a contract, as every contract has at least two parties; instead, it refers to the number of parties to the contract who are making promises or performing acts. A **bilateral contract** is one in which *two parties have made promises of some kind to each other.* The promise could be for the payment of money or for the performance of some act such as painting a house. Because both parties make promises, both are bound or obligated under the contract from the onset of the contract.

The real estate sales contract is bilateral because it is based on the exchange of promises whereby the seller will sell and the buyer will buy. Other examples of bilateral contracts in real estate are mortgages, listings, leases, and land contracts (contracts for deed).

Unilateral Contracts

The "uni" in unilateral means "one." Again, this does not refer to the number of parties to a contract but, instead, to the number of promises made by the parties to a contract. In a **unilateral contract,** *one party makes a promise in order to induce a second party to do something.* The party making the promise is bound and obligated under the contract. The other party, however, has made no promise and thus is not bound or obligated in any way to perform or act.

An example of a unilateral contract outside of real estate is an offer for a reward for the return of a pet. No one is obligated to look for and return the pet. If someone does return the pet, however, the one who promised the reward is obligated to pay.

The typical unilateral contract in the real estate business is an option contract. Under an **option,** the *owner of the property (optionor) promises to sell her land to another (optionee) at a certain price for a certain time period.* The optionee is not obligated to purchase the land; however, if the optionee does desire to purchase the land, the optionor is obligated to sell on the terms promised. The optionor cannot legally sell the land to any other person during the term of the option.

Executory Contracts

A *contract that is not yet fully performed or completed* is called an **executory contract.** In real estate, most contracts begin as executory. A mortgage is a contract whereby the borrower pays money over a term of years to the lender. The action yet to be done—the monthly payments—will go on for years. A lease is a contract whereby the tenant will pay rent on an ongoing basis or face eviction. A listing contract sets a definite time period during which the real estate broker tries to sell the property and activity continues during the term of the listing.

Executed Contracts

A *contract that has been fully performed* is an **executed contract.** An example in the real estate business is an offer to purchase in which all contingencies and conditions have been met and closing takes place. After the closing, nothing more is to be performed under the offer to purchase.

PUTTING IT TO WORK

Although a real estate sales contract becomes executed upon closing, it often gives rise to many other ongoing contracts. Closing may present a new mortgage, an insurance contract, and a homeowner's warranty, all of which are executory.

Valid Contracts

A **valid contract** is one that is *binding and enforceable on all parties to it.* It contains all the essential elements of a contract (discussed later in this chapter). The parties to a valid contract are legally obligated to abide by the terms and conditions of the contract. If a party to a valid contract defaults in performing an obligation under the contract, that individual is subject to legal action by the nondefaulting party in a court of law. In drawing up contracts, every effort should be made to create a valid contract.

Unenforceable Contracts

An **unenforceable contract** is one that *appears to meet the requirements for validity but would not be enforceable in court.* Parties to the contract would not be able to sue for performance of contract. Even though the contract would not be enforceable in court, unenforceable contracts may still be considered valid between the parties if they wish to complete performance.

Void Contracts

A **void contract** has *absolutely no legal force or effect even though all of the essential elements for a contract exist.* The phrase "null and void" is often used to mean "does not exist in the eyes of the law." Five circumstances cause a contract to be void:

1. *The purpose of the contract is illegal.* A contract between two people to murder a third person for money is void. The purpose of the contract is illegal. Neither party is obligated by the terms agreed to. No contract exists.

2. *The contract is impossible to complete because of an act of God or operation of law.* Parties to a real estate sales contract may agree on the price and terms of purchase, yet if the state condemns the property for a highway, neither party can sue the other for failing to complete the contract. The contract is impossible to complete under the operation of law. The same impossibility to complete can occur if the object of the contract is destroyed by fire, flood, tornado, or other natural causes. If the contract is impossible to complete, it is void; it does not exist. Impossibility to complete a contract is more common than illegal contracts in real estate.

3. *The contract is forged.* If someone forges George's name to a contract, the contract cannot be enforced against George. The contract is void and does not exist in the eyes of the law. Forged checks, forged deeds, and other forged documents are also void.

4. *The contract lacks consideration.* In order to be valid, a contract must have consideration. For example, Anita's parents wish to give her a piece of real estate. The attorney that draws up the legal documents will place a nominal dollar amount, say $10, in the deed. The deed will state that the property is being conveyed from Anita's parents for the good consideration of love and affection and the valuable consideration of $10. The amount of consideration does not matter, only that some form of valuable consideration changed hands. Consideration is discussed in detail later in this chapter.

5. *The contract is entered into with a person adjudged to be insane.* Parties that are insane or lack mental capacity cannot enter into contracts. A contract that has been entered into with an insane person is void. It is up to each individual party to determine if the other party has the capacity to enter into a contract.

Voidable Contracts

A **voidable contract** may or may not be enforceable between the parties. It *results from the failure of the contracting parties to meet some legal requirement in negotiating the agreement.* Usually in the voidable contract situation, one party to the contract is the victim of wrongdoing by the other party. For example, Mr. Smith contracts to buy property owned by Mrs. Brown; Mrs. Brown states that the property has no defects when she knows the septic system does not function properly; Mr. Smith relies on Mrs. Brown's statement and buys the property. Mrs. Brown has committed fraud (intentional lying); thus, Mr. Smith can choose to complete the contract or to nullify the contract.

The parties to a voidable contract are not required to set aside or void the contract. The parties may fulfill their obligations under the contract and receive their benefits. A voidable contract can be voluntarily performed by the parties. At any time prior to complete performance of the contract, however, the party that is wronged can elect to discontinue. Contracts that lack genuine assent are voidable also. Situations that make a contract lack genuine assent are minority status of a party, intoxication of a party, fraud, misrepresentation, mutual mistake, undue influence, and menace or duress. These items are discussed later in this chapter.

Essential Elements of Contracts

The first step in understanding contract law is to recognize when a contract exists and, conversely, when it does not exist. The essential elements required for the existence of a contract are:

1. offer and acceptance (meeting of the minds)
2. consideration
3. legal capacity of the parties
4. reality of consent
5. legality of object
6. possibility to complete

In analyzing any controversy concerning real estate, the first step should be to run down the checklist of elements of a contract to ascertain that in fact a contract exists.

Offer and Acceptance

For a contract to exist, an offer and an unconditional acceptance of the offer must be present. Another name for **offer and acceptance** is *meeting of the minds.* Meeting of the minds is evident when the *parties to the contract reach agreement on the terms to be included in the contract. Agreement of the parties* is also called **mutual assent.** The party making the offer is the offeror, and the party to whom the offer is made is the offeree.

In the typical real estate sales contract, the buyer begins as the offeror. An offer that has not been accepted can be withdrawn at any time prior to acceptance and the notification of that acceptance. Once the offeror (or his agent) has knowledge of the acceptance, the offer may not then be withdrawn.

The offer must be *definite and specific* in its terms. If the offer is vague and indefinite and, therefore, subject to various interpretations, its acceptance will not result in a valid contract. For example, if an offer is made to Seller A to purchase a home in the Executive Heights Subdivision without setting out a specific address, and Seller A owns three houses in that subdivision, the offer is vague, and an acceptance will not result in the creation of a valid contract.

Putting It to Work

> In real estate, the agreement should be complete as it relates to the details. To be truly complete, an offer to buy will include price, terms, financing, performance, dates, closing costs, warranties, and many other details.

The offer *must not be illusory* in nature. An offer that is indefinite and totally in the control of the offeror is illusory. For example, an offer to buy a home in Security Estates, when and if the offeror decides to move, is too indefinite and totally within the offeror's control. The offer is not binding upon the offeror and thus is illusory. Acceptance of an illusory offer will not result in the creation of a valid contract.

If the offer is clear and definite, the offeree has the right to accept unconditionally, reject, or counteroffer. The contract comes into existence only at the time unconditional acceptance of the offer is communicated to the offeror or to the offeror's agent.

An acceptance that varies in any way from the offer as presented will not qualify as an acceptance. An *acceptance that varies from the offer* is a **counteroffer.** If the seller makes a counteroffer, no contract exists regarding the first offer. The making of a counteroffer terminates and destroys the original offer, much like rejection of the offer. The seller has now become the offeror, and the buyer is the offeree. In the typical real estate transaction, where many offers and counteroffers can be made before consummating the deal, the parties switch "hats" of offeror and offeree often.

A unilateral offer may be accepted only by performance of the action specified in the offer—for example, a promise to pay money upon the delivery of goods. Acceptance of this unilateral offer is made by delivery of the goods. A bilateral offer is accepted by an agreement to do the things requested in the offer. Acceptance of a bilateral offer must be communicated to the offeror for a contract to be created. The acceptance must be absolutely unconditional in the case of either the unilateral or bilateral offer.

Sometimes an offer specifies the manner in which acceptance of the offer must be communicated to the offeror by the offeree. In the absence of any specific provision in this regard, the offeree should communicate acceptance in the same manner as the offer. If the offer is made in writing, the acceptance should be made in writing. If acceptance is by mail, the communication is effective and a contract is created at the time the offeree deposits the acceptance in the mail.

Offers may be terminated in the following ways:

1. expiration of a time limit specified by the offeror prior to acceptance
2. death or insanity of either the offeror or the offeree prior to acceptance
3. revocation of the offer by the offeror prior to acceptance and notification of that acceptance
4. expiration of a reasonable period of time after the offer is made without an acceptance
5. failure of the offeree to comply with the terms of the offer as to the specific manner in which the acceptance must be communicated
6. rejection of the offer
7. acceptance of the offer, at which time the offer becomes a contract

When the offer is accepted, a contract is created, and the buyer acquires an interest in the land known as equitable title. The seller retains legal title until transfer by deed to the buyer. **Equitable title** is *an interest in real estate of sufficient worth for court protection of that interest,* although this may not be anywhere near ownership.

Consideration

Consideration is *the giving of something of value.* For a contract to be valid, consideration must be present. The two classifications of consideration are good consideration and valuable consideration. Good consideration consists of love and affection and is derived from a moral obligation. A mother's love is good consideration. However, courts often find good consideration to be insufficient to support a contract between parties and will require valuable consideration, which may consist of money, goods, services, a promise to do something, or forbearance.

One of the most common errors real estate licensees make is stating that for an offer to purchase to be valid, the buyer must pay earnest money. Buyers almost always give earnest money in an offer to purchase, but earnest money is not required. The buyer's promise in the offer to buy the property is sufficient consideration for a valid contract.

In the case of a unilateral contract, a promise is made in exchange for the performance of a specified act. A bilateral contract entails mutual promises for future performance. Each party must promise simultaneously. If one party promises to make a gift to another party, a valid contract does not exist because the other party has made no promise in return. There must be consideration from both sides. This is called *mutuality of contract.* Each party to a contract must do something or promise to do something.

Legal Capacity of the Parties

For a contract to be valid, the parties to the contract must have the capacity to enter into a contract. Age is one consideration in the legal capacity of a party. Minors—those who have not reached the age of majority as established by statutory law—do not have the legal capacity to contract. Illinois citizens reach the age of majority at 18. An exception for minors is made in some jurisdictions for those who are married or for minors who are contracting for essential services such as housing or medical care.

Legal capacity of a party also is determined by **competence,** *the mental or emotional capacity to enter into contracts.* A person adjudged to be insane does not have legal capacity to contract.

The legal capacity of a person to contract also can be affected by alcohol and drugs. An individual who is intoxicated or under the influence of drugs to the extent that she does not understand what is happening is temporarily incompetent to contract. Any contract signed under these conditions is not enforceable against the person who was temporarily incompetent.

Contracts entered into by parties lacking legal capacity are voidable by the party lacking capacity. In the case of minors, the contract is voidable at the option of the minor. The minor may hold an adult to a contract, but the adult cannot legally hold the minor to the contract. The contract is not legally enforceable against the minor. If a minor fulfills the terms of the contract and does not take steps to terminate the contract prior to reaching the age of majority or soon after, the individual is said to have ratified the contract as an adult and thus is bound.

The legal capacity of entities other than individuals also must be considered. Entities that may enter into contracts include corporations, partnerships, churches, schools, towns, cities, and other governmental agencies. The legal capacity of these entities does not involve age, insanity, or drunkenness. The legal capacity of entities created by the statutes of the state is determined by the documents and instruments that create the entities. For example, in a corporation, the bylaws of the corporation determine which actions must be taken and which officers or directors must sign contracts for validity.

Reality of Consent

For a valid contract to be created, the parties must enter into it voluntarily. They must mutually agree to the terms and conditions in the contract. If a person enters into a written contract, as evidenced by his signature on the contract, the individual is presumed to have assented to the terms and conditions of the contract.

The consent of the parties to enter into a contractual agreement must be a real consent. **Reality of consent** is *based on the parties having an accurate knowledge of the facts concerning the terms and conditions of the contract.* If one or both parties does not have full knowledge or accurate knowledge, the contract will fail to be valid because of the lack of mutual assent. Typical factors causing the lack of mutual consent are fraud, misrepresentation, mutual mistake, undue influence, and duress. Any of these factors can defeat the voluntary assent of the parties and, therefore, invalidate the contract and make it voidable.

Fraud (Actual Fraud)

Fraud is *intentional deceit or lying,* a misstatement of material facts to induce someone to rely on the erroneous facts and enter into a contract. A false statement is deemed to be fraudulent when (a) the party making the statement knows it to be false or (b) the party making the statement does not know in fact whether the statement is true or false but proceeds without determining its truth or falsehood.

For example, prospective buyer Alice asks Julio, the real estate agent or the owner of real property, if the house has termites. Actually knowing that the house has termites, either by his own personal inspection or by a report from an independent inspector, Julio tells Alice that there are no termites. Julio has committed fraud. Based upon this misstatement of facts, Alice may rescind any contract entered into. Julio also could be held personally liable to Alice for any damages arising from the falsehood or could face disciplinary action.

Misrepresentation (Negative Fraud)

Misrepresentation is the *unintentional misstatement of facts,* the result of a misunderstanding of the facts by the person making the misrepresentation. A party to a contract who has relied on the misrepresented facts is legally entitled to rescind the contract. It is voidable.

For example, prospective buyer Joseph asks Lillian, the real estate agent for the owner of real property, how much land the seller owns. Upon checking the local records, Lillian finds that the owner owns 50 acres. The owner, however, is selling only 10 acres. Lillian has unintentionally misled Joseph, and he makes an offer assuming that the sale will be of 50 acres and not 10 acres. The confusion is innocent. Joseph will be able to invalidate or void the contract.

Both fraud and misrepresentation involve the material representation of facts that may turn out to be false or misleading. The difference is in the intent.

Mutual Mistake

A **mutual mistake,** *a mistake of material fact by both parties,* may nullify a contract. For example, if an incorrect street address is used, the contract is voidable.

Mutual mistake does not cover a misunderstanding of the law by one party or the other, only a mistake of fact. Mistake of law will not invalidate an otherwise valid contract. An example of mistake of law may occur in an offer to purchase. The prospective buyer has in mind to open a beauty shop at a given address. The buyer does not state in the offer that the purchase is conditional upon proper zoning. After the offer is accepted, the buyer finds that local zoning will not allow a beauty shop. The buyer does not have the right to invalidate the contract.

Undue Influence

Undue influence is *any improper or wrongful control or influence by one person over another.* As a result, the will of one person is overpowered so that he is induced to act or prevented from acting of his own free will. Undue influence occurs when one person takes advantage of another person's lack of knowledge or takes advantage of a special relationship between the parties. Such a relationship may exist between a legal advisor and a client or between employer and employee. If a person is induced to enter into a contract as a result of undue influence, the contract is voidable.

Menace and Duress

Menace is *the threat of force.* The essential element of menace is physical fear or threat of force against a person. **Duress** is *the use of force.* The presence of menace or duress in contract negotiations renders the contract voidable by the victim. It defeats the requirements of a voluntary meeting of the minds.

Legality of Object

Legality of object means that the contract must be for a legal purpose. A contract for an illegal purpose is void. Examples of illegal contracts include contracts in restraint of trade, contracts to stifle or promote litigation, and contracts in restraint of marriage.

Possibility to Complete

The parties must be able to complete the contract without interference from operation of law or acts of God. A contract that is impossible to complete is void. Examples of contracts that are impossible to complete arise in times of national emergency. A steel company may have contracted to deliver steel to a manufacturer of household appliances, but because of a declaration of war, the steel company is ordered by the government to send all steel to battleship manufacturers. Examples of contracts that are impossible to complete in times of natural disaster are those affected by tornadoes, hurricanes, fires, and floods. A contract to paint a house on a certain day is impossible to complete if the house is destroyed by hurricane or other act of God.

STATUTE OF FRAUDS

Nowhere in the list of essential elements for a valid contract is a requirement for writing. In most cases an oral contract is just as valid as a written contract. Both oral and written contracts are express contracts. The difficulty with oral contracts lies in the chance for misunderstanding as to the parties' rights and obligations. Terms of an oral contract may be extremely difficult to prove in a court proceeding if that becomes necessary.

Because of the potential for misunderstandings in oral contracts, all states have adopted the **Statute of Frauds.** This law states that *contracts involving the creation of an interest in real property or the conveyance of an interest in real property must be written to be enforceable.* "Enforceable" means that a party to the contract may ask the court to order that the terms of the contract be carried out.

The Statute of Frauds requires that real estate contracts be written and contain all of the essential elements for a valid contract. Oral testimony (parol evidence) is not sufficient to create a contract involving the transfer of title to real property. A primary purpose of the Statute of Frauds is to prevent presentation of fraudulent proof of an oral contract. This issue is also addressed by a concept known as the **parol evidence rule,** which essentially states that *oral explanations can support the written words of a contract but cannot contradict them.* (Oral contracts entered into after a written contract, however, can be considered a "new" contract or modifications to the prior written contract.)

The statute does not require any particular form of writing. To satisfy the requirements of the statute, the writing may be a short memorandum, a telegram, a receipt, or similar document. The contract need not necessarily be contained in one document. It can be a series of letters or invoices. The best format, however, is to have the entire contract in one writing and signed by all parties.

All real estate contracts fall under the Statute of Frauds, including contracts to buy and sell real estate, options, contracts for deeds, and contracts for the exchange of real estate. Lease contracts also fall under the Statute of Frauds, but an exception exists for leases of short duration. In Illinois, a lease whose term is for more than one year falls under the Statute of Frauds and must be in writing to be enforceable. Leases with shorter terms are enforceable even if not written.

ILLINOIS RESIDENTIAL REAL PROPERTY DISCLOSURE ACT

The Illinois **Residential Real Property Disclosure Act** requires that all sellers of residential properties of four units or less make prospective buyers *aware of known material defects* of the property with a residential real property disclosure form. This form consists of 22 statements to which the seller must respond regarding the condition of certain aspects of the property, based on the seller's actual knowledge of any known defects in the residential property. While this form does not constitute a warranty by the seller, the buyer may rely on the information in choosing to purchase and defining the terms of the offer. The seller is responsible for completing the disclosure form. Real estate salespeople and even the seller's attorneys should refrain from assisting in the completion of the disclosure form.

The following persons or entities are exempt from this act: transfers pursuant to a court order, including, but not limited to, transfers ordered by a probate court in administration of an estate; transfers between spouses resulting from a judgment of dissolution of marriage or legal separation; transfers pursuant to an order of possession; transfers by a trustee in bankruptcy; transfers by eminent domain; and transfers resulting from a decree for specific performance. Also exempt are transfers from a mortgagor to a mortgagee by deed in lieu of foreclosure or consent judgment, transfer by judicial deed issued pursuant to a foreclosure sale to the successful bidder or the assignee of a certificate of sale, transfer by a collateral assignment of a beneficial interest of a land trust, or transfer by a mortgagee or a successor in interest to the mortgagee's secured position or a beneficiary under a deed in trust who has acquired the real property by deed in lieu of foreclosure, consent judgment, or judicial deed issued pursuant to a foreclosure sale. Exemptions are further extended to transfers by a fiduciary in the course of the administration of a decedent's estate, guardianship, conservatorship, or trust. Transfers from one co-owner to one or more co-owners, transfers pursuant to testate or intestate succession, and transfers made to a spouse or to a person or persons in the lineal line of consanguinity of one or more of the sellers are exempt. Transfers from an entity that has taken title to residential real property from a seller for the purpose of assisting in the relocation of a seller, so long as the entity makes available to all prospective buyers a copy of the disclosure form furnished to the entity by the seller, are exempt. Transfers to or from a government entity and transfers of newly constructed residential property that has not been occupied are exempt.

The act requires that the written disclosure statement be delivered to the prospective buyer before the signing of a contract to purchase. If a material defect is revealed by the disclosure after an accepted offer, the prospective buyer may, within three business days after receipt of the report, terminate the contract without liability or recourse. No right to terminate the contract exists once the property has been conveyed. The buyer has no right to terminate the contract if the report is delivered before the prospective buyer enters into a contract for the conveyance of the property.

No action can be taken under this act later than one year from the earlier of the date of possession, date of occupancy, or date of recording of the deed. However, this one-year limit applies only to actions available under the act, not to a cause of action that would take place under common law.

FEDERAL LEAD-BASED PAINT DISCLOSURE REGULATIONS

New federal regulations announced March 6, 1996, require the disclosure of lead-based paint hazards in the sale or rental of residential properties built before 1978. Owners of 1–4 unit residential dwellings must comply with the requirements by December 6, 1996. Owners of properties containing more than 4 residential units must comply by September 6, 1996.

Under the federal regulations, sellers and lessors of residential properties built before 1978:

- must disclose the presence of known lead-based paint or lead-based paint hazards in the housing

- must provide prospective buyers or tenants with any records or reports pertaining to the presence of lead-based paint or lead-based paint hazards
- must provide a lead hazard information pamphlet that must be given to the buyer or lessee
- must include required statutory disclosure and acknowledgment language in sales and lease agreements
- must provide purchasers with a 10-day opportunity to conduct risk assessment or inspection for the presence of lead-based paint or lead-based paint hazards, prior to the purchaser's becoming obligated under any purchase contract

The real estate salesperson must ensure compliance with these requirements. States that have existing lead-based paint disclosure laws may combine the state requirements with federal requirements to satisfy both laws. Some states require the testing, abatement, or removal of lead-based paint. The federal law only requires disclosure.

Discharge of Contracts

Contracts can be discharged or terminated by (a) agreement of the parties, (b) full performance, (c) impossibility of performance, or (d) operation of law.

Agreement of the Parties

Just as contracts are created by agreement of the parties, any executory contract can be terminated by agreement of the parties. This is typically called a *release of contract*. The release is itself a contract and thus must have consideration to be valid. The consideration is found in the relief from the obligations under the original contract. The release also must be voluntarily given and with full knowledge of all material facts.

In some instances a contract is terminated not by agreed release but by **accord and satisfaction,** *a new agreement between the parties,* often the result of a negotiated compromise. An example of accord and satisfaction is when one party to the contract wishes to be released but the other party desires money for the attempted default. The parties enter into a new contract for the payment of money as a substitution for performance of the contract. In real estate, the typical example of accord and satisfaction occurs when the buyer of property wishes to be relieved from the contract to buy and the seller agrees to take the earnest money in place of selling the property.

Another form of agreement that discharges or terminates contracts is **novation,** *the substitution of a new contract for a prior contract or the substitution of a new party for an old party.* It typically involves the substitution of parties in the contract. A new party to the contract agrees to satisfy the former contracting party's obligation. Upon reaching the agreement to substitute parties, the novation or new contract is created, terminating the original contract and the original party's liability.

Complete Performance

The usual and most desirable manner of terminating contracts is by **complete performance** of all terms of the contract. The contract is said to be executed when *all parties fully perform all terms.*

Impossibility of Performance

The general rule is that even if a party to a contract is unable to perform obligations under the contract, the party is still liable. The reasoning is that the one who cannot perform should have provided against this possibility by including a provision in the contract for relief in the event of impossibility.

There are exceptions to the general rule. One is in the case of personal service contracts. If a person contracts to render services such as mowing a yard, but is unable to complete the services as a result of death or incapacity, the obligated person is relieved of liability. This is one of the few instances in which death or incapacity affects contractual obligations. In most other contract cases, death does not affect the contract obligation or rights.

Another exception to the general rule is when the performance of an obligation under a contract becomes illegal as a result of a change in law after the contract was created, such as contracting for the drainage of farmland that has been recently designated as wetlands. The prohibition against drainage of wetlands renders the contract between the parties impossible to complete through no fault of either party, and the obligated parties are relieved of responsibility.

Operation of Law

The term **operation of law** describes *the manner in which the rights and liabilities of parties may be changed by the application of law without cooperation or agreement of the parties affected.* Contracts can be terminated or discharged by operation of law. Examples of discharge of contracts by operation of law are:

1. *Statute of limitations.* If a party to a contract *fails to bring a lawsuit against a defaulting party within a time period set by statute,* the injured party loses the right of remedy because of operation of law or **laches.** The mere passage of time and expiration of the statutory time period affect the injured party's right to recover. Every state limits by statute the time to bring legal action against a party; in Illinois this period is seven years.

2. *Bankruptcy.* The filing of a petition in bankruptcy under federal law may have the effect of terminating contracts in existence as of the date of filing the bankruptcy petition. The purpose of bankruptcy law is to relieve the bankrupt from liability of outstanding contracts and to provide a fresh start.

3. *Alteration of contract.* The intentional cancellation or alteration of a written agreement has the effect of discharging the agreement. The alteration must be material and intentional. This frequently involves negotiable instruments such as checks, stocks, and bonds in which the date of payment, amount of payment, or changes in interest rates are altered.

Illinois Uniform Vendor and Purchaser Risk Act

Under the **Uniform Vendor and Purchaser Risk Act,** *if the property suffers destruction, the seller bears the risk once the contract has been signed but before title has passed or possession has taken place.* The contract cannot be enforced, and the seller must give back any earnest money. Once title has transferred or the buyer has taken possession, the contract is valid and enforceable. The full purchase price must be paid even if the property has been partially or totally destroyed. A buyer who has taken possession under a contract for deed, but has not received title, must bear the loss.

ASSIGNMENT OF CONTRACT RIGHTS

Contract rights are considered a personal property right. The contract itself may concern real estate, and thus the ownership of contract rights is ownership of a stick in the bundle of sticks of that real estate. Either party to a contract may transfer or sell the contract rights unless the contract specifically prohibits such a sale or transfer. The *transfer or sale of contract rights* is called **assignment.** *The party assigning or transferring her rights* is the **assignor.** *The party receiving the rights* is the **assignee.**

Any assignment of contract rights is only of the rights and does not eliminate the contract obligations. For the contract obligations to be eliminated, a release or novation must occur.

A typical assignment in real estate happens when a landlord sells rental property to a new owner. Sale of the property does not terminate the lease; thus, the new owner not only owns the real estate but also has been assigned the old owner's rights under the lease to rent. Another assignment in real estate transactions is more commonly called "mortgage assumption." For example, Mr. Adams owns a house with a mortgage owed to a local bank. Mr. Adams sells to Mr. and Mrs. Brown, who assume the mortgage of Mr. Adams. The contract rights belonging to Mr. Adams concerning monthly payments and interest rate are transferred to Mr. and Mrs. Brown. Mr. Adams, however, is still obligated under the mortgage contract in the event Mr. and Mrs. Brown do not make the monthly payments.

INTERPRETATION OF CONTRACTS

A contract that is clear, concise, and unambiguous will require no interpretation by a court. When a contract is not clear and is instead ambiguous or confusing, the court has certain rules for interpretation. The court will not use the rules of contract construction and interpretation to make or amend a contract for the parties. If the parties do not have all of the essential elements of a contract, the court will hold that no contract exists. The court will only interpret and enforce a contract that does exist.

If a contract exists, the court will enforce the contract in accordance with what is typical and customary, giving it a practical interpretation, if possible, and considering the circumstances leading to the contract. The court will look to the intent of the parties making the contract. The court will look to the entire contract as a whole but will stay within the "four corners" of the document. The court cannot add terms to the contract.

Any ambiguity in a contract is construed *against* the party preparing the contract. This has been established as good public policy so that the one providing the confusing contract cannot benefit from the ambiguity. Any ambiguity in the contract will work against the party the licensee represents.

If a printed contract form, such as a listing or real estate sales contract, is used, with blanks filled in by the parties, the handwritten words supersede the printed words if a conflict exists. The same is true of typewritten words in a preprinted contract.

Real estate contracts that contain blanks to be filled in after signing are not allowed in Illinois. Additions, deletions, or alterations of any signed documents cannot be made without the written consent of all parties to the contract. All additions, deletions, or alterations must be initialed by all parties to the contract. True copies are to be delivered to all partices to the contract within 24 hours of signing or initialing.

Illinois licensees are not allowed to draft contracts or riders. Licensees may fill in the blanks of a preprinted contract or attach an approved rider that is in general use in the areas in which they do business. Licensees are not allowed to prepare legal documents or give legal advice. They may add to or delete only factual material. An attorney should be recommended for such matters. It is a violation of the Illinois Real Estate License Act for a broker who is also an attorney to legally represent either party when the attorney is acting as a broker or salesperson in the transaction.

CONTRACT REMEDIES

In some cases, a party to a contract *fails to complete the contract or fails to perform for no legal cause*. This is **breach of contract.** Breach of contract is also called *default*. The effect of breach of contract by a party is to terminate that party's contract rights. The breach, however, does not terminate the contract obligations of the breaching party. The nondefaulting party has the following legal remedies against the defaulting party. The remedies are obtained by filing suit in a court of law.

1. specific performance
2. rescission
3. compensatory damages
4. liquidated damages

Specific Performance

Every piece of real estate is unique. No piece can be substituted for another and have an exact match. As a result, a party contracting to buy a parcel of real estate does not have to accept a similar, or even almost identical, parcel. Because of the unique nature of real estate, the remedy of specific performance is available to nondefaulting parties. An order from the court requiring **specific performance** means that *the contract will be completed as originally agreed.*

For example, Buyer B has contracted to buy 123 Hickory Lane from Seller H. Seller H attempts to convey 456 Hickory Lane, which is an exact mirror image of 123 Hickory Lane. Buyer B does not have to accept the substitute and files suit for specific performance. The court orders Seller H to deed 123 Hickory Lane to Buyer B.

Rescission

This remedy is the opposite of specific performance. **Rescission** means *to take back, remove, annul, or abrogate.* A marriage of short duration is rescinded or annulled. This contract remedy is applied when a contract has not been performed by either party and when it has been breached by a party. Upon suit for rescission, the court orders the parties placed back in their original positions as if the contract had never existed.

For example, Vendor Smith enters into a contract for deed (land contract) with Vendee Black, date of possession to be immediately. Within two months, Vendee Black loses his job, tells Vendor Smith that he will not move out or pay the agreed payments, and refuses to sign a release of contract. Vendor Smith files suit for rescission of the contract. The court order places Vendor Smith in possession and control and shows that Vendee Black has no interest in the real estate, just as before the contract. If Vendee Black had paid a down payment, the down payment would be ordered returned to Vendee Black, minus a fair amount for rental during the period Vendee Black had possession of the premises.

Compensatory Damages

When a contract is breached, one party usually suffers monetary loss as a result of the contract breach. The *amount of money actually lost is the amount of* **compensatory damages** *the court will award.*

The amount of compensatory damages should be an amount sufficient to put the nondefaulting party in the same economic position that she would be in if the contract had not been breached. The amount ordered paid should total what the injured party lost from the contract breach. The amount must be able to be calculated with some certainty. For example, Landlord T must evict Tenant G for failure to pay rent in the amount of $500. Upon inspection of the premises, damage to windows, walls, and appliances has been done in the amount of $850. In addition, Landlord T must move and store Tenant G's belongings at the cost of $235. The compensatory damage award should be a total of $500 plus $850 plus $235 plus any court costs to file suit.

The items usually included are lost rent, unpaid taxes, repair cost to the premises, title search fees, lost interest, commissions, and lost profits. Traditionally, attorney fees incurred to litigate the contract breach are not included in calculating compensatory damages. Some states, however, including Illinois, have passed laws that allow attorney fees to be recoverable as part of compensatory damages for contract breach.

Punitive damages or exemplary damages are not typically allowed in breach of contract cases. Punitive or exemplary damages are *awarded for extremely bad behavior by a party.* They are to punish and send a message to society that the bad behavior will not be tolerated. An award of punitive damages is made most often in cases in which one party has taken fraudulent advantage of another.

Liquidated Damages

Instead of compensatory damages or in addition to compensatory damages, the parties to the contract can stipulate in the contract an amount of money to be paid upon certain breaches of the contract. *Damages agreed to be paid in the contract* are called **liquidated damages.** Liquidated damages usually consist of forfeiture of some money or late fees held by one party in the event of breach.

Courts do not favor forfeiture. Thus, for liquidated damages to be collectible and enforced by the court, the amount must be reasonable as compared to the damage caused by the breach. To be enforceable, the amount must not appear to be a penalty.

Examples of liquidated damage clauses exist in many real estate contracts. The most typical one is the forfeiture of earnest money by the buyer to the seller in the event the real estate sales contract is not completed for legal cause. Another example is found in the typical real estate sales contract. The buyer and the seller agree on a date of possession; they also agree what amount of money the seller will pay the buyer if possession is not given as agreed. A further example is the late fee agreed to be paid in leases and mortgages in the event of late payments.

AUCTION SALES

The sale of real estate by auction is becoming more and more common. Sellers who wish a quick sale with the greatest potential for interested buyers are turning to the services of an auctioneer.

Even at an auction sale, the issue of contract existence and terms of the contract are present. In most types of auctions, the seller places the property for sale with reserve unless specifically stated otherwise. **With reserve** means *the seller does not have to accept any bids.* In this type of auction, the bidder is the offeror. The auctioneer, as agent for the seller, may accept the bid and thus form the contract. After bidding begins and before acceptance, however, the seller or the auctioneer may remove the property from the sale. If the property is removed, no contract exists. Likewise, prior to accepting a bid at auction, the bidder may withdraw his offer. Thus, no contract will exist.

If the sale is without reserve or an absolute auction, the seller is the offeror. Any bid will result in acceptance of the offer and thus form a contract. Once the bidding has begun, no property may be removed from a sale without reserve or absolute auction.

Under an auction sale, the seller and the auctioneer, as agent for the seller, can disclaim all warranties as to the property except:

1. The seller and the auctioneer warrant that what is claimed to be sold is in fact being sold.
2. The seller and the auctioneer have the legal right to sell the property and transfer title.

LISTING CONTRACTS AND PRACTICES

Definition and Purpose

The first contract in the real estate business is usually the listing contract. A **listing contract** is one whereby *the owner of the property engages a real estate broker to find a buyer for her property.* Under common law, this contract creates an agency relationship in which the seller is the principal and the broker is the special agent of the seller. Also under common law, if a buyer hires a broker to locate property that he may purchase, the broker is the agent of the buyer and the buyer is the principal. Illinois, however, follows the Brokerage Relationships in Real Estate Transactions Law, discussed extensively in Chapter 4. Under this law, with the broker and consumer lacking another agreement to the contrary, the broker is the designated agent of the consumer (buyer or seller) with whom she is working. While other sections of the Illinois Real Estate License Act refer to listings, the newer Brokerage Relationships section of the act refers to brokerage agreements. Brokerage agreement is a term that better reflects consumers' trend toward buyer brokerage, seeking someone to represent the buyer in a real estate transaction. The following discussion refers to listing agreements under which brokers represent sellers in the sale of their properties.

Under a listing contract, no transfer of interest in real property is going to occur. No title will pass between seller and broker. Most states require the listing contract to be in writing because listing contracts relate to the sale of real property and the broker's eligibility to receive a commission.

In many cases, the broker must prove the existence of an employment contract. A written contract clearly spells out that the broker actually has been hired by the seller, and it sets forth all the terms and conditions of employment. Written listings substantially reduce lawsuits between brokers and property owners concerning matters of the broker's employment. In Illinois, a definite expiration date is required for a written listing; a clause automatically extending the listing date is not allowed.

Commission Entitlement

The broker's entitlement to commission is determined by two tests:

1. **Ready, willing, and able.** If the broker brings to the seller a *buyer who is ready to buy, is willing to buy, and is able (financially) to buy under the terms and conditions of the listing contract,* the broker is legally entitled to the commission. The broker has done the job he was hired to do in the listing contract—find a buyer who will pay the listed price in cash or other specified, accepted terms. When the broker does this, the commission has been earned under the ready, willing, and able test. Whether the owner actually agrees to sell the property to the prospective buyer does not matter. The seller may reject any offer, but rejection of an offer that conforms to the terms of the listing contract does not remove the duty to pay the commission.

2. **Acceptance.** If the *broker brings a buyer that the seller accepts,* the broker is legally entitled to the commission, as she has been instrumental in procuring a buyer for the property. Acceptance is based on some price or terms other than the listed price in cash. For example, the listing contract may specify $80,000 to be payable in cash.

A broker may bring an offer to the seller of $78,500. This offer may not be for payment in cash but instead may be subject to the buyer's assuming the seller's existing mortgage. If the seller accepts this offer, the broker is legally entitled to the commission on the basis of acceptance. The broker has brought the seller a buyer who is acceptable to the seller.

Fulfillment of both tests is not required. This is an either/or situation. The broker earns a commission either on the basis of having brought a ready, willing, and able buyer or on the basis of having brought an offer the seller accepts. In Illinois, a broker may use the closing of the sale as proof in court that she has procured that specific buyer and earned a commission.

Putting It to Work

In reality, most listings do not attract offers at full list price and terms (a mirror offer). Usually an offer is somewhat less than the asking price or on slightly different terms. Thus, the second test is met more often.

Types of Listings

The three types of listing contracts in general use are the open listing, the exclusive agency listing, and the exclusive right-to-sell listing. Each of these contracts gives different rights to the broker and the seller. All written listings in Illinois must contain six items: the property's listing price, the amount of commission, and time of payment, duration of the listing agreement, broker and seller names, and the address or legal description of the property, and signatures of the parties (see Figure 5.1). Any of the different listing types may be placed, with the owner's permission, into the MLS. Antitrust laws prohibit the MLS Board from limiting the types of listings accepted.

Open Listing

Under an **open listing,** the *seller lists a property with the assistance of one or more brokers.* The broker effecting the sale is entitled to the commission. If the owner sells the property (to a prospect not generated by any broker), however, the owner owes no commission.

This type of listing is not overly beneficial to the owner or to the broker. Usually a broker cannot afford to spend advertising dollars and sales staff on such an uncertain listing. The broker is competing rather than cooperating with the owner and every other broker who has an open listing on the property. This type of listing also can lead to disputes over commissions between brokers and can present legal problems for the owner. The lack of protection for the broker provides little incentive for aggressive marketing.

Exclusive Agency Listing

In an **exclusive agency listing,** the *property is listed with one broker as the only agent.* If the broker effects sale of the property, he is legally entitled to the commission agreed upon, but if the owner sells the property, the broker earns no commission.

This type of listing is somewhat better than the open listing in that only one broker is involved, but the broker is still competing with the owner. The broker's advertising

FIGURE 5.1
Illinois written listing agreement requirements.

1. Property listing price
2. Commission amount and when due
3. Duration of listing agreement
4. Broker and seller names
5. Legal description of the property or address
6. Signatures of parties

programs, including a "for sale" sign on the property, may generate prospects for the owner.

PUTTING IT TO WORK

If the owner already has commenced negotiations with a prospect, she may still grant an exclusive agency listing. The owner does not have to pay a commission if that prospect purchases the home. An alternative solution would be to list with an exclusive right-to-sell with a clause excluding by name only those persons with whom the owner is currently negotiating.

Exclusive Right-to-Sell Listing

An **exclusive right-to-sell listing** contract is recommended by the National Association of REALTORS®. Under this listing contract, the *property is listed with only one broker, and if anyone else sells the property during the term of the listing contract, the broker is legally entitled to the commission.* The seller is legally obligated to pay the broker's commission if the broker or the seller or some third party effects a sale of the property during the term of the listing contract.

The exclusive right-to-sell listing contract benefits the owner because the broker is secure enough in the opportunity to earn a commission that he can afford to spend time and advertising dollars to effect a quick and satisfactory sale of the listed property.

Listing Contract Provisions

A sample listing contract or cooperative marketing agreement is shown in Figure 5.2. The sample is an express bilateral contract. Under most listings, the seller agrees to cooperate with the broker and to pay a commission if the listed property is sold, and the broker agrees to make her best efforts to procure a sale of the listed property. Specific provisions must be included to make the terms of the contract between the seller and the broker clear and unambiguous. Examples of the specific provisions are found in Figure 5.1.

It is a violation of the Illinois Real Estate License Act to induce a party to a contract to break this contract for the purpose of substituting a new contract with a third party. If a licensee is aware of a written exclusive listing agreement, the licensee may not negotiate directly with the property owner without written authority from the listing broker. There are two conditions under which a future listing agreement may be discussed with a seller who is listed with another broker: (a) if the seller requests or (b) if the listing broker fails to respond to a written request for information as to the type and expiration date of the listing within 10 days of such request, and if this information cannot be obtained from another source. If the information is not received by the 14th day after the request, the broker can contact the seller directly.

Real Estate Contracts 103

FIGURE 5.2
A sample listing contract.

CHICAGO ASSOCIATION OF REALTORS®/MLS
EXCLUSIVE LISTING AGREEMENT

1. TO: _____ ADDRESS: _____

2. In consideration of your efforts to secure a Purchaser for the property (together with its undivided interest in the common elements, and accumulated reserves, if a condominium),

3. **FIXTURES AND PERSONAL PROPERTY.** Seller agrees to transfer to Purchaser by a Bill of Sale, all heating, electrical, and plumbing systems together
4. with the following: *(check or enumerate applicable items)*
5. ___T.V. Antenna   ___Washer   ___Central air conditioner   ___Electronic garage door(s)
6. ___Refrigerator   ___Dryer   ___Window air conditioner   with ___ remote units(s)
7. ___Oven/Range   ___Sump pump   ___Electronic air filter   ___Fireplace screen and equipment
8. ___Microwave   ___Water softener (if not rental) ___Central humidifier ___Fireplace gas log
9. ___Dishwasher   ___Wall to wall carpeting, if any ___Ceiling fan   ___Firewood
10. ___Garbage disposal ___Built-in or attached shelving ___Outdoor Shed ___Existing storms & screens
11. ___Trash compactor ___Smoke and carbon monoxide detectors ___All planted vegetation ___Attached book cases and cabinets
12. ___Window shades, attached shutters, draperies & curtains, hardware & other window treatments ___Radiator covers
13. ___Security system (if not leased)
14. Other items included: _____
15. Items excluded: _____
16. Address _____ Unit # _____
17. City _____ IL. Zip Code _____
18. I (hereinafter called Seller) do hereby give you (hereinafter called Broker) the sole and exclusive right to sell for a period commencing _____,
19. 19___ and terminating at midnight of _____, 19___, and the authority to offer for sale, to promote and advertise as Broker deems
20. appropriate, and to place for sale signs thereon where permitted by law, for a price of $_____ or on such other terms as Seller may agree
21. to accept.
22. **POSSESSION.** Seller shall surrender possession and remove all debris and Seller's personal property not conveyed to Purchaser no later than
23.
24. **SELLER AGREES:**
25. To cooperate fully with Broker (and Seller's Designated Agent) and refer all inquiries to Broker (and Seller's Designated Agent), to allow inspection of
26. property and entry at convenient times by Broker and/or cooperating Brokers whether alone or accompanied by Broker, for the purpose of showing it
27. to prospective Purchasers, to conduct all negotiations through Broker, to pay Broker a commission or compensation in the amount of
28. _____ in the event Broker produces a Purchaser ready, willing and able to purchase the premises on the terms herein provided;
29. or if the property is sold, gifted, exchanged, optioned (and such option is exercised before or subsequent to the termination of this agreement), a joint
30. venture is contracted, or the property is exchanged through or as a result of Broker's efforts, or Seller's, or any other person or persons during
31. the period of this agreement; or if the property is sold, gifted, optioned, joint ventured, or exchanged within _____ after termination
32. of this agreement to any person to whom the property was submitted during the term of this agreement, provided however, if the property is residential
33. property of four units or less and if a valid, bonafide, written listing agreement is entered into with another licensed real estate broker during such period,
34. no commission or compensation shall be due and owing pursuant to the terms of this agreement. For property which is not residential property of four
35. units or less, if the property is listed with another broker during such period, Seller shall be liable for only one commission, the allocation thereof to be
36. determined by the Brokers.
37. Broker(s) and Seller(s) hereby agree that _____, sales associate(s) affiliated with Broker, is (are) being
38. named as Seller's exclusive designated legal agent(s) under Seller's Exclusive Listing Agreement with Broker. Seller(s) understands and agrees that the
39. Seller's Designated Agent(s) will be Seller's exclusive legal agent pursuant to the Exclusive Listing Agreement with Broker and Seller(s) will be free to
40. enter into agreements with prospective buyers as legal agents of those buyers. Seller(s) also understands and agrees that neither Broker nor other sales
41. associates affiliated with Broker will be acting as legal agents of the Seller(s). The above named Broker and Designated Agent (herein after sometimes
42. referred to as "Licensee") may undertake a dual representation (represent both the seller or landlord and the buyer or tenant) for the sale or lease of your
43. property or properties they may show you. The undersigned acknowledge they were informed of the possibility of this type of representation. Before
44. signing this document, please read the following:
45. Representing more than one party to a transaction presents a conflict of interest since both clients may rely upon licensee's advice and the client's
46. respective interests may be adverse to each other. Licensee will undertake this representation only with the written consent of ALL clients in the
47. transaction. Any agreement between the clients as to a final contract price and other terms is a result of negotiations between the clients acting in their
48. own best interests and on their own behalf. You acknowledge that licensee has explained the implications of dual representation, including the risks
49. involved, and understand that you have been advised to seek independent advice from your advisors or attorneys before signing any documents in this
50. transaction.
51. **WHAT A LICENSEE CAN DO FOR CLIENTS WHEN ACTING AS A DUAL AGENT:**
52. 1. Treat all clients honestly. 2. Provide information about the property to the buyer or tenant. 3. Disclose all latent material defects in the property that are known
53. to Licensee. 4. Disclose financial qualification of the buyer or tenant to the seller or landlord. 5. Explain real estate terms. 6. Help the buyer or tenant to arrange
54. for property inspections. 7. Explain closing costs and procedures. 8. Help the buyer compare financing alternatives. 9. Provide information about comparable
55. properties that have sold so both clients may make educated decisions on what price to accept or offer.
56. **WHAT A LICENSEE CANNOT DISCLOSE TO CLIENTS WHEN ACTING AS A DUAL AGENT:**
57. 1. Confidential information that Licensee may know about the clients, without that client's permission. 2. The price the seller or landlord will take other than
58. the listing price without permission of the seller or landlord. 3. The price the buyer or tenant is willing to pay without permission of the buyer or tenant. 4. A
59. recommended or suggested price the buyer or tenant should offer. 5. A recommended or suggested price the seller or landlord should counter with or accept.
60. If either client is uncomfortable with this disclosure and dual representation, please let Licensee know. You are not required to accept this section unless you
61. want to allow the Licensee to proceed as a Dual Agent in this transaction.
62. By checking "Yes", initialing and signing below, you acknowledge that you have read and understand this section and voluntarily consent to the Licensee acting
63. as a Dual Agent (that is, to represent BOTH the seller or landlord and the buyer or tenant) should that become necessary. ___Yes ___No *(check one)*
64. _____ *(initial here)*
65. In the event the property is leased during the term of this Agreement, Seller agrees to pay Broker a rental commission of _____ plus expenses.
66. In the event the property is purchased by the lessee, or an option to purchase is granted to lessee which is then exercised by lessee, then in addition to
67. a rental commission, the sales commission or compensation shall be paid to Broker as set forth above.
68. ADDITIONAL TERMS OR INFORMATION. Seller hereby represents the following information to be true and correct:
69. a) Real Estate tax for 19___ is $_____   Homeowner's Exemption ___Yes / ___No
70.   Senior Citizen's Exemption ___Yes / ___No
71. b) Current monthly assessment $_____ includes _____
72. c) Percentage of interest in common elements is ___%. Waiver of Right of First Refusal necessary ___Yes / ___No
73. d) Seller is___ is not___ *(check one)* aware of a proposed special assessment. Seller shall keep Broker informed of all Board of Directors/Managers
74. actions. Seller shall keep Broker informed of all changes to the above.
75. e) If applicable, the amount of special assessment is $_____ with a remaining balance due of $_____
76. f) The lot size is approximately _____. If condo, approximate square feet _____
77. g) Title information: Torrens System ___Yes / ___No   Land Trust ___Yes / ___No
78. h) Heating Cost Information: $_____/Month $_____/Year.
79. i) Insulation Information:
80.   If this property is new construction, the following information is required:
81.   R Factor   Thickness   Type
82.   Exterior Walls _____
83.   Interior Walls _____
84.   Ceiling _____
85.
86.
87. j) If income property, Seller shall provide Broker with accurate copies of all leases, income and expense statements, a rent roll and relevant information
88. necessary to market the property.
89. THIS AGREEMENT IS SUBJECT TO THE PROVISIONS APPEARING ON THE REVERSE SIDE HEREOF.

DATED: _____
SELLER _____ ADDRESS _____

Type or Print Name   (Social Security #)   (City)   (State)   (Zip Code)
Telephone: Home_____ Work_____ Facsimile_____
SELLER _____ ADDRESS _____

Type or Print Name   (Social Security #)   (City)   (State)   (Zip Code)
Telephone: Home_____ Work_____ Facsimile_____
SELLER _____ ADDRESS _____

Type or Print Name   (Social Security #)   (City)   (State)   (Zip Code)
Telephone: Home_____ Work_____ Facsimile_____
BROKER _____
By: _____

Revised 10/95

Illinois requires that if the amount of commission or time of commission payment is changed, this change must be stated in writing and signed by all parties. If the listing agreement states that in case of buyer default the seller does not receive the earnest money, this statement must be in letters larger than those generally used in the listing agreement. Listing agreements may contain a protection period for the broker known as a carryover, extender, or safety clause. The protection period is a length of time agreed to by the sellers during which they agree to pay a commission if the property is sold to the broker's prospect during the listing period. In Illinois, if a valid, written listing agreement is entered into with another broker during the protection period, no commission shall be paid on residential properties with four units or fewer to the broker with the expired listing. The first broker has a protection period only if the seller does not enter into a valid listing with another broker. All listings must include this statement: "It is illegal for either the owner or the broker to refuse to sell or show property to anyone because of race, color, religion, national origin, sex, or physical disability."

Key provisions of the sample listing contract shown in Figure 5.2 are:

- Section 1 states the name of the seller, the beginning and expiration dates of the listing contract, and the address or legal description of the property. Additionally, personal property (if any) is described in this section as well as the listed sales price.
- Section 2 sets forth the broker's commission rate and provides for a safety or carry-over clause.
- Section 3 explains designated agency and appoints a designated agent or agents of the seller. Relationship of agents to buyers is also explained.
- Section 4 offers a dual agency option and provides the statutory language required for creation of a dual agency under the Illinois Brokerage Relationships in Real Estate Transactions Law.
- Section 5 provides for the seller's written permission or denial of a dual agency relationship with the broker.
- Section 6 deals with general provisions of the listing agreement such as the time of payment of the commission and the revocation of the listing. The disbursement of the earnest money in the event of a default is also discussed.
- Section 7 informs the seller that it is illegal to violate the Civil Rights Act in regard to discrimination.
- Section 8 calls for additional property and real estate tax information. This section also provides for the signatures of the agent and the owners. If the property is owned by a married couple, both husband and wife must sign the listing. Even if the property is owned in severalty by a married person, both the husband and wife should sign to avoid any later homestead claims.

The rear of the form (not shown) lists additional provisions of the listing.

Data Sheet

As a part of the listing contract, the broker attaches a data sheet with detailed information on the specific property listed. A sample data sheet is found in Figure 5.3. The information contained on the data sheet is to be gathered from personal inspection and measurement by the broker; from contacts with government offices to verify taxes, zoning, assessed value, age, lot size, type of ownership, and deed restrictions; and from contacts with the seller's mortgage company to verify the existing loan terms. Information on the data sheet usually is included in all multiple listing information, and, thus, all member brokers rely upon it. This is added reason for the reported information to be accurate.

The Illinois Residential Real Property Disclosure Act, effective October 1, 1994, requires sellers of residential property to deliver to prospective buyers, prior to sale, a

FIGURE 5.3
A sample data sheet.

written disclosure statement on the property that alerts the buyer to any possible defects.

Illinois licensees are not subject to a cause of action for failure to disclose that an occupant of the property is affected with HIV or that the property was the site of an act of violence that had no physical effect on the property or its environment.

Termination

Listing contracts terminate after expiration of the time period agreed to by the seller and the broker in the listing or sale of the property. They also terminate upon the death or incapacity of the seller, destruction of the listed property, condemnation of the listed property, bankruptcy of the seller, revocation of the broker's license, mutual agreement of the seller and the broker, or breach of the listing terms by either the seller or the broker. In Illinois, listing agreements that do not contain a definite termination date are void, and clauses automatically extending the listing period are not allowed.

PUTTING IT TO WORK

Termination should be handled on a case-by-case basis in situations of material change in the property, such as damage to the property, a zoning change, or discovery of minerals. The change may or may not terminate a listing. Obviously, some renegotiation or pricing changes should be considered.

Competitive Market Analysis

Part of the listing process involves recommending to the owner a market price that will be the listed price. This price should be determined by a competitive market analysis, which compares the listed property with other similar properties that have sold recently. No two properties are exactly alike; however, many are comparable or similar in quality, location, and utility. In comparing the listed property and the selected comparables, allowances are made for differences in things such as lot size, age, number of rooms, square footage, and so on.

A minimum of three comparables is desirable. Comparables should be as similar as possible in all respects to the listed property. Comparables are found in office real estate files, in county assessor files, in MLS closed sales data, and from appraisers. The more recent the date of sale of the comparable, the more valuable the comparable is to the analysis. Also of great importance is the extent of similarity of physical characteristics of the comparable and location of the comparable in relation to the listed property. A sample of a competitive market analysis is found in Figure 5.4.

> **PUTTING IT TO WORK**
>
> In addition to knowing what has sold recently, the seller should be shown what is currently available. Knowing the competition may influence pricing and marketing strategies.

SALES CONTRACTS AND PRACTICES

Real Estate Sales Contract

The parties to an accepted real estate sales contract are the buyer and the seller, also called offeror and offeree, respectively. This contract is the road map for the real estate transaction. The contract relationship between the parties is described as "arms length." The parties are not in an agency relationship; they are assumed to have equal bargaining power and equal ability from opposing viewpoints.

The purchase contract is a bilateral express contract. The buyer promises to buy the property if certain terms and conditions are met; the seller promises to convey marketable title to the property as prescribed by the real estate sales contract. The consideration given consists of the promises made by the parties. Although most real estate sales contracts are accompanied by earnest money, earnest money is not legally required for a valid real estate sales contract. **Earnest money** *is given (a) to show sincerity of the buyer, (b) to demonstrate her financial capability to raise the money called for in the agreement, and (c) to serve as possible liquidated damages to the seller in the event of default by the buyer.*

All terms and conditions of sale of the property are contained in the real estate sales contract. They include sales price, type of financing, interest rate (if a mortgage is to be obtained or if seller financing is to be used), inspections required, proration of taxes and insurance, listing of personal property to be included in the purchase, designated party with risk of loss from fire, flood, and other causes, time periods for possession and transfer of title, type of deed to be used, type of title acceptable to buyer, amount of earnest money, liquidated damages upon breach, and period of time for acceptance or rejection.

> **PUTTING IT TO WORK**
>
> Many brokerages use prepared addenda to cover supplemental issues of the agreement. Some examples are personal property lists, homeowner's warranties, pre-sale or post-sale rental agreements, and contingency clauses.

If the real estate sales contract is written clearly and concisely, the parties should be able to close the deal without controversy. Conversely, if the real estate sales contract is unclear or ambiguous, the road to closing will be difficult.

FIGURE 5.4 A competitive market analysis of a subject property and three comparables.

COMPETITIVE MARKET ANALYSIS

Prepared especially for:
John and Susan Mitchell

Prepared by:
Grace Sanford,
Levittown Real Estate

Date:
January 9, 1997

Medium Range Adj ADDRESS PROXIMITY	SUBJECT 2735 Hawthorne Carriage Estates	COMPARABLE 1 of 3 2815 Hemingway Carriage Estates		COMPARABLE 2 of 3 3270 Melville Heath Heights		COMPARABLE 3 of 3 4520 Thoreau Ct. Foxpointe	
Style	Ranch/Rambler	Ranch/Rambler		Ranch/Rambler		Ranch/Rambler	
Construction	Fr Stucco	Ced Stone	0	Brick	0	Brick	0
Date Sold		July 1996	238	Nov 1996	856	Sept 1996	907
Effective Age	12	12	0	14	1,000	11	(500)
Sq Ft Total	1,544	1,442		1,654		1,608	
Sq Ft Main	1,544	1,442	2,040	1,654	(2,200)	1,608	(1,280)
Sq Ft Up	0	0	0	0	0	0	0
Sq Ft Down	0	0	0	0	0	0	0
Pct Down Finished	0	0		0		0	
Acreage/Lot Size	120 x 80	120 x 85		125 x 80		115 x 97	
Value of Lot	$4,500	$4,500	0	$4,500	0	$4,500	0
Price/Sq Ft Inc Lot	$60 (Adj Ave)	$66		$56		$57	
Price/Sq Ft Exc Lot	$57 (Adj Ave)	$62		$54		$54	
Bedrooms Total	3	3	0	3	0	3	0
Bedrooms Main	3	3		3		3	
Bedrooms Up	0	0		0		0	
Bedrooms Down	0	0		0		0	
Bath Total	2.0	2.0	0	2.5	(1,000)	2.0	0
Baths Main	2.0	2.0		2.5		2.0	
Baths Up	0.0	0.0		0.0		0.0	
Baths Down	0.0	0.0		0.0		0.0	
Fireplaces	1	1	0	1	0	1	0
Air Conditioning	Central	Central	0	Central	0	Central	0
Garage	2.0	2.0	0	2.0	0	2.0	0
Swimming Pool	0	0	0	0	0	0	0
Semi Annual Tax	852.16	697.12	0	691.04	0	820.51	0
Assessment	22360	21400	0	22060	0	25530	0
Fenced Yard	Privacy		0	Privacy	0	Privacy	0
Double Storage Blg			0		0		0
Fruit Trees			0		0		0
Listed Price		$94,500 Adjustment		$96,000 Adjustment		$93,500 Adjustment	
Sales Price		$94,500	$2,278	$93,000	($1,344)	$92,000	($873)
ADJ SALES PRICE		$96,778		$91,656		$91,127	

Comp 1: 35% × $96,778 = $33,872
Comp 2: 25% × $91,656 = $22,914
Comp 3: 40% × $91,127 = $36,451

Reconciled Price: $33,872 + $22,914 + $36,451 = $93,237

In accordance with the Statute of Frauds, the real estate sales contract is required to be in writing. It is not a contract until the seller unconditionally accepts it. Unlike the listing contract, an accepted real estate sales contract does obligate the seller to sell the property or face litigation for specific performance. The real estate sales contract is binding on the heirs and estates of the buyer and the seller. Upon the seller's acceptance of the real estate sales contract, the buyer has equitable title in the real estate, which is an interest such that a court will take notice and protect the rights of the owner of the equitable title.

Because most real estate sales contracts contain specific deadlines to be met, parties to the contract or agents of the parties must keep close track of the calendar. If it appears a deadline is not going to be met, all parties to the contract, to keep the contract in force, must agree to any extension and initial the extension as written on the real estate sales contract. Failure to meet all of the conditions in the real estate sales contract excuses the buyer and the seller from the obligations of the contract. If failure to meet all of the conditions in the real estate sales contract was outside the seller's control and not caused by the seller, the seller will be excused from payment of a commission per the listing contract.

Discharge or termination of the real estate sales contract occurs when all terms and conditions are met and the seller conveys title to the buyer. Discharge or termination also occurs when all of the terms and conditions are not met or when the deadlines set out in the real estate sales contract expire with no extension acknowledged by the parties. Termination occurs, too, when the property is condemned under right of eminent domain; when the property is destroyed by fire, flood, or other natural disaster; or when insanity or incapacity of either party occurs.

The Uniform Vendor and Purchaser Risk Act adopted in Illinois provides that once a contract has been signed, the seller bears the risk of loss before title or possession has been transferred to the buyer. If the buyer has taken title or possession and a loss occurs, the buyer is required to pay the full contract price.

A sample real estate contract is found in Figure 5.5 The specific provisions are outlined below.

- Section 1 states the name of the seller, the date of the offer, the purchase price, personal property included, amount of earnest money, and who is to hold the earnest money.

- Section 2, the financing section, includes a financing contingency for the buyer and the amounts of loan, term, and interest rate on which the contingency is based.

- Section 3 calls for the seller to convey ownership via a warranty deed. It also states the encumbrances that the purchaser will accept with the property and calls for a proration of real estate taxes.

- Section 4 deals with the possession of the property after the closing and provides a per diem charge for each day the seller remains in the property after the closing.

- Section 5 provides a space for buyer and seller to initial to acknowledge that permission was granted for dual agency (if dual agency is applicable) required under the Illinois Brokerage Relationships in Real Estate Transactions Law.

- Section 6 calls attention to and makes a part of the contract the provisions listed on the opposite side of the contract (not shown) and any riders that are attached. This section also provides for an attorney's approval contingency by either the seller's or the buyer's attorney. The attorney is prohibited from changing the sales price, broker's commission, and the dates in the contract.

- Section 7 provides for an inspection of the property by an outside inspector who is not a party to the contract. The purchaser agrees to pay for the inspection.

- Section 8 provides spaces for the seller's and purchaser's names, addresses, and signatures.

Real Estate Contracts 109

FIGURE 5.5
A sample real estate sales contract.

CHICAGO ASSOCIATION OF REALTORS®/MLS
REAL ESTATE SALE CONTRACT — RESIDENTIAL

1. TO:_____ SELLER   DATE:_____

2. I/We offer to purchase the property known as _____
(Address) (City) (State) (Zip)

3. lot approximately _____ feet, together with improvements thereon, including the following, if any, now on
4. premises for which a Bill of Sale is to be given: Heating, central cooling, ventilating, plumbing and electrical fixtures; screens and storms for windows
5. and doors; shades, awnings, blinds, draperies, curtain and drapery rods; radiator covers,; attached exterior TV antenna; attached mirrors,
6. shelving, interior shutters, cabinets and bookcases; planted vegetation, washer/dryer; fireplace screens; dishwasher; disposal, _____ oven/
7. range(s):_____refrigerator(s);____window air conditioner(s); ceiling fans, garage door opener; and _____
8. _____ but excluding _____

9. 1. Purchase Price $_____
10. 2. Initial earnest money $_____, in the form of _____ shall be held by
11. _____, to be increased to 10% of purchase price within _____days after acceptance
12. hereof. Said initial earnest money shall be returned and this contract shall be void if not accepted by Seller on or before
13. _____, 19____. Earnest money shall be deposited by _____, as escrowee, for the
14. benefit of the parties hereto in an established escrow account in compliance with the laws of the State of Illinois. An original of this contract
15. shall be held by Listing Broker.

16. 3. The balance of the purchase price shall be paid at the closing, plus or minus prorations, as follows (STRIKE THROUGH INAPPLICABLE
17. SUBPARAGRAPHS):
18.   (a) Cash, Cashier's check or Certified Check or any Combination Thereof.
19.   (b) Assumption of Existing Mortgage (See Rider 7, if applicable).
20.   (c) Mortgage Contingency. This contract is contingent upon Purchaser securing by _____ (date) a written commit-
21. ment for a fixed rate mortgage, or an adjustable rate mortgage permitted to be made by a U.S. or Illinois savings and loan association or bank,
22. for $_____, the interest rate (or initial interest rate if an adjustable rate mortgage) not to exceed _____%
23. per annum, amortized over _____ years, payable monthly, loan fee not to exceed _____%, plus appraisal and credit report fee, if any.
24. If said mortgage has a balloon payment, it shall be due no sooner than _____ years. Purchaser shall pay for private mortgage insurance if
25. required by lending institution. If Purchaser does not obtain such commitment, Purchaser shall notify Seller in writing by the aforesaid date.
26. If Seller is not so notified, it shall be conclusively presumed that Purchaser has secured such commitment or will purchase said property
27. without mortgage financing. If Seller is so notified, Seller may, within an equal number of additional days, secure a mortgage commitment for
28. Purchaser upon the same terms, and shall have the option of extending the closing date up to the same number of days. Said commitment
29. may be given by Seller or a third party. Purchaser shall furnish all requested credit information, sign customary documents relating to the
30. application and securing of such commitment, and pay one application fee as directed by Seller. If Purchaser notifies Seller as above provided,
31. and neither Purchaser nor Seller secures such commitment as above provided, this contract shall be null and void and all earnest money shall
32. be returned to Purchaser.
33.   If an FHA or VA mortgage is to be obtained, Rider 8 or 9 is hereby attached as applicable.
34.   (d) Purchase Money Note and Trust Deed or Article of Agreement for Deed. See Rider 10.

35. 4. At closing, Seller shall execute and deliver to Purchaser, or cause to be executed and delivered to Purchaser, a recordable Warranty Deed
36. with release of homestead rights (or other appropriate deed if title is in trust or in an estate), or Articles of Agreement, for such a deed if that
37. portion of subparagraph 3(d) is applicable, subject only to the following, if any: covenants, conditions, and restrictions of record; public and
38. utility easements; existing leases and tenancies; special governmental taxes or assessments for improvements not yet completed; unconfirmed
39. special governmental taxes or assessments; general real estate taxes for the year 19____ and subsequent years; the mortgage or trust deed set
40. forth in paragraph 3 and/or Rider 7. Seller represents that the 19____ general real estate taxes are $_____.

41. 5. Closing or escrow payout shall be on _____, 19____ (except as provided in paragraph 3(c) above), provided title has been shown to be
42. good or is accepted by Purchaser, at the office of Purchaser's mortgagee or at _____

43. 6. Seller agrees to surrender possession of said premises on or before _____, provided this sale has been closed.
44.   (a) Use and Occupancy. At closing, Seller shall pay to Purchaser $_____ per day for use and occupancy commencing the first day
45. after closing up to and including the date possession is to be surrendered or on a monthly basis, whichever period is shorter. Purchaser shall
46. refund any payment made for use and occupancy beyond the date possession is surrendered.
47.   (b) Possession Escrow. At closing, Seller shall deposit with escrowee designated in paragraph 2 above a sum equal to 2% of the purchase
48. price to guarantee possession on or before the date set forth above, which sum shall be held from the net proceeds of the sale on escrowee form of
49. receipt. If Seller does not surrender possession as above, Seller shall pay to Purchaser in addition to the above use and occupancy, the sum of 10%
50. of said possession escrow per day up to and including day possession is surrendered to Purchaser plus any unpaid use and occupancy to the date
51. possession is surrendered, said amounts to be paid out of escrow and the balance, if any, to be turned over to Seller. Acceptance of payments
52. by Purchaser shall not limit Purchaser's other legal remedies. Seller and Purchaser hereby acknowledge that escrowee will not distribute the
53. possession escrow without the joint written direction of the Seller and Purchaser or their authorized agent. If either Seller or Buyer objects to the
54. disposition of the possession escrow, then the parties hereto agree that the escrowee may deposit the possession escrow with the Clerk of the
55. Circuit Court by the filing of an action in the nature of an Interpleader. The parties agree that escrowee may be reimbursed from the possession
56. escrow for all costs, including reasonable attorney's fees, related to the filing of the Interpleader and do hereby agree to indemnify and hold
57. escrowee harmless from any and all claims and demands, including the payment of reasonable attorney's fees, costs and expenses.

58. **7. PURCHASER ACKNOWLEDGES RECEIPT OF SELLER'S RESIDENTIAL REAL PROPERTY DISCLOSURE REPORT.**

59. 8. DUAL AGENCY CONFIRMATION OF CONSENT: The undersigned confirm that they have previously consented to _____
60. _____ (Licensee) acting as a Dual Agent in providing brokerage services on their behalf and specifically
61. consent to Licensee acting as a Dual Agent in regard to the transaction referred to in this document.

62. _____ _____
    Seller(s) initials   Buyer(s) initials

63. 9. THIS CONTRACT IS SUBJECT TO THE PROVISIONS APPEARING ON THE REVERSE SIDE AND THE FOLLOWING RIDERS
64. ATTACHED HERETO AND MADE A PART HEREOF _____

65. 10. The Real Estate Brokers named below shall be compensated in accordance with their agreements with their clients and/or any offer of
66. compensation made by the Listing Broker in a multiple listing service in which the listing and Cooperating Broker both participate.

67. 11. It is agreed by and between the parties hereto that their respective attorneys may make modifications to the contract other than sales price,
68. broker's compensation and dates, mutually acceptable to the parties. If within _____ days after acceptance of the Contract, it
69. becomes evident agreement cannot be reached by the parties hereto regarding the proposed modifications of their attorneys and written notice
70. thereof is given to either party within the period specified herein, then this Contract shall become null and void and all monies paid by the
71. Purchaser shall be refunded upon joint written direction of both parties to escrowee. IN THE ABSENCE OF WRITTEN NOTICE WITHIN THE
72. TIME SPECIFIED HEREIN, THIS PROVISION SHALL BE DEEMED WAIVED BY ALL PARTIES HERETO, AND THIS CONTRACT SHALL
73. BE IN FULL FORCE AND EFFECT.

74. 12. Purchaser's obligation to purchase under the Contract is subject to the inspection and approval of the condition of the property by the
75. Purchaser or Purchaser's agent, at Purchaser's expense, within _____ days from the date of acceptance of this Contract.
76. Purchaser shall indemnify Seller from and against any loss or damage to the property caused by the acts or omissions of Purchaser or Purchaser's
77. agent performing such inspection. In the event the condition of the property is not approved, written notice shall be given to the Seller or Seller's
78. agent by the Purchaser within the time specified for approval, and thereupon, Seller's obligation to sell and Purchaser's obligation to Purchase
79. under this contract shall become null and void and all monies paid by the Purchaser shall be refunded upon joint written direction of both parties
80. to escrowee. IN THE ABSENCE OF WRITTEN NOTICE WITHIN THE TIME SPECIFIED HEREIN, THIS PROVISION SHALL BE DEEMED
81. WAIVED BY ALL PARTIES HERETO, AND THIS CONTRACT SHALL BE IN FULL FORCE AND EFFECT.
    PURCHASER _____ ADDRESS _____

    (Print Name) (Social Security #) (City) (State) (Zip Code)
    PURCHASER _____ ADDRESS _____

    (Print Name) (Social Security #) (City) (State) (Zip Code)
    ACCEPTANCE OF CONTRACT BY SELLER
    This _____ day of _____, 19____. I/We accept this contract and agree to perform and convey title or cause title to be
    conveyed according to the terms of this contract.
    SELLER _____ ADDRESS _____

    (Print Name) (Social Security #) (City) (State) (Zip Code)
    SELLER _____ ADDRESS _____

    (Print Name) (Social Security #) (City) (State) (Zip Code)
    FOR INFORMATIONAL PURPOSES:
    Listing Office _____ Address _____
    Seller's Designated Agent Name _____ Phone _____

    Cooperating Office _____ Address _____
    Buyer's Designated Agent Name _____ Phone _____

Revised 10/94

Installment Agreement/Contract for Deed

An **installment agreement** is also called a **contract for deed,** an **installment land contract,** an agreement of sale, or articles of agreement for warranty deed. The essence of this contract is that the *buyer is contracting to obtain legal title to the property by paying the purchase price in installments, and the seller is agreeing to transfer the legal title to the buyer by delivery of a deed* upon buyer's full payment of the purchase price. The seller is deferring receipt of payment of the purchase price from the buyer over the term of the contract. Figure 5.6 is a sample installment agreement.

The parties to an installment agreement are the vendor and the vendee. Under this contract the vendor is the seller and the vendee is the buyer. An installment agreement is an express bilateral executory contract. The vendor promises to give possession to the vendee during the contract, accept payments toward the purchase price, and convey marketable title to the vendee upon payment of the full purchase price. The vendee promises to make the agreed-upon payments, pay taxes, obtain insurance on the property, and maintain the property in good condition during the term of the contract. The vendor's security for payment of the purchase price is retention of legal title until all payments are made. Upon execution of the installment agreement, the vendee has equitable title in the real estate.

In accordance with the Statute of Frauds, an installment agreement must be in writing to be enforceable. The installment agreement also must include the legal description of the property sold. An installment agreement is recorded in the locality where the real estate is situated. This provides constructive notice to the world of the vendee's equitable title and vendor's legal title and right to payment from vendee.

Illinois does not allow clauses that forbid the recording of the contract or a penalty for recording the contract in an installment agreement. Also prohibited is the statement that recording does not constitute notice. Notice of violation of a building code received within the past 10 years or the fact that none has been received must be a part of, or attached to, the contract when selling real property of 12 or fewer units. If such notice is not provided, the contract is voidable at the buyer's option. When purchasing residential property with six or fewer units from a land trust, the buyer must be told prior to the signing of the contract the names of the beneficiaries of the trust. If the names are not revealed, the contract is voidable. An installment agreement is binding on the heirs and estates of the parties. It is discharged by payment in full by the vendee with conveyance of the title by deed from the vendor. It also may be discharged by suit for breach of contract by the parties or mutually agreed release of the contract.

This type of contract originally was used to purchase relatively inexpensive pieces of land, but it can be used for any type of property. It has major advantages to the buyer, particularly in times of tight credit (high interest rates) markets or when the buyer does not qualify for conventional loans. In these cases, the seller may be willing to provide the financing, especially because this form of contract puts the seller in a strong position.

Most mortgage documents today contain a "due on sale" clause, specifying that the entire principal balance due on the mortgage must be paid in full if a sale of the property is to take place. An installment agreement must never be used to circumvent these loan assumption clauses. The lending institution holding the mortgage may declare the execution of an installment agreement a sale of the property and thereby require the seller to pay off the mortgage.

Consultation with legal counsel prior to creating the installment agreement is advised for the protection of all parties.

Real Estate Contracts 111

FIGURE 5.6 A sample installment agreement, also called a contract for deed.

UNILATERAL CONTRACTS AND PRACTICES

Options

An **option** is *a contract wherein an optionor (owner) sells a right to purchase the property to a prospective buyer, called an optionee, at a particular price for a specified time period.* An option is an express unilateral contract. Only one party to the option contract makes a promise. The optionor promises to allow the optionee the sole right to purchase the real estate during the specified time. The optionee pays for this right but makes no promise to purchase the real estate. The optionee is merely "buying time" to decide or arrange financing. The money the optionee pays to the optionor for the option right may or may not apply to the purchase price of the property. The parties to the option will negotiate this matter.

> **PUTTING IT TO WORK**
>
> Many times an option to purchase is a viable alternative when a buyer is serious but does not have the required down payment or cannot qualify for a loan. After renting for a certain amount of time, the buyer will have accumulated the down payment, or the financing situation may have changed, or both, allowing the transaction to complete to the satisfaction of buyer and seller.

In accordance with the Statute of Frauds, options to purchase must be in writing to be enforceable. Options to purchase are binding on the heirs and estates of the parties. All owners of the real estate must sign the option.

If the optionee desires to complete the purchase, she exercises the option right. At this point, the option becomes a purchase agreement as in any other real estate transaction. Because an option can become a purchase agreement between the parties, the original option should be specific as to type of title to be conveyed, terms of financing if other than cash, and any other provisions typically contained in an offer to purchase. These issues should not be left to be addressed at the time of exercise. Options to purchase are discharged by expiration of the time period agreed upon in the option or by exercise of the option by the optionee.

A sample option is found in Figure 5.7. The various sections of this document are outlined here.

- Section 1 gives the name and address of the optionor and optionee and the price paid for the option.

- Section 2 sets forth the legal description of the property that is the subject of the option.

- Section 3 states the price to be paid for the property, the length of the option, the manner of payment, and method of exercising the option.

- Section 4 specifies the obligations of the optionor if the option to purchase has been initiated. This section provides for the time period within which proof of title and delivery of deed shall take place and the conditions under which the optionee may terminate the contract and be reimbursed for monies paid upon default of the optionor to furnish good title.

- Section 5 warrants that no notice of a dwelling code violation has been received within 10 years of the date of the execution of this instrument.

- Section 6 provides a space for the signature of the optionor(s).

FIGURE 5.7
A sample option to purchase.

The Optionor, _____,
of _____, in consideration of the sum of
_____ Dollars,
receipt whereof is hereby acknowledged by the Optionor, (which sum shall _____ be applied as part of the price hereinafter specified), does hereby grant to the Optionee, _____
_____, of _____,
the option to purchase the following described real estate in _____ County, Illinois, to-wit:

1

Permanent Real Estate Index Number(s): _____

Address(es) of real estate: _____

2

for the price of _____ Dollars
payable as follows:

    The option hereby granted shall be exercised by the Optionee by (a) written notice to that effect delivered to the Optionor at _____ and
(b) payment to the Optionor of the price or portion thereof specified, and (c) the delivery of any note and mortgage or trust deed above provided for, on or before _____, 19___. At the Optionee's election to be made expressly in said notice, said payment of the price or portion thereof and the delivery of any note and mortgage or trust deed may be made to _____
as escrow agent under its usual form of deed and money escrow agreement with modifications necessary to make it conform with this instrument, which agreement the Optionor and the Optionee shall promptly sign; anything in this instrument to the contrary notwithstanding, payment of the price and delivery of deed shall be made through the escrow and this instrument and all sums paid or payable hereunder shall be deposited in the escrow; and the cost of the escrow shall be divided equally between the Optionor and the Optionee.
    If said option is not exercised on or before the date specified, said option shall expire and the Optionee shall have no rights or privileges under this instrument.

3

    If the Optionee exercises the option hereunder in the manner and within the time hereinabove specified, the Optionor shall at his expense, within thirty days after such exercise, furnish to the Optionee:
       (1) Title insurance policy of _____
           in the amount of the price, or the usual preliminary report on title of such company, in either event covering the date of such exercise*
       (2) Certificate of title of the Registrar of Titles of Cook County, Illinois and a certificate of tax search covering the date of such exercise*
       (3) Merchantable abstract of title covering the date of such exercise*
showing good title in the Optionor on the date of such exercise, subject only to the following: (1) existing leases expiring _____; (2) special taxes or assessments for improvements not yet completed; (3) installments not due at the date of such exercise of any special tax or assessment for improvements theretofore completed; (4) general taxes for the year _____ and subsequent years; (5) building, building line and use or occupancy restrictions, conditions and covenants of record; (6) zoning and building laws or ordinances; (7) party wall rights or agreements, if any; (8) roads and highways, if any;

Within five days after the Optionor has furnished evidence of title as hereinabove provided, the Optionor shall convey good title to said real estate to the Optionee by a good and sufficient _____ deed, with release of dower and homestead rights, subject nevertheless to the exceptions and objections hereinabove specified. If the Optionor fails or is unable to furnish evidence of title in accordance with this instrument, the Optionee may terminate the contract resulting from the exercise of said option and require the return of the price, including the sum paid for said option, and all instruments and documents relating thereto.
    If, prior to delivery of deed hereunder, the improvements on said real estate shall be destroyed or materially damaged by fire or other casualty, this instrument shall, at the election of Optionee, become null and void, and all sums paid and instruments delivered by the Optionee hereunder shall be returned to him.
    Time is of the essence of this instrument. This instrument shall be binding upon and inure to the benefit of the heirs, executors, administrators, successors and assigns of each of the Optionor and the Optionee. This instrument shall not be recorded or filed in any public office. If either the Optionor or the Optionee consists of more than one person, this instrument shall be applicable to all such persons, irrespective of the use of verbs and pronouns importing the singular number.

4

    Optionor warrants to Optionee that no notice from any city, village or other governmental authority of a dwelling code violation which existed in the dwelling structure before the execution of this contract has been received by the Optionor, his principal or his agent within 10 years of the date of execution of this instrument.

5

    IN WITNESS WHEREOF, the Optionor has signed and sealed this instrument this _____ day of _____, 19___.

                                _____(SEAL)

                                _____(SEAL)

6

PUTTING IT TO WORK

An option is often tied to a lease. If this is the case, additional issues must be addressed. For example, does any of the rent apply toward the purchase price? Who bears the expense of repairs? If the tenant breaches the lease, how does that affect the option?

Right of First Refusal

A **right of first refusal** is another type of unilateral contract whereby the *property owner agrees to give an individual the first right to refuse the property if and when it is offered.* This contract is very different from the option to purchase, in that the owner does not promise to sell the property to the individual, nor is a price established for sale. The owner merely promises to give the individual first chance to purchase the property at whatever price and terms anyone else offers for the property, if it is sold.

This is an express unilateral contract. To be enforceable under the Statute of Frauds, it must be in writing. It will be binding on the heirs and estate of the owner of the real estate. The right of first refusal is discharged upon sale of the property to the named individual or upon the named individual's refusal to purchase the property when offered for sale.

This type of contract is often found in real estate transactions when a family member has gifted property or sold property to another family member. In an effort to control ownership of the property, the right of first refusal is given to the original owner.

IMPORTANT POINTS

1. A contract is an agreement between competent parties, upon legal consideration, to do or abstain from doing some legal act.
2. An express contract is spoken or written. An implied contract is one inferred from the actions of the parties.
3. Bilateral contracts are based on mutual promises. Unilateral contracts are based on a promise by one party and an act by another party.
4. An executed contract has been fully performed. An executory contract has provisions yet to be performed.
5. A contract is created by the unconditional acceptance of a valid offer. Acceptance of bilateral offers must be communicated. Communication of the acceptance of unilateral offers results from the performance of an act by the promisee.
6. Contracts that have an illegal purpose or are missing an element are void.
7. A voidable contract is one that may not be enforceable at the option of one of the parties to the contract.
8. The requirements for contract validity are (a) competent parties, (b) reality of consent, (c) offer and acceptance, (d) consideration, (e) legality of object, and (f) possibility to complete.
9. An offer must not be indefinite or illusory.
10. An offeror may revoke an offer at any time prior to acceptance.
11. Consideration is anything of value, including a promise.
12. Illinois citizens reach the age of majority at age 18.
13. Reality of consent is defeated and a contract made voidable by (a) misrepresentation, (b) fraud, (c) mutual mistake, (d) undue influence, or (e) duress or menace.

14. After the signing of a contract, but prior to title passing or possession taking place, under the Illinois Uniform Vendor and Purchaser Risk Act, the seller bears the risk if the property suffers destruction.
15. Contracts are assignable in the absence of a specific prohibition against assignment in the contract.
16. Real estate contracts in Illinois cannot contain any blanks to be filled in after the signing. True copies of the contract must be given to all parties within 24 hours of the signing of said contract.
17. Illinois real estate licensees may not draft or write contracts.
18. When acting as a broker or salesperson in a transaction, an attorney cannot represent either party to the transaction in a legal capacity.
19. The remedies for breach of contract are (a) compensatory damages, (b) liquidated damages, (c) specific performance, and (d) rescission.
20. If a contracting party defaults in the performance of contractual obligations, the injured party may sue for damages in a suit for breach of contract. If the contract is for the purchase and sale of real property, an alternative remedy in the form of a lawsuit for specific performance is available to the injured party.
21. A listing contract is one in which a property owner employs a broker to find a buyer for his property. The contract creates an agency relationship wherein the seller is the principal and the broker is the special agent of the seller.
22. In Illinois, a written listing must include: property list price, commission and when due, listing term, seller's and broker's names, address of property, and signatures of parties.
23. Commission rates are negotiable, and the amount or percentage rate must be clearly stated in the listing agreement.
24. In Illinois, if the listing agreement states that in case of buyer default the seller does not receive the earnest money, this statement is to be in letters larger than those used in the listing agreement.
25. Listing agreements that do not contain a definite termination date are considered void in Illinois.
26. Licensees may not negotiate a possible future listing with a property owner who has an exclusive listing agreement with another broker without that broker's written authority or unless contacted directly by the owner.
27. Illinois license law requires that all earnest money be deposited in a federally insured, non-interest-bearing special account no later than the next business day following acceptance of the contract.
28. A protection period is allowed in a listing agreement; however, in Illinois no commission is paid to the broker with expired residential (1-4 units) listing if the property is listed with another broker and sold during that time period.
29. In Illinois, contracts for the sale of real estate that are meant to be legal and binding may not be entitled "offer to purchase."
30. An installment agreement is also called a contract for deed, a conditional sales contract, or a land contract. It is a contract of sale and a method of financing by the seller for the buyer. Legal title does not pass until the buyer pays all or some specified part of the purchase price. The contract buyer holds equitable title until transfer of legal title.
31. An installment agreement cannot contain a provision forbidding the buyer to record or state that recording does not constitute notice.
32. An option provides a right to purchase property under specified terms and conditions. During the option term, the contract is binding on the optionor but not on the optionee. When an option is exercised, it becomes a contract of sale and is, therefore, binding on both parties.
33. The Illinois Residential Real Property Disclosure Act affects the sale of residential properties of four units or fewer. The seller must complete a disclosure statement consisting of 22 statements.

Review Questions

Answers to these questions are found in the Answer Key section at the back of the book.

1. A contract in which mutual promises are exchanged at the time of signing (execution) is termed:
   a. multilateral
   b. unilateral
   c. bilateral
   d. promissory

2. Termination of a contract by mutual agreement of the parties is called:
   a. partition
   b. patent
   c. rescission
   d. reintermediation

3. For contracts in general, all of the following are essential elements EXCEPT:
   a. competent parties
   b. offer and acceptance
   c. legality of object
   d. writing

4. All of the following statements about contracts are true EXCEPT:
   a. a contract may be an agreement to do a certain thing
   b. contracts may arise out of implication
   c. a contract may be an agreement not to do a certain thing
   d. all contracts must be based upon an express agreement

5. All of the following statements are true in Illinois EXCEPT:
   a. Illinois citizens reach the age of majority at age 18
   b. a lease for more than one year must be in writing to be enforceable in court
   c. blanks in real estate contracts may be filled in after all parties have signed the contract
   d. Illinois licensees are not allowed to draft real estate contracts

6. Which of the following is the basis of duress?
   a. fear
   b. mistake
   c. indefiniteness
   d. illusion

7. An otherwise valid contract that cannot be enforced by legal action because of lack of compliance with the Statute of Frauds is:
   a. voidable by either party
   b. void on its face
   c. voidable by the offeree
   d. unenforceable

8. A contract to sell real property may be terminated by all of the following EXCEPT:
   a. complete performance
   b. death
   c. mutual assent
   d. breach of contract

9. Which of the following has the effect of terminating contracts?
   a. consideration
   b. bankruptcy
   c. exercise
   d. assignment

10. A listing contract creates an agency relationship between:
    a. buyer and seller
    b. buyer and lender
    c. broker and seller
    d. broker, seller, and buyer

11. Brown has listed a house for sale for $90,000. Cox makes a written offer of $86,500, which Brown accepts. Under the terms of this agreement:
    a. Brown was the offeror
    b. Cox was the offeree
    c. there was a meeting of the minds
    d. a unilateral contract was created

12. A contract between an adult and a minor is usually:
    a. voidable by either party
    b. voidable by the minor
    c. voidable by the adult
    d. void on its face

13. An owner employs a broker to market the owner's property and agrees to pay the broker a percentage of the sales price if the property is sold by anyone during the specified time period of the broker's employment. This agreement is:

    a. exclusive right-to-sell listing
    b. net listing
    c. exclusive agency listing
    d. open listing

14. Deliberate misrepresentation of a material fact, made with the intent that the other party act upon it to his detriment, is:

    a. misrepresentation
    b. undue influence
    c. fraud
    d. duress

15. The clause in the listing contract that protects the broker's commission entitlement beyond the listing period in the event of sale by the owner to a prospect who was in fact introduced to the property by the broker or another agent of her listing firm is called:

    a. forfeiture clause
    b. carryover clause
    c. settlement clause
    d. exclusive right clause

16. All of the following should always be present in offers and contract of sale EXCEPT:

    a. date of final settlement
    b. date possession will be given purchaser
    c. date of commission payment
    d. date of contract inception

17. Which of the following most accurately describes an agreement wherein a property owner agrees to convey title to the property when another party satisfies all obligations agreed to in the contract?

    a. lease contract
    b. listing contract
    c. level contract
    d. land contract

18. When a purchaser and seller have a valid contract for the sale of real property, the purchaser has:

    a. legal title
    b. no title
    c. equitable title
    d. constructive title

19. When a party purchases an option, the optionee is purchasing:

    a. contract liability
    b. time
    c. land
    d. exercise

20. Owner Appleton has given Miller an option for 30 days to purchase Appleton's farm at a specified price. Under the terms of an option, which of the following statements would NOT be correct?

    a. Appleton is the optionor
    b. Miller is the optionee
    c. Miller can require Appleton to sell at any time during the 30 days
    d. Appleton can require Miller to purchase within 30 days

21. All of the following are requirements of options EXCEPT:

    a. must be in writing to be enforceable
    b. must contain a description of the property
    c. must be exercised
    d. must contain a recital of consideration

22. Upon the receipt of a buyer's offer, the seller accepts all of the terms of the offer except the amount of earnest money; the seller then agrees to accept an amount 50 percent higher than the buyer had offered. This fact is promptly communicated to the offeree by the real estate agent. Which of the following most accurately describes these events?

    a. the communication created a bilateral contract
    b. the seller accepted the buyer's offer
    c. the seller conditionally rejected the buyer's offer
    d. the seller rejected the buyer's offer and made a counteroffer to the buyer

23. The Illinois Residential Real Property Disclosure Act affects the sale of:

    a. commercial properties with underground storage tanks
    b. residential properties with underground storage tanks
    c. residential properties of four or fewer units
    d. residential properties of more than four units

24. Under the Illinois Residential Real Property Disclosure Act, if the buyer receives the completed disclosure form before entering into a contract to purchase, the recission period is:

   a. three days if a defect is revealed on the form
   b. three days regardless of whether or not a defect is revealed on the form
   c. five days if a defect is revealed on the form
   d. there is no recission period

25. Which of the following would not be required to complete a disclosure statement under the Illinois Residential Real Property Disclosure Act?

   a. an owner who has not lived in the property in the past 12 months
   b. an owner who has always used the property as a rental
   c. a builder selling a new property that has never been occupied
   d. a seller of a four-unit residential property

CHAPTER 6

Important Terminology

abstract of title
acknowledgment
administrator/administratrix
adverse possession
alienation
baseline
benchmark
beneficiary
bequest
block
bona fide purchaser
certificate of title opinion
chain of title
codicil
constructive notice
contract buyer's policy
covenant against encumbrances
covenant for further assurances
covenant of quiet enjoyment
covenant of right to convey
covenant of seisin
covenant of warranty
datum
deed of confirmation
deed of gift
deed of release
deed of surrender
delivery and acceptance
descent
devise/devisee
executor/executrix
general warranty deed
grant, bargain, and sale deed
grant deed
grantee/grantor
granting clause

habendum clause
Illinois Affordable Housing Act
involuntary alienation
judicial deeds
Land Trust Recordation
   and Transfer Tax Act
leasehold policy
lien foreclosure sale
marketable (merchantable) title
metes and bounds
mortgagee's policy
owner's policy
permanent index numbers
plat
point of beginning (POB)
principal meridian
probate
quitclaim deed
range line
recordation
rectangular (government)
   survey system
section
sheriff's sale
special warranty deed
subdivision, lot, block, and tract
subrogation of rights
tacking
testator/testatrix
title examination
title insurance
title transfer taxes
Torrens system
township
township line
voluntary alienation

Transfer of Title to Real Property

IN THIS CHAPTER   The transfer of real property between buyer and seller is the goal of the typical real estate deal. Assuring the transfer of good title requires knowledge of the recording system, legal descriptions, abstracts of title, title insurance, surveys, deeds, and the requirements to be a bona fide purchaser. *Transfer of title to real property* is described in law as **alienation.** In a transfer, the property owner is alienated or separated from the title. Transfer may be during an owner's life or upon the owner's death. **Involuntary alienation** occurs when *an individual must relinquish title to real property due to a court action.* **Voluntary alienation** is usually accomplished by *the delivery of a valid deed by the grantor to the grantee while both are still alive,* or by an executor or administrator delivering the deed as directed by a testator in a will.

METHODS OF TRANSFERRING TITLE

Intestate Descent

When a person dies and leaves no valid will, the laws of **descent** determine *the order of distribution of property to heirs.* The typical order of descent is to spouses, children, parents, siblings, and then more remote lineal and lateral descendants. State statutes enacted for this purpose are called intestate succession statutes because a person dying without leaving a valid will has died intestate. In Illinois, this statute is the Illinois Law of Descent and Distribution (see Figure 6.1).

Escheat occurs when no one is eligible to receive the decedent's property as provided by statute. In Illinois, if a diligent search fails to reveal qualified heirs as specified by the statute, the property escheats to the county in which the property is located. This means that in the absence of heirs, the county takes title to the deceased's property. Because the deceased has no control over the transfer of title to the county, this results in an involuntary alienation after death. This is the only form of involuntary alienation after death. (In most states, property escheats to the state rather than the county.)

The *person appointed by a court to distribute the property of a person dying intestate,* in accordance with provisions of the statute, is called an **administrator** (male) or **administratrix** (female).

Testate Descent

A person who dies and leaves a valid will is said to have died testate. The deceased is called a **testator** if a man and a **testatrix** if a woman. A *person appointed in a will to* *carry out provisions of the will* is called an **executor** (man) or an **executrix** (woman). **Probate** is the *judicial determination of the validity of a will* by a court of competent jurisdiction *and subsequent supervision* over distribution of the estate. *A gift of real property by will* is a **devise,** and *the recipient of the gift of real property by will is the* **devisee.** *A gift of personal property by will* is a **bequest,** and the *recipient of the gift of personal property* is the **beneficiary.**

Wills in Illinois may be written by persons of sound mind who are 18 years of age or older. The will must be signed by the maker and witnessed by two or more persons who are not beneficiaries under the will. Nuncupative (oral deathbed) or holographic (written by maker entirely in hand without the necessary witnesses) wills are not recognized in Illinois. Wills can only be changed by a **codicil,** *a separate amendment to the will,* which also must be witnessed. A statutory right to renounce the will is given to a surviving spouse should the decedent spouse disinherit the surviving spouse.

Putting It to Work

Although wills are relatively simple documents, certain absolute requirements must be met or the will may be declared invalid. Wills always should be drafted by an attorney specializing in estate planning. After all, when it is discovered that a will has been inadequately drawn, it is too late to change it.

Voluntary Alienation

Voluntary transfer is the type of alienation that is of primary importance to the real estate business. Voluntary alienation is accomplished by the delivery of a valid deed by the grantor to the grantee during the life of both of them. The contract for sale of real property is consummated when the grantor delivers to the grantee a valid deed as required in the contract. Voluntary alienation may also take place by delivery of a deed by an executor or an administrator pursuant to a will.

Figure 6.1 Illinois descent and distribution.

IF THE DECEASED HAS LEFT NO VALID WILL AND HAS:	THE HEIRS WILL INHERIT THE FOLLOWING:
A spouse, and no children or descendants of children	The spouse inherits all of the real estate.
A spouse, and children or descendants of children	The spouse inherits half of each parcel; the children share the remaining half.
No spouse, but children or descendants of children	The children, or descendants of children, receive equal shares of the real estate.
No spouse or descendants	The parents each receive one part, and siblings or their descendants receive equal shares of the remainder. If one parent is deceased, the surviving parent gets the deceased parent's share.
No spouse, descendants, siblings, or parents	Heirs will be traced.
No traceable heirs	The property will escheat to the county where the property is located.

Involuntary Alienation

During the life of an owner, title to real property may be transferred by involuntary alienation through operation of law. Such court actions include foreclosure sales, adverse possession, petitions in bankruptcy, eminent domain, partition suits, execution sales enforcing judgments, and quiet title suits. The only form of involuntary alienation after death is the escheat of real property to the county.

Lien Foreclosure Sale and Sheriff's Sale

In Chapter 3 we discussed the concept that real property may be sold at public auction to satisfy a specific or general lien against the property. The **lien foreclosure sale** is *without consent of the property owner who incurred the debt resulting in a lien.*

In some states, including Illinois, another *option to satisfy a specific or general lien against a property* is a **sheriff's sale.** A sheriff's sale is ordered by the court, and the successful bidder receives a certificate of sale. If the owner redeems the property, the owner must repay the holder of the certificate of sale the redemption money plus interest from the date of sale. There is no right of redemption after the sale of the property.

Adverse Possession

A *person other than the owner can claim title to real property,* under **adverse possession,** if the other person makes use of the land under the following conditions:

1. The possession or occupation must be open and well-known to others (notorious).
2. Possession of the property must be under color of title (possession based on a written document) or claim of title (possession based on some claim against the title); that is, the occupant of the property must have some reasonable basis to believe that he is entitled to possession of the property. This basis typically is in the form of a defective deed or a quitclaim deed (discussed later).
3. The possession must be without the permission of the true owner and must be exclusive (not shared with the true owner). Thus, co-owners cannot adversely possess against each other.
4. The possession must be continuous and uninterrupted for a period of 20 years. The continuous use of the property refers to successive interests in the property. For instance, "A" lives on the property for 10 years and sells the property to "B," who lives there for eight years. If "B" sells the property after the eight years, the purchaser can claim title by adverse possession after only two more years. The *adding up of successive interests to reach the 20 years* is called **tacking.** Tacking is permissible in Illinois.

Illinois provides by statute a shorter period of time if possession is under color of title rather than when possession is under a claim of title. Adverse possession can take place with color of title by paying the real estate taxes for a seven-year period. Government property and property registered in Torrens (see discussion later in this chapter) cannot be adversely possessed.

To perfect the claim and obtain a title to the property, the claimant must satisfy the court that he has fulfilled the requirements of the adverse possession statute of Illinois in an action to quiet title. If the court is satisfied that the statutory requirements have been met, the court will award the title to the claimant under adverse possession.

Filing of Bankruptcy

If the owner of real estate files a bankruptcy petition under Chapter 7 of the United States Code, title to the real estate is transferred by operation of bankruptcy law to the bankruptcy trustee. Any further conveyance requires the approval and execution of documents by the bankruptcy trustee.

Condemnation Under Eminent Domain

The federal government, states and their agencies, counties, cities, towns, and boroughs have the power of eminent domain. This power confers the right to condemn, or take private property for public use. The condemned property must be for the use and benefit of the general public. The property owner must be compensated for the fair market value of the property lost through condemnation. The condemning authority must adhere to due process of law (that is, adequately notify the property owner of the condemnation by filing a suit for condemnation), and the property owner must have the right to appeal the value of the property as established by the condemning authority through the court system. The property owner, however, cannot prevent the condemnation and, therefore, the loss of title is involuntary.

DEEDS

Essential Elements of a Valid Deed

Various requirements are necessary to create a valid deed and convey title. These are discussed in the following pages. The minimum requirements for a valid deed in Illinois are shown in Figure 6.2.

In Writing

The deed must be in writing. As required by the Statute of Frauds, every deed must be written. An oral conveyance is ineffective. The written form of the deed must meet the legal requirements of the state in which the property is located.

Grantor

The **grantor,** *the one conveying the title,* must be legally competent; the individual must have the capacity to contract. This is the same requirement that exists for all parties to a valid contract. The grantor must have reached the age of majority (in Illinois, age 18), and must be mentally competent at the time of deed execution. Also, the grantor must be named with certainty; it must be possible to positively identify the grantor.

A corporation may receive, hold, and convey title to real property in the corporate name. Therefore, a corporation may be a grantor. If the conveyance of title by the corporation is in the corporation's ordinary course of business, the deed may be executed

FIGURE 6.2
Minimum requirements of a valid deed in Illinois.

1. In writing
2. A legally competent grantor
3. The grantor's name
4. The grantee's name and current address
5. The property's legal description
6. A stated consideration
7. A granting clause (words of conveyance)
8. The grantor's signature (acknowledgment)
9. Delivery and acceptance of the deed

on behalf of the corporation by the corporate president or vice president and countersigned by the secretary or assistant secretary. If the transfer of title is not in the ordinary course of the corporation's business, the board of directors of the corporation authorizing the transfer of title must make a resolution authorizing the conveyance. When the resolution has been made, the signatures of the individuals named above are sufficient. A partnership may receive, hold, and convey title to real property in the partnership name, in the name of an individual general partner, or in the name of a trustee acting for the partnership for this purpose.

Title to real property may be held in an assumed name, and it can be transferred under that name. Examples are titles in the name of a corporation or partnership. Title may be held by or transferred to a person with a fictitious name, but title cannot be held by or transferred to a fictitious person.

Grantee

The **grantee,** *the person receiving title,* does not have to have legal capacity; a minor or a mentally incompetent person can receive and hold title to real property. These people, however, cannot convey title on their own, because they are not qualified to be grantors. To effect a conveyance of title held in the name of an incompetent, a guardian's deed must be executed by the incompetent's guardian as grantor. The conveyance by the guardian may be accomplished only with court authority.

Grantees must be named with certainty, and Illinois requires the grantee's current address. It must be possible to identify the grantee. The grantee must actually exist and be either a natural person or an artificial person such as a corporation or partnership. The grantee must be alive at the time of delivery of the deed. A dead person cannot be a grantee.

Property Description

The deed must contain an adequate formal legal description of the property. The three methods of providing this description are discussed later in this chapter.

Consideration

The deed must provide evidence that consideration (something of value, such as money) is present. In Illinois, the deed does not have to recite the actual amount of consideration (money) involved; thus, a phrase such as "ten dollars, and other consideration" is sufficient to accomplish this purpose. This is called *nominal* consideration.

Good consideration is often present in gift or charitable conveyances. In Illinois, the phrase "for love and affection" or "for the continued use of the [charity]" is acceptable in a deed.

Words of Conveyance

The deed must contain *words of conveyance demonstrating that it is the grantor's intention to transfer the title to the named grantee.* These words of conveyance are contained in the **granting clause.** In the case of warranty deeds, typical wording is "as given, granted, bargained, sold, and conveyed."

PUTTING IT TO WORK

The words of the granting indicate the type of deed. "Conveys and warrants to" indicates a warranty deed. "Quits any and all claims to" indicates a quitclaim deed.

In addition to the granting clause, the deed sometimes contains a **habendum clause,** which *describes the estate granted and always must be in agreement with the granting clause.* Illinois does not require a habendum clause. If included, this clause begins with the words "to have and to hold." A typical habendum clause in a deed conveying a fee simple title reads, "to have and to hold the above described premises with all the appurtenances thereunto belonging, or in anywise appertaining, unto the grantee, his heirs, and/or successors and assigns forever." By contrast, the typical habendum clause in a deed conveying a life estate reads, "to have and to hold the premises herein granted unto the grantee for and during the term of the remainder of the natural life of the herein named grantee."

If the property is being sold subject to specific encumbrances of record, such as an easement or a mortgage lien, the habendum clause recites these encumbrances. Two points in regard to encumbrances are:

1. Transfer of fee simple absolute title does not mean an absence of encumbrances.
2. The warranty against encumbrances in a deed, discussed below, is only a warranty against encumbrances that have not been disclosed (those not on record).

Execution

Proper execution of the deed means that it must be signed by each grantor conveying an interest in the property. Only the grantors execute the deed. The grantee does not sign. In a minority of states, but not in Illinois, proper execution includes execution under seal.

Witnessing

Illinois does not require witnessing, although a few states require it for the deed to be valid.

Acknowledgment

In many states, but not in Illinois, for a deed to be eligible for recording, it must have an **acknowledgment.** A g*rantor must appear before a public officer* such as a notary public, who is eligible to take an acknowledgment, *and state that signing of the deed was done as a voluntary act.* In these states a deed is perfectly valid between grantor and grantee without an acknowledgment. Without the acknowledgment, however, the grantee cannot record the deed and thereby have protection to title against subsequent creditors or purchasers of the same property from the same grantor who record their deed. Acknowledgment allows the deed to be presented as evidence in a court of law. The grantee should insist upon receiving a deed that has been acknowledged.

Delivery and Acceptance

To effect a transfer of title by deed, there must be **delivery and acceptance**. The *grantor must deliver a valid deed to the grantee, and the grantee must accept the deed.* Delivery may be directly to the grantee or to an agent of the grantee. The agent for this purpose is typically the grantee's attorney, real estate broker, or the lending institution providing the mortgage loan to finance purchase of the property. In almost every case there is a presumption of acceptance by the grantee. This presumption is especially strong if the deed has been recorded and the conveyance is beneficial to the grantee.

Types of Deeds

Many types of deeds result from the various forms of warranty of title contained in the deed, and many variations are based on the special purpose for which the deed is drawn. The various types of deeds are discussed next, both by type of warranty and by special purpose.

General Warranty Deed

The **general warranty deed** (Figure 6.3) *contains the strongest and broadest form of guarantee of title of any type of deed* and therefore provides the greatest protection to

FIGURE 6.3
A sample general warranty deed.

the grantee. The general warranty deed usually contains six covenants, as discussed below. Exact wording of these covenants may vary. In Illinois, the covenants in a general warranty deed are implied by statute.

1. **Covenant of seisin.** Typical wording of this covenant is, "Grantor covenants that he is seised of said premises in fee." This covenant, like the others in the general warranty deed, is a specific covenant and provides *an assurance to the grantee that the grantor holds the title that he or she specified in the deed* that he or she is conveying to the grantee. In the example cited, the grantor promises the grantee that he or she has fee simple title to the property.

2. **Covenant of right to convey.** This covenant, which usually follows the covenant of seisin in the general warranty deed, typically reads, "and has the right to convey the same in fee simple." By this covenant the grantor provides *an assurance to the grantee that the grantor has legal capacity to convey the title and also has the title to convey.*

3. **Covenant against encumbrances.** This covenant typically states that, "said premises are free from encumbrances (with the exceptions above stated, if any)." The grantor assures the grantee that there are *no encumbrances against the title except those set forth in the deed itself.* Typical encumbrances that are acceptable to grantees are a lien of a mortgage when grantee is assuming grantor's existing mortgage, recorded easements, and restrictive covenants.

4. **Covenant of quiet enjoyment.** This covenant typically reads, "the grantee, his or her heirs and assigns, shall quietly and peaceably have, hold, use, possess, and enjoy the premises." This covenant is an *assurance by the grantor to the grantee that the grantee shall have quiet possession and enjoyment of the property being conveyed* and will not be disturbed in the use and enjoyment of the property because of a defect in the title being conveyed by the grantor. In warranty deeds not containing a specific covenant of quiet enjoyment, the covenant of warranty itself assures the grantee of quiet enjoyment of the property.

5. **Covenant for further assurances.** This covenant typically reads, "that the grantor will execute such further assurances as may be reasonable or necessary to perfect the title in the grantee." Under this covenant, *the grantor must perform any acts necessary to correct any defect in the title being conveyed and any errors or deficiencies in the deed itself.*

6. **Covenant of warranty.** The warranty of title in the general warranty deed provides that the grantor "will warrant and defend the title to the grantee against the lawful claims of all persons whomsoever." This is the *best form of warranty for protecting the grantee* and contains no limitations as to possible claimants protected against, because the grantor specifies that he or she will defend the title against "the lawful claims of all persons whomsoever." The covenant of warranty is the most important of all the covenants.

PUTTING IT TO WORK

In many states, including Illinois, the form of warranty deed may not specifically outline in words what is warranted. These promises, or warranties, are merely implied with the word "warrants" in the granting clause, but still would be recognized in the event of a dispute over title.

If the covenant of seisin or the covenant of warranty is broken, a grantee may recover from the seller any financial loss up to the price paid for the property. If the covenant against encumbrances is broken, the grantee may recover from the grantor any expenses incurred to pay off the encumbrance. The amount the grantee may recover in this case also is limited to the price paid for the property.

The covenant of quiet enjoyment is not considered broken unless the grantee is actually dispossessed of the property. The mere threat or assertion of a claim by another party to some right in the property does not constitute a breach of the covenant of quiet enjoyment. In the case of dispossession, the grantee may recover from the grantor an amount up to the price paid for the property.

The covenant for further assurances is not broken until the grantor has to execute some instrument to perfect the grantee's title. Neither the covenant of quiet enjoyment nor the covenant of warranty is broken until the grantee actually is evicted from the property by someone holding a superior title.

Special Warranty Deed

In the **special warranty deed,** the warranty is *limited to claims against the title arising out of the period of ownership of the grantor.* This warranty goes back in time only to the date when the grantor acquired the title, as contrasted with the general warranty deed, in which the warranty is against defects in the title going back for an unlimited time.

Putting It to Work

The special warranty deed usually is used by a non-owner acting on behalf of the true owner. Examples include the executor or administrator of an estate, guardian, custodian, trustee, receiver, or anyone acting in a fiduciary capacity.

Quitclaim Deed

The **quitclaim deed** contains no warranties whatsoever. It is simply a *deed of release.* It will release or convey to the grantee any interest, including title, that the grantor may have. The grantor, however, does not state in the deed that she has any title or interest in the property and certainly makes no warranties as to the quality of title. Execution of the quitclaim deed by the grantor prevents the grantor from asserting any claim against the title at any time in the future.

Quitclaim deeds may be used to clear a cloud on a title. This terminology describes the situation when someone has a possible claim against a title. As long as this possibility exists, the title is clouded and therefore not a good and marketable title. To remove this cloud and create a good and marketable title, the possible claimant executes a quitclaim deed as grantor to the true titleholder as grantee.

Putting It to Work

Common clouds include lingering spousal claims (particularly after a divorce), liens that appear to have been paid but not released (mortgages and mechanics' liens), and claims of relatives after estate probation.

Quitclaim deeds also are used in community property states to enable a married individual to own property purchased during the marriage in severalty.

The granting clause in the quitclaim deed shown in Figure 6.4 contains the words "convey and quitclaim" instead of "convey and warrant," as used in the warranty deed shown in Figure 6.3.

FIGURE 6.4
A sample quitclaim deed.

QUIT CLAIM DEED
Statutory (ILLINOIS)
(Individual to Individual)

CAUTION: Consult a lawyer before using or acting under this form. Neither the publisher nor the seller of this form makes any warranty with respect thereto, including any warranty of merchantability or fitness for a particular purpose.

THE GRANTOR

of the _____ of _____ County of _____ State of _____ for the consideration of _____ DOLLARS, _____ in hand paid, CONVEY ___ and QUIT CLAIM ___ to

(NAME AND ADDRESS OF GRANTEE)

(The Above Space For Recorder's Use Only)

all interest in the following described Real Estate situated in the County of _____ in the State of Illinois, to wit:

hereby releasing and waiving all rights under and by virtue of the Homestead Exemption Laws of the State of Illinois.

Permanent Real Estate Index Number(s): _____

Address(es) of Real Estate: _____

DATED this _____ day of _____ 19 ___

PLEASE PRINT OR TYPE NAME(S) BELOW SIGNATURE(S)

_____(SEAL) _____(SEAL)

_____(SEAL) _____(SEAL)

State of Illinois, County of _____ ss. I, the undersigned, a Notary Public in and for said County, in the State aforesaid, DO HEREBY CERTIFY that

IMPRESS SEAL HERE

personally known to me to be the same person ___ whose name _____ subscribed to the foregoing instrument, appeared before me this day in person, and acknowledged that ___ h ___ signed, sealed and delivered the said instrument as _____ free and voluntary act, for the uses and purposes therein set forth, including the release and waiver of the right of homestead.

Given under my hand and official seal, this _____ day of _____ 19 ___

Commission expires _____ 19 ___   _____
NOTARY PUBLIC

This instrument was prepared by _____
(NAME AND ADDRESS)

MAIL TO:
(Name)
(Address)
(City, State and Zip)

OR   RECORDER'S OFFICE BOX NO. _____

SEND SUBSEQUENT TAX BILLS TO:
(Name)
(Address)
(City, State and Zip)

AFFIX "RIDERS" OR REVENUE STAMPS HERE

Grant, Bargain, and Sale Deed

The **grant, bargain, and sale deed** may be with or without covenants of warranty. In Illinois this type of deed conveys a fee simple title and warrants that the title is free from encumbrances made by the grantor, except those named in the deed, and warrants quiet enjoyment.

Grant Deed

The **grant deed** is a special form of statutory deed used in western states where warranty deeds are rarely used. Rather than being expressly set forth in the deed, *the warranties are implied from state statute.* These implied warranties include a warranty against encumbrances created by the grantor or anyone claiming title under his deed and a warranty that the grantor has not previously conveyed the same title to anyone else. The form of an individual grant deed is the simplest of all the various types of deeds.

Deed of Confirmation

The **deed of confirmation,** also called a deed of correction, is *used when a deed contains an error that requires correction.* Examples of the types of errors corrected by this type of deed are errors in names of the parties, errors in the property description, and mistakes made in execution of the deed.

Deed of Release

The **deed of release** is *used primarily to release a title from the lien of a mortgage when the debt secured by the mortgage has been paid in full* or, in the case of a blanket mortgage, to release individual parcels of land from the lien of the blanket mortgage. A deed of release also is used to release a dower right in property.

Deed of Surrender

A life tenant may use the **deed of surrender** *to convey an estate to the reversionary interest or to the remainder interest,* depending on the form of the life estate. This same result may be accomplished through a quitclaim deed.

Deed of Gift

A **deed of gift** of *real property may be conveyed by either general warranty deed or quitclaim deed.* If using the warranty deed, the grantee cannot enforce the warranties against the grantor; the grantor received no consideration for conveying the title to the grantee, as the conveyance was a gift. Either a warranty deed or a quitclaim deed conveys the property provided the grantor has title to convey.

Judicial Deed

Execution of **judicial deeds** *results from a court order to the official executing the deed.* The various types of judicial deeds receive their names from the title of the official executing the deed. They include sheriff's deed (in some states, referee's deed in foreclosures), tax deed, guardian's deed, commissioner's deed (in some states, referee's deed in partition), executor's deed, and administrator's deed. Judicial deeds contain no warranties.

Transfer Taxes

Illinois Real Estate Transfer Tax Act

At the time of this writing, most states, including Illinois, impose *a tax on the conveyance of title to real property.* Illinois uses the term **title transfer taxes,** though the name of the tax varies from state to state. State statutes usually require the seller to pay this tax. The amount of tax is based on the consideration the seller receives in selling the property.

The amount of tax charged on the purchase price varies by state. Illinois excludes from the tax the amount of any mortgage being assumed, which is called "old money," and therefore charges the tax only on the "new money" brought into the transaction above the amount of the assumed loan. A mortgage note taken back by the seller is considered part of the total consideration, and the tax is paid on the full sales price. Personal property included in the sale is also exempt from the tax in Illinois.

The transfer tax on the new money is charged at the rate of $.50 per each $500 or fraction thereof. In addition, a county transfer tax is charged at the rate of $.25 per each $500 or fraction thereof. The total state and county transfer tax charge equals $.75 per each $500 or fraction thereof. The formula for computing transfer tax is shown in Figure 6.5. No tax is required if the total actual consideration is less than $100. Many municipalities, such as Chicago, also have imposed a transfer tax.

Transfer tax stamps are affixed to the deed before recording. An examination of tax stamps only provides an indication of the new money, which will be less than the sales price if a mortgage was assumed.

When a deed is presented for recording it must be accompanied by the Real Estate Transfer Declaration, otherwise known as the "green sheet." Falsifying or omitting any required data on the transfer declaration is a Class B misdemeanor, which could result in up to six months imprisonment.

Illinois Affordable Housing Act of 1989

The **Illinois Affordable Housing Act** is *designed to assist low-income families with affordable housing.* The program is administered by the Illinois Housing Development Authority (IHDA). The governor appoints a 15-member advisory commission that works with the IHDA in implementing affordable housing programs. The program is funded from income received from transfer taxes. Of every $.50 the state receives from the sale of transfer tax stamps, $.25 is allotted to the IHDA for affordable housing programs.

FIGURE 6.5 Formula for figuring transfer tax.

Example: A property is selling for $90,000 and $50,000 is being assumed.

Amount property selling for:	$90,000
Amount being assumed, *if any*:	$50,000 (subtract from sales price)
Amount of personal property, *if any*:	$ 0 (subtract from sales price)
Amount subject to transfer tax	$40,000 ($40,000 ÷ 500 = 80)
Amount of taxable units	80
Amount of state transfer tax	$ 40 (80 × .50 = $40)
Amount of county transfer tax	$ 20 (80 × .25 = $20)

Land Trust Recordation and Transfer Tax Act

The **Land Trust Recordation and Transfer Tax Act** *provides for the payment of transfer taxes on the transfer of a beneficial interest in a land trust.* The trustee records a facsimile of the assignment of beneficial interest.

Inspection Ordinances

Many municipalities have enacted ordinances requiring inspection of properties being transferred. If violations are found, the seller is usually required to pay for repairs needed for compliance. Transfer stamps may not be issued until the building inspector has issued a certificate of compliance.

TITLE ASSURANCE

Title Examination

Before the title can be transferred, the seller must provide evidence of **marketable or merchantable title,** one that is *readily salable in a locality.* Marketable title is not perfect title. It is not necessarily title free of all liens. In the case of a sale with mortgage assumption, the buyer has bargained for and will accept seller's title with the present mortgage as a lien on the title.

Evidence of marketable title through **title examination** can be provided by a commercially hired search or by a personal *search of the records that may affect real estate titles.* The records searched include public records of deeds, mortgages, long-term leases, options, installment agreements, easements, platted subdivisions, judgments entered, deaths, marriages, bankruptcy filings, mechanics' and materialmen's liens, zoning ordinances, real and personal property taxes, miscellaneous assessments for improvements, mortgage releases, and lis pendens notices.

PUTTING IT TO WORK

Given the extent and complexity of records to be searched, as well as future legal implications, use of a skilled service, such as a title insurance company or an abstractor, is recommended for title examination.

The search of the records on a given piece of real estate will establish a **chain of title,** which must be unbroken for the title to be good and, therefore, marketable. It involves *tracing the successive conveyances of title* starting with the current deed and going back an appropriate time (typically 40 to 60 years), quite often researching back to original title (the last instance of government ownership).

PUTTING IT TO WORK

Any missing links in the chain of title create uncertainty as to the path of ownership and proof thereof. These missing links could be the result of oversight (failing to record a deed), fraud, or a dispute between parties. Any of these uncertainties is of sufficient concern to a buyer to threaten the marketability of title. If these missing links can be bridged by obtaining proper title-clearing documents, the transaction may safely occur. If not, the sale should not close.

The two most often used forms of commercial title evidence are abstract of title with attorney opinion and policy of title insurance.

Abstract of Title with Attorney Opinion

An **abstract of title** is a *condensed history of the title,* setting forth a summary of all links in the chain of title plus any other matters of public record affecting the title. The abstract contains a legal description of the property and summarizes every related instrument in chronological order. An abstract continuation is an update of an abstract of title that sets forth memoranda of new transfers of title. The preparer of the abstract certifies that all recorded matters relating to the real estate in question are included in the abstract. When the abstract is completed, an attorney must examine it to assure that the chain of title is unbroken and clear. The attorney then gives a written **certificate of title opinion** as to *what person or entity owns the real estate and the quality of title.*

The abstractor certifies that the public records have been searched. The attorney certifies that the abstract has been examined and states the quality of title and exceptions, if any, to clear title.

Policy of Title Insurance

A **title insurance** policy is a contract of insurance that *insures the policy owner against financial loss if title to real estate is not good.* Title insurance policies are issued by the same companies that prepare abstracts of title. The company issuing the insurance policy checks the same public records as abstractors do, to determine if it will risk insuring the title.

The typical title insurance policy requires the title insurance company to compensate the insured for financial loss up to the face amount of the policy resulting from a title defect (plus cost of litigation or challenge). The policy protects the insured only against title defects existing at the time of transfer of title. If a claim is filed and the title insurance company pays the claim, it may have the right to bring legal action against the grantor for breach of warranties in the deed. The title insurance company has obtained from the insured grantee this right to file suit by payment of the claim. The *substitution of the title insurance company in the place of the insured for filing a legal action* is called **subrogation of rights.**

Like any other insurance policy, a title insurance policy has a list of risk items that are included and excluded. A typical title insurance policy does not cover financial loss from adverse possession, adverse parties in possession, easements by prescription, or any other unrecorded documents. A title insurance policy does insure against financial loss by forgery of any document affecting real estate. A title insurance policy also may include special endorsements that increase the areas of coverage. Typical endorsements in commercial real estate, particularly, are to insure ingress and egress and proper zoning.

The title insurance policy is issued only upon an acceptable abstract or title opinion. A title that is acceptable to the title insurance company is called *insurable title.* The premium for a title insurance policy is a one-time premium paid at the time the policy is placed in effect. The four forms of title insurance policies are: owner's policy, mortgagee's policy, leasehold policy, and contract buyer's policy.

Owner's Policy

The **owner's policy,** *for the protection of the new owner,* is written for the amount the new owner paid for the property. The amount of coverage remains the same for the life of the policy. The policy remains in effect for the duration of the insured's ownership of the property and continues in effect after the death of the owner to benefit heirs receiving an interest in the property.

Mortgagee's Policy

A **mortgagee's policy** *protects only the mortgagee.* Under the terms of the policy, the mortgagee is insured against defects in the title to property pledged as security in the mortgage. The mortgagee's insurable interest is only to the extent of the outstanding loan balance at any given time. Therefore, the mortgagee's policy decreases in face amount as the loan principal decreases but always provides coverage equivalent to the amount of the loan balance.

Leasehold Policy

The **leasehold policy** *protects the lessee (leaseholder) and/or a mortgagee against defect in the lessor's title.* This policy is issued to a mortgagee when the mortgagor has pledged a leasehold interest instead of a fee simple title as security for the mortgage debt.

Contract Buyer's Policy

A **contract buyer's policy** *protects the contract buyer against defects in the contract seller's title* prior to the contract. This policy is issued when an installment agreement (contract for deed) is executed between vendor and vendee.

Recordation

Title insurers, abstractors, and attorneys all rely on recorded documents concerning real estate. **Recordation** *provides protection for the owner's title against subsequent claimants.* This protection is provided by the theory of **constructive notice:** *All of the world is bound by knowledge of the existence of the conveyance of title if evidence of the conveyance is recorded.* Illinois does not require that deeds be recorded to be valid, but in practice most deeds are recorded. If a deed is to be recorded, it should be acknowledged.

Constructive notice is not the same as actual notice. Constructive notice is binding on everyone, even though they have not actually read the deed, because recording it gives notice to the world. Actual notice requires that the person in fact knows about and sees the document. Constructive notice, provided by recording, protects the title for the grantee. This protection is against everyone with a later claim, including other purchasers of the same property from the same grantor.

A buyer of property who relies on the records and is unaware of an unrecorded prior document is called a **bona fide purchaser** (BFP). A bona fide purchaser's real estate title is protected because of recording.

Figure 6.6 illustrates the possible effects of a grantee's failure to record a deed and the protection provided to a grantee who does record a deed. In the figure, title is transferred effectively from Grantor Charlie to Edna (Grantee #1), but the title is defeated by Edna's failure to record the deed. Charlie then conveys the same title to Sasha (Grantee #2), who records the deed. Sasha now holds the title, and Edna has the right to sue Charlie to recover her money. This right may be worth pursuing provided that Charlie can be found and has money or property. For Edna to sue Charlie, Sasha must be a bona fide purchaser for value, completely unaware of the prior conveyance to Edna, and must have paid fair market value for the property.

In summary, Figure 6.6 illustrates that a valid conveyance of title can take place between grantor and grantee without the deed being recorded. Nevertheless, the deed must be recorded to protect a grantee's title from third parties, such as purchasers from the grantor, subsequent creditors, or other lienholders of the grantor.

FIGURE 6.6
The possible effects of failure of grantee to record a deed.

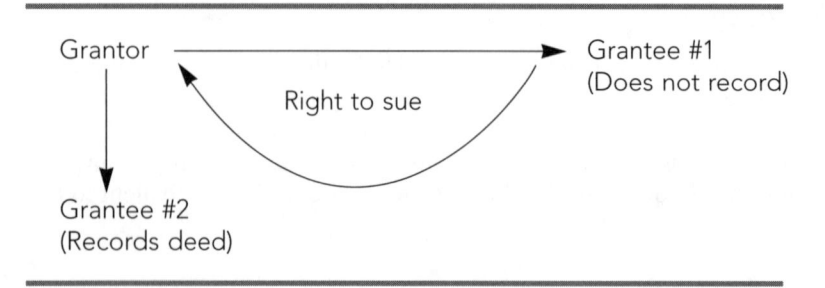

Title Registration/Torrens System

In addition to the regular method of recording titles, a special form of recording called the **Torrens system** of title recordation was previously used in Cook County. Under the Torrens system the *titleholder applies to the court to have property registered.* The court orders the title to be examined by official title examiners, who report the examination results to the court. If results of the examinations are satisfactory, the court issues instructions to the Register of Titles to record the title and issues certificates of registration of title after giving adequate public notice so anyone contesting the title has ample opportunity to appear. Cook County began to phase out Torrens in January 1992. Property is removed from Torrens as documents are presented for filing. After January 1, 1997, all properties remaining in Torrens will be automatically transferred to the unified system of recording.

The certificate of registration of title contains the type of title the applicant has and sets forth any encumbrances against the title. One certificate is issued to the Register of Titles and the other to the titleholder who applied for registration of the title. The certificate of registration provides conclusive evidence of the validity of the title, and it cannot be contested except for fraud. Title to properties recorded under the Torrens system cannot be obtained by adverse possession. Though the Torrens system has been abolished in Illinois, it still exists in approximately 10 states.

Property Description

For effective and accurate title transfers, title insurers, abstractors, and attorneys rely on an accurate legal description of the land. The legal description for title transfer must be a formal description. Informal descriptions, such as street addresses or assessor's tax numbers, are acceptable on listing agreements, but unacceptable for documents transferring or encumbering title.

Putting It to Work

If a legal description and informal reference do not identify the same property, the legal description is recognized and the informal reference is ignored. Because most people readily recognize street addresses and do not recognize legal descriptions, it is essential to verify that both describe the same property.

Monuments and Markings

In the early days of the U.S., descriptions of land were created by observation. Natural and artificial markings or monuments were an integral part of early land descriptions.

Natural monuments consisted of rivers, streams, lakes, trees, rocks, and other such phenomena. Artificial monuments consisted of such landmarks as fences, walls, houses, streets, alleys, and drainage ditches. There were frequently problems when fences were removed, streets widened or closed, trees knocked down, rocks moved about, or other alterations made.

Since the earliest settlers had no governmental office in which to record their descriptions, the owner would walk the land with his son, pointing out all the land that the son would someday inherit using landmarks and monuments to delineate this parcel. Land was passed down from generation to generation in this manner. Problems arose when owners of abutting lands did not agree with the position of the monuments.

To improve the accuracy of land descriptions, three methods were developed: metes and bounds; the government or rectangular survey system; and subdivision, lot block, and tract. Illinois uses all three methods; however, every parcel in Illinois is described using the rectangular survey system.

Metes and Bounds

The first 13 colonies in the U.S. were surveyed using the metes and bounds method, as were the states of Kentucky, Tennessee, Maine, Vermont, Texas, and parts of Ohio. Illinois uses the metes and bounds method in conjunction with the rectangular survey system when describing small or irregular shaped parcels. In a **metes and bounds** description, the **metes** are *the distances from point to point in the description,* and the **bounds** are *the directions from one point to another.* An example of a metes and bounds description is given in Figure 6.7.

A metes and bounds description is made from a survey performed by a state licensed and registered land surveyor. One of the most important aspects of metes and bounds description is the selection of the starting point or **point of beginning (POB).** The POB should be reasonably easy to locate and well-established. After starting at the POB, the surveyor sights the direction to the next point. The next point might be described as "north 45 degrees 3 east." The surveyor will sight the exact direction using increments of minutes and seconds (60 minutes in a degree and 60 seconds in a minute). A description might read something like "north 45 degrees 30'10" east." This bearing is illustrated in Figure 6.7. A metes and bounds description must always close (end) at the point of beginning.

PUTTING IT TO WORK

The Illinois Plat Act requires that all parcels of land divided into two or more parts, any of which is less than five acres, must be surveyed and a plat of subdivision recorded. This rule has some exceptions, about which the county recorder should be consulted.

Government Rectangular Survey System

The metes and bounds system was adequate in the early days of the country, but as the United States incorporated large tracts of land, it was clear that a more uniform system of land description was necessary. In 1784, at the suggestion of Thomas Jefferson, who was a land surveyor, the rectangular survey system was devised. With the Louisiana Purchase in 1803, the United States doubled in size. In 1805, the government officially adopted the rectangular survey system.

The **rectangular (government) survey system** is *used to describe large, regularly shaped tracts of real estate, such as rectangles and squares.* In this system, the

138 *Chapter 6*

FIGURE **6.7** A sample metes and bounds description in conjunction with a description by reference.

An example of a typical metes and bounds description and the plat resulting from that description follow.

*Being all of Lot No. 20 of the subdivision of a portion of the property of Mortgage Heights Land Company, Inc., as shown by plat thereof prepared by Worley and Gray, Consulting Engineers, dated October 1, 1965, and recorded in Book 5, page 40, Records of Plats for Buncombe County, and more particularly bounded and described as follows:

**BEGINNING on a stake in the northeast margin of Amortization Drive, south corner of Lot No. 20 of the subdivision or a portion of the property of Mortgage Heights Land Company, Inc., and running thence North 6° 18' East 215.2 feet to a stake; thence North 8° 49' West 241.0 feet to a stake, common corner of Lot Nos. 20 and 19 of said subdivision; thence with the dividing line between said Lot Nos. 19 and 20, South 87° 50' West 138.5 feet to a stake in the east margin of a cul-de-sac; thence with the east margin of said cul-de-sac in a southwesterly direction along a curve with the radius of 50.0 feet, 61.2 feet to a stake in said margin; thence with the east margin of a drive leading to Amortization Drive, South 5° 19' West 132.8 feet to a stake in the point of intersection of said margin of said drive with Amortization Drive; thence with the northeast margin of said Amortization Drive, South 51° 17' East 84.7 feet to a stake in said margin; thence still with said margin of said drive, South 42° 27' East 47.2 feet to a stake in said margin; thence still said margin of said drive, South 29° 36' East 199.9 feet to the BEGINNING.

*Description by reference.
**Description by metes and bounds.

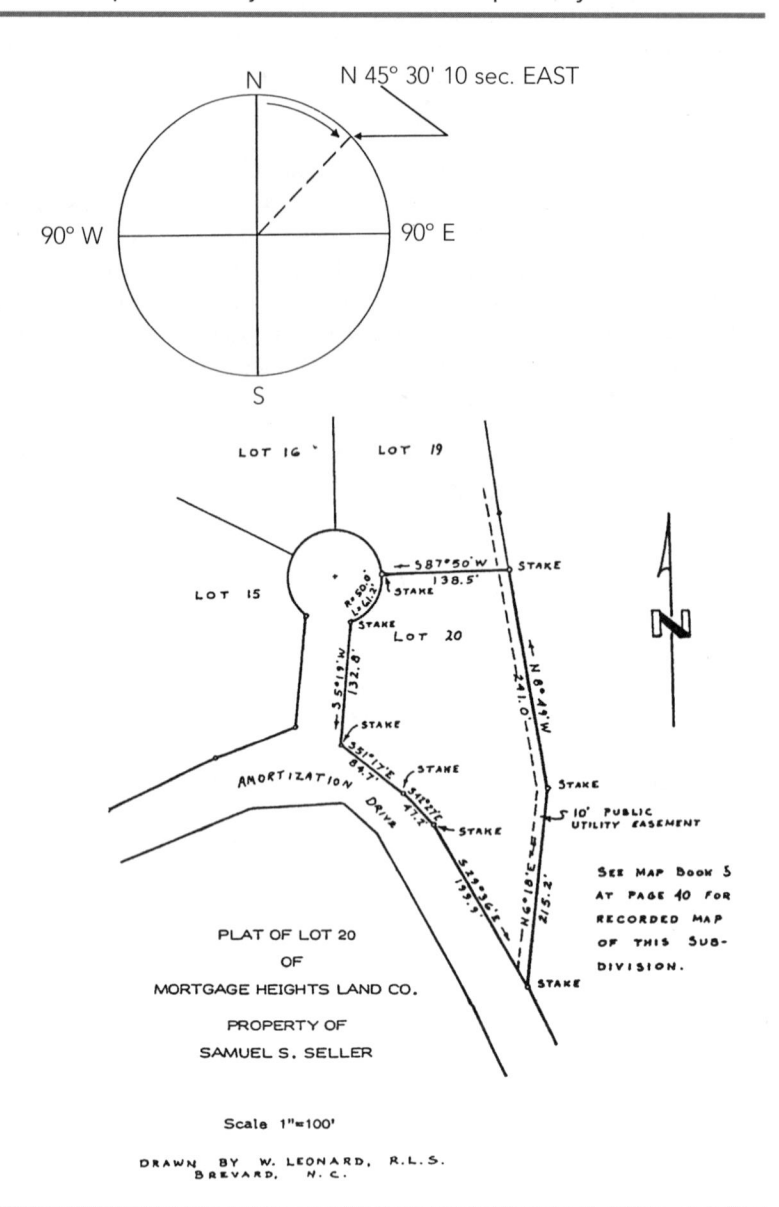

country is divided by *36 north-south lines* called **principal meridians** and *32 east-west lines* called **baselines.** In Illinois, land is referenced by the 2nd, 3rd, and 4th principal meridians, as shown in Figure 6.8.

Dividing the land into smaller sections are range and township lines. **Range lines,** located *every six miles east and west of the principal meridians,* form rows of land called ranges, which are numbered east and west of the principal meridians as Range 1 East (R1E), Range 2 East (R2E), and so forth. **Township lines** are located *every six miles north and south of the baselines.* These township rows are numbered every mile north and south of the baseline as Township 1 South (T1S), Township 2 South (T2S), and so on.

As shown in Figure 6.9, *the range lines and township lines cross to form squares of six miles by six miles (36 square miles)* called **townships.** Due to the curvature of the earth, all townships are not a perfect six miles square. As range lines extend northward, they grow closer together, and townships become smaller. The township is kept as close to six miles wide as possible by designating every fourth township north of

FIGURE 6.8 The principal meridians (2nd, 3rd, and 4th) and baselines that divide Illinois and Indiana.

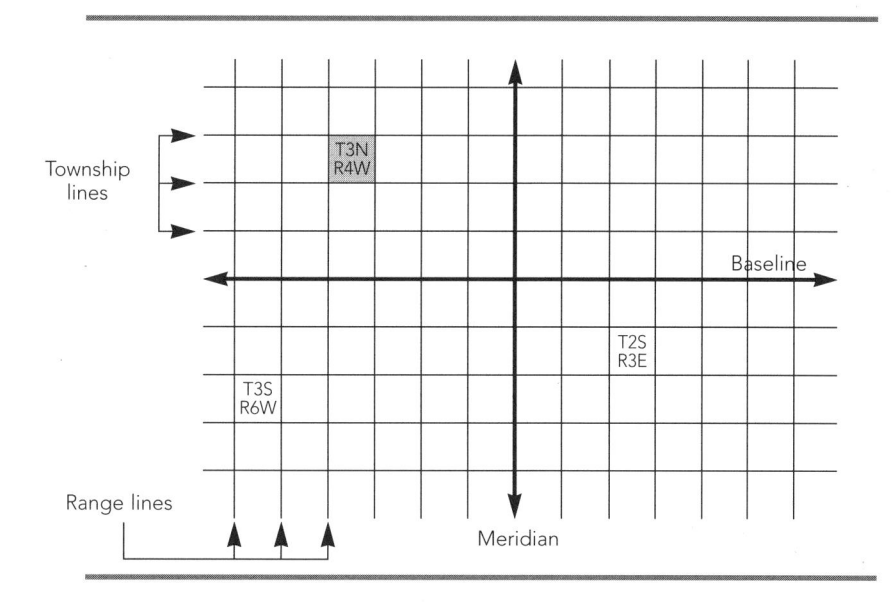

FIGURE 6.9 Range and township lines cross to form squares called townships. Each township square is six miles by six miles.

the baseline as a correction line. Every fourth township, the distance between range lines is measured to a full six miles.

Townships are divided into 36 sections, as illustrated in Figure 6.10. A **section** is *one mile wide by one mile wide* (one square mile). The numbering of sections begins with the northeast section as section 1, and counts westward through the six sections, then drops south to the next section and moves east again through the next six sections, and so on through the township. Originally, section 16 was set aside for school and school revenue–generating purposes.

Each one-mile square section consists of 640 acres that can be continuously subdivided. As illustrated in Figure 6.11, a section can be divided in half so there is a north half and a south half. Each of these halves is 320 acres. The north half can be divided into half again so that it contains an east half and a west half. This is actually two quarters of a section, each containing 160 acres. Dividing the west quarter into quarters results in four parcels of 40 acres each. This could continue into even smaller parcels in a process of continuous subdivision. Western movies sometimes depicted a farmer saying, "I'm going to go plow the back 40," or a rancher saying, "I'm going to check the fences on the north 40." The back 40 or north 40 were parcels delineated by the rectangular survey system.

The legal description of the parcel described above and shown in Figure 6.12 is: the southwest quarter of the northwest quarter of section 25, Township 3 North, Range 4 West of the third principal meridian, Cook County, Illinois. Given such a description, the parcel could be found by working from the latter part of the description to the

140   Chapter 6

FIGURE 6.10
There are 36 sections in each township, each measuring one mile by one mile (one square mile).

Township 3 North, Range 4 West

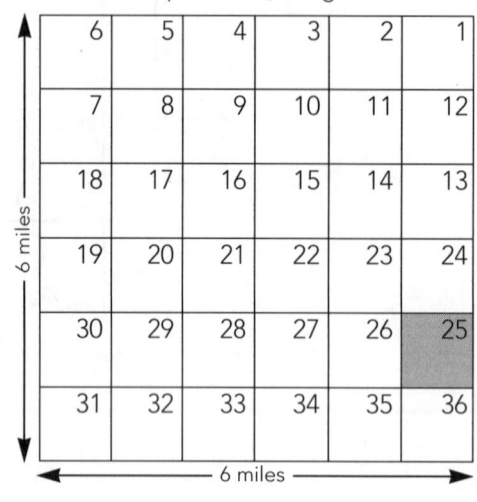

6	5	4	3	2	1
7	8	9	10	11	12
18	17	16	15	14	13
19	20	21	22	23	24
30	29	28	27	26	25
31	32	33	34	35	36

←—— 6 miles ——→
6 miles (vertical)

FIGURE 6.11
Each one-mile square section contains 640 acres that can be further subdivided.

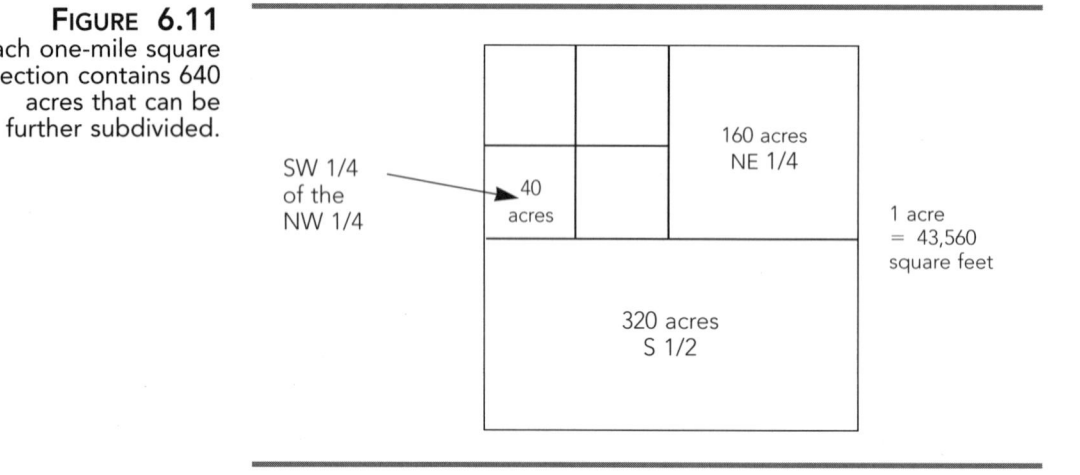

SW 1/4 of the NW 1/4 → 40 acres

160 acres NE 1/4

1 acre = 43,560 square feet

320 acres S 1/2

FIGURE 6.12
Finding a specific parcel from a legal description.

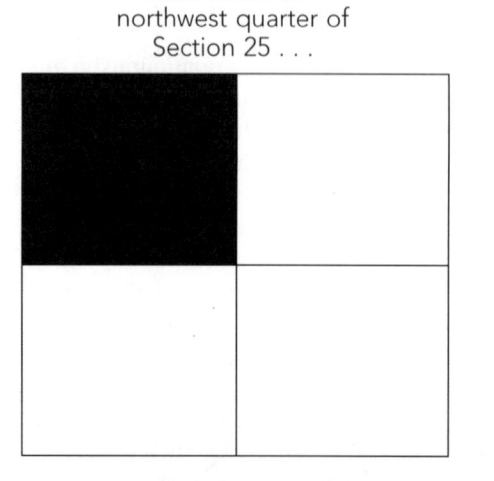

First locate the northwest quarter of Section 25 . . .

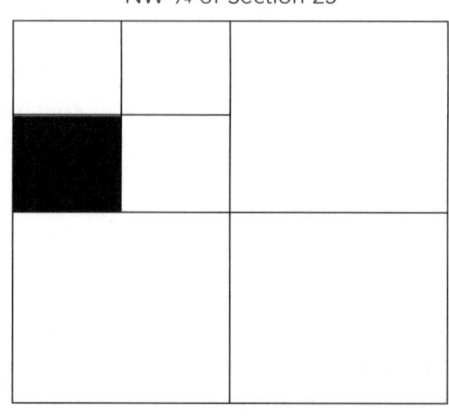

. . . then find the southwest quarter of the NW 1/4 of Section 25

beginning—from the general to the specific—as shown in Figure 6.12. In the description of the southwest quarter of the northwest quarter of section 25, first find section 25. Then continuing to work from the end to the beginning of the description, next find the northwest quarter of the section and then the southwest quarter of that.

Subdivision, Lot, Block, and Tract

A third method of land description is the **subdivision, lot, block, and tract** method, which *defines a parcel of land by reference to where it can be found in a tract book.* This method is used on smaller parcels of land. Land surveyed by the rectangular survey and metes and bounds systems is then divided into blocks. Each **block** of *land is divided into a number of contiguous lots.* This *survey map,* or **plat,** is then delivered to the recorder's office. The recorded plat is placed in the appropriate plat book. These parcels are then referenced by their tract book, lot, block numbers, the name of the subdivision, and their reference to the rectangular survey system. A subdivision, lot, block, and tract description is illustrated in Figure 6.13.

Assessor's Parcel Numbers

County assessors have derived another *method of distinguishing parcels from one another* called **permanent index numbers.** These numbers are used to aid the assessors' appraisal of properties and the county collector's gathering of taxes. They are not appropriate for the conveying of title.

Types of Lots

There are several types of lots, as indicated in Figure 6.14. A **cul-de-sac** is *usually located at the end of a street (dead end) and is irregular in shape.* The cul-de-sac lot will have a curved front lot line. A corner lot is located on a corner, while inside lots are not located on a corner. A T-lot is the lot that is at the end of a T-intersection. These are often considered the key lots, or the least desirable lots, in a subdivision.

Contour Maps

A **contour map** *shows the topography (elevations) of a site.* Contour maps are helpful in determining a suitable use for a particular lot and in calculating the amount of fill a site must have brought in or removed. The plat map in Figure 6.15 has contour lines. The closer these lines are together, the higher the relative elevation.

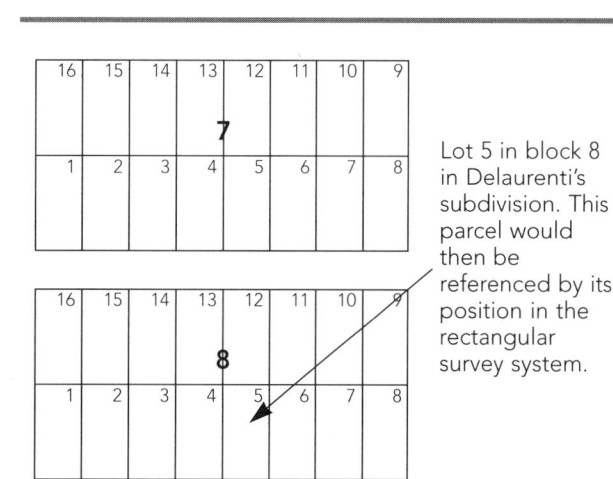

FIGURE 6.13
A subdivision, lot, block, and tract description.

Lot 5 in block 8 in Delaurenti's subdivision. This parcel would then be referenced by its position in the rectangular survey system.

FIGURE 6.14
Types of lots.

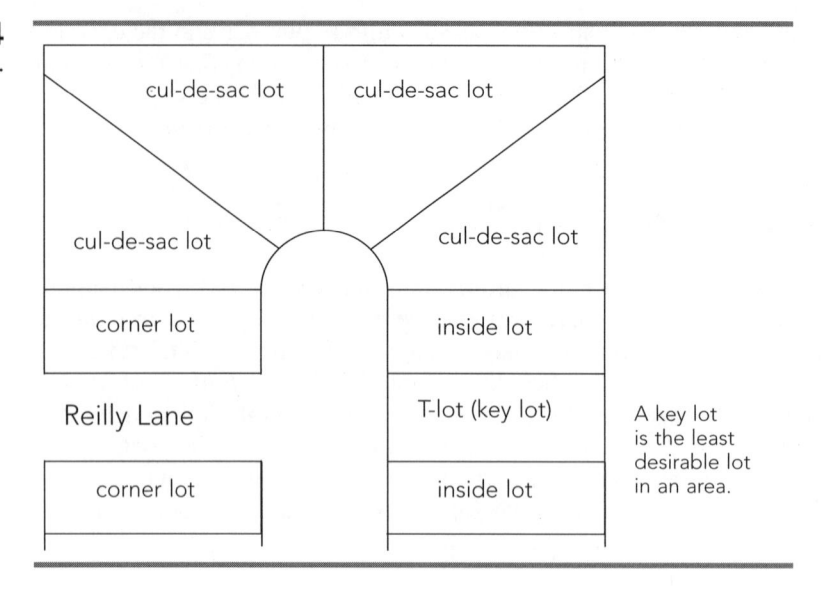

FIGURE 6.15
A plat map with contour lines.

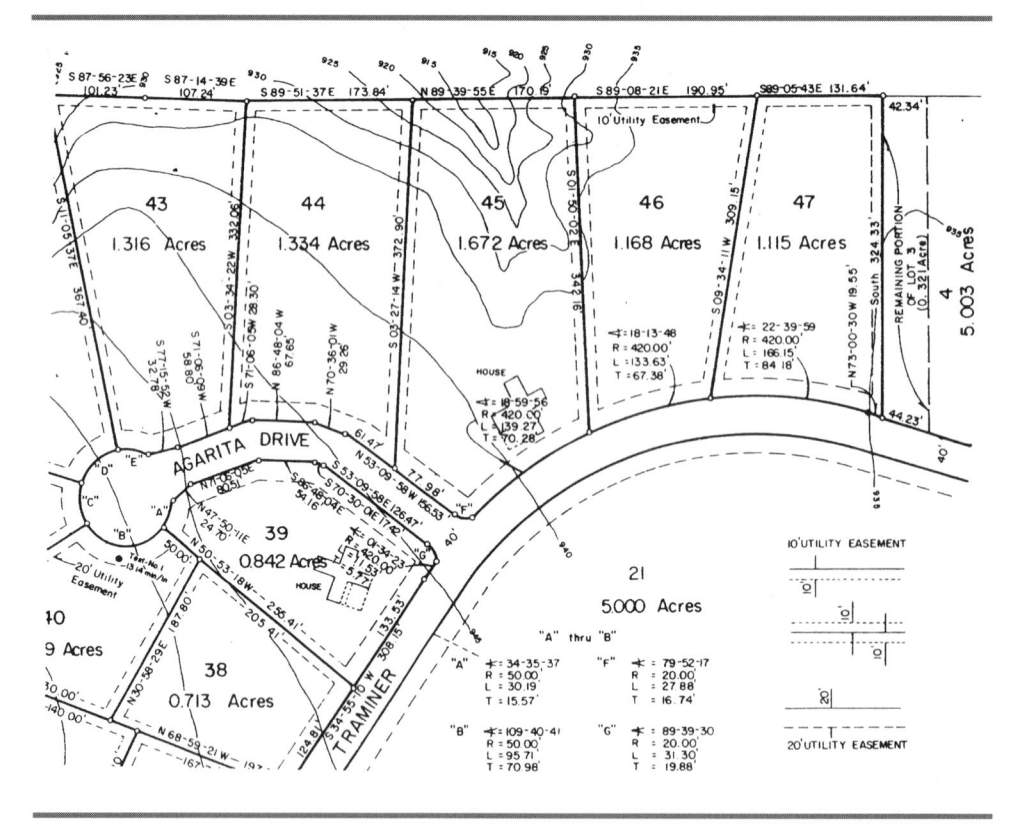

Vertical Land Description

The metes and bounds, rectangular survey, and subdivision, lot, block, and tract systems are used in the measurement of land surfaces. Condominium ownership, however, does not include any land: a condominium purchaser purchases an air lot. In order to precisely define the condominium owner's air space, a vertical survey of the unit must be completed, making reference to the datum and benchmarks. A **datum** is *the primary reference point for vertical measurement*. A **benchmark** is *a secondary reference point for vertical measurement*. The official datum for the entire country is the United States Geological Survey Datum, based on mean sea level at New York Harbor, although some cities, such as Chicago, have their own city datum. Vertical surveys, therefore, reference the land elevation, or how far above or below sea level a point is. Knowledge of land elevations is needed for road building construction and for such things as making sure new sewers have been installed so that they flow downhill.

IMPORTANT POINTS

1. Transfer of title is termed alienation. Involuntary alienation occurs during life as a result of adverse possession, lien foreclosure sale, or condemnation under the power of eminent domain. Involuntary alienation after death is escheat. Voluntary alienation after death is by will or descent. Voluntary alienation during life can occur only by delivery of valid deed.
2. In Illinois, property of those who die intestate (without a will) is distributed according to the Illinois Law of Descent and Distribution.
3. Real property of those who die without a will and without any heirs escheats to the county in which the property is located.
4. Adverse possession of real property can take place after 20 years of continuous, uninterrupted use that is hostile to the true owner's claim. Adverse possession also can occur by payment of the real estate taxes for a period of seven years, along with a claim and color of title.
5. The requirements for deed validity are (a) deed in writing, (b) competent grantor, (c) competent or incompetent grantee, (d) grantor and grantee named with certainty, (e) adequate property description, (f) recital of consideration, (g) words of conveyance, (h) habendum clause, (i) proper execution by grantor, (j) witnessing (in some states), and (k) delivery and acceptance to convey title.
6. In most states, to be eligible for recording in the public record, a deed must be acknowledged. Illinois does not require an acknowledgment. Recording protects the grantee's title against creditors of the grantor and subsequent conveyances by the grantor.
7. A general warranty is the strongest and broadest form of title guarantee. The general warranty deed typically contains six covenants: seisin, right to convey, against encumbrances, quiet enjoyment, for further assurances, and warranty.
8. A quitclaim deed is a deed of release and contains no warranties. It will convey any interest the grantor may have. The quitclaim deed is used mainly to remove a cloud from a title.
9. The Illinois Real Estate Transfer Tax Act imposes a tax on the transfer of real estate in which the consideration is more than $100. The state transfer tax is $.50 per each $500 or fraction of the sales price. The county transfer tax is $.25 per each $500 or fraction thereof. If a mortgage is being assumed by the buyer, the amount of the assumed mortgage is subtracted from the sales price and the tax is figured on the remaining balance. Personal property included in the sale would also be substracted prior to tax computation.
10. Of every $.50 the state collects in transfer taxes, $.25 is allotted to the Illinois Housing Development Authority for affordable housing programs.
11. The purpose of a title examination is to determine the quality of a title. The examination must be made by an attorney or a title company. Only an attorney can legally give an opinion as to the quality of a title.
12. A title insurance policy protects the insured against financial loss caused by a title defect. The four types of policies are owner's, mortgagee's, leasehold, and contract buyer's.

144 Chapter 6

13. The three methods of formal property description in use in the United States are metes and bounds, reference, and rectangular survey.
14. Cook County was the only county in Illinois using the Torrens system, but it will be phased out by January 1997.

REVIEW QUESTIONS

Answers to these questions are found in the Answer Key section at the back of the book.

1. Voluntary alienation may occur by:
   a. condemnation
   b. will
   c. escheat
   d. adverse possession

2. Voluntary alienation during life may occur only through a:
   a. will
   b. foreclosure sale
   c. deed delivery
   d. devise

3. Essential elements of a valid deed include all of the following EXCEPT:
   a. acknowledgment
   b. writing
   c. competent grantor
   d. execution by grantor

4. The purpose of a deed being acknowledged is to:
   a. make the deed valid
   b. make the deed eligible for delivery
   c. allow the deed to be presented as evidence in court
   d. identify the grantee

5. The type of notice provided by recording is:
   a. actual
   b. reasonable
   c. protective
   d. constructive

6. Of the following types of deeds, which provides the grantee with the greatest assurance of title?
   a. special warranty
   b. deed of confirmation
   c. sheriff's deed
   d. general warranty

7. Which of the following covenants assures the grantee that the grantor has the legal capacity to transfer title?
   a. covenant of quiet enjoyment
   b. covenant of right to convey
   c. covenant of seisin
   d. covenant for further assurances

8. A deed in which the wording in the granting clause is "remise and release" is a:
   a. quitclaim deed
   b. special warranty
   c. grant deed
   d. bargain and sale deed

9. Either a general warranty deed or a quitclaim deed is equally suitable for a:
   a. judicial deed
   b. deed of confirmation
   c. official deed
   d. deed of gift

10. A grantor left a deed for the grantee to find after the grantor's death. The result was to convey:
    a. the title during the grantor's life
    b. the title after the grantor's death
    c. no title as the deed was not delivered
    d. no title as the deed was not recorded

11. The type of deed used to remove a mortgage lien when the debt is satisfied is:
    a. deed of surrender
    b. grant deed
    c. deed of release
    d. special warranty deed

12. A deed passes title upon:
    a. delivery and acceptance
    b. execution
    c. recordation
    d. acknowledgment

13. A claim of title by adverse possession may be defeated by the property owner by:
    a. permission
    b. confirmation
    c. will
    d. condemnation

14. The type of deed that guarantees the title against defects that were created only during the grantor's ownership is:
    a. bargain and sale
    b. special warranty
    c. surrender
    d. release

15. A mortgagee's title insurance policy protects:
    a. owner
    b. lending institution
    c. seller
    d. grantee

16. The successive conveyances of a title are called:
    a. releases
    b. remises
    c. links in the chain of title
    d. abstracts of title

17. Which of the following is a system of title recording?
    a. abstract continuation
    b. records of liens
    c. record of acknowledgment
    d. Torrens

18. A title insurance policy may be written to protect all of the following EXCEPT:
    a. owner
    b. licensee
    c. lessee
    d. mortgagee

19. A title insurance policy protects the insured against loss caused by defects in the title:
    a. existing at the time the insured acquired title
    b. created during the insured's ownership
    c. created in the past 40 years
    d. created by the assumed mortgage

20. All of the following are examples of involuntary alienation EXCEPT:
    a. devise
    b. lien foreclosure sale
    c. eminent domain
    d. execution by judgment creditor

21. The NE 1/4 of the NE 1/4 of Section 12 describes:
    a. 40 acres
    b. 160 acres
    c. 320 acres
    d. 640 acres

22. The Illinois Affordable Housing Program is administered by:
    a. HUD
    b. IHDA
    c. IDR
    d. IHP

23. J lives in a property for 12 years and sells the property to K, who lives in the property for 6 years. K sells the property to L, who holds the property for the next 2 years and claims the property by adverse possession. This adding of successive interests is called:
    a. tacking
    b. Cohen rule
    c. injunctive relief
    d. subrogation

24. Which of the following is INCORRECT regarding title insurance?
    a. the mortgagee's policy is generally for the loan amount
    b. the mortgagee's policy is assignable
    c. the mortgagor's policy is assignable
    d. title insurance is available to contract sale purchasers

25. Q inspects a property that is for sale. Upon inspection of the property, Q finds R, who is not the owner, living on the property. Which of the following statements is true?
    a. R is giving actual notice of his interest in the property
    b. R is giving constructive notice of his interest in the property
    c. Q need not be concerned with R's occupancy of the property
    d. Q cannot purchase the property until R moves out of the property

CHAPTER 7

Important Terminology

- acceleration clause
- alienation clause
- amortizing
- arrears
- conforming loans
- deed in lieu of foreclosure
- deed of trust
- defeasance clause
- deficiency judgment
- disintermediation
- due-on-sale clause
- equity of redemption
- Fannie Mae (FNMA)
- foreclosure
- Freddie Mac (FHLMC)
- Ginnie Mae (GNMA)
- hypothecate
- Illinois Mortgage Foreclosure Law
- interest
- intermediate theory
- judicial foreclosure
- lien theory
- liquidity
- mortgage
- mortgage assumption
- mortgage banker
- mortgage broker
- mortgagee
- mortgagor
- nonrecourse note
- prepayment penalty
- principal
- promissory note
- right of assignment
- savings and loan association (S&L)
- secondary mortgage market
- strict foreclosure
- title theory
- trustee
- trustor

Real Estate Finance Principles

IN THIS CHAPTER This chapter focuses on financing instruments, such as mortgages and deeds of trust, and the various sources of real estate funds. Because cash sales are unusual, knowledge or lack of knowledge of the ways to finance a sale makes the difference between a successful or unsuccessful career in real estate. Federal government regulation of lending institutions that make mortgage loans and the secondary mortgage market are also covered.

NOTES

In making a mortgage loan, the lender requires the borrower to sign a **promissory note,** or bond in some states. *The note, which must be in writing, provides evidence that a valid debt exists.* The note contains a promise that the borrower will be personally liable for paying the amount of money set forth in the note and specifies the manner in which the debt is to be paid. Payment is typically in monthly installments of a stated amount, commencing on a certain date. The note also states the annual rate of interest to be charged on the outstanding principal balance.

PRINCIPAL, INTEREST, AND PAYMENT PLANS

Understanding the terms *interest* and *principal* is essential to understanding notes, mortgages, deeds of trust, and all real estate financing methods. **Interest** is the *money paid for using someone else's money.* The **principal** is the *amount of money on which interest is either paid or received.* In the case of an interest-bearing note, principal is the amount of money the lender has lent the borrower and on which the borrower will pay interest to the lender.

The note can be an interest-only note on which interest is paid periodically until the note matures and the entire principal balance is paid at maturity. Construction notes are usually of this type. Or the note can be a single-payment loan that requires no payments on either principal or interest until the note matures, and the entire principal and interest is paid at maturity. This is seen more frequently in short-term notes. The note also can be an amortizing note in which periodic payments are made on both principal and interest until such time as the principal is completely paid. Most mortgage loans are of this type.

The original principal is the total amount of the note. This amount remains the same in an interest-only or a one-payment loan until the entire principal is paid.

In an **amortizing** loan, *periodic payments are applied first toward the interest and then toward the principal.* As the principal portions of these payments are applied, the amount of principal gradually decreases. As each successive payment is made, the interest is applied to the declining principal balance; therefore, with each successive payment, the interest portion of the payment decreases and the principal portion increases. The first payment is applied mostly toward interest, and the last payment is applied mostly toward principal. The payments can be set at a fixed rate for the life of the loan, or they can fluctuate based on a specified index, or they can change at set intervals according to a set formula. This subject is covered in more detail under types of mortgages in Chapter 8.

Simple interest is usually used for mortgage loan interest. This means the annual rate of interest is used to calculate payments even though payments normally are made monthly. Payments sometimes are set up to be paid quarterly or annually. Recently, a payment plan in which payments are made every two weeks (biweekly) has become popular because it reduces the term of the loan and saves a significant amount of interest over the life of the loan. A current loan can sometimes be switched to this payment plan.

Mortgage loan interest almost always is calculated in arrears, although it sometimes is calculated in advance. If interest is calculated in **arrears,** *a monthly payment due on the first of the month includes interest for using the money during the previous month.* If interest is calculated in advance, a monthly payment due on the first of the month includes interest for the month in which the payment is due. When paying off or assuming a loan, one must know if the interest is paid in advance or in arrears to determine the amount of interest owed or to be prorated at closing. Interest must be paid in arrears on all loans sold in the secondary mortgage market.

MORTGAGE AND DEED OF TRUST

Typically, the borrower's personal promise to pay the debt is not enough security for the large amount of money involved in a mortgage loan. The lender therefore requires the additional security of the property itself as collateral for the loan. *Pledging property as security for the loan* (**hypothecating**) is accomplished through the mortgage or deed of trust instrument. Therefore, every mortgage loan has two instruments: (a) the note (a personal IOU), and (b) the mortgage or deed of trust (a pledge of real property). Pledging the property does not require the borrower to give up possession except in case of default.

The main lending practices, or theories of financing, are:

1. **Lien (or mortgage) theory,** in which the *loan constitutes a lien against the real property.* The mortgage is a two-party instrument between the lender and the borrower.
2. **Title theory** (granting theory), in which *a disinterested third party actually holds legal title to the property in security for the loan* through a **deed of trust.**
3. **Intermediate theory,** adopted by some states including Illinois, is a modification of the title and lien theories. In accordance with this intermediate theory, the *borrower holds legal title subject to the lien created by the mortgage.* Illinois is considered an intermediate theory state.

In all states the mortgage or deed of trust creates a lien against the property pledged to secure payment of the note.

A **mortgage** is a *two-party instrument in which the borrower gives a piece of paper (mortgage) to the lender in return for the borrowed funds.* The *borrower who gives the mortgage* is called the **mortgagor.** The *lender who receives the mortgage* is known as the **mortgagee.** The borrower (mortgagor) retains title to the property, but this title is encumbered by the lien created by the mortgage in favor of the lender (mortgagee). If the lender is not paid according to terms of the mortgage and note, the lender can execute the lien through foreclose.

In contrast, the title theory of finance requires the mortgagor (borrower) to convey title to the property to a **trustee,** *a type of third-party referee,* through a deed of trust also called a *trust deed.* When the mortgagor completes paying off the debt, the trustee is required to return title to the **trustor,** the *borrower,* by executing a *deed of release.* If the borrower defaults in his or her obligation to pay back the funds, the lender (mortgagee) may instruct the trustee to sell the title to recover the lender's funds. Because the lender therefore benefits from the trust title, he or she is also known as the *beneficiary.*

The **Illinois Mortgage Foreclosure Law** enacted July 1, 1987, *requires that mortgage foreclosures be brought about through a court proceeding.* In a judicial foreclosure state, such as Illinois, a deed of trust is treated like a mortgage and is subject to the mortgage foreclosure rules.

Putting It to Work

The concepts of note and mortgage might become clearer by giving them "plain English" titles. The note's title would be, "I promise to pay you back." The mortgage or deed of trust would be titled, "And if I break any rules of our agreement, this is what you can do to me."

Requirements for Validity of a Mortgage or Deed of Trust

1. The mortgage or deed of trust must be in *writing,* as required by the Statute of Frauds, because the mortgage or deed of trust pledges or conveys title to real property to secure payment of the note.
2. The mortgagor in a mortgage or the trustor (borrower) in the deed of trust must have *contractual capacity.* This is the same requirement of competency necessary for creation of a valid contract as discussed in Chapter 5, on contracts. Illinois citizens reach contractual capacity at age 18.
3. The mortgagee or trust beneficiary in a deed of trust and the trustee must have contractual capacity.
4. There must be a *valid debt* to be secured by the mortgage or deed of trust. The existence of the valid debt is evidenced by the note.
5. To secure the debt in the mortgage or deed of trust, the mortgagor or trustor must have a *valid interest* in the property pledged or conveyed.
6. A legally acceptable *description of the property* must be included.
7. The mortgage or deed of trust must contain a *mortgaging clause.* In an intermediary theory state such as Illinois, the mortgagor is the owner of the property. The mortgaging clause provides that the title is subject to the defeasance clause and, upon repayment of the debt, a release of mortgage must be given to the mortgagor.
8. The mortgage or deed of trust has to contain a *defeasance clause* that defeats the lien and conveyance of title when the mortgage debt is fully satisfied.
9. The *borrower must properly execute* the mortgage or deed of trust. Only the mortgagor or trustor signs the deed of trust. The lender does not sign.
10. The mortgage or deed of trust must be *delivered* to and *accepted* by the mortgagee or trust beneficiary (lender).

Mortgage Clauses and Covenants

Examples of the various clauses and covenants that may be included in a mortgage or deed of trust are presented next.

1. The mortgage is dated and contains the names of mortgagor and mortgagee. If the deed of trust form is used, the borrower's name appears, identified as trustor, grantor, or mortgagor. The name of the trustee or grantee and the name of the lender, who is both the trust beneficiary and the noteholder, also appear.

2. The note executed by the borrower is reproduced in the mortgage or deed of trust. The note includes an **acceleration clause** *enabling the lender to declare the entire balance remaining immediately due and payable if the borrower is in default.*

3. The note may provide that the borrower is permitted to pay off the loan any time prior to expiration of the full mortgage term without incurring a financial penalty for the early payoff, or it may provide for *a penalty to be imposed on the borrower* (**prepayment penalty**) *if the debt is satisfied prior to expiration of the full term.* FHA, VA, and conforming loans (discussed in Chapter 8) cannot have a prepayment penalty.

In Illinois, on loans with an 8 percent interest rate or higher and which are secured by residential real estate, lenders cannot charge a prepayment penalty.

4. The mortgage requires the borrower to pay all real property taxes and assessments on a timely basis, keep the buildings in a proper state of repair and preservation, and protect the buildings against loss by fire or other casualty by an insurance policy written in an amount at least 80 percent of the value of the structures. Many lenders also require insurance for 100 percent of the loan value minus the lot value.

5. The mortgage contains a **defeasance clause** *giving the borrower the right to defeat and remove the lien by paying the indebtedness in full.*

6. The mortgage provides the right of foreclosure to the lender if the borrower fails to make payments as scheduled or fails to fulfill other obligations as set forth in the mortgage.

7. In the deed of trust form, a clause gives the lender irrevocable power to appoint a substitute trustee or trustees, without notice and without specifying any reason, by recording an *instrument of appointment* on the public record where the deed of trust is recorded.

8. In both the mortgage form and the deed of trust form, a covenant always specifies that the mortgagor has a good and marketable title to the property pledged to secure payment of the note.

9. The mortgage or deed of trust may contain an **alienation** or **due on sale clause** entitling *the lender to declare the principal balance immediately due and payable if the borrower sells the property during the mortgage term and making the mortgage unassumable* without the lender's permission. Permission to assume the mortgage at an interest rate prevailing at the time of assumption can be given at the lender's discretion. The alienation clause may provide for release of the original borrower from liability if an assumption is permitted. This release is sometimes referred to as a *novation.*

10. The mortgage or deed of trust always provides for execution by the borrower.

11. The mortgage or deed of trust provides for acknowledgment by the borrower to make the document eligible for recording on the public record for the lender's protection.

12. Illinois requires that a release of mortgage must be delivered to the mortgagor upon full payment of the mortgage. The mortgagee may be liable to pay a $200 penalty if the release is not delivered to the mortgagor within one month after full repayment of the mortgage loan. The release must state in bold letters: "FOR THE PROTECTION OF THE OWNER, THIS RELEASE SHALL BE FILED WITH THE RECORDER OR THE REGISTRAR OF TITLES IN WHOSE OFFICE THE

MORTGAGE OR DEED OF TRUST WAS FILED." The borrower has the responsibility to record the release to clear the record of the mortgage lien.

Recordation

Recordation gives order to the system of land ownership and transfer. Recorded documents affecting real estate can be found in public records in the county in which the property is located. Documents do not have to be acknowledged or notarized to be valid. Documents can be recorded without acknowledgment in Illinois. Recording an invalid document does not make it valid.

Mortgages and deeds of trust should always be recorded. This protects those with any present or future interest in the property by providing constructive notice to the general public of ownership and any other interest in the property. Real estate documents do not have to be recorded to be valid between the parties. If they are not recorded, however, someone obtaining and recording a future interest in the property may have an interest superior to that of the person who gained an interest earlier but did not record the document.

Priority and Subordination

Priority usually is established by the time (date and hour) the lien is recorded. The priority of certain liens, such as property tax liens, special assessment liens, and mechanics' or materialmen's liens, is not based on the time of recording but on other factors, as discussed in Chapter 3. In the event of a foreclosure sale, the holder of the first lien has the first claim against the sale proceeds, and that debt must be fully satisfied before the holder of the second lien is fully satisfied, and so on down the line of priorities. In some instances, the order of priority can be modified by a subordination agreement, whereby an earlier lender may be willing to subordinate (take a back seat) to a later lender. Typically a lender will only subordinate his mortgage to another mortgage if he is certain the property value is sufficient to pay off both mortgages should foreclosure become necessary. An example of subordination is the lien holder on a building lot subordinating his mortgage lien to the construction mortgage lien.

Releases

Recording a release of a mortgage, note, claim, or deed of trust is just as important as recording the original document. Failure to do so may cloud the title to the property.

RIGHTS OF THE BORROWER

1. The borrower has the right to possession of the property during the mortgage term as long as the borrower is not in default.
2. The defeasance clause gives the borrower the right to redeem the title and have the mortgage lien released at any time prior to default by paying the debt in full.
3. The borrower has the right of **equity of redemption.** After default, the *borrower can redeem the title pledged or conveyed to secure a mortgage debt up to the time of a foreclosure sale by paying the debt, interest, and costs* (discussed later in the chapter).

Rights of the Lender

1. The lender has the right to take possession of the property (after foreclosure) if the borrower defaults in mortgage payments.
2. The lender has the right to foreclose on the property if the borrower defaults in the payments. The property may be sold at a foreclosure sale, and the proceeds of the sale, after certain other items are paid, are applied to satisfy the mortgage debt.
3. The lender has the right to assign the mortgage or deed of trust. This enables the lender to sell the mortgage, if he or she so desires, and thereby free the money invested. The **right of assignment** provides liquidity to mortgages because *the lender can sell the mortgage at any time and obtain the money invested rather than wait for payment* of the loan over an extended time.

Foreclosure

If the borrower (mortgagor) does not make the payments as required, he or she is in default on the loan. The lender's ultimate power is to foreclose. **Foreclosure** is the *liquidation of title to the real property pledged, to recover funds to pay off the mortgage debt.*

The Illinois Mortgage Foreclosure Law now includes long-term installment agreements that are payable for more than five years if the unpaid balance is less than 80 percent of the purchase price. Details concerning installment agreements in Illinois were discussed in Chapter 5.

Judicial Foreclosure

Judicial foreclosure *requires the lender to bring a lawsuit against the borrower and obtain a judgment for the amount of debt the borrower owes.* When the judgment is obtained, the lender requests the court to issue an execution instructing the sheriff to take possession of the mortgaged property and sell it for cash at public auction to the highest bidder. Title is conveyed to the purchaser by a sheriff's deed or a trustee's deed.

Equity of Redemption

After default, and up to the time a foreclosure sale is held, the borrower has an equitable right to redeem his or her property by paying the principal amount of the debt, accrued interest, and lender's costs incurred in initiating the foreclosure. The borrower's equity of redemption cannot be defeated by a mortgage clause. This right is terminated by the foreclosure sale. In Illinois, the defaulting owner may (a) cure and reinstate the loan within 90 days after the service of summons (statutory right of reinstatement), or (b) pay the principal balance, interest, and other fees prior to the sale (equitable right of redemption), or (c) be able to redeem the property within seven months from the service of summons or three months from the date of judgment of foreclosure, whichever is later. If the property is redeemed, the sale does not occur.

Statutory Foreclosure

Some states recognize statutory foreclosure. In statutory foreclosure, the borrower is granted the right to pay the debt plus accrued interest and costs in full after the foreclosure sale and thereby recover the property. However, Illinois does *not* allow a borrower to redeem a property after the foreclosure sale.

Illinois law may allow the defaulting owner to remain in possession until after judgment. Following judgment and confirmation of the sale, payment of rent is due to the holder of the certificate of sale. The holder of the certificate of sale may take possession of the property on the 31st day after judgment.

Strict Foreclosure

Under **strict foreclosure,** the *lender may file a foreclosure petition with a court after the mortgagor is in default.* The court then issues a decree requiring the mortgagor to satisfy the mortgage debt within a stated period of time or lose his or her equitable right to redeem the title. Once this right is lost, the mortgagor cannot assert any rights in the title, which passes to the mortgagee. This type of foreclosure is not in favor in the United States.

Deed in Lieu of Foreclosure

In a measure sometimes called a friendly foreclosure but more formally a **deed in lieu of foreclosure,** a *borrower in default simply conveys the title to the property to the lender,* to avoid record of foreclosure. The disadvantage is that it does not eliminate other liens against the property. Furthermore, the lender may lose the right to claim against mortgage insurance or guarantee programs such as FHA or VA.

Distribution of Sale Proceeds

Proceeds of the mortgage foreclosure sale are distributed in the following order of priority:

1. All expenses of the sale are paid. These include court costs, trustee's fee, advertising fees, legal fees, accounting fees, and the like.
2. Next, any real property tax liens and assessment liens against the property are paid. Some localities sell these properties subject to the tax lien, thereby requiring the new buyer to pay the tax lien in addition to the sales price.
3. If there are no other lienholders with liens having priority over the lien of the mortgage or deed of trust, the lender is paid. In Illinois, mechanics' liens attach as of the date of contract or when work is started.
4. Any other creditors holding liens against the property are paid; however, creditors who are not secured by the foreclosed property are not paid from sale proceeds. Illinois homestead laws protect a limited amount of equity in a home from unsecured creditors, as discussed in Chapter 3.
5. Any remaining moneys after items 1 through 4 have been satisfied are paid to the borrower.

Deficiency Judgment

The borrower in a mortgage loan is personally liable for payment of the note. Therefore, if the proceeds of a foreclosure sale are not sufficient to satisfy the balance due the lender, the lender can sue for a **deficiency judgment** on the note. A deficiency judgment is *a court order stating that the borrower still owes the lender money and is a general lien against the debtor.*

Nonrecourse Note

One situation in which deficiency judgments are not available to the lender is in the case of a **nonrecourse note.** This type of note typically is used in mortgage loans secured by commercial property. Nonrecourse means the *borrower assumes no personal liability for paying the note;* therefore, the lender may look only to the property pledged in the mortgage to obtain the money owed in the case of default by the borrower.

Types of Sales Transactions

Cash Sales

Although cash sales are the exception in real estate, they are perhaps the simplest real estate transaction to process. They can be as simple as the seller providing a deed and the buyer providing the cash. Unfortunately, the simplicity of these cash transactions may cause an inexperienced real estate salesperson to make costly mistakes. No mortgage company is involved in the transaction demanding an appraisal, a survey, a wood-destroying insect inspection, a structural inspection, deed recordation, payment of taxes or transfer fee, title search, and so on. Nonetheless, real estate practitioners have an obligation to make a reasonable effort to know and disclose to the buyer anything materially affecting the value of the property. Whether the transaction is closed by an attorney or an escrow, abstract, or title company, brokers are responsible for safeguarding the interests of their clients and for fairness to the other party.

New Financing

Most real estate transactions require new financing. To help buyers choose the most advantageous method of new financing, today's real estate practitioner needs a thorough knowledge of real estate finance. Knowledge of down payments, closing cost regulations, amounts of allowable seller or third-party contributions, and methods of structuring the best possible payment plans is essential to a successful real estate transaction involving new financing. These aspects of finance and closing are discussed more fully in Chapters 8 and 9.

Mortgage Assumption

Although most conventional fixed-rate real estate loans are not assumable, some are, along with some FHA-insured and VA-guaranteed loans. When a purchaser assumes the seller's existing mortgage, the purchaser assumes liability for the mortgage and personal liability for payment of the note. Therefore, purchasers who default in mortgage payments are subject to lose their property as a result of a foreclosure sale and also are subject to a possible deficiency judgment obtained by the lender.

In a **mortgage assumption,** the *seller whose mortgage was assumed remains liable for the mortgage and payment of the note* unless specifically released from liability by the lender. If the purchaser defaults and the proceeds of a foreclosure sale are insufficient to pay off the mortgage, the seller whose mortgage was assumed may be subject to a possible deficiency judgment by the lender. The lender can foreclose against the current titleholder and possibly sue the original borrower, or anyone who has assumed the mortgage, for a deficiency judgment if the proceeds of the foreclosure sale do not satisfy the mortgage debt. The seller's agent has a responsibility to inform the seller of a property sold under a loan assumption of any liability and recommend that the seller obtain a release of liability from the lender at the time of sale if possible.

Taking "Subject to" a Mortgage

If property is sold and title is conveyed subject to the lien of an existing mortgage (but that lien is not actually assumed), the lender can still foreclose against the property in the event of a default in mortgage payments. In taking title subject to a mortgage, the purchaser does not become liable for payment of the note. Therefore, the lender cannot sue the purchaser for a deficiency judgment but may only obtain a deficiency judgment against the seller, who remains personally liable for paying the debt as evidenced by the note.

Primary Sources of Real Estate Finance

Savings and Loan Associations

Savings and loan associations (S&Ls) lend money to construct housing, to purchase existing housing, and to effect improvements in existing housing. Traditionally, these organizations supplied more money for financing the purchase and construction of single-family dwellings than any other type of lending institution. During the late 1980s, however, S&Ls encountered a great deal of difficulty, losing billions of dollars. Hundreds of S&Ls merged or closed, and the government took over hundreds more. Costs to taxpayers is in the billions of dollars, and the effects on the economy will be felt for years to come. Nevertheless, these institutions continue to invest a larger portion of their assets in residential real estate than any other type of institution. Commercial banks, however, recently have surpassed S&Ls in actual number of mortgage loans originated and the amount of money invested in mortgage loans. Savings institutions, including S&Ls and savings banks, continue to provide more funds for one- to four-family housing than commercial banks provide; however, the gap has been steadily narrowing during the past several years.

Savings and loan associations may be state chartered or federally chartered; however, the practical difference has been blurred by passage of the Financial Institutions Reform, Recovery, and Enforcement Act (FIRREA) in 1989. This act, passed to curb the abuses and problems that led to the S&Ls' problems, affects all federally insured depository institutions. This legislation substituted (a) the Office of Thrift Supervision for the Federal Home Loan Bank Board and (b) the Savings Association Insurance Fund for the Federal Savings and Loan Insurance Corporation. The Federal Deposit Insurance Corporation (FDIC) now regulates both banks and S&Ls; however, the insuring funds are maintained separately.

Some S&Ls have changed their names to "savings banks" to avoid the negative connotations associated with S&Ls in the late 1980s. Although some of these S&Ls changed their structure and function, others changed only their names. These savings banks differ from mutual savings banks (discussed below), some of which also have changed their names to savings banks.

The primary purposes for which savings and loan associations exist are (a) to encourage thrift (hence the term "thrifts") and (b) to provide financing for residential properties. In 1991 almost one-third fewer S&Ls were in existence than in 1986; however, thrifts in general have had several profitable years. S&Ls reported profits of $1.2 billion in 1994 and $1.8 billion in 1995. They continue to play a major role in residential real estate.

Mutual Savings Banks

Mutual savings banks are similar to savings and loan associations, as their main objectives are to encourage thrift and to provide financing for housing. These organizations are chartered and regulated by the state in which they are located. Mutual savings banks play a prominent role in financing housing in many states.

During the late 1970s and the 1980s, regulatory changes allowed these institutions to branch out into other types of loans and to become more like commercial banks. They now are more commonly called savings banks. These depositor-owned institutions currently differ from other depositor institutions primarily in form of ownership: They are still depositor-owned.

Commercial Banks

Commercial banks can be either federally chartered or state chartered. In both cases, commercial banks are sources of mortgage money for construction, purchase of existing housing, and home improvements. Their loan policies usually are more conservative than those of other types of lending institutions. Commercial banks have steadily increased their mortgage holdings in recent years.

Mortgage Bankers

Mortgage bankers, also called mortgage companies, *make mortgage loans for the construction of housing and purchase of existing housing.* They often specialize in FHA-insured loans and VA-guaranteed loans, although most also make conventional loans.

A mortgage banker and a mortgage broker are quite different. A mortgage banker makes and services mortgage loans. A **mortgage broker** *brings together a lender and a borrower for a fee paid by the lending institution,* just as a real estate broker brings together a buyer and seller of real property for a fee. Mortgage brokers generally work with and represent many lending institutions.

Rural Economic and Community Development

The United States Department of Agriculture Reorganization Act of 1994 mandated the USDA to create new ways to provide services to rural areas. The act created the Rural Economic and Community Development (RECD) mission area within the USDA. The RECD would administer many of the programs formerly administered by the Farmers Home Administration (FmHA).

The Guaranteed Rural Housing Loan Program is administered from 26 Illinois RECD field offices. The programs give moderate income home buyers the opportunity to purchase, build, or improve a home. Other programs offer rental assistance. More than 125 Illinois lenders participate in this program.

Life Insurance Companies

At one time a number of life insurance companies were active in making loans directly to individual mortgage borrowers. Today, they provide funds to lending institutions to lend to individual borrowers and to provide funds for the purchase or construction of large real estate projects such as apartment complexes, office buildings, and shopping malls.

PUTTING IT TO WORK

Currently, some life insurance companies are experimenting with the concept of mortgage divisions geared to residential borrowers. This is likely to be an area of expansion for insurance companies in the future.

Credit Unions

Credit unions may be an excellent source of mortgage money for their members. Usually, credit unions offer mortgage loans to their membership at an interest rate below the commercial rate at any given time. To be financially able to make long-term mortgage loans, the credit union must be of substantial size. The Federal Employees Credit Union, a state employees credit union, and the credit union of a major industry are examples of large credit unions.

Real Estate Investment Trusts (REITs)

Real estate investment trusts (REITs) make loans secured by real property. REITs are owned by stockholders and enjoy certain federal income tax advantages. They provide financing for large commercial projects, such as second-home developments, apartment complexes, shopping malls, and office buildings. REITs may invest in properties as owners and managers, known as equity REITs, or they may choose to lend money on projects owned by others, known as mortgage REITs.

Individual Investors

Individuals in every area invest in mortgages. These investors usually are an excellent source for second mortgage loans. The seller of real property is definitely not to be overlooked as an individual investor. These sellers may finance the sale of their properties by taking a regular second mortgage, taking a second mortgage in the form of a wraparound, taking a purchase money first mortgage, or financing by means of a contract for deed. (These concepts are discussed in Chapter 8.) In times of extremely high interest rates, a sale often cannot be made unless the seller provides a substantial part of the financing for the buyer.

SECONDARY MORTGAGE MARKET

The primary mortgage market consists of lending institutions that make loans directly to borrowers. By contrast, the **secondary mortgage market** *buys and sells mortgages created in the primary mortgage market.* One of the requirements for mortgage validity is that it be assignable. This assignability feature allows the lender holding the mortgage to assign or sell the rights in the mortgage to another; thus, the money invested in the mortgage is freed without waiting for the borrower to repay the debt over the long mortgage term.

Sale of the mortgage by the lender does not in any way affect the borrower's rights or obligations. The original mortgagor may not even be aware that the mortgage has been sold, because the original lending institution often continues to service the loan for the purchaser of the mortgage and the mortgagor continues to make the necessary mortgage payments to the same lending institution that made the mortgage loan. If the purchaser of the mortgage prefers to service the mortgage itself, the original lender simply notifies the mortgagor to make payments to a different lender at a different address.

The secondary mortgage market benefits lending institutions and, in turn, the borrowing public, by providing **liquidity** to mortgages. The mortgage is a liquid asset because it *can be readily converted to cash* by the lending institution selling the mortgage in the secondary market. Sale of the mortgage by the lender is especially beneficial in low-yield mortgages—those mortgages for which the lender receives a lesser return on his or her investment in terms of both discount and interest rate, expressed as an annual percentage rate. The lender may get the money out of these mortgages to reinvest in new mortgage loans at current higher yields. This provides stability in the supply of money for making mortgage loans. Therefore, the secondary mortgage market benefits the borrowing public by enabling lending institutions to make money available for loans to qualified applicants.

Mortgage liquidity available in the secondary market reduces the impact of disintermediation on lending institutions. **Disintermediation** is the *loss of funds available to lending institutions for making mortgage loans, caused by the withdrawal of funds by depositors for investment in higher-yield securities in times of higher interest rates.* Without the secondary mortgage market, disintermediation would result in funds available to lenders "drying up" to the extent that these loans would be practically unavailable.

Secondary Market Activities

Some lending institutions limit their mortgage loans to their own assets rather than participate in the secondary mortgage market. For lenders that do participate in the secondary market, two types of markets are available: (a) the purchase and sale of mortgages between lending institutions and (b) the sale of mortgages by lending institutions to three organizations that provide a market for this purpose (FNMA, GNMA, and FHLMC, discussed on the following pages).

Activities Between Lending Institutions

A major activity of the secondary mortgage market is the purchase and sale of mortgages by and between lending institutions. In this way, the market facilitates movement of capital from institutions that have available funds to invest to lenders that do not have enough money for this purpose.

For example, at any given time the demand for mortgage loans may be low in a given locality. Institutions with funds available for making loans in those areas are unable to invest these funds in the local market by making primary mortgage loans. Their funds should be invested in mortgages where they could earn interest instead of lying idle. At this same time, another part of the country may have a high demand for mortgage loans. A lender in that area may have a short supply of available funds to lend to qualified loan applicants. The problems of both of these lending institutions can be solved if the institution whose funds are in short supply sells its existing mortgages on hand to a lender in another area having a surplus of available funds and a low demand for mortgage loans. As a result, the lender with otherwise idle funds has them invested in mortgages earning interest as they should be, and the lender in short supply of money frees up capital invested in mortgages to meet the high demand for new mortgage loans in that area.

The direct sale of loans from investor to investor is legal and occurs relatively frequently, especially among small investors who sell to larger investors to make "pools." Much more likely are sales to organizations that buy and sell mortgages, as discussed in the following paragraphs.

Sale to Organizations

The three organizations that actively participate in purchasing mortgages from financial institutions are the Federal National Mortgage Association (FNMA), the Government National Mortgage Association (GNMA), and the Federal Home Loan Mortgage Corporation (FHLMC).

Federal National Mortgage Association (FNMA). The **FNMA** usually is referred to by its nickname **Fannie Mae.** It is the *oldest secondary mortgage institution and the single largest holder of home mortgages.* Fannie Mae was created in 1938 as a corporation completely owned by the federal government to provide a secondary market for residential mortgages. By 1968, it had evolved into a privately owned corporation. It is a profit-making organization, and its stock is listed on the New York Stock Exchange.

As a government-owned corporation, Fannie Mae was limited to purchasing FHA-insured mortgages and VA-guaranteed mortgages. As a privately owned corporation, it now may also purchase conventional mortgages, which currently are a major portion of its business.

Fannie Mae buys mortgages regularly. Mortgage bankers are major sellers of mortgages to Fannie Mae. Savings and loan associations, mutual savings banks, commercial banks, and life insurance companies also sell mortgages to Fannie Mae. Fannie Mae sells interest-bearing securities (bonds, notes, and debentures) to investors. These securities are backed by specific pools of mortgages purchased and held by Fannie Mae.

Government National Mortgage Association (GNMA). The popular name for **GNMA** is **Ginnie Mae.** It was established in 1968, when Fannie Mae was fully converted to a private corporation. Ginnie Mae, *an agency of the Department of Housing and Urban Development* (HUD), *purchases mortgages to make capital available to lending institutions.* As a government agency, Ginnie Mae is *limited to the purchase of VA and FHA mortgages.*

Ginnie Mae guarantees the "Ginnie Mae Pass-Through," a mortgage-backed security providing participation in a pool of FHA-insured or VA-guaranteed mortgages. The pass-throughs are originated by lending institutions, primarily mortgage bankers. Ginnie Mae guarantees these securities and thereby makes them highly secure investments for purchasers. The yield on each pass-through issue is guaranteed by the full faith and credit of the U.S. government; the pass-throughs are secured by the FHA-insured and VA-guaranteed loans; and the lending institution originating the pass-through provides a guarantee as well. The government does not guarantee that investors in Ginnie Mae securities will make or not lose money on their investments. It only guarantees the loans backing the securities. If the interest rates change dramatically, the investor can either make or lose money as a result of these fluctuations.

Federal Home Loan Mortgage Corporation (FHLMC). Like the other organizations, **FHLMC** has a nickname, **Freddie Mac,** and likewise *exists to increase the availability of mortgage credit and provide greater liquidity for savings associations.* It achieves these objectives by purchasing mortgages.

Freddie Mac was created by Congress in 1970 *primarily to establish a reliable market for the sale of conventional mortgages.* Fannie Mae then purchased only a small number of conventional mortgages, although this number has now increased, and Ginnie Mae may not purchase conventional mortgages. Therefore, prior to Freddie Mac, lending institutions holding conventional mortgages were fairly well limited to the purchase and sale of these mortgages among themselves.

Freddie Mac sells mortgage-participation certificates (PCs) and guaranteed-mortgage certificates (GMCs). These are securities that represent an undivided interest in specific pools of mortgages. Freddie Mac guarantees payment of principal and interest to purchasers of PCs and GMCs.

Freddie Mac was part of, and was wholly owned by, the Federal Home Loan Bank (FHLB) System. When Freddie Mac began, approximately 3,000 savings and loan associations held its stock. In 1988, these associations released the stock for sale, which provided another source of funds for Freddie Mac's operations. Any member of the system and any other financial institution whose deposits or accounts are insured by an agency of the federal government is eligible to sell mortgages to Freddie Mac. Although Freddie Mac purchases residential conventional mortgages primarily from savings and loan associations, it also purchases residential conventional mortgages from mutual savings banks and commercial banks.

Other Aspects of the Market

Primary lenders wishing to sell mortgages to Fannie Mae or Freddie Mac must use uniform loan documents that meet criteria established by FNMA and FHLMC. Loans *processed on uniform loan forms and according to FNMA/FHLMC guidelines* are called **conforming loans.** For example, these organizations will not purchase any mortgage containing a **prepayment penalty,** an *extra charge for paying off a mortgage sooner than specified in its terms*. This requirement is particularly advantageous to individual borrowers when they are required to pay off their mortgage as a condition of a contract of sale. In some cases, prepayment penalties on nonconforming loans are extremely high and, therefore, pose a real hardship to sellers.

In late 1980, Fannie Mae announced a program that is highly beneficial to home sellers who are willing to finance the sale for a buyer by taking a purchase money first mortgage (discussed in Chapter 8). Under the Fannie Mae program, the seller can have the mortgage prepared by a lending institution qualified to sell mortgages to Fannie Mae using uniform FNMA and FHLMC documents. The lending institution will close the transaction between seller and buyer and continue to service the loan for the seller for a fee. The institution collects the payments of principal and interest from the buyer and forwards them to the seller. In this way, sellers have an on-site expert to protect their interests and rights in the mortgage.

An important aspect of this Fannie Mae program is Fannie Mae's guarantee to purchase the mortgage if the sellers/mortgagees desire to sell and get their money out without waiting to complete a series of payments over the mortgage terms. Prior to this, sellers holding purchase money first mortgages had no reliable market for these mortgages if they wished to sell. This Fannie Mae program should provide additional incentive to home sellers to take purchase money first mortgages.

Important Points

1. The purpose of a mortgage or deed of trust (trust deed) is to secure the payment of a promissory note.
2. The three legal theories regarding a mortgage or deed of trust are the lien theory, title theory, and intermediate theory. Illinois subscribes to the intermediate theory.
3. A mortgage is a two-party instrument. A deed of trust is a three-party instrument.
4. The requirements for mortgage or deed of trust validity are: (a) writing, (b) competent parties, (c) valid debt, (d) valid interest, (e) property description, (f) mortgaging clause, (g) defeasance clause, (h) execution by borrower, (i) delivery to and acceptance by lender.
5. The borrower's rights are (a) possession of the property prior to default, (b) defeat of lien by paying debt in full prior to default, (c) statutory right of reinstatement, and (d) equity right of redemption.
6. The lender's rights are: (a) possession of the property upon default, (b) foreclosure, and (c) right to assign the mortgage.
7. A buyer assuming a seller's mortgage assumes liability on both the mortgage and the note. The seller remains liable on the note unless specifically released by a mortgage clause or by the lender. A buyer taking title subject to an existing mortgage has no liability on the note.
8. A fully amortizing mortgage requires payments of principal and interest that will satisfy the debt completely over the mortgage term.
9. The major sources of residential financing are savings and loan associations, mutual savings banks, commercial banks, mortgage bankers and mortgage brokers. Of these, S&Ls have traditionally provided more funds for one- to four-family housing than any other single source, though the gap between savings institutions and commercial banks narrowed significantly after the S&L shake-up in the 1980s. When all types of mortgages (residential, commercial, and farm) are considered, commercial banks hold more mortgage loans than do savings institutions.

10. The primary mortgage market is the activity of lending institutions making loans directly to individual borrowers. The secondary market is the activity of lending institutions selling and buying existing mortgages. The secondary market consists of the purchase and sale of mortgages between lenders and the sale of mortgages by lenders to Fannie Mae (FNMA), Ginnie Mae (GNMA), and Freddie Mac (FHLMC). The market provides liquidity to mortgages, thereby reducing the effect of disintermediation for the benefit of lending institutions and borrowers as well.

REVIEW QUESTIONS

Answers to these questions are found in the Answer Key section at the back of the book.

1. All of the following statements are applicable to promissory notes EXCEPT:
   a. they must be written
   b. the borrower is personally liable for payment
   c. they provide evidence of a valid debt
   d. they are executed by the lender

2. Which of the following statements concerning a mortgage is correct?
   a. the purpose of a mortgage is to secure the payment of a promissory note
   b. a mortgage is a lien on real property
   c. a mortgage is a two-party instrument
   d. all of the above

3. Which of the following is NOT a right given to lenders by a deed of trust?
   a. assignment
   b. possession after default
   c. foreclosure
   d. equity of redemption

4. The clause that makes a mortgage unassumable is:
   a. defeasance
   b. alienation
   c. mortgaging
   d. prepayment

5. Which of the following gives the borrower the right to pay the debt in full and remove the mortgage lien at any time prior to default?
   a. defeasance
   b. prepayment
   c. equity of redemption
   d. foreclosure

6. A promissory note:
   a. secures a mortgage
   b. provides evidence of a loan
   c. cannot be recorded
   d. is confidential between the lender and the borrower

7. A deed in lieu of foreclosure conveys a title to:
   a. lender
   b. borrower
   c. trustee
   d. mortgagor

8. Which of the following is paid first from the proceeds of a foreclosure sale?
   a. mortgage debt
   b. real property taxes
   c. mortgagee's equity
   d. sale expenses

9. A deficiency judgment may be available to:
   a. mortgagee
   b. mortgagor
   c. trustee
   d. trustor

10. A buyer assumed the seller's mortgage without providing release of liability and subsequently defaulted. Which of the following is correct?
    a. only the buyer is personally liable for payment of the note
    b. only the seller is personally liable for payment of the note
    c. both the buyer and the seller may be personally liable for payment of the note
    d. neither the buyer nor the seller is personally liable for payment of the note

11. Which of the following traditionally has provided more financing for the purchase or construction of single-family, owner-occupied dwellings than any other type of lending institution?

    a. mortgage bankers
    b. commercial banks
    c. mutual savings banks
    d. savings and loan associations

12. The activity of lending institutions making mortgage loans directly to individual borrowers is:

    a. secondary mortgage market
    b. money market
    c. institutional market
    d. primary mortgage market

13. Which of the following is a government-owned corporation that purchases FHA and VA mortgages?

    a. Fannie Mae
    b. Ginnie Mae
    c. Freddie Mac
    d. Maggie Mae

14. The major benefit of the secondary mortgage market is to reduce the effect of:

    a. amortization
    b. liquidity
    c. disintermediation
    d. expensive settlement charges

15. Which of the following statements is true?

    a. Illinois is a lien theory state
    b. Illinois is a title theory state
    c. Illinois is an intermediate theory state
    d. Illinois is not a theory state

CHAPTER 8

Important Terminology

adjustable rate mortgage (ARM)
annual percentage rate (APR)
appraisal
balloon mortgage
blanket mortgage
certificate of reasonable value (CRV)
construction mortgage
conventional mortgage loan
cooling-off period
disclosure statement
discount points
Equal Credit Opportunity Act (ECOA)
escrow account
Federal Housing Administration (FHA)
FHA-insured loan
good faith estimate
graduated payment adjustable mortgage
graduated payment mortgage (GPM)
growing equity mortgage (GEM)
impound account
junior mortgage
leasehold mortgage
loan origination fee
loan-to-value ratio
margin
mortgage insurance premium (MIP)
negative amortization
open-end mortgage
package mortgage
participation mortgage
prepaid items
prepayment penalty
private mortgage insurance (PMI)
purchase money mortgage
Real Estate Settlement Procedures Act (RESPA)
Regulation Z
release clause
release of liability
settlement
shared appreciation mortgage (SAM)
substitution of entitlement
take-out loan
term mortgage
Truth-in-Lending Simplification and Reform Act (TILSRA)
underwriting
VA-guaranteed loan
wraparound mortgage

Real Estate Finance Practices

IN THIS CHAPTER In this chapter we discuss the various loans the buyer may use to finance the purchase of real property with a lending institution. The types of mortgage loans that may be obtained from lending institutions can be divided into two groups:

1. Conventional loans, which are not backed by an agency of the federal government.
2. FHA or VA mortgage loans, which the federal government participates in either by insuring the loan to protect the lender (FHA-insured loans) or by guaranteeing that the loan will be repaid (VA-guaranteed loans).

CONVENTIONAL MORTGAGE LOANS

An owner's *equity* or financial interest in the real property consists of the present value of the property minus any outstanding debt against it. The equity increases as the debt is reduced. Equity is also increased through the appreciation of the property.

A **conventional mortgage loan,** one that has *no participation by an agency of the federal government,* can be either uninsured or insured. In the uninsured conventional loan, the borrower's equity in the property provides sufficient security for the lender to make the loan; therefore, insurance to protect the lender in case of the borrower's default is not required. In most cases, the borrower obtains a loan that does not exceed 75 to 80 percent of the property value and has an equity of 20 or 25 percent. An insured conventional loan typically is a conventional loan in which the borrower has a down payment of only 5 percent or 10 percent and therefore borrows 90 to 95 percent of the property value. In these cases, *insuring repayment of the top portion of the loan to the lender is necessary in the event the borrower defaults.* The insurance is called **private mortgage insurance (PMI),** and private insurance companies issue the policies. Today, private mortgage insurance companies insure more mortgage loans than the FHA does. The premiums and features of private mortgage insurance have grown more varied and complex in recent years. The examples that follow are just that—examples.

In the case of the 90 percent insured loan, repayment of the top 20 percent of the loan is insured. In the 95 percent insured loan, the top 25 percent of the loan is insured. This generally assures the lender that he will recoup the investment by means of the insurance proceeds and the foreclosure proceeds should the borrower default. The borrower pays the premium for the insurance. The premium varies from state to state and according to the insurance company. In the 90 percent loan, the premium due at closing is typically ½ percent the amount of the loan. With the 95 percent loan, it is usually 1 percent. The insurance also has an annual renewal premium, paid monthly.

When the borrower's equity in the property reaches 20 percent as a result of appreciation and loan pay-down, the individual may request a reappraisal of the property by the lender and discontinuation of the insurance requirement. This request may be granted if the equity has reached 20 percent or more. Again, these are examples only; premiums and features vary widely.

Types of Conventional Mortgage Loans

Conventional mortgages can take many shapes with varied terms. In the early 1980s, more innovations appeared in the types of mortgages than in the preceding 50 years combined because of inflation and the accompanying increases in interest rates. Often these increases were radical and on very short notice. As a result and for their protection, lending institutions shifted the burden resulting from rapid increases in interest rates from themselves to the borrowing public by making substantial innovations in mortgage loans. We discuss here the various types of mortgages, including those of longstanding duration and those that have come into existence recently.

Many of these mortgages can exist as the only mortgage on a property (or properties, in the case of a blanket mortgage) or as one of two or more mortgages on the same property or properties. If more than one mortgage exists on the same property or properties, one of them is the first mortgage and all others are junior mortgages. We discuss the junior mortgage first, although, in essence, it describes priority rather than a type of mortgage.

Junior Mortgage

Junior mortgage describes *any mortgage that is subordinate (lower in priority) to another mortgage.* A junior mortgage may be a second mortgage, a third mortgage, a fourth mortgage. Each of these is subordinate to any prior mortgage secured by the same property. The second mortgage is subordinate to a first mortgage, the third mortgage is subordinate to the second, and so on. Junior mortgages are usually for a shorter term and at a higher interest rate because they pose a greater risk to the lender than a first mortgage.

Second mortgages, the most common form of junior mortgages, frequently are used to finance part of the difference between the purchase price of a property and the loan balance being assumed in a purchase involving assumption of the seller's existing mortgage. The seller often offers a short-term (5-, 7-, or 10-year) purchase money second mortgage to the buyer for part of the difference when the buyer does not have the funds to pay the full amount. Second mortgages also are available from finance companies, credit unions, and other sources.

Term Mortgage

In a **term mortgage,** *the borrower pays interest only for a specified term; at the end of the term, the borrower is required to pay the principal.* This was the type of mortgage generally in use before and during the depression of the 1930s. Many borrowers were unable to pay the principal when it came due, and lenders were unable to refinance the principal for the borrower as they had done in more prosperous times. As a result, many homeowners lost their property through foreclosure.

Amortizing Mortgage

The **Federal Housing Administration (FHA)** was created by the National Housing Act of 1934 for the purpose of *insuring mortgage loans to protect lending institutions in case of borrower default.* FHA will insure only amortizing mortgages (mortgages that retire the debt). As a result of this and of the potential hardship for borrowers under the term mortgage, the typical home mortgage loan today is the amortizing mortgage whether the loan is FHA, VA, or conventional.

As explained in Chapter 7, amortization provides for paying a debt by installment payments. A portion of each payment is applied first to the payment of interest and the remainder to reduction of principal. The interest always is applied against only the outstanding principal balance due at the time of an installment payment.

The rate of interest is an annual percentage rate as specified by the note and mortgage. The interest rate is calculated by multiplying the annual percentage rate by the unpaid principal balance and dividing the result by 12 (months) to determine the amount of interest due and payable for any monthly installment.

After deducting the interest, the remainder of the payment goes to reduce the principal balance. Therefore, the amount of interest paid with each installment declines because the interest rate is applied against a smaller and smaller amount of principal.

FIGURE 8.1
Qualifying income for a conventional loan.

Before approving a conventional mortgage loan, the lender must determine if the borrower will be able to meet the financial obligation of monthly house payments. Most often, the lender requires that the monthly home payments not exceed 28% of the borrower's gross monthly income and that the total of all long-term obligations not exceed 36% of this income; this is referred to as the 28/36 rule.

For example, assume a sales price of $125,000, a loan amount of $100,000* and an annual interest rate of 8.5% with a 30-year loan term. (Please use the amortization chart in Figure 8.2 if you don't have a financial calculator.) Tax and insurance escrow numbers are given. In this case, the formula would be applied as follows:

1. The lender will first calculate the total monthly payments:

   $769.00   (P & I)
    116.80   for tax escrow (T)
     54.00   for insurance escrow (I)
   $939.80   P.I.T.I. (total monthly payment)

2. Next the borrower's gross monthly income will be calculated by dividing the annual household salary by 12:

   $55,000 ÷ 12 = $4,583.33

3. The ratio of home payments to gross monthly income is then determined by dividing the payment by monthly income:

   $939.80 ÷ $4,583.33 = 20.5%

   The first part of the 28/36 rule has been satisfied since this ratio is under 28%.

4. All other long-term expense payments are then added to determine the borrower's other long-term debt:

   $340.00   car payments
     75.00   credit card payments
    100.00   personal loan
   $515.00   total monthly payment for long-term debt

5. Add this total to the house payment:

   $ 515.00
      939.80
   $1,454.80

6. Divide this total by monthly income to determine the ratio of long-term debt:

   $1,454.80 ÷ $4,583.33 = 31.7%

   The borrower will qualify for the loan since this ratio is under 36%.

   *This is an 80% loan-to-value ratio; therefore, it requires no private mortgage insurance (PMI). A higher loan-to-value ratio requires PMI to be included in payments.

FIGURE 8.2
An abbreviated amortization chart.

AMORTIZATION CHART (Monthly payments per $1,000)

Annual interest rate	\multicolumn{4}{c}{Years to fully amortize loan}
	15	20	25	30
6.50	8.71	7.46	6.75	6.32
6.75	8.85	7.60	6.91	6.49
7.00	8.99	7.75	7.07	6.65
7.25	9.13	7.90	7.23	6.82
7.50	9.27	8.06	7.39	6.99
7.75	9.41	8.21	7.55	7.16
8.00	9.56	8.36	7.72	7.34
8.25	9.70	8.52	7.88	7.51
8.50	9.85	8.68	8.05	7.69
8.75	9.99	8.84	8.22	7.87
9.00	10.14	9.00	8.39	8.05
9.25	10.29	9.16	8.56	8.23
9.50	10.44	9.32	8.74	8.41
9.75	10.59	9.49	8.91	8.59
10.00	10.75	9.65	9.09	8.78

Note: This is an abbreviated amortization chart intended for example and learning purposes. Most real estate salespersons find it easier to use a calculator to compute and compare payments and to quickly solve other real estate math problems.

In this way, the loan is amortized so that the final payment in a fully amortizing mortgage will pay any remaining interest and principal.

The payment may be a fixed amount and remain the same over the life of the loan, or it may be a graduated payment. Possibly the payment may change as a result of a varying interest rate specified in the note and mortgage.

Fifteen-Year Mortgage

The 15-year mortgage has gained popularity in recent years. In reality, this is a regular fully amortized mortgage with a 15-year term. By cutting the loan term from 30 years to 15 years, the borrower greatly reduces the interest paid, and therefore the cost of funds, for a moderate increase in monthly payment. The shorter term also provides for faster equity accumulation in the property.

Balloon Mortgage

The **balloon mortgage** *provides for installment payments that are not enough to pay off the principal and interest over the term of the mortgage, so the final payment (called a balloon payment) is substantially larger than any previous payment, to satisfy the remaining principal and interest.* If this balloon payment is to be a substantial amount, the note may provide for refinancing by the lender to provide the funds to the borrower if he or she cannot otherwise make the final payment.

Open-End Mortgage

An **open-end mortgage** *may be refinanced without rewriting the mortgage* or incurring additional closing costs. The original mortgage provides the security for additional funds to be advanced to the borrower after the loan balance has been reduced to a specified amount and sometimes functions as a line of credit. This is not the typical residential first mortgage, but the home equity loans that became instantly popular in 1987 with the new tax law may be considered in this category. These loans are currently a popular form of junior financing.

Graduated Payment Mortgage (GPM)

In the **graduated payment mortgage (GPM)**, the *monthly payments are lower in the early years of the mortgage term and increase at specified intervals* until the payment amount is sufficient to amortize the loan over the remaining term. The monthly payments are kept down in the early years by not requiring the borrower to pay all the interest, which is added to the principal balance.

The purpose of this type of mortgage is to enable individuals to buy homes because they are able to afford the lower initial monthly payments. An outstanding example of this type of mortgage loan is the FHA 245 graduated payment mortgage, discussed later in this chapter.

PUTTING IT TO WORK

Although GPM loans do make qualifying for a loan easier, the greater financial burden of the "peak" payments actually may make default more likely. In addition, adding unpaid accrued interest to the balance may cause owners to find themselves "upside down" in the property, meaning that they owe more than the property may be worth.

Adjustable Rate Mortgage (ARM)

To say that the 1980s and 1990s have been turbulent decades for real estate finance would be an understatement. In the late 1970s, no sage would have predicted that interest rates would soar from 9 percent to 18 percent or higher. Who would have predicted in 1982 the 7.5 percent rates seen in mid-1986 and again in 1996? Nevertheless, such was to be history. Given these circumstances, the motivation of lending institutions to shift the burden of unpredictability from themselves to the mortgagor is easier to understand. We therefore can appreciate the adjustable rate mortgage from the lender's standpoint. Suppose you had $50,000 to commit to a 30-year, fixed-rate loan. What interest would you accept?

The **adjustable rate mortgage (ARM)** (or *variable rate mortgage*) evolved as one solution to the uncertainty of future financial rates. With the ARM, the *parties agree to float mortgage rates based on the fluctuations of a standard index*. Common indices include the cost of funds for savings and loan institutions, the national average mortgage rate, and the more popular one-year rate for the government's sale of Treasury Bills.

An ARM designates an index and then adds a **margin** (*measure of profit*) above this index. For example, if the Treasury Bill (T-Bill) index were 7 and the lender's margin were 2.50, the ARM would call for an interest rate of 9.5. (Margins sometimes are expressed in terms of basis points, each basis point being $1/100$ of a percent, or 250 basis points in the above example.)

The ARM has definite advantages for some buyers, especially for the short-term owner who expects to sell the home in the near future, perhaps because of an employment transfer. Long-term owners may fear the possibility of an ever-increasing mortgage rate, but apprehension should be moderated by the understanding that economic cycles rise and fall and, in the case of inflation, the value of the property likely will rise as well. The potential long-term buyer may choose an ARM with a conversion feature allowing him or her to convert to a fixed-rate mortgage when interest rates are more favorable.

A significant concern in an ARM is the possibility of **negative amortization.** When the index rises while the payment is fixed, it may cause the payments to fall below the amount necessary to pay the interest required by the index. This shortfall is added back into the principal, causing the principal to grow larger after the payment.

FIGURE 8.3 Understanding loan payments.

(a) Using the amortization chart.

Example: Assume a home purchase price of $87,500 with a conventional mortgage of 80% of the sales price at an annual interest rate of 8.5% for 30 years.

1. Calculate the amount of the loan:
 $87,500 × 80% = $70,000

2. Figure 8.2 lists a factor for each $1,000 of a loan. Divide $70,000 (our loan amount) by $1,000 (as per Figure 8.2) to determine the number of units of $1,000, which is 70. Jot down this figure before completing step 3.

3. Go to the 8.5% row (our annual interest rate) on Figure 8.2. Read across to the 30-year column (our loan term). The factor listed is 7.69. This is the payment per month per $1,000 of the loan.

4. Multiply the 70 from step 2 by the 7.69 figure from step 3 to arrive at $538.30. This is the monthly payment of principal and interest (P & I) needed to amortize (pay off) a loan of $70,000 at 8.5% for 30 years.

(b) Calculating interest paid per month.

Use the data from (a) to calculate how much of the payment (P & I) went toward interest (I).

1. Interest (I) equals the principal (P) times the rate (R) times the period of time (T) you have had the money, or:
 I = P × R × T

2. In our example,
 I = $70,000 × 8.5% × 1/12 of one year, or
 I = $70,000 × 0.085 = $5,950.00 ÷ 12 = $495.83

3. Therefore, of the total payment of $538.30 in the first month, $495.83 went to interest.

(c) Calculating principal reduction per payment.

How much did this monthly payment of $538.30 reduce the loan principal? Subtract the amount that went toward interest from the total payment amount; the remainder went to principal:

$538.30   (P & I)
− 495.83   (I)
$ 42.47   (P)

(d) Calculating principal balance after one payment.

1. Calculate the amount that went to principal: $42.47

2. Subtract this amount from the previous balance:
 $70,000.00
 − 42.47

3. The remainder is the new principal balance: $69,957.53

(e) Calculating total interest paid over the life of this loan.

1. Calculate the monthly payment: $538.30

2. Calculate the total number of months to be paid; in this case:
 30 (years) × 12 (months per year) = 360 payments

3. Multiply the monthly payment times the total number of months to be paid to calculate the total of the payments:
 $538.30 × 360 payments = $193,788 total payback

4. Subtract the amount of the loan borrowed from the total payback to calculate the amount that went toward interest:
 $193,788.00
 − 70,000.00
 $123,788.00 total interest paid

FIGURE 8.4 Comparing monthly payments and interest paid between a 15-year and a 30-year loan.

As we determined in Figure 8.3, the monthly payment needed to amortize an 8.5% interest loan of $70,000 in 30 years (360 payments) is $538.30.

Using the same formula, we can determine that the monthly payment to amortize an 8.5% interest loan of $70,000 in 15 years (180 payments) is $689.50. With these two figures, we can now make the following comparisons:

30-year loan		15-year loan
$ 538.30	Monthly payment	$ 689.50
× 360	Number of payments	× 180
$193,788.00	Total $ paid over life of loan	$124,110.00
− 70,000.00	Minus amount of original loan	− 70,000.00
$123,788.00	TOTAL INTEREST PAID	$ 54,110.00

Thus, with the 30-year loan, the borrower paid $69,678 more interest.

Note: While this is a substantial savings in actual dollars, the benefit may be reduced by several factors:
1. The borrower will have less of a tax deduction for interest paid.
2. The dollars paid in extra principal each month could possibly earn more money if invested elsewhere.
3. Due to inflation, dollars paid toward the mortgage in later years are actually worth less than those paid in early years.

The effect of these factors varies depending upon an individual's tax bracket, his or her expertise at investing money, and the rate of inflation.

In some ARMs, this event is expected if the payment contract rate falls below the internal accrual rate by ½ percent.

Modern ARMs are structured with caps (ceilings) that limit both the annual adjustment and the total adjustment during the lifetime of the loan. For example, annual increases could be limited to perhaps 1 or 2 percent interest, and the lifetime of the loan cap might be no higher than perhaps 5 or 6 percent. Many modern ARMs also prohibit negative amortization.

FHA has authorized adjustable rate mortgages for several years. HR 939, signed into law October 1992, authorized the Department of Veteran Affairs to offer an ARM similar to the one offered by FHA. Veterans will have to qualify for these loans on the basis of the second-year interest rate.

Graduated Payment Adjustable Mortgage

Another innovation in mortgage loans was approved in July 1981 by the Federal Home Loan Bank Board in the form of a **graduated payment adjustable mortgage.** This is a *combination of the graduated payment mortgage and the variable rate mortgage.* Its purpose is to make more borrowers eligible for mortgage loans by keeping the payments down in the early years as a result of the graduated payment and the variable rate features.

Federal regulation of lending institutions has been liberalized in an effort to protect financial institutions making long-term loan commitments from the extreme fluctuations in short-term interest rates. These institutions borrow funds at the short-term rate but lend money on a long-term basis. As a result, they sometimes are caught in a situation in which the price they must pay in the form of interest for use of money is more than the interest they earn on a long-term basis from making mortgage loans. The addition of ARMs, GPMs, and combinations of the two has shifted some of the burden of fluctuating interest rates from lending institutions to mortgage loan borrowers.

Shared Appreciation Mortgage (SAM)

The **shared appreciation mortgage (SAM)** *allows the lender to benefit from the appreciation of property value in exchange for a lower rate of interest to the borrower.* Typically, for a one-third share in appreciation, the lender makes the loan at a rate one-third less than the going rate for a fixed-term conventional loan at the time the loan is created.

The increase in value that the lender shares is demonstrated by the price for which the borrower sells the property, as compared to the price paid for the property. Federal regulations require that if the property is not sold within 10 years, the property must be appraised and the lending institution must receive its one-third share of the value increase as shown by the appraisal. This could result in a substantial hardship for the borrower who does not sell within the 10-year term. This borrower may have to refinance to obtain the money to pay the lender the one-third share of value increase.

Growing Equity Mortgage (GEM)

The **growing equity mortgage** is *a loan in which the monthly payments increase annually, with the increased amount applied directly toward the loan's principal,* thus allowing the loan to be paid off more quickly.

Participation Mortgage

Participation mortgage describes two different types of mortgages.

1. *A mortgage in which two or more lenders participate in making the loan.* The participation agreement between the lenders may provide that each participating lender owns a pro rata share of the mortgage and each will receive his or her share of the mortgage payment of principal and interest as it is made. Another option would be for one lender to make a substantial portion of the loan, and another lender to lend a small amount of the loan. In this case, the larger lender receives first priority in the security pledged in the mortgage.
2. *A mortgage in which the lender participates in the profits generated by a commercial property used to secure payment of the debt in the mortgage loan.* The borrower agrees to the lender's participation in the net income as an inducement for the lender to make the loan. This allows the lender to receive interest as well as a share of the profits.

Wraparound Mortgage

A **wraparound mortgage** is *a second mortgage for an amount larger than the existing balance owed on a first mortgage against the same property.* This mortgage "wraps around" the existing first mortgage, which stays in place. The seller of the property makes a wraparound loan to the buyer, who takes title to the property subject to the existing first mortgage. The seller continues to make the payments on the first mortgage, and the buyer makes the payments to the seller on the wraparound.

The wraparound mortgage can be beneficial to both seller and buyer. The seller makes payments on the existing first mortgage at an old and often lower interest rate and on a smaller initial loan amount. The seller receives the buyer's payments on a substantially larger loan amount at a higher rate of interest than the seller is paying on the existing first mortgage. In this way, the seller receives principal payments on the second mortgage and earns interest income on the amount by which the interest received on the wraparound exceeds the interest being paid on the existing first mortgage. In addition, the wraparound may enable the seller to effect a sale that otherwise may not have been accomplished in times of high interest rates and tight money. The benefits to the buyer in this situation include purchasing the property with a small down payment and obtaining seller financing at a rate usually several percentage points below the prevailing market rate for new financing at that time.

Wraparounds work only when the existing first mortgage is assumable. If the existing first mortgage contains a due on sale or alienation clause, a wraparound mortgage cannot be used. The alienation clause provides that the existing first mortgage must be paid in full if the title to the property is transferred by the first mortgage borrower without the lender's authorization. Lenders will usually give their approval provided the interest rate on the existing mortgage is increased to the current rate charged by the lender.

Package Mortgage

In a **package mortgage,** *personal property in addition to real property is pledged to secure payment of the mortgage loan.* Typical examples of these items are washer and dryer, range and oven, dishwasher, and refrigerator. The package mortgage is used frequently in sales of furnished condominium apartments and includes all furnishings in the units.

Blanket Mortgage

In a **blanket mortgage,** *two or more parcels of real estate are pledged as security for payment of the mortgage debt.* The blanket mortgage usually contains a **release clause** that *allows certain parcels of property to be removed from the mortgage lien if the loan balance is reduced a specified amount.* The mortgage always should provide that sufficient property value remain subject to the mortgage lien to secure the remaining principal balance at any given time.

Real estate developers typically use blanket mortgages with release clauses. In this way, the mortgagor can obtain the release of certain parcels from the lien of the mortgage and convey clear title to purchasers to generate a profit and provide the funds to make future mortgage payments.

Construction Mortgage

The **construction mortgage** is a form of *interim, or temporary, short-term financing for creating improvements on land.* The applicant for a construction loan submits, for the lender's appraisal, the plans and specifications for the structure to be built and the property on which the construction is to take place. The lender makes the construction loan based on the value resulting from an appraisal of the property and the construction plans and specifications. The loan contract specifies that disbursements will be made as specified stages of the construction are completed; for example, after the foundation is laid or upon framing. Interest is not charged until the money has actually been disbursed. Upon completion, the lender makes a final inspection and closes out the construction loan, which is then converted to permanent, long-term financing or replaced by financing obtained by a buyer of the property.

Often the lender requires the builder to be bonded for completion of the property. The bond is made payable to the lender in the event the builder goes bankrupt and is unable to complete the structure. In this way, the lender can obtain the funds to complete the construction and have a valuable asset to sell and recover the monies extended under the construction loan.

If the mortgage commitment is strictly a short-term construction loan, permanent financing (for example, 30 years) will have to be established. *Permanent financing on a short-term construction loan* is known as a **take-out loan.** This commitment is necessary to assure long-term financing within the mortgagor's means.

Purchase Money Mortgage

The **purchase money mortgage** is a *mortgage given by a buyer to the seller to cover part of the purchase price.* Here, the seller becomes the mortgagee and the buyer, the mortgagor. The seller conveys title to the buyer, who immediately reconveys or pledges it as security for the balance of the purchase price. The seller is financing the sale of his or her property for the buyer in the amount of the purchase money mortgage. The purchase money mortgage may be a first mortgage, a typical junior mortgage, or a junior mortgage in the form of a wraparound.

Installment Agreement

As discussed in Chapter 5, the installment agreement (or contract for deed) is both a contract of sale and a financing instrument. The seller provides a method of purchasing the property, and the buyer makes installment payments.

The distinction between the installment agreement and the purchase money mortgage method of financing between buyer and seller is that in the purchase money mortgage, the seller conveys title to the buyer, who pledges it as security for payment of the mortgage debt. In the installment agreement, no title passes until the buyer completes the required installment payments totaling the purchase price, unless the installment agreement stipulates that the title pass at some other specified time.

Leasehold Mortgage

The **leasehold mortgage** *pledges a leasehold estate rather than a freehold estate to secure payment of a note.* The leasehold acceptable to the lender is a long-term estate for years. The usual case is a lease for vacant land whereon the lessee is to construct an improvement such as a shopping mall, a hotel, or an office building as an investment.

FHA-Insured Mortgage Loans

Part of the mission of the Federal Housing Administration (FHA), created during the Depression of the 1930s, was to make home ownership available to more people, to improve housing construction standards, and to provide a more effective and stable method of financing homes. It succeeded in this mission and provided the leadership to standardize procedures for qualifying buyers, appraising property, and evaluating construction. FHA has been an agency of the U.S. Department of Housing and Urban Development (HUD) since 1968.

FHA does not make mortgage loans. Instead, **FHA-insured loans** *protect lenders against financial loss.* The buyer pays for this insurance protection by paying an upfront mortgage insurance premium at closing and an annual mortgage insurance premium prorated monthly and paid with the monthly mortgage payment (discussed later in this section). This insurance enables lenders to provide financing when the loan-to-value ratio is high. **Loan-to-value ratio** *compares the loan amount to the property value.* With a high ratio, the borrower has to make only a small down payment. The amount of insurance protection to the lender is always sufficient to protect the lender from financial loss in the event of a foreclosure sale because these loans are insured for 100 percent of the loan amount.

Many of the FHA programs available in the past are no longer available or are no longer widely used. The most popular program still in existence is the FHA 203(b) loan, which allows an owner-occupant to purchase a one- to four-family dwelling with an FHA-insured loan. The FHA 245 graduated payment mortgage, the FHA 203(b)(2) FHA-VA mortgage, and the FHA 234(c) condominium loan also are available when circumstances warrant.

Types of FHA Mortgage Loans

FHA 203(b) Regular Loan Program

The FHA 203(b) regular loan program is the original and still the basic FHA program. It provides for insuring loans for the purchase or construction of one- to four-family dwellings. FHA does not set a maximum sales price, only a maximum loan amount. A buyer may purchase a home for more than the FHA maximum loan amount, but he or she will have to pay anything above the maximum loan amount in cash. FHA maximum loan amounts vary by county. Contact the local HUD office to determine loan maximums in your area. The maximum loan amount to an individual is based on the acquisition cost, which is the combination of the FHA's appraised value of the property or its sales price, whichever is less, plus the buyer's closing costs that FHA will allow to be financed. Of course, the resultant loan amount cannot be greater than the loan maximum for the area.

FHA 245 Graduated Payment Loan

Under the graduated payment plan, the payments are lower in the early years and increase at specified intervals until the payment reaches an amortizing basis. The monthly payment is kept lower in the early years of the mortgage term by not requiring the borrower to pay all the interest due in those years. The unpaid interest, however, is added back to the principal. As a result, the principal increases during those years (negative amortization). Under an FHA 245 loan, the principal may not increase to an amount in excess of 97 percent of the appraised value or acquisition cost. A larger down payment usually will be required to prevent the loan amount from exceeding the above limit.

PUTTING IT TO WORK

> This program is relatively unused in times of low interest rates because qualifying for a loan is easier at these rates. When interest rates get higher (13–18 percent), programs such as this are often the only viable way for buyers to obtain new financing.

The borrower may select any one of five plans. Three are 5-year plans, and two are 10-year plans. Under the 5-year plans, payments are at an amortizing level (level at which part of each payment is applied to the principal) beginning with the sixth year of the 30-year term. Under the 10-year plans, the amortizing level begins with the 11th year. The 10-year plans are rarely used.

The FHA graduated payment loan is available for purchasing or constructing a single-family dwelling to be occupied by the borrower. The original borrower and anyone assuming the borrower's loan during the graduated phase must sign a certification that she is aware of the annual increases in monthly payments.

The borrower may refinance an FHA graduated payment loan at any time to a level-mortgage payment plan insured by the FHA; however, a borrower with a level-payment FHA loan may never refinance to a graduated payment FHA loan. The maximum loan amount is slightly lower under this program than for a regular FHA 203(b) loan to prevent the maximum principal balance from exceeding 97 percent of the appraised value or acquisition cost during the years of graduated payments.

FHA 203(b)(2) FHA-VA Loan

The FHA 203(b)(2) program is available to veterans of military service. It is not related in any way to the regular VA loan program. Use of this program by a veteran does not affect his or her eligibility for a loan under the VA program. The advantage of this program is that no down payment is required on the first $25,000 of acquisition cost.

FHA 234(c) Condominium Loan

The FHA 234(c) loan is similar to the FHA 203(b) loan except that it insures loans for individual condominium units. The condominium complex must meet FHA requirements for construction, number of units, owner occupancy, and homeowner association structure.

FHA Mortgage Insurance Premium (MIP)

In 1990, the U.S. Congress revised FHA **mortgage insurance premium (MIP)** calculations again. In July 1991, the 3.8 percent MIP, which was *calculated on the base loan amount and paid at closing or added to the loan amount,* was renamed an up-front mortgage insurance premium (UFMIP). The amount of this UFMIP decreased to 3.0 percent in October 1992 (the beginning of fiscal year 1993) and again in April 1994 to 2.25 percent. It is not affected by the term of the loan or the loan-to-value ratio. An additional annual MIP is charged at the rate of .5 percent, applied to the average unpaid principal balance. This amount is divided by 12 to arrive at the premium to be paid monthly. The length of time this annual MIP must be paid depends upon the loan-to-value ratio and the fiscal year in which the loan is made.

FHA Loan Qualification

FHA loan qualification procedures changed dramatically on December 1, 1989, when FHA changed from a net income to a gross income approach. This change simplified qualifying a buyer for an FHA loan. Under these guidelines, the monthly housing expenses composed of principal, interest, taxes, homeowner's insurance, MIP paid monthly, and homeowners' association dues or assessments, if any, cannot exceed 29 percent of gross income. These expenses, plus any recurring monthly debts which will either extend for six months or more or have payments of more than $100 per month, cannot exceed 41 percent of effective gross income. See Figure 8.5 for an FHA loan qualification worksheet.

FHA Maximum Loan Amount

Several changes in legislation and regulations from 1990 until late 1992 have affected FHA maximum loan amount calculations. The net effect of the changes is that the determination of maximum loan amount is now a two-step process. In the first step, the loan amount calculation is based on acquisition cost (or mortgage basis), which consists of the FHA appraised value or sales price, whichever is lower, plus 100 percent of the buyer's allowable closing cost. These loan amounts are 97 percent of the first $25,000 of acquisition cost, 95 percent of the acquisition cost between $25,001 and $125,000, and 90 percent of acquisition cost above $125,000. A special case exists if the adjusted sales price or appraised value is $50,000 or under. The 97 percent loan-to-value ratio is applied to the whole acquisition cost, even that amount between $25,000 and $50,000. The loan amounts discussed in this paragraph cannot exceed the

FIGURE 8.5 Qualifying income worksheet for an FHA loan.

Gross Monthly Income
Borrower's base pay, monthly $_____
  (gross weekly × 52 ÷ 12)
Co-borrower's base pay, monthly $_____
Other earnings (overtime, child
  support, bonus, etc.) $_____
TOTAL MONTHLY EFFECTIVE GROSS INCOME $_____ (A)

Total Monthly Debts
Revolving charge accounts $_____
  (monthly minimum payment)
Installment accounts (auto, personal $_____
  student loans, etc. with more than
  6 remaining payments)
Child care $_____
TOTAL MONTHLY PAYMENTS $_____ (B)

RATIOS
Gross monthly income (A) × 29% = $_____ (C) Housing ratio
Gross monthly income (A) × 41% = $_____ (D) Housing & debt ratio
(D) − (B) = _____ (E) Compare (E) to (C). Use the lower figure of (E) or (C) for the monthly mortgage payment (PITI).
LOWER OF (E) OR (C) = _____ PITI
              PITI: _____
          − TAXES: _____
       − INS./DUES: _____
            = P & I: _____

area's FHA loan limit, which equals 95 percent of the area's median home price or 75 percent of the loan amount allowed by Fannie Mae and Freddie Mac, whichever is lower.

The second step in the maximum loan amount calculations applies a 97.75 percent maximum loan-to-value ratio to the appraised value, excluding closing costs, if the value is over $50,000 and 98.75 percent if the value is $50,000 or less. The lesser amount derived from step 1 and step 2 is the maximum loan amount. The calculation of maximum loan amounts shown in Figure 8.6 is current as of late 1996; however, real estate practitioners are advised to keep abreast of changes in this area.

Maximum loan amounts are available for dwellings that are more than one year old or, if less than one year old, were built to FHA specifications and under FHA supervision or with an acceptable 10-year homeowner warranty. If the dwelling is less than one year old and not built to specifications and under supervision or with an acceptable 10-year homeowner warranty, the loan amount is 90 percent of the total acquisition cost. These guidelines require that the borrower must occupy the property.

FHA Loan Assumption Policies

In 1986, FHA began changing its policies toward assumptions of FHA-insured loans. FHA mortgages originated before December 1, 1986, are freely assumable without qualification by owner-occupants and investors alike. For loans originating between

FIGURE 8.6
Examples of FHA maximum loan amount calculation.

Example 1: Based on a $90,000 FHA appraisal and estimated closing cost of $2,000 to be paid by the buyer. Appraised value is the same as the sales price in this example.

Calculation 1

Lesser of sales price or appraised value	$ 90,000
Buyer's total closing cost	+ 2,000
Total	$ 92,000
97% of first 25,000, 95% of remainder	× 97/95%
97% × $25,000 = $24,250	
95% × $67,000 = $63,650	
Total = $87,900	
Maximum loan amount (excluding UFMIP)	$ 87,900

*Calculation 2**

Appraised value	$ 90,000
Maximum loan-to-value ratio	× 97.75%
Maximum loan amount (excluding UFMIP)	$ 87,975

The maximum loan amount (excluding UFMIP) is $87,900, which is the lesser of calculations 1 and 2. Maximum loan amount is always rounded down to the nearest $50 increment.

Example 2: Based on a $45,000 FHA appraisal and estimated closing cost of $1,350 to be paid by the buyer. Appraised value is the same as the sales price in this example. Because adjusted acquisition cost and appraised value is under $50,000, only the 97% maximum loan-to-value ratio is used in calculation 1, and 98.75% maximum loan-to-value ratio is used in calculation 2.

Calculation 1

Lesser of sales price or appraised value	$ 45,000
Buyer's total closing cost	+ 1,350
Total	$ 46,350
	× 97%
Maximum loan amount (excluding UFMIP)	$ 44,959

Calculation 2

Appraised value	$ 45,000
Maximum loan-to-value ratio (1990 housing legislation)	× 98.75%
Maximum loan amount (excluding UFMIP)	$ 44,437

The maximum loan amount (excluding UFMIP) is $44,400, which is the lesser of calculations 1 and 2, rounded down to the nearest $50 increment.

Although space does not permit an example of all variations, the above examples illustrate the basic method of calculating FHA maximum loan amounts. When calculating, consider the following factors and adjust calculations and loan limits as required:

(1) Maximum loan amounts on single-family homes vary by area from $67,500 to $151,725. (2) When loan basis is above $125,000, use 97/95/90 percent in calculation 1. (3) Closing costs are never included in calculation 2. (4) Any part of normal closing costs paid by seller for buyer cannot be added to the sales price to determine mortgage basis. (5) If seller pays over 6 percent of sales price for financing concessions including closing costs for buyer, any amount over 6 percent must be subtracted from sales price before determining mortgage basis. (6) If seller pays prepaid items such as taxes and insurance for buyer, the amount of these items must be subtracted from sales price before determining mortgage basis.

*Note: Closing cost is never included in calculation 2.

December 1, 1986, and December 15, 1989, the buyer's creditworthiness had to be approved for a loan assumption or the original borrower was liable for any default for five years from the loan origination date. The Housing and Urban Development Reform Act of 1989 effectively stopped new investor loans and nonqualifying loan assumptions. A creditworthiness review is required for the assumption of all FHA loans originated after December 15, 1989. This requirement remains in effect throughout the life of the loan.

FHA Changes

Significant changes have taken place in the FHA home loan program since its inception, but especially since 1983. Salespeople must understand these changes because they will likely be selling properties purchased with FHA loans that originated under rules different from those currently in effect. When such a property is listed, the salesperson should obtain copies of the documents relating to the original sale to determine what rules apply to the sale in the case of either a loan assumption or a loan payoff. Rules for loan assumption qualification, release of liability, notification and time of payoffs, and possible partial refunds of mortgage insurance premiums are important, and these differ according to when the loan was underwritten.

PUTTING IT TO WORK

> Comprehensive changes pertaining to FHA loans have occurred in the past decade. Changes during the past two years have been frequent and especially difficult for inexperienced salespeople to understand. Salespeople must remain current regarding FHA guidelines. To keep aware of changes as they occur, they can look to their broker-in-charge, the firm's training or loan processing department, a trade publication, or a mortgage lender.

Contract Requirement

If a sales contract contingent upon the buyer's obtaining any FHA-insured loan is created prior to an FHA appraisal and commitment to insure, the contract must contain the following wording, as required by the FHA:

> It is expressly agreed, that notwithstanding any other provisions of this contract, the purchaser shall not be obligated to complete the purchase of the property described herein or to incur any penalty by forfeiture of earnest money deposit or otherwise unless the seller has delivered to the purchaser a written statement issued by the Federal Housing Commissioner setting forth the appraised value of the property (exclusive of closing costs) of not less than $_____, which statement seller hereby agrees to deliver to the purchaser promptly after such appraised value statement is made available to the seller. The purchaser shall, however, have the privilege and option of proceeding with the consummation of this contract without regard to the amount of the appraised valuation made by the Federal Housing Commissioner.
>
> The appraised valuation is arrived at to determine the maximum mortgage the Department will insure. HUD does not warrant the value or the condition of the property. The purchaser should satisfy himself/herself that the price and the condition of the property are acceptable.

DEPARTMENT OF VETERAN AFFAIRS GUARANTEED LOAN PROGRAM

Whereas the FHA programs insure loans, the Department of Veteran Affairs (VA) offers a guaranteed loan program. Under a **VA-guaranteed loan,** the VA *guarantees repayment of the top portion of the loan to the lender in the event the borrower defaults.* Unlike the FHA, the VA does not set maximum loan amounts.

The VA-guaranteed loan is a 100 percent loan. The loan amount may be 100 percent of the VA appraisal of the property set forth in the VA **certificate of reasonable value (CRV)** or 100 percent of the sales price, whichever is less. The VA provides this certificate, sometimes informally called the VA appraisal, to the lending institution as a basis for making the loan. VA-guaranteed loans are available for the purchase or construction of one- to four-family dwellings. The VA does not have a program for loans in which the veteran borrower will not occupy the property being purchased or constructed. When obtaining the loan, the veteran must certify in writing that he or she will occupy the property being purchased with the loan proceeds. (If veteran is on active duty, spouse must occupy.) If the property is a multi-family dwelling (maximum of four units), the veteran must occupy one of the apartments.

Eligibility

For the borrower to be eligible for a VA-guaranteed loan, he or she must qualify as a veteran under requirements of the Department of Veteran Affairs. Three groups of qualifying periods are as follows:

Group I

Qualification in this group consists of at least 90 days of active duty during any one of four wartime periods:

- World War II: September 16, 1940, to July 25, 1947
- Korean: June 27, 1950, to January 31, 1955
- Vietnam: August 5, 1964, to May 7, 1975
- Persian Gulf: August 2, 1990, to present

The veteran must have been discharged or released from duty under conditions other than dishonorable or may still be on active duty.

Group II

The three periods in Group II fall between the wars and after Vietnam until September 8, 1980. To qualify in any of these groups, the veteran must have served at least 181 days of active duty and must have been discharged or released under conditions other than dishonorable or still be on active duty. (The period between September 8, 1980, and August 2, 1990, is covered under Group III even though it is technically between the Vietnam and the Persian Gulf Conflicts.)

- Post-World War II: July 26, 1947, to June 26, 1950
- Post-Korean: February 1, 1955, to August 4, 1964
- Post-Vietnam: May 8, 1975, to September 8, 1980

Group III

From September 8, 1980 (enlisted) or October 17, 1981 (officers) to August 2, 1990, 24 months on active duty are required if the veteran is no longer on active duty.

During this time, the veteran could get a VA loan after 181 days on active duty as long as he or she was on active duty at the time of the loan or was discharged for a service-connected disability, the convenience of the government, or hardship.

The not-remarried spouse of a deceased veteran who had qualified under any group and died as a result of a service-connected disability or in the line of duty is qualified as the veteran would have been. Eligibility is not allowed for spouses who remarry, children, or spouses in cases when the deceased veteran did not die as a result of service.

In October 1992, President Bush signed HR 939 into law. This legislation provides for VA entitlement to certain members of the National Guard and the military reserves with over six years of service. These individuals will have to pay a higher VA funding fee, and their entitlement will end in October 1999.

If a contract of sale subject to the buyer's obtaining a VA-guaranteed loan is created prior to an appraisal and commitment by the VA, the contract must contain the following statement, as required by the VA:

> It is expressly agreed that, notwithstanding any other provisions of this contract, the purchaser shall not incur any penalty by forfeiture of earnest money or otherwise be obligated to complete the purchase of the property described herein, if the contract purchase price or cost exceeds the reasonable value of the property established by the Veterans Administration. The purchaser shall, however, have the privilege and option of proceeding with the consummation of this contract without regard to the amount of the reasonable value established by the Veterans Administration.

Qualifying for VA Loans

In mid-1986, the VA announced new qualification standards for loan applications after October 1, 1986. The new standards require borrowers to be creditworthy and qualify under both a net family support standard and a gross monthly income ratio.

VA Loan Analysis Form 26-6393 is used to organize information on estimated home payments, long-term debts (six months or longer), family dependents, and to evaluate the reliability of monthly income. Net take-home pay is determined by taking the gross monthly income minus federal taxes, state taxes, social security tax, and other pension plans or deductions. This net income then is reduced by the amount of the estimated home payments and long-term debts to determine a residual balance available for family support. This residual balance must meet regional standards established by the VA. A family of four must have a monthly residual balance of $986 in the Northeast, $964 in the Midwest, $964 in the South, and $1,113 in the West.

The next step in the qualification is to compare the total of home payments, special assessments, homeowners' association dues, and debts that either will extend for six months or more or will have payments of more than $100 per month to the gross monthly income. This ratio is limited to 41 percent. The VA loan analysis form shown in Figure 8.7 is used to organize information on income and long-term debts to determine if the 41 percent ratio will be met.

PUTTING IT TO WORK

> Qualifying a veteran for a VA loan is not difficult; however, it requires consulting several tables to determine various taxes, maintenance costs, residual requirements, and child care expenses. Military pay tables for active duty veterans also are helpful. VA qualification can be time-consuming. Even though all practitioners should understand this qualification process, using a computer program to perform the qualification is highly recommended. Many inexpensive, easy-to-use programs incorporating these tables are available.

FIGURE 8.7
VA qualification worksheet.

Gross Monthly Income (weekly pay × 52 ÷ 12)		$_____	
Additional Monthly Income (commission, overtime, bonus average for two years)		$_____	
TOTAL MONTHLY INCOME	(A) =	$_____	
Multiply (A) by 41% (.41)			×.41
	(B) =	$_____	
Total monthly payments for auto, school, installment, personal loans, credit cards, child care	(C) =	$_____	

_____   _____   _____ PITI
     B   −   C   =   D

This figure (D) is the monthly mortgage payment you should use for qualifying the customer. This payment includes principal and interest, taxes, and insurance.

Anyone can assume a VA loan. The person assuming the loan does not have to be a veteran. He or she can either be an owner-occupant or an investor and can provide release of liability in both situations. Only an owner-occupant can substitute entitlement. All VA loans after March 1, 1988, require qualification and release of liability.

Restoration of Eligibility

When a veteran is discharged from the service, he or she receives a certificate of eligibility. This certificate states the maximum entitlement in effect at the time the veteran is discharged. Regardless of when they were in the service, all vets qualifying will have an eligibility of $36,000 on loans of $144,000 or less and $50,750 on loans of more than $144,000. There is no maximum VA loan amount, but generally a lender will lend a veteran four times the entitlement (4 × $50,750 = $203,000) with no money down. If a veteran has used either full or partial eligibility in obtaining a VA loan, he or she may have that eligibility fully restored in one of the two following ways:

1. The loan is paid in full and the veteran has disposed of the property.
2. The veteran purchaser who has as much remaining eligibility as the original veteran used to obtain the loan and also satisfies the VA requirements for income, credit, and occupancy assumes the VA loan from the original veteran borrower. The assuming veteran must meet the same requirements as an original VA loan applicant and agree to substitute his or her entitlement for that of the original veteran purchaser.

A mere **release of liability** by the lender and the VA does not in itself restore eligibility. Anyone can assume a VA loan; however, only a qualified veteran can give a **substitution of entitlement.** As pointed out in item 1 above, simply *paying the loan in full is not sufficient to restore the entitlement; the veteran must no longer own the property.*

Real Estate Finance Practices   **183**

PUTTING IT TO WORK

There is a widespread misunderstanding that VA financing is a once-in-a-lifetime loan. This is not true. The VA entitlement may be fully restored (see above) or any remaining partial guarantee may be used (see below).

Unused Eligibility

If a veteran has used part of his or her eligibility and sold the property to a nonqualifying veteran or nonveteran who assumed the loan, the veteran may still have eligibility remaining. For example, if the veteran obtained the loan between May 1968 and December 1974, the maximum guarantee in effect was the lesser of $12,500 or 60 percent of the loan amount. Even if the veteran used all eligibility at that time by obtaining a loan for $50,000 (all of the entitlement would have been used at that time for any loan of $20,833.33 or above), the remaining eligibility is $23,500 to $38,250, depending on the loan amount. These numbers are derived by subtracting the maximum eligibility of $12,500 existing at the time the loan was made from the current two-tiered maximums of $36,000 or $50,750.

History of Loan Guarantees

The loan guarantee the Department of Veteran Affairs gives to lenders making VA loans has steadily increased over the years from the lesser of $2,000 or 50 percent of the loan amount, when the program was first initiated in 1944, to the present multilayered system outlined in Figure 8.8. In all, there have been eight increases since the initial program.

On December 18, 1989, the VA changed its guarantee to the lender to the present structure (see Figure 8.9). These guarantees are the same as the guarantees put into effect February 1, 1988, except for the addition of a $50,750 guarantee for loans of more than $144,000. This change complicates the calculation of remaining entitlement when a veteran has used part of his or her entitlement. Because the loan amount determines whether the remaining entitlement is based on $36,000 or $50,750, the loan amount must be determined before it is known whether all or any of the extra $14,750 ($50,750 - $36,000) can be used.

DATE	MAXIMUM ENTITLEMENT	PERCENTAGE
June 22, 1944	$ 2,000	50
December 28, 1945	$ 4,000	50
July 12, 1950	$ 7,500	60
May 7, 1968	$12,500	60
December 31, 1974	$17,500	60
October 1, 1978	$25,000	60
October 1, 1980	$27,500	60
February 1, 1988	$36,000	*
October 13, 1994	$50,750	*

*Loan guarantees are now on a multitiered system according to the loan amount. See Figure 8.9.

FIGURE 8.8
A record of VA entitlements as they have increased by year.

FIGURE 8.9 VA loan guarantees.

LOAN AMOUNT	PERCENT OR AMOUNT OF GUARANTEE
$45,000	50% of loan amount
$45,001 to $144,000	40% of loan amount or $36,000, whichever is less
$144,001 to $203,000	25% of loan amount or $50,750, whichever is less

OTHER ASPECTS OF FHA AND VA LOANS

Escrow Account

These loans require that the borrower maintain an **escrow account** (also called an **impound account**) with the lending institution. The *borrower must pay into this account an impound each month to accumulate money to pay the annual real property tax bill and the annual homeowner's insurance policy premium.* In addition, if the loan is used to purchase a condominium apartment, escrow deposits may include an amount to pay the property owner's assessment.

Mortgage loans on single-family, owner-occupied residential properties without assistance or insurance by the Illinois state or federal government come under the Illinois Mortgage Escrow Account Act. At the time of closing any real estate-secured mortgage, including FHA-insured loans, the lender must give the borrower written notice of the provision of this act. The act provides that (a) the lender may not require an escrow of more than 150% of the previous year's real estate taxes, except in the first year; (b) when the principal balance reaches 65 percent of its original amount, the borrower may terminate the escrow account; (c) at any time, the borrower may choose to pledge an interest-bearing deposit to cover the future tax bills and insurance premiums in lieu of an escrow account. Federally related mortgages cannot require an initial deposit into escrow of more than an amount to pay the estimated used-up portion of annual taxes and insurance premiums in addition to two months of escrowed funds.

At closing, the borrower must put money into the account to get it started and provide a head start for accumulating the necessary funds. This includes two months' payments toward the next hazard insurance premium, several months toward payment of the real property tax bill, and, if the loan is insured by the FHA, the equivalent of one month's FHA mortgage insurance premium. The number of months of property tax placed in escrow usually is determined by the lender, depending upon the length of time since the last payment of taxes. These *insurance and tax moneys deposited at the time of closing* are called **prepaid items** and are not a part of the borrower's actual closing costs; they are in excess of the closing costs.

The FHA requires the borrower to pay these prepaid items but allows the seller to pay buyer closing costs within the limits specified and stated above under FHA loans, provided that these closing costs are taken into consideration in determining maximum loan amount. Under the VA program, sellers are permitted, if they agree, to pay the closing costs and prepaid items for the buyer.

Down Payment

If the VA certificate of reasonable value is less than the price the veteran is willing to pay for a home, the veteran still may obtain the VA loan and make a down payment for the difference between the loan amount and the purchase price. In this case, as well as in the down payment required under an FHA-insured loan program, the borrower may not finance the down payment unless it is secured by other collateral. The borrower must have these funds on hand and certify in writing that he or she has not borrowed this money, and is under no obligation to repay the money if the money is a gift.

Miscellaneous

The maximum term of either an FHA or a VA loan is 30 years. Both of these types of loan are assumable, although with qualification after certain dates, and at the interest rate at which the loan was originally created. The presence or absence of qualification requirements and the dates they became effective are given under each loan type. Mortgages securing these loans may not contain a due on sale or alienation clause as long as the purchaser meets the qualification requirements in effect at the time the loan was made and the loan is transferred in accordance with applicable regulations. In either an FHA or a VA assumption, the difference between the loan amount assumed and the purchase price can be financed, although the loan payment on the amount financed must be considered in the qualification process on loan assumptions requiring release of liability. FHA and VA mortgages never require a **prepayment penalty,** a *charge for paying off the loan before the end of the mortgage term.*

As of October 1, 1992, all FHA loans require that the borrower sign a lead-based paint notice if the property was built before 1978. This notice must be signed on or before date of contract of sale. Lead-based paint disclosure regulations applicable to all 1–4 residential properties are discussed in Chapter 5. Properties sold after May 20, 1996 require FHA borrowers to receive a one-paragraph form explaining the benefit of a home inspection and noting the cost of an inspection up to $200 can be financed as part of the mortgage.

RESIDENTIAL LENDING PRACTICES AND PROCEDURES

Loan Origination

Application

Once a borrower has contracted to purchase a home, the process of arranging for mortgage financing commences. The main document in the loan origination process is the loan application. Customarily, the borrower and the lender's representative meet, and the borrower completes the loan application at this initial meeting. Figure 8.10 shows the standard form of residential loan application that all lenders adopted after 1986.

Authorizations

At the time of loan application, the borrower is required to sign the following authorization forms so that the lender can verify the data the borrower gives on the loan application:

1. verification of employment or if the borrower is self-employed, the most recent two years' tax returns (personal and business)
2. verification of rent or mortgage
3. verification of bank account balance
4. verification of outstanding loans
5. verification of sales contract deposit
6. verification of pension (if applicable)
7. authorization to release information
8. consent to credit check and verification

Sometimes substitute documentation may be used in place of verifications. For example, pay stubs or employee year-end W-2 statements may be used in place of

FIGURE 8.10 The standard form of a residential loan application.

Uniform Residential Loan Application

This application is designed to be completed by the applicant(s) with the lender's assistance. Applicants should complete this form as "Borrower" or "Co-Borrower", as applicable. Co-Borrower information must also be provided (and the appropriate box checked) when ☐ the income or assets of a person other than the "Borrower" (including the Borrower's spouse) will be used as a basis for loan qualification or ☐ the income or assets of the Borrower's spouse will not be used as a basis for loan qualification, but his or her liabilities must be considered because the Borrower resides in a community property state, the security property is located in a community property state, or the Borrower is relying on other property located in a community property state as a basis for repayment of the loan.

I. TYPE OF MORTGAGE AND TERMS OF LOAN

Mortgage Applied for: ☐ VA ☐ FHA ☐ Conventional ☐ FmHA ☐ Other: | Agency Case Number | Lender Case No.

Amount $ | Interest Rate % | No. of Months | Amortization Type: ☐ Fixed Rate ☐ GPM ☐ Other (explain): ☐ ARM (type):

II. PROPERTY INFORMATION AND PURPOSE OF LOAN

Subject Property Address (street, city, state, & zip code) | No. of Units

Legal Description of Subject Property (attach description if necessary) | Year Built

Purpose of Loan ☐ Purchase ☐ Refinance ☐ Construction ☐ Construction-Permanent ☐ Other (explain): | Property will be: ☐ Primary Residence ☐ Secondary Residence ☐ Investment

Complete this line if construction or construction-permanent loan.

Year Lot Acquired | Original Cost $ | Amount Existing Liens $ | (a) Present Value of Lot $ | (b) Cost of Improvements $ | Total (a + b) $

Complete this line if this is a refinance loan.

Year Acquired | Original Cost $ | Amount Existing Liens $ | Purpose of Refinance | Describe Improvements ☐ made ☐ to be made Cost: $

Title will be held in what Name(s) | Manner in which Title will be held | Estate will be held in: ☐ Fee Simple ☐ Leasehold (show expiration date)

Source of Down Payment, Settlement Charges and/or Subordinate Financing (explain)

III. BORROWER INFORMATION

Borrower

Borrower's Name (include Jr. or Sr. if applicable)

Social Security Number | Home Phone (incl. area code) | Age | Yrs. School

☐ Married ☐ Unmarried (include single, divorced, widowed) ☐ Separated | Dependents (not listed by Co-Borrower) no. ages

Present Address (street, city, state, zip code) ☐ Own ☐ Rent ____No. Yrs.

Co-Borrower

Co-Borrower's Name (include Jr. or Sr. if applicable)

Social Security Number | Home Phone (incl. area code) | Age | Yrs. School

☐ Married ☐ Unmarried (include single, divorced, widowed) ☐ Separated | Dependents (not listed by Borrower) no. ages

Present Address (street, city, state, zip code) ☐ Own ☐ Rent ____No. Yrs.

If residing at present address for less than two years, complete the following:

Former Address (street, city, state, zip code) ☐ Own ☐ Rent ____No. Yrs. | Former Address (street, city, state, zip code) ☐ Own ☐ Rent ____No. Yrs.

Former Address (street, city, state, zip code) ☐ Own ☐ Rent ____No. Yrs. | Former Address (street, city, state, zip code) ☐ Own ☐ Rent ____No. Yrs.

IV. EMPLOYMENT INFORMATION

Borrower

Name & Address of Employer ☐ Self Employed | Yrs. on this job | Yrs. employed in this line of work/profession

Position/Title/Type of Business | Business Phone (incl. area code)

Co-Borrower

Name & Address of Employer ☐ Self Employed | Yrs. on this job | Yrs. employed in this line of work/profession

Position/Title/Type of Business | Business Phone (incl. area code)

If employed in current position for less than two years or if currently employed in more than one position, complete the following:

Name & Address of Employer ☐ Self Employed | Dates (from - to) | Monthly Income $ | Name & Address of Employer ☐ Self Employed | Dates (from - to) | Monthly Income $

Position/Title/Type of Business | Business Phone (incl. area code) | Position/Title/Type of Business | Business Phone (incl. area code)

Name & Address of Employer ☐ Self Employed | Dates (from - to) | Monthly Income $ | Name & Address of Employer ☐ Self Employed | Dates (from - to) | Monthly Income $

Position/Title/Type of Business | Business Phone (incl. area code) | Position/Title/Type of Business | Business Phone (incl. area code)

Freddie Mac Form 10/92 ITEM 7300L1 (9210) Page 1 of 4 pages "I/We acknowledge that the information provided on this page is true and correct ______." Fannie Mae Form 1003 10/92

(continued)

Real Estate Finance Practices 187

FIGURE 8.10
Continued.

V. MONTHLY INCOME AND COMBINED HOUSING EXPENSE INFORMATION

Gross Monthly Income	Borrower	Co-Borrower	Total	Combined Monthly Housing Expense	Present	Proposed
Base Empl. Income*	$	$	$	Rent	$	
Overtime				First Mortgage (P&I)		$
Bonuses				Other Financing (P&I)		
Commissions				Hazard Insurance		
Dividends/Interest				Real Estate Taxes		
Net Rental Income				Mortgage Insurance		
OTHER (before completing, see the notice in "describe other income," below)				Homeowner Assn. Dues		
				Other:		
Total	$	$	$	Total	$	$

*Self Employed Borrower(s) may be required to provide additional documentation such as tax returns and financial statements.

Describe Other Income Notice: Alimony, child support, or separate maintenance income need not be revealed if the Borrower (B) or Co-Borrower (C) does not choose to have it considered for repaying this loan.

B/C		Monthly Amount
		$

VI. ASSETS AND LIABILITIES

This Statement and any applicable supporting schedules may be completed jointly by both married and unmarried Co-Borrowers if their assets and liabilities are sufficiently joined so that the Statement can be meaningfully and fairly presented on a combined basis; otherwise separate Statements and Schedules are required. If the Co-Borrower section was completed about a spouse, this Statement and supporting schedules must be completed about that spouse also.

Completed ☐ Jointly ☐ Not Jointly

ASSETS Description	Cash or Market Value	LIABILITIES — Liabilities and Pledged Assets. List the creditor's name, address and account number for all outstanding debts, including automobile loans, revolving charge accounts, real estate loans, alimony, child support, stock pledges, etc. Use continuation sheet, if necessary. Indicate by (*) those liabilities which will be satisfied upon sale of real estate owned or upon refinancing of the subject property.	Monthly Payt. & Mos. Left to Pay	Unpaid Balance
Cash deposit toward purchase held by		Name and address of Company	$ Payt./Mos.	$
List checking and savings accounts below				
Name and address of Bank, S&L, or Credit Union				
		Acct. no.		
Acct. no.	$	Name and address of Company	$ Payt./Mos.	$
Name and address of Bank, S&L, or Credit Union				
		Acct. no.		
Acct. no.	$	Name and address of Company	$ Payt./Mos.	$
Name and address of Bank, S&L, or Credit Union				
		Acct. no.		
Acct. no.	$	Name and address of Company	$ Payt./Mos.	$
Name and address of Bank, S&L, or Credit Union				
		Acct. no.		
		Name and address of Company	$ Payt./Mos.	$
Acct. no.	$			
Stocks & Bonds (Company name/number & description)	$			
		Acct. no.		
		Name and address of Company	$ Payt./Mos.	$
Life insurance net cash value	$			
Face amount: $				
Subtotal Liquid Assets	$			
Real estate owned (enter market value from schedule of real estate owned)	$	Acct. no.		
Vested interest in retirement fund	$	Name and address of Company	$ Payt./Mos.	$
Net worth of business(es) owned (attach financial statement)	$			
Automobiles owned (make and year)	$			
		Acct. no. Alimony/Child Support/Separate Maintenance Payments Owed to:	$	
Other Assets (itemize)	$	Job Related Expense (child care, union dues, etc.)	$	
		Total Monthly Payments	$	
Total Assets a.	$	Net Worth (a minus b) → $	Total Liabilities b.	$

Freddie Mac Form 65 10/92   Page 2 of 4 pages   "I/We acknowledge that the information provided on this page is true and correct _____."   Fannie Mae Form 1003 10/92

(continued)

FIGURE 8.10
Continued.

VI. ASSETS AND LIABILITIES (cont.)

Schedule of Real Estate Owned (If additional properties are owned, use continuation sheet.)

Property Address (enter S if sold, PS if pending sale or R if rental being held for income)	▼	Type of Property	Present Market Value	Amount of Mortgages & Liens	Gross Rental Income	Mortgage Payments	Insurance, Maintenance, Taxes & Misc.	Net Rental Income
			$	$	$	$	$	$
		Totals	$	$	$	$	$	$

List any additional names under which credit has previously been received and indicate appropriate creditor name(s) and account number(s):

Alternate Name	Creditor Name	Account Number

VII. DETAILS OF TRANSACTION

a. Purchase price	$
b. Alterations, improvements, repairs	
c. Land (if acquired separately)	
d. Refinance (incl. debts to be paid off)	
e. Estimated prepaid items	
f. Estimated closing costs	
g. PMI, MIP, Funding Fee	
h. Discount (if Borrower will pay)	
i. Total costs (add items a through h)	
j. Subordinate financing	
k. Borrower's closing costs paid by Seller	
l. Other Credits (explain)	
m. Loan amount (exclude PMI, MIP, Funding Fee financed)	
n. PMI, MIP, Funding Fee financed	
o. Loan amount (add m & n)	
p. Cash from/to Borrower (subtract j, k, l & o from i)	

VIII. DECLARATIONS

If you answer "yes" to any questions a through i, please use continuation sheet for explanation.

	Borrower Yes	Borrower No	Co-Borrower Yes	Co-Borrower No
a. Are there any outstanding judgments against you?	☐	☐	☐	☐
b. Have you been declared bankrupt within the past 7 years?	☐	☐	☐	☐
c. Have you had property foreclosed upon or given title or deed in lieu thereof in the last 7 years?	☐	☐	☐	☐
d. Are you a party to a lawsuit?	☐	☐	☐	☐
e. Have you directly or indirectly been obligated on any loan which resulted in foreclosure, transfer of title in lieu of foreclosure, or judgment? (This would include such loans as home mortgage loans, SBA loans, home improvement loans, educational loans, manufactured (mobile) home loans, any mortgage, financial obligation, bond, or loan guarantee. If "Yes," provide details, including date, name and address of Lender, FHA or VA case number, if any, and reasons for the action.)	☐	☐	☐	☐
f. Are you presently delinquent or in default on any Federal debt or any other loan, mortgage, financial obligation, bond, or loan guarantee? If "Yes," give details as described in the preceding question.	☐	☐	☐	☐
g. Are you obligated to pay alimony, child support, or separate maintenance?	☐	☐	☐	☐
h. Is any part of the down payment borrowed?	☐	☐	☐	☐
i. Are you a co-maker or endorser on a note?	☐	☐	☐	☐
j. Are you a U.S. citizen?	☐	☐	☐	☐
k. Are you a permanent resident alien?	☐	☐	☐	☐
l. **Do you intend to occupy the property as your primary residence?** If "Yes," complete question m below.	☐	☐	☐	☐
m. Have you had an ownership interest in a property in the last three years?	☐	☐	☐	☐
(1) What type of property did you own - principal residence (PR), second home (SH), or investment property (IP)?				
(2) How did you hold title to the home - solely by yourself (S), jointly with your spouse (SP), or jointly with another person (O)?				

IX. ACKNOWLEDGMENT AND AGREEMENT

The undersigned specifically acknowledge(s) and agree(s) that: (1) the loan requested by this application will be secured by a first mortgage or deed of trust on the property described herein; (2) the property will not be used for any illegal or prohibited purpose or use; (3) all statements made in this application are made for the purpose of obtaining the loan indicated herein; (4) occupation of the property will be as indicated above; (5) verification or reverification of any information contained in the application may be made at any time by the Lender, its agents, successors and assigns, either directly or through a credit reporting agency, from any source named in this application, and the original copy of this application will be retained by the Lender, even if the loan is not approved; (6) the Lender, its agents, successors and assigns will rely on the information contained in the application and I/we have a continuing obligation to amend and/or supplement the information provided in this application if any of the material facts which I/we have represented herein should change prior to closing; (7) in the event my/our payments on the loan indicated in this application become delinquent, the Lender, its agents, successors and assigns, may, in addition to all their other rights and remedies, report my/our name(s) and account information to a credit reporting agency; (8) ownership of the loan may be transferred to successor or assign of the Lender without notice to me and/or the administration of the loan account may be transferred to an agent, successor or assign of the Lender with prior notice to me; (9) the Lender, its agents, successors and assigns make no representations or warranties, express or implied, to the Borrower(s) regarding the property, the condition of the property, or the value of the property.

Certification: I/We certify that the information provided in this application is true and correct as of the date set forth opposite my/our signature(s) on this application and acknowledge my/our understanding that any intentional or negligent misrepresentation(s) of the information contained in this application may result in civil liability and/or criminal penalties including, but not limited to, fine or imprisonment or both under the provisions of Title 18, United States Code, Section 1001, et. seq. and liability for monetary damages to the Lender, its agents, successors and assigns, insurers and any other person who may suffer any loss due to reliance upon any misrepresentation which I/we have made on this application.

Borrower's Signature	Date	Co-Borrower's Signature	Date
X		X	

X. INFORMATION FOR GOVERNMENT MONITORING PURPOSES

The following information is requested by the Federal Government for certain types of loans related to a dwelling, in order to monitor the Lender's compliance with equal credit opportunity, fair housing and home mortgage disclosure laws. You are not required to furnish this information, but are encouraged to do so. The law provides that a Lender may neither discriminate on the basis of this information, nor on whether you choose to furnish it. However, if you choose not to furnish it, under Federal regulations this Lender is required to note race and sex on the basis of visual observation or surname. If you do not wish to furnish the above information, please check the box below. (Lender must review the above material to assure that the disclosures satisfy all requirements to which the Lender is subject under applicable state law for the particular type of loan applied for.)

BORROWER

☐ I do not wish to furnish this information

Race/National Origin: ☐ American Indian or Alaskan Native ☐ Asian or Pacific Islander ☐ White, not of Hispanic origin ☐ Black, not of Hispanic origin ☐ Hispanic ☐ Other (specify) ______

Sex: ☐ Female ☐ Male

CO-BORROWER

☐ I do not wish to furnish this information

Race/National Origin: ☐ American Indian or Alaskan Native ☐ Asian or Pacific Islander ☐ White, not of Hispanic origin ☐ Black, not of Hispanic origin ☐ Hispanic ☐ Other (specify) ______

Sex: ☐ Female ☐ Male

To be Completed by Interviewer	Interviewer's Name (print or type)	Name and Address of Interviewer's Employer
This application was taken by:	Interviewer's Signature / Date	
☐ face-to-face interview ☐ by mail ☐ by telephone	Interviewer's Phone Number (incl. area code)	

Freddie Mac Form 65 10/92 Page 3 of 4 pages Fannie Mae Form 1003 10/92

(continued)

Real Estate Finance Practices

FIGURE 8.10
Continued.

Continuation Sheet/Residential Loan Application		
Use this continuation sheet if you need more space to complete the Residential Loan Application. Mark B for Borrower or C for Co-Borrower.	Borrower:	Agency Case Number:
	Co-Borrower:	Lender Case Number:

I/We fully understand that it is a Federal crime punishable by fine or imprisonment, or both, to knowingly make any false statements concerning any of the above facts as applicable under the provisions of Title 18, United States Code, Section 1001, et. seq.

Borrower's Signature	Date	Co-Borrower's Signature	Date
X		X	

Freddie Mac Form 65 10/92   Page 4 of 4 pages   Fannie Mae Form 1003 10/92 employment verification; bank account statements for two months prior to loan application may substitute for bank account verification. In addition to the documents listed, most lenders require a copy of the borrower's driver's license and social security card for identification purposes. The loan origination documentation, along with the purchase contract, the borrower's check to cover the cost of the credit report and the property appraisal, and an application fee, is delivered to the lender's loan processing department for action.

PUTTING IT TO WORK

Many lending institutions have implemented a "one-button" loan application process whereby most loans can be approved or declined by confidential computer analysis, without upfront human processing. Check to see if lenders in your area offer this service.

Loan Processing

Appraisal

The first step in loan processing is to order out the file. This involves ordering an appraisal and a credit report.

An **appraisal,** *an evaluation of the subject property by a qualified professional,* normally is ordered from an appraiser who has obtained recognized training and experience through membership in a professional appraisal organization. For most lending that requires appraisals, the appraiser now must be licensed or certified according to state regulations. A uniform appraisal report form has been created to standardize appraisals nationally (see Chapter 10, Figure 10.1).

The appraisal should contain the following exhibits:

1. certification and Statement of Limiting Conditions, wherein the appraiser gives his or her opinion subject to certain limitations and indicates his or her qualifications, including licensure or certification, educational background, professional ratings, and previous experience
2. an area map reflecting the location of the subject property and comparable sales
3. a floor plan sketch clearly showing all perimeter dimensions and room locations, including interior partitions and door locations; should show living area calculations sufficient to allow a reviewer to calculate the total living area
4. color photographs of the subject property, including front, back, street scene, all improvements, and buildings
5. color photographs of the front of each comparable property, showing the property address wherever possible
6. a copy of flood hazard map (where applicable), showing the flood area and subject property location
7. a copy of the real estate listing sheet on the subject property
8. addenda explanations of any adjustments to value that vary from standard guidelines or of any negative comments concerning the neighborhood
9. a copy of the zoning ordinance relative to nonconforming properties
10. legal description
11. environmental disclaimer statement

Credit Report

In ordering a credit report, the reporting agency must contact at least two national repositories of accumulated credit records covering each residence of the borrower over the prior two-year period. Several national credit organizations meet the repository definition: Trans Union, TRW, Credit Bureau, Chilton Corporation, Associated Credit Services, and Associated Credit Bureau Service. All information on the credit report must be verified from sources other than the borrower; otherwise, the credit agency must report that it is unable to verify or that the credit source refused to verify. The borrower may be required to provide other explanations or documentation concerning these accounts. As other requirements, the credit report must:

1. identify the reporting agency by name, address, and telephone number
2. be an original report
3. identify the party requesting the report
4. reflect the names of the national repositories that provided information
5. list all credit inquiries made within the last 90 days
6. include a certification of compliance with FNMA, FHLMC, FHA, and VA standards as prescribed for a residential mortgage credit report
7. contain all credit and legal activity for the past seven years
8. note dates of last creditor account update
9. verify employment where obtainable
10. verify previous employment and income if employment changed within the last two years
11. include all available public records information
12. note acceptable or unacceptable payment status

Also included in ordering out the file are:

1. mailing verification forms as required to verify bank deposits and employment
2. completing and mailing the Truth-in-Lending disclosure if it was not completed at the time of application

Once these ordered-out data have been returned, the application review stage begins.

Application Review

The purpose of loan processing is to verify all data the borrower presents in the loan application. This is done by comparing the verified information with the application data. The borrower must explain items that do not match and must obtain additional verification or data. For example, employment income, bank deposit, and outstanding debts must be the same on the credit report as on the loan application.

Although the loan processor is not the loan underwriter, the processor sometimes may decline the loan before submitting to underwriting if the borrower clearly will not qualify because of excessive debts or insufficient income, or if the property fails to meet the lender's standards as to condition or value.

Loan Underwriting

Once all information has been verified and the loan documentation assembled, the loan processor submits the loan to **underwriting.** The underwriter is responsible for *reviewing the loan documentation and evaluating the borrower's ability and willingness to repay the loan and the sufficiency of the collateral value of the property.* The underwriter may be someone on the lender's staff or, in the case of a loan designated for sale, someone on the investor's staff. In the case of FHA and VA loans, these agencies have delegated underwriting responsibility to the lender. For conventional loans over 80 percent loan-to-value and requiring mortgage insurance, an underwriting submission also must be made to the private mortgage insurance company.

Many factors govern loan underwriting. The following are only representative of the basic factors that must be considered in the loan approval process. Loan underwriting can be divided into three categories: buyer ability to pay, buyer willingness to pay, and property evaluation.

Buyer Ability to Pay

The buyer's ability to pay consists of the following considerations:

1. *Employment.* Borrower employment for the past two years is verified as evidence of ability to pay. Also, the underwriter must determine the probable stability and continuance of that employment. Job hopping without advancement does not reflect stability, but recent college graduates beginning work in their fields of endeavor should be able to look forward to continued and stable employment.

2. *Income.* Even if employment is stable, income may not be. Borrowers who are self-employed, work on commission, or are employed by a close relative must submit signed federal income tax returns for the most recent two years. Income reported on the past tax returns is averaged with current verified income to reflect a stable income figure. In reaching a stable income figure, self-employed or commissioned employees with declining incomes must be evaluated especially against offsetting factors.

Overtime and bonus income usually is not counted unless the borrower verifies stability over the prior two years. Part-time income can be counted if the borrower has held the job continually for the past two years and seems likely to continue in the job. Seasonal employment is counted if it is uninterrupted over a two-year history and prospects for continued employment are evident.

3. *Closing funds.* The borrower has to show sufficient funds on hand to close the mortgage transaction. The verified borrower's deposit on the sales contract plus verified bank balances must equal the down payment plus closing costs and prepaid items. The underwriter must look for the possibility of last-minute unsecured borrowed funds being used for all or part of the required closing costs (evidenced by large, unexplained recent bank deposits).

Sales contract deposits of more than 2 percent must be checked to verify that an actual deposit was made and that no seller or third-party concessions were made that would violate the underwriting requirements for the specified loan involved. FHA, VA, and conventional loans all have different rules as to what can be paid by others.

Gift funds from a family member are acceptable to meet cash requirements for closing FHA or VA loans if they are actually transferred to the borrower and verified. With conventional loans, the borrower must invest 5 percent of the sales price from his or her own funds; the family member may put up additional money required over that 5 percent.

Stocks and bonds also are acceptable as closing funds if the market value can be verified and a 5 percent borrower cash down payment is made. A separate appraisal must be made of the securities, along with a property record search to verify ownership.

4. *Debt ratio.* The underwriter must calculate the borrower's two debt ratios: (a) monthly housing expense to income and (b) total payment obligations to income. These ratios determine the borrower's ability to meet home ownership responsibilities. The ratios most lenders in the secondary market recognize are shown in Figure 8.11.

Monthly housing expense includes: fixed mortgage payment plus escrow deposits for hazard insurance premium; real estate taxes and mortgage insurance premium; owners' or condominium association charges, less the utility charge portion; any ground rents or special assessments; and payments under any secondary financing on the subject property.

FIGURE 8.11 Secondary mortgage market ratios.

LOANS	MONTHLY HOUSING EXPENSE	TOTAL OBLIGATIONS
Conventional		
Fixed-rate	28%	36%
Adjustable-rate	28%	36%
FHA	29%	41%
VA	None	41%

These ratios do not constitute absolute requirements. For example, compensating factors allow for approval of a borrower with higher housing expense and total obligations ratios than set forth here. Some factors or conditions allowing for higher ratios are:

1. For straight-mortgage loans with 20 percent or larger down payment:
   - Borrower demonstrates ability to delegate a higher percentage of income to mortgage payments.
   - Borrower demonstrates ability to accumulate savings (high cash or net worth position) combined with good and debt-free credit history.
   - Borrower's property qualifies as an energy-efficient dwelling.
   - Borrower has potential for higher long-term earnings because of education, training, or initial entry into job market.

2. For straight-mortgage loans with less than 20 percent down payment, the lender has risks in addition to the above ratios; therefore, the underwriter must determine that:
   - Borrower will have adequate cash reserves after closing, usually the equivalent of two months' mortgage payments.
   - Borrower has the ability to make mortgage payments in excess of his or her previous housing expense.
   - Borrower has demonstrated an ability to accumulate savings and to properly manage debt.
   - Borrower has maintained an excellent credit history.
   - Borrower has a capability for future increased earnings and savings.

3. For adjustable rate mortgages with less than 20 percent down payment, the debt ratio usually is calculated based on the fully indexed adjustable rate (loan margin plus index), not the initial rate, which in most instances can be up to 2 percent lower. Thus, when mortgage rates are at 10 percent, the borrower may have to qualify on the basis of 10 percent.

4. For adjustable rate mortgages with greater than 20 percent down payment, the borrower under an ARM may well qualify on the basis of the lower first-year rate. Thus, under the same interest rate conditions, a buyer might qualify on the basis of 8 percent if he or she has the larger down payment.

Buyer Willingness to Pay

The buyer's willingness to pay is reflected by credit history. This can be demonstrated by the borrower's mortgage payment record, number and amount of outstanding credit obligations, and payment history on other credit obligations.

In determining the acceptability of borrower credit, the underwriter examines the total credit history, the borrower's written explanations of any problems, and offsetting factors. Borrowers who have substantial debts with slow pay, steadily increasing obligations not offset by income increases, or a history of periodic refinancing or debt consolidation to cure debts are considered higher credit risks.

Bankruptcy and prior poor credit history are not disqualifying factors (a) if they are caused by extraordinary circumstances, such as health problems, or (b) if in the two-year period prior to loan application, the borrower has reestablished credit and demonstrated an ability to now manage his or her financial affairs.

Property Evaluation

The property appraisal is a mere estimate of value that the underwriter must evaluate. Some of the major considerations the underwriter must include in this evaluation process are: site analysis, improvements, economic life, and valuation. Property evaluation and each of these factors are discussed in detail in Chapter 10.

Based on the gathered data, the appraiser makes a final reconciliation of value. This is the appraised value, and the underwriter, after totally reviewing and evaluating the appraisal, makes his or her own conclusion as to value.

Discount Points

In making mortgage loans, lending institutions may charge **discount points.** The purpose is to increase the yield to the lender by raising the effective interest rate in an amount exceeding a maximum rate that may be charged under certain conditions. *Each point that the lender charges costs someone* (either the buyer or the seller, depending upon the situation) *1 percent of the loan amount,* paid at the time of loan closing. And, each point charged has the effect of increasing the lender's yield by ⅛ of a percent (see Figure 8.12).

Lenders may charge discount points in making conventional loans. These situations have no prohibition against the borrower paying the points, and the borrower usually is the one who pays. In times of high interest rates and short supply of money for making mortgage loans, lenders often charge one or two points in making 90 percent and 95 percent conventional loans. In Illinois, there is no limit on the rate of interest that a lender may charge on a mortgage loan when the loan is secured by real estate. The Illinois usury laws were terminated in 1981. Borrowers sometimes volunteer to pay discount points to "buy down" a mortgage interest rate at the time the loan is made.

Sellers traditionally have had to pay discount points in order for a veteran buyer to purchase their home using a VA loan when the maximum VA rate was below the current market rate. As of October 28, 1992, HR 939 abolished the ceiling on VA interest rates and made both interest rates and discount points negotiable between buyer and seller and between buyer and lender. FHA discount points are also negotiable and can be paid by buyer or seller.

FIGURE 8.12 Discount points figured as charges and yields.

Discount points calculated as *charges*
One discount point = 1% of the loan amount
For example, if the loan amount is $40,000 and the lender charges:

1 point	=	.01	x	$40,000	=	$ 400
2 points	=	.02	x	$40,000	=	$ 800
3 points	=	.03	x	$40,000	=	$ 1,200
4 points	=	.04	x	$40,000	=	$ 1,600

Discount points calculated as increase in *yield to lender*
One discount point = ⅛% increase

1 point	=	⅛% increase in yield
2 points	=	²⁄₈% or ¼% increase in yield
3 points	=	³⁄₈% increase in yield
4 points	=	⁴⁄₈% or ½% increase in yield

Closing or Settlement Costs

At the time of **settlement** or *closing of a real estate transaction*, both the buyer and the seller must satisfy the various expenses and obligations incurred in the transaction. If this is a new first mortgage from a lending institution, the buyer's cost typically is at least 3 percent of the loan amount plus discount points. The seller's closing cost varies widely depending on the obligations that must be satisfied at the closing. One substantial obligation that the seller may have is the requirement to satisfy an existing first mortgage against the property.

PUTTING IT TO WORK

At various points in the process, the salesperson provides the buyer or the seller, or both, with an estimate of closing costs. This typically occurs during the prequalification process and again as needed when offers or counteroffers are presented. At the time of listing the property, and again when offers are presented, the salesperson usually gives the seller an estimate of net proceeds.

Typical buyer costs in closing a new loan and real estate transaction include:

1. Discount points paid to obtain a conventional loan or to buy down the interest rate on a conventional loan.
2. The *financing charge required by the lender*, called the **loan origination fee** or loan service charge, ranges from 1 to 3 percent of the loan amount.
3. The appraisal fee the lender charges to estimate the market value of the property to be pledged as security in the mortgage or deed of trust. (Appraisal is the topic of Chapter 10.)
4. Attorney's fee for title examination and document preparation.
5. Survey fee. Usually a seller charge.
6. Credit report charge.
7. Assumption fee charged by the lender if the buyer is assuming the seller's existing mortgage.
8. Mortgage guarantee insurance premium required in conventional insured loans when the loan-to-value ratio exceeds 80 percent.
9. Title insurance premium.
10. Cost of termite inspection and certification.

The various closing or settlement costs buyers and sellers incur in real estate transactions are discussed in detail in Chapter 9.

Financing Legislation

Truth-in-Lending Simplification and Reform Act (TILSRA)

The Truth-in-Lending law is part of the Federal Consumer Credit Protection Act, which became effective July 1, 1969. It subsequently was amended and became known as the **Truth-in-Lending Simplification and Reform Act (TILSRA)** of 1980.

The Truth-in-Lending Act empowered the Federal Reserve Board to implement regulations in the act. TILSRA now *requires four chief disclosures: annual percentage rate, finance charge, amount financed, and total of payments.* The Federal Reserve Board implemented these regulations by establishing Regulation Z. The law is enforced by the Federal Trade Commission (FTC).

Regulation Z does not regulate interest rates but instead *provides specific consumer protections in mortgage loans for residential real estate.* It covers all real estate loans for personal, family, household, or agricultural purposes. The regulation does not apply to commercial loans. Regulation Z also standardizes the procedures involved in residential loan transactions and requires that the borrower be fully informed of all aspects of the loan transaction. In addition, the regulation addresses any advertisement of credit terms available for residential real estate.

Disclosure

At time of application or within three days thereafter, the lender must provide the borrower with a **disclosure statement.** The disclosure *must set forth the true, or effective, annual interest rate on a loan,* called the **annual percentage rate (APR).** This rate may be higher than the interest as expressed in the mortgage. For example, when certain fees and discount points charged by the lender are subtracted from the loan amount, the result is an increase in the true rate of interest. As a result of the subtraction, the borrower receives a smaller loan amount and pays interest on a larger amount. Therefore, the effect is to increase the interest rate being paid.

In addition to stating the true or effective annual interest rate on the loan, the disclosure statement must specify the finance charges, which include loan fees, interest, and discount points. The finance charges do not have to include things such as title examination, title insurance, escrow payments, document preparation fees, notary fees, attorney fees, or appraisal fees.

PUTTING IT TO WORK

> The APR provides a method for consumers to compare costs when lenders charge quite differently. For example, a loan for which a lender charges 8½ percent interest with a 2 percent origination fee and 4 discount points may be more costly than a 9 percent loan with only a 1 percent origination fee and no points. The APR allows the true loan cost to be accurately compared.

Cooling-Off Period

If the borrower is refinancing an existing mortgage loan or obtaining a new mortgage loan and is pledging a principal residence already owned as security for the loan, the disclosure statement must provide for a **cooling-off period,** or *three-day right of rescission for the loan transaction.* The borrower must exercise the right to rescind, or cancel, the loan prior to midnight of the third business day after the date the transaction was closed. The three-day right of rescission *does not* apply if the loan is to finance the purchase of a new home, or to finance the construction of a dwelling to be used as a principal residence, or to refinance an investment property.

Advertising

Regulation Z also applies to advertising the credit terms available in purchasing a home. The only specific thing that may be stated in the advertisement without making a full disclosure is the annual percentage rate, spelled out in full, not abbreviated as APR. If any other credit terms are included in the advertisement, it must provide a full disclosure. For example, an advertisement mentioning a down payment triggers the requirement to make a complete disclosure of all of the following credit terms: cash price of the property, annual percentage rate, amount of down payment, amount of each payment, date when each payment is due, and total number of payments over the mortgage term. If the annual percentage rate is not a fixed rate but is instead a variable rate, the ad must specify the rate to be a variable or adjustable rate.

Statements of a general nature regarding the financing may be made without a full disclosure. Statements such as "good financing available," "FHA financing available," and "loan assumption available" are satisfactory. Real estate agents must take special care not to violate advertising requirements of Regulation Z.

Penalties

Violators of Regulation Z are subject to criminal liability and punishment by fine up to $5,000, imprisonment for up to a year, or both. If the borrower suffers a financial loss as the result of the violation, he or she may sue the violator under civil law in federal court for damages.

Real Estate Settlement Procedures Act (RESPA)

Congress enacted the **Real Estate Settlement Procedures Act (RESPA)** in 1974. It *regulates lending activities of lending institutions in making mortgage loans for housing.* RESPA is administered by HUD.

While most of RESPA deals with lender requirements and responsibilities, some provisions of RESPA directly affect brokers and the way they do business. Loans covered by RESPA include funds for purchase, refinancings, lines of credit, or other home-equity loans made by a federally related financial institution. Not covered are second mortgages, home improvement loans, installment contracts, and assumptions. If a lender requires that a particular settlement provider be used, the lender must disclose the provider and state whether the provider has a business relationship with the lender (ownership in the provider, promise of referral fees from the provider, etc.).

Purpose of RESPA

RESPA has the following purposes:

1. to effect specific changes in the settlement process resulting in more effective advance disclosure of settlement costs to home buyers and sellers
2. to protect borrowers from unnecessarily expensive settlement charges resulting from abusive practices
3. to ensure that borrowers are provided with more information, on a more timely basis, on the nature and cost of the settlement process
4. to eliminate referral fees or kickbacks that increase the cost of settlement services. In this regard, lenders are permitted to charge for only those services that are actually provided to home buyers and sellers, and in an amount that the service actually costs the lender

RESPA Requirements

RESPA requires:

1. *Good faith estimate.* Within three working days of receiving a completed loan application, the lender is required to provide the borrower with a **good faith estimate** of the *costs likely to be incurred at settlement.* A sample form is shown in Figure 8.13.

FIGURE 8.13
A lender's good faith estimate of settlement costs.

GOOD FAITH ESTIMATE OF BORROWER'S SETTLEMENT COSTS

APPLICANT ("You", "Your")	LENDER ("We")

Date of this Estimate Estimated Closing Date Loan Officer

Loan Program

Term ; Rate %; Origination Fee %; Discount Fee %

Purchase Price / Value $ Loan Amount $ Loan to Value %

Property Address

The information provided below reflects estimates of the charges which you are likely to incur at the settlement of your loan. The fees listed are estimates - the actual charges may be more or less. Your transaction may not involve a fee for every item listed.

The numbers listed beside the estimates generally correspond to the numbered lines contained in the HUD-1 or HUD-1A settlement statement which you will be receiving at settlement. The HUD-1 or HUD-1A settlement statement will show you the actual cost for items paid at settlement.

800. ITEMS PAYABLE IN CONNECTION WITH LOAN:

801. Loan Origination Fee % $
802. Loan Discount Fee % $
803. Appraisal Fee $
804. Credit Report $
805. Lender's Inspection Fee $
806. Mortgage Insurance Application Fee $
807. Assumption Fee $
808. $
809. $
810. $
811. $
812. $
813. $
814. $
815. $

900. ITEMS REQUIRED BY LENDER TO BE PAID IN ADVANCE:

901. Interest from
to at $ /day $
902. Mortgage Insurance Premium $
903. Hazard Insurance Premium $
904. $
905. $

1000. RESERVES DEPOSITED WITH LENDER:

1001. Hazard Insurance Premium $
months at $ /month
1002. Mortgage Insurance $
months at $ /month
1003. City Property Taxes $
months at $ /month
1004. County Property Taxes $
months at $ /month
1005. Annual Assessments $
months at $ /month
1006. $
1007. $
1008. $
1009. $

1100. TITLE CHARGES:

1101. Settlement Fee $
1102. Abstract or Title Search $
1103. Title Examination $
1104. Title Insurance Binder $
1105. Document Preparation Fee $
1106. Notary Fee $
1107. Attorney's Fee $
1108. Title Insurance $
1111. $
1112. $
1113. $

1200. GOVERNMENT RECORDING AND TRANSFER CHARGES:

1201. Recording Fees $
Deed $; Mortgage $;
Release $
1202. City / County Tax / Stamps $
Deed $; Mortgage $;
Release $
1203. State Tax / Stamps $
Deed $; Mortgage $
1204. $
1205. $

1300. ADDITIONAL SETTLEMENT CHARGES:

1301. Survey $
1302. Pest Inspection $
1303. $
1304. $
1305. $

1400. TOTAL ESTIMATED SETTLEMENT CHARGES: $

EST. MONTHLY PMT.:	PPD. INT. & ESCROWS:	ANNUAL AMOUNT:	ANALYSIS OF ESTIMATED SETTLEMENT CHARGES:
P & I	Ppd. Interest		1400. Total Estimated Settlement Charges: $
R.E. Taxes	R.E. Taxes	R.E. Taxes	
Hazard Ins.	Hazard Ins.	Hazard Ins.	Less: Prepaid Interest and Escrows $
Flood Ins.	Flood Ins.	Flood Ins.	
Mtg. Ins.	Mtg. Ins.	Mtg. Ins.	= Other Estimated Settlement Charges: $
Other	Other	Other	
Total Pmt.	**Total Ppds.**		

THIS SECTION TO BE COMPLETED ONLY IF A PARTICULAR PROVIDER OF SERVICE IS REQUIRED. Listed below are providers of service which we require you use. The charges or ranges indicated in the Good Faith Estimate above are based upon the corresponding charge of the below designated providers.

Item No. Name / Address
Telephone Relationship? ☐ Yes ☐ No Nature of Relationship:
Item No. Name / Address
Telephone Relationship? ☐ Yes ☐ No Nature of Relationship:
Item No. Name / Address
Telephone Relationship? ☐ Yes ☐ No Nature of Relationship:

AGREEMENT:
You acknowledge you have received a copy of the HUD Special Information Booklet "Settlement Costs", if your application is to purchase residential real property and the Lender will take a first lien on the property.
If for any reason the loan you have applied for does not close, and if permitted by applicable law, you agree to reimburse the **lender** for any and all costs incurred to process your application including but not limited to appraisal, survey and title insurance.
These estimates are provided pursuant to the Real Estate Settlement Procedures Act of 1974, as amended (RESPA). Additional information can be found in the HUD Special Information Booklet, which is to be provided to you by your mortgage broker or lender, if your application is to purchase residential real property and the lender will take a first lien on the property.

APPLICANT DATE APPLICANT DATE

APPLICANT DATE APPLICANT DATE

AUTHORIZED OFFICIAL

2. *Homebuyer's Guide to Settlement Costs.* At the time of loan application, the lender must provide the borrower with this booklet, which contains the following information:
   a. clear and concise language describing and explaining the nature and purpose of each settlement cost
   b. an explanation and sample of the standard real estate settlement forms required by the act
   c. a description and explanation of the nature and purpose of escrow/impound accounts
   d. an explanation of choices available to borrowers in selecting persons or organizations to provide necessary settlement charges
   e. Examples and explanations of unfair practices and unreasonable or unnecessary settlement charges to be avoided

3. *HUD Form No. 1.* In making residential mortgage loans, lenders are required to use a standard settlement form designed to clearly itemize all charges to be paid by borrower and by seller as part of the final settlement. The form (see Figure 8.14), which has become known as HUD Form No. 1, or the HUD 1, must be made available for the borrower's inspection at or before final settlement. This form is not required for assumptions and nonresidential loans.

4. *Prohibition against kickbacks.* No person or entity can receive payment, fees, referral fees, commissions, or other things of value in connection with a RESPA-regulated mortgage loan without performing an actual service.
   a. *Controlled business arrangement (CBA):* If a real estate broker or lender has a financial interest or ongoing business relationship in a provider of settlement services, such as title insurance, home inspection, or pest inspection, disclosure of this relationship must be made in writing to the borrower. Borrowers must also be informed that they are free to select other settlement service providers.
   b. *Computerized loan origination (CLO):* Computerized loan origination (CLO) systems typically consist of a computer terminal in a broker's office that is linked via a modem to a lender or group of lenders. The broker usually starts the application from his office, cutting the time necessary to receive a loan approval. Real estate brokers are allowed to use a CLO system to originate a mortgage loan and may charge a fair fee for this service. This fee must be disclosed in writing and be paid directly by the borrower, not the lender.

HUD's New Escrow Rules

In late 1994, HUD instituted new escrow regulations that ban the most popular method lenders use to calculate mortgage escrows and allow lenders up to the end of 1997 to revise their accounting on loans that existed in 1994. Under the new rules governing monthly escrows, the lender cannot charge more than $\frac{1}{12}$ per month of combined property tax, insurance, and other recurring expenses "that are reasonably anticipated" to come due in the next 12 months. The lender is allowed to maintain a cushion of two months' worth of the estimated charges. These new rules do not mandate the payment of interest on escrow balances, nor do they allow a borrower to be relieved from paying into an escrow account if her principal balance starts at, or drops below, a certain loan amount or percentage.

Illinois Mortgage Escrow Account Act

The Illinois Mortgage Escrow Account Act affects mortgages for which single-family, owner-occupied homes are the collateral. The act allows a borrower that has reduced

FIGURE 8.14 HUD Form No. 1, required by RESPA for settlement cost calculations.

A. U.S. DEPARTMENT OF HOUSING AND URBAN DEVELOPMENT SETTLEMENT STATEMENT	B. TYPE OF LOAN	OMB No. 2502-0265
	1. ☐ FHA 2. ☐ FMHA 3. ☐ CONV. UNINS.	
	4. ☐ VA 5. ☐ CONV. INS.	
	6. FILE NUMBER: 7. LOAN NUMBER:	
	8. MORTGAGE INS. CASE NO.:	

C. NOTE: This form is furnished to give you a statement of actual settlement costs. Amounts paid to and by the settlement agent are shown. Items marked "(p.o.c.)" were paid outside the closing; they are shown here for informational purposes and are not included in the totals.

D. NAME OF BORROWER:
   ADDRESS OF BORROWER:

E. NAME OF SELLER:
   ADDRESS OF SELLER:

F. NAME OF LENDER:
   ADDRESS OF LENDER:

G. PROPERTY
   LOCATION:

H. SETTLEMENT AGENT:
   PLACE OF SETTLEMENT:

I. SETTLEMENT DATE:

J. SUMMARY OF BORROWER'S TRANSACTION		K. SUMMARY OF SELLER'S TRANSACTION	
100. GROSS AMOUNT DUE FROM BORROWER:		**400. GROSS AMOUNT DUE TO SELLER:**	
101. Contract sales price		401. Contract sales price	
102. Personal property		402. Personal property	
103. Settlement charges to borrower: (from line 1400)		403.	
104.		404.	
105.		405.	
ADJUSTMENTS FOR ITEMS PAID BY SELLER IN ADVANCE:		ADJUSTMENTS FOR ITEMS PAID BY SELLER IN ADVANCE:	
106. City/town taxes to		406. City/town taxes to	
107. County taxes to		407. County taxes to	
108. Assessments to		408. Assessments to	
109.		409.	
110.		410.	
111.		411.	
112.		412.	
120. GROSS AMOUNT DUE FROM BORROWER:		**420. GROSS AMOUNT DUE TO SELLER:** ▶	
200. AMOUNTS PAID BY OR IN BEHALF OF BORROWER:		**500. REDUCTION IN AMOUNT DUE TO SELLER:**	
201. Deposit or earnest money		501. Excess deposit (see instructions)	
202. Principal amount of new loan(s)		502. Settlement charges to seller (line 1400)	
203. Existing loan(s) taken subject to		503. Existing loan(s) taken subject to	
204.		504. Payoff of first mortgage loan	
205.		505. Payoff of second mortgage loan	
206.		506.	
207.		507.	
208.		508.	
209.		509.	
ADJUSTMENTS FOR ITEMS UNPAID BY SELLER:		ADJUSTMENTS FOR ITEMS UNPAID BY SELLER:	
210. City/town taxes to		510. City/town taxes to	
211. County taxes to		511. County taxes to	
212. Assessments to		512. Assessments to	
213.		513.	
214.		514.	
215.		515.	
216.		516.	
217.		517.	
218.		518.	
219.		519.	
220. TOTAL PAID BY/FOR BORROWER:		**520. TOTAL REDUCTIONS IN AMOUNT DUE SELLER:** ▶	
300. CASH AT SETTLEMENT FROM/TO BORROWER:		**600. CASH AT SETTLEMENT TO/FROM SELLER:**	
301. Gross amount due from borrower (line 120)		601. Gross amount due to seller (line 420)	
302. Less amount paid by/for borrower (line 220)	( )	602. Less total reductions in amount due seller (line 520)	( )
303. CASH ( ) FROM ( ) TO BORROWER:		603. CASH ( ) TO ( ) FROM SELLER: ▶	

SUBSTITUTE 1099-S: This form may be used as the written statement to the Transferor. This is important tax information and is being furnished to the Internal Revenue Service. If you are required to file a return, a negligence penalty will be imposed on you if this item is required to be reported and the IRS determines that it has not been reported. See Substitute 1099-S Information Sheet.

Previous Edition is Obsolete

SB-4-3538-000-1
HUD-1 (3-86)
RESPA, HB 4305.2

(continued)

Real Estate Finance Practices   201

FIGURE 8.14
Continued.

L.	SETTLEMENT CHARGES		PAID FROM BORROWER'S FUNDS AT SETTLEMENT	PAID FROM SELLER'S FUNDS AT SETTLEMENT
700.	TOTAL SALES/BROKER'S COMMISSION: BASED ON PRICE $ @ % =			
	DIVISION OF COMMISSION (LINE 700) AS FOLLOWS:			
701.	$ to			
702.	$ to			
703.	Commission paid at settlement			
704.				
800.	ITEMS PAYABLE IN CONNECTION WITH LOAN:			
801.	Loan Origination fee %			
802.	Loan Discount %			
803.	Appraisal Fee to:			
804.	Credit Report to:			
805.	Lender's Inspection fee			
806.	Mortgage Insurance application fee to			
807.	Assumption fee			
808.				
809.				
810.				
811.				
812.				
813.				
814.				
815.				
900.	ITEMS REQUIRED BY LENDER TO BE PAID IN ADVANCE:			
901.	Interest from to @ $ /day			
902.	Mortgage insurance premium for mo. to			
903.	Hazard insurance premium for yrs. to			
904.	Flood Insurance Premium for yrs. to			
905.				
1000.	RESERVES DEPOSITED WITH LENDER:			
1001.	Hazard insurance months @ $ per month			
1002.	Mortgage insurance months @ $ per month			
1003.	City property taxes months @ $ per month			
1004.	County property taxes months @ $ per month			
1005.	Annual assessments months @ $ per month			
1006.	Flood Insurance months @ $ per month			
1007.	months @ $ per month			
1008.	months @ $ per month			
1009.	months @ $ per month			
1100.	TITLE CHARGES:			
1101.	Settlement or closing fee to			
1102.	Abstract or title search to			
1103.	Title examination to			
1104.	Title insurance binder to			
1105.	Document preparation to			
1106.	Notary fees to			
1107.	Attorney's fees to			
	(includes above items Numbers:)			
1108.	Title insurance to			
	(includes above items Numbers:)			
1109.	Lender's coverage $			
1110.	Owner's coverage $			
1111.				
1112.				
1113.				
1200.	GOVERNMENT RECORDING AND TRANSFER CHARGES:			
1201.	Recording fees: Deed $; Mortgage $; Releases $			
1202.	City/county tax/stamps: Deed $; Mortgage $			
1203.	State tax/stamps: Deed $; Mortgage $			
1204.				
1205.				
1300.	ADDITIONAL SETTLEMENT CHARGES:			
1301.	Survey to			
1302.	Pest inspection to			
1303.				
1304.				
1305.				
1306.				
1307.				
1400.	TOTAL SETTLEMENT CHARGES (Enter on line 103, Section J - and - line 502, Section K) ▶			

I have carefully reviewed the HUD-1 Settlement Statement and to the best of my knowledge and belief, it is a true and accurate statement of all receipts and disbursements made on my account or by me in this transaction. I further certify that I have received a copy of HUD-1 Settlement Statement.

Borrowers _____   Sellers _____

The HUD-1 Settlement Statement which I have prepared is a true and accurate account of this transaction. I have caused or will cause the funds to be disbursed in accordance with this statement.
Settlement Agent _____   Date _____

WARNING: It is a crime to knowingly make false statements to the United States on this or any other similar form. Penalties upon conviction can include a fine or imprisonment. For details see: Title 18 U.S. Code Section 1001 and Section 1010.

PAGE 2

his loan to a balance of 65 percent of the initial loan amount to terminate his escrow account. The act also allows a borrower to open an interest-bearing pledge account to cover the amount of taxes and insurance. The lender must provide a written notice of these escrow procedures to the borrowers.

Equal Credit Opportunity Act (ECOA)

The **Equal Credit Opportunity Act (ECOA)** was enacted by Congress in 1975 *to prevent lending institutions from discriminating in the loan process.* The act requires financial institutions that make loans to do so on an equal basis to all creditworthy customers without regard to discriminatory factors. The Equal Credit Opportunity Act is implemented by Regulation B of the Federal Reserve Board.

This act makes it unlawful for any creditor to discriminate against any loan applicant in any aspect of a credit transaction:

1. on the basis of race, color, religion, gender, national origin, marital status, or age (unless the applicant is a minor and, therefore, does not have the capacity to contract)
2. because part of the applicant's income is derived from a public assistance program, alimony, or child support
3. because the applicant has in good faith exercised any right under the Federal Consumer Credit Protection Act of which the Truth-in-Lending Law (Regulation Z) is a part

Compliance with the Equal Credit Opportunity Act is enforced by different agencies depending on which agency has regulatory authority over the type of financial institution.

IMPORTANT POINTS

1. Methods of financing include insured and uninsured conventional mortgage loans, FHA-insured loans, VA-guaranteed loans, and the various types of seller financing.
2. Conventional loans are not required to be insured if the loan amount does not exceed 80 percent of the property value. Most conventional insured loans are 90 percent and 95 percent loans. The insurance is called private mortgage insurance (PMI). The premium is paid by the borrower.
3. Various types of mortgages include junior, term, amortizing, balloon, open-end, graduated payment, adjustable or variable rate, shared appreciation (SAM), growing equity (GEM), participation, wraparound, package, blanket, construction, purchase money, and leasehold mortgages.
4. FHA and VA loans are made by specifically qualified lending institutions.
5. The FHA-insured programs include 203(b), 245, 203(b)(2), and the 234(c). FHA insurance, called mortgage insurance premium (MIP), protects the lender from financial loss in the event of foreclosure. The borrower pays the premium. FHA establishes a maximum loan amount.
6. VA loans are guaranteed loans. The current guarantee is a multitiered system. VA loans may be made for up to 100 percent of the sales price or of the property value established by a VA appraisal and stated in the Certificate of Reasonable Value (CRV), issued by the VA, whichever is less.
7. FHA and VA loans require escrow accounts and are for 30-year terms or shorter. Both are assumable with certain restrictions and do not impose a prepayment penalty. The down payment can be borrowed if it is secured by collateral.

8. Either the buyer or seller may pay FHA or VA discount points.
9. The Illinois Mortgage Escrow Account Act applies to mortgage loans on single family owner-occupied residential property without assistance from or insurance by the Illinois state or the federal government.
10. Federal laws that regulate lending institutions in making consumer loans include Regulation Z, RESPA, and ECOA.

REVIEW QUESTIONS

Answers to these questions are found in the Answer Key section at the back of the book.

1. Insurance for the protection of lending institutions making conventional loans is called:
   a. mutual mortgage insurance
   b. conventional mortgage insurance
   c. institutional insurance
   d. private mortgage insurance

2. The FHA programs are for:
   a. making housing loans
   b. guaranteeing housing loans
   c. purchasing housing loans
   d. insuring housing loans

3. The FHA bases its commitment on a percentage of:
   a. certificate of reasonable value
   b. purchase price
   c. selling price
   d. acquisition cost

4. Which of the following FHA programs provides for lower monthly payments in the early years of the mortgage term by not requiring the borrower to pay all the interest at that time?
   a. 203(b)
   b. 203(b)(2)
   c. 234(c)
   d. 245

5. Which of the following statements about VA loans is correct?
   a. repayment of 100 percent of VA loans in the event of borrower default is guaranteed to the lender
   b. VA loans may be for 100 percent of the property value established by the VA
   c. a veteran can use his or her VA entitlement to purchase a single-family home for use as a rental property
   d. once a veteran has purchased one home using a VA loan, he can never get another VA loan

6. All of the following statements about FHA and VA loans are correct EXCEPT:
   a. they are assumable with qualifying
   b. they require a prepayment penalty
   c. the maximum term is 30 years
   d. they require an escrow account

7. Which of the following statements about discount points is correct?
   a. points increase the lender's yield on the loan
   b. each point charged by the lender costs 1 percent of the loan amount
   c. buyers can pay points on VA, FHA, and conventional loans
   d. all of the above

8. All of the following statements about Regulation Z are correct EXCEPT:
   a. it applies to commercial mortgage loans
   b. it requires lenders to furnish a disclosure statement to the borrower
   c. it provides for a three-day right of rescission if a residence already owned is pledged
   d. it regulates the advertising of credit terms of property offered for sale

9. RESPA requires the lender to furnish the borrower all of the following EXCEPT:

   a. homebuyer's guide to settlement costs
   b. good faith estimate
   c. standard settlement form
   d. three-day right of rescission

10. ECOA requires lenders to make consumer loans without regard to all of the following EXCEPT:

    a. age
    b. occupation
    c. gender
    d. marital status

11. The type of mortgage requiring the borrower to pay only interest during the mortgage term is:

    a. balloon
    b. open
    c. term
    d. closed

12. The amount of interest paid in an amortizing mortgage for a month in which the principal balance is $73,000 and the rate is 12 percent is:

    a. $876
    b. $730
    c. $600
    d. $1,369

13. A mortgage that is not on a fully amortizing basis and, therefore, requires a larger final payment is called:

    a. graduated mortgage
    b. balloon mortgage
    c. open mortgage
    d. flexible mortgage

14. The type of mortgage in which the lender reduces the interest rate for a part of the profit realized when the property is sold is a:

    a. participation mortgage
    b. price-level adjusted mortgage
    c. wraparound mortgage
    d. shared appreciation mortgage

15. A mortgage in which two or more parcels of land are pledged is called:

    a. blanket
    b. package
    c. all-inclusive
    d. wraparound

16. A mortgage that is subordinate to another is called:

    a. leasehold
    b. blanket
    c. junior
    d. participation

17. A mortgage given by buyer to seller to secure payment of part of the purchase price is a(n):

    a. purchase money mortgage
    b. earnest money mortgage
    c. participation mortgage
    d. graduated payment mortgage

18. Which of the following statements regarding wraparound mortgages is true?

    a. it is a junior mortgage in an amount larger than the existing first mortgage
    b. it is not necessary that the existing first mortgage is assumable
    c. both a and b are true
    d. neither a nor b is true

19. A lender is making loans at 7.25 percent. If a borrower desired a 7 percent loan, how many points would the buyer have to pay?

    a. one
    b. two
    c. four
    d. eight

20. Which of the following would be considered an advertising trigger term under Regulation Z?

    a. low down payment
    b. easy monthly payment
    c. VA and FHA financing available
    d. zero down

CHAPTER 9

Important Terminology

accrued expenses
closing statement
credits
debits
escrow instructions
impound accounts

perc test
prepaid expenses
proration
reconciliation
vendor's affidavit

Closing Real Estate Transactions

IN THIS CHAPTER Closing is the consummation of the sales effort that began when the broker or salesperson obtained a listing. Closing includes settlement, passing of papers, and coming out of escrow. At the closing, the buyer receives a deed and the seller receives payment for the property. In Illinois, an attorney (usually present at the title company) and a lending institution (when a new loan is involved) perform the functions necessary for closing a real estate transaction.

This chapter covers the various methods of closing, items required at closing, and proration calculations. Four examples and four closing problems allow practice in preparing for closing.

METHODS OF CLOSING

Face-to-Face Closing

At the *face-to-face closing,* the parties and other interested persons meet to review the closing documents, execute the closing documents, pay money, receive money, and receive title to real estate. The face-to-face closing typically is held at the office of the lender, attorney for one of the parties, or title company. Those present at this type of closing are buyers, sellers, real estate agents, and lender representatives. Before executing the closing documents and disbursing the closing funds, the parties should assure themselves that the conditions and contingencies of the purchase agreement have all been met. In a face-to-face closing, the title to the real estate is transferred upon execution and delivery of the deed.

Escrow Closing

In Illinois, some real estate transactions are closed in escrow. The expenses of closing in escrow usually are shared by both parties.

In an *escrow closing* a disinterested party is authorized to act as the closing or escrow agent, in charge of all closing documents, moneys, and activities. The escrow agent may be any of the following:

1. attorney
2. title company
3. escrow company
4. escrow department of a lending institution
5. trust company

Prior to selecting the escrow agent, the buyer and seller often execute **escrow instructions** in a detailed offer to purchase, *outlining the escrow agent's authority and what must occur prior to and at closing.*

> **PUTTING IT TO WORK**
>
> The escrow instructions should exactly parallel the offer and acceptance. Reference should be made in the escrow instructions to include the terms, conditions, contingencies, and addenda of the sales contract.

After the escrow agent is chosen, the earnest money, escrow instructions, and all pertinent documents are delivered to the escrow agent for completion of the transaction. The documents provided to the escrow agent by buyer and seller are all executed by the providing party prior to or upon delivery. This means that the seller executes the deed and delivers it to escrow, where it is held by the escrow agent until all contingencies and conditions of the offer to purchase have been met. Title to the real estate technically transfers when the deed is deposited with the escrow agent. Thus, death of either the buyer or the seller prior to completing the conditions of the offer to purchase will *not* invalidate the deal.

The escrow agent has the authority and obligation to examine the title evidence to assure marketable title. When marketable title is shown and all other contingencies of the escrow instructions are met, the escrow agent disburses the purchase price to the seller minus all charges and expenses attributable to the seller. The escrow agent also records the deed, mortgage, deed of trust, and any other documents set out in the escrow instructions.

If the seller cannot give marketable title or if any contingencies of the offer are not able to be met and the buyer will not accept title or waive the contingency, the escrow instructions provide that the closing will not be completed. The buyer then reconveys title to the seller, and all moneys are returned to the buyer or handled in accordance with the sales contract and escrow instructions.

Title and Escrow Companies

Title and escrow companies selected as the escrow or closing agents schedule the closing, assure that the escrow instructions are completed accurately, prepare all documents needed to close the transaction, deposit and disburse moneys, and record all documents to transfer title and secure any debt. Title or escrow companies usually are paid for their work and expertise based upon a percentage of the moneys handled at closing. The escrow agent is liable for any damages resulting from an improperly handled closing, either in disbursement of funds or inaccurate documents. Title and escrow companies also are responsible for preparing the 1099-S form to report the sale of real estate to the Internal Revenue Service.

PRELIMINARIES TO CLOSING

Before closing, the closing agent must assure that all conditions and contingencies of the real estate sales contract are met. Some typical items or documents of concern for the closing agent are described next.

Putting It to Work

The obligation for paying various costs is determined by local custom, state law, and the type of financing incurred, if any. Local closing officers should be consulted to determine who bears responsibility for each item. Many closing costs are negotiable and should be discussed as such with clients.

Parties

The legal names and marital status of the parties must be identified prior to closing. This is to assure accurate completion of the closing documents to transfer title and secure debt.

Survey

In Illinois, the seller usually is required to furnish the buyer a recent survey; thus, the seller pays for the survey.

Pest Inspection

Often the buyer or the buyer's lender requires proof that no wood-destroying pest, infestation, or damage is present. The cost of this inspection is typically the seller's. If infestation is found, the seller has to pay for treating and repairing any damage.

Title Examination, Insurance, and Defects

The seller must provide evidence of marketable title for transfer. This proof can be provided by the update of an abstract of title or by issuance of a title insurance binder. The seller bears the cost of either.

If an updated abstract of title is provided, the buyer must hire an attorney to prepare an opinion as to the quality of title shown in the abstract. If title defects are found, the seller is responsible for the cost of curing or removing the defects. Until marketable title is available, closing will not likely be completed.

If the buyer is borrowing money from an institutional lender, a mortgagee's title insurance policy also is needed. The buyer bears the cost of this title insurance policy.

Because abstract updates and title insurance binders typically are issued several days or weeks before closing, an update of the abstract or title binder should be obtained prior to closing with an effective date to the date of closing. In addition, the seller may be required to sign a **vendor's affidavit,** a *document stating that the seller has done nothing since the original title evidence to adversely affect title.*

Property Inspection

Usually the buyer wants to inspect the premises prior to closing. The inspection most often is performed by a professional inspection company. This is called a whole house inspection. The inspection report indicates any mechanical, electrical, plumbing, design, or construction defects. The buyer bears the cost of this inspection.

In addition to the professional inspection, the buyer usually arranges for a final walk through the day of closing or immediately prior to closing. This is to ensure that no damage has been done since the offer to purchase and that no fixtures have been removed.

Many Illinois municipalities have a building inspection ordinance that applies when title is transferred. The seller pays for this inspection and the repair costs, if any, necessary for compliance. Likewise, along with this ordinance, a proof of a certificate of compliance from the building inspector may be required before transfer tax stamps will be issued.

Insurance

Prior to closing, the buyer usually provides homeowner's fire and hazard insurance on the real estate being purchased. If the buyer is borrowing money for the purchase, the lender/mortgagee is listed on the policy as an additional insured. The cost of this insurance is the buyer's, and it must be purchased to cover the lender.

Perc and Soil Tests

If the property is not connected to a public sewer, the seller is required to provide the results of what is commonly called a **perc test,** an *inspection on percolation of the septic system to assure proper functioning and drainage and to show compliance with local and state health codes.* In addition, if the property is for commercial purposes, the seller is responsible for a soil test to assure the absence of hazardous waste or EPA problems.

Soil bearing tests measure the pressure that can be exerted on soil or soil rock without the soil yielding to the pressure. This test will determine the suitability of a lot for building purposes. Will the soil, and at what depth, support a foundation and structure?

Additional Documents

Any of the following documents may be involved in closing the real estate transaction. Accurate preparation of all relevant documents must be completed before closing.

- bill of sale of personal property
- certificate of occupancy
- closing or settlement statement (HUD Form No. 1)
- contract for deed
- deed
- deed of trust or mortgage
- note
- disclosure statement
- estoppel certificate
- homeowner's policy or hazard insurance policy
- lease
- lien waivers
- mortgage guarantee insurance policy
- option and exercise of option
- sales contract
- flood insurance policy

Not all of the above are applicable at each closing, but each is possible at typical real estate closings.

PRORATIONS AT CLOSING

Items Prorated

A closing sometimes involves the *division of expense between buyer and seller* for items such as rent, taxes, insurance, interest, and homeowner's association dues. This division, called **proration,** is necessary to ensure fair apportioning of expenses between buyer and seller. Prorated items are either accrued or prepaid. **Accrued expenses** are *costs the seller owes at the day of closing but the buyer will eventually pay.* The seller therefore gives the buyer a credit for these items at closing. Typical accrued items to be prorated are:

1. unpaid real estate taxes
2. rent collected by the seller from the tenant
3. interest on seller's mortgage assumed by the buyer

Prepaid expenses are *costs the seller pays* in advance and are not fully used up. At closing, these items are shown as a credit to the seller and a debit to the buyer. Typical prepaid items to be prorated are:

1. prepaid taxes and insurance premiums
2. rent paid by the seller under lease assigned to the buyer
3. utilities billed and paid in advance

Proration Rules and Methods

Methods for prorating expenses and the calculations involved follow.

1. Either the buyer or the seller may pay the costs of the day of closing. In Illinois, the day of closing belongs to the seller.

2. Mortgage interest, taxes, insurance, and like expenses are prorated using one of three acceptable methods: (a) actual number of days (365 or 366 during leap year; this is the most accurate method); (b) the statutory month, whereby the yearly charge is divided by 12 to arrive at the monthly amount and the monthly amount is divided by 30 to determine the daily amount using a 360-day year; or (c) a variation, in which the yearly charge is divided by 12 to arrive at the monthly amount and the monthly charge is then divided by the actual number of days in the month of closing to determine the daily charge for that month. In Illinois, any method agreed to by the parties is acceptable. Because mortgage interest usually is paid in arrears, parties to the transaction must understand that the mortgage payment for August, for example, will include interest for the month of July.

Some mortgage terms in Illinois may provide that the interest is paid in advance (at the beginning of the month). If the buyer assumes a mortgage on which interest is paid in advance, the prepaid portion from the date of closing to the end of the month must be credited to the seller and debited to the buyer. Mortgage interest paid in arrears would be a debit to the seller and a credit to the buyer. In some areas, taxes are paid in advance, requiring the seller to receive reimbursement at closing for the days of the year after closing.

In Illinois, taxes are paid in the year after they are levied. Any unpaid billed installment will be credited to the buyer and debited to the seller. A proration also will be necessary to credit the buyer with the current year's taxes and debit the seller with the current amount owed.

Special assessments typically are due on January 2 of each year. The buyer and the seller may agree upon the payment of special assessments. Usually the owner of record on the billing date pays the full amount.

212 Chapter 9

3. Accrued real estate taxes that are assessed but not yet due are typically prorated to the day of closing, with the seller having a debit and the buyer a credit for the amount owed as of the day of closing.

4. In prorating rent, the seller typically receives the rent for the day of closing.

5. Personal property taxes may be prorated between buyer and seller, or they may be paid entirely by the seller. In the calculations here, personal property taxes are not prorated.

6. Although other date prorations are acceptable (see number 2 above), in this book and on the Illinois Real Estate Licensing Exam every year is considered to have 360 days; every month has 30 days.

The arithmetic for proration is discussed completely in Chapter 17. Basically, the computation involves determining a yearly, monthly, or daily charge for the item being prorated. This charge then is multiplied by the number of months or days of the year for which reimbursement or payment is to be made. A synopsis of the method is set out in Figure 9.1.

FIGURE 9.1 Exercises for determining prorated costs.

EXERCISE 1

Accrued Items: The closing of a property is to be held on October 14. The real estate taxes of $895 for the year have not been paid and are due at the end of the year. What entry will appear on the seller's and buyer's closing statement?

January 1   October 14   December 31
_____/_____

Accrued period of taxes owed by seller at closing:
    895 ÷ 12 = $74.58 taxes per month
    74.58 ÷ 30 = $2.49 taxes per day

       74.58   plus   2.49
×   9 full months   ×   14 days
    $671.22   plus $34.86   = $706.08

Thus, the accrued taxes owed by seller at closing are $706.08. This will be a seller debit and a buyer credit at closing.

EXERCISE 2

Prepaid Items: The closing of a sale of a rental is to be held March 10. The seller has received the rent for March in the amount of $500. What entry will appear on the seller's and buyer's closing statement?

March 1   March 10   March 30
_____/_____

                                        Prepaid period not earned by seller
                                        prior to closing and assigned
                                        to buyer at closing

    500 ÷ 30 = $16.67 rent per day

      16.67
×   20 days not used
    $333.40 unused rent

Thus, the prepaid rent credited to the buyer at closing is $333.40. This will be a seller debit and a buyer credit at closing.

PREPARATION OF CLOSING STATEMENTS

A **closing statement** is a historical document prepared in advance. The statement is prepared before the closing, but it records what must happen at closing. The statement *sets forth the distribution of moneys involved in the transaction*—who is to pay a specific amount for each expense and who is to receive that amount. The closing statement is to be prepared by the person in charge of disbursing moneys at closing. This could be an escrow agent, an attorney, a broker, a lender, or a title company. In Illinois, the seller's attorney usually prepares the closing statement, and the buyer's lender or a title insurance company prepares the RESPA closing statement. Illinois real estate licensees are limited to preparing a statement in regard to escrow funds (for example, earnest money) being held or funds paid out for the benefit of both parties.

Format and Entries

The first step in preparing statements is to list all items in the transaction. Some of these items involve both the buyer and the seller, other items are of concern only to the buyer, and still others are of concern only to the seller. Entries that involve both parties will appear on the settlement statement of both parties. Items that involve only the buyer will appear only on the buyer's settlement statement. Those that involve only the seller will appear only on the seller's settlement statement.

Items included on the settlement statement fall into one of two categories: debits or credits. *Items that are owed* are **debits.** Those to be paid by the buyer are called buyer debits, and those owed and to be paid by the seller are seller debits. *Moneys received* are **credits.** Items representing money to be received by the buyer are called buyer credits. Items representing money to be received by the seller are called seller credits.

In the RESPA settlement statement form shown in Chapter 8 (Figure 8.14), the areas for debits and credits have been marked. Although real estate agents typically do not have to complete that form, they should be sufficiently familiar with the format to explain the entries to buyer and seller. For purposes of the examples and practice problems at the end of this chapter, a simplified, basic buyer and seller statement is used.

The typical debits and credits of buyer and seller are set out in Figure 9.2.

Handling Closing Funds

At the closing, the moneys the buyer owes are to be received by the closing agent. The moneys owed to the seller are to be disbursed by the closing agent. All other expenses of the sale are to be paid from the closing proceeds and disbursed by the closing agent. The closing agent basically begins with an empty account, receives money, disburses money, and ends with an empty account.

The money available for disbursement must equal the amount to be disbursed. The closing agent should perform a **reconciliation,** *a check of the money available and money owed prior to closing.* A reconciliation of a sample closing is shown on page 219.

CASH SALE STATEMENT

Our first illustration and analysis is the cash sale statement. This statement is usually the least complex of the four types because it has fewer items. The items involved in the transaction are listed below, developed from the real estate sales contract between buyer and seller, expenses incurred prior to closing, and expenses owed at closing.

FIGURE 9.2 Buyer and seller debits and credits.

Buyer Debits

Purchase price
Hazard or homeowner's insurance
Preparation of loan documents (mortgage and note)
Mortgagee's title insurance
Credit report
Loan origination fee
Mortgage assumption fee
Prepaid mortgage interest
Mortgage insurance
Buyer's discount points
Service points
Real estate property taxes paid in advance by seller
Recording of deed
Recording of mortgage documents
Overpaid (by seller) taxes

Seller Debits

Seller's discount points
Unpaid real property taxes prorated
Delinquent real property taxes
Existing mortgage and accrued interest
Deed preparation
Contract for deed balance
Purchase money mortgage taken back from buyer
Termite inspection and treatment
Soil test (perc test)
Unpaid utility bills
Mortgage interest on assumed loan
Transfer tax on transfer of real estate (Illinois state and county transfer tax, and municipal transfer tax, if any, are paid according to mandate or per agreement of the parties)
Survey
Broker's fee
Balance due to seller at closing (this is a balancing entry only, as seller gets this money)

Seller Credits

Purchase price
Overpaid real property taxes
Overpaid insurance premium
Sale of personal property
Escrow balance on assumed loan

Buyer Credits

Earnest money deposit
New mortgage money
Purchase money mortgage
Assumed mortgage and accrued interest on mortgage
Contract for deed balance
Unpaid real property taxes prorated
Balance due from buyer at closing (this is a balancing entry only, as buyer owes this money)

The statement prepared from this list and shown in Figure 9.3 is a typical example of a cash sale statement. The subsequent analysis, when related to each entry in the figure, should clarify the cash sale statement.

Closing date: February 15, 19XX
Sales price: $100,000
Earnest money deposit: $3,000
Annual insurance premium paid by buyer: $435
Annual real property taxes, unpaid: $1710
Deed preparation: $25
Recording fee: $13.32
Owner's title insurance policy: $445
Transfer taxes charged on transfer of real estate: $150
Broker's commission due (7%): $7,000

FIGURE 9.3   A cash sale closing statement.

Settlement Date: February 15, 19XX	Summary of Buyer's Transaction		Summary of Seller's Transaction	
	Debit	Credit	Debit	Credit
Purchase Price	$100,000.00	$	$	$100,000.00
Earnest Money		3,000.00		
Insurance Premium	435.00			
Prorated Real Property Tax		213.75	213.75	
Deed Preparation			25.00	
Deed Recording	13.32			
Title Search			445.00	
Transfer Taxes			150.00	
Commission Due			7,000.00	
Balance Due from Buyer		97,234.57		
Proceeds Due Seller			92,166.75	
Totals	$100,448.32	$100,448.32	$100,000	$100,000

Analysis of the Cash Sale Statement

Settlement Date

The settlement date shown for this transaction is February 15, 19XX. This is the date on which the closing took place, and this date becomes the calendar basis for all prorations involved in the closing statement. In making prorations, the day of closing or settlement date is charged to the seller. Expenses for this date in a prorated item are to be paid by the seller. For purposes of this book and most licensing examinations, all prorations are performed on the basis of a 360-day year.

Purchase Price

Both buyer and seller are involved with the purchase price. The buyer is paying, and the seller is receiving. Because the buyer is paying, this is a debit on the buyer's statement. The seller is receiving, and thus it appears as a credit on the seller's statement. This is a double-entry item; it shows up in both seller's and buyer's statements.

Earnest Money

When the buyer entered into the contract for purchase with the seller, he made a deposit of $3,000 in the form of earnest money, escrow money, or binder, as it is called. The buyer receives credit in his statement for having paid this amount. This money usually is held in the broker's trust or escrow account until closing. The broker brings a check for the $3,000 to the closing for the benefit of the buyer. This money is available at the closing, to be applied to the buyer's debits. This affects only the buyer.

Hazard Insurance Premium

Buyers want to be protected against financial loss resulting from total or partial destruction of their property. Therefore, the buyer has in force at closing a hazard or homeowner's insurance policy. This policy is for the buyer's benefit and thus is a debit to the buyer. This affects only the buyer.

Real Property Taxes

The annual real property taxes in the cash sale example are $1,710, and these taxes are not paid. This is an accrued item. At the end of the year, when the tax bill is due, the property will belong to the buyer, and thus the buyer will have to pay the taxes. The unpaid taxes constitute a specific lien on the real estate. To make an equitable division of these taxes at closing, seller should pay the taxes from January 1 through February 15. The seller owes the prorated tax bill, and thus it is a seller debit. The money is owed to the buyer for use at the end of the year and thus is a buyer credit. The seller's share for the 45 days is $4.75 per day, or a total of $213.75 for entry on the settlement statement. This affects both parties.

Title Insurance and Deed Preparation

In the offer to purchase, the seller agreed to convey a marketable title to the buyer. To accomplish this conveyance, she must provide a title insurance policy or updated abstract. In this example, the seller provided title insurance at a cost of $445. This is an expense solely of the seller, to be paid to the title company at closing. It is a seller debit.

Once marketable title is provided, the seller must complete the conveyance by execution of a deed. Because the deed is necessary to complete the seller's promise in the offer to purchase, the seller is responsible for the cost of deed preparation. This is a seller debit only.

Deed Recording

The purpose of recording a deed is to protect the title for the buyer. Therefore, the buyer usually pays the recording fee. This is a buyer debit only.

Transfer Taxes

Illinois and most of the other states impose a tax on the conveyance of real estate, based on the consideration that the seller receives in the transaction. Although who pays the tax varies by mandate or per agreement of the parties, the seller usually pays these taxes; therefore, this item appears as a seller debit on the settlement statement.

Broker's Fee (Commission Due)

In the listing contract, the seller has hired the broker to market the property and agreed to pay the broker a fee or commission of 7 percent of the final sales price of the property. Therefore, an entry of $7,000 is made as seller debit. This affects only the seller.

In Illinois, the commission owed to the broker usually is paid out of the earnest money being held in the broker's escrow account. Any escrow funds being held in excess of the broker's commission will be paid to the seller by the broker at closing or will be disbursed in accordance with the terms of the contract. If the broker's commission exceeds the amount of earnest money being held in escrow, the balance of the commission is paid at closing out of the seller's proceeds, if any, or from other seller funds.

Balance Due from Buyer

The balance due from the buyer is the amount the buyer must bring to closing to fulfill his obligations in the transaction. The combination of the $3,000 earnest money and the $97,234.57 balance due from the buyer will fulfill the financial responsibility. The balance due from the buyer is determined by totaling the buyer debits and subtracting the buyer credits. The total debits are $100,448.32. The total credits are $3213.75. The difference is $97,234.57. The buyer has $97,234.57 more debits than credits; thus, the buyer must pay this amount at closing to satisfy his obligations. This amount is entered in the buyer credit column because he must bring this amount and pay it at closing.

Balance Due to Seller

In this illustration, the seller has only one credit, the purchase price. We subtract the seller's debits from this credit to arrive at the balance due the seller at closing. The difference is $92,166.75. The seller has $92,166.75 more in credits than debits. Therefore, to satisfy the obligations due her at closing, she must receive a check in the amount of $92,166.75. Because she received this check at closing, it is entered as a debit. With the entry of the amount due the seller, the seller debit and credit columns are equal.

Other Comments

Notice that the totals of the buyer's statement and seller's statement in the illustration are different. This is because the two statements are not completely interrelated. The buyer has certain expenses and credits that the seller does not, and the seller has certain expenses that the buyer does not. For this reason, the two statements are not the same.

A typical entry on a seller's statement that did not appear in this example is the payoff of an existing mortgage. In the example, if the seller had a mortgage on the property, the seller would have to pay off the mortgage balance to convey clear title to the buyer. The cost of paying off the mortgage would be a debit to the seller only.

PURCHASE MONEY MORTGAGE STATEMENT

This type of closing statement involves the use of a mortgage given by the buyer to the seller for part of the purchase price. The seller is financing the sale of her property to the extent of the amount of the purchase money mortgage taken back from the buyer. In the discussion of this type of statement and in the next two statements, various terms are used to identify mortgage. These are: mortgage, deed of trust, and trust deed. For purposes of the closing statement, these terms are interchangeable.

Typical items for a settlement statement involving a purchase money mortgage are listed below. Figure 9.4 shows closing statements for buyer and seller that would result from the following list of information.

Settlement date: September 27, 19XX
Sales price: $60,000
Earnest money: $2,000
Insurance policy: on Jan. 31, the seller paid $240 for a full year in advance. At closing, the buyer is purchasing the remaining portion of the policy from the seller
Annual real property tax: $536 unpaid
Seller's existing mortgage: $5,000

FIGURE 9.4 Purchase money mortgage closing statement.

Settlement Date: September 27, 19XX	Summary of Buyer's Transaction		Summary of Seller's Transaction	
	Debit	Credit	Debit	Credit
Purchase Price	$60,000.00	$	$	$60,000.00
Earnest Money		2,000.00		
Insurance Prorated	82.00			82.00
Real Property Tax		397.53	397.53	
Purchase Money Mortgage		45,000.00	45,000.00	
Seller's Existing Mortgage			5,000.00	
Deed Preparation			40.00	
Mortgage and Note Preparation	45.00			
Deed Recording	3.50			
Mortgage Recording	4.50			
Title Insurance			300.00	
Commission Due			3,600.00	
Balance Due from Buyer		12,737.47		
Proceeds Due to Seller			5,744.47	
Totals	$60,135.00	$60,135.00	$60,082.00	$60,082.00

Purchase money mortgage: $45,000
Deed preparation: $40
Mortgage and note preparation: $45
Deed recording: $3.50
Mortgage recording: $4.50
Owner's title insurance policy: $300
Broker's commission: 6 percent of the sales price

Analysis of Purchase Money Mortgage Statement

In the following analysis of the purchase money mortgage statement, only the entries that were not in the cash sale statement are discussed.

Prorated Insurance Premium

In the example, the seller has paid for a full year's premium in advance, and the buyer is purchasing the unused portion of the policy. This is a prepaid item requiring proration.

On January 31, the seller paid $240 for one year, but used only a portion of the year. She used the full months of February through August, which is 7 x 30 = 210 days, plus 27 days of September, for a total of 237 days. The total of unused days is 360 − 237 = 123. Thus, the buyer owes the seller for 123 days. This is a seller credit and a buyer debit on the settlement statement. It is a double-entry item in the amount of 123 x $.6666 = $82 (rounded).

Purchase Money Mortgage

The buyer is given credit for having given the seller a purchase money mortgage at closing. A purchase money mortgage simply means the seller lends the buyer the money to purchase the property by agreeing to wait for the actual cash to be paid over a period of time. The seller is not going to get the cash at closing. This is treated just as if the buyer had given the seller $45,000 in cash toward the purchase price of $60,000 and thus is placed as a buyer credit. The fact that the seller received this mortgage results in an offsetting entry in the seller's debit column. This affects both parties.

Seller's Existing Mortgage

To have clear title to convey to the buyer, the seller must satisfy the existing mortgage. Because this is a seller expense, the payoff amount appears as a seller debit.

Cost of Preparing Mortgage

The buyer must have the purchase money mortgage to deliver to the seller; therefore, the buyer will pay for the preparation of the mortgage and note. This is a buyer debit.

Other Comments

All other entries appearing in Figure 9.4 are similar to those in Figure 9.3 for the cash sale statement. If you are unclear as to the other entries, refer to Figure 9.3 and the discussion of Figure 9.3.

Reconciliation

A good check to perform on statements for both buyer and seller is to verify that the money available for disbursement equals the expenses and money to be disbursed. The closing agent is to begin with a zero balance and, after disbursements at closing, end with a zero balance. To recap the reconciliation for the purchase money mortgage sample for the buyer and seller immediately preceding:

Money Available	
Earnest money	$ 2,000.00
Balance due from buyer	$12,737.47
Total available	$14,737.47
Money to Disburse	
Preparation of note and mortgage	$ 45.00
Deed recording	3.50
Mortgage recording	4.50
Title insurance binder	300.00
Seller's existing mortgage	5,000.00
Preparation of deed	40.00
Broker's commission	3,600.00
Proceeds due seller	5,744.47
Total to disburse	$14,737.47

The money available and the money to be disbursed to pay expenses and the seller are equal. The closing statement figures have been reconciled, and the closing agent can be assured that at the closing the exact funds needed will be available.

MORTGAGE ASSUMPTION STATEMENT

In the next example (see Figure 9.5), the buyer is assuming the seller's existing mortgage. The buyer is paying part of the purchase price by the assumption of this mortgage. In assuming the seller's existing mortgage, the buyer is agreeing to make the payments of the principal and interest as well as assuming the responsibility for the other conditions set out in the mortgage contract between the seller and seller's lender. In the illustration, $49,000 of the $65,000 purchase price is paid by the buyer's assumption.

> Closing date: November 13, 19XX
> Sales price: $65,000
> Earnest money deposit: $1,500
> Annual premium for new homeowner's insurance: $280
> Annual real property taxes: $300 prepaid
> Mortgage to be assumed by buyer: $49,000
> Interest rate on mortgage to be assumed: 9 percent
> Mortgage assumption fee: $135
> Deed preparation: $50
> Recording fee: $3.50
> Broker's commission: 6.5 percent

Analysis of Mortgage Assumption Statement

Prorated Real Property Taxes

The closing date in this sample is November 13, 19XX. The seller is responsible only for the real property taxes through the date of closing. Because the seller has paid the

FIGURE 9.5   A mortgage assumption closing statement.

Settlement Date: November 13, 19XX	Summary of Buyer's Transaction Debit	Summary of Buyer's Transaction Credit	Summary of Seller's Transaction Debit	Summary of Seller's Transaction Credit
Purchase Price	$65,000.00	$	$	$65,000.00
Earnest Money		1,500.00		
Insurance Premium	280.00			
Prorated Real Property Tax	39.17			39.17
Assumed Mortgage Balance		49,000.00	49,000.00	
Mortgage Interest Nov. 1–13		159.25	159.25	
Mortgage Assumption Fee	135.00			
Deed Recording	3.50			
Cost of Preparing the Deed			50.00	
Commission Due			4,225.00	
Balance Due from Buyer		14,798.42		
Proceeds Due to Seller			11,604.92	
Totals	$65,457.67	$65,457.67	$65,039.17	$65,039.17

taxes for the entire year, the seller will be reimbursed for 30 + 17 days of taxes. The amount represented by 47 days is $39.17 (rounded). This will appear as a credit to the seller and a debit to the buyer.

PUTTING IT TO WORK

Examples of items commonly paid outside closing (POC) include appraisal, credit report, loan application fee, and hazard insurance premium.

Mortgage Interest Through November 13

In transactions involving the buyer's assumption of the seller's existing mortgage, the interest rate is important in calculating the monthly interest. Monthly interest must be prorated to the date of closing for an equitable division between buyer and seller for the interest owed. Most mortgage loans are set up for the interest to be paid in arrears rather than in advance. In this illustration, the seller's interest was paid in arrears. The mortgage payment owed by the buyer on December 1 will include interest for the month of November. The seller is responsible for 13 days of the interest in November. Therefore, the buyer will be credited with 13 days of interest. A corresponding debit will appear in the seller's statement. The accrued interest will be a double-entry item. The calculation is:

$49,000 (mortgage assumed) × .09 (interest rate) = $4,410.00 annual interest
$4410.00 ÷ 12 = $367.50 monthly interest
$367.50 ÷ 30 = $12.25 daily interest
$12.25 × 13 = $159.25 owed by seller

Mortgage Assumption Fee

Lending institutions typically charge a fee to transfer the mortgage record from the seller to the buyer. The buyer who is assuming the mortgage pays the fee. Therefore, it appears as a single-entry buyer debit on the closing statement.

Other Comments

If the seller has a mortgage escrow account with the lender for the purpose of accumulating funds to pay the annual tax and insurance bills when they come due, the escrow account balance must be considered at the closing and shown on the closing statement. One way to handle this on the closing statement is to have the buyer purchase the account from the seller on a dollar-for-dollar basis. The entry on the closing statement would be a double entry for a prepaid item. The buyer would have a debit, and the seller would have a credit for the amount of the escrow account.

An alternative method would be for the buyer to establish *a new escrow account with the lender.* These accounts are also called **impound,** budget, or reserve **accounts.** The buyer then would make her own contributions to the account. This would require an entry as a buyer debit for the amount to be contributed to the new account at closing. The old escrow account could be refunded to the seller at closing or after the closing. If the refund is at the closing, the seller will have a credit for the amount of the account. If the refund is to be after the closing, no entry will appear.

(See Practice Problem 1: Mortgage Assumption on page 224 for an opportunity to apply the information studied in this section.)

NEW FIRST MORTGAGE STATEMENT

A new first mortgage statement represents a transaction in which the buyer is obtaining a new loan from a lending institution. The security for this loan is a first mortgage given by the buyer to the lending institution.

> Closing date: August 20, 19XX
> Sales price: $94,000
> Earnest money deposit: $2,500
> Annual premium for new insurance: $382
> New first mortgage: 80 percent of the sales price
> Annual real property taxes: $1,128 unpaid
> Seller's existing mortgage: $46,000
> Deed preparation: $60
> Mortgage preparation: $55
> Lender's title insurance: $2.50 per $1,000 of loan amount
> Credit report: $35
> Survey: $175
> Termite inspection: $50
> Loan origination fee: $752
> Deed recording: $7
> Mortgage recording: $10.50
> Broker's commission: 7 percent of sales price

Analysis of New First Mortgage Statement

The new first mortgage is shown as an entry only on the buyer's statement (see Figure 9.6). It is shown as a credit because this money is available to the buyer to be applied to the satisfaction of his obligations in the transaction. In this illustration, three sources of funds contribute to payment of the buyer's cost: earnest money, new first mortgage, and balance of money due from the buyer at closing. Several new expenses are reflected as buyer debits; these are additional expenses associated with the new first mortgage. The other entries have been covered in prior analysis.

(See Practice Problem 2: New First Mortgage on page 225 for an opportunity to apply the information studied in this section.)

FIGURE 9.6 New first mortgage closing statement.

Settlement Date: August 20, 19XX	Summary of Buyer's Transaction		Summary of Seller's Transaction	
	Debit	Credit	Debit	Credit
Purchase Price	$94,000.00	$	$	$94,000.00
Earnest Money		2,500.00		
Insurance Premium	382.00			
Real Property Taxes, Prorated		720.67	720.67	
First Mortgage		75,200.00		
Mortgage Preparation	55.00			
Title Insurance	188.00			
Credit Report	35.00			
Survey			175.00	
Loan Origination	752.00			
Deed Recording	7.00			
Mortgage Recording	10.50			
Existing Mortgage			46,000.00	
Deed Preparation			60.00	
Termite Inspection			50.00	
Commission Due			6,580.00	
Balance Due from Buyer		17,008.83		
Proceeds Due to Seller			40,414.33	
Totals	$95,429.50	$95,429.50	$94,000.00	$94,000.00

IMPORTANT POINTS

1. In Illinois, the seller usually is required to furnish and pay for a recent survey.
2. Taxes in Illinois are paid in arrears (the year following their levy).
3. An attorney, the lender, or a title company prepares the settlement statement in Illinois. Illinois real estate licensees are only allowed to prepare a statement in regard to escrow funds being held or paid out to the benefit of both parties.
4. Illinois does not have a personal property tax assessment.
5. The broker's earned commission usually is paid out of the earnest money being held in the broker's escrow account.

PRACTICE PROBLEM 1: MORTGAGE ASSUMPTION

Use the following information to prepare statements on the provided worksheet. The solution to this practice problem is found at the end of the chapter.

Settlement date: July 10, 19XX
Purchase price: $69,500
Earnest money deposit: $4,500
New insurance policy premium: $278
Annual real property taxes: $900 unpaid
Assumed mortgage balance: $42,000
Mortgage interest rate for July: 9% paid in advance
Mortgage assumption fee: $50

Purchase money second mortgage from buyer to seller: $9,000
Seller's escrow account for taxes and insurance (to be purchased by buyer at closing): $735
Deed preparation: $25
Second mortgage preparation: $30
Recording of deed and second mortgage: $8
Title insurance binder: $320
Lighting allowance given to buyer by seller for fixtures being removed by seller: $180
Broker's commission: 7½%

PRACTICE PROBLEM 1 Worksheet.

Settlement Date:	Summary of Buyer's Transaction		Summary of Seller's Transaction	
	Debit	Credit	Debit	Credit
Totals				

PRACTICE PROBLEM 2: NEW FIRST MORTGAGE

Use the following information to prepare statements on the provided worksheet. The solution to this practice problem is found at the end of the chapter.
Settlement date: July 18, 19XX
Purchase price: $140,000
Earnest money deposit: $10,000
New insurance premium: $497
New mortgage: 90% of the purchase price; 4 points to be paid by buyer
Annual real property taxes: $1,700 unpaid
Additional property assessment: $1,540 unpaid to be prorated

Seller's existing mortgage: $83,760
Private mortgage insurance: 1% of the loan
Deed preparation: $60
Deed of trust preparation: $50
Credit report: $50
Survey: $225
Termite clearance: $650
Loan service charge: 1% of the loan
Mortgagee's title insurance: $385
Recording fees: $12
Broker's commission: 6% of the sales price
Owner's title insurance: $785

PRACTICE PROBLEM 2 Worksheet.

Settlement Date:	Summary of Buyer's Transaction		Summary of Seller's Transaction	
	Debit	Credit	Debit	Credit
Totals				

SOLUTION TO PRACTICE PROBLEM 1: MORTGAGE ASSUMPTION

Settlement Date: July 10, 19XX	Summary of Buyer's Transaction Debit	Summary of Buyer's Transaction Credit	Summary of Seller's Transaction Debit	Summary of Seller's Transaction Credit
Purchase Price	$69,500.00	$	$	$69,500.00
Earnest Money Deposit		4,500.00		
Insurance Premium	278.00			
Prorated Real Property Taxes		475.00	475.00	
Assumed Mortgage		42,000.00	42,000.00	
Mortgage Interest	210.00			210.00
Mortgage Assumption Fee	50.00			
Purchase Money Second Mortgage		9,000.00	9,000.00	
Seller's Escrow Account	735.00			735.00
Cost of Preparing the Deed			25.00	
Cost of Preparing Second Mortgage	30.00			
Cost of Recordings	8.00			
Cost of Title Abstract			320.00	
Light Fixture Allowance		180.00	180.00	
Commission Due			5,212.50	
Balance Due from Buyer		14,656.00		
Proceeds Due to Seller			13,232.50	
Totals	$70,811.00	$70,811.00	$70,445.00	$70,445.00

SOLUTION TO PRACTICE PROBLEM 2: NEW FIRST MORTGAGE

Settlement Date: July 18, 19XX	Summary of Buyer's Transaction		Summary of Seller's Transaction	
	Debit	Credit	Debit	Credit
Purchase Price	$140,000.00	$	$	$140,000.00
Earnest Money		10,000.00		
Insurance Premium	497.00			
First Mortgage		126,000.00		
Discount Points	5,040.00			
Real Property Taxes		935.00	935.00	
Assessment		847.00	847.00	
Existing Mortgage			83,760.00	
P.M.I.	1,260.00			
Deed Preparation			60.00	
Deed of Trust	50.00			
Credit Report	50.00			
Survey			225.00	
Termite Clearance			650.00	
Loan Origination	1,260.00			
Owner's Title Insurance			785.00	
Mortgagee's Title Insurance	385.00			
Recording Fees	12.00			
Commission Due			8,400.00	
Balance Due from Buyer		10,772.00		
Proceeds Due to Seller			44,338.00	
Totals	$148,554.00	$148,554.00	$140,000.00	$140,000.00

Review Questions

Answers to these questions are found in the Answer Key section at the back of the book.

1. The amount of an assumed mortgage appears on the buyer's statement as a:
   a. credit
   b. debit
   c. reconciliation
   d. format

2. The amount of the earnest money deposit appears as a:
   a. seller's debit
   b. seller's credit
   c. buyer's debit
   d. buyer's credit

3. If property was listed for sale at $30,000 and sold for $28,500, the 6 percent broker's fee would appear in the seller's statement as a:
   a. debit of $1,800
   b. credit of $1,800
   c. debit of $1,710
   d. credit of $1,710

4. The cost of preparing a deed appears as a:
   a. seller's debit
   b. seller's credit
   c. buyer's debit
   d. buyer's credit

5. If the closing date is June 30 and seller's real property taxes of $664 for the calendar year are unpaid, the appropriate entry on the buyer's statement would be a:
   a. credit of $332
   b. debit of $664
   c. debit of $332
   d. credit of $664

6. The proper entry on the closing statements for a transaction closed on April 15, in which the buyer is purchasing the seller's insurance policy for which the seller paid an annual premium of $156 on November 30, would be:
   a. credit to seller of $97.50
   b. debit to buyer of $58.50
   c. debit to seller of $97.50
   d. credit to buyer of $58.50

7. A buyer purchased a rental property and closed the transaction on July 20. The tenant had paid rent for the month of July in the amount of $540 on July 1. The rent should be shown as a:
   a. debit to seller of $180
   b. debit to buyer of $180
   c. debit to seller of $360
   d. credit to buyer of $360

8. A purchase money mortgage appears as:
   a. credit to seller
   b. debit to seller
   c. debit to buyer
   d. prepaid by seller

9. The cost of recording a deed appears as a:
   a. debit to the buyer
   b. debit to the seller
   c. credit to the buyer
   d. credit to the seller

10. The test to determine a parcel's ability to support a septic system is:
    a. soil-bearing test
    b. percolation test
    c. EPA test
    d. radon test

CHAPTER 10

Important Terminology

- anticipation
- appraisal
- arm's-length transaction
- balance
- book value
- capitalization rate (cap rate)
- change
- chronological age
- comparable
- comparison approach
- competition
- conformity
- contribution
- correlation
- cost
- cost approach
- cubic-foot method
- depreciation
- economic obsolescence
- effective age
- FIRREA
- fixed expenses
- four agents of production
- functional obsolescence
- gentrification
- gross effective income
- GRM (gross rent multiplier)
- highest and best use
- historical cost index method
- income approach
- increasing and decreasing returns
- investment value
- market data method
- market value
- net operating income
- operating expenses
- operating statement
- progression
- quantity survey method
- regression
- replacement cost
- replacement reserve
- reproduction cost
- square-foot method
- substitution
- supply and demand
- surplus productivity
- transferability
- unit-in-place method
- USPAP
- utility
- vacancy rate
- value

Property Valuation

IN THIS CHAPTER Appraising is not an exact science. Uniformity in appraising, however, has developed by applying proven appraisal techniques developed by appraisal organizations such as the Society of Real Estate Appraisers and the Institute of Real Estate Appraisers, now merged to form the Appraisal Institute. These organizations offer continuing education programs for members to assure high quality standards of appraisers and the appraisals they produce. Specialized designations and certifications have been available to members for many years.

In 1989, President Bush signed into law the **Financial Institutions Reform, Recovery, and Enforcement Act (FIRREA),** more commonly known as the savings and loan bailout bill. Title XI of FIRREA *requires that appraisers completing appraisals for federally related financial transactions be licensed or certified and also mandates that the states set up licensing and certification programs.* Federally related financial transactions include loans made by institutions insured by the FDIC or loans sold to Ginnie Mae, Freddie Mac, Fannie Mae or any other governmental secondary mortgage market agency. FIRREA also requires all appraisals to meet the Uniform Standards of Professional Appraisal Practice (**USPAP**), *a constantly evolving document of new and revised requirements setting the standards to which appraisals must be performed.* It is incumbent on appraisers to keep up to date with USPAP.

In keeping with the federal mandate, Illinois has adopted Article II of the Illinois Real Estate License Act. Article II calls for the voluntary licensing or certification of appraisers. Therefore, in Illinois, if the appraisal assignment does not involve a federally related financial transaction, licensing or certification of the one doing the appraisal is not required. An appraiser in Illinois is not required to have a broker or salesperson license.

Professional fee appraisers concentrate their time, knowledge, and skill in appraising real estate. Even though real estate brokers and salespersons are not required to be professional appraisers, they need to have a working knowledge of the approaches to determining value of property to be listed and sold.

This chapter covers the various types of value that can be established by appraisals, factors and forces affecting appraisals, and the three approaches used in arriving at the appraised value.

DEFINING APPRAISAL AND VALUATION

An **appraisal** is *an estimate of value, based on factual data, on a particular property, at a particular time, for a particular purpose.* It is an objective opinion as to the worth of a given property. The opinion must be supported in writing with collected data and logical reasoning. The reasoning must follow one or more of the three appraisal approaches discussed later in the chapter. As the definition implies, the date of the appraisal affects the opinion of value

The purpose of an appraisal is to estimate some type of value, for instance, market value or investment value. There are several other types of value, which are explained later in this chapter. Generally **value** is the *quantity of one item given in exchange for another item.* The function of an appraisal is the use the appraisal is to be put to, such as property settlement in a divorce, protesting of real estate taxes, or pledging collateral for a loan.

Valuation Versus Evaluation

Valuation of a property establishes an opinion of value utilizing a totally objective approach. The person assigned to perform the valuation must base her opinion wholly upon facts relating to the property, such as age, square footage, location, cost to replace, and so on. A valuation is done to determine the market value of the property. **Market value** is defined by USPAP as:

> The most probable price in terms of money which a property will bring in a competitive and open market under all conditions requisite to a fair sale, the buyer and seller, each acting prudently, knowledgeably and assuming the price is not affected by undue stimulus.

Market value is the most probable price a property will bring if:

1. Buyer and seller are equally motivated.
2. Both parties are well informed or well advised, and each is acting in what the individual considers his own best interest.
3. A reasonable time is allowed for exposure in the open market.
4. Payment is made in cash or its equivalent.
5. Financing, if any, is on terms generally available in the community at the specified date and typical for the property type in its locale.
6. The price represents a normal consideration for the property sold, unaffected by special financing amounts or terms, services, fees, costs, or credits incurred in the transaction.

Implied in the definition of market value is an **arm's-length transaction,** which *is the standard under which two unrelated parties, each acting in her own best interest, would carry out a particular transaction.* For instance, a sale of property from a parent to a child or the sale of a property by an owner about to be foreclosed on are probably not arm's-length transactions. Whether these transactions are arm's-length transactions can only be determined by ascertaining what price the properties would bring if sold to a disinterested third party and without any undue urgency to sell, such as pending foreclosure.

Evaluation, on the other hand, is a study of the usefulness or utility of a property without reference to the specific estimate of value. Evaluation studies take the form of land utilization studies, highest and best use studies, marketability studies, and supply and demand studies. Evaluation of a property does not result in an estimate of value of the property.

Types of Value

The usual purpose of an appraisal is to estimate the market value of the particular property. In addition to market value, the following values are often the subject or purpose of an appraisal:

Assessed value
Investment value
Liquidation value
Value in use
Insurance value
Condemnation value
Book value

Assessed Value

The assessed value of real property is determined by a local official. It is the value to which a local tax rate is applied to establish the amount of tax imposed on the property. The assessed value, as set by statute or local ordinance, is normally a percentage of market value. This percentage may be up to 100 percent. Therefore, a combination of the rate of assessment and the equalization factor and the tax rate applied to the property is what determines the annual tax bill. Assessed value is calculated by using the formula: market value × assessment rate × equalization factor = equalized assessed value.

Investment Value

Market value was defined in part as the value to a typical purchaser. Investment value is defined as *the value to a specific purchaser.* Consider two prospective purchasers contemplating the purchase of the same 12-unit apartment building. Based on the purchasers' individual financial and income tax situations and investment requirements, the building will possibly have a different value to each of them.

Liquidation Value

Liquidation value is the price an owner is compelled to accept if the property cannot be adequately exposed in the marketplace.

Value in Use

Value in use is the value to an owner based on the productivity derived from the property. This is a subjective value based on the income or amenities associated with the owner's use of the property.

Insurance Value

In estimating the value of property as a basis for determining the amount of insurance coverage necessary to adequately protect the structure against loss by fire or other casualty, the insurance company is concerned with the cost of replacing or reproducing structures in the event of a total loss caused by an insured hazard. **Insurance value** is *the cost of replacing or reproducing the structure in the event of a total loss.* This cost is calculated by multiplying a square-foot replacement cost by the number of square feet in the structure, or it may involve more detailed analysis of component costs. Land value is not included in calculating insurance value.

Condemnation Value

When real property is taken under the power of eminent domain, the property owner is entitled to receive the fair market value of the property to compensate for the loss. Condemnation value in the case of condemnation of the entire property is not difficult to estimate. In the case of a partial condemnation, however, it becomes more complex. In this case, the property owner is entitled to be compensated for the difference in the market value of the property before and after condemnation. This amount is typically an amount greater than the value of the portion of property condemned as a percentage of the entire property value.

Book Value

Book value is *an artificial value used for accounting or tax purposes, in connection with establishing a depreciation schedule* for a property based on the property's useful life. Often, this useful life has nothing to do with the actual useful life of the property. In 1980 the tax schedule assumed a property had a useful life of 40 years; in 1981 this became 15 years, later 18 years, then 19 years, and now the useful life is 27.5 years for residential properties and 39 years for nonresidential.

Assuming a property currently may be assigned a tax life of 27.5 years, this provides a straight-line depreciation of 3.64 percent per year. If the property is 8 years old, the depreciation claimed is 3.64% × 8, or 29%; thus 71% (100% − 29%) has not depreciated. If the original cost of the property is $100,000, the present book value is $71,000.

Original cost	$100,000
8 years' depreciation	−29,000
Present book value	$ 71,000

APPRAISAL VERSUS COMPETITIVE MARKET ANALYSIS

An appraisal is an estimate of property value using the collected data in applying the three appraisal approaches: market data approach, cost approach, and income approach. Each of these three approaches may yield a different value. The appraiser then reconciles the differing values, applying accepted appraisal principles and methods. In some cases, one or more of the approaches may not be utilized in the reconciliation (such as ignoring the income approach in appraising single-family residential property).

A competitive market analysis (also called CMA) is an analysis of the competition in the marketplace that a property will face upon sale attempts. This procedure is not an appraisal. A CMA takes into consideration other properties currently on the market, properties taken off the market (expired listings), and properties that have recently sold. A CMA is similar to the market data approach of a true appraisal, which is only one of the three approaches to the value applied in each appraisal. A CMA is a comparison of properties and is prepared in the same fashion as the market data approach described later in this chapter. An example of a CMA is found later in this chapter in Figure 10.3.

BASIC REAL ESTATE APPRAISAL CONCEPTS

Characteristics of Real Property

An appraisal is an opinion of value. For property to have value, it must have certain legal and economic characteristics. These characteristics basic to all real property are:

1. utility
2. scarcity
3. transferability
4. effective demand

Utility

For the property to have value, it must have **utility,** *the ability to satisfy a need.* A property must be useful. It must be possible to use or adapt the property for some legal purpose. If a property cannot be put to some beneficial use to fill a need, it will not have value; nobody will want it.

Scarcity

The characteristic of scarcity is based on the supply of the property in relation to the effective demand for the property. The more abundant the supply of property in comparison with the effective demand for property, the lower the value. Conversely, the fewer properties available on the market in comparison with the effective demand or bidding for these properties, the greater the value of the properties.

Transferability

Transferability is a legal concept that must be present for a property to have value. The owner must *be able to shift the ownership interests to a prospective buyer.* These ownership interests include all of those previously discussed in the bundle of rights theory.

PUTTING IT TO WORK

Examples of property that may not have transferability include property in probate proceedings, property held in trust, property with options against it or with defeasible conditions, and co-owned properties.

Effective Demand

Effective demand is a desire or need for property together with the financial ability to satisfy the need. In times of excessively high interest rates, many people with a strong desire and substantial need for housing are priced out of the mortgage market; therefore, the demand for the property is *not* effective. The people who wish to buy do not have the ability to satisfy the demand. In creating housing or other types of properties, such as office buildings, shopping malls, and hotels, a developer must take into consideration not only the need for these types of property but also the financial ability of prospective tenants or purchasers to satisfy their needs.

Factors Affecting Value

Once a property is shown to be of value because it has utility, scarcity, transferability, and effective demand, many factors affect the value of the property in a negative or a positive way. These factors are divided into four categories: physical, economic, social, and governmental.

Physical Factors

The forces in this category are both natural and manmade. Natural physical factors that affect value are things such as land topography, soil conditions, mineral resources, size, shape, climate, and location. Manmade physical factors include public utilities, streets, highways, available public transportation, and access to streets and highways.

Economic Factors

Economic factors are typically separate from the real property being appraised. They include employment levels, median family income, interest rates, inflation, recession, and availability of credit.

Social Factors

Social factors include rates of marriage, births, divorces, and deaths; the rate of population growth or decline; and public attitudes toward things such as education, cultural activities, and recreation. The racial composition of an area is not a factor affecting value.

> **PUTTING IT TO WORK**
>
> In compliance with Fair Housing regulations, questions or comments regarding race and ethnicity are not appropriate in either the appraisal or marketing of property.

Governmental Factors

Governmental factors affecting value include regulations such as zoning laws, building codes, subdivision control ordinances, fire regulations, and city or county planning.

BASIC ECONOMIC VALUATION PRINCIPLES

Many economic principles may affect the value of real property. In establishing an estimate of value, an appraiser considers these principles.

Highest and Best Use

A property is valued at its **highest and best use,** which is the *use that gives the property its highest value.* Therefore, one of the appraiser's first considerations involves determining the highest and best use of a property. The appraiser determines the highest and best use of a property as if the land were vacant, even if a structure is currently on the land. To determine the highest and best use of the land, the appraiser must apply the following four tests:

1. *Physically possible.* The physical characteristics of the site and the proposed structure must be considered.
2. *Legally permissible.* The use must be legal under existing zoning, government planning, deed restrictions, and so on.
3. *Financially feasible.* There must be a need for the use, and the projected or anticipated need must be great enough to financially support the use.
4. *Maximally productive.* This is the ultimate test of highest and best use. There are probably several uses for a site that would meet the first three tests. However, only one of these possible uses will be maximally productive.

At a given point in time, a site can have only one highest and best use, which may change over a period of time. Determining the highest and best use of a property requires knowledge of the subject property, community, market forces, and principles of land utilization.

> **PUTTING IT TO WORK**
>
> A common example of changing conditions dictating change to a higher and better use is an older home in a downtown area being converted to professional office space for an attorney's office.

To accomplish the highest income and the highest present value of land, care must be taken not to create an overimprovement or an underimprovement. An overimprovement represents an added investment in property that does not yield a return to the owner. For example, creating too many apartment units with a high cost of maintenance may not yield sufficient income after paying capital and labor costs. Investment in the improvement exceeds the ability of the improvement to provide sufficient net income to cover the priority demands and still leave a residual income that will result in the highest land value. The same result occurs from underimprovement—insufficient investment in improving property. For example, if an insufficient number of apartment units are constructed, the improvement will not produce sufficient income to result in a net income to create maximum land value.

Either an underimprovement or an overimprovement will result in loss of property value (or failure to realize the property's full potential). Therefore, in adhering to the principle of highest and best use, the owner not only must establish a feasible use but also a use capable of supporting the improvements constructed plus a return of investment to the owner.

The principle of highest and best use also can be applied to the construction of a single-family residence. For example, if a house costs $125,000 to construct in a neighborhood of $75,000 houses, the result is an overimprovement. Conversely, a $50,000 house constructed in an area of homes valued at $125,000 and higher is an underimprovement. The principle of conformity, discussed later, also applies to this example.

Substitution

Under the principle of **substitution,** the *highest value of a property has a tendency to be established by the cost of purchasing or constructing another property of equal utility and desirability,* if the substitution can be made without unusual delay. Therefore, if two properties are on the market, each having the same degree of desirability and utility, one priced at $95,000 and the other at $100,000, a buyer would substitute the $95,000 property instead of purchasing the $100,000 property. The buyer will select the property that gives him or her the same amenities at the lesser price. Both the cost approach and the market data approach are heavily based upon the principle of substitution.

Supply and Demand

The economic principle of **supply and demand** is applicable to the real estate industry just as it is to other economic activities in the free enterprise system. This principle states that *the greater the supply of any commodity in comparison with the demand for that commodity, the lower the value will be.* Conversely, the smaller the supply and the greater the demand, the higher the value will be. Therefore, factors influencing the demand and supply of real estate affect property values either positively or negatively.

Conformity

Conformity means *"like kind" or compatible uses of land within a given area.* Adhering to the principle of conformity results in maximum property values. Failure to adhere to the principle results in inharmonious and incompatible uses of land within the area, with the consequence of depreciating property values. In residential subdivisions, conformity is achieved through restrictive covenants. In other areas, conformity is accomplished through zoning laws and subdivision ordinances. An example of a noncompatible use might be a "dome" home or "submerged home" in a subdivision of all ranch-style houses.

Progression and Regression

If a property fails to conform to an area, either regression or progression may be the result. **Regression** occurs *when the worth of a better property is diminished by the presence of a lesser quality property.* An example is a large, elegant home in a neighborhood of modest ranch-style homes. **Progression** signifies *an increase in the worth of a lesser property because of its location near higher quality properties.* An example is an older, smaller home in an area of new construction of larger homes.

Anticipation

Under the principle of **anticipation,** *property value is based on the expectation of future benefits of ownership.* The future, not the past, is what is important in estimating property value. Changes in the expected demand for property can stem from various improvements such as schools, shopping centers, freeways, or other developments deemed beneficial to the area. Therefore, real estate licensees and appraisers have to be aware of plans for future development in their local market area. Other changes adversely affect the expected demand for property. Changes in surrounding land use patterns, such as re-routing of traffic via a by-pass, have an adverse effect on future demand. Changes producing an increase in demand increase property value; changes leading to a reduction in demand cause a loss in value. The income approach is heavily based on the principle of anticipation.

Contribution

The principle of **contribution** states that *various elements of a property add value to the entire property.* For example, if a typical buyer is willing to pay $5,500 more for a property with a garage than for the same property without the garage, we infer that the element (garage) adds a value of $5,500 by itself.

The market data approach to valuing property utilizes this principle. To establish value, adjustments are made for differences between the comparable properties and the property that is being appraised. For example, the appraisal property has a fireplace—the element of contribution—whereas a comparable does not. The appraiser must estimate the value the fireplace contributes to the property as a whole and compare it to the value the property has in the absence of the fireplace. The appraiser extracts the contributed value from comparisons of properties in the market with and without the element. The values extracted will vary from area to area.

> **PUTTING IT TO WORK**
>
> An element's contribution may not be related to its cost. For example, a fireplace upgrade in a new home may cost $3,500, but when the home is resold, the buying market may be willing to pay only an additional $2,000 for the improvement. The contribution of the fireplace is thus $2,000.

Increasing and Decreasing (Diminishing) Returns

Under the principle of increasing and decreasing (or diminishing) returns, an improvement to a structure is not valued as a separate element. The cost of the improvement is compared to the increase in value to the property after the improvement is completed. Under **decreasing returns,** *the increase in value is less than the cost of the improvement.* Under **increasing returns,** *the increase in value is more than the cost of the improvement.*

This principle becomes important when a property owner is considering placing property for sale. Any fix-up expenses the owner incurs prior to sale should have an increasing return effect. If the fix-up cost is greater than the potential increase in sales price, the owner may not want to do the fix-up.

Competition

The principle of **competition** states that *when the net profit a property generates is great (excessive), others will be drawn to produce similar properties.* Excessive profits are generated when demand exceeds supply. For example, if a growth area contains only one or two properties of a certain type, such as apartment complexes, these properties will produce excess profits because of the high demand. Competitors who build apartment complexes will come to the area eager to share in the market and profits. Competition will work to reduce excess profits, and the supply of competing services will increase until excess profits are finally eliminated.

Balance

The principle of **balance** holds that *a property's value is affected by the balance of the four agents of production.* The **four agents of production** consist of *labor or wages, capital, management or coordination, and land.* This principle applies to the costs of production of both personal and real property. The various components of the agents of production are all related and must be maintained in an economic balance.

In real properties, the most important element of balance is the relationship between the improvements (labor, capital, and management) and the land. For instance, someone does not build a $500,000 house on a $15,000 lot. The improvements are out of balance. Likewise, someone should not build a $100,000 house on a $100,000 lot. Again, the agents are out of balance.

After labor, capital, and management have been satisfied, the amount remaining is called **surplus productivity.** This amount is imputed to the land; that is, it is the value of the land. This is the source of the axiom *the value of the land is residual.*

Change

The principle of **change** states that *constantly differing conditions affect land use and therefore continually impact the value.* Every property and every area are constantly undergoing change. Nothing remains the same. The only constant is that change will occur. Change may cause a value to go up (appreciate) or go down (depreciate). Change may come from a physical or an economic condition relating to the property or surrounding property.

Growth, Equilibrium, and Decline

The principle of growth, equilibrium, and decline acknowledges that properties and neighborhoods go through life cycles. The *growth stage,* also known as the integration or development stage, is the stage during which the neighborhood is being built up. There is a great deal of new construction taking place. Prospective buyers consider the area a "hot area." Prices in the area rise faster than in surrounding areas due to a shortage of listings to satisfy demand. Buyers will find themselves in bidding wars, driving up prices.

After a while, this neighborhood will cease to be considered the most desirable, and new hot areas will spring up. Values during this *equilibrium stage* will tend to rise because of housing inflation, rather than because of high appreciation rates caused by bidding wars.

Finally, the area and individual properties will suffer a period of *decline.* This period is identified by properties that are deteriorating due to deferred maintenance. Owners patch a leaky roof rather than replace it. The owners believe that if they pay to replace the roof, they will not sufficiently recover the roof's cost from the property when it is sold. After a neighborhood has been in decline for some time, it is likely that the neighborhood will attract entrepreneurs that will begin speculating in the area's housing. If these first speculators are successful, the area is on its way to **gentrification,** *the upgrading of a neighborhood to a more affluent one.*

Age

Every structure may have two different ages: chronological and effective. The **chronological age** of a structure is measured by *the number of years the structure has existed.* This is similar to the age of a person. The **effective age** refers to *the age that the structure appears to be.* If a property is well maintained, it may seem to be younger than it actually is chronologically. Conversely, the effective age may be greater than the chronological age if adequate maintenance and modernization measures have not been taken.

APPRAISAL METHODOLOGY

An appraisal is an estimate of property value based on factual data. In estimating property value, an organized and systematic program must be followed. The following steps provide an orderly progression of the appraisal process.

1. Define the appraisal problem or purpose. This includes determining the purpose of the appraisal and the type of value to be estimated. The purpose of the appraisal may prescribe the approaches to be implemented. If the appraisal is for repairs from fire damage, the cost approach may be more appropriate. For a lender's appraisal, the market data approach makes more sense.

2. Obtain a complete and accurate description of the property that is to be appraised. The appraisal report must contain a legal description of the property to precisely locate and identify the property. The identification must specifically define the limits of the area included in the appraisal.
3. Inspect the surrounding area and the property to be appraised. Determine which properties in the area will be used in comparison.
4. Collect the specific data required as the basis for the value estimate. This information will be gathered from several sources including government offices, recent real estate sales records, zoning changes, and so on.
5. Analyze the data and consider the three approaches of market, cost, and income. Arrive at a value estimate by each of these three appraisal methods if each can be applied.
6. Correlate and reconcile the results obtained by each of the three methods. The reconciliation will determine the estimate of value.
7. Prepare the appraisal report. A sample uniform residential appraisal report form is shown in Figure 10.1.

APPROACHES TO VALUE: MARKET, INCOME, COST

Market Data or Comparison Approach

The **market data method,** or **comparison approach,** is the primary appraisal approach for estimating the value of single-family, owner-occupied dwellings and vacant land. It involves *comparing the property that is the subject of the appraisal (subject property) with other properties offering similar utility that have sold recently.* These are called **comparables,** or comps. No two properties are exactly alike; however, many are similar in desirability and utility. Adjustments are made for the differences by following the principle of contribution.

A minimum of three comparables is generally used in an appraisal. However, an appraiser will use as many comparables as necessary to support the appraised value. Comparables may be found in real estate office files of closed sales, in the closed sales data of a multiple listing service, in the county clerk or recorder's office, in the assessor's office, and from other appraisers. The more recent the date of sale of the comparable, the more valuable the comparable is to the appraisal process. Also of great importance is the degree of similarity of physical characteristics of the comparables and the location of the comparables.

In selecting the comparables, certain property characteristics and nonproperty characteristics of each comparable must be specifically identified. Property characteristics include things such as size, type of construction, age, design, special features, and location. Nonproperty characteristics include the date of sale, verified sales price, method of financing, length of time on the market, and the seller's motivation in the sale.

Before using the market data comparison shown in Figure 10.3, an important point to understand is that the data values assigned as adjustments are the result of careful analysis of appraiser records. The numbers are not pulled arbitrarily from the air but, rather, derive from comparable sales analysis data from the appraiser's files. The appraiser should verify all comparable data provided by a party involved in the sales transaction. The number used in the adjustments is not the cost to build the element being compared. **Cost** is defined as *the dollars needed to construct the element,* market value is defined as what the market will pay for the element. This is an application of the principle of contribution. Cost is not the same as market value. To arrive at the value of an element, the agent must constantly determine from the marketplace

FIGURE 10.1
A uniform residential appraisal report.

Property Description **UNIFORM RESIDENTIAL APPRAISAL REPORT** **File No.**

SUBJECT

Property Address | City | State | Zip Code
Legal Description | County
Assessor's Parcel No. | Tax Year | R.E. Taxes $ | Special Assessments $
Borrower | Current Owner | Occupant: ☐ Owner ☐ Tenant ☐ Vacant
Property rights appraised ☐ Fee Simple ☐ Leasehold | Project Type ☐ PUD ☐ Condominium (HUD/VA only) | HOA$ /Mo.
Neighborhood/Project Name | Map Reference | Census Tract
Sale Price $ | Date of Sale | Loan charges/concessions to be paid by seller $
Lender/Client | Address
Appraiser | Address

NEIGHBORHOOD

Location	☐ Urban	☐ Suburban	☐ Rural	**Predominant occupancy**	**Single family housing** PRICE $ (000) / AGE (yrs)	**Present land use %**	**Land use change**
Built up	☐ Over 75%	☐ 25-75%	☐ Under 25%			One Family	☐ Not Likely ☐ Likely
Growth Rate	☐ Rapid	☐ Stable	☐ Slow	☐ Owner	Low	2-4 family	☐ In process
Property values	☐ Increasing	☐ Stable	☐ Declining	☐ Tenant	High	Multi-family	To:
Demand/supply	☐ Shortage	☐ In balance	☐ Over supply	☐ Vacant (0-5%)	Predominant	Commercial	
Marketing time	☐ Under 3 mos.	☐ 3-6 mos.	☐ Over 6 mos.	☐ Vacant (over 5%)			

Note: Race and the racial composition of the neighborhood are not considered reliable appraisal factors.

Neighborhood boundaries and characteristics:

Factors that affect the marketability of the properties in the neighborhood (proximity to employment and amenities, employment stability, appeal to market, etc):

Market conditions in the subject neighborhood (including support for the above conclusions related to the trend of property values, demand/supply, and marketing time -- such as data on competitive properties for sale in the neighborhood, description of the prevalence of sales and financing concessions, etc.):

PUD

Project Information for PUDs (If applicable) -- Is the developer/builder in control of the Home Owners' Association (HOA)? ☐ Yes ☐ No
Approximate total number of units in the subject project . Approximate total number of units for sale in the subject project .
Describe common elements and recreational facilities:

SITE

Dimensions | Topography
Site area | Corner Lot ☐ Yes ☐ No | Size
Specific zoning classification and description | Shape
Zoning compliance ☐ Legal ☐ Legal nonconforming (Grandfathered use) ☐ Illegal ☐ No zoning | Drainage
Highest & best use as improved: ☐ Present use ☐ Other use (explain) | View

Utilities	Public	Other	**Off-site Improvements**	Type	Public	Private	
Electricity	☐		Street		☐	☐	Landscaping
Gas	☐		Curb/Gutter		☐	☐	Driveway Surface
Water	☐		Sidewalk		☐	☐	Apparent easements / FEMA Special Flood Hazard Area ☐ Yes ☐ No
Sanitary sewer	☐		Street lights		☐	☐	FEMA Zone / Map Date
Storm sewer	☐		Alley		☐	☐	FEMA Map no.

Comments (apparent adverse easements, encroachments, special assessments, slide areas, illegal or legal nonconforming zoning, use, etc.):

DESCRIPTION OF IMPROVEMENTS

GENERAL DESCRIPTION	EXTERIOR DESCRIPTION	FOUNDATION	BASEMENT	INSULATION
No. of Units	Foundation	Slab	Area Sq. Ft.	Roof ☐
No. of Stories	Exterior Walls	Crawl Space	% Finished	Ceiling ☐
Type (Det./Att.)	Roof Surface	Basement	Ceiling	Walls ☐
Design (Style)	Gutters & Dwnspts.	Sump Pump	Walls	Floor ☐
Existing/Proposed	Window Type	Dampness	Floor	None ☐
Age (Yrs.)	Storm/Screens	Settlement	Outside Entry	Unknown ☐
Effective Age (Yrs.)	Manufactured House	Infestation		Adequacy ☐

ROOMS	Foyer	Living	Dining	Kitchen	Den	Family Rm.	Rec. Rm.	Bedrooms	# Baths	Laundry	Other	Area Sq. Ft.
Basement												
Level 1												
Level 2												

Finished area **above** grade contains: Rooms; Bedroom(s); Bath(s); Square Feet of Gross Living Area

SURFACES Materials/Condition	HEATING	KITCHEN EQUIP.	ATTIC	AMENITIES	CAR STORAGE:
Floors	Type	Refrigerator ☐	None ☐	Fireplace(s) # ☐	None ☐
Walls	Fuel	Range/Oven ☐	Stairs ☐	Patio ☐	Garage # of cars
Trim/Finish	Condition	Disposal ☐	Drop Stair ☐	Deck ☐	Attached
Bath Floor	COOLING	Dishwasher ☐	Scuttle ☐	Porch ☐	Detached
Bath Wainscot	Central	Fan/Hood ☐	Floor ☐	Fence ☐	Built-In
Doors	Other	Microwave ☐	Heated ☐	Pool ☐	Carport
	Condition	Washer/Dryer ☐	Finished ☐		Driveway

COMMENTS

Additional features (special energy efficient items, etc.):

Condition of the improvements, depreciation (physical, functional, and external), repairs needed, quality of construction, etc.:

Adverse environmental conditions (such as, but not limited to, hazardous wastes, toxic substances, etc.) present in the improvements, on the site, or in the immediate vicinity of the subject property.:

Freddie Mac Form 70 6-93 | 12 CH. | PAGE 1 OF 2 | Fannie Mae Form 1004B 6-93

(continued)

FIGURE 10.1
Continued.

Valuation Section

UNIFORM RESIDENTIAL APPRAISAL REPORT

File No.

COST APPROACH

ESTIMATED SITE VALUE .... = $

ESTIMATED REPRODUCTION COST-NEW-OF IMPROVEMENTS

Dwelling ______ Sq. Ft @ $ ______ = $ ______

______ Sq. Ft @ $ ______ = ______

= ______

= ______

Garage/Carport ______ Sq. Ft @ $ ______ = ______

Total Estimated Cost New .... = $ ______

Less | Physical | Functional | External

Depreciation ______ = $ ______

Depreciated Value of Improvements .... = $ ______

"As-is" Value of Site Improvements .... = $ ______

INDICATED VALUE BY COST APPROACH .... = $ ______

Comments on Cost Approach (such as, source of cost estimate, site value, square foot calculation, and for HUD, VA and FmHA, the estimated remaining economic life of the property): ______

SALES COMPARISON ANALYSIS

ITEM	SUBJECT	COMPARABLE NO. 1		COMPARABLE NO. 2		COMPARABLE NO. 3	
Address							
Proximity to Subject							
Sales Price	$		$		$		$
Price/Gross Liv. Area	$ ⌀	$ ⌀		$ ⌀		$ ⌀	
Data and/or Verification Sources							
VALUE ADJUSTMENTS	DESCRIPTION	DESCRIPTION	+(-) $ Adjustment	DESCRIPTION	+(-) $ Adjustment	DESCRIPTION	+(-) $ Adjustment
Sales or Financing Concessions							
Date of Sale/Time							
Location							
Leasehold/Fee Simple							
Site							
View							
Design and Appeal							
Quality of Construction							
Age							
Condition							
Above Grade Room Count	Total Bdrms Baths	Total Bdrms Baths		Total Bdrms Baths		Total Bdrms Baths	
Gross Living Area	Sq. Ft.	Sq. Ft.		Sq. Ft.		Sq. Ft.	
Basement & Finished Rooms Below Grade							
Functional Utility							
Heating/Cooling							
Energy Efficient Items							
Garage/Carport							
Porch, Patio, Deck Fireplaces, etc.							
Fence, Pool, etc.							
Net Adj. (total)		+ -	$	+ -	$	+ -	$
Adjusted Sales Price of Comparable		Gross % Net %	$	Gross % Net %	$	Gross % Net %	$

Comments on Sales Comparison (including the subject property's compatibility to the neighborhood, etc.): ______

ITEM	SUBJECT	COMPARABLE NO. 1	COMPARABLE NO. 2	COMPARABLE NO. 3
Date, Price and Data Source for prior sales within year of appraisal				

Analysis of any current agreement of sale, option, or listing of the subject property and analysis of any prior sales of subject and comparables within one year of the date of appraisal:

INDICATED VALUE BY SALES COMPARISON APPROACH .... $ ______

INDICATED VALUE BY INCOME APPROACH (If Applicable) Estimated Market Rent $ ______ /Mo. x Gross Rent Multiplier ______ = $ ______

RECONCILIATION

This appraisal is made ☐ "as is" ☐ subject to the repairs, alterations, inspections or conditions listed below ☐ subject to completion per plans and specifications.

Conditions of Appraisal: ______

Final Reconciliation: ______

The purpose of this appraisal is to estimate the market value of the real property that is the subject of this report, based on the above conditions and the certification, contingent and limiting conditions, and market value definition that are stated in the attached Freddie Mac Form 439/Fannie Mae Form 1004B (Revised ______).

I (WE) ESTIMATE THE MARKET VALUE, AS DEFINED, OF THE REAL PROPERTY THAT IS THE SUBJECT OF THIS REPORT, AS OF ______ (WHICH IS THE DATE OF INSPECTION AND THE EFFECTIVE DATE OF THIS REPORT) TO BE $ ______.

APPRAISER:		SUPERVISORY APPRAISER (ONLY IF REQUIRED):	
Signature		Signature	☐ Did ☐ Did Not Inspect Property
Name		Name	
Date Report Signed		Date Report Signed	
State Certification #	State	State Certification #	State
Or State License #	State	Or State License #	State

Freddie Mac Form 70 6-93 12 CH. PAGE 2 OF 2 Fannie Mae Form 1004B 6-93

FIGURE 10.2 Approaches to determining value (appraisal methods).

1. The Market Data Method:
   Compares subject to similar properties and makes appropriate adjustments.

2. The Income Method:
   Applies capitalization formula to forecasted income or income produced (rent).

3. The Cost Method:
   Theoretically rebuilds the structure new, and then adjusts to its present condition by subtracting depreciation.

PUTTING IT TO WORK

Many people are frustrated by the adjustments appraisers make for differences in features; they often think the adjustments are too low or too high. No book or single resource says, "Bathroom: $1,500" or "Garage: $2,500." Instead, the appraiser's files, experience, and expertise justify the adjustment figures.

what the average buyer will pay for the element being compared. This value is based upon facts determined to exist in the area of the subject property and the comparables.

All data used in making adjustments between the comparable properties and the subject property must be laid out in the orderly, detailed, and accurate manner shown in Figure 10.3. The comparison sets forth all the property and nonproperty characteristics utilized in this specific value estimate.

As can be seen, plus and minus adjustments are made to the comparable properties to reconcile the differences and arrive at a value estimate for the subject property on the basis of the prices for which the comparables sold (see Figure 10.4). A plus adjustment to a comparable is made when the comparable is deficient in some respect when compared to the subject property. This is illustrated in Figure 10.3 by the square footage main adjustment of plus $2,040 in Comparable #1, made because of less square footage in the main floor of Comparable #1. The adjustment indicates that Comparable #1 would have sold for $2,040 more if its main floor had been as large as the subject property.

A minus adjustment is made to a comparable when it contains an additional feature that the subject property does not, rendering the comparable superior to the subject property. For example, an adjustment of minus $1,000 is made to Comparable #2 because it has 2.5 bathrooms instead of the 2.0 in the subject property. Therefore, if Comparable #2 had only 2.0 bathrooms, theoretically it would have sold for $1,000 less.

After making all adjustments, the net adjustment amount for each comparable is calculated and the result is applied to the price for which the comparable sold, to arrive at an adjusted price. The adjusted price is an estimate of the price for which the comparable would have sold if all features and factors had been the same as the subject property. The three adjusted prices are correlated or reconciled to arrive at an indicated market value for the subject property. This reconciliation is reached by calculating a weighted average, in which comparables with a high degree of similarity are given more weight than comparables with less similarity. In Figure 10.3, Comparable #3 is given the greatest weight because it requires the fewest adjustments. Next in order of similarity is Comparable #1, which is located in the same subdivision as the subject property. Comparable #2 is given the least weight because it is located in a different subdivision.

Property Valuation   245

FIGURE 10.3   The market data approach.

Prepared Especially for:
John and Susan Mitchell

Prepared by:
Grace Sanford,
Levittown Real Estate

Date:
January 9, 1997

Medium Range Adj	SUBJECT	COMPARABLE 1 of 3	COMPARABLE 2 of 3	COMPARABLE 3 of 3
ADDRESS	2735 Hawthorne	2815 Hemingway	3270 Melville	4520 Thoreau Ct.
PROXIMITY	Carriage Estates	Carriage Estates	Heath Heights	Foxpointe
Style	Ranch/Rambler	Ranch/Rambler	Ranch/Rambler	Ranch/Rambler
Construction	Fr Stucco	Ced Stone 0	Brick 0	Brick 0
Date Sold		July 1996 238	Nov 1996 856	Sept 1996 907
Effective Age	12	12 0	14 1,000	11 (500)
Sq Ft Total	1,544	1,442	1,654	1,608
Sq Ft Main	1,544	1,442 2,040	1,654 (2,200)	1,608 (1,280)
Sq Ft Up	0	0 0	0 0	0 0
Sq Ft Down	0	0 0	0 0	0 0
Pct Down Finished	0	0	0	0
Acreage/Lot Size	120 x 80	120 × 85	125 x 80	115 x 97
Value of Lot	$4,500	$4,500 0	$4,500 0	$4,500 0
Price/Sq Ft Inc Lot	$60 (Adj Ave)	$66	$56	$57
Price/Sq Ft Exc Lot	$57 (Adj Ave)	$62	$54	$54
Bedrooms Total	3	3 0	3 0	3 0
Bedrooms Main	3	3	3	3
Bedrooms Up	0	0	0	0
Bedrooms Down	0	0	0	0
Baths Total	2.0	2.0 0	2.5 (1,000)	2.0 0
Baths Main	2.0	2.0	2.5	2.0
Baths Up	0.0	0.0	0.0	0.0
Baths Down	0.0	0.0	0.0	0.0
Fireplaces	1	1 0	1 0	1 0
Air Conditioning	Central	Central 0	Central 0	Central 0
Garage	2.0	2.0 0	2.0 0	2.0 0
Swimming Pool	0	0 0	0 0	0 0
Semi Annual Tax	852.16	697.12 0	691.04 0	820.51 0
Assessment	22360	21400 0	22060 0	25530 0
Fenced Yard	Privacy	0	Privacy 0	Privacy 0
Double Storage Blg		0	0	0
Fruit Trees		0	0	0
Listed Price		$94,500 Adjustment	$96,000 Adjustment	$93,500 Adjustment
Sales Price		$94,500 $2,278	$93,000 ($1,344)	$92,000 ($873)
ADJ. SALES PRICE		$96,778	$91,656	$91,127

Comp 1:   35% × $96,778 = $33,872
Comp 2:   25% × $91,656 = $22,914
Comp 3:   40% × $91,127 = $36,451

Reconciled price: $33,872 + $22,914 + $36,451 = $93,237

FIGURE 10.4 Adjusting comparables to subject property.

When adjusting comparables to subject property, an appraiser must add to inferior properties and subtract from superior comparables to arrive at an adjusted comparison. In this example, the inferior property has no garage, the subject property has a one-car garage, and the superior property has a two-car garage. The appraiser must adjust for these discrepancies.

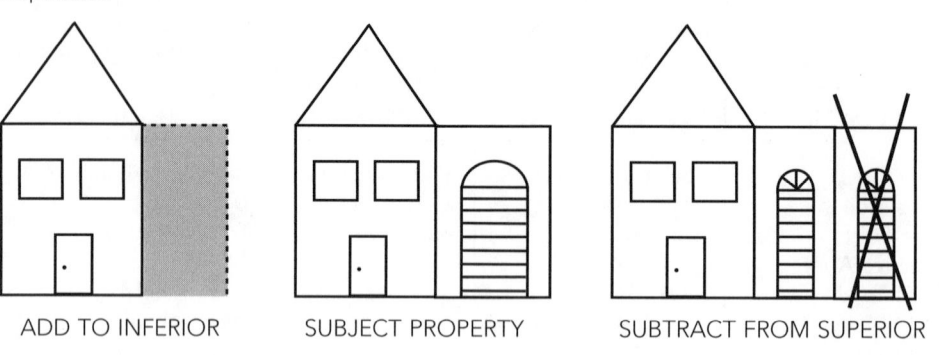

ADD TO INFERIOR — SUBJECT PROPERTY — SUBTRACT FROM SUPERIOR

Income Approach

The **income approach,** also called appraisal by capitalization, is the primary method used to estimate the present value of properties that produce income. Properties included in this category are apartment complexes, single-family rental houses, mobile home parks, office buildings, shopping malls, parking lots, leased industrial plants, and any individual properties occupied by commercial tenants. The *value of the property is estimated by converting net annual income into an indication of present value by application of a capitalization rate.* This procedure is illustrated in Figure 10.5 and the accompanying analysis. It shows an **operating statement** *stating income, vacancy rate, and expenses.* The information provided is used in the analysis, which applies the **capitalization formula:**

Value × capitalization rate = annual net income

Analysis of Operating Statement

The apartment complex has a potential gross income of $1,350,000. This is the income that would be produced if every apartment were rented 100 percent of the time at $450 per month for a 12-month period. To expect any rental property to be occupied 100 percent of the time on a continuing basis is unrealistic. Therefore, the potential gross income must be reduced by the **vacancy rate** and credit loss. This example estimates the vacancy rate at 6 percent. The credit loss may include uncollected rent from defaulting tenants. In the example, the vacancy and credit losses are expected to reduce the gross potential income by $81,000.

This apartment complex has other income generated by vending machines and laundry facilities that the tenants use. This income is projected to be $25,000 per year. *Any income added to the rental income yields the* **gross effective income.** The gross effective income in our example is $1,294,000. This is the amount of money the complex may realistically be expected to generate in a 12-month period.

To arrive at the net income, which is the number used in the capitalization formula, various expenses must be subtracted from the gross effective income. These expenses are categorized into fixed expenses, operating expenses, and replacement reserve.

Fixed expenses are *costs that do not fluctuate with the operating level of the complex.* They will remain the same whether the occupancy rate is 95 percent or 50 percent. These include real property taxes, insurance, licenses, and permits. The fixed

OPERATING STATEMENT

250 unit apartment complex with rent schedule of $450 per month per unit.

Potential Gross Income: 250 × $450 × 12		$1,350,000
Less Vacancy and Credit Losses (6%)		(81,000)
Plus Other Income		25,000
Gross Effective Income		$1,294,000
Less Expenses		
Fixed Expenses:		
Property Insurance	$24,500	
Property Taxes	95,300	
Licenses and Permits	1,200	($121,000)
Operating Expenses:		
Maintenance	$106,000	
Utilities	103,200	
Supplies	16,000	
Advertising	7,500	
Legal & Accounting	15,000	
Wages & Salaries	90,000	
Property Management	64,700	($402,400)
Replacement Reserve:		($ 25,000)
Total Expenses		$548,400
Net Operating Income		$745,600

FIGURE 10.5
A sample operating statement.

expenses in the illustration total $121,000 and are 9.35 percent of the gross effective income.

Operating expenses, or variable expenses, in general *fluctuate with the operating level* or occupancy of the property. As in the example, maintenance is the major operating expense, totaling $106,000. This expense varies with level of operation and is related to the age and condition of the property. Older properties naturally have more expenditures for maintenance than newer properties do. The property manager's fee also is an operating expense. Property managers typically are paid on a percentage of gross income. This fee increases with high occupancy and decreases with lower occupancy. Total operating expenses of the sample complex are $402,400, or 31.1 percent of the gross effective income. Of the three types of expenses, operating expenses typically represent the largest dollar amount.

A **replacement reserve** represents *an amount of money set aside to replace equipment* and make improvements. Replaced equipment may be hot water heaters, ranges, ovens, dishwashers, and disposals, for example. Typical improvements are pavement and roofs. Setting aside an amount of money for this purpose each year enables the project to avoid the impact of substantial expenditures in any given year when a number of the items must be replaced. In the illustration, the replacement reserve is $25,000.

The total of the three types of expenses equals $548,400, which represents 42.38 percent of the gross effective income. For appraisal purposes, debt service (mortgage principal and interest payments) is not included in the list of expenses. Debt service is considered a personal obligation of the property owner. Thus, the appraisal process puts all comparable properties on the same basis by eliminating items that vary substantially from one property to another and one owner to another.

Also not included is any tax or accounting depreciation on the building. These items do not reflect expenditures that will adjust the cash flow. **Net operating income** is determined by *subtracting the expenses from the gross effective income.* The annual net operating income in the illustration is $745,600.

The final step in estimating the value of the property by the income approach is to apply the capitalization formula given earlier. This involves dividing the annual net income by the capitalization rate. The difficulty lies in arriving at the proper capitalization rate. A number of complex methods are used to establish this rate. They are beyond the scope of this discussion and typically are not covered in pre-licensing courses. In essence, the **capitalization rate**, or **cap rate**, is *the rate that other investors are achieving on like investments in the same area*. This is called direct or market capitalization.

In the illustration of the apartment complex, we will use the capitalization rate of 12 percent. Dividing the annual net operating income by 0.12 yields a value estimate of $6,213,333. The numbers used in our example are estimates, based on projection and speculation that the property and economy will continue to perform as in the past. These figures and assumptions are not guaranteed. Further, the computations do not account for the investor's income tax or financing efforts.

Capitalization rates are made up of two elements: the return *of* the investment and the return *on* the investment. If $100 is deposited into a passbook account paying 3 percent at a local bank, at the end of the year the depositor will be entitled to $103. The $100 is the return *of* the investment, and the $3 is the return *on* the investment. Real estate is considered a wasting asset, meaning that it is supposed to wear out, although it probably increases in value. Therefore, the capitalization rate must be high enough for the owner to have recovered the original investment, the return *of* the investment, before the end of the economic life of the property.

The capitalization rate must also be high enough to include a return *on* the investment, which includes a safe rate, risk rate, management rate, and nonliquidity rate. The passbook account paying 3 percent represents a safe rate. However, investors will not invest in real estate to yield only a safe rate. They must also be compensated for the risk involved in a real estate investment. However, there are many alternative investments that will compensate the investor for a higher risk with a higher return. If all the investment will yield is a rate equal to the alternative investment, an investor will not get involved in a real estate investment. To become involved in a real estate investment, the investor will also need to be compensated for management. There is little or no management to a passbook account or similar investment. However, the investor must manage or hire a manager to manage the real estate investment. In addition, a real estate investment is not very liquid. The investor cannot go to the property and withdraw $100. He will have to either refinance the property or sell it, both of which cost time and money in fees. If the capitalization rate is not high enough to attract investors, money goes out of the real estate market into other investments.

The importance of selecting a proper capitalization rate cannot be overemphasized. Even a slight variation in this rate will result in a substantial change in the estimate of value. For example, if a 13 percent rate had been used in the foregoing example, the value estimate would be $5,735,385, which represents a reduction in estimated value of 7.69 percent. The higher the capitalization rate, the lower the estimated value; the lower the capitalization rate, the higher the estimated value. Other examples applying the capitalization rate are found in Chapter 17, on real estate mathematics.

Gross Rent Multiplier

A simplified variation from the capitalization appraisal is found in the gross rent multiplier (GRM) or the gross income multiplier (GIM). This approach is not truly a part

Figure 10.6 Computation and application of gross rent multiplier.

A. $\dfrac{\text{Comparable's Sales Price}}{\text{Rent}} = \text{GRM}$

B. Subject's Rent × GRM = Estimate of Subject's Value

of the income approach but may be used to estimate income-producing properties by sales comparison. **GRM** is *a factor calculated from comparing sales of 1–4 unit residential income-producing properties and the gross rental income of said properties.* GIM is the same factor applied to commercial or industrial properties or residential properties of five or more units. GIM may also include sources of income other than rent.

This method has a degree of unreliability because calculations are based on the gross income rather than the net income. If the property is managed efficiently, the gross income provides a reliable basis for calculating an estimate of value. If expenses are extraordinary, however, gross income does not accurately reflect the property value.

Gross rent multipliers are calculated by dividing the price for which a property sold by the monthly rental income. A gross income multiplier uses the gross annual income in calculations on larger residential (more than 1–4 family), commercial, and industrial properties.

In estimating the value on an income-producing property, gross rental incomes may be obtained for comparable income-producing properties that have sold recently. An average of the gross rent multipliers obtained can be used as a multiplier for the monthly gross (or annual gross) income produced by a property that is being valued. Figure 10.7 illustrates sales prices and monthly gross income of several income-producing properties. The calculation of the GRM is also shown. If the GRM in Figure 10.7 is applied to a subject property with $99,000 gross monthly income, the estimated value would be:

$99,000 × 58 = $5,742,000

Cost Approach or Approach by Summation

The **cost approach** in appraisal is the *main method for estimating the value of properties that have few, if any, comparables and are not income-producing.* Examples of the type of structures appraised by this method are schools, owner-occupied factories, fire stations, hospitals, government office buildings, and libraries. Virtually any new construction can be appraised by the cost approach also.

The first step in the cost approach is to estimate the value of the site as if it were vacant. The site value is estimated by the market data approach, which uses comparable parcels of land to arrive at the value estimate. As a basis for the land value, the site is compared to comparable parcels of land that have sold recently.

The second step in the cost approach is to estimate the cost of reproducing or replacing the structure. Replacement cost and reproduction cost are different. **Reproduction cost** is the *price to construct an exact duplicate of the property when it was new.* **Replacement cost** is *based on constructing a building of comparable utility using modern building techniques and materials.* If the subject property was constructed many years ago, estimating the cost of reproducing that property today may

COMPARABLE	PRICE	MONTHLY GROSS	GRM/ MONTH	ANNUAL GROSS	GRM/ YEAR
No. 1	$6,213,000	$107,833	58	1,294,000	4.8
No. 2	5,865,000	101,000	58	1,212,000	4.8
No. 3	5,125,000	90,000	57	1,080,000	4.7
No. 4	6,060,000	103,000	59	1,236,000	4.9
No. 5	7,250,000	125,000	58	1,500,000	4.8
No. 6	6,588,000	111,000	59	1,332,000	4.9
Average GRM			58		4.8

FIGURE 10.7
Calculating gross rent multipliers.

be impossible. The materials and craftsmanship may not be available. Therefore, the basis of the cost approach for older structures is replacement cost new. Reproduction cost new may be used for properties that have been constructed recently.

Methods of estimating reproduction or replacement costs include the quantity survey method, the unit-in-place method, the square-foot or cubic-foot method, and the historical cost index. Of these, the quantity survey method is the most accurate but is also the least practical. Each of these methods is discussed below.

1. The **quantity survey method** involves *the detailed determination of the exact quantity of each type of material to be used in the construction and the necessary material and labor costs applicable to each unit.* The final estimate includes a profit to the builder.

2. In the **unit-in-place method,** *the cost of each component of the structure is calculated, including material, labor, and overhead costs plus a profit to the builder.* Components consist of foundation, roofing, rough framing, electrical, plumbing, heating, and other such items. These components are usually installed by a subcontractor. The total of the bids from each of these subcontractors combined with an amount for the builder's overhead and profit will add up to the cost to build the property. The unit-in-place method is often called the segregated cost method or the builder's method.

3. In the **square-foot method,** *the cost is calculated by multiplying the number of square feet in the structure being appraised by the cost per square foot to construct the building, using the current cost per square foot.*

4. The **cubic-foot method** is *mathematically similar to the square-foot method except the measurement is of the volume of the structure.* This method is most applicable to warehouse or storage space.

5. The **historical cost index method** *requires that the appraiser know how much the home originally cost to build and multiplies the cost to build by an appropriate factor.* The historical cost index will provide a factor by which to multiply the original cost. A house that had an original cost to build of $4,500 in 1950 will have a current cost of $4,500 × 14.37 (factor) or $64,665.

The estimated cost figures employed in any of these methods are available through construction cost services that publish construction cost estimates for various types of structures and structural components.

The third step in the value estimate by the cost approach is to deduct from the estimated cost of replacing or reproducing the property with new construction any observed depreciation existing and resulting from any of the three forms of depreciation. (See discussion of depreciation below.) Deduction of the dollar amount of depreciation provides the depreciated value of the structure as it exists at present.

Fourth, the depreciated value of any other site improvements is added to the value of the structure to provide an estimate of the total depreciated value of all improvements.

The estimate of the land value by the market data approach is added to the estimate of the total depreciated value of the improvements to provide a value estimate for the total property by the cost approach.

The various steps and calculations employed in the cost approach are illustrated by the example of the cost approach calculations in Figure 10.8.

Depreciation

Depreciation is defined as *a loss in value from any cause.* The loss in value is estimated by the difference in the present market value and the cost to build new. Depreciation results from the following: physical deterioration, functional obsolescence, and economic obsolescence. Each of these three types of depreciation is caused by forces having an adverse effect on structure.

Replacement or reproduction cost:		
21,000 square feet @ $52.50 sq. ft.		$1,102,500
Less structure depreciation:		
Physical deterioration	$33,075	
Functional obsolescence	44,100	
Economic obsolescence	-0-	77,175
Depreciated value of structure		1,025,325
Plus depreciated value of other improvements:		
Retaining walls	10,000	
Paved drive and parking	15,000	
Exterior lighting	2,000	
Fencing	1,500	28,500
Depreciated value of all improvements		1,053,825
Land value by market data approach		253,000
Total Property Value		$1,306,825
Rounded down		$1,306,800

FIGURE 10.8 Cost approach calculations.

Physical Deterioration

Physical deterioration, or erosion in the condition of property, is caused by:

- unrepaired damage to the structure caused by fire, explosion, vandalism, windstorm, or other action of the elements, and damage caused by termites or other woodboring insects
- wear and tear resulting from normal use of the property and lack of adequate maintenance measures to keep the property in good condition

Functional Obsolescence

Functional obsolescence refers to *flawed or faulty property, rendered inferior because of advances and change,* such as:

- inadequacy or superadequacy of things such as wiring and plumbing, heating and cooling systems, and insufficient or oversufficient number of bathrooms, closets, and other facilities
- equipment that is out of date and not in keeping with current style and utility
- exposed wiring or plumbing, lack of automatic controls for things such as furnaces and hot water heaters, and inadequate insulation
- faulty design resulting in inefficient use of floor space, poor location of various types of rooms in relation to other types such as bathrooms in relation to bedrooms, and too-high ceilings

Economic Obsolescence (External, Environmental, or Locational)

Economic obsolescence refers to *property that is adversely affected for external, environmental, or locational reasons,* such as:

- changes in surrounding land-use patterns resulting in increased vehicular traffic, air pollution, noise pollution, inharmonious land uses, and other hazards and nuisances adversely affecting the quality of the area
- changes in zoning and building regulations that adversely affect property use

- reduction in demand for property in the area caused by local economic factors, changes in growth patterns, population shifts, and other economic factors adversely affecting property value

Physical deterioration and functional obsolescence result from forces at work within the property and may be curable or incurable. Depreciation is curable if it can be fixed and if it makes economic sense to do so. For example, the exterior of a home needs scraping and painting. The increase in value as a result of paying someone to scrape and paint the home will be greater than the cost of the work. In this example, the scraping and painting were physically curable. Fixing a cracked foundation, however, will probably not increase the value of a home by the cost of the foundation repairs. Buyers expect to get a sound foundation under a home. They do not pay extra to get a sound foundation. The foundation problem therefore would be considered incurable physical deterioration. Curable functional obsolescence may consist of an out-of-date bath. The owner has the bath remodeled with new fixtures, floor, and wall coverings, and the resultant increase in value is greater than the cost of the remodeling. Incurable functional obsolescence might consist of a home without a fireplace. If the cost of remodeling to add a fireplace is greater than the contributory value the fireplace adds to the value of the home, the lack of a fireplace is considered incurable.

Economic obsolescence is caused by forces outside the property. Economic obsolescence is never curable by the property owner. The owner has no control over properties others own and therefore is not able to take necessary corrective measures.

CORRELATION AND RECONCILIATION

In making an appraisal, a professional appraiser uses as the primary appraisal method the most relevant approach to the value estimate. The most relevant method depends on the type of property that is the subject of the appraisal. For example, in estimating the value of an existing single-family, owner-occupied dwelling, the most relevant method is the market data approach. In addition, the qualified appraiser also estimates the property value by each of the other two methods. In the case of the single-family dwelling, the appraiser treats the property as if it were rental property and estimates the value using the income approach. Last, the appraiser arrives at a value estimate by the cost approach. As a practical matter, the results obtained by these three methods will not be identical. To provide the most reliable estimate of value, there must be a correlation or reconciliation of the three different results.

In the **correlation** or reconciliation process, three factors are taken into consideration:

1. *The relevancy of each of the three methods to the subject property.*
2. *The reliability of the data on which each estimate is based.*
3. *The strong points and weak points of each method.*

After considering these factors, the greatest weight should be given to the estimate resulting from using the most appropriate or relevant method for the type of property that is the subject of the appraisal.

If the property is an office building, the most relevant approach, and the one to receive the greatest weight, is the income approach. Even though the results obtained by the different approaches will not be exactly the same, they should be reasonably close. Therefore, each approach provides a check on the other two. If the result by one method varies considerably from the others, it indicates a calculation error, an error in the data used as a basis, or inappropriateness of the method.

The final step in the appraisal process is to prepare the appraisal report. The report contains the appraiser's opinion of value based on observation of the results obtained by the three methods and the appraiser's reasons for adopting the final estimate of value. The appraisal report may be in narrative form or may be a form report. The narrative report provides all the factual data about the property and the elements of judgment the appraiser used in arriving at the estimate of value. When a standard form is used to report the various property data and the appraisal method employed, it is called a form report. A form report does not contain narrative information as does the narrative report but simply sets forth various facts and figures used in the appraisal process and correlation of the final estimate of market value.

PUTTING IT TO WORK

The most common appraisal form in use today is the URAR, or uniform residential appraisal report. This form gives a brief recap of the property and the site, a neighborhood analysis, and a fairly detailed analysis of the mathematics of all three approaches. On the URAR form, the most attention and emphasis is given to the market data, or sales comparison, approach.

IMPORTANT POINTS

1. Illinois follows a system of voluntary licensing or certification of appraisers. FIRREA, however, requires all appraisals for federally related financial transactions to be completed by a licensed or certified appraiser.
2. The purpose of an appraisal is to estimate value, for instance, market value or investment value. The function of the appraisal is the use to which the appraisal is to be put.
3. An appraisal is an estimate (not a determination) of value based on factual data at a particular time for a particular purpose on a particular property.
4. Market value is the amount of money a typical buyer will give in exchange for a property.
5. In an arm's-length transaction, the parties are unrelated to each other, act in their own best interests, and are not under duress.
6. The various types of value include market value, assessed value, insurance value, liquidation value, investment value, value in use, condemnation value, and book value.
7. Property value is dependent on utility, scarcity, transferability, and effective demand.
8. The highest and best use of a property is the use that gives the property its highest value. There are four tests for determining the highest and best use: physically possible, legally permissible, financially feasible, and maximally productive.
9. The basic valuation principles are: balance, substitution, supply and demand, conformity, anticipation, contribution, increasing and decreasing returns, competition, change, depreciation, and age.
10. Depreciation is the loss in value from any cause. In structures, the causes of depreciation are physical deterioration, functional obsolescence, and economic obsolescence.
11. The market data or comparison approach to value estimate is the most relevant appraisal method for estimating the value of single-family, owner-occupied dwellings and vacant land.
12. The income approach, or appraisal by capitalization, is the most appropriate appraisal method for estimating the value of property that produces rental income.

13. The capitalization rate is made up of the return *on* and the return *of* the investment. The return *on* the investment consists of the safe rate, the risk rate, the management rate, and the nonliquidity rate.
14. A gross rent multiplier may be appropriate for estimating the value of rental property.
15. The cost approach is the main appraisal method for estimating the value of property that does not fall into the other categories. These properties, known as special-use properties, include museums, hospitals, schools, and churches, as well as new construction.
16. An appraisal report provides a value estimate based on a correlation of the estimates obtained by all three approaches.

REVIEW QUESTIONS

Answers to these questions are found in the Answer Key section at the back of the book.

1. The basis of market value is most typically:
   a. utility value
   b. book value
   c. subjective value
   d. value determined between a willing buyer and willing seller

2. All of the following characteristics must be present for a property to have value EXCEPT:
   a. utility
   b. obsolescence
   c. transferability
   d. effective demand

3. The amount of money a property will bring in the marketplace for sale in an area is called:
   a. extrinsic value
   b. intrinsic value
   c. market value
   d. GRM factor

4. Applying the principle of conformity results in:
   a. depreciation
   b. minimizing value
   c. maximizing value
   d. competition

5. The cost of constructing a building of comparable utility using modern techniques and materials is:
   a. reproduction cost
   b. operating cost
   c. unit cost
   d. replacement cost

6. Physical deterioration is caused by all of the following EXCEPT:
   a. unrepaired damage
   b. lack of adequate maintenance
   c. inefficient floor plan
   d. inadequate exterior maintenance

7. Functional obsolescence results from:
   a. faulty design and inefficient use of space
   b. changes in surrounding land-use patterns
   c. inadequate exterior maintenance
   d. extensive and poorly planned urban redevelopment

8. Which of the following causes of depreciation is NOT curable by the property owner?
   a. economic obsolescence
   b. functional obsolescence
   c. competitive obsolescence
   d. physical deterioration

9. The principle followed in making adjustments to comparables in an appraisal by the market data approach is:
   a. competition
   b. change
   c. contribution
   d. conformity

10. An appraisal is:
    a. estimate of value
    b. appropriation of value
    c. correlation of value
    d. determination of value

11. All of the following are approaches to value EXCEPT:
    a. cost approach
    b. contribution approach
    c. income approach
    d. comparison approach

12. The primary appraisal method for estimating the value of vacant land is:
    a. cost approach
    b. market data approach
    c. income approach
    d. appraisal by capitalization

13. All of the following are important data in selecting comparables EXCEPT:
    a. size of the lot
    b. income of the owners
    c. location of the properties
    d. condition of the properties

14. Using the capitalization formula, the income used as a basis for estimating value is:
    a. monthly net
    b. annual gross effective
    c. monthly gross effective
    d. annual net

15. If the income used in the appraisal by capitalization is $480,000, and the capitalization rate is 11 percent, which of the following will be the estimate of property value?
    a. $2,290,000
    b. $2,990,000
    c. $4,363,636
    d. $5,280,000

16. All of the following are deductible from gross effective income in arriving at net operating income for appraisal purposes EXCEPT:
    a. maintenance
    b. legal fees
    c. replacement service
    d. debt service

17. In the income approach, which of the following is deducted from gross potential income to calculate gross effective income?
    a. fixed expenses
    b. vacancy loss
    c. other income
    d. replacement service

18. If a property produces a gross income of $103,000 and the GIM is 7.5, which of the following is the indication of value?
    a. $137,333
    b. $772,500
    c. $927,000
    d. $1,373,333

19. Which of the following would use the cost approach as the primary method of appraisal if comparable sales are not available?
    a. shopping mall
    b. courthouse
    c. parking garage
    d. condominium apartment

20. All of the following are methods used for estimating replacement cost EXCEPT:
    a. quantity survey
    b. square foot
    c. unit in place
    d. quality survey

CHAPTER 11

Important Terminology

aesthetic zoning
building codes
bulk zoning
certificate of occupancy
cluster zoning
conditions
covenant
cumulative zoning
declaration of restrictions
deed restrictions
directive zoning
enabling acts
Environmental Policy Act
Environmental Protection Agency (EPA)
exclusive-use zoning
flood hazard area
general plan
home rule

Illinois Environmental Protection Act
Illinois Plat Act
Illinois Responsible Party Transfer Act
Interstate Land Sales Full Disclosure Act
National Flood Insurance Program
nonconforming use
planned unit development (PUD)
property report
restrictive covenant
setback
spot zoning
subdivision regulation
variance
zoning map
zoning ordinance

Land Use Controls

IN THIS CHAPTER Understanding land use controls is important to real estate salespeople. Almost every property is subject to some form of control, whether it is the result of city zoning ordinances, general subdivision restrictions, deed restrictions unique to one parcel of land, or federal legislation. Any of these forms of land control may have a major impact on the owner's rights.

Real estate salespersons are obligated to be knowledgeable regarding existing public and private land use controls within their market area and must keep abreast of changes in requirements as they happen. Lack of knowledge in these areas may subject real estate salespeople to civil liability and even possible criminal liability under certain state and federal laws.

HISTORICAL DEVELOPMENT OF LAND USE CONTROLS

Private control of land use was the forerunner of public controls. In 1848, U.S. courts first recognized and enforced restrictive covenants regulating land use in residential subdivisions. Not until 1926, however, when the U.S. Supreme Court upheld the validity of zoning ordinances, did public land use controls become legally reliable. Before these two important legal events, a developer or governmental unit had no way to regulate land use, even though the need for controls was readily apparent.

The need for land use controls has increased along with the increasing population density. Abuse by even one property owner in the use of land can have a substantial adverse effect on the rights of other property owners and cause severe depreciation of their properties.

Private land use controls, discussed later in this chapter, are limited in scope. Only a specific area can be subject to private use controls. For example, property owners in a subdivision with private controls have absolutely no control over surrounding land uses. Therefore, a subdivision may be affected adversely by uncontrolled use of an adjoining property outside the subdivision. As people became aware of the need for planning and land use controls for larger areas of land, zoning ordinances came into being, the first of which was enacted in 1916. The U.S. Supreme Court in 1926 upheld the legality of zoning laws.

Public Land Use Controls

Local Controls

Home Rule

Illinois allows municipalities to establish **home rule** units of government, which *give municipalities unlimited authority to exercise police power and pass laws governing the use of land.* Municipalities with a population of more than 25,000 automatically create a home rule unit. The municipality may elect, by referendum, not to be a home rule unit.

Non-home rule municipalities derive their limited authority to pass land use controls from enabling statutes. Municipalities with fewer than 25,000 people may become a home rule unit by referendum.

Townships are not allowed to be home rule units. They also cannot pass building codes or subdivision controls.

Zoning

Zoning begins with city or county planning; zoning laws implement and enforce the plan. Violations of zoning laws can be enforced by fines, corrected by a court injunction requiring the violation to be discontinued, or corrected by extreme measures such as demolishing an unlawful structure.

Zoning ordinances consist of two parts: (a) the **zoning map,** which *divides the community into various designated districts* and (b) the text of the **zoning ordinance,** which *sets forth the type of use permitted under each zoning classification and specific requirements for compliance.* The extent of authority for zoning ordinances is prescribed by the enabling acts passed by state legislatures. These acts specify the types of uses subject to regulation. They also limit the area subject to the ordinances to the geographic boundaries of the government unit enacting the zoning laws. For example, city zoning ordinances may not extend beyond city limits into the county. A county government, however, sometimes authorizes the extension of city zoning for some specified distance into the county, and in some cases the state empowers cities to specifically extend zoning beyond the city limits.

Several types of zones may be established by local ordinances:

1. residential, which can be subdivided into single-family homes and various levels of multi-family dwellings
2. commercial
3. light manufacturing
4. heavy industrial
5. *multiple use* or **cluster zoning**
6. **planned use development (PUD)**

The last classification of zoning, the PUD, generally is *a mixed-use development that does not meet any of a municipality's zoning classifications.* Developers may wish to develop a large tract of land with a mix of condominiums, single-family homes, and an area for small retail stores. Because the development does not fit into any zoning classification, the developer will bring the plans for development before the city council for approval. If approved, the city council will provide the site with a PUD plan number. Usually, the municipality will require construction to start within a year of the plan's approval. Most often, a PUD will enable a developer to build a higher density of housing units.

Zoning ordinances may provide for either exclusive-use zoning or cumulative-use zoning. In **exclusive-use zoning,** *property may be used only in the ways specified for that specific zone.* For example, if the zone is commercial, residential uses will not be permitted. In contrast, **cumulative zoning** *may permit uses that are not designated in the zone.* For instance, if an area is zoned commercial, a residential use could still be made of the property. In cumulative zoning, however, uses are placed in an order of priority: residential, commercial, industrial. A use of higher priority may be made in an area where the zoned use has a lower priority.

Directive zoning ordinances *follow the municipality's urban growth plan. The plan will use different zoning classifications to provide an orderly growth of residential, commercial, and industrial properties to create a well-balanced tax base.* **Aesthetic zoning** *requires that buildings adhere to a certain style of architecture.* For instance, structures in an area may be required to be English Tudor or French Provincial.

Zoning laws also define certain standards and requirements that must be met for each permitted type of use. **Bulk zoning** requirements include things such as *minimum side yards, front and rear yards, and height restrictions.* Bulk zoning requirements also include **setbacks,** or *distances from the property line to the building line.* Zoning may include regulations or restrictions to prevent interference with the passage of sunlight and air to other properties, requirements for off-street parking, and many other regulations.

PUTTING IT TO WORK

A strip of land separating one land use from another is called a buffer zone. An example would be a strip of land planted with grass and trees separating a residential area from a shopping center.

Nonconforming use. When zoning is first imposed on an area or when property is rezoned, the zoning authority generally cannot require the property owners to discontinue a current use that does not now conform to the new zoning ordinance. A **nonconforming use** occurs when a *preexisting use of property in a zoned area is different from that specified by the zoning code for that area.* The nonconforming use must be permitted because requiring the property owners to terminate the nonconforming use would be unconstitutional. In these cases, the property owner is permitted to lawfully continue a nonconforming use. This is called a *preexisting nonconforming use* or a use "grandfathered" in.

Although nonconforming use is permitted under these circumstances, the nonconforming user is subject to certain requirements designed to gradually eliminate the nonconforming use. Examples are:

1. If the property owner abandons the nonconforming use, the owner cannot resume that type of use at a later date but may then use the property only in a manner that conforms to the zoning ordinance.
2. The property owner may not make structural changes to the property to expand the nonconforming use. The owner is permitted to make only normal necessary repairs to the structure.
3. The nonconforming use cannot be changed from one type of nonconforming use to another type of nonconforming use.
4. If a nonconforming structure is destroyed in fire or other casualty, it cannot be replaced by another nonconforming structure without specific approval.
5. Some ordinances provide for a long-term amortization period, during which the nonconforming owner is permitted to continue the nonconforming use. At the end of this period, the owner must change the property use to conform with the zoning ordinance, rebuilding the structure if necessary. This long-range "notice" to the owner should allow sufficient time to relocate or modify the use without causing an economic shock to the owner.

6. Nonconforming uses may or may not be transferable to another owner. This may depend on who the acquiring owner is (for example, a relative) or on local ordinances.

Variance. A **variance** is a *permitted deviation from specific requirements of the zoning ordinance.* For example, if an owner's lot is slightly smaller than the minimum lot size restrictions set by zoning ordinances, the owner may be granted a variance by petitioning the appropriate authorities.

Variances are permitted where the deviation is not substantial, where variance will not severely impact neighboring owners, and where strict compliance would impose an undue hardship on the property owner. The hardship must be applicable to one property only and must be a peculiar or special hardship for that property under the zoning law. The special hardship does not exist where all of the property owners in the zoned area have the same difficulty.

Spot zoning. With **spot zoning**, a *specific property within a zoned area is rezoned to permit a use different from the zoning requirements for that zoned area.* If the rezoning of a property is solely for the benefit of the property owner and has the effect of increasing the land value, the spot zoning is illegal and invalid; however, when spot zoning is used for the benefit of the community and not for the benefit of a certain property owner (or owners), the spot zoning is not illegal and is valid even though the owner may benefit. An example of legal spot zoning occurs in residential urban areas when lots are rezoned to allow retail shops for the benefit of the community.

Urban and Regional Planning

The purpose of planning is to provide for the orderly growth of a community that will result in the greatest social and economic benefits to the people in the community. Over the years, state legislatures have passed **enabling acts** that *provide the legal basis for cities and counties to develop long-range plans for growth.* Planning and zoning are based on the police power of government to enable it to protect the health, safety, and welfare of the people.

In urban planning, the first step is typically to develop a master plan to determine the city make-up. This is done through a survey of the community's physical and economic assets. This information serves as a basis for developing a master plan for orderly growth. The resulting plan designates the various uses to which property may be put in specific areas.

Regional planning has its origins in the grassroots of a community. This planning may occur in communities located in unzoned county areas where property owners see the need to plan for orderly community growth; thus, they adopt and enforce a plan through zoning ordinances. In the absence of this planning, haphazard development often ensues. A plan created and based on a strong consensus of property owners in the community is the result of community-based planning. Along with the plan, the community agrees on certain zoning requirements. The proposal is presented by referendum to all of the property owners in the community. If a substantial majority of the community endorses the plan and zoning, the county government adopts the plan and enacts the necessary zoning ordinances to enforce the plan as conceived by the property owners.

Building Codes

Building codes provide another form of land use control to protect the public. These codes *regulate things such as materials used in construction, electrical wiring, fire and safety standards, and sanitary equipment facilities.* Building codes require a permit from the appropriate local government authority before constructing or renovating a commercial building or residential property. While construction is in progress, local government inspectors perform frequent inspections to make certain that code requirements are being met.

After a satisfactory final inspection, a **certificate of occupancy** is issued, *permitting occupation of the structure by tenants or the owner.* Many cities today require a certificate of occupancy, based upon satisfactory inspection of the property, prior to occupancy by a new owner or tenant of any structure even though it is not new construction or has not been renovated. Inspection is required to reveal any deficiencies in the structure requiring correction before the city will issue a certificate of occupancy to protect the new purchaser or tenant.

Subdivision Regulations

States may empower local government, cities, and counties, through **subdivision regulations,** *to protect purchasers of property within the subdivisions and taxpayers in the city or county from an undue tax burden* resulting from the demands for services that a new subdivision generates. Subdivision ordinances typically address the following requirements:

1. Streets must be of a specified width, be curbed, have storm drains, and not exceed certain maximum grade specifications.
2. Lots may not be smaller than a specified minimum size.
3. Dwellings in specified areas must be for single-family occupancy only. Specific areas may be set aside for multi-family dwellings.
4. Utilities, including water, sewer, electric, and telephone, must be available to each lot, or plans must include easements to later provide utilities.
5. All houses must be placed on lots to meet specified minimum standards for setbacks from the front property line, as well as from interior property lines.
6. Drainage must be adequate for runoff of rainfall to avoid damage to any properties.

After adopting a subdivision ordinance, developers must obtain approval from the appropriate officials before subdividing and selling lots. Compliance with most subdivision ordinances requires the platting of land into lots. Then the subdivision plat is recorded on the public record and development can begin.

State Controls

Illinois Plat Act

The **Illinois Plat Act** *requires that a survey of each parcel and a plat of subdivision be recorded whenever an owner divides a parcel of land into two or more parts, any of which is less than five acres.* Some exemptions to this rule are allowed. A county recorder or an attorney should be consulted regarding the act.

Putting It to Work

Until the subdivision plat is approved and recorded, a subdivision reference may not be used in a legal description. Once approved, this lot, block, and subdivision type of description is acceptable.

Illinois Land Sales Registration Act

Subdivided land that is sold or promoted within Illinois is regulated by the Illinois Land Sales Registration Act of 1989. A person who sells or promotes the subdivided land of another, if the person is a resident of Illinois or from an office located in Illinois, must have an Illinois real estate broker's license. Subdividers promoting the sale or rental of land divided into 25 or more lots are required to register with the OBRE. The subdivider files a public property report (PPR) with the OBRE, and all prospective buyers must be given a copy of the PPR that contains complete disclosure regarding the land and its location, tax status, financing, and associated liens. If a prospective purchaser receives a copy of the PPR before signing a contract, the purchaser has seven days from the signing of the agreement to cancel the contract. If a purchaser does not receive the PPR before signing a contract, the purchaser has two years from the date of signing to cancel. OBRE may revoke the subdivider's certification or registration if an investigation determines that any misrepresentation or fraudulent statements have been made in the offering, advertising, or sale of the subdivided land.

There are six exemptions to the offering or dispositions. The act does not apply (a) if promotional costs, including commissions, do not exceed 20 percent of the sales price; (b) when purchasing for one's own account in a single transaction; (c) if the lot contains a building or provision to have a building constructed within two years; (d) to the purchase of cemetery lots; (e) when 10 or fewer buyers purchase the total land; and (f) to lots of 20 or more unimproved acres or to lots of 10 or more acres if each lot has access to a road maintained by the county.

PUTTING IT TO WORK

> The Illinois Land Sales Registration Act regulates the sale or promotion within the state of Illinois of some subdivided land, irrespective of where the land is located. Persons selling or promoting land from offices within Illinois must hold an Illinois broker's license. Persons selling or promoting land without entering the state of Illinois do not need licensing.

Illinois Environmental Protection Act

The **Illinois Environmental Protection Act** *creates two agencies to control and regulate noise, air, water, and land pollution.* The Illinois Pollution Control Board, composed of five members appointed by the governor, is located in Chicago. This board is responsible for issuing permits and for investigation of potential violations. It adopts regulations and standards of emission and waste and sets the state's air quality standards. The board can grant variances and impose civil penalties of up to $10,000 for each violation plus $1,000 for each day the violation continues. Criminal penalties of up to $1,000 or one year in jail, or both, for each violation also can be imposed.

The Illinois Environmental Protection Agency, located in Springfield, administers the board's certification and permit systems and keeps track of sources of contamination. The Illinois EPA also conducts research, development, and experimentation and proposes regulations to the board.

Illinois Responsible Property Transfer Act

The **Illinois Responsible Property Transfer Act,** which became effective November 1, 1989, affects the sale of all commercial and industrial property, as well as residential property with underground storage tanks. The purpose of the act is to elicit complete disclosure of existing environmental liabilities associated with the property ownership. Within 30 days following execution of a written contract, if any, for transfer of the property, the transferor must complete and deliver to the transferee and to the lender, if any, an environmental disclosure document for transfer of real property.

If all parties to the transfer agree in writing, the time period for disclosure may be waived, but the disclosure document must be delivered to all parties on or before the date of transfer of the real property. If environmental defects are revealed that previously were unknown to the parties, or if the transferor fails to comply with the disclosure as required in the act, any of the parties to the transfer may at their discretion, within 10 days after demand for or receipt of the disclosure statement, void any obligation to accept a transfer or to finance a transfer that has yet to be finalized.

Under this act, owners of real property may be held liable for costs related to the release of hazardous substances. Owners of the property must provide regulatory information during current ownership and site information about the previous owners or persons leasing or managing the property.

The proper disclosure document must be recorded in the county in which the property is located within 30 days after the property is transferred. This is also filed with the EPA.

Persons failing to comply with disclosure as required are liable for civil penalties not to exceed $1,000 plus $1,000 for each day the violations continue. Any person or transferor who with actual knowledge makes any false statement, representation, or certification is liable for civil penalties not to exceed $10,000 plus $10,000 for each day the violations continue. Persons who fail to record a disclosure document are liable for civil penalties not to exceed $10,000. Persons who suffer damage as a result of a violation of this act may bring an action against the violators.

Federal Controls

Interstate Land Sales Full Disclosure Act

The federal **Interstate Land Sales Full Disclosure Act** *regulates interstate* (across state lines) *sale of unimproved lots.* It became effective in 1969 and was made more restrictive by a 1980 amendment. The act is administered by the Secretary of Housing and Urban Development (HUD) through the office of Interstate Land Sales Registration. Its purpose is to prevent fraudulent marketing schemes that may transpire when land is sold sight unseen. The act requires that a developer file a statement of record with HUD before offering unimproved lots in interstate commerce by telephone or through the mails. The statement of record requires disclosure of information about the property as specified by HUD.

Developers of these properties also are required to provide each purchaser or lessee of property with a printed **property report,** which *discloses specific information about the land* before the purchaser or lessee signs a purchase contract or lease. Information required on these property reports includes things such as the type of title a buyer will receive, number of homes currently occupied, availability of recreation facilities, distance to nearby communities, utility services and charges, and soil or other foundation problems in construction. If the purchaser or lessee does not receive a copy of the property report prior to signing a purchase contract or lease, the purchaser may have grounds to void the contract. If a prospective purchaser receives a copy of the property report before signing a contract, the purchaser will have seven days to cancel the contract. If the purchaser does not receive the report, he will have two years to cancel.

The act provides for several exemptions, the most important of which are:

1. subdivisions in which the lots are five acres or more
2. subdivisions consisting of fewer than 25 lots
3. lots offered for sale exclusively to building contractors
4. lots on which a building exists or where a contract obligates the lot seller to construct a building within two years

If a developer offers only part of the total tract owned and thereby limits the subdivision to fewer than 25 lots to acquire an exemption, the developer may not then sell additional lots within the tract. HUD considers these additional lots a part of a "common plan" for development and marketing, thereby eliminating the opportunity for several exemptions for the developer as a result of piecemeal development of a large tract in sections of fewer than 25 lots at a time.

The act provides severe penalties for violation by a developer or a real estate licensee who participates in marketing the property. The developer or the real estate licensee, or both, may be sued by a purchaser or a lessee for damages and are potentially subject to a criminal penalty by fine of up to $5,000 or imprisonment for up to five years or both. Therefore, prior to acting as an agent for the developer in marketing the property, real estate salespersons must be certain to ascertain that a developer has complied with or is exempt from the law.

FEMA Flood Hazard Areas

In 1968, Congress passed the National Flood Insurance Act, which created the **National Flood Insurance Program (NFIP)** *to reduce losses through flood plain management and to provide insurance to property owners already located in flood plains.* A flood plain or **flood hazard area** is *the natural storage area for excess water from rain or melting snow.* In other words, water from melting snow or heavy rainfall will settle in the lowest area of a community. This low-lying area is called the flood plain. Location away from bodies of water is no guarantee of being out of a flood plain.

The Federal Emergency Management Agency (FEMA) has identified more than 20,000 communities across the United States as having flood-prone or flood hazard areas. Properties in a flood hazard area must meet certain flood plain management building requirements. One such requirement requires that any new construction in a flood plain would have to be built at least one foot above the 100-year flood plain mark.

Homeowners that borrow money from a federally insured lender (FDIC-insured) or a lender that sells its loans on the secondary mortgage market are required to buy a federal flood insurance policy as a condition of getting that loan if the property used as collateral is in a flood hazard area. The flood insurance is purchased through any of the private insurance companies. To find out if a property is located in a flood plain, flood plain maps can be viewed at a local municipal hall.

Environmental Protection Legislation

The National **Environmental Policy Act** of 1969 *requires filing an environmental impact statement with the* **Environmental Protection Agency (EPA)** *prior to changing or initiating a land use or development,* to ensure that the use will not adversely affect the environment. Typical subject areas regulated by the act include air, noise, and water pollution, as well as chemical and solid waste disposal.

Since 1969, several amendments and companion pieces of legislation have been passed to more clearly define the EPA's role in land use. The Resource Conservation and Recovery Act (RCRA), passed in 1976, defined hazardous substances. Then, in 1980, Congress passed the Comprehensive Environmental Response, Compensation and Liability Act (CERCLA) to provide solutions to the environmental problems created over the years by uncontrolled disposal of wastes. Under CERCLA, a program was created to identify sites containing hazardous substances, ensure that those sites were cleaned up by the parties responsible or by the government, and establish a procedure to seek reimbursement for clean-up from the party responsible for placing the hazardous substance.

In 1986, CERCLA was amended by the Superfund Amendments and Reauthorization Act (SARA). The amendments imposed stringent clean-up standards and expanded the definition of persons liable for the costs of clean-up. Under CERCLA and SARA, every landowner is potentially affected.

In addition to federal legislation, some states now require full disclosure, prior to title transfer by deed, if real estate is listed by a federal or state agency as contaminated by hazardous substance.

More recent environmental issues include protection of habitats for wildlife, wetlands, shorelines, and endangered species, as well as issues such as lead-based paint, radon, formaldehyde, and asbestos. These topics are discussed in Appendix B.

PRIVATE LAND USE CONTROLS

Individual owners have the right to place private controls on their own real estate. These restrictions take the form of individual deed restrictions or subdivision restrictive covenants affecting the entire subdivision.

Individual **deed restrictions** are *in the form of covenants or in the form of conditions*. A **covenant** may be included in a deed *to benefit property that is sold or to benefit a property that is retained when an adjoining property is sold*. For example, an owner who retains one property and sells an adjoining property may provide in the deed that a structure may not be erected in a certain area of the property being sold, to protect the view from the retained property or to prevent loss of passage of light and air to the retained property. These restrictions are covenants that run with the land (move with the title in any subsequent conveyance). Covenants may be enforced by a suit for damages or by injunction. *Restrictions that provide for a reversion of title if they are violated* are called **conditions.** If a condition is violated, ownership reverts to the grantor. These conditions thus create a defeasible fee estate.

Restrictive covenants are *limitations placed on the use of land by the developer of a residential subdivision*. The purpose of these covenants is to preserve and protect the quality of land in subdivisions and to maximize land values by requiring the homogeneous use of the land by purchasers. The covenants are promises by those who purchase property in the subdivision to limit the use of their property to comply with requirements of the restrictive covenants; therefore, they are negative easements. The deed conveying title to property in the subdivision contains a reference to a recorded plat of the subdivision and a reference to recording of the restrictive covenants; or the restrictions may be recited in each deed of conveyance. Restrictions must be reasonable, and they must benefit all property owners alike.

PUTTING IT TO WORK

Subdivision restrictions typically address issues to maintain quality and consistency of the subdivision. These may be concerns of a relatively minor nature, such as exterior lighting and clean-up of rubbish, or things such as speed limits, landscaping, and even construction and architectural review and approval.

If the subdivision is in a zoned area, restrictive covenants have priority over the zoning ordinance to the extent that the covenants are more restrictive than the zoning requirements. For example, if the zoning permits multi-family dwellings and the restrictive covenants do not, the restrictive covenants will be enforced. If restrictive covenants are contrary to public law and public policy, they will not be enforced. For example, a restrictive covenant requiring discrimination on the basis of race, religion, gender, or national origin is invalid. Also, restrictive covenants are not valid unless they are recorded on the public record in the county in which the land is located.

Typical Restrictive Covenants

Restrictive covenants provide a **general plan** *setting forth development of a subdivision.* Prior to beginning development, the developer establishes a list of *rules each lot purchaser will be required to adhere to in use of the property,* as recorded in an instrument called **declaration of restrictions.** The declaration is recorded simultaneously with the plat and includes a reference to the plat. Examples of typical restrictive covenants are:

- Only single-family dwellings may be constructed in the subdivision.
- Dwellings must contain a specified minimum number of square feet of living area.
- Only one single-family dwelling may be constructed on a lot.
- No lot may be subdivided.
- Dwellings must be of a harmonious architectural style. To ensure this, a site plan and plans and specifications for the structure must be submitted to and approved by a committee prior to start of construction.
- Structures must be set back a specified distance from the front property line and a specified distance from interior property lines.
- Temporary structures may not be placed on any lot.
- Covenants may be enforced by any one property owner or several property owners of land within the subdivision by taking appropriate court action.
- The covenants will remain in effect for a specified time period. (Restrictive covenants, in some cases, are subject to automatic renewal periods, which may be changed by a vote of the property owners.)

Putting It to Work

Real estate licensees must be aware of restrictive covenants in subdivisions in which they are selling property. The salesperson should provide prospective buyers with a copy of the covenants, which may be obtained from the developer, if he or she is still on the site, or from the office of title registration in the county in which the property is located. In preparing offers to purchase in the subdivision, the real estate licensee should include a provision that the offeror acknowledged receipt of a copy of the restrictive covenants.

Enforcement of Covenants

Private land use controls are enforced by public law. This is accomplished by an action of a court known as an injunction. An injunction prevents a use contrary to the restrictions of record, or orders the removal of any such uses that have been implemented. In a practical sense, the individuals who bear primary responsibility for making sure the restrictions are enforced are the other owners of property in the affected area. Their failing to enforce the restrictions on a timely basis might lead to the eventual loss of the right to enforce the restrictions at all.

Enforcement of covenants is not limited to the original purchasers of property in the subdivision. Subsequent purchasers must abide by and may enforce the restrictive covenants until such time as the covenants may be terminated, as previously discussed. In this sense, the restrictions run with the land.

Termination of Covenants

Restrictive covenants may be terminated in the following ways:

1. The time period for which the covenants were created expires.
2. The property owners vote unanimously to end the restrictions, unless the restrictions provide for termination by vote of a smaller number of landowners.
3. Changes in the character of the subdivision render it unsatisfactory to continue the type of use specified by the restrictions. For example, if property owners in a subdivision fail to restrict it to single-family residential use, the area might gradually change to commercial use; consequently, the subdivision is no longer suitable for limitation to residential use.
4. The property owners abandon the original plan and thus violate their restrictions, in many instances participating in the violations. As a result, a court may rule that the property owners have abandoned the original general plan and therefore the court will not enforce the restrictions.
5. Restrictions are not enforced on a timely basis. Owners cannot sit by idly and watch someone complete a structure in a subdivision in violation of the restrictive covenants and then attempt to enforce the restrictions by court action. If property owners do not act to enforce restrictive covenants on a timely basis, the court will not apply the restriction against the violator and it will be terminated. Termination of a covenant in this manner is an application of the doctrine of laches, which states that if landowners are lax in protecting their rights, they may lose them.

IMPORTANT POINTS

1. The plan for development is enforced by zoning ordinances. Planning and zoning are an exercise of police power.
2. Types of zones include residential, commercial, planned unit developments (PUDs), industrial, and agricultural.
3. Zoning may be either exclusive-use or cumulative-use.
4. In addition to specifying permitted uses, zoning ordinances define standards and requirements that must be met for each type of use.
5. A nonconforming use is one that differs from the type of use permitted in a certain zone. The nonconforming use may be lawful or unlawful.
6. A variance is a permitted deviation from specific requirements of a zoning ordinance because the property owner would be subject to a special hardship imposed by the strict enforcement.
7. Spot zoning occurs when a certain property within a zoned area is rezoned to permit a use that is different from the zoning requirements for that area. Spot zoning may be valid or invalid.
8. The purpose of planning is to provide for the orderly growth of a community that will result in the greatest social and economic benefits to the people.
9. Subdivision ordinances regulate the development of residential subdivisions to protect property purchasers as well as taxpayers in the area from increased tax burdens to provide essential services to the subdivisions.
10. The Illinois Plat Act requires owners to file a survey or plat of subdivision when dividing a parcel of land into two or more parts, any of which is five acres or smaller.
11. Subdivided land sold or promoted within Illinois is regulated by the Illinois Land Sales Registration Act. An Illinois real estate broker's license also is required. Subdividers promoting land divided into 25 or more lots must be registered with the OBRE. This act has some exemptions.

12. Building codes require certain standards of construction. The codes are concerned primarily with electrical systems, fire and safety standards, and sanitary systems and equipment.
13. The Interstate Land Sales Full Disclosure Act regulates sale of unimproved lots in interstate commerce to prevent fraudulent schemes in selling land sight-unseen.
14. Borrowers purchasing a property in a FEMA-designated flood plain are required to buy flood insurance to receive a loan from a federally insured depository or from a lender that sells its loans on the secondary mortgage market.
15. Environmental protection legislation is a form of land use control to protect the public against abuses of the environment in the development of real estate.
16. Illinois has an Environmental Protection Agency and a Pollution Control Board that control and regulate noise, air, water, and land pollution.
17. The Responsible Property Transfer Act affects the sale of all commercial and industrial property and residential property with underground storage tanks. Environmental disclosure documents for transfer of real property must be completed and delivered to all parties on or before the date of transfer of the real property.
18. Highway access controls regulate entry onto and exit from certain highways to protect the public using the highways.
19. Private land use controls are in the form of deed restrictions and restrictive covenants.
20. Restrictive covenants must be reasonable and must be equally beneficial to all property owners.
21. Restrictive covenants are recorded on the public record in an instrument called a declaration of restrictions. These covenants are not legally effective and enforceable unless they are recorded.
22. Restrictive covenants are enforced by court injunction upon petition by the property owners on a timely basis.

REVIEW QUESTIONS

Answers to these questions are found in the Answer Key section at the back of the book.

1. All of the following statements about land use controls are correct EXCEPT:
    a. deed restrictions are a form of private land use control
    b. public land use controls are an exercise of police power
    c. enforcement of private restrictions is by injunction
    d. public land use controls are limited to state laws

2. Deed restrictions that run with the land are:
    a. covenants
    b. variances
    c. declarations
    d. nonconforming

3. All of the following statements about restrictive covenants are correct EXCEPT:
    a. they must be reasonable
    b. they are enforceable even though not recorded
    c. they are not enforceable if contrary to law
    d. they provide for a general plan for development

4. The instrument used for recording restrictive covenants is called:
    a. plat
    b. master deed
    c. covenant
    d. declaration of restrictions

5. Restrictive covenants may be terminated in all of the following ways EXCEPT:
   a. expiration
   b. transfer of title
   c. failure to enforce on a timely basis
   d. abandonment

6. Restrictive covenants are enforced by:
   a. zoning
   b. injunction
   c. police power
   d. condemnation

7. The type of zoning that permits a higher priority use in a lower priority zone is called:
   a. exclusive use
   b. nonconforming use
   c. amortizing use
   d. cumulative use

8. Rezoning of an area caused the use by one property owner to be in noncompliance with the new zoning ordinance. If the owner continues this use, it is called:
   a. variance
   b. lawful nonconforming use
   c. spot zoning
   d. unlawful nonconforming use

9. A permitted deviation from the standards of a zoning ordinance is called:
   a. variance
   b. nonconforming use
   c. spot zoning
   d. unlawful nonconforming use

10. Rezoning of a specific property for the owner's benefit is called:
    a. variance
    b. nonconforming use
    c. spot zoning
    d. unlawful nonconforming use

11. A purpose of subdivision ordinances is to protect:
    a. taxpayers from increased taxes caused by increased demand for services to subdivisions
    b. developers during the development period from excessive costs and thereby encourage residential development
    c. homeowners in existing subdivisions from an oversupply of residential property
    d. developers from excessive building code requirements

12. When the initiative for zoning and planning ordinances comes from property owners, it is called:
    a. owner planning
    b. community-based planning
    c. general planning
    d. exclusive-use planning

13. Building codes require:
    a. property report
    b. PUDs
    c. certificate of occupancy
    d. statement of record

14. Which of the following statements concerning the Interstate Land Sales Full Disclosure Act is NOT correct?
    a. it regulates sales of unimproved lots across state lines
    b. it is administered by HUD
    c. the developer is required to record a property report in the local recorder's office
    d. subdivisions of fewer than 25 lots are not subject to the law

15. Exemptions to the Interstate Land Sales Full Disclosure Act include all of the following EXCEPT:
    a. subdivisions of fewer than 25 lots
    b. lots offered only to building contractors
    c. lots on which there is a building
    d. subdivisions in which the lots are 2 acres or more

16. The Illinois Environmental Protection Agency:
    a. administers the Pollution Control Board's certification and permit systems
    b. keeps track of sources of contamination
    c. conducts research and development
    d. does all of the above

17. The Responsible Property Transfer Act affects the sale of:

    a. commercial property with underground tanks
    b. industrial property with underground tanks
    c. residential property with underground tanks
    d. all of the above

18. An owner of a parcel of land plans to subdivide the parcel into four parts with each part consisting of four acres. Which of the following statements is true, relating to the Illinois Plat Act?

    a. the owner must have the land surveyed
    b. the owner must file a plat of subdivision
    c. the Illinois Plat Act does not affect this division of land
    d. both a and b are required

19. The Illinois Land Sales Registration Act regulates the sale of land in subdivisions of:

    a. 25 lots or fewer located out of state, marketed to people in Illinois
    b. 25 lots or fewer located in or out of state, marketed to people in Illinois
    c. 25 lots or more located out of state, marketed to people in Illinois
    d. 25 lots or more located in or out of state, marketed to people in Illinois

20. All of the following are true regarding the Federal Flood Insurance Program EXCEPT:

    a. it requires all lenders to require flood insurance on any loan secured by a property in a flood plain
    b. it requires that new properties built in a flood plain meet flood plain management building codes
    c. it is administered by the Federal Emergency Management Agency (FEMA)
    d. it affects only those properties near a river or stream

CHAPTER 12

IMPORTANT TERMINOLOGY

administrative law judge (ALJ)
Americans with Disabilities Act
blockbusting
Civil Rights Act of 1866
Civil Rights Act of 1968
disability
Discrimination in Sale of Real Estate Act

discriminatory advertising
Fair Housing Act of 1968
Fair Housing Amendments Act of 1988
familial status
Illinois Human Rights Act
redlining
steering

Fair Housing

IN THIS CHAPTER Two federal laws prohibit discrimination in housing: (a) the Civil Rights Act of 1866 and (b) the Fair Housing Act of 1968, together with its important 1974 and 1988 amendments. The 1866 law prohibits all discrimination based on race in both real and personal property. The Fair Housing Act of 1968 and its subsequent amendments apply specifically to housing.

CIVIL RIGHTS ACT OF 1866

The first significant statute affecting equal housing opportunity is the federal **Civil Rights Act of 1866.** Far from being obsolete, this statute has had a major impact on fair housing concepts, through a landmark case in 1968, the year the Federal Fair Housing Act became law. Although the 1968 statute, discussed later, provides for a number of exemptions, the 1866 law has no exemptions and contains the blanket statement that *all citizens have the same rights to inherit, buy, sell, or lease all real and personal property.* This statute is interpreted to prohibit all racial discrimination.

In the case of *Jones* v. *Alfred H. Mayer Company,* the U.S. Supreme Court applied the Civil Rights Act of 1866 to prohibit any racially based discrimination in housing. The ruling provides an interesting interplay between the 1866 act and the 1968 amendments to the Federal Fair Housing Act, because the exemptions provided for in the 1968 law cannot be used to enforce any racial discrimination.

Enforcement

If discrimination on the basis of race occurs, the aggrieved party can file an action in federal district court for an injunction and damages.

FEDERAL FAIR HOUSING ACT OF 1968

Originally enacted by Congress as Title VIII of the Civil Rights Act of 1968, the **Fair Housing Act** *prohibits discrimination in housing on the basis of race, color, religion, or national origin.* An amendment in the Housing and Community Development Act of 1974 added the prohibition against discrimination on the basis of sex. The **Fair Housing Amendments Act of 1988** added *provisions to prevent discrimination based on mental or physical handicap or familial status.*

Real estate brokers should be aware of an amendment to the 1968 law that requires all offices to prominently display the Fair Housing Poster, shown in Figure

12.1. Upon investigation of a discrimination complaint, failure to display the poster could be conclusive proof of failure to comply with the federal law.

1988 Amendments to Fair Housing Act

Although the Fair Housing Act of 1968 established broad responsibilities in providing fair housing for the nation, it essentially lacked teeth for enforcement. Until 1988, the role of the U.S. Department of Housing and Urban Development (HUD) was limited to that of a negotiator, trying to effect a voluntary conciliation between the affected parties through the force of persuasion. Although aggrieved parties could always take their complaints to a federal court and seek civil damages, this often was not a reality because of the burden of legal expense on the discriminated party.

In addition, Congress found that although racial complaints were becoming less frequent, a major problem was discrimination against families with young children and against people with disabilities. To address these concerns, Congress passed sweeping amendments to the act that became effective March 12, 1989. Here is a synopsis of those amendments.

1. Protected classes now include individuals with **disabilities,** *mental or physical impairments that impede any of their life functions.* Landlords must allow a tenant with disabilities to make reasonable modifications to an apartment, at the tenant's expense, to accommodate special needs. Tenants, for example, must be allowed to install a ramp or widen doors to accommodate a wheelchair, or install grab bars in a bathroom. At the end of their tenancy, the premises must be returned to their original condition, also at the tenant's own expense.

FIGURE 12.1 Poster for equal housing opportunity.

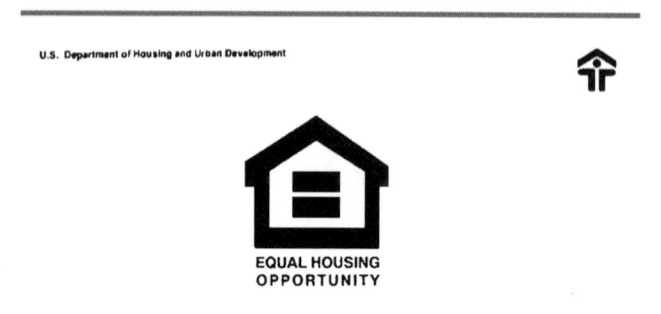

Also, new multi-family construction to be occupied two years from the effective date of the 1988 amendments must provide certain accommodations for people with disabilities—for example, switches and thermostats at a level that can be operated from a wheelchair, reinforced walls to install grab bars, and kitchen space that will permit maneuverability in a wheelchair.

2. Another added protected class is **familial status.** Familial status is defined as *an adult with children under 18, a person who is pregnant, one who has legal custody of a child or who is in the process of obtaining such custody*. Thus, landlords are prohibited from advertising "adults only" in most circumstances. The amendments, however, provide for elderly housing if (a) all units are occupied by individuals age 62 or older or (b) 80 percent of the units have persons age 55 or older and the facility has services to accommodate the physical and social needs of the elderly.

In December 1995, an amendment was passed removing the requirement for "facilities and services to accommodate the physical and social needs of the elderly." The amendment clarified the requirements for the exemption. To qualify as "55 or older housing" the complex must have at least one person 55 or older in 80 percent of its units and the association or owners must have a written policy of intent to serve residents 55 and over. The amendment protects real estate professionals from being sued in cases where in "good faith" they act on the written word of a housing association that the complex meets the "55 and over" criteria and later find that it does not.

3. The 1988 amendments added major enforcement provisions. Previously, HUD could use only persuasion, but now HUD can file a formal charge and refer the complaint to an **administrative law judge (ALJ)** unless the aggrieved party or the charged party elects a jury trial in a civil court. The ALJ, who *hears complaints regarding violations of the 1988 amendments,* can impose substantial fines from $10,000 to $50,000 for subsequent offenses.

4. Enforcement is further strengthened by the expanding role of the U.S. Attorney General to initiate action in the public interest that could result in fines of as much as $50,000 on the first offense. This will occur only upon the finding of a pattern of discrimination. The Attorney General will take the role of the aggrieved party, freeing the actual aggrieved party from the legal expense of pursuing the case.

Prohibited Acts

As the law presently exists, discrimination on the basis of race, color, religion, sex, national origin, handicap, or familial status is illegal in the sale or rental of housing or residential lots, advertising the sale or rental of housing, financing housing, and providing real estate brokerage services. The act also makes blockbusting and racial steering illegal.

A few special exemptions are available to owners in renting or selling their own property (examined later in the chapter). In the absence of an exemption, the following specific acts are prohibited:

1. Refusing to sell or rent housing, or to negotiate the sale or rental of residential lots on the basis of discrimination because of race, color, religion, sex, national origin, disability, or familial status. This includes representing to any person on discriminatory grounds "that any dwelling is not available for inspection, sale, or rental when in fact such dwelling is available." It is also illegal "to refuse to sell or rent after the making of a bona fide offer, or to refuse to negotiate for the sale or rental of, or otherwise make unavailable or deny a dwelling to a person" because of race, color, religion, sex, national origin, disability, or familial status. Examples of violations of these prohibited acts are:

   - advising a prospective buyer that a house has been sold, because of the prospect's national origin, when it has not

- refusing to accept an offer to purchase because the offeror is a member of a certain religion
- telling a rental applicant that an apartment is not available for inspection because the applicant is a female (or male) when the apartment is actually vacant and available for inspection
- refusing to rent to a person who uses a wheelchair or make reasonable modifications (at the tenant's expense) to an apartment to accommodate the wheelchair
- refusing to rent to a family with children

2. The act makes it illegal "to discriminate against any person in the terms, conditions, or privileges of sale or rental of a dwelling, or in the provision of services or facilities in connection therewith, because of race, color, religion, sex, national origin, disability, or familial status." Examples of prohibited acts in this category are:

    - requiring tenants to have a security deposit in an amount equal to one month's rent, except when the rental applicant is Hispanic, in which case the required deposit is increased to two months' rent
    - restricting use of the apartment complex swimming pool to white tenants only
    - including in the purchase of a condominium apartment a share of stock and membership in a nearby country club, provided the purchaser is not Jewish
    - charging a larger deposit to a couple with young children
    - charging a higher rent to a person in a wheelchair

Blockbusting

The act specifically makes **blockbusting** illegal. This practice is defined as: *to induce or attempt to induce any person to sell or rent any dwelling by representations regarding the entry or prospective entry into the neighborhood of a person or persons of a particular race, color, religion, sex, national origin, disability or familial status."* Blockbusting occurs when real estate salespersons induce owners to list property for sale or rent by telling them that persons of a particular race, color, national origin, sex, religion, disability, or familial status are moving into the area. Blockbusting also occurs when real estate firms sell a home in an area to a person of a particular race, color, national origin, sex, religion, disability, or familial status with the sole intent to cause property owners in the neighborhood to panic and place their property for sale at reduced or distressed prices.

Steering

In **steering,** another violation resulting from the acts of licensees, real estate licensees *direct prospective purchasers, especially minority purchasers, toward or away from specific neighborhoods to avoid changing the racial or ethnic makeup of neighborhoods.* The prohibition against steering falls under the general prohibition of refusing to sell, rent, or negotiate the sale or rental of housing or residential lots. Examples of steering are:

- showing a white prospect properties only in areas populated only by white people
- showing African American prospects properties only in integrated areas or areas populated only by African Americans
- showing Polish prospects properties only in areas populated by Poles

Discriminatory Advertising

Discriminatory advertising, that which *shows preference based on race, color, religion, sex, national origin, disability, or familial status*, is illegal. The act specifies that it is illegal to make, print, or publish, or cause to be made, printed, or published any notice, statement, or advertisement, concerning the sale or rental of a dwelling, that indicates any preference, limitation, or discrimination based on race, color, religion, sex, national origin, disability, or familial status. Examples of violations are:

- a series of advertisements for the sale of condominium units or rental apartments containing pictures that show owners or tenants on the property of only one race
- an advertisement stating that the owner prefers tenants who are male college students
- a for sale sign specifying "no Puerto Ricans"
- a statement to prospective white tenants by a real estate salesperson that black tenants are not permitted
- an apartment advertisement stating "adults only"

Putting It to Work

Most people can clearly recognize the negative discrimination in advertising that states "no children" or "no blacks." Equally illegal, however, are advertisements that show discriminatory practices such as "Catholics preferred" or "mature couple." "Adult community" also is forbidden unless the community meets strict federal guidelines.

Redlining

In the past, areas populated by minorities were redlined. Prior to enactment of the Fair Housing Act, some lending institutions circled certain local areas with a red line on the map, refusing to make loans within the circled areas based upon some characteristic of property owners in the area. The act prohibits lending institutions from **redlining,** or *refusing to make loans to purchase, construct, or repair a dwelling by discriminating on the basis of race, color, religion, sex, national origin, disability or familial status.*

The Fair Housing Act does not limit the prohibition to the refusal to make loans. The prohibition against discrimination applies to those who deny a loan or who deny financial assistance to a person applying for the purpose of purchasing, constructing, improving, repairing, or maintaining a dwelling. The prohibition also extends to individuals who discriminate in fixing terms of the loan, including interest rates, duration of loan, or any other terms or conditions of the loan.

Putting It to Work

The Federal Equal Credit Opportunity Act prohibits lenders from discriminating on the basis of race, religion, national origin, sex, marital status, age, or because the applicant receives public assistance. Applicants whose loan applications are rejected must be informed in writing within 30 days of the main reason for the rejection.

Discrimination in Providing Brokerage Services

The act prohibits discrimination in providing real estate brokerage services and states "it is unlawful to deny any person access to or membership or participation in any multiple listing service, real estate broker's organization, or other service relating to the business of selling or renting dwellings, or to discriminate against him in the terms or conditions of such access, membership or participation on account of race, color, religion, sex, national origin, disability or familial status." This provision of the Fair Housing Law makes illegal the denial of membership or special terms or conditions of membership in any real estate organization on discriminatory grounds. The prohibition extends to access to a multiple listing service.

Exemptions

The Fair Housing Law provides exemptions to property owners under certain conditions. Exemptions from the 1968 Fair Housing Act as amended are available as follows:

1. An owner of no more than three single-family dwellings at any one time is exempt. Unless the owner was living in or was the last occupant of the dwelling sold, he or she is limited to only one exemption in any 24-month period.
2. An owner of an apartment building containing up to four units is exempt in rental of the units provided the owner occupies one of the units as a personal residence.
3. Religious organizations are exempt as to properties owned and operated for the benefit of their members only and not for commercial purposes *provided that* membership in the organization is not restricted on account of race, color, national origin, sex, disability, or familial status.
4. A private club not open to the public is exempt as to the properties the club owns to provide lodging for the benefit of the membership and not for commercial purposes.

None of these exemptions is available if either of the following has occurred:

1. Discriminatory advertising has been used.
2. The services of a real estate broker, associate, salesperson, or any person in the business of selling or renting dwellings are used. A person is deemed to be in the business of selling or renting dwellings if:

    - The individual has, within the preceding 12 months, participated as principal in three or more transactions involving the sale or rental of any dwelling or any interest therein.
    - The person has, within the preceding 12 months, participated as agent (excluding the sale of personal residence) in providing sales or rental facilities or services in two or more transactions involving the sale or rental of any dwelling or any interest therein.
    - The individual is the owner of any dwelling designed or intended for occupancy by five or more families.

Enforcement and Penalties

The Fair Housing Act may be enforced in three ways:

1. By administrative procedure through HUD's Office of Equal Opportunity. HUD may act on its own information and initiative. HUD must act in response to complaints. If a state or local law where the property is located is substantially equivalent, HUD must refer the complaint to the state or local authorities. Complaints must be in writing and state the facts upon which an alleged violation is based. If HUD or the state organization is unable to obtain voluntary conciliation, a charge will be filed and the case referred to an administrative law judge, unless either party elects to have the case tried in a civil court.

The ALJ may impose a civil penalty of up to $10,000 for a first offense, $25,000 if another violation occurs within five years, and $50,000 if two or more violations occur in seven years. An individual can be fined $25,000 or $50,000 without limitation of time periods if he or she engages in multiple discriminatory practices.

2. The aggrieved party, with or without filing a complaint to HUD, may bring a civil suit in federal district court within one year of the alleged violation of the act unless a complaint has been filed with HUD, in which case the period is two years. If the aggrieved party wins the case, the court may issue an injunction against the violator and award actual damages and punitive damages with no limitation by the statute.

3. The U.S. Attorney General may file a civil suit in any appropriate U.S. district court where the Attorney General has reasonable cause to believe that any person or group is engaged in a pattern of violation of the act and, as such, raises an issue of general public importance. The court may issue an injunction or restraining order against the person responsible and impose fines up to $50,000 to "vindicate the public interest." A first-time fine of $50,000 may be imposed where a "pattern of practice" of discrimination is discovered.

4. Due process, whether judicial or administrative, is accorded to all parties. This includes the right of appeal. A jury trial can be requested where monetary demands are involved.

COMMUNITY REINVESTMENT ACT

The Community Reinvestment Act was passed by Congress in 1977 and requires that financial institutions conduct activities and provide services to meet the credit and deposit needs of all members of their communities. Examples of such services would be offering basic checking as an alternative to currency exchange fees for those persons on public assistance and helping low- to moderate-income families pay their property taxes with a one-time property tax loan to be repaid within 12 to 24 months. A federal supervisory agency prepares a written evaluation of an institution's compliance with the Community Reinvestment Act.

ILLINOIS HUMAN RIGHTS ACT

The **Illinois Human Rights Act** *prohibits discrimination against a person because of race, color, religion, national origin, ancestry, age, sex, marital status, physical or mental disability, perceived disability, unfavorable discharge from the military service, or familial status.* It prohibits discrimination in the sale or rental of real estate against families with children under the age of 18 or against people with vision, hearing, or physical impairments who require a guide, hearing, or support animal, although a charge can be made for actual damages to the property caused by the animal. Further, no discrimination is allowed against persons with these disabilities in the terms, conditions, privileges, provision of services or facilities, or extra charge in a lease or sales contract.

In states like Illinois that have a law substantially equivalent to the federal fair housing law, a complaint based on the federal law may be referred to the Illinois Human Rights Commission. the case may be heard by the Illinois Human Rights Commission or, if either party so elects, by a state circuit court.

Contracts relating to real property are void and in violation of civil rights if they forbid or restrict the conveyance, encumbrance, occupancy, or lease of, or limit use of or right of entry on the basis of race, color, religion, or national origin. In addition, the law forbids a refusal to sell or rent and prohibits discriminatory differences in price, terms, or other conditions of a real estate transaction, as well as in financing of the transaction. Property operated, supervised, or controlled by religious institutions or charitable organizations and used for religious or charitable purposes can limit the use of such properties.

Exemptions

The Illinois Human Rights Act has six exemptions:

1. The sale of a single-family home by its owner is exempt as long as:
   a. The owner does not have beneficial interest in more than three single-family homes at the time of the sale.
   b. The owner or a member of the family was the last resident.
   c. The home is sold by the owner without the use of any real estate licensees or agents of licensees, sales, or rental facilities.
2. Apartments in buildings for not more than five families are exempt if the lessor or a member of the family lives in one of the apartments.
3. Room(s) in a private home where the owner or a member of the family lives or expects to live within one year are exempt.
4. Restricting the rental or sale of housing to persons of a certain age group is allowed when the housing is authorized, approved, financed, or subsidized for the benefit of that age group by any form of government or when the duly recorded initial declaration of a condominium or community association limits housing to elderly persons, provided that the owner or a member of the owner's immediate family was not in violation prior to recording as long as they continue to own or reside in such housing.
5. If membership in a religion is not restricted on account of race, color, or national origin, the religious organization or any nonprofit institution may limit the sale, rental, or occupancy of a property that it owns or operates, for other than commercial purposes, to persons of the same religion or give preference to such persons.
6. Restricting the rental of rooms in a housing accommodation to persons of the same sex is permitted.

Fair housing laws also are enacted in many cities and counties, such as in Cook County in Illinois. These are enforced on the local level.

Enforcement and Penalties

Enforcement of state laws typically is through injunctive relief or damages, or both, after a hearing or negotiated settlement. The amount of damages is determined by a civil court. The state also may require a person found guilty of violating the state laws to take affirmative action. The affirmative action could be in the form of community service, advertisements concerning fair housing, sponsorship of a seminar on fair housing, or the like. An Illinois licensee who is found guilty of illegal discrimination will have his or her license revoked or suspended unless the adjudication or the order is in the appeal process. OBRE may also impose a fine of up to $10,000.

EQUAL HOUSING OPPORTUNITY TODAY

Many people have the idea that the issue of fair housing has long been resolved through actions such as the civil rights movements of the 1960s. Despite the intention of both the 1866 and the 1968 civil rights acts to provide equal housing opportunity for all citizens, this goal has not been achieved in practice. Although the Fair Housing Act has been in effect for many years, recent HUD studies find that minorities are still confronted with discrimination in purchasing homes and in leasing rental units.

Many proposals have been developed to correct this situation. One means of enforcing the law is through an organized program of testing by civil rights groups. In 1968 the administration supported a Fair Housing Initiative Program (FHIP) to provide funding for testers. The National Association of REALTORS® negotiated an agreement with HUD to ensure that the funded testing will be objective, reliable, and controlled, and then it endorsed the program.

To address attitudes against discrimination, NAR developed a Voluntary Affirmative Marketing Program. NAR encourages its affiliates and members to adopt the program by signing an affirmative marketing agreement. Provisions of the agreement pledge signatories to adopt affirmative advertising, recruitment, and educational programs. As each April is celebrated with observances of passage of the Fair Housing Act of 1968, it is hoped that the spirit and intention of the law will be fulfilled.

PUTTING IT TO WORK

> Salespersons should be well-informed on the laws of Illinois as they apply to discrimination issues. Not only is discrimination socially offensive, but it also can jeopardize a transaction or one's license and expose one to legal liability.

DISCRIMINATION IN SALE OF REAL ESTATE ACT

In 1967, the Illinois General Assembly passed the **Discrimination in Sale of Real Estate Act** (DSREA). DSREA prohibits real estate solicitations and inducements to sell or purchase by reason of race, color, religion, national origin, ancestry, creed, disability, or sex. It also prohibits the solicitation of homeowners who have given notice not to be solicited. A solicitation can be a personal visit, telephone call, direct mail, mailbox insert, or doorknob hanger. It can also be the offer of a competitive market analysis or an inquiry to determine whether a homeowner or homeowner's acquaintance will be selling now or in the future. Nonsolicitation lists are usually organized by a homeowners' group. The names collected are then provided to brokers' offices. The office has, therefore, been given notice and cannot solicit anyone on the list in any fashion. Conviction of violation of the Illinois Real Estate Solicitation Statute may result in the revocation of a real estate licensee's license.

AMERICANS WITH DISABILITIES ACT

The **Americans with Disabilities Act,** which took effect on January 26, 1992, specifically *protects the rights of individuals with disabilities.* **Disability** is defined in USC 42, Sec. 12101, as a *physical or mental impairment that substantially limits one or more of the major life activities of a person.* Individuals with AIDS, alcoholism, or mental illness are included in this category.

Under this law, individuals with disabilities cannot be denied access to public transportation, any commercial facility, or public accommodation. This act applies to all owners and operators of public accommodations and commercial facilities, regardless of the size or number of employees. It also applies to all local and state governments.

Public accommodations are defined as private businesses that affect commerce and trade, such as inns, hotels, restaurants, theaters, convention centers, bakeries, laundromats, banks, barber shops, attorneys' offices, museums, zoos, places of education, day care centers, and health clubs. Commercial facilities are those intended for nonresidential use and affect commerce, such as factories.

To comply with this law, public accommodations and commercial facilities are to be designed, constructed, altered to meet the accessibility standards of the new law if readily achievable. "Readily achievable" means easily accomplishable and able to be carried out without much difficulty or expense. Considerations in determining if the commercial facility or public accommodation can be made accessible are:

1. nature and cost of the needed alteration
2. overall financial resources of the facility involved and number of persons employed
3. type of operation of the entity

Public accommodations must remove structural, architectural, and communication barriers in existing facilities if the removal is readily achievable. Examples of barriers to be removed or alterations to be made include placing ramps, lowering telephones, making curb cuts in sidewalks and entrances, widening doors, installing grab bars in toilet stalls, and adding raised letters on elevator controls. Commercial facilities are not required to remove the barriers in existing facilities.

In the construction of new public accommodations and commercial facilities, all areas must be readily accessible and usable by individuals with disabilities as of January 26, 1993. The Americans with Disabilities Act is enforced by the U.S. Attorney General. Punishment for violating this law includes injunctions against operation of a business, a fine up to $50,000 for the first offense, and a fine of $100,000 for any subsequent offense.

Important Points

1. The Civil Rights Act of 1968, as amended, prohibits discrimination in housing because of race, color, religion, sex, national origin, disability, or familial status.
2. Discrimination is prohibited in (a) sale or rental of housing, (b) advertising the sale or rental of housing, (c) financing of housing, and (d) provision of real estate brokerage services. The act also makes blockbusting illegal.
3. Four exemptions are provided to owners in selling or renting housing under the federal act: (a) owners who do not own more than three houses, (b) owners of apartment buildings with not more than four apartments and owner occupies one of the apartments, (c) religious organizations, as to properties used for the benefit of members only, provided that membership in the organization or club is not discriminatory, and (d) private clubs, as to lodging used for the benefit of members only. The owners' exemptions are not available if the owner used discriminatory advertising or the services of a real estate broker.
4. In addition to the four exemptions provided by the federal law, Illinois also exempts certain situations involving rental of private rooms and rental to persons of a specific age group, under certain restrictions.
5. Enforcement of Title VIII of the 1968 Civil Rights Act was amended significantly in 1988. Enforcement procedures now include: (a) administrative procedure through the Office of Equal Opportunity of HUD, which first attempts voluntary conciliation and then can refer the case to an administrative law judge, who can impose financial penalties of $10,000 to $50,000; (b) civil suit in federal court; and (c) action by the U.S. Attorney General, who may file a suit in federal court and impose penalties of up to $50,000 on the first offense in a "pattern of discrimination."
6. The Civil Rights Act of 1866 only prohibits discrimination on the basis of race. The prohibition is not limited to housing but includes all real estate transactions. The act may be enforced only by civil suit in federal court. This law has no exemptions.
7. The Illinois Real Estate Solicitation Statute prohibits the solicitation of homeowners who have given notice not to be solicited.

8. The Illinois Human Rights Act prohibits discrimination against a person because of race, color, religion, national origin, ancestry, age, sex, marital status, physical or mental disability, perceived disability, unfavorable discharge from military service, or familial status.
9. Discrimination is not allowed in the sale or rental; in the pricing, conditions or terms; or in the financing of a real estate transaction.
10. The Americans with Disabilities Act provides that individuals with disabilities cannot be denied access to public transportation, any commercial facility, or public accommodation. Barriers in existing buildings must be removed if readily achievable. New buildings must be readily accessible and usable by individuals with disabilities.

REVIEW QUESTIONS

Answers to these questions are found in the Answer Key section at the back of the book.

1. Sam Seller refuses to accept an offer to purchase his home from Juan Pedro from Spain because Sam considers the $50 of earnest money insufficient. Which of the following is correct?
    a. Sam is in violation of the Fair Housing Act of 1968 because he has discriminated on the ground of national origin.
    b. Sam refused the offer because of the small amount of earnest money, so he is not in violation of the 1968 act.
    c. Sam is in violation of the Civil Rights Act of 1866 because he discriminated on the basis of race.
    d. Sam is guilty of redlining.

2. Which of the following is not a basis of discrimination prohibited by the 1968 Act?
    a. race
    b. sex
    c. occupation
    d. religion

3. Larry Landlord refuses to rent one of five apartments in his building to Barbara Barrister, an attorney. Which of the following statements about Larry's refusal is correct?
    a. if Larry's refusal to rent to Barbara is because she is an attorney, he is not in violation of the 1968 act
    b. if Larry's refusal to rent to Barbara is because she is female, Larry is not in violation of the 1968 act
    c. if Larry's refusal to rent to Barbara is because she is a female, he is guilty of redlining
    d. it doesn't matter what Larry's reason is because he can claim an exemption

4. The Our Town Multiple Listing Service refuses to accept a listing because the home's owner is Russian. Which of the following is correct?
    a. an MLS does not come under the 1968 act because it is a private nonprofit organization
    b. the 1968 act does not prohibit discrimination against Russians
    c. the listing broker's membership in the MLS may be terminated for taking the listing
    d. the MLS is in violation of the 1968 act for denying access to the service because of the owner's national origin

5. A property manager refuses to rent an office because the rental applicant is an African American. The applicant has legal recourse under the:
    a. Civil Rights Act of 1968
    b. Civil Rights Act of 1866
    c. Civil Rights Act of 1988
    d. Civil Rights Act of 1974

6. In an advertisement offering her only house for sale, the owner states that she will give preference to cash buyers who are female and members of the Catholic religion. The owner subsequently refuses a cash offer because the offeror is a male Presbyterian. Which of the following is correct?
    a. because the seller only owns one house, she is exempt from the 1968 act
    b. because the advertisement only stated a preference, it is not discriminatory
    c. because the seller's main purpose was to obtain cash, the refusal is not discriminatory
    d. because the advertisement was in fact discriminatory, the seller's exemption is lost and she has violated the 1968 act in two ways

7. A real estate salesperson shows white prospects homes only in all-white areas. This discriminatory practice is called:

   a. redlining
   b. blockbusting
   c. steering
   d. directing

8. Ella, who owns and occupies a single-family home in Illinois, restricts the rental of rooms in her home to women only. Ella has:

   a. not violated any civil rights acts
   b. violated the Illinois Human Rights Act
   c. violated the Civil Rights Act of 1968
   d. violated the Civil Rights Act of 1974

9. Which of the following is exempt from the provisions of the 1968 act?

   a. an owner of four houses
   b. an owner occupying one of four apartments in his building
   c. a religious organization renting one of 16 apartments it owns and operates for commercial purposes
   d. an owner who has listed a residential lot for sale with a real estate broker

10. The Swansons own no real property other than their home and wish to sell the home by themselves and move to Wisconsin Rapids. They will be in violation of the Illinois Human Rights Act if they:

    a. sell only to family members
    b. sell only to persons of Norwegian descent
    c. sell only to Lutherans
    d. prohibit sale of the property to persons of Swedish descent by placing this restriction in a deed

11. The Civil Rights Act of 1968 as amended in 1988 may be enforced by all of the following EXCEPT:

    a. a civil suit for damages in federal court
    b. administrative procedures through HUD
    c. action by the U.S. Attorney General
    d. arbitration with the National Labor Relations Board

12. A homeowner avails herself of the exemption provided by the 1968 act and refuses to accept an offer because the offeror is a white person. The offeror may:

    a. bring suit in federal district court under the Civil Rights Act of 1866
    b. bring suit in federal district court under the Civil Rights Act of 1968
    c. bring suit in federal district court under the Civil Rights Act of 1988
    d. ask for arbitration with HUD

13. Salesperson Williams, an Illinois licensee, took a listing from Seller Michaels that prohibits sale of the property to persons with disabilities. Salesperson Williams:

    a. may not show the property to persons with disabilities
    b. is in violation of the Illinois Human Rights Act
    c. is in violation of the Illinois Real Estate License Act
    d. is in violation of both the Illinois Human Rights and Illinois Real Estate License Act

14. The following ad appears in a local paper: "Home for rent; limited to mature persons; 2 bedrooms; 1 bath." Which of the following is correct?

    a. the ad is in compliance with the Fair Housing Act of 1968 as amended in 1988
    b. the ad violates the Civil Rights Act of 1866
    c. the ad is in compliance with the Civil Rights Act of 1974
    d. the ad violates the Fair Housing Amendments of 1988

15. A person who uses a wheelchair requests that an apartment be modified to meet his physical needs. Which of the following is correct?

    a. the owner must make appropriate modifications at the owner's expense
    b. at the end of the tenancy, the renter must pay for returning the premises to their original condition
    c. the owner may refuse to rent to the tenant because of the needed modifications
    d. the owner may charge increased rent because of the disability and the needed modifications

16. Sonja, a single person, owns five single-family homes and plans to sell her home. She will be in violation of the Illinois Human Rights Act if she:

    a. restricts the sale to only females
    b. uses the services of a real estate broker
    c. advertises the sale of the property to females only
    d. refuses to sell to a married couple

17. Jay is telephone surveying homeowners in an area near his office to determine if they plan to move or know someone who is planning to move. Kraig, a homeowner called by Jay, tells Jay in an angry voice that his name is on a non-solicitation list and he is going to report Jay to the state's attorney. Jay may have violated the:

    a. Equal Housing Rights Act
    b. Federal Fair Housing Act
    c. Illinois Human Right Act
    d. Illinois Real Estate Solicitation Statute

18. The following phrase in a real estate ad would be considered discriminatory:

    a. mother-in-law apartment
    b. bachelor's apartment
    c. master bedroom
    d. mature couple preferred

19. An African American tries to lease a storefront for the business that she intends to open. The lessor refuses to rent the space to her due to her race. The lessor is in violation of the:

    a. Illinois Landlord–Tenant Act
    b. Federal Fair Housing Act of 1989
    c. Civil Rights Act of 1866
    d. Americans with Disabilities Act

20. Under the Americans with Disabilities Act, which of the following is NOT a public accommodation?

    a. hotel
    b. bakery
    c. factory
    d. school

CHAPTER 13

Important Terminology

- escalated lease
- eviction
- fixed lease
- graduated lease
- gross lease
- ground lease
- holdover tenant
- Illinois Security Deposit Return Act
- index lease
- lease
- lessee
- lessor
- negligence
- net lease
- option to renew
- percentage lease
- periodic lease
- privity of contract
- quiet enjoyment
- reappraisal lease
- reversionary interest
- sale and leaseback
- security deposit
- self-help
- sublease
- surrender

Landlord and Tenant (Leasehold Estates)

IN THIS CHAPTER Landlord–tenant law revolves around the lease contract. The basic law of contracts, discussed in Chapter 5, applies to the leases discussed in this chapter. The history of landlord–tenant law is vast. Most of the law prior to recent time was established by court decisions called common law. Today, many new statutes drastically change the relationship of landlord and tenant. This chapter defines and explains the parties in a lease agreement: the essential elements of a valid lease; duties, obligations, and rights of the parties to the lease agreement; and various legal leaseholds.

DEFINITIONS CONCERNING THE LANDLORD/TENANT RELATIONSHIP

A **lease** is a *contract between the owner of the property and the tenant.* Under the lease agreement, the owner transfers to the tenant a property interest, possession, for a prescribed period of time. The *owner of the property* is called the *landlord* or **lessor.** The *tenant placed in possession* is called the **lessee.** The tenant is to have quiet enjoyment of the premises, and the landlord is to receive money plus a **reversionary interest** in the property; *possession of the property will go back to the owner at the end of the lease.*

Under a lease, the lessor and lessee agree to the terms of possession and the rent to be paid. The benefit of the lease runs both to the lessor and the lessee, so either the lessor or lessee can demand to receive the contracted benefit. The *right to demand and receive the specific benefit* is based upon **privity of contract** that exists only between lessor and lessee.

Individuals who are not a party to the lease contract cannot demand to receive any benefit from the lease contract. For example, a guest of the lessee has no right to bring legal action against the lessor for lessor's breach of the lease; the guest does not have privity of contract. A person who receives the rights of the lessee by assignment, however, has privity of contract to bring suit against the lessor. Assignment of contract rights transfers the privity of contract necessary for suit.

ESSENTIAL ELEMENTS OF A LEASE

In creating a lease, the requirements of offer, acceptance, legal capacity, legal purpose, consideration, and reality of assent apply, just as they do in any contract.

Property Description

A formal legal description of the property is not required. A street address or other informal reference that is sufficiently identifying to both parties is acceptable. If the lease is for a long term, a formal legal description is recommended to accommodate recordation of the contract.

Term

The term of the lease is the period of time for which the lease will exist between landlord and tenant. The term should be specified in a sufficiently clear fashion so that all parties will know the date of expiration and the method to terminate. The term may be cut short prematurely by breach of the lease by one of the parties or by mutual agreement.

Rent

Rent is the consideration the tenant pays to the landlord for possession of the premises. In addition to possession, the rent paid assures the tenant quiet enjoyment of the premises (explained later in the chapter).

The due date of the rent should be stated in the lease. If the lease does not state when the rent it due, then the rent will be due at the end of the rental term: on a one-year lease the rent would be due in one single payment at the end of the year; on a 10-year lease it would be due in a single payment at the end of the tenth year. This concept of payment in arrears is from common law, where the traditional thought is that a user should be able to use something before being obligated to pay for it. Lessors are usually very careful to stipulate in the lease when the rent is due.

Other Lease Provisions

Leases may contain additional provisions setting out specific agreements of the landlord and tenant. One common provision is an **option to renew** the lease. This *sets forth the method for renewal and the terms* by which the renewed lease will exist. The parties also may include in the lease an option to buy. This provision allows the tenant to purchase the leased premises for a certain price for a certain period of time. In commercial leases, a right of first refusal often is given to a tenant to allow an opportunity to expand into additional space before it is leased to another tenant. This option may be at a different rental rate than originally agreed upon.

In most written leases, provisions stating who has the responsibility for maintenance and repair are included. Also, the landlord usually includes a provision prohibiting assignment of lease rights or subleasing of the premises by the tenant (discussed later in the chapter) without the landlord's approval. Examples of these provisions are found in the sample lease in Figure 13.1.

Written or Oral Provisions

The Statute of Frauds in Illinois requires that leases for a period longer than one year be in writing to be enforceable by the court. Oral leases for one year or less can generally be enforced by the courts. If a written lease is used, it is good business practice for both the lessor and lessee to sign the lease. However, common law requires only the lessor to sign the lease. The lessee acknowledges or confirms the lease by taking possession of the property.

Landlord and Tenant (Leasehold Estates) **289**

FIGURE 13.1 A sample lease.

THIS INDENTURE, Made this _____ day of _____, 19___ Between _____, Lessor, and _____, Lessee.

WITNESSETH, that Lessor has demised and leased to Lessee the Premises, situated in _____ County of _____ and State of Illinois, known and described as follows:

TO HAVE AND TO HOLD the same, unto Lessee, from the _____ day of _____ 19___ until the _____ day of _____ 19___. And Lessee in consideration of said demise, does covenant and agree with Lessor as follows:

FIRST. — To pay to Lessor at _____ as rent for the Premises for said term the sum of: _____ Dollars ($_____) payable in advance in equal monthly installments upon the first day of each and every month during the term hereof.

SECOND. — That he has examined and knows the condition of the Premises; and has received the same in good order and repair, and that he will keep the Premises in good repair during the term of this lease, at his own expense; and upon the termination of this lease will yield up the Premises to Lessor in good condition and repair (loss by fire and ordinary wear excepted).

THIRD. — That he will not sublet the Premises, nor any part thereof, nor assign this lease without the prior written consent of Lessor.

FOURTH. — To pay (in addition to the rents above specified) all water rents taxed, levied or charged on the Premises, for and during the time for which this lease is granted.

Lessee hereby irrevocably constitutes _____ or any attorney of any Court of Record, attorney for Lessee in Lessee's name, on default by Lessee of any of the covenants herein, to enter Lessee's appearance in any such Court of Record, waive process and service thereof, and trial by jury, and confess judgment against Lessee in favor of Lessor or Lessor's assigns for forcible detainer of the Premises, with costs of said suit; and also to enter the appearance in such court of Lessee, waive process and service thereof, and confess judgment from time to time, for any rent which may be due to Lessor or Lessor's assigns by the terms of this lease, with costs, and reasonable attorney's fees, and to waive all errors and all right of appeal, from said judgment and judgments; and to file a consent in writing that a writ of restitution or other proper writ of execution may be issued immediately; Lessee hereby expressly waives all right to any notice or demand under any statute in this state relating to forcible entry and detainer.

In case the Premises shall be rendered untenantable by fire or other casualty, Lessor, may, at his option, terminate this lease, or repair the Premises within thirty days, and failing so to do or upon the destruction of the Premises by fire, the term hereby created shall cease and determine.

All the parties to this lease agree that the covenants and agreements herein contained shall be binding upon, apply and inure to, their respective heirs, executors, administrators and assigns.

WITNESS the hands and seals of the parties hereto the day and year first above written.

IN PRESENCE OF

_____ (SEAL)

_____ (SEAL)

_____ (SEAL)

GUARANTEE

For value received _____ hereby guarantee the payment of the rent and the performance of the covenants and agreements of Lessee in the within Lease, in manner and form as in said Lease provided.

Witness _____ hand _____ and seal _____ this _____ day of _____, 19___

_____ (SEAL)

ASSIGNMENT AND ACCEPTANCE

For value received _____ hereby assign all _____ right, title and interest in and to the within Lease unto _____ heirs and assigns, and in consideration of the consent to this assignment by the Lessor _____ guarantee the performance by said _____ of all the covenants on the part of Lessee in said Lease mentioned.

Witness _____ hand _____ and seal _____ this _____ day of _____, 19___

_____ (SEAL)

_____ (SEAL)

In consideration of the above assignment and the written consent of Lessor thereto, _____ hereby assume and agree to make all payments and perform all the covenants and conditions of the within Lease, by Lessee to be made and performed.

Witness _____ hand _____ and seal _____ this _____ day of _____, 19___

_____ (SEAL)

CONSENT TO ASSIGNMENT

_____ hereby consent to the assignment of the within Lease to _____ on the express condition, however, that the assignor shall remain liable for the prompt payment of the rent and performance of the covenants on the part of Lessee as therein mentioned, and that no further assignment of said Lease or subletting of the premises or any part thereof shall be made without written assent first had thereto.

Witness _____ hand _____ and seal _____ this _____ day of _____, 19___

_____ (SEAL)

LESSOR'S ASSIGNMENT

In consideration of One Dollar to _____ in hand paid, _____ hereby transfer, assign and set over to _____ and assigns _____ interest in the within Lease, and the Rent thereby secured

Witness _____ hand _____ and seal _____ this _____ day of _____, 19___

_____ (SEAL)

_____ (SEAL)

Recordation

Most short-term leases are not recorded, but for ground leases (discussed later), leases of more than one year in duration, and leases with an option to buy, it is in the best interest of the tenant to record the lease in the jurisdiction where the property lies. Possession of the property by the tenant also provides actual notice. Recordation provides constructive notice of the tenant's rights in the event of sale or death of the landlord.

Obligations of Landlord and Tenant

The common law of leases, which is the law set by past court decisions, has established the obligations of landlord and tenant in many states. In recent years, however, with an increase in the number of residential tenants, some states have passed specific legislation setting out the obligations of landlord and tenant. The most widely used statute is called the Uniform Landlord and Tenant Act. As of 1991, 13 states have adopted this law totally or with modifications. Illinois does not have such an act. However, many cities including Chicago, have adopted their own landlord and tenant act.

Whether under the common law or under specific statute, terms of the lease control the obligations and duties of landlord and tenant. Without a lease agreement to indicate which party is responsible for certain items, common law or the specific state law dictates the responsible party.

Mutual Obligations

Under contract law, the validity of a contract can be challenged if both parties are not bound or if both parties have not received consideration. Under a lease, the landlord's consideration is receipt of rent. The tenant's consideration is possession of the premises and the right of quiet enjoyment. The landlord's obligation to give possession of the premises to the tenant is directly tied to the tenant's payment of rent. If one party fails in his or her responsibility (consideration), the other party may be relieved of his or her duty. (Because of the interplay of many of the rights and duties—payment, maintenance, liquidated damages, and so on—one should never assume the relief of one's duties without court support of this position.)

Landlord's Duties

The landlord is required to put the tenant in possession of the premises. The tenant is entitled to **quiet enjoyment** of the premises, meaning that *no one will interrupt the tenancy or invade the premise without the tenant's consent.* This includes the landlord. The landlord does not have an automatic right to inspect the leased premises although the tenant may agree, in the lease, to the landlord's right to inspect. The landlord also has the right to enter the premises in an emergency, such as in the case of fire or burst water pipes, to protect the premises.

In the case of residential property, the landlord usually is obligated to have the premises in *habitable*, or *livable*, condition at the beginning of the lease and to maintain the premises in habitable shape during the term of the lease. (The concept of an implied warranty of habitability was confirmed by the Illinois Supreme Court in 1972.) The requirement for maintenance may be shifted to the tenant by agreement of the parties. The landlord also is required to warn the tenant of any dangers that are not obvious (latent dangers) such as electrical circuit problems, loose floor boards or steps, or holes in the floor hidden by carpet.

Unless the lease agreement specifically states the contrary, the lease allows for the tenant to assign his lease or to sublease. In an assignment, the assignor (original lessee) transfers all his rights to the assignee without retaining a reversion or remainder in the lease. In a **sublease**, *the sublessor (original lessee) gives the sublessee his rights in the lease while retaining an interest in the lease.* We refer to this lease as a sandwich lease and the sublessor as the sandwich man.

Tenant's Duties

The tenant's basic obligation under any lease (apart from the payment of rent) is to maintain the premises in the same condition as at the beginning of the lease, with ordinary wear and tear excepted. This is the usual deterioration caused by normal living circumstances. The tenant will be held responsible for damage or waste. During occupancy, the tenant is expected to use the premises only for legal purposes and to conform to all local laws.

The tenant is obligated, of course, to pay the agreed-upon rent in a timely fashion. Under common law, rent is due at the end of the lease period unless the lease agreement states otherwise. Because this is typically unacceptable to the landlord, lease agreements usually require rent to be paid in advance on a month-to-month basis.

At the end of the lease, the tenant is obligated to vacate the premises without the need for legal eviction by the landlord.

If the tenant has guests (invitees) or customers (licensees), the tenant must warn them of any hidden dangers that might cause harm.

PUTTING IT TO WORK

Because of the many variables involved and the subjective nature of the words "reasonable" and "wear and tear," the lease should outline specifics such as "lawn maintained in present condition," "carpets cleaned by tenant annually," and so on.

Law of Negligence

Negligence is defined as a *failure to use that care that a reasonable person would use in like circumstances.* The term is relative and depends on the circumstances of each case. Under the law of negligence, a person is liable for damages that result to another person if a duty to that person is owed and the duty is not performed in a reasonable fashion.

Under landlord–tenant law, the landlord is responsible for damage that occurs to the tenant, tenant's guests or clients, or tenant's possession only if the landlord has a duty to that person and the landlord fails to perform that duty. An example of landlord negligence is if the landlord assures the tenant that all plumbing apparatus is properly maintained at the premises and the plumbing then ceases to function because of improper maintenance, and as a result of the faulty plumbing, the tenant's possessions are damaged. Negligence law does not apply where, through no lack of maintenance, the plumbing ceases to function or if the plumbing ceases to function as a result of the tenant's action and damage occurs to the tenant's possessions.

The duty of care imposed upon the landlord is the care that a reasonable and prudent person would exercise under like conditions. A landlord's liability also may be created by failure to comply with basic safety codes and laws. Examples of this might be failure to install a smoke alarm or porch railing. Any injury because of the absence of these features results in liability on the part of the landlord.

The law of negligence also applies to tenants. If tenants do not exercise reasonable care in their use of the premises and damage occurs to the landlord's property, the tenant is liable for the resulting damages.

Lead Paint Disclosures

The Illinois Lead Poisoning Prevention Act requires the owners of residential rental units constructed before 1978 to provide tenants with a brochure prepared by the Department of Public Health concerning lead paint. Unless the owner has corrected the problem and received a certificate of compliance, the owners of any rental cited for lead paint must give prospective tenants written notice of the citation. EPA/HUD lead-based paint regulations that became effective in 1996 are discussed in Chapter 5.

Withholding Rent

In some cases, the tenant can claim *constructive eviction* and thus be relieved of the obligation to pay rent. In such cases, through the landlord's lack of care, the tenant has been evicted, for all practical purposes, because enjoyment of the premises is not available. This usually happens when heat and water are not available to the tenant because of the landlord's lack of care. To claim constructive eviction in most states, however, the tenant must actually vacate the premises while the conditions that make the premises uninhabitable still exist. The lease is terminated under the claim of constructive eviction. This is not an automatic right that the tenant can assume; it may have to be litigated.

Security Deposits

Most landlords require the tenant to deposit a certain *sum of money that will be refunded at the end of the lease* based upon the condition of the premises. This **security deposit** often is negotiated as one month's rent. The money is intended for repair of only that damage the tenant causes beyond ordinary wear and tear, and the landlord is not to use it for basic cleaning and repainting. However, the landlord is allowed to charge the tenant a separate sum for cleaning and repainting if it was agreed to in the lease. In some cases the landlord is to pay interest to the tenant for the moneys held as deposits.

The **Illinois Security Deposit Return Act** *provides that persons leasing residential property containing five or more units cannot withhold any part of a security deposit for compensation for property damage unless an itemized statement of the damage along with the estimated or actual cost of repairs is provided to the lessee.* The statement must be provided within 30 days of the date the lessee vacated the premises and can be delivered in person or by mail. Actual receipts must accompany the statement or must be delivered within 30 days of the estimate. If the lessor does not meet any of the provisions, the lessee must be given the full amount of the security deposit within 45 days of vacating the premises. The lessor may utilize his or her own labor to repair any damages the lessee caused and include the reasonable cost of his or her labor to repair the damage.

For residential properties with 25 or more units, the lessor must pay interest on security deposits at an interest rate equal to the rate on the minimum passbook account of the largest commercial bank in Illinois. The security deposit must have been held for more than six months. A penalty may be imposed on landlords who do not pay the interest as required.

If the landlord fails to comply with any and all requirements, the tenant may collect double the security deposit plus court costs and attorney fees.

Other Laws Affecting the Rental of Property

The Civil Rights Act of 1968 and the Americans With Disabilities Act (ADA) are just two laws that have a significant impact on the rental of property. Fair housing laws and the ADA are discussed in Chapter 12. In addition, many local municipalities have passed their own landlord–tenant acts and fair housing laws. Chicago, for one, has a very extensive landlord–tenant act. When involved in the rental of property, the owner or manager should inquire about any additional rental law requirements with the municipality in which the property is located.

Termination and Eviction Remedies

A lease may terminate in a variety of ways. The simplest way is for the lease term to expire. At expiration of the lease, if proper notice to terminate the lease was given (see Figure 13.2) and no renewal agreement is reached, the duties and rights of the landlord and tenant terminate. The tenant vacates the premises, and possession reverts to the landlord.

The landlord and tenant also can mutually agree to cancel a lease prior to expiration of the term. This is called **surrender**. Mutual cancellation also terminates the parties' duties and rights. Possession reverts to the landlord. Because cancellation of the lease is by mutual agreement, it may occur after a breach of the lease by either party.

Destruction of the premises may or may not terminate a lease. Leases that include building and land (single-user properties such as a single-family homes, freestanding stores, or freestanding industrial buildings) typically do not terminate with the destruction of the premises. The lease for one unit in a multi-unit building would be terminated upon the destruction of the premises. A renter in an apartment building, therefore, would have her lease terminated and would no longer be responsible for the rent. A renter of a single-family home, however, could find himself responsible for the remainder of the lease.

The lease also can be terminated by the landlord's evicting the tenant. This can occur during the term of the lease if the tenant breaches the agreement—for example, by failing to pay rent. It also can occur *after the lease agreement expires and the tenant fails or refuses to vacate the premises.* At this point, the tenant is called a **holdover tenant,** and the landlord requests ouster of the tenant and his or her belongings and return of possession of the premises. In some cases, the landlord requests a landlord's lien on the tenant's belongings as security for payment of rent owed. This type of lien on personal property falls under the Uniform Commercial Code (UCC).

An Illinois landlord may serve a tenant who defaults on the rent with a five-day written notice of demand for payment of the rent. If the tenant does not pay the rent, the landlord may terminate the lease automatically and sue for possession without further notice.

If a tenant defaults on terms of the lease, including failure to pay the rent, a 10-day written notice may be served on the tenant. This notice terminates the lease and demands possession of the property. If the default is cured after the 10-day period following notice, the landlord may still sue for possession without further notice. If nonpayment of rent was the only default and the landlord thereafter accepts rent, he or she has waived the right to proceed with the suit. Illinois allows both the 5- and 10-day notices to be served by personal delivery to the tenant or to anyone 14 years or older residing on the premises. The notice can also be sent by certified or registered mail or may be posted on the premises.

Eviction is a *legal action in the court system for removal of the tenant and his or her belongings and a return of possession of the premises to the landlord.* Eviction is different from **self-help,** in which *the landlord, without the aid or control of the court system, physically removes the tenant and his or her belongings from the premises or* *takes action to prevent tenant access to the premises.* This is a violation of common law by the landlord. Illinois does not allow self-help.

Landlords in Illinois may file a suit for forcible entry and detainer action in the circuit court of the county where the property is located. The landlord names an appearance date in the complaint, and the tenant is required to appear in court not fewer than 7 days or more than 40 days after the service of summons.

The tenant may request a jury trial; if not requested, the trial is held on the appearance date. If the court finds in favor of the landlord, a judgment for possession and moneys owed will be entered. An order of possession will be issued. If after a judgment the tenant refuses to leave the premises, the order will be delivered to the sheriff, who will forcibly evict the tenant.

A landlord seeking eviction is well-advised to hire an attorney to handle an eviction proceeding or to obtain a copy of the court rules and forms to assure compliance.

As set out earlier, a lease also can be terminated by the tenant's claim of constructive eviction. This claim is limited to residential properties.

A lease also can terminate if the tenant abandons the premises and the landlord reenters to accept return of possession of the premises. This is similar to cancellation of the lease. Upon the tenant's abandonment, the landlord does not have to accept return of the premises; instead, he or she can pursue the tenant for rent under the lease. If the landlord does accept return of the premises, he or she may still pursue the tenant for lost rent under the old lease. The landlord must use his or her best efforts to re-rent the premises. This is called *mitigating damages.*

A lease agreement does not always terminate upon the death of the landlord or the tenant. The type of leasehold existing between the landlord and tenant determines whether the lease survives at death of a party. These leaseholds are discussed next. The lease agreement does not terminate upon a landlord's selling the premises. The new owner is bound by the terms of the lease.

Leasehold (Nonfreehold) Estates

Leasehold (nonfreehold) estates were discussed initially in Chapter 2, in conjunction with the bundle of rights in ownership of real estate. A leasehold estate is also called a rental estate. These estates are less than a lifetime. Leasehold estates are created by a contract providing contractual rights and duties to both parties, as discussed earlier in this chapter. Leasehold estates provide possession, but not title, to the tenant. The owner retains the title and the right of reversion of possession upon termination of the lease. The relationship of landlord and tenant exists between the parties. These estates may be called estates, tenancies, or leaseholds and are more fully described below.

Estate for Years

The key feature of the estate, tenancy, or leasehold for years is that it exists for only a fixed period of time. The term "years" is misleading in that the estate does not have to

Figure 13.2 Illinois requirements regarding notice to terminate a periodic estate.

TYPE OF TENANCY	NOTICE REQUIRED TO TERMINATE:
Year-to-year	60 days written notice
Month-to-month	30 days written notice (if for a period shorter than a year but longer than a week)
Week-to-week	7 days written notice
Farm tenancy year-to-year	4 months written notice

FIGURE 13.3 Leasehold (nonfreehold) estates.

LEASEHOLD (NONFREEHOLD) ESTATES

An interest in real estate that is of limited duration and provides the right of possession and control but not title.

Estate at will	Estate at sufferance	Estate for years	Periodic estate
A leasehold estate that may be terminated at will by either party.	Describes the situation in which the tenant continues to occupy property after lawful authority has expired.	A leasehold estate of definite duration that terminates automatically.	A leasehold estate that automatically renews itself for successive tenancy unless one party terminates.

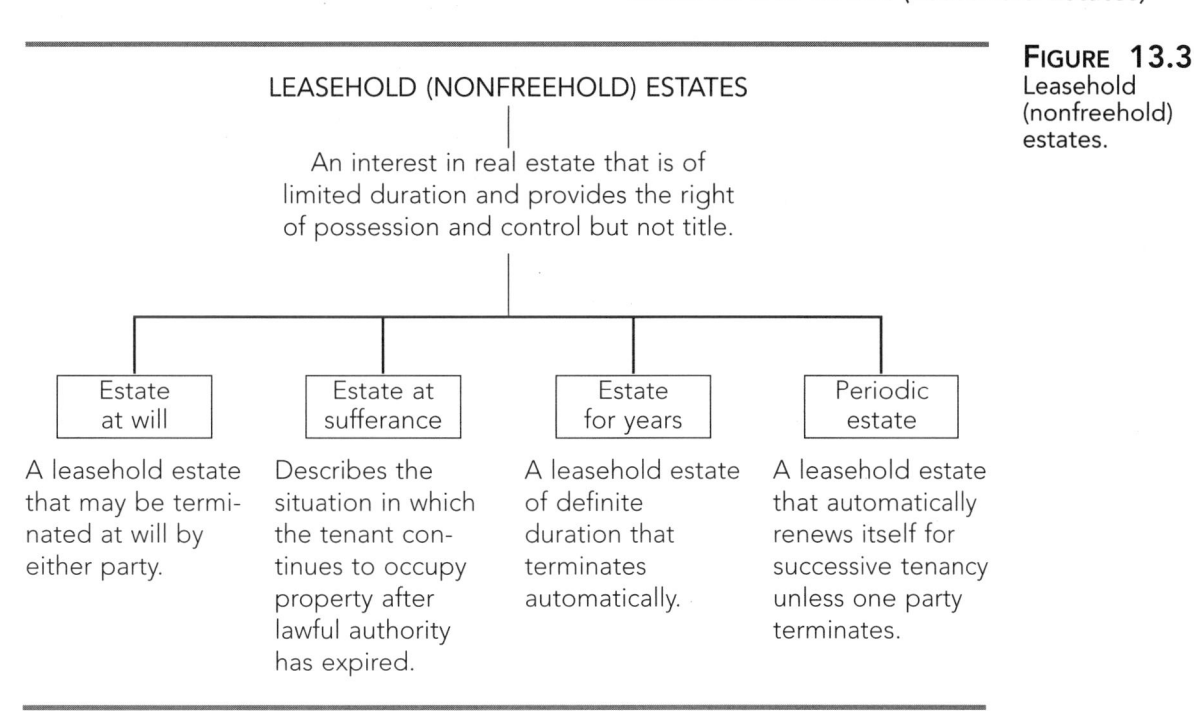

be in effect for a year or more but simply for a fixed period, which can be as short as a week or even one day. At the end of that stated time, the estate (rental agreement) terminates automatically without any need for either party to give notice to the other. If any uncertainty exists about the duration of the lease, it is not an estate for years.

Illinois requires that if this estate is for more than one full year, the lease must be in writing to be valid. The lease does not have to be recorded to be valid. The tenant's rights are established by possession of the property. If the property is sold with a tenant in possession at the time of sale, the purchaser will have to honor the lease. At the death of either the landlord or the tenant, heirs of the deceased party are bound by the terms of the lease. The lease is considered to be inheritable because the obligations and rights of the lease pass to the estate or heirs of the decedent.

Periodic Estate (Tenancy from Year-to-Year)

The estate, tenancy, or leasehold from year-to-year is commonly known as a periodic tenancy. The term "year-to-year" is misleading in that the estate does not have to be in effect for one year or more. The period length can be a week, a month, or any other negotiated time period. The key feature of a **periodic lease** is that it *automatically renews itself for another period at the end of each period unless one party gives notice to the other* at the prescribed time prior to the end of the lease. This notice period may be one to three months, depending upon the state of residence. For example, if the required notice period is one month and the parties enter the last 30 days of the lease without notifying the other of any change, a new lease is created automatically for another period at the same terms. (See Figure 13.2.) At the death of either the landlord or the tenant, heirs of the deceased party are bound by terms of the lease, including giving notice if the heirs wish to terminate.

Estate (Tenancy) at Will

In the estate at will, duration of the term is completely unknown at the time the estate is created, because either party may terminate the lease simply by giving notice to the other party. This type of leasehold is typical in a casual arrangement, such as a family setting in which a parent rents to an adult child. At the death of either the landlord or the tenant, this leasehold terminates, unlike the estate for years and the periodic lease.

Estate (Tenancy) at Sufferance

An estate at sufferance is not truly an estate that the parties voluntarily establish. This term is used simply to describe a tenant who was originally in lawful possession of another's property but refuses to leave after his right to possession terminates. This might be upon termination of any of the three previously discussed leases. The term "estate at sufferance" differentiates between the tenant at sufferance, who originally was in lawful possession of the property, and someone who has been on the property illegally from the beginning (trespasser). The estate at sufferance continues until the property owner brings a legal action to evict the person wrongfully holding over or until the one holding over vacates voluntarily. During this period, the occupier is called a tenant at sufferance. A tenant at sufferance is not a trespasser. The legal action to remove a tenant at sufferance is eviction, not an action in trespass.

PUTTING IT TO WORK

Rights and duties of the parties regarding notice, termination, and inheritance are determined first by which of the four leaseholds exists. The difference between the leaseholds is not in how long they last but, rather, in the agreement as to when and how termination is established. The termination may be at a fixed date (estate for years), at the end of a recurrent period (periodic estate), or open-ended (estate at will).

TYPES OF LEASES

Gross and Net Leases

The two primary classifications of leases, based on arrangement of payment of expenses of the rental property, are gross lease and net lease. A **gross lease** provides for *the owner (lessor) to pay all expenses,* such as real property taxes, insurance, and maintenance. In a **net lease,** *the tenant (lessee) pays some or all of the expenses.* Sometimes the net lease is referred to as net, double net, or triple net, depending upon how many property expenses the tenant pays. Certain other expenses of the property, such as income taxes, depreciation, and mortgage payments, are not considered operating expenses. These are the owner's personal expenses, not expenses of the building.

Variations of the standard lease are discussed next. Any of these variations can be either gross or net. The arrangement for paying property expenses is the determining factor.

Graduated Lease

A **graduated lease** is one in which the *rental amount changes from period to period* over the lease term. The lease contract specifies the change in rental amount, which usually is an increase in stair-step fashion. This type of lease could be utilized for a new business tenant whose income is expected to increase with time.

Escalated Lease

An **escalated lease,** usually a gross lease, *provides for rental changes in proportion to changes in the lessor's cost of ownership and operation of the property.* As the lessor's obligations for the real property taxes and operating expenses change, the lease rent changes in specified proportions.

Index Lease

In an **index lease,** the *rental amount changes in proportion to changes in the government cost of living index or some other index* agreed to by the parties.

Fixed Lease

A **fixed lease** is one in which the *rental amount remains constant during the term of the lease.* This is sometimes called a flat lease.

Reappraisal Lease

With a **reappraisal lease,** *changes in rental amount are based on changes in property value, as demonstrated by periodic reappraisals of the property.* These appraisals may occur at three- or five-year intervals in the case of a long-term lease. The rent changes a specified percentage of the previous year's rent as spelled out in the lease.

Percentage Lease

Many retail commercial leases are percentage leases. A **percentage lease** has *a base rent plus an additional monthly rent that is a percentage of the lessee's gross sales.* Most commercial leases in cases where the lessee is using the property to conduct a retail business are percentage leases. This is especially true of shopping malls. The percentage lease provides the lessor with a guaranteed monthly rental plus the opportunity to participate in the lessee's sales volume on a percentage basis.

Ground Lease

A **ground lease** is a *lease of unimproved land,* usually for construction purposes. The ground lease normally contains a provision that the lessee will construct a building on the land. Ownership of the land and improvements is separated. The ground lease is typically a long-term lease to allow the lessee sufficient time to recoup the cost of improvements. This type of lease also is typically a net lease in that the lessee is required to maintain the improvements, pay the property taxes, and pay the expenses of the property.

Oil and Gas Leases

In oil and gas leases, the landowner usually receives a one-time lease payment in exchange for giving the oil and gas company the right to drill for oil or gas for a long period of time. If no drilling occurs but the oil and gas company wishes to continue the lease, it typically pays a small flat monthly or annual fee. If no drilling occurs and the company does not make any further payments, the lease expires and terminates.

Sale and Leaseback

A **sale and leaseback** is a *transaction wherein a property owner sells a property to an investor and the investor agrees to immediately lease back the property to the seller.* This type of transaction usually is used by an owner of business property who wishes to free capital invested in the real estate and still retain possession and control of the property under a lease.

Important Points

1. A lease is created by contract between the owner of property and the tenant. The landlord or owner is the lessor; the tenant is the lessee.
2. The landlord and tenant are bound by contractual rights and obligations created by the lease agreement.
3. The transfer of the entire remaining term of a lease by the lessee is an assignment. A transfer of part of the lease term with a reversion to the lessee is a subletting.
4. In a lease of residential property, the landlord has the duty to provide habitable premises to the tenant.
5. The tenant has a duty to maintain and return the premises to the landlord, at expiration of the lease, in the same condition as at the beginning of the lease, ordinary wear and tear excepted.
6. The tenant can make a claim of constructive eviction when the premises become uninhabitable because of the landlord's lack of maintenance. A claim of constructive eviction will terminate the lease.
7. The Illinois Lead Poisoning Prevention Act requires the owners of residential rental units constructed before 1978 to provide tenants with a brochure concerning the health hazards associated with lead paint.
8. Leases are terminated by (a) expiration of lease term, (b) mutual agreement, (c) breach of condition, (d) self-help, (e) court-ordered eviction, or (f) constructive eviction. The law does not favor self-help.
9. The return of security deposits in the leasing of residential properties containing five or more units is regulated by the Illinois Security Deposit Return Act. No part of the security deposit can be withheld for compensation of damages unless an itemized statement of the damages, along with the estimated or actual cost of the repairs, is provided within 30 days of the date of vacation of the premises.
10. A tenant who defaults on the rent may be served with a five-day written notice for demand of payment of the rent. If not paid, the landlord may terminate the lease and sue for possession without further notice.
11. If in default on nonpayment of the rent or other terms of a lease, a 10-day notice may be served on the tenant. This notice terminates the lease and demands possession of the property. Even if the default is cured, the landlord may sue for possession of the property.
12. Leases are nonfreehold estates. A tenant at sufferance is not a trespasser.
13. Landlords may file a forcible entry and detainer action to begin eviction proceedings.
14. Illinois requires that leases for more than one year be in writing to be enforceable in a court.
15. The two main classifications of leases are gross lease and net lease. Under a gross lease, the landlord pays the real property taxes, insurance, and maintenance of the property. Under a net lease, the tenant pays some or all of these expenses.
16. Types of lease include the graduated lease, escalated lease, index lease, fixed lease, reappraisal lease, percentage lease, ground lease, oil and gas leases, and sale and leaseback.

REVIEW QUESTIONS

Answers to these questions are found in the Answer Key section at the back of the book.

1. A transaction in which a lessee transfers the remainder of a lease term without reversion is a(n):
   a. assignment
   b. option to renew
   c. sandwich lease
   d. sublease

2. Which of the following leaseholds has the characteristic of a definite termination date agreed upon by the parties?
   a. periodic estate
   b. estate for years
   c. estate at will
   d. estate at sufferance

3. A tenant at sufferance is:
   a. the owner of a freehold estate
   b. a trespasser
   c. a holdover tenant
   d. a lessor in possession

4. When a lease terminates with no right to renew and the tenant fails to vacate, the tenant is holding a(n):
   a. estate for years
   b. estate at will
   c. estate at sufferance
   d. periodic estate

5. According to the Statute of Frauds, an oral lease for five years is:
   a. enforceable
   b. unenforceable
   c. assignable
   d. renewable

6. A lease with a term from January 1 to July 1 of the same year is a(n):
   a. estate for years
   b. estate at will
   c. estate at sufferance
   d. periodic estate

7. The right of the lessee to uninterrupted use of the leased premises is called:
   a. conveyance
   b. quiet enjoyment
   c. quiet commencement
   d. letting the premises

8. If cost of maintenance is increasing and rents are increasing, a fixed lease arrangement for a long term is advantageous to:
   a. the tenant
   b. the landlord
   c. both landlord and tenant
   d. neither landlord nor tenant

9. Mr. A buys a building owned by Ms. X. Ms. X has leased the building to ABC Company for seven years. Mr. A must:
   a. renegotiate the lease with ABC
   b. evict ABC to get possession
   c. share the space with ABC
   d. honor the lease agreement

10. Which of the following lease arrangements is designed to allow the lessee to receive her capital investment from the leased property?
    a. percentage lease
    b. index lease
    c. step-up lease
    d. sale and leaseback

11. A lease from period to period will not be terminated by:
    a. mutual agreement of the lessor and lessee
    b. eviction by the court
    c. death of the lessor
    d. abandonment by lessee and acceptance by lessor

12. Paul, an 18-year-old musician, has entered into an oral lease for an apartment in Chicago for two years. Under the circumstances, which of the following statements is true?
    a. Paul may not enter into a valid lease contract
    b. Paul's lease is not enforceable in court
    c. Paul's lease is enforceable in court
    d. Paul may cause damage to the property without recourse

13. When a tenant under a valid lease gives up possession of the leased premises to the landlord prior to expiration of the lease, it is called:

    a. novation
    b. abatement
    c. abandonment
    d. renunciation

14. A lease that provides for an adjustment in rent to cover the lessor's operating expenses is called:

    a. escalated
    b. accelerated
    c. sufferance
    d. gross lease

15. Under a residential lease, if the lessor does not provide habitable premises, the lessee can claim:

    a. eviction
    b. constructive eviction
    c. habitability damages
    d. mitigation of damages

16. Joan Delaurenti, a tenant in a six flat owned by Bill Reilly, caused considerable damage to the unit she rented. Under the Illinois Security Deposit Return Act, Reilly must do all of the following except:

    a. provide Delaurenti with an itemized list of estimated repairs with in 30 days
    b. provide the actual receipts for repairs within 30 days of the estimate
    c. allow the tenant to make the repairs
    d. return any of the security deposit not needed to pay for the repairs

17. If a lease does not state when the rent is due, then the rent automatically will be due:

    a. on the first of the month
    b. on the fifteenth of the month
    c. at the end of the month
    d. at the end of the lease term

18. Louis rents an apartment in Springfield, Illinois. Louis is two months behind in his rent payment. The landlord, who wishes to sue for payment must first:

    a. serve Louis with a 5- or 10-day written notice demanding payment
    b. terminate the lease
    c. notify the sheriff
    d. lock Louis out of the apartment

19. A lease with a fixed low base rent plus an additional amount based upon gross receipts of the lessee is a(n):

    a. percentage lease
    b. gross lease
    c. net lease
    d. escalated lease

20. The final tenant in sale and leaseback is the:

    a. seller
    b. buyer
    c. lessor
    d. mortgagor

21. Under a lease, the reversionary interest is owned by the:

    a. lessor
    b. lessee
    c. tenant for years
    d. life tenant

22. At the death of the landlord under an estate for years, the lease is:

    a. terminated
    b. expired
    c. not affected
    d. cancelled

23. Kendra's apartment in a large apartment complex is destroyed in an explosion. Which of the following is correct?

    a. Kendra's lease is terminated
    b. Kendra must accept an apartment elsewhere in the complex for the remainder of her lease
    c. Kendra must find a place to live until the building is repaired and is then obligated for the remaining months still on her lease
    d. Kendra must follow the directives of the property manager regarding relocation

24. The Illinois Security Deposit Return Act requires the lessor of properties containing 25 or more units to pay interest on security deposits at a rate:

    a. of 5 percent
    b. 1.5 percent below the 12 month average of treasury bills
    c. equal to the minimum passbook account of the largest commercial bank in Illinois
    d. equal to the cost of funds index published by the Federal Home Loan Bank Board

25. The Illinois Lead Poisoning Prevention Act requires owners of residential units constructed before 1978 to:

   a. remove all substances containing lead
   b. test each unit for lead paint
   c. post notices of lead paint contamination at each entry of the unit
   d. provide tenants with a brochure concerning lead paint

CHAPTER 14

Important Terminology

anchor store
capital reserve budget
coinsurance clause
corrective maintenance
endorsement
extended coverage
face amount
fire insurance policy
homeowner's policy
homeowner's warranty (HOW)
insurable interest
leasing agent license

management agreement
management proposal
operating budget
package policy
preventive maintenance
property management
property management report
property manager
resident manager
risk management
stabilized budget
strip center

Property Management and Insurance

IN THIS CHAPTER Property management is one of a number of specializations within the real estate industry. A **property manager** is *a person who manages properties as an agent for owners.* In acting as an agent, the property manager is a fiduciary and therefore owes all the obligations imposed by the law of agency to each owner-principal. The discussion in this chapter centers on the functions and purpose of property managers. Property insurance and homeowner's warranty (HOW) policies also are explained.

THE BASICS OF PROPERTY MANAGEMENT

By applying real estate knowledge and expertise, a property manager strives to produce the greatest net return possible for the owner. He or she is responsible for protecting the owner's investments. Because the property manager acts as the owner's agent in managing and, typically, renting, leasing, and perhaps selling the property, the property manager must have a real estate license in Illinois, as in other states. In 1995, the Illinois legislature created a new classification of license, the **leasing agent license,** *a limited scope license that restricts the licensee working under the supervision of a broker to leasing and collecting rent from residential properties.* The Illinois Real Estate License Act allows for a grace period of 120 days in which a prospective licensee may complete a 15-hour class qualifying her to take the state examination required for leasing agents. More information on the leasing agent license can be found in Chapter 16.

In addition to a license, the property manager also must have comprehensive, specialized training to be able to satisfactorily perform the functions expected under the typical contract with the property owner. Some of this knowledge may be acquired through courses provided by the Institute of Real Estate Management, an affiliate of the National Association of REALTORS®. After completing this program, individuals receive the professional designation of Certified Property Manager (CPM). Other associations for property managers include the National Apartment Association, the National Association of Residential Property Managers, the Building Owners and Managers Institute, and the Community Association Institute.

A **resident manager** is *a person living on the premises who is a salaried employee of the owner or the managing broker.* In Illinois and some other states, this person is not required to have a real estate license if he or she is employed directly by the owner or the managing broker. Illinois allows nonlicensed residential lessees to receive fees or compensation for referring prospective tenants to the lessor. The prospective tenants must be seeking a unit in the same building or complex as the lessee. The lessee cannot refer more than three prospective tenants in a 12-month period. In a 12-month period, the lessee may receive compensation of no more than one month's rent or $1,000, whichever is less. The tenant may not show a unit or discuss the terms or conditions of a lease with a prospective tenant.

Expert management is often needed for income property to be a profitable investment. Competent **property management** provides a *comprehensive, orderly program, on a continuing basis, analyzing all investment aspects of a property to ensure a financially successful project.* The need for property management has increased in recent years as a result of the trend toward absentee ownership by investors and larger and more complicated properties in need of management. As a result, many brokerage firms have separate staffs of property managers.

Types of Properties and Management

Many different types of properties can benefit from real estate management services, including (a) residential property management, which includes apartments, condominiums, single-family homes, and vacation property; (b) retail or commercial property management, which includes offices, small retail stores, office condominiums, and large shopping malls; (c) industrial property management, including industrial parks and industrial warehouses; (d) farm property management; and (e) management by homeowners' association, which provides physical property management.

Residential Property Management

Residential property includes apartments, single-family housing, multi-family housing, condominiums, vacation houses, and mobile home parks. The concerns of a property manager when selecting tenants for residential properties include credit history of tenants, past landlord references, and employment status. The manager also must be involved with maintenance and repair of the premises and eviction of tenants. The manager has to be in tune with the local housing market.

PUTTING IT TO WORK

Although the manager's function is to represent the owner in most situations regarding the property (with tenants, repair people, city officials, and so on), the manager may not be able to represent the owner in court proceedings such as evictions. These actions may require an attorney. Consult your local law.

Retail Property Management

Most retail properties managed by a property manager are in strip centers, neighborhood shopping centers, and regional malls. A **strip center** consists of *more than four stores located conveniently and with easy access to a main roadway.* Neighborhood shopping centers usually are made up of several buildings grouped together with common parking and common access. Regional malls typically are under one roof and include several *nationally recognized stores* called **anchor stores.** A manager of these properties must select tenants suitable for this type of center. The manager also must be aware of the desires of retail tenants as to noncompetition from like tenants, group or common advertising, and common area maintenance.

Industrial Property Management

Based upon the desired economic growth of many cities and towns, industrial developments and industrial parks are common. These are often handled by a professional manager. Property managers must be aware of the transportation systems and utility services available in the area. In addition, they must be knowledgeable about tax rates, tax incentives, available labor force, commercial financing, and community services.

Farm Property Management

Farm property can consist of grain crops, animal production, dairy production, or a combination of these. Besides understanding accounting methods, the property manager must be familiar with crop production, commodity prices, soil types, environmental controls, and soil conservation. As more and more farms are owned by corporations, the property manager becomes indispensable.

Management by Homeowners' Associations

Although not always involved with leasing or renting, a manager for a condominium, townhome, or PUD association is tremendously involved in the physical management of property for owners and occupants. The responsibility begins with budgeting expenses and collecting assessments and progresses to coordinating common facility maintenance, landscaping, security, and enforcement of the association's regulations.

THE OWNER–MANAGER RELATIONSHIP

Authority

The owner–manager relationship is formalized by a **management agreement.** This contract creates *an agency relationship wherein the owner is the principal and the property manager is the agent* for the purposes specified in the agreement. This relationship imposes the same serious fiduciary duty as demanded of listing agents toward their principals in the sale of a home.

Provisions of the typical property management agreement include:

1. inception date and names of the parties.
2. property location and description of the premises
3. duration of the agency
4. method of termination by either party
5. agent's fee (a base fee plus a percentage of the rent actually collected is common)
6. agent's authority
7. agent's covenants
8. owner's covenants
9. handling of security deposits, rents, and expenses by agent
10. execution of the agreement by owner and agent

The authority of the manager comes from and must be explicitly set out in the management agreement. The management agreement creates a general agency and should be in writing. This agreement creates the responsibility in the property manager to realize the highest return on the property while obeying the owner's instructions and the laws of agency and landlord–tenant relations.

Duties

One of the first duties of a prospective property manager is to submit a **management proposal** to the property owner, *setting forth the commitments of the manager* if employed by the owner.

A typical proposal includes:

1. a complete description of the land and all improvements
2. a listing of all maintenance required and existing curable obsolescence
3. information regarding maintenance records and accounting procedures the manager will use
4. schedules of property inspections and owner conferences
5. a thorough operating budget, capital improvement budget, and stabilized budget (all discussed later)
6. a document citing the management fee

Fees

The property manager's fee is negotiated between the property owner and the manager. It commonly consists of a base fee and/or a percentage of the rents actually collected.

PRINCIPAL FUNCTIONS OF PROPERTY MANAGERS

Although renting space, collecting rents, and paying expenses are basic functions of property managers, their functions and responsibilities go far beyond these activities. In essence, the property manager's overall responsibilities are (a) to produce the highest possible net operating income from the property and (b) to maintain and increase the value of the principal's investment. The property manager fulfills these responsibilities by performing the specific activities discussed next.

Rental Schedule

In setting the rental rates, the property manager must be aware of the owner's goals for return on investment, as well as the current market for rental rates. Consideration must be given to current rates in like properties. Supply and demand for rental properties and present vacancy rates also must be considered. Adjustments in rental rates should be made only after a careful survey and analysis of the factors affecting rental.

PUTTING IT TO WORK

Many owners justify increasing rents by citing increased expense. In fact, this is often the only allowable increase for rent-controlled units. In a free rental market, however, rental rates are totally independent of expense level. An owner may want to raise rent 12 percent because expenses have increased by that percentage. Tenants, however, may not accept the increase if comparable lower-cost space is available elsewhere.

Budget

Before rental of a project can be organized and structured, an operating budget, capital reserve budget, and stabilized budget should be established. The budgets are always subject to adjustments, particularly in the first months of a project. The **operating budget** is *an annual budget and includes only the items of income and expense expected for week-to-week operation.* The **capital reserve budget** is *a projected budget over the economic life of the improvements of the property* for variable expenses such as repairs, decorating, remodeling, and capital improvements. The **stabilized budget** is *a forecast of income and expenses as may be reasonably projected over a short term*, typically five years.

PUTTING IT TO WORK

The budgeting practices described above are common, expected, and necessary on larger projects. With smaller buildings, however, budgets may be subject to extreme fluctuations as expenses are not always predictable. For example, if three of four air conditioners fail in a four-plex in a single year, this could completely exhaust the typical repair budget.

Marketing

The manager's strategy of marketing available rental space is shaped by the present demand for space, newness of the project, and the tenant selection process. In designing and implementing any marketing activity, managers must comply with all federal, state, and local fair housing laws.

Handling Funds

The property manager collects or attempts to collect all moneys owed to the owner. Any moneys collected are to be held in a trust account for the benefit of the owner. The only moneys taken from the account are to be used for expenses in the property management budget. In handling security deposits, the property manager must comply with local laws with regard to collecting and retaining security deposits.

PUTTING IT TO WORK

Illinois real estate license law requires that all rental security deposits be placed in an escrow account. The broker must be scrupulous in maintaining records and must avoid commingling and conversion.

Legal Actions

If the property manager is careful in selecting tenants, legal actions for eviction and collection of rents will be minimal. Effective property managers attempt to resolve any disputes before they result in a lawsuit. If a lawsuit is necessary, the property manager's file must show his or her compliance with all terms of any lease agreement with the tenant.

In filing a suit, the property manager must be familiar with local court rules and procedure. Some courts require that the property manager be represented by an attorney. If so, the property manager should consult with legal counsel prior to any court date to assure that any witnesses will attend and that all exhibits for the hearing are available.

Maintenance

One of the most important functions of a property manager is to supervise physical property maintenance. Efficient maintenance requires accurate analysis of the building's needs, coupled with consideration of the costs of any work done. Maintenance can include preventive maintenance, corrective maintenance, and construction.

Preventive maintenance requires a *periodic check of mechanical equipment* on the premises, to *minimize excessive wear and tear from improper operation.* An example of preventive maintenance is changing the air filters on air conditioners and furnaces.

Corrective maintenance, the most difficult to predict and budget for, is the *work performed to fix a nonfunctioning item* that the tenant has reported. An example of this type of maintenance is the repair of a leaky faucet.

Construction is done after money has been budgeted for remodeling, interior redecorating, or new capital improvements. Renovation often increases a property's desirability and thus can lead to increased income.

Records

The property manager should provide a *periodic* (usually monthly) *accounting of all funds received and disbursed.* This accounting is called a **property management report.** It contains detailed information of all receipts and expenditures for the period covered (plus the year-to-date) and relates each item to the operating budget for the period. In addition to the reports to the owner, the manager should maintain whatever records are necessary for compliance with local laws on fair housing, security deposits, trust accounts, and so on.

Basic Insurance Concepts and Terminology

The modern term **risk management** *embodies the concern for controlling and limiting risk in property ownership.* Ownership and use of real estate necessarily entail risk, but the questions are how the risk is to be controlled and whether some risk can be transferred by means of an insurance policy. The manager should find a competent insurance agent who is familiar with the type of property to be insured. Written specifications by the manager to competing agents will ensure comparable quotes for consideration. The insured property will be the property being managed. The person or entity insured will be the person or entity who owns the property.

Property Insurance

Most insurance policies in the United States are based on the New York standard fire policy form as revised in 1943. This **fire insurance policy** *indemnifies the insured against loss caused by fire.* If the insured wishes to have protection against losses from other hazards, he or she must obtain an extended coverage endorsement to the fire policy. This endorsement, in the form of a rider attached to the fire policy, requires an additional premium. The **extended coverage** endorsement *usually includes coverage for losses resulting from hail, explosion, wind storm, aircraft, civil commotion,* *vehicles, and smoke from friendly fires.* A fire confined to the place where it is intended to be, such as a fireplace or furnace, is a friendly fire; otherwise it is a hostile fire.

Liability Insurance

Public liability insurance covers the risks an owner assumes when the public enters the premises. Payments under this coverage are to pay claims for medical expenses incurred by the person injured on the property as a result of the landlord's negligence.

Package Policy (Homeowner's Policy)

A **package policy** is available to homeowners. This form of policy, called a **homeowner's policy,** provides *coverage for the structure and its contents* (casualty insurance). A homeowner's policy provides coverage against loss by fire, wind storm, hail, dust, surface waters, waves, frozen plumbing, vandalism, and industrial smoke damage, and provides personal financial liability coverage to the policyholder for personal injury and property damage caused by the policyholder.

STANDARDIZED HOMEOWNER'S INSURANCE POLICIES

Standardized homeowner's policies are identified as HO-1, HO-2, HO-3, HO-4, HO-5, and HO-6. An HO-4 is a tenant's policy, and HO-6 is designed for condominiums and cooperatives. HO-1, HO-2, HO-3, and HO-5 cover owners of single-family dwellings.

Every hazard insurance policy must contain a description of the insured property. The street address usually is adequate, although some insurers require a full legal description. Specific provisions of the various homeowner's policies are:

HO-1	"Named perils." Perils covered are damage or loss from fire at the premises.
HO-2	"Broad form." Coverage extends to loss or damage as a result of fire, vandalism, malicious mischief, wind, hail, aircraft, riot, explosion, and smoke.
HO-3	A special "all risk" policy. It covers loss for damage resulting from anything not specifically excluded from coverage.
HO-4	"Tenant's broad form." Its coverage is like HO-2 except it applies only to the tenant's contents at the premises.
HO-5	A special "all risk" policy offering automatic replacement cost for contents and dwelling.
HO-6	Like a tenant's broad form but applies to condominium owners and cooperative owners covering their contents. (The structure would be insured by the association.)

The HO-2, 3, 4, 5, and 6 are all package policies that include medical payments coverage and personal liability coverage for negligence.

SELECTED LEGAL ISSUES

Insurable Interest

To be eligible for insurance coverage of any type, the insured must have a *legitimate financial interest,* known as an **insurable interest,** in the property. In the absence of an insurable interest, the policy is void. Examples of people with insurable interests are buyer and seller in a contract of sale or land contract, owner, owner of a partial interest, trustee, receiver, life tenant, mortgagor, and mortgagee. A mortgagee is an individual, a group of individuals, or an insurable organization with interest in the property based upon lending money. The mortgagee usually requires, in the mortgage, that the borrower maintain adequate hazard insurance coverage on the property to satisfy the debt in the case of destruction. The policy is issued in the names of both the mortgagee and the mortgagor. The policy protects the mortgagee up to the amount of the principal balance owed on the loan if within the coverage limits the policy provides. In the event of partial loss, the insurance company pays mortgagors so they may make the appropriate repairs. In the event of total loss, the mortgagee is paid first up to the amount of the mortgage debt still outstanding, and the mortgagor receives any surplus.

Coinsurance

Every homeowner's insurance policy contains a **coinsurance clause** *requiring the property owner to insure for at least 80 percent of the property value for the face amount.* **Face amount,** typically set out on the first page of the policy, is *the maximum amount of coverage specified in the policy* and sets the insurance company's maximum liability. Some policies require 90 or 100 percent, but 80 percent is the typical requirement in policies insuring an owner-occupied residence. If the coverage is for less than 80 percent of value, the policy will pay only part of the loss in proportion to the percentage of value insured by the policy owner.

For example: A structure is worth $100,000, the coinsurance clause is 80 percent, and the insurance carried is only $60,000. In the event of a partial loss of $30,000, the insurance company's liability is only $22,500. The amount of the insurance company's liability is calculated using the following formula:

$$\frac{\text{Insurance carried}}{\text{Insurance required}} \times \text{loss} = \text{company's limit of liability}$$

$$\frac{\$60,000}{\$80,000} \times \$30,000 = \$22,500$$

If the loss had been $80,000 or more, the insurance company's liability would be the amount of insurance carried. If the loss equals or exceeds the amount of insurance required by the coinsurance clause, the company pays the face amount of the policy. This is illustrated by the following example:

Value of structure	$100,000
Insurance required (80%)	80,000
Insurance policy amount	60,000
Loss	90,000

$$\frac{\text{Insurance carried}}{\text{Insurance required}} \times \text{loss} = \text{company's limit of liability}$$

$$\frac{\$60,000}{\$80,000} \times 90,000 = 67,500 \quad \text{but because the policy was for only } \$60,000, \text{ the company pays only } \$60,000$$

Because the loss equals or exceeds the amount of insurance required by the coinsurance clause, the insurance company pays the policy amount even though the requirement of the coinsurance clause is not met. In no event, however, will the policy pay an amount in excess of the amount of coverage specified in the policy.

Unoccupied Building Exclusion

Insurance coverage available on a property varies depending upon whether the premises are unoccupied or occupied. If occupied, the homeowner's coverages set out above apply. If unoccupied, the maximum coverage available is similar to the HO-1 "named perils." The premises are insured against loss from fire at the premises only.

PUTTING IT TO WORK

Many insurance policies cover vacant properties for a maximum of 30 days, after which time the coverage lapses.

Policy Interpretation

Insurance policies generally are assignable with the written consent of the insurance company. Often a seller assigns his or her interest in a hazard insurance policy to a buyer of the property as of the date of closing, and the premium is prorated between buyer and seller. The assignment is not valid, however, without the *written consent of the insurer*. This consent typically is evidenced by the insurance company's **endorsement** to the policy, *changing the name of the insured*.

Homeowner's Warranty (HOW) Policies

The **homeowner's warranty (HOW) policy** *protects home buyers against certain defects in a house they purchase*. In the case of a new house, the builder provides the policy through the National Association of Home Builders. The policy extends a one-year warranty against defective workmanship, a ten-year warranty against major structural defects, and a two-year warranty against defects in mechanical and electrical systems.

In the resale of an existing house, the seller may transfer the policy to the buyer if the warranty is still in effect. If the policy is no longer in force or if the house was never protected by a HOW policy, policies are available through many insurance companies as well as many real estate brokerages. The premium usually is paid by the seller, who transfers the policy to the home buyer.

Several real estate franchise companies also provide warranties to purchasers. These buyer protection programs are attractive and effective marketing tools. The salesperson, seller, and buyer have to realize that these warranties are not coverage from foundation to roof. Instead, the coverage has many exclusions of which the agent must be keenly aware in discussions with customers and clients. Overrepresenting the warranty's provisions can result in personal liability to the agent.

PUTTING IT TO WORK

Generally, the builder's warranties regarding new homes are much more comprehensive than HOWs offered by third-party insurers on resale properties.

Important Points

1. Property managers are agents engaged in the management of property for others and, therefore, must have a real estate license. Illinois exempts from licensing those property managers who reside on the property they are managing and are employed by the property's owner or a managing broker.
2. Illinois has a limited scope license classification for residential leasing agents. The license allows a leasing agent to lease residential property and collect rents.
3. The management agreement is a contract in which a property owner employs a property manager to act as his or her agent.
4. The property manager's basic responsibilities are (a) to produce the best possible net operating income from the property and (b) to maintain and increase the value of the principal's investment.
5. Properties that may require management are condominiums, cooperatives, apartments, single-family rental houses, mobile home parks, office buildings, shopping malls, industrial property, and farms.
6. Property managers fulfill their basic responsibilities by formulating a management plan, soliciting tenants, leasing space, collecting rent, hiring and training employees, maintaining good tenant relations, providing for adequate maintenance, protecting tenants, maintaining adequate insurance, keeping adequate records, and auditing and paying bills.
7. The property management report is a periodic accounting provided by a property manager to the property owner.
8. A fire insurance policy indemnifies the insured against loss by fire. Protection from losses by other hazards may be obtained by an extended coverage endorsement.
9. Package policies, called homeowner's policies, provide all the usual protections in one policy. These policies are available to both homeowners and renters.
10. To be eligible for insurance, the applicant must have an insurable interest in the property, such as buyer and seller in a contract, owner, part owner, trustee, receiver, tenant, mortgagor, and mortgagee.
11. Every hazard insurance policy contains a coinsurance clause requiring the property owner to insure the property for at least 80 percent of the property value to recover up to the face amount of the policy in the event of a partial loss. If the loss equals or exceeds the amount of coverage required by the coinsurance clause, however, the insurance company will pay the policy amount even though the requirement of the coinsurance clause is not met.
12. Insurance policies usually are assignable with the written consent of the insurance company. The consent is evidenced by an endorsement to the policy.
13. Homeowner's warranty policies (HOWs) are available to purchasers of newly constructed houses and of existing houses. These policies insure against many, but not all, structural and mechanical defects.

Review Questions

Answers to these questions are found in the Answer Key section at the back of the book.

1. All of the following statements about property management are correct EXCEPT:
   a. property management is a specialized field within the real estate industry
   b. a property manager acts as an agent of the property owner
   c. the terms *property manager* and *resident manager* always have the same meaning
   d. a property manager is a fiduciary

2. Martin Kim manages an apartment building for the Ace Apartment Rental Company. Martin uses one of the apartments in the building he manages for his principal residence. Under these circumstances, Martin:
   a. is not required to hold an Illinois real estate license
   b. is required to hold an Illinois real estate license
   c. is required to hold an Illinois real estate license because he does not own the building he manages
   d. cannot manage a building he does not own

3. A budget based on a forecast of income and expense anticipated over a period of years is called a(n):
   a. stabilized budget
   b. projected budget
   c. anticipated budget
   d. operating budget

4. When building occupancy reaches 98 percent, this tends to indicate that:
   a. rents should be lowered
   b. rents should be raised
   c. management is ineffective
   d. the building needs remodeling

5. An HO-4 insurance policy offers coverage for:
   a. condominium's contents
   b. cooperative's contents
   c. tenant's contents
   d. owner's contents

6. Which of the following statements about hazard insurance policies is NOT correct?
   a. they are not assignable
   b. they contain a coinsurance clause
   c. there must be an insurable interest
   d. they protect only the person or persons named in the policy

7. If a home valued at $200,000 and insured for $120,000 by a policy with an 80 percent coinsurance clause suffers a loss of $175,000 from an insured hazard, what amount will the insurance company pay?
   a. $96,000
   b. $120,000
   c. $160,000
   d. $175,000

8. Which of the following identifies a policy insuring against loss caused by structural defects?
   a. fire and extended coverage
   b. HOW
   c. HO-1
   d. HO-6

9. All of the following are true regarding Illinois referral fees paid by property manager or owner to an unlicensed tenant EXCEPT:
   a. the tenants referred must be seeking a unit in the same building or complex
   b. the lessee cannot refer more than three prospective tenants in a 12-month period
   c. the lessee can show the unit, but cannot discuss the terms or conditions of the lease
   d. the lessee can receive compensation of no more than $1,000 or one month's rent each 12-month period

10. An agency relationship exists between the:
    a. property manager and tenant
    b. property manager and owner
    c. property manager, tenant, and owner
    d. property manager and janitor

CHAPTER 15

Important Terminology

accelerated depreciation
acquisition debt
adjusted basis
age-55-and-over exclusion
blue sky laws
boot
capital gain
deductible expenses
depreciation
economic depreciation
fix-up expenses
gross operating income
home-equity debt
income shelter
inheritance basis

installment sale
investment syndicate
like-kind property
multiple exchange
net operating income
Revenue Reconciliation Act of 1993 (RRA)
rollover rule
Starker exchange/Starker trust
straight-line depreciation
tax basis
tax-deferred exchange
tax depreciation
unlike-kind property

Federal Income Taxation of Real Estate

IN THIS CHAPTER Although all real estate licensees must have basic knowledge and understanding of the federal income tax laws affecting real property, they must not give tax advice to buyers and sellers. Because each taxpayer's situation is different, only competent professional tax consultants who are familiar with the taxpayer's position should give advice of this nature. Real estate licensees should recommend that buyers and sellers seek this specialized expertise when appropriate.

This chapter presents the fundamentals of tax implications in the ownership and sale of a principal residence and business and investment property. It illustrates and explains the special tax benefits provided to owners and sellers of real property to enable you to understand these advantages.

REVENUE RECONCILIATION ACT OF 1993

The **Revenue Reconciliation Act (RRA) of 1993** brought with it several changes; some benefit the real estate industry and some do not. The act *eased the passive activity loss regulations on certain real property trades or businesses* (as discussed below), *but it also raised tax rates to 39.6 percent for wealthier taxpayers and phased out some exemptions and itemized deductions.*

Capital Gain

Older laws provided for long-term **capital gain** treatment that allowed investors to exclude 60 percent of their *gain (profit) on real estate investments* from taxation on a qualifying transaction. An investor who realized a gain of $100,000 could exclude 60 percent and be taxed only on the 40 percent, or $40,000, at a maximum rate of 50 percent of this income, for a tax of $20,000. The Tax Reform Act (TRA) of 1986 reduced this beneficial capital gain treatment: The same investor now pays a straight 28 percent on the entire $100,000, or $28,000—a 40 percent increase in tax ($8,000 increase divided by the original $20,000 tax). Many had hoped Congress would bring back the capital gain exclusion with the RRA of 1993; however, this did not occur. The good news is that the maximum tax rate for capital gain is still only 28 percent, even though tax brackets for ordinary income (other than capital gain) may be as high as 39.6 percent.

Depreciation

Depreciation is *an allowance deducted from the net income of a property before taxes are assessed, which is determined by the property's loss in value.* (Tax shelters are discussed later in this chapter.) A little historical background will help put recent changes in depreciation allowances into perspective.

Under the Tax Act of 1981, the Accelerated Cost Recovery System (ACRS) established a schedule that allowed **accelerated** (or front-loaded) **depreciation:** *Higher deductions were taken in early years and lower deductions in later years,* an obvious benefit to investors. The TRA of 1986, however, disallowed accelerated depreciation on real property; **straight-line depreciation** is once again the standard so *deductions are taken in equal amounts each year.*

Prior to the TRA of 1986, depreciation was allowed over 15 years, later modified to 18 and then 19 years. The TRA of 1986 set the depreciation schedule at 27½ years for residential property and 31½ years for nonresidential properties. The RRA of 1993 has further tightened depreciation allowances by expanding the depreciation period for nonresidential properties to 39 years. Real estate does not have the tax benefits it had in the early 1980s, when accelerated depreciation was allowed and depreciation schedules were shorter.

Passive Income

The passive activity rules enacted under the TRA of 1986 allowed tax losses from investment properties to be offset only by income from passive activities, any trade or business in which the taxpayer does not materially participate. If the taxpayer materially participates, the income derived is not passive income. A taxpayer is considered a material participant if during a tax year he or she satisfies one of the following tests:

1. participates more than 500 hours
2. is the only participant in the activity
3. participates 100 hours, and no other participant has more hours involved
4. participates materially for any five years in a 10-year period
5. the activity is a personal service activity, such as health fields, engineering, architecture, accounting, and actuarial service

Under this law, if excess passive losses existed in any tax year, they could be carried over to later years and deducted then, if passive income was available, or claimed when the asset was sold. Passive losses could not be used to offset nonpassive income such as wages, interest, or dividends.

With the advent of the RRA of 1993 (effective for tax years beginning after December 31, 1993), however, certain taxpayers who are involved in real property trades or businesses are no longer subject to passive activity loss (PAL) rules. This means that the taxpayers who meet the special requirements are able to use rental real estate losses against nonpassive income. To be eligible for this special treatment the taxpayer's material performance must be:

1. more than 50 percent of taxpayer's personal service
2. more than 750 hours of service

Real property trade or business is defined as any real property development, redevelopment, construction, reconstruction, acquisition, conversion, rental, operation, management, leasing, or brokerage trade or business. Material participation requires that the individual be involved in the operations of the activity on a regular and continuous basis. Limited partners cannot be considered material participants. For purposes of the RRA of 1993, the activities may be considered individually or aggregated into like groups.

The $25,000 rule still applies to all other taxpayers who do not meet the special eligibility requirements. Taxpayers with adjusted gross incomes of up to $100,000 may shelter up to $25,000 in rental property losses. This exception phases out as the taxpayer's adjusted gross income reaches $150,000, after which no deduction is allowed unless the taxpayer falls under the new rules of RRA of 1993. Certain deductions for real property, such as most mortgage interest and property taxes, are maintained. These deductions apply to both a principal residence and a second home.

PUTTING IT TO WORK

As a result of lost deductions for consumer interest on cars and credit cards, many taxpayers are borrowing against the equity in their homes (which may be fully deductible) to pay off nondeductible interest debts. The risk in this, however, is that the home may be lost if payments are not made per the loan agreement; this risk is not typically associated with failure to pay monthly credit card installments per a credit agreement.

TAX IMPLICATIONS OF HOME OWNERSHIP

The tax-deductible expenses involved in home ownership are mortgage interest (not principal) and real property taxes paid to local taxing authorities. In addition, taxpayers who can deduct mortgage interest usually find it advantageous to itemize and take advantage of other tax-deductible expenses not associated with home ownership. The combination of mortgage interest and other itemized expenses provides greater tax relief than is available by taking the more modest standard deduction.

Let's assume a home buyer purchases a residence for $100,000 with a $10,000 down payment and finances the balance for 30 years at 11½ percent interest. The monthly payment of principal and interest necessary to fully amortize the remaining $90,000 over a 30-year period is $891.26. During the first 12 months of loan payments, the borrower will pay a total of $10,331.21 in mortgage interest. This interest is available as a tax deduction for the year in which it is paid.

Rollover Rule or Deferred Reporting

The federal tax laws provide that *a gain realized from the sale of a main residence is not taxed in the year of the sale provided the seller buys or constructs another residence, within 24 months before or after the sale, for a price equal to or greater than the adjusted sales price of the home sold.* If the transaction qualifies under the requirements set forth above, the **rollover rule** is mandatory. The taxpayer does not have a choice but must indefinitely defer the tax on the gain.

A taxpayer may be involved in a number of qualifying transactions, and therefore many mandatory rollovers of tax, during his or her lifetime. Any gain in the sale of a residence that is not taxed under the rollover rule is used to reduce the **tax basis** of the new residence purchased (as discussed below). The tax basis is essentially *the original cost of the property plus any improvements that increase its value.* The tax basis of the new residence is reduced by the untaxed amount. This results in a lower tax basis for the new property in calculating the gain when that home is sold.

If the transaction does not qualify under the rollover rule, the gain realized in the sale of the residence is taxable for the tax year in which the sale transpires, not when the 24-month period has expired. The taxpayer will have to pay the tax due for the year of sale plus any statutory IRS interest. An example of the rollover provision and the computation of gain is provided later in this chapter.

To compute gain or loss in the sale of a principal residence, the first step is to establish the owner's tax basis in the property. Tax is owed only on the gain and not on the full sales price. Gain is determined by subtracting the tax basis of the property from the sales price of the property.

```
  Sales price
− Tax basis
       Gain
```

The tax basis consists of the price paid for the property, less any gain realized in the sale of the previous residence on which the payment of tax was deferred under a prior rollover, plus expenses incurred in acquiring the property (other than those incurred in arranging financing), plus the cost of any capital improvements (not repairs) made during ownership. It is important that accurate records of any major improvements made to the home be kept by the taxpayer.

In addition, certain costs of acquiring the property may be added to the basis. It is to the homeowner's advantage to have as large a basis as possible to reduce the tax gain realized when the property is eventually sold. Alternatively, the gain is reduced by being able to deduct certain items from the sales price. If the basis is higher than the adjusted sales price and results in a loss, the loss is *not* deductible. Personal residence losses are not deductible. Losses on the sale of investment property may be deductible. An actual example of computing gain is provided later in this chapter.

Effect of Purchase and Sale

In the purchase and sale of a personal residence, both the buyer and the seller have certain expenses. Examples of these expenses and their application to buyer and seller in calculating taxable gain are offered below.

 1. The premium paid for a title insurance policy may be subtracted from the selling price if the seller pays it. If the buyer pays that premium, the amount paid is added to the buyer's basis.

 2. Transfer taxes, ordinarily paid by the seller at the transfer of the real estate, are based upon the seller's equity or sales price. They may be deducted by the seller from the selling price. If the tax is paid by the buyer, however, the amount is added to the buyer's basis.

 3. Attorney fees paid by the seller are deductible from the selling price. Attorney fees paid by the buyer are added to the buyer's basis. Attorney fees incurred by the buyer to obtain financing, however, may not be added to the buyer's basis.

 4. If the seller pays the attorney's fee for preparation of a deed, the seller may deduct this fee from the selling price. If the buyer pays the fee for drawing the deed, it may be added to the buyer's basis.

 5. Buyer's closing costs that are allocable to purchasing the property may be added to the buyer's basis. Expenses of borrowing the purchase price, however, may not be added to the buyer's basis. Expenses involved with obtaining the loan include things such as appraisal fees, mortgage insurance premiums, charges by the lender's attorney, and credit report cost.

 6. The seller often pays the discount points charged by many lending institutions in making home loans. Discount points charged by lending institutions may be deducted from the selling price if the seller pays them to enable the buyer to obtain a loan. These discount points are not deductible as interest by the seller because the seller has not borrowed the money and therefore has no obligation to repay. However, recent legislation retroactive to December 31, 1990, allows *buyers* to deduct, as interest, any discount points paid by the seller on the buyer's behalf. Discount points paid

by the buyer are also deductible as interest by the buyer for the year in which the points are paid.

PUTTING IT TO WORK

In 1986, the IRS ruled that discount points paid by the owner to refinance an existing loan have to be spread out over the term of the loan. The essential difference is that a buyer who pays $2,000 in points for a new home can deduct all $2,000 in the year paid. If refinancing the present loan for 20 years, however, the owner can deduct only $100 per year. If a mortgage loan is not obtained to purchase or improve a principal residence, deduction of the discount points as interest must be spread out over the life of the loan. For example, if a borrower pays $2,000 in discount points to obtain a 20-year conventional loan to purchase an apartment building, the discount points are deductible at a rate of $100 per year for 20 years.

7. If the borrower pays a loan origination fee or a loan processing fee, typically 1 percent of the amount of the loan, the fee is not deductible as interest because the fee is for loan services and not for use of the money borrowed. Also, the borrower may not add the cost of a loan origination or processing fee to the basis of the property because this is an expense of borrowing the purchase price rather than a cost for obtaining the property. Loan origination fees paid by the seller are a selling expense and may be deducted from the sales price in arriving at the amount realized.

8. Other expense items, such as surveys, escrow fees, title abstracts, recording fees, and advertising costs, may be added to the buyer's basis if paid by the buyer, or subtracted from the selling price if paid by the seller.

9. The real estate commission a seller pays may be deducted, but only from the selling price. The commission paid is not deductible from the seller's ordinary income.

10. **Fix-up expenses** are *costs the seller incurs in preparing a residence for sale.* To qualify as adjustments from the amount realized to establish the adjusted sale price, these costs must have been incurred within 90 days prior to signing the contract of sale that results in the completed sale of the home and must be paid for within 30 days after the sale. Fix-up expenses, however, are not deductible unless the seller purchases or builds a new home within the limits specified by the rollover rule. Also, these expenses are deductions only to determine the amount of gain on which tax is to be postponed and may not be used as deductions in arriving at gain.

11. A financial penalty required by a lender for early payoff of a mortgage loan (a prepayment penalty) is deductible as interest by the borrower for the year in which the prepayment penalty is paid.

12. Moving expenses are deductible if the taxpayer itemizes and the expenses are incurred while moving to a new job that would require 50 miles increased travel one way without the move. A deduction is available for employees and for self-employed taxpayers. Although buying and selling expenses (items 1 through 10) at one time were allowed as moving expense deductions from taxable income, the RRA of 1993 now allows them only as deductions toward arriving at the adjusted basis of the old or new residence for determining capital gain.

Other deductible moving expenses are used to calculate net taxable income and are deductible in the year of the sale. These expenses may include transportation of furniture and effects, and expenses of transportation and lodging when moving from the former home to the new home. Auto expenses on a personal car, gas, oil, repairs, tolls, and parking (but not depreciation) during the move are deductible.

Moving expenses no longer deductible include premove house-hunting trips and even meals during the move. It should be noted that if the employer reimburses the employee for expenses, provides temporary living quarters, or reimburses the employee for a loss on the sale of the home, the IRS will treat this as compensation (pay), and the employer must issue a W-2 for the amount.

The Age-55-and-Over Exclusion

The **age-55-and-over exclusion** is available to sellers of a principal residence provided the seller is age 55 or over. The *seller may exempt from tax up to $125,000 (effective July 20, 1981) of gain in the sale of a principal residence.* The seller must have used the property as his or her principal residence for at least three of the five years immediately preceding the date of the sale. The tax on any gain in excess of the $125,000 exemption must be deferred under the rollover rule, if applicable.

This is a once-in-a-lifetime exemption. After it is used, it is gone. This is true even if the exclusion is taken on a gain of only $40,000. The seller does not have an additional $85,000 to exempt in another sale of property in the future.

An unmarried co-owner of property used as his or her principal residence qualifies for the exclusion. In this case, the qualifying owner may take the exemption even though the other does not qualify. If they both qualify, one may elect to take the exclusion for his or her portion of the gain, and the other may elect not to do so. Single owners in severalty also qualify for the $125,000 exclusion.

If the property is owned by a married couple, only one spouse has to be at least age 55 for the transaction to qualify for the exemption. If a married couple takes the exemption, even if only one spouse qualifies, it is binding upon both of them. If they are divorced after the sale in which the exemption is taken and both subsequently acquire a new spouse, the fact that each of them took the exclusion previously disqualifies the new spouse in each case as well, even if the new spouse would have qualified otherwise.

A good question to ask when considering a proposal of marriage after age 55 is: "Have you taken your $125,000 exemption?" A married taxpayer filing a separate tax return may exclude a maximum of $62,500 of gain on the sale. Each spouse filing separately may exclude a maximum of $62,500.

A taxpayer who has been in the house for less than three years does not normally qualify for the exclusion. In meeting the ownership and use tests, the taxpayer may add the time he or she owned and lived in a previous home destroyed by fire or other casualty or condemned under eminent domain to the time he or she owned and lived in the home for which he or she desires to exclude a gain under the age-55-and-over exclusion.

Computation of Gain

Figures 15.1 and 15.2 illustrate the steps taken in computing taxable gain and arriving at the **adjusted basis** for a new residence. Figure 15.1 depicts the situation in which the homeowner purchases a new home for a price greater than the amount realized on the sale of his previous residence. The gain realized in the sale is calculated by subtracting the adjusted basis from the amount realized (the sales price minus expenses of the sale). The original cost (basis) of the old home has been increased by a portion of the closing costs to obtain it, as well as the costs of improvements to the property.

The most noteworthy feature of Figure 15.1 is the $40,000 proceeds the seller received from the old home. Because the seller is purchasing a new $110,000 home with a VA loan (no down payment), he does not have to actually invest any of the cash proceeds in the new purchase. Therefore, the seller has $40,000 cash tax-free to use as desired. The seller has not totally escaped the consequences of this profit, however, as the basis of the new home is reduced by the $40,000. If, in the future, this new home sells for the same $110,000 amount and the seller does not purchase another home, he will be subject to taxation on $40,000.

Figure 15.2 illustrates a situation in which the homeowner does not purchase a new home for a price greater than the amount realized on the sale of her previous residence. The taxable gain for the year of the sale is $3,400 and not the full gain of $25,800. The taxable gain in the year of sale is incurred because the price of the new residence was not equal to or greater than the adjusted basis of the old home. The tax on the gain postponed, $22,400, is deferred indefinitely under the mandatory rollover rule. The gain postponed, however, is used to reduce the tax basis of the new residence purchased and is the tax basis for the new residence when it is sold some time in the future. Therefore, the tax basis of the new residence to the purchaser will be $53,600 ($76,000 − $22,400). Had the taxpayer purchased a new residence costing $79,400 or more, all of the gain realized would have been postponed.

FIGURE 15.1 The rollover rule applied to a more expensive new home.

Selling price of old home	$85,000
Less: Selling expenses	− 7,000
Amount realized	$78,000
Basis of old home	$35,000
Plus: Closing costs	+ 1,000
Improvements	+ 2,000
Adjusted basis of old home	$38,000
Amount realized	$78,000
Less: Adjusted basis	−38,000
Gain realized	$40,000
Cost of new home	$110,000
Less: Gain postponed	−40,000
Basis of new home	$70,000

FIGURE 15.2 The rollover rule applied to a less expensive new home.

Selling price of old home	$85,000
Less: Selling expenses	− 5,600
Amount realized on old home	$79,400
Basis of old home	$52,400
Plus: Capital improvements	+ 1,200
Adjusted basis of old home	$53,600
Amount realized on old home	$79,400
Less: Adjusted basis	−53,600
Gain on old home	$25,800
Amount realized on old home	$79,400
Less: Cost of new home	−76,000
*Gain not postponed	$ 3,400
Gain on old home	$25,800
Less: Gain not postponed	− 3,400
Gain postponed	$22,400
Cost of new home	$76,000
Less: Gain postponed	−22,400
Basis of new home	$53,600

*Taxable for year of sale.

The rollover rule does not require that the seller use the same funds received in the sale of his or her old principal residence to buy or build a new home. The seller may invest a lesser amount of cash and obtain a larger mortgage loan with which to purchase another qualifying residence.

> **PUTTING IT TO WORK**
>
> Taxpayers and real estate licensees alike often misunderstand the fundamental provision of the tax code regarding rollovers. The issue is so important in selling (and repurchasing) decisions that the licensee should be clearly versed on the technical rules applied. They are not difficult, but they are important.

Inheritance Basis

The tax basis for all real property received by heirs is the *market value of the property on the date of the decedent's death,* not the price the decedent paid. As a result of this stepped-up **inheritance basis,** any tax on gains deferred under the rollover rule during the decedent's lifetime is eliminated. Therefore, gains deferred under the rollover rule are not taxed in the decedent's estate or final tax return. The only time these deferred taxes must be paid is in the event of the sale of the property during the taxpayer's lifetime that does not qualify for tax deferment under the rollover rule and also does not qualify for the $125,000 once-in-a-lifetime exclusion, discussed earlier.

Mortgage Interest Deduction

The one major tax break that remains for the average homeowner is the tax deductibility of mortgage interest. Mortgage interest remains deductible on both a primary residence and a second or vacation home. If a home was purchased, refinanced, or incurred additional debt after October 13, 1987, the home falls into two categories of debt: acquisition debt and home-equity debt. **Acquisition debt** is *debt that is secured by a primary residence or a second home and that derives from purchasing, building, or improving a home.* Acquisition debt is limited to $1,000,000. **Home-equity debt** is *debt that is secured by a primary or a second home and that is borrowed for reasons other than the purchasing, building, or improving of a home.* Home-equity debt is limited to $100,000 ($50,000 if married and filing separately) or the property's market value, whichever is less. If a person owns two homes, the cap on the home-equity debt may still not exceed $100,000 ($50,000 if married and filing separately). Loans made before October 1987 are under a different set of rules. Contact an accountant for the most recent IRS regulations.

Points

Points remain deductible in the year the home is purchased and the points are paid. However, points paid in a refinancing and loans on second homes are not deductible in the current tax year. The IRS requires the points paid in a refinancing or second home to be deducted over the life of the loan. If the loan is paid off early, the remaining points can be deducted in that year. Points (or fees) used to pay for appraisal fees, preparation of a note or deed of trust, settlement fees, notary fees, abstract or title insurance fees, commissions, and recording fees may not be deducted.

Vacation Homes

Under the TRA of 1986, homeowners are allowed to deduct mortgage interest on both a principal residence and a second home, such as a vacation property. Special rules apply in classifying this second property. The vacation property is considered a second home if it is occupied for personal use more than 14 days per year or 10 percent of its useful rental period. In this case, the mortgage interest and property taxes on both the principal residence and the second home can be deducted to the extent the mortgages do not exceed the original purchase price of the properties plus improvements.

If, however, personal use of the second property is limited to less than 14 days or 10 percent of the useful rental period, the home is treated as a business property. In this case, it is eligible for the 27½-year depreciation schedule and repairs and maintenance deductions, as well as a deduction for the mortgage interest and property taxes less a percentage of these expenses that must be allocated to the owner's personal use. The proper ratio for allocating the expenses is (a) the number of days the property is used divided by (b) the total number of days the property is rented.

INSTALLMENT SALES

The subject of installment sales is included at this point because tax law applications in installment sales apply both to a personal residence and to property held for investment or for use in a trade or business. An owner may sell his or her principal residence on an **installment sale** basis, in which *at least one payment is received by the taxpayer in a tax year after the sale,* and avoid the total impact of the tax in one year. The typical installment sale is by contract for deed or land contract. If the seller does not plan to purchase a new residence within the time period required for the rollover rule and also does not qualify for the $125,000 maximum tax exemption, an installment sale can be used to provide tax relief.

Installment sales may be used to spread the impact of federal income taxes on gains over several years or to postpone taxes to a future year or years as the principal is received. This enables the taxpayer to avoid the impact of tax on gain in the sale of property in a single year. Installment sale rules apply to the sale of real property, businesses, securities, and personal property.

The TRA of 1986 makes the installment sale method much less attractive than under previous laws. Retroactive to March 1986, for installment sales of business property it is assumed that the seller has received a minimum cash payment each year. This means the payment is recognized for tax purposes, regardless of whether any cash is actually received during that year.

INVESTMENT PROPERTY

As we have seen, ownership and sale of a principal residence have special tax benefits. Ownership and sale of real property held as an investment or for use in a trade or business also have special tax benefits including depreciation, deductible expenses, and tax-free exchanges of like-kind property. **Like-kind property** is *property of the same nature and character, such as real property for real property, depreciable personal property for depreciable personal property, and so on.*

Depreciation

The two types of depreciation are (a) tax depreciation and (b) economic depreciation. **Economic depreciation** *results from physical deterioration of property caused by* *normal use, damage caused by natural and other hazards, and failure to adequately maintain the property.* **Tax depreciation** is a provision of the tax law, applicable to certain types of assets, that permits a property owner to take an *ordinary business deduction for the amount of annual depreciation.* This permits the owner to recover the cost or other basis of an asset over the period of the asset's useful life. Tax depreciation is a deduction from net income in calculating taxable income.

PUTTING IT TO WORK

Tax depreciation is an accounting concept only. The property being "depreciated" actually may be appreciating in value. When the property is sold, tax may have to be paid on the "real" appreciation plus recapture of the "artificial" tax depreciation.

The Tax Reform Act of 1986 established two depreciation schedules for real property: 27½ years straight-line for residential property and 31½ years straight-line for nonresidential property. Under the RRA of 1993 the depreciable lives of nonresidential property increased from 31½ years to 39 years for properties placed in service on or after May 13, 1993. Under the TRA of 1986, the amount of claimed investment losses must equal an amount no more than the income received from similar passive activities. For example, if an investor loses $35,000 on her properties but the properties' income is only $21,000, the investor can claim only $21,000 in loss this tax year. The excess loss of $14,000 ($35,000 − $21,000) cannot be used in the year of the loss. The excess loss may be carried over to future tax years. The RRA of 1993 changed this situation somewhat for those taxpayers who meet the eligibility requirements.

A limited exception to this rule applies to owners with adjusted gross income of less than $100,000 who actively manage their own property. These owners may shelter up to $25,000 of other wages or active income in the same tax year. Passive investors who do not actively manage their own property cannot apply excess losses to other active income in the same tax year. In the above example, if the investor manages her own properties and has an adjusted gross income of $70,000, she can use the $14,000 excess loss to reduce the adjusted gross income to $56,000.

Depreciable property includes assets such as buildings, equipment, machinery, and other things that are used in business to produce income (other than inventories) or that are held as an investment. Assets held for personal use, including a personal residence, are not depreciable assets. Also, land is not a depreciable asset. Therefore, the value of the land and the value of structures on the land must be separated to arrive at a basis for determining depreciation. This basis normally is the cost of acquiring the property reduced by the estimated salvage value of the property at the end of its useful life.

When a depreciable asset is sold, *the basis of the asset used to compute the taxable gain from the sale is the depreciated value.* For example, if a depreciable asset is purchased for $100,000 and the purchaser had taken $40,000 of tax depreciation at the time the property was sold for $130,000, the taxable gain is $70,000 ($130,000 sales price minus $60,000 depreciated value = $70,000 taxable gain). In essence, the basis of a depreciable asset is reduced by any depreciation deduction taken.

Income Shelter

Deductible allowances from net income of property to arrive at taxable income and tax losses allowed to offset passive and active income are **income shelters** for individual taxpayer owners. Examples of expenses and allowances deductible from gross income include depreciation, operating expenses, real estate taxes, and mortgage interest.

To see the benefit of this concept, reconsider the operating statement for an apartment building introduced in Chapter 10 (Figure 10.5) and further discussed in Chapter 14. The subject property was purchased for $6,200,000. Because land does not depreciate, an allocation between the land and the improvement (the building) was made. If 15 percent of the price is allocated to the land, the depreciable property becomes 85% × $6,200,000, or $5,270,000. Because the property can be depreciated over a 27½-year period, one year's depreciation is ¹⁄₂₇th or $191,636, which may be used to offset (shelter) income from the property itself. Further interest on the debt service is deductible. The final figures are illustrated in Figure 15.3.

Viewed another way, if the property owner is in a 28 percent tax bracket, the exclusion (sheltering) of the depreciation allowance of $191,636 means that she saved 28 percent of this figure, or potentially $53,658 in federal income taxes, without having to "write a check" for the depreciation.

Deductible Expenses

Unlike the expenses of operating property held for personal use, such as a personal residence, the *costs of operating property held for use in business or as an investment* are **deductible expenses.** These operating costs may be deducted from gross income in arriving at net income. Before deducting operating expenses, *losses from vacancies and credit losses are deducted from gross scheduled rental income* to arrive at **gross operating income.** Operating expenses are deducted from gross operating expenses. Examples of operating expenses are:

accounting and legal fees	services
advertising	maintenance and repairs
property management fee	supplies
property insurance	taxes
licenses and permits	utilities
wages and salaries	

The *result of deducting operating expenses* is **net operating income.** Mortgage interest and depreciation are deducted from net operating income to arrive at net taxable income. This otherwise taxable income may be completely or partially sheltered from tax liability as a result of the depreciation allowance. Consequently, the building may have no taxable income.

Tax-Deferred Exchanges

The Internal Revenue Code provides that, in cases of qualified exchange of property, some or all of the gain may not have to be recognized for tax purposes. The property exchanged must be investment property or business property. In a qualified **tax-deferred exchange,** *the tax on the gain is postponed, and the deduction of a loss also must be postponed.* These requirements are not discretionary with the taxpayer or the

Net Operating Income	$745,600
Less: Interest	−463,836
Depreciation	−191,636
Net Taxable Income	$ 90,128

FIGURE 15.3
Determination of net taxable income.

government. If a transaction qualifies as an exchange, no gain or loss may be recognized in the year of the exchange. The basis of the property each exchangor received is treated as if it were the same basis as the property each owned prior to the exchange, plus any additional expenditures on the new property. Tax-deferred exchanges are barred, however, if the property to be received is not identified on or before 45 days after the transfer or if it is not received within 180 days after the transfer or by the due date (with extensions) of the tax return for the year of transfer if earlier.

Like-Kind Property

To qualify as an exchange, the properties must be like-kind. Essentially, this involves exchanging personal property for other personal property or real property for other real property. Exchanges of like-kind real property may be an office building for a shopping mall, an apartment house for a tract of land, or an office building for an apartment building. Examples of personal property exchanges are a truck for a machine or an automobile for a truck. Personal residences and foreign property do not qualify for an exchange.

Business or Investment Property

The property exchanged must be held for use in business or as an investment. Property held for personal use does not qualify. An exchange of residences by homeowners does not qualify as a tax-deferred exchange but is treated as a sale and a purchase and thus may qualify for the rollover rule.

Property Not Held for Sale

The property exchanged must not be held for sale to customers in the regular course of business, such as lots held for sale by a developer.

Boot

If an exchangor receives cash or some other type of nonqualifying property in addition to like-kind property, the transaction may still partially qualify as a tax-deferred exchange. The recipient of *the cash in the exchange*, called the **boot,** or other nonqualifying property must include tax liability on the boot or other unlike-kind property in the calendar year of the exchange. **Unlike-kind property** is *property that is not similar in nature and character to the property exchanged.*

Basis

The basis of the property an exchangor receives is the basis of the property given up in exchange plus new expenditures or debt incurred. Therefore, an exchangor does not change the basis of an asset as a result of the exchange. For example, Exchangor #1 trades a property with a market value of $100,000 and a basis of $20,000 for another property also worth $100,000. The property Exchangor #1 receives also is considered to have a basis of $20,000 plus any new debt assumed and cash paid, regardless of the other exchangor's basis.

Multiple Exchange

A **multiple exchange** is one in which *more than two properties are exchanged in one transaction.* Usually, multiple exchanges are three-way exchanges. For example, A, B, and C each own like-kind real property held for business purposes of investment. In the exchange, A acquires the property owned by C, B acquires the property owned by A, and C acquires the property owned by B. Multiple exchanges qualify as tax-deferred exchanges in the same way two-way exchanges do. An exchangor does not have to receive property from the same person with whom he or she is exchanging property.

Starker Exchange (Starker Trust)

In the case for which the Starker exchange was named, Starker sold land to a corporation. The purchaser, however, withheld the purchase price until Starker subsequently found a suitable property to be purchased with proceeds from the sale. The U.S. Circuit Court of Appeals in 1979 held that the **Starker exchange** qualified for treatment as a tax-deferred exchange because the sale proceeds were held beyond the control of the taxpayer seeking the tax-deferred exchange. The court viewed the exchange as one continuous transaction.

Therefore, *if the proceeds of a sale of property are held beyond the seller's control until the seller can locate the like-kind property in which to invest the proceeds, the transaction may constitute a tax-free exchange. Proceeds from a Starker exchange* are held in a **Starker trust.** Some time limitations apply. The property for exchange must be identified in writing within 45 days of the time the Starker trust is established (first closing date), and the closing on the property must be within 180 days of establishment of the Starker trust, or April 15, whichever comes first.

INVESTMENT SYNDICATES

As a result of the tax implications and advantages in owning real estate, many people want to invest in real estate. To achieve maximum purchasing power, some investors pool their resources in a real estate **investment syndicate,** *a joint venture typically controlled by one or two persons hoping for return to all investors.* Profit for investors is generated when the syndicate buys, sells, and develops real estate.

To protect investors from fraud by syndicate promoters, the federal and state governments have enacted securities laws and regulations. Because these laws are *designed to protect investors from buying "blue sky,"* they are commonly referred to as **blue sky laws.**

The Security Act of 1933 was the first federal securities law. This law regulated companies' initial issuance of securities, outlined fraudulent practices, and required registration of securities prior to sale. Since that time, many additional laws have been passed requiring further disclosure, regulating insider trading, and requiring disclosure of any conflicts of interest.

The Illinois Securities Law of 1953 was enacted to protect the public when buying securities. A person who buys into a syndication owns a security. State and federal securities laws both require full disclosure of any and all material facts concerning the security. Securities, unless exempt, must be registered with the Securities and Exchange Commission (SEC). Illinois also requires registration with the Securities Division of the Secretary of State. Exemption from Federal Registration does not necessarily exempt a security from registration in Illinois.

Persons selling securities in Illinois must pass at least one of the series of exams administered by the National Association of Securities Dealers, Inc. (NASD). Dealers, salespersons employed to sell securities, and investment advisors also must register with the Illinois secretary of state.

Securities requiring registration, whether federal or state, must make complete disclosure via a document entitled a *prospectus.* Full disclosure is required even if the security is exempt from registration.

The goals of the 1933 law and subsequent laws are to protect the investing public. The act requires full disclosure by companies wishing to issue and sell stock to the public. Companies also are required to file a registration statement with the Securities and Exchange Commission (SEC). In all sales, a pamphlet or prospectus must be provided to all potential investors. The SEC does not pass judgment on the quality of the investment. It merely requires all disclosures necessary for investors' full knowledge.

In certain situations, securities legislation provides for exemptions from the registration process. Exemptions from the registration of securities and dealers are generally granted to issuers selling their own securities or making offerings to a small number of people, for a short period of time, and without general solicitation. Large organizations that require very little monitoring are often exempt from registration. More typical exemptions relate to minimum number of investors and minimum amount of money to be pooled by the investors. If a pool of investors (syndicate) does not comply with federal and state securities laws, the penalty is a fine up to $10,000 and imprisonment of up to five years.

IMPORTANT POINTS

1. Real estate licensees should be knowledgeable about tax legislation but must refrain from giving tax advice.
2. Depreciation is a deductible allowance from net income in arriving at taxable income. Therefore, it provides a tax shelter for the property owner.
3. A homeowner's real estate property taxes and mortgage interest are deductible expenses in calculating federal income tax liability.
4. Losses incurred in the sale of a personal residence are not tax deductible.
5. The rollover rule is mandatory for purchasing a new personal residence, and it enables the owner to postpone taxation on the gain from the former personal residence if the purchase price of the new home is equal to or greater than the adjusted sales price of the home sold.
6. The amount of gain on which taxes are deferred under the rollover rule is used to reduce the tax basis of the new home purchased.
7. The age-55-and-over exclusion allows an exemption of up to $125,000 of gain in the sale of a principal residence occupied for at least three of the last five years immediately preceding the sale. The exclusion may be taken only once.
8. The installment sale laws for taxation apply to the principal residence as well as to business and investment properties.
9. Depreciation enables the owner of business or investment property to recover the cost or other basis of the asset.
10. Land is not depreciable. Only structures on the land are depreciable real property.
11. Depreciation for real property is now calculated at 27½ years for residential property and 39 years for nonresidential property.
12. When a depreciable asset is sold, the basis of the asset used to compute taxable gain is the depreciated value, not the price the seller pays for the property.
13. Expenses of operating a business or investment property are deductible expenses in arriving at taxable income.
14. To qualify as a tax-deferred exchange, like-kind property must be exchanged. An exchangor receiving cash (boot) or other unlike-kind property in addition to like-kind property is taxed on the value of the boot or other unlike-kind property received.
15. To qualify as a tax-deferred exchange, the property exchanged must have been held for use in business (other than inventory) or as an investment. Property held for personal use does not qualify.
16. The Illinois blue sky laws require complete disclosure in regard to the sale of securities. Sellers must be registered with the SEC and the secretary of state and must have passed one exam administered by NASD.

REVIEW QUESTIONS

Answers to these questions are found in the Answer Key section at the back of the book.

1. Which of the following is a tax-deductible expense resulting from home ownership?
   a. operating expenses
   b. depreciation
   c. mortgage interest
   d. energy use

2. The rollover rule providing for deferment of an otherwise taxable gain in qualifying transactions is:
   a. optional
   b. mandatory
   c. conditional
   d. flexible

3. Discount points paid by a borrower to obtain a conventional mortgage loan to purchase a principal residence:
   a. are not deductible by the borrower as interest
   b. are deductible by the borrower as interest
   c. increase the basis of the new residence
   d. decrease the basis of the new residence

4. A real estate commission paid by a seller:
   a. may be deducted from the selling price as a selling expense in calculating the amount realized in the sale of a principal residence
   b. is deductible from ordinary income (wage income) by the seller when itemizing tax deductible expense
   c. increases the basis of the residence sold
   d. decreases the basis of the residence sold

5. A mortgage prepayment penalty paid by a borrower as a requirement for early loan payoff:
   a. may be deducted as interest in the year paid
   b. may be deducted as interest over a five-year period
   c. may only be deducted from selling price as a selling expense
   d. may not be taken as a deduction for any purpose

6. The amount of gain on which tax is postponed under the rollover rule is used to:
   a. increase the basis of the new residence
   b. reduce the basis of the new residence
   c. increase the allowable moving expenses
   d. reduce the inheritance basis of the new residence

7. The age-55-and-over exclusion provides all of the following EXCEPT:
   a. the choice of excluding from taxation up to $125,000 of gain resulting from the sale of a principal residence
   b. the exclusion may be taken only once in lifetime and, if taken by a married person, is binding on the other spouse even though the other spouse did not qualify
   c. the choice of excluding from taxation up to $125,000 of gain resulting from the sale of business property
   d. the exclusion is available only on sale of real estate that has been the principal residence three of the last five years

8. Which of the following is a benefit depreciation provides?
   a. tax credit
   b. tax deduction
   c. tax evasion
   d. tax deferment

9. Deductible expenses for a business property include all of the following EXCEPT:
   a. advertising
   b. utilities
   c. mortgage principal
   d. insurance

10. Raul Ramirez and Sarah Gildar trade office buildings. In the trade, Raul receives $20,000 in cash in addition to Sarah's office building. With regard to this transaction, which of the following is correct?

    a. the transaction does not qualify as a tax-free exchange
    b. the cash Raul receives is called boot and is taxable for the year in which the exchange occurs
    c. the exchangors, Raul and Sarah, exchange basis in the traded properties
    d. the cash Raul receives is deductible for the year the exchange occurs

11. The basis of property received in a tax-free exchange is:

    a. the basis as it was to the prior owner at the time of the exchange
    b. the average of the difference in the basis of all properties exchanged
    c. the same basis as the basis of the property given up in the exchange plus any debt assumed and cash paid
    d. the value of the property received in the exchange

12. In 1993, Ed and Margaret take advantage of the low interest rates to refinance their existing 30-year, 13.5 percent mortgage with a 15-year, 9.5 percent mortgage on their present home. They pay $1,500 in discount points to refinance this loan. How will the cost of these points be treated in their income tax?

    a. the cost is added to the basis of their home
    b. since all discount points are fully deductible in the year paid, they may deduct the $1,500 from their 1993 income
    c. they may deduct only $100 per year
    d. there is no deduction benefit at all

13. Bill and Betty purchase a home for $40,000 and later add a new room to the home at a cost of $5,000. They subsequently sell this home for $60,000 minus a 6 percent real estate commission. What will be the minimum purchase price of their new home in order to postpone taxation from all of the gain on the old home?

    a. $40,000
    b. $45,000
    c. $56,400
    d. $60,000

14. Victor and Valerie own a vacation property at the beach, which they use only one week per year. The property is rented out at fair market value the rest of the year. Which items of this property can they deduct?

    a. mortgage principal only
    b. mortgage interest only
    c. mortgage interest, repairs, depreciation, maintenance, and property taxes
    d. mortgage interest and property taxes only

15. Charles and Maria own two properties. One is their principal residence, and the other is a vacation cottage they use three weeks of the year and rent out the rest. What items can they deduct for the cottage?

    a. mortgage interest and property taxes
    b. depreciation only
    c. repairs
    d. nothing, as it is a vacation home

CHAPTER 16

IMPORTANT TERMINOLOGY

Appraisal Administration Fund
broker
Chief of Real Estate Investigations
continuing education requirement
inoperative license
leasing agent
Office of Banks and Real Estate (OBRE)
pocket card
Real Estate Administration and Disciplinary Board

Real Estate Appraisal Committee
Real Estate Education Advisory Council
Real Estate License Administration Fund
Real Estate Recovery Fund
Real Estate Research and Education Fund
real estate sponsor cards
reciprocity
salesperson

Illinois Real Estate License Law

IN THIS CHAPTER Today, all states require people engaged in the real estate business to be licensed by the state. The state's authority to require licenses falls under its police power—the power of every state that enables it to fulfill its obligation to protect the health, safety, welfare, and property of citizens of the state.

The purpose of license law legislation is to protect the general public. License laws require a licensee to possess the necessary knowledge and skill and a reputation for honest, fair-dealing, and ethical conduct before entering the real estate business. License laws also govern the conduct of licensees in their real estate business activities.

Although license law legislation varies from state to state, the most important provisions are similar, if not identical, and are based on the model recommended by the National Association of REALTORS® (NAR). Substantial uniformity in the major provisions of license law statutes also has resulted from efforts of the Association of Real Estate License Law Officials (ARELLO). Organized in 1930, ARELLO consists of license law officials representing every state. ARELLO and the NAR have made substantial contributions to license law legislation that have elevated the standards of the real estate industry.

ILLINOIS REAL ESTATE LICENSE ACT

The Illinois Real Estate License Act of 1983, ILL. Rev. Stat. 1989 (Chapter 111, Paras. 5801-5836.24, as amended effective 7/1/95) contains four articles: (a) real estate licensing, (b) appraiser certification, (c) continuing education, and (d) brokerage relations. This act is intended to evaluate the competency and regulate the business of those engaged in real estate activity for the protection of the public.

Article I: Real Estate Licensing

Governing Bodies

The governor of Illinois appoints the commissioner of the **Office of Banks and Real Estate (OBRE).** The commissioner *appoints an executive director of real estate to head the real estate unit and oversee the licensing of real estate brokers and salespersons.* The executive director must have a valid broker's license, which is surrendered to the OBRE. The executive director, who reports to the commissioner, has the following duties:

1. chairperson of the board, ex-officio, without vote

2. liaison between the real estate unit, the profession, and real estate organizations and associations
3. preparation and circulation of informational material to licensees
4. appointment of necessary committees
5. supervision of the real estate unit subject to administrative approval of the commissioner of the OBRE

Section 17 of the act authorizes the director to employ one full-time **Chief of Real Estate Investigations** and not fewer than one full-time investigator and one full-time auditor for every 15,000 licensees.

The governor appoints a nine-member **Real Estate Administration and Disciplinary Board,** which is created by Section 9 of the Illinois Real Estate License Act. The recommendations of members and organizations of the profession are considered, as well as geographic representation. Composition of the board is subject to the following conditions:

1. All members must be residents and citizens of Illinois for at least six years.
2. Six members must be active brokers or salespersons in the business for at least 10 years.
3. Three of the members are to be from the general public, unlicensed, whose spouses, if any, are unlicensed and without any interest in any real estate business.

A member's term is four years, with a lifetime maximum of eight years. Terms are staggered so that no more than two members' terms expire in any one year. Appointments may be terminated by the governor for just cause or simply for missing four board meetings per year. Members are paid a per-diem stipend as well as necessary expenses in the performance of their duties.

The board considers and makes recommendations regarding standards of professional conduct and discipline, suggests rules for administering and enforcing the act, and prescribes forms for use in accordance with the act. The board oversees examinations, hearings, registration of licensees, certification of schools offering real estate courses, and promulgation of the rules and regulations of the license act.

Section 20 of the act authorizes the board to conduct hearings on proceedings to suspend or revoke or to refuse to issue or renew licenses. The board can have actions of the accused investigated upon the verifiable written complaint of any person or upon a motion of either the OBRE or the board.

The governor also appoints a five-member **Real Estate Education Advisory Council,** which *makes recommendations to the board on rules and regulations relating to pre-license and continuing education.* The council is composed of three members from the board, one member from a real estate-related trade organization, and one member from an approved sponsor of real estate courses. This council also is responsible for reviewing and approving all applications for sponsors of licensing courses as well as real estate education instructors.

Activities Requiring a License

A license is required for anyone who, for another person and for compensation, sells, offers to sell, exchanges, negotiates, purchases, rents, or leases; lists, offers to list, deals in options on real estate or improvements thereon; collects, offers, or agrees to collect rents; advertises or represents himself or herself as being engaged in the business; assists or directs in procuring prospects or negotiating any transaction intended to result in the sale, exchange, lease, or rental of real estate. Section 3 of the Illinois Real Estate License Act makes it unlawful for any person, corporation, or partnership to act as a broker or salesperson without a properly issued sponsor or pocket card.

The Illinois Real Estate License Act requires that all officers of a corporation acting as a real estate broker hold a broker's license and that all their employees who engage in the real estate business hold real estate licenses. All general partners in a partnership who engage in real estate activities must have broker's licenses, and all their employees who act as salespersons must be licensed.

Exemptions. Illinois exempts the following persons from licensing:

1. persons performing real estate activities relating to their own property
2. attorneys-in-fact and attorneys-at-law in performance of their duties
3. persons acting under a court order or under authority of a will or trust
4. persons employed as resident managers who reside on the premises
5. officers or employees of a federal agency or state government in the conduct of their official duties
6. multiple listing services or referral systems wholly owned by a not-for-profit organization or association of real estate brokers

Fines and Disciplinary Action

Complaints against a licensee are reviewed by a subcommittee of the board, which makes a recommendation to the full board as to whether to proceed with formal disciplinary proceedings. Accused persons found guilty of an Illinois Real Estate License Act violation may appeal to the circuit court. If found guilty there, an appeal may be made to the Illinois Supreme Court.

Action against a licensee for a violation of the act must be taken within five years of the occurrence of the alleged violation.

Unlicensed persons engaging in real estate activities are considered harmful to the public and a public nuisance. A cease-and-desist action and criminal penalties may be brought against them.

The major portion of license law legislation pertains to standards of conduct. These standards are substantially uniform throughout the states and reinforce licensees' obligations to the principal and to the general public. Violation of these statutory requirements by a licensee subjects the licensee to disciplinary procedures.

Section 18 of the Illinois Real Estate License Act provides for probation, suspension, revocation of license, refusal to issue or renew, and reprimand or a civil penalty not to exceed $10,000 for the causes listed below.

1. obtaining or seeking to obtain a license by false or fraudulent representation

FIGURE 16.1 Penalties for criminal violations of the Illinois Real Estate License Act.

	VIOLATOR	VIOLATION	PENALTY
Section 3	Individual	Class A misdemeanor	Fined up to $1,000 for 1st offense; prison up to 1 year
	Individual	Class 4 felony	Fined not less than $10,000 nor more than $25,000 for 2nd or subsequent offenses
	Corporation	Business offense	Fined up to $10,000 for a 1st offense; fined not less than $10,000 nor more than $25,000 for a 2nd or subsequent offense
Section 18	Individual	Class C misdemeanor	Fined up to $500, prison up to 30 days for a 1st offense
	Individual	Class A misdemeanor	Fined up to $1,000, prison up to 1 year for a 2nd or subsequent offense
	Corporation	Business offense	Fined up to $2,000 for a 1st offense; fined up to $5,000 for a 2nd or subsequent offense

2. conviction of a felony in this state or a crime of a similar nature in another state
3. adjudged to be mentally insane
4. performing or attempting to practice real estate from an office not separate and distinct from a retail business
5. discipline by another state if one of the grounds for the discipline is the same as or equal to grounds set forth in this act
6. engaging in real estate activity without an operative license
7. cheating or subverting or aiding another to cheat or subvert on the real estate examination
8. engaging in real estate and found guilty of:
   - substantial misrepresentation or untruthful advertising
   - false promises likely to influence, persuade, or induce
   - continued and flagrant misrepresentation or making of false promises
   - misleading advertising or representing oneself as a member of any real estate organization of which one is not a member
   - acting for more than one party in a transaction without providing written notice to all parties and obtaining consent of all parties
   - representing or attempting to represent other than the licensee's employing broker
   - failing to account for or to remit moneys or documents
   - failing to maintain and deposit all escrow in a special account until the transactions are consummated or terminated; special account must be non-interest-bearing unless required by law or written instructions by the principals that deposits be placed in an interest-bearing account
   - failing to make all records required in the practice of real estate available to the OBRE
   - failing to provide copies of real estate–related documents to all parties to the transaction
   - paying a commission to anyone for activities in violation of the act
   - unworthiness or incompetency
   - commingling funds
   - evading licensing requirement for payment of commission by employing a person on a temporary basis or for a single deal
   - allowing broker's license to be used to operate a brokerage without broker's actual participation
   - dishonest dealing or conduct of any such nature
   - advertising in any manner or displaying a "for sale" or rental sign on any property without the written consent of the owner(s)
   - failing to provide, within 30 days, information requested by the OBRE
   - disregarding or violating, aiding, or abetting in the disregarding or violating of this act or the rules and regulations promulgated to enforce this act
   - failing to use the name of the firm in any advertising or the use of a blind ad
   - offering a guaranteed sales plan other than as defined in the act
   - promoting the continuance or maintenance of racially or religiously segregated housing
   - violating the Illinois Human Rights Act
   - interfering with a sales contract or listing contract for the purpose of substituting a new sales contract or listing agreement
   - negotiating with an owner whom licensee knows has a written exclusive listing with another broker

- acting as both real estate agent and attorney in the same transaction
- failing to disclose in advertisements, if any, conditions or obligations necessary for receiving free merchandise or services
- disregarding or violating the Illinois Real Estate Time-Share Act
- violating terms of a disciplinary order issued by the OBRE
- paying a commission directly to a licensee employed by another broker

Failure to file a tax return or to pay moneys due as required by any tax act administered by the Illinois Department of Revenue may result in the OBRE refusing to issue or renew a license or suspending a license.

The license of Illinois brokers or salespersons is not jeopardized for failure to disclose that a property was occupied by an HIV-infected person or that acts (e.g., physical violence, suicide) were committed that do not affect the physical or environmental aspects of the property.

Licensees who have been adjudged to have committed illegal discrimination while engaging in real estate activities may be subject to disciplinary action unless the adjudication is in the appeal process.

Classification of Licenses

Illinois has three classifications of real estate licenses: real estate broker, real estate salesperson, and leasing agent. The definition of real estate broker and the definition of real estate salesperson are substantially uniform in the various state licensing laws. A broker is licensed to participate in real estate activities as described in the license act. A **broker** *may own and operate a brokerage business and employ broker associates or salespersons or both. A broker's license is required to manage a real estate office.*

A **salesperson** is *licensed to engage in real estate activities under the employment of a broker as described in the license act.* The salesperson is either an independent contractor or an employee depending upon state laws and the written employment contract. A salesperson may have a written employment agreement with only one employing broker at a time.

In 1995, the Illinois legislature created a new classification of license: the **leasing agent** license, *a limited-scope license that restricts the licensee working under the supervision of a broker to leasing and collecting rent from residential properties.* A person 18 years old or older may engage in residential leasing activities for a period of 120 consecutive days without being licensed as long as the broker notifies OBRE that the person is pursuing licensure. Educational requirements consist of 15 hours of OBRE-approved coursework and the successful completion of a state exam for leasing agents. The 15 hours may be applied toward a salesperson or broker license.

Application for Licensure

Applicants for licensure must be at least 21 years of age, be of good moral character, and have a high school diploma or a GED equivalency. There is one exception: Candidates who are 18 to 20 years old and have successfully completed at least four semesters of college with a major emphasis on real estate, in a school approved by the board, may be eligible for licensure.

A salesperson candidate must show proof of successful completion of 30 hours of real estate courses approved by the board or evidence of a baccalaureate degree with minor courses involving real estate from a college or university approved by the board.

A broker candidate must have 90 hours of real estate course work approved by the board or evidence of a baccalaureate degree with minor courses involving real estate from a college or university approved by the board. Active licensing as a salesperson for one of the prior three years also is required.

Attorney applicants who are in active standing and admitted to practice law by the Supreme Court of Illinois are exempt from the above-named educational requirements but not from the examination.

Generally, real estate coursework is good only for 5 years. The 30 hours transactions class will expire 5 years from its completion, unless the individual applies for and maintains a real estate salesperson license. The broker coursework will also expire in 5 years unless the individual applies for and maintains a broker license. The saleperson's real estate transaction coursework and the broker's coursework will be valid indefinitely as long as they have no lapse in licensing. If they do not get licensed, the coursework will expire for both salespersons and brokers.

Reciprocity

Illinois grants **reciprocity,** or *the mutual exchange of privileges,* to brokers and salespersons licensed in another state that has entered into a reciprocal agreement with the OBRE under the following conditions:

1. The broker is licensed and maintains a place of business in his or her home state.
2. Registration standards are equal to Illinois' minimum standards.
3. The broker has been actively licensed for at least two years prior to date of application.
4. The broker submits the proper fees and provides verification of an active license in another state that is in good standing and has no pending complaints.
5. The salesperson is under contract to a broker with an Illinois license and resides in the same state as that broker.

Applicants have to agree in writing to abide by all of the provisions of the Illinois Real Estate License Act.

Brokerage Office

Brokers in Illinois must maintain an office within the state that is separate and distinct from all other retail establishments. A highly visible identification sign must be displayed on the outside of the office. The broker's license or certificate and the certificates of all licensees in his or her employ must be conspicuously displayed in the broker's office.

A broker may own more than one office. One of the offices must be designated as the main office; all of the other offices are called *branch offices.* The name of the branch office must be the same as that of the main office or have some identifiable relationship to the main office. A broker is allowed to be in direct operational control of only one office; thus, a *branch manager* must be appointed to manage each branch office. Only brokers can manage branch offices. The principal broker–owner must have a written employment contract with each of the branch managers.

The Office of Banks and Real Estate is to be notified immediately upon the change of address of a broker's main office or a branch office. A written request for authorization to continue operation of an office or a branch, in the case of death or disability of an employing broker or loss of a managing broker, must be sought from the OBRE within 10 days of the loss. Authorization, if granted, is valid for no more than 30 days unless extended by the OBRE.

Escrow accounts. Brokers who receive escrow funds—moneys belonging to others—must place these funds in an escrow or special account. Unless specified by the principals, Illinois requires that all escrow funds be placed in a non-interest-bearing special account in a federally insured depository. Principals, however, may state in writing that funds are to be placed in an interest-bearing account. The written agreement must specify to whom the interest is to be disbursed. Escrow funds are to be deposited not later than the next business day following acceptance of the contract or receipt of funds from a branch office. Branch offices may maintain a special account. If they do not, escrow funds must be delivered or mailed to the main office not later than the next business day following acceptance of the contract. Rental deposits are considered escrow funds and as such are to be placed in an escrow account. Escrow money includes moneys a licensee receives on a property in which he is only a partial owner. On properties for which a licensee acts as a property manager, rental deposits must be placed into an escrow account unless this requirement is waived by the tenant. Withdrawals from special accounts take place as agreed to by the principals. Earned brokerage commission may be withdrawn on the day of, but no later than the next business day following, the contract consummation or termination.

Brokers must maintain a journal for each special account, showing the receipts and disbursements in chronological order. A ledger also must be maintained, containing pertinent facts regarding receipt and disbursement of the funds.

OBRE is to be notified of each account and of any changes in the account within 10 days of a change and is authorized to examine and audit each special account. Brokers are to reconcile each account within 10 days of receipt of the bank statement. Records are to be maintained for at least three years from the date of reconciliation. Brokers who do not receive escrow funds need not maintain an escrow account.

Sponsor cards. Section 12.1 of the Illinois Real Estate License Act requires that employing or managing brokers issue a **real estate sponsor card** to each newly employed sales associate. A real estate sponsor card *acts as a 45-day temporary work permit and allows the holder to engage in real estate activities under the sponsoring broker.* The employing broker and the associating salesperson each receive a copy of the permit.

A duplicate of the sponsor card and an application for licensure (for new candidates) or an invalidated certificate from the previous broker, along with the proper fees, must be sent to the OBRE within 24 hours of issuance of the card. Upon receipt of the license application and the proper fees, the OBRE will issue the license (wall certificate) and a **pocket card** to the licensee.

PUTTING IT TO WORK

Licensees are required to carry their current pocket card or sponsor card while engaging in real estate activities.

A candidate who has passed the state exam is eligible for licensing by a sponsoring or employing broker. The employing broker may issue a sponsor card to candidates who have received a "pass" notice without any restrictions or conditions that require further explanation. Qualified candidates—those who have passed the state exam—must apply for their license within one year of passing the licensing examination. If application is not made within that time, the candidate must retake the state exam and pass it again to become eligible again for licensing.

Illinois regards salespersons as either independent contractors or employees and requires brokers to have a written contract with each licensee in their employ. The agreement must cover the areas of supervision, duties, compensation, and termination. When contracts designate salespersons as independent contractors, this is for tax purposes only.

Termination of employment. Upon termination of a sales associate's employment, the terminating broker signs the licensee's wall certificate. The licensee receives the original endorsed license; the broker retains a copy for her files until the expiration date and sends a copy to the OBRE within two days of the termination.

When a salesperson leaves the employ of a broker, he takes the endorsed wall certificate, which renders his license inoperative. The endorsed certificate is presented to a new employing broker, who sends it along with a new broker sponsor card to the OBRE within 24 hours, via certified mail. Any listings the salesperson has belong to the broker and do not go along to the salesperson's new office.

Advertising. The broker's business name must appear in any and all advertising. Advertising cannot be false or misleading. An operative licensee must advertise in the name of the employing broker (even when advertising the licensee's own property) and disclose her status in writing as a licensee as well as any interest she may have in the subject property.

Putting It to Work

Only inoperative licensees may advertise "for sale by owner." Disclosures that the property is agent- or broker-owned must appear on yard signs as well as any other advertising to market the property. A person whose license is being held by a broker is considered an operative licensee and cannot advertise her property "for sale by owner."

Before placing a "for sale" sign on the property or advertising the property in any way, the written permission of all owners must be obtained. Placing the property in a multiple listing service also requires written permission.

When advertising free merchandise or services, the conditions or obligations necessary to receive said free merchandise or services must also be disclosed in the advertisement.

Contracts. Illinois licensees are prohibited from practicing law and cannot draft legal instruments. The Quinlan and Tyson cases established authorization for brokers to complete the blanks in a preprinted sales contract generally used in the area where the broker does business. Illinois brokers also may add facts and business details to contracts and riders that are approved for use in their community.

After the signing, no blanks are to be filled in. Any and all changes to a signed contract must be at the direction of all the signing parties, with all changes signed or initialed by all parties. Within 24 hours of the signing, all copies of the contract, original or corrected, must be delivered to all signing parties.

Contracts that are binding on the parties must so state in large, bold headings, for example, REAL ESTATE SALES CONTRACT. Contracts designated "Offer to Purchase" cannot be used if the form is to be used as a binding real estate contract.

All listing contracts must have a definite termination date. Any listing contract not containing a provision for an automatic expiration date is void.

Putting It to Work

Illinois does not have an inactive status for licensees. A licensee who is not broker sponsored is considered inoperative. If licensees do not renew with a sponsoring broker by the time their license is up for renewal, their license will be considered nonrenewed.

License Renewal

The salesperson license is renewed every two years, during March of the odd-numbered years. The renewal fee for an unexpired salesperson license is $25 per year. The broker license is renewed every two years, during January of the even-numbered years. The renewal fee for an unexpired broker license is $50 per year. A branch office or corporation renews at $50 per year.

The OBRE must be notified in writing of:

- a change in place of business or branch immediately; A fee of $25 is required to issue a license with a change of location

- any change in the operation of an escrow account, within 10 days of such change
- the termination of sales associates; the terminating broker sends a copy of the sales associate's invalidated license to the OBRE within two days of the termination

> **PUTTING IT TO WORK**
>
> Any request for issuance of duplicate license with a change, other than during the renewal period, is $25.

Nonrenewed licenses may be reinstated if the license has not been inoperative for more than five years. The fee to renew an inoperative license is $50 plus all lapsed renewal fees. Continuing education missed must also be completed. A license that has been nonrenewed between three and five years may be reinstated upon proof of successful completion of at least a 15-hour refresher course and payment of the required fees. A license that has been nonrenewed for more than five years will not be reinstated.

Distribution of Fees

The initial salesperson or broker licensing fee is $100 of which the $85 processing fee deposited in the **Real Estate License Administration Fund** is *used for the operating expenses of the OBRE and the board in administering the Illinois Real Estate License Act.*

The $10 fee deposited in the **Real Estate Recovery Fund** is *used to reimburse aggrieved persons who suffer loss from a licensee's violation of the act.* These persons may recover, after having exhausted all other avenues of recovery, no more than $10,000 from any one violation plus costs and attorney's fees up to a maximum of 15 percent of the amount of recovery. The maximum liability for any one violation arising out of the activities of any one single licensee is $50,000. Automatic termination of one's real estate license occurs from payment out of the Real Estate Recovery Fund on one's behalf. The licensee may contest this procedure.

Fines and penalties are also deposited in the Real Estate Recovery Fund. If the balance in the fund is less than $1,250,000 on December 31 of any year, an additional fee of $10 will be charged to all licensees at the time of the next renewal.

The moneys deposited in the **Real Estate Research and Education Fund** are *used for the operating expenses of the Office of Real Estate Research at the University of Illinois.* A scholarship fund for persons of minority racial origin wishing to pursue a course of study in the field of real estate receives $1 of every $5 deposited in this fund.

See Figure 16.2 for distribution of fees. The real estate recovery fund will receive $10, and the real estate research and education fund will receive $5 from both the initial sales and broker license fees and their renewals.

Article II: Real Estate Appraiser Certification

Article II of the Illinois Real Estate License Act provides for the voluntary licensing and certification of appraisers to enable real estate appraisers to conduct appraisals required of Title XI of the federal Financial Institutions Reform, Recovery, and Enforcement Act (FIRREA) of 1989. Real estate appraisers licensed or certified under this act shall practice in accordance with Uniform Standards of Professional Appraisal Practice. (See Figure 16.3.) The state-certified or -licensed appraiser's certificate number is to be placed adjacent to or below the appraiser's title on all reports.

Nothing in this act precludes a person who is not certified or licensed under this act from appraising real estate in Illinois for compensation. *Application and renewal fees are to be deposited* in the **Appraisal Administration Fund.**

FIGURE 16.2
Breakdown of Illinois licensing fees.

	Initial Fee	Processing Fee	Real Estate Recovery Fund	Real Estate Research and Education Fund
Salesperson	$100	$85	$10	$5*
Broker	$100	$85	$10	$5*
Corporation or partnership	$100	$85	$10	$5*
Branch office	$100	$95	—	$5*

*$1 goes to the Minority Racial Origin Scholarship Fund.

FIGURE 16.3
Real estate appraiser qualifications and fees in Illinois.

TYPE OF LICENSE	FEES	QUALIFIED TO APPRAISE	REQUIREMENTS
Licensed Real Estate Appraiser	$100, application; $450, initial license $450, renewal	1–4 units	• 75 classroom hours • No experience, but 500 hours required for the second renewal • Pass the appraisal examination
Certified Residential Real Estate Appraiser	$150, application; $450, initial license $450, renewal	All types of residential property	• 120 classroom hours • 2 years experience, 50% relating to residential property • Pass the appraisal examination
Certified General Real Estate Appraiser	$150, application; $450, initial license $450, renewal	All types of real estate	• 165 classroom hours • 2 years experience, 50% relating to nonresidential property • Pass the appraisal examination

Note: In 1998, new, stricter experience requirements take effect.

Nonresident Certification and Reciprocity

The Illinois Real Estate License Act allows for nonresident certification by complying with all the provisions and conditions required for certification in Illinois. Those certified in another state are entitled to receive certification provided that the laws of that state grant reciprocity to Illinois and provided that no proceeding is pending or unresolved against such appraiser. Such nonresident shall maintain an active place of business in the state of domicile.

A nonresident who is licensed or certified in another state may apply for a temporary appraisal practice permit by filing with the OBRE. The temporary permit is valid for 60 days from date of issuance. It may be extended for 30 days. Each applicant is limited to two temporary appraisal practice permits in any calendar year. The nonrefundable fee is $80. Applicants may not advertise, solicit, or otherwise represent themselves as being state licensed or certified.

Appraisal Administrator

An appraisal administrator is appointed by the commissioner. This person's current, valid, certified general real estate appraisal certificate has to be surrendered during the term of office. Duties consist of:

1. direct liaison between the OBRE and real estate appraisers and assistance to the

Real Estate Appraisal Committee in carrying out its functions and duties under this article
2. direct liaison between the OBRE and the real estate appraiser and the real estate appraisal organizations and real estate–related organizations
3. supervision of the appraisal unit of the OBRE, subject to administrative approval of the commissioner
4. preparation and circulation to a licensed and certified appraiser, of educational and informational materials as the OBRE deems necessary for guidance or assistance
5. appointment of any committees necessary to assist in performing the OBRE's functions and duties under this article

---

PUTTING IT TO WORK

All licenses and certificates of appraisers expire on September 30 of each odd-numbered year. A minimum of 10 hours of continuing education per year is required.

Appraisal Violations

The OBRE may suspend, revoke, place on probation, reprimand, or discipline the certificate of any state-certified or -licensed appraiser for any of the following:

1. attempting to procure or receiving certification or licensing by misrepresenting, bribery, supplying false or fraudulent information, or failing to meet the minimum qualifications for certification
2. criminal conviction or dishonest, fraudulent, and misrepresentative acts related to the performance of appraisal activities
3. violation of standards in the development or communication of appraisals; failing to use reasonable diligence, negligence, or incompetence in the development, preparation, or communication of an appraisal report
4. willful disregarding or violating the provisions or rules and regulations of this article
5. providing an appraisal whereby the fee is contingent upon the report

Real Estate Appraisal Committee

A committee of 10 members is appointed by the governor. Consideration is to be given to geographic and demographic areas as well as recommendations of real estate brokerage and appraisal organizations. The appraisal administrator is a member without a vote. Composition of this committee is as follows:

1. Seven members must be real estate appraisers who have engaged in real estate appraising within the state of Illinois for not fewer than five years immediately preceding their appointments.
   At least two of the seven shall be representative of the statewide real estate industry. After the date when federal law requires real estate appraisals for federally related transactions in Illinois to be performed, at least two of the real estate appraisers must hold a valid certificate and all noncertified members must have a valid license.
2. One member has to be a representative of a financial institution.
3. Two members must be from the general public.

The **Real Estate Appraisal Committee** *conducts hearings on charges against state-certified or -licensed appraisers; makes recommendations on rules and regulations to* *be followed by state-certified or -licensed appraisers; recommends standard of professional conduct, discipline, precertification, and continuing education; and submits renewal procedures and examination requirements.*

Article III: Salesperson and Broker Continuing Education

Article III of the Illinois Real Estate License Act establishes the **continuing education requirement** for real estate licensees. *Within the 24 months preceding license renewal (prerenewal period), licensees are required to complete 12 hours of continuing education courses.*

Exempt from the continuing education requirement are: (a) individuals who submitted an application to obtain a license under the act on or before December 31, 1976, and whose license was issued by the OBRE on or before April 1, 1977; (b) licensees who are in their first renewal period (whether as a broker or a salesperson); and (c) attorneys who are also real estate licensees.

At least six hours of credit must be earned in the mandatory category. All 12 hours can be earned within this category. Mandatory courses cover license law and escrow, antitrust, fair housing, and agency.

A maximum of six hours can be earned in the elective category. Elective courses include appraisal, property management, residential brokerage, farm property management, rights and duties of buyers and sellers and brokers, commercial brokerage and leasing, financing, and others as approved by the Real Estate Education Advisory Council.

Each course must be a minimum of three hours in length. Licensees must score a minimum of 70 percent on a 25-question examination given immediately following the course. Credit for a duplicate course can be earned if the course is taken from different continuing education sponsors.

Continuing education credit can be earned only from approved coursework offered by an OBRE-approved continuing education sponsor.

REAL ESTATE LICENSING INFORMATION

Q: How do I become licensed?
A: Application for licensure must be made to the OBRE. All applicants must be at least 21 years of age (or qualify under the 18–20 exception rule), be of good moral character, and have successfully completed high school or have acquired a GED equivalency.

Q: What are the qualifications for application?
A: To qualify, applicants for licensure must have proof of successfully completing the proper coursework and have passed the real estate licensing examination as administered by the OBRE.

Q: What are the qualifications for taking the real estate examination?
A: To qualify to take the state examination, salesperson applicants must successfully pass a 30-hour real estate transaction course in an OBRE-approved school or qualify under the baccalaureate degree exception. Broker applicants must have successfully completed 90 hours of coursework or qualify under baccalaureate degree, or the licensed attorney exception as approved by the OBRE, and have an active salesperson license for at least one year of the last three.

Q: How do I find an approved school?
A: In Illinois, more than 100 schools are approved to offer real estate courses in subjects preparing candidates for fitness to receive a license. Courses are offered by

private and vocational schools, high school districts, and local colleges and universities. For a list of approved schools, call the OBRE at (217) 785-9300 or (312) 793-8704.

Q: What does the Illinois real estate examination consist of?
A: The Illinois portion of the real estate examination consists of 30 items or questions for the salesperson candidate and 40 items for the broker candidate. The examination covers Illinois real estate law, the Illinois Real Estate License Act, the rules and regulations of the act, and other aspects of real estate practice relevant to Illinois. The national or uniform portion of the examination consists of 80 questions for both salespersons and brokers. In addition, the candidate will be required to answer a number of pretest questions, which will not be scored. (The candidate handbook contains general content and state content outlines.)

Q: How do I make a reservation to take the state examination?
A: The OBRE has authorized Assessment Systems, Inc. (ASI) to administer the real estate examination and to issue score reports to all qualified candidates. A State of Illinois *Real Estate Candidate Handbook* is available from the OBRE and from the approved schools. You may make a reservation by telephone or by fax to take the examination; walk-in testing is not available.

By telephone: Dial (800) 274-0404 between 7:00 A.M. and 10:00 P.M. Central Time, Monday through Friday, or between 7:00 A.M. and 3:00 P.M. on Saturday. Be prepared to give your social security number and to write down a confirmation number, which you must take with you on the day of the examination. Candidates must call at least three business days before the examination date desired.

By fax: Use the form in the handbook and fax it to ASI at (610) 617-9303, 24 hours a day, 7 days a week. The fax must be received no less than four business days before the examination date desired.

Note: Broker candidates must have received a certificate of examination eligibility to make a reservation (see "Prior Approval" in the candidate handbook).

Q: When is the examination given?
A: Some assessment centers in Illinois are available for testing every day, Tuesday through Saturday. Other assessment centers test on Saturday only. Testing begins at 8:00 A.M. and at 1:00 P.M.

Q: What is the examination fee?
A: An examination fee of $52 is paid when you report to the test center to take your examination. *Cash and personal checks are not accepted.* You will have to bring a money order or cashier's check. Examination fees are nonrefundable. You may transfer the fee without penalty to another test date if you call four business days prior to your test appointment date. If you call later than that to reschedule, or if you are absent, you will be billed for two examinations when you register again.

Review Questions

Answers to these questions are found in the Answer Key section at the back of the book.

1. The Illinois Real Estate License Act allows licensed real estate salespersons to do all of the following EXCEPT:
   a. list commercial real estate
   b. list residential real estate
   c. sell all types of real estate
   d. manage a real estate brokerage

2. Which of the following activities requires a real estate license?
   a. selling your own real estate
   b. selling real estate under a court order
   c. acting as a resident property manager
   d. selling real estate for another for compensation

3. The Real Estate Administration and Disciplinary Board is responsible for which of the following?
   a. setting the commission rate
   b. enforcing the Real Estate License Act
   c. setting the interest rate
   d. running the multiple listing service

4. The court decision limiting real estate salespeople to filling in the blanks between the words on a preprinted contract and prohibiting them from drafting any document is the:
   a. Statute of Frauds
   b. Illinois Fraud and Deceptive Practices Act
   c. Clayton vs. Coldwell Banker decision
   d. Quinlan and Tyson decision

5. The youngest an Illinois licensed salesperson could be is:
   a. 16 years old
   b. 18 years old
   c. 21 years old
   d. 25 years old

6. The Real Estate Recovery Fund:
   a. provides sales associates with lost commissions
   b. provides a way for aggrieved persons to recover losses
   c. pays out an unlimited amount per each act of a licensee
   d. receives $5 from each licensee's registration fee

7. Real estate licensees are in violation of the Real Estate License Act when they:
   a. represent only one broker
   b. provide copies of all real estate documents to all parties
   c. account for all moneys entrusted to them
   d. act as a real estate agent and an attorney in the same transaction

8. Broker licensees may:
   a. pay a commission to any licensee
   b. be in direct operational control of more than one real estate branch
   c. promote racially segregated housing
   d. advertise their listings in the firm's name

9. Real estate licensees must disclose all of the following EXCEPT:
   a. dual agent representation
   b. their ownership interest in listed property
   c. amount of their commission
   d. receipt of funds from all parties

10. Jane Jones owns and manages a real estate brokerage. Jane:
    a. may not employ brokers as salespersons
    b. may have more than one special account
    c. may not own more than one real estate brokerage
    d. may not have two offices with the same name

11. Which of the following statements is NOT true concerning a broker sponsor card?
    a. it is a temporary 45-day work permit
    b. it must be displayed in the broker's office
    c. a copy must be sent to the OBRE within 24 hours of issuance
    d. a managing broker can issue a sponsor card

12. Which of the following is INCORRECT regarding the licensing of residential leasing agents?

    a. leasing agents have a grace period of 120 days before being required to have a license
    b. Leasing agents have a grace period of 180 days before being required to have a license
    c. leasing agents may apply their 15 hours of coursework toward either a broker or salesperson license
    d. leasing agents must be employed by a broker

13. Which of the following statements is true in regard to escrow accounts and escrow funds?

    a. escrow funds must be placed in an interest-bearing account
    b. escrow funds must be placed in a special account no later than the next business day after acceptance of the contract
    c. branch offices cannot have escrow accounts
    d. brokers receive the interest earned from escrow accounts

14. All of the following statements are true EXCEPT:

    a. records are to be maintained for three years following reconciliation
    b. accounts must be reconciled within 10 days after receipt of the bank statement
    c. the OBRE must be notified of all special accounts
    d. all brokers must maintain special accounts

15. Which of the following statements is true in regard to real estate contracts?

    a. licensees may fill in the blanks in a preprinted form
    b. licensees may draft contracts
    c. blanks in a contract may be filled in after the signing by all parties
    d. binding sales contracts must be designated "Offer to Purchase"

16. All of the following statements are true regarding a real estate salesperson's licensure candidate EXCEPT:

    a. licensees must have reached the age of 21
    b. licensees must have a high school diploma or GED equivalent
    c. licensees must have successfully completed 30 hours of a real estate transaction course
    d. licensees must have at least one year of real estate experience

17. A real estate broker candidate must:

    a. have three years of experience
    b. have a college degree
    c. have 90 hours of real estate coursework
    d. be sponsored by another broker

18. An inoperative license can be all of the following EXCEPT:

    a. an unsponsored license
    b. renewed between three and five years upon completing a minimum of 15 hours of coursework
    c. renewed after five years after successfully passing another state examination
    d. used to list and sell real estate

19. Which of the following statements is true regarding reciprocity?

    a. Illinois grants reciprocity only to bordering states
    b. Illinois grants reciprocity to licensees in any state
    c. Illinois extends reciprocity to states with equal standards of registration
    d. Illinois extends reciprocity only to states with greater standards of registration

20. Upon the loss of a branch manager, the broker has how much time to notify the OBRE?

    a. must do so immediately
    b. 24 hours
    c. 3 days
    d. 10 days

21. Which of the following statements is true regarding real estate appraisers?

    a. Illinois requires all appraisers to be licensed or certified
    b. all licenses and certifications expire on September 30 of odd-numbered years
    c. a certified general appraiser can appraise only commercial properties
    d. licensed appraisers must have two years experience

22. All of the following licensees are exempt from meeting the continuing education requirement for renewal EXCEPT those who:
    a. applied for a license before January 1, 1977, and received a license before April 1, 1977
    b. are renewing a license for the first time
    c. hold a broker's license
    d. are also admitted to practice law before the Illinois Supreme Court

23. All of the following are mandatory continuing education courses EXCEPT:
    a. financing
    b. agency
    c. fair housing
    d. license law and escrow

24. The Real Estate Recovery Fund will pay a maximum of:
    a. $10,000 per aggrieved individual
    b. $10,000 per broker
    c. $50,000 per aggrieved individual
    d. $100,000 per broker

25. A licensee must provide information or documents requested by the OBRE within:
    a. 24 hours
    b. 10 days
    c. 30 days
    d. 60 days

CHAPTER 17

Real Estate Math

IN THIS CHAPTER Mathematics plays an important part in every real estate transaction. The mathematics normally involved in real estate transactions consists of nothing more than simple arithmetic applied to mathematical formulas. All that is required is the ability to determine what mathematical formula is involved, and then add, subtract, multiply, or divide. These calculations are made with whole numbers, fractions, and decimal numbers.

A difficulty some people have in solving real estate mathematics problems is converting word problems into mathematical symbols illustrating the calculations to be performed. For example, the word "of" is translated into a multiplication sign meaning "to multiply." If something is one-half of something else, this means that the solution requires multiplying the fraction ½ times the other unit. "Is" or "represents" always translates into an equal sign. Saying, "Two thousand dollars represents a 10% profit" means $2,000 = a 10% profit.

This chapter sets out the different real estate formulas for finance, appraisal, closing, commissions, profit, loss, square feet, acreage, prorations, and income tax. It also provides practice problems and examples in each area.

APPLICATIONS OF REAL ESTATE MATH

Finance

Typical arithmetic calculations pertaining to real estate finance include annual interest, debt service on a loan, loan-to-value ratios in qualifying for a loan, and amortization of a loan.

Annual interest on a loan is calculated by multiplying the rate of interest as a percentage times the loan balance (also known as the principal balance). The number resulting from the multiplication is the annual interest.

The annual interest calculation also may be used in amortizing a loan on a monthly basis. The annual interest is divided by 12 (number of months in a year) to determine the monthly interest. The monthly interest then is subtracted from the monthly loan payment to determine what amount of the monthly payment paid applies to reduce the loan principal.

Debt service is the annual amount to be paid to retire or regularly reduce a loan or mortgage balance. The annual debt service on a mortgage is the monthly mortgage payment times 12 (number of months in a year).

Lending institutions use loan-to-value ratios to determine the maximum loan to be issued on a given parcel of real estate. The loan-to-value ratio also can be stated as a percentage of the value of the real estate; in fact, the ratio is much more commonly expressed as a percentage. Some lending institutions lend only up to 90% of the appraised value of the property (a 9:10 ratio). If a lending institution approved a loan of 100% of the value, the loan-to-value ratio would be 1:1. If a lending institution approved a loan that was only 70% of the value, the loan-to-value ratio would be 7:10.

Appraisal

Typical arithmetic calculations involved in real estate appraisal include depreciation on improvements, comparison of properties based upon gross income, and the capitalization rate (rate of return an investor can achieve on a property based upon the present annual net income).

Depreciation on improvements is a reduction in value based upon age. The percentage of value lost each year is determined by dividing the number 1 by the number of years the improvements will last. For example, if a fence will last 15 years, the percentage lost each year is 1 divided by 15, or 6.7%. The percentage lost from passage of time multiplied by the original value shows the amount in dollars lost each year to depreciation. This is called straight-line depreciation.

Gross income on a property is the total income. Net income is the income remaining after subtracting the operating expenses of an investment from the gross income. Operating expenses are the normal day-to-day costs of the property, such as insurance, taxes, and management, but not the debt service or tax depreciation.

Capitalization rate is the percentage of the investment the owner will receive back each year from the net income from the property. This rate is based upon the dollars invested and the annual net income from the property. The capitalization formula is by far the most utilized formula for investment real estate. Investors project the rate of return of money invested based upon present value and present annual net income. Investors also can use the capitalization calculation to project the purchase price of property based upon the present annual net income and a stated desired rate of return. The capitalization formula is:

investment (value) $\times$ rate of return = annual net income.

Closing

In closing a real estate transaction, the closing agent may be involved in proration of rents, interest, insurance premiums, and other shared expenses. Also at the closing, preparation of the closing statement requires an understanding of bookkeeping entries and balancing of debits and credits.

Miscellaneous Calculations

In addition to a basic understanding of finance, appraisal, and closing arithmetic principles, real estate licensees need a general understanding of commission calculations, square and cubic footage calculations, acreage calculations, profit and loss on sale of real estate, estimating net to the seller after payment of expenses of sale, basic income taxation, and ad valorem taxes.

GENERAL PRACTICE IN REAL ESTATE MATHEMATICS

Percentages

In the real estate brokerage business, many arithmetic calculations involve percentages. For example, a real estate broker commission is a percentage of the sales price. A percentage is simply a number that has been divided by 100. To use a percentage in an arithmetic calculation, change the percentage to its decimal equivalent. The rule for changing a percentage to a decimal is to remove the percent sign and move the decimal point two places to the left (or divide the percentage by 100). Examples of converting a percentage to a decimal are:

$$98\% = 0.98 \qquad 1\tfrac{1}{2}\% = 1.5\% = 0.015$$
$$1.42\% = 0.0142 \qquad 1\tfrac{1}{4}\% = 1.25\% = 0.0125$$
$$0.092\% = 0.00092 \qquad \tfrac{3}{4}\% = 0.75\% = 0.0075$$

To change a decimal or a fraction to a percentage, simply reverse the procedure. Move the decimal point two places to the right and add the percent sign (or multiply by 100). Some examples of this operation are:

$$1.00 = 100\% \qquad \tfrac{1}{2} = 1 \div 2 = 0.5 = 50\%$$
$$0.90 = 90\% \qquad \tfrac{3}{8} = 3 \div 8 = 0.375 = 37.5\%$$
$$0.0075 = 0.75\% \qquad \tfrac{2}{3} = 2 \div 3 = 0.667 = 66.7\%$$

Formulas

Almost every arithmetic problem in a real estate transaction uses the format of something × something = something else. In mathematics language, factor × factor = product. Calculating a real estate commission is a classic example:

sales price paid × percentage of commission = commission
$80,000 × 7% = $5,600

In most real estate arithmetic problems, two of the three numbers are provided. Calculations to find the third number are required. If the number missing is the product, the calculation or function is to multiply the two factors. If the number missing is one of the factors, the calculation or function is to divide the product by the given factor.

Solving for product: **Answers:**

43,500 × 10.5% = _____   (43,500 × 0.105 = 4,567.50)
100,000 × 4% = _____   (100,000 × 0.04 = 4,000)
51.5 × 125 = _____   (6,437.50)

Solving for factor: **Answers:**

43,500 × _____ = 4,567.50   (4,567.50 ÷ 43,500 = 0.105 = 10.5%)
_____ × 4% = 4,000.00   (4,000.00 ÷ 0.04 = 100,000)
51.5 × _____ = 6,437.50   (6,437.50 ÷ 51.5 = 125)

Commission Problems

Problems involving commissions are readily solved by the formula:

sales price × rate of commission = total commission

Sales

1. A real estate broker sells a property for $90,000. Her rate of commission is 7%. What is the amount of commission in dollars?

   Solution: sales price × rate = commission
   $90,000 × 0.07 = _____
   product missing: multiply

   Answer: $6,300 commission

2. A real estate broker earns a commission of $6,000 in the sale of a residential property. His rate of commission is 6%. What is the selling price?

   Solution: sales price × rate = commission
   _____ × 0.06 = $6,000
   factor missing: divide
   $6,000 ÷ 0.06 = _____

   Answer: $100,000 sales price

3. A real estate broker earns a commission of $3,000 in the sale of property for $50,000. What is her rate of commission?

   Solution: sales price × rate = commission
   $50,000 × _____ = $3,000
   factor missing: divide
   $3,000 ÷ $50,000 = _____

   Answer: 6% rate

Rentals

4. A real estate salesperson is the property manager for the owner of a local shopping center. The center has five units, each renting for $24,000 per year. The center has an annual vacancy factor of 4.5%. The commission for rental of the units is 9% of the gross rental income. What is the commission for the year?

   Solution: gross rental × rate = commission
   gross rental = $24,000 × 5 minus the vacancy factor
   vacancy factor = $120,000 × 0.045 = $5,400
   $120,000 − $5,400 = $114,600
   $114,600 × 0.09 _____ = _____
   product missing: multiply

   Answer: $10,314 commission

Splits

5. A real estate salesperson sells a property for $65,000. The commission on this sale to the real estate firm with whom the salesperson is associated is 7%. The salesperson receives 60% of the total commission paid to the real estate firm. What is the firm's share of the commission in dollars?

Solution: sales price × rate = commission
$65,000 × 0.07 = _____
product missing: multiply
$65,000 × 0.07 = $4,550
100% − 60% = 40% is the firm's share
$4,550 × 0.40 = $1,820

Answer: $1,820 firm's share of commission

6. A broker's commission is 10% of the first $50,000 of sales price of a property and 8% of the amount of sales price over $50,000. The broker receives a total commission of $7,000. What is the total selling price of the property?

Solution:
Step 1: sales price × rate = commission
$50,000 × 0.10 = _____
product missing: multiply
$50,000 × 0.10 = $5,000 commission on first $50,000 of sales price

Step 2: total commission − commission on first $50,000 = commission on amount over $50,000
$7,000 − $5,000 = $2,000 commission on selling price over $50,000

Step 3: sales price × rate = commission
_____ × 0.08 = 2,000
factor missing: divide
$2,000 ÷ 0.08 = $25,000

Step 4: $50,000 + $25,000 = $75,000

Answer: $75,000 total selling price

Estimating Net to Seller

The formula used to estimate the net dollars to the seller is:

sales price × percent to seller = net dollars to seller

The percent to the seller is 100% minus the rate of commission paid to the real estate agent.

7. A seller advises a broker that she expects to net $80,000 from the sale of her property after the broker commission of 7% is deducted from proceeds of the sale. For what price must the property be sold?

Solution: 100% = gross sales price
100% − 7% = 93%
93% = net to owner
$80,000 = 0.93 × sales price
factor missing: divide
$80,000 ÷ 0.93 = _____

Answer: $86,022 sales price (rounded)

Estimating Partial Sales of Land

8. A subdivision contains 400 lots. If a broker has sold 25% of the lots and his sales staff has sold 50% of the remaining lots, how many lots are still unsold?

Solution: 0.25 × 400 = 100 sold by broker
400 − 100 = 300
300 × 0.50 = 150 sold by sales force
400 − 250 sold = 150 unsold

Answer: 150 lots still unsold

Profit/Loss on Sale of Real Estate

Profit or loss is always based upon the amount of money invested in the property. The formula for profit is:

investment × percent of profit = dollars in profit

The formula for loss is:

investment × percent of loss = dollars lost

9. Mr. Wong buys a house for investment purposes for $48,000. He sells it six months later for $54,000 with no expenditures for fix-up or repair. What is Mr. Wong's percentage of profit?

   Solution: Investment × percentage of profit = dollars in profit
   $48,000 × _____ = $6,000
   Factor missing: divide and convert decimal to percentage
   $6,000 ÷ $48,000 =

   Answer: 12.5%

10. Ms. Clary purchases some property in 1987 for $35,000. She makes improvements in 1988 costing her $15,500. In 1990 she sells the property for $46,000. What is her percentage of loss?

    Solution: Investment × percentage lost = dollars in loss
    $50,500 × _____ = $4,500
    Factor missing: divide and convert decimal to percentage
    $4,500 ÷ $50,500 = _____

    Answer: 8.91%, rounded to 9%

AREA CALCULATIONS

Determine the size of an area in square feet, cubic feet, number of acres, and so forth. In taking a listing, the broker should determine the number of square feet of heated area in the house. To establish the lot size, the number of square feet should be determined so it may be translated into acreage, if desired. Table 17.1 provides a list of measures and formulas.

The area of a rectangle or square is determined by simply multiplying the length times the width. In a square, the length and width are the same. The area of a triangle is calculated by multiplying one-half times the base of the triangle times the height of the triangle.

Formula for rectangle: area = length × width or A = L × W
Formula for square: area = side × side or A = S × S
Formula for triangle: area = 0.5 × base × height

> **FIGURE 17.1**
> Measures and formulas.

Linear Measure
12 inches = 1 ft
3 ft = 1 yd
16½ ft = 1 rod, 1 perch, or 1 pole
66 ft = 1 chain
5,280 ft = 1 mile

Square Measure
144 sq inches = 1 sq ft
9 sq ft = 1 sq yd
30¼ sq yd = 1 sq rod
160 sq rods = 1 acre
43,560 sq ft = 1 acre
640 acres = 1 sq mile
1 sq mile = 1 section
36 sections = 1 township

Formulas
1 side × 1 side = area of a square
width × depth = area of a rectangle
1/2 base × height = area of a triangle
1/2 height × (base$_1$ + base$_2$) = area of a trapezoid
1/2 × sum of the bases = distance between the other two sides at the mid-point of the height of a trapezoid
length × width × depth = volume (cubic measure) of a cube or a rectangular solid

Cubic Measure
1,728 cubic inches = 1 cubic foot
27 cubic feet = 1 cubic yard
144 cubic inches = 1 board foot
   (12" × 12" × 1")

Circular Measure
360 degrees = circle
60 minutes = 1 degree
60 seconds = 1 minute

Tax Valuation
Per $100 of Assessed Value: Divide the AV by 100, then multiply by tax rate.

$$\frac{\text{assessed value}}{100} \times \text{tax rate}$$

Per Mill: Divide the AV by 1000, then multiply by tax rate.

$$\frac{\text{assessed value}}{1000} \times \text{tax rate}$$

Acreage

1. An acre of land has a width of 330 feet. If this acre of land is rectangular in shape, what is its length? (Each acre contains 43,560 square feet.)

    Solution: A   =   L   × W
    43,560 = _____ × 330
    factor missing: divide
    43,560 ÷ 330 = _____

    Answer: 132 foot long lot

2. If a parcel of land contains 32,670 square feet, what percent of an acre is it?

    Solution: 32,670 square feet is what % of an acre?
    32,670 = _____% × 43,560
    factor missing: divide and convert decimal to percent
    32,670 ÷ 43,560 = 0.75

    Answer: 75% of an acre

Square Footage

3. A rectangular lot measures 185 feet by 90 feet. How many square feet does this lot contain?

    Solution: A   = L × W
    _____ = 185 × 90

    Answer: 16,650 sq ft

358   Chapter 17

4. A room measures 15 feet by 21 feet. We want to install wall-to-wall carpeting and need to calculate the exact amount of carpeting required.

   Solution: Carpeting is sold by the square yard, so we need to convert square feet to square yards. The number of square feet per square yard is 3 x 3 = 9 square feet per square yard. Therefore, to convert size in square feet to size in square yards, we need to divide by 9.

   Area × 15 × 21 = 315 sq ft

   sq yd = 315 ÷ 9 = _____

   Answer: 35 sq yd of carpeting

5. A new driveway will be installed, 115 feet by 20 feet. The paving cost is $0.65 per square foot. What will be the minimum cost to pave the new driveway?

   Solution:

   Step 1:   A = L × W
              A = 115 × 20
              A = 2,300 sq ft

   Step 2:   cost = 2,300 × $0.65

   Answer: $1,495

6. A house measures 28 feet wide by 52 feet long and sells for $64,000. What is the price per square foot?

   Solution:

   Step 1:   calculate the area
              A = 28 × 52 = 1,456 sq ft

   Step 2:   divide the sales price by the area
              $64,000 ÷ 1,456 = _____

   Answer: $43.96 per sq ft

Cost/Size

7. A triangular lot measures 200 feet along the street and 500 feet in depth on the side perpendicular to the front lot line. If the lot sells for 10 cents per square foot, what is the selling price?

   Solution: .5   × base × height   = area
                    area   × $.10   = selling price
                    .5   × 200   × 500   = 50,000 sq ft
                    50,000   × $.10   = _____

   Answer: $5,000 selling price

8. A property owner's lot is 80 feet wide and 120 feet long. The lot is rectangular. The property owner plans to have a fence constructed along both sides and across the rear boundary of his lot. The fence is to be 5 feet high. The property owner has determined that the labor cost to construct a fence will be $2.25 per linear foot. The material cost will be $6.00 per square yard. What is the total cost of constructing the fence?

   Solution:

   Step 1:   determine the linear footage to establish the labor cost
              (2 × 120 ft) + 80 ft   = 320 linear ft
              320 ft × $2.25 per linear ft = $720 labor cost

Step 2: establish the number of square yards to determine material cost
5 ft × 320 ft = 1,600 sq ft
1,600 sq ft ÷ 9 (9 sq ft in 1 sq yd) = 177.78 sq yds (rounded)
177.78 × $6.00 per sq yd = $1,066.68 material cost

Step 3: total cost
$1,066.68 + $720 = $1,786.68

Answer: $1,786.68 total cost

9. A new driveway will be installed, 120 feet by 18 feet. The paving cost is $.75 per square foot. What will be the minimum cost to pave the new driveway?

Solution:

Step 1: Area = length × width
A = 120 × 18
A = 2,160 square feet

Step 2: Cost = 2,160 × $.75

Answer: $1,620.00

10. A house measures 28 feet wide by 52 feet long and sells for $64,000. What is the price per square foot?

Solution:

Step 1: Calculate the area
A = 28 × 52 = 1,456 square feet

Step 2: Divide the sales price by the area
$64,000 ÷ 1,456 =

Answer: $43.96 per square foot

AD VALOREM PROPERTY TAXES

Certain terms must be understood to solve problems involving real property taxes. Assessed value is the value established by a tax assessor. The tax value or assessed value usually is a percentage of the estimated market value of the property and may be up to 100 percent of market value. The assessed value is multiplied by the equalization factor to arrive at the equalized assessed value. The amount of tax is calculated by multiplying the equalized assessed value by the tax rate, which is expressed either in dollars per $100 of assessed value or in mills (one mill is one-tenth of a cent) per $1,000 of assessed value. The formula for calculating property tax is:

Assessed value × tax rate × equalization factor = annual taxes

1. If the assessed value of the property is $80,000 and the tax value is 100% of the assessed value, what is the annual tax if the tax rate is $1.50 per $100 and the equalization factor is 1.5?

Solution: assessed value × tax rate × equalization factor = annual taxes
$80,000 × $\frac{1.50}{100}$ × 1.5 = _____

product missing: multiply
$80,000 × .0150 = $1,200 × 1.5 = $1,800

Answer: $1,800 annual taxes

2. A property sells at the assessed value. The annual real property tax is $705.56 at

a tax rate of $1.15 per $100 of tax value, with an equalization factor of 1.2. The property is taxed at 80% of assessed value. What is the selling price?

Solution: assessed value × tax rate × equalization factor = annual taxes
　　　　　　　　　　　　× $\frac{1.15}{100}$ × 1.2 = annual taxes

factor missing: divide
　$706.56　÷　.0115　=　$61,440 ÷ 1.2　=　$51,200
　$51,200　=　.80　×　_____

factor missing: divide
　$51,200　÷　.80　=　selling price

Answer: $64,000 is selling price

3. If the assessed value of property is $68,000 and the annual tax paid is $1,105 and the equalization factor is 1.3, what is the tax rate?

Solution: assessed value × tax rate × equalization factor = annual taxes
　$68,000　×　_____　×　1.3　=　$1,105

factor missing: divide
　$1,105　÷　1.3　=　$850 ÷ $68,000　=　$1.25

Answer: tax rate $1.25 per $100 of tax value

4. If the market value is $70,000, the tax rate is 120 mills, and the equalization factor is 1.5, and the assessment is 80%, what is the semiannual tax bill? (To get mills, divide by 1000).

Solution:
　assessed value　=　.80　×　$70,000
　assessed value　=　$56,000
　assessed value　× tax rate × equalization factor = annual taxes
　$56,000　× 120 mills =　$6,720 × 1.5　=　$10,080
　annual tax bill　=　$10,080
　semiannual tax bill　=　$10,080 ÷ 2

Answer: $5,040 semiannual tax bill

5. The real property tax revenue required by a town is $197,120. The assessed valuation of the taxable property is $12,800,000. The tax value is 100% of the assessed value with an equalization factor of 1.4. What must the tax rate be per $100 of assessed valuation to generate the necessary revenue?

Solution: assessed value × tax rate × equalization factor = annual taxes
　$12,800,000　×　_____　×　1.4　=　$140,800

factor missing: divide and convert to per $100 of value
　$197,120　÷　1.4　=　$140,800 ÷ 12,800,000
　　=　.011 (rate per $1.00)
　$.011　×　100　=　$1.10 per $1000

Answer: tax rate $1.10 per $100 of assessed value

TRANSFER TAX CALCULATIONS

When title to real estate is conveyed in Illinois, a tax on the conveyance is imposed as a result of the Illinois Real Estate Transfer Tax Act. The amount subject to taxation is the sales price minus any personal property included in the sales price, and minus any assumed mortgage or mortgage taken "subject to." The amount remaining is subject to the tax which is figured at the rate of .50 per $500 or fraction thereof, as a state tax, and .25 per $500 or fraction thereof, as a county tax. If the total amount of consideration is less than $100 no tax is required.

1. A property sold for $125,000. The purchaser assumed a mortgage on the property in the amount of $37,450. What is the total amount of transfer tax?

   Solution:

   Step 1: determine the taxable amount
   sales price − assumed mortgage = taxable amount
   $125,000 − $37,450 = $87,550

   Step 2: determine the taxable units; $87,550 should be rounded to the nearest 500 so as to include the "fraction thereof."
   $87,550 rounded = $88,000
   88,000 ÷ 500 = 176 taxing units

   Step 3: determine the state tax
   tax units × state tax rate = amount of state tax
   176 × .50 = $88

   Step 4: determine the county tax
   tax units × county tax rate = amount of county tax
   176 × .25 = $44

   Step 5: determine the total amount of transfer tax
   state tax + county tax = total amount of transfer tax
   $88 + $44 = $132

   Answer: $132 total amount of transfer tax

PRORATIONS AT CLOSING

Prorations at closing involve the division between seller and buyer of annual real property taxes, rents, homeowner's association dues, and other items that may have been paid or must be paid. Proration is the process of dividing something into respective shares.

In prorating calculations, the best method is first to draw a time line with the beginning, ending, and date of proration, then decide which part of the time line you need to use. In calculating prorations for closing statements, the amount is figured to the day of closing. Every month is assumed to have 30 days. Therefore, in problems that require calculating a daily rate, the monthly rate is divided by 30, even though the month may be February.

An alternative approach to proration is to reduce all costs to a daily basis. Assuming 30 days in every month and 12 months per year, we can assume 360 days per year for our purposes (and most standard exams). One other rule to remember in prorating various costs for closing statements is that the day of closing is charged to the seller. In the "real world," be sure to check with an attorney about local customs regarding prorations.

1. In preparing a statement for a closing to be held August 14, a real estate broker determines that the annual real property taxes in the amount of $360 have not been paid. What will the broker put in the buyer's statement as her entry for real property taxes?

   Solution:
   $360 ÷ 12 = $30/mo
   $30/mo ÷ 30 days = $1/day
   7 mos × $30 = $210
   $210 + $14 = $224

Answer: $224 buyer credit (this is the seller's share of the real property taxes to cover the 7 months and 14 days of the tax year during which he owned the property).

2. A sale is closed on September 15. The buyer is assuming the seller's mortgage, which has an outstanding balance of $32,000 as of the date of closing. The annual interest rate is 8%, and the interest is paid in arrears. What is the interest proration on the closing statements the broker prepares?

Solution: $32,000 × 0.08 = $2,560 annual interest
$2,560 ÷ 12 = $213.33 interest for September (rounded)
½ × $213.33 = $106.67 interest of ½ mo
or
$2,560 ÷ 24 = $106.67 interest for ½ mo

Answer: $106.67 buyer credit
$106.67 seller debit

Because the interest is paid in arrears, the buyer is required to pay the interest for the full month of September when making the scheduled monthly payment on October 1. Therefore, the buyer is credited with the seller's share of a half-month's interest for September in the amount of $106.67. The entry in the seller's closing statement is a debit in this amount.

FINANCIAL CALCULATIONS

Typical arithmetic calculations pertaining to real estate finance include annual interest, debt service on a loan, loan-to-value ratios in qualifying for a loan, and amortization of a loan.

Annual interest on a loan is calculated by multiplying the rate of interest as a percentage times the loan balance (also known as the principal balance). The number resulting from the calculation is the annual interest. The annual interest calculation also may be used in amortizing a loan on a monthly basis. The annual interest is divided by 12 (number of months in a year) to determine the monthly interest. The monthly interest then is subtracted from the monthly loan payment to determine what amount of the monthly payment paid applies to reduce the loan principal.

Debt service is the annual amount to be paid to retire or regularly reduce a loan or mortgage balance. The annual debt service on a mortgage is the monthly mortgage payment times 12 (number of months in a year). Lending institutions use loan-to-value ratios to determine the maximum loan to be issued on a given parcel of real estate. The loan-to-value ratio also can be stated as a percentage of the value of the real estate; in fact, the ratio is much more commonly expressed as a percentage. Some lending institutions lend up to only 90% of the appraised value of the property (a 9:10 ratio). If a lending institution approved a loan of 100% of the value, the loan-to-value ratio would be 1:1. If a lending institution approved a loan that was only 70% of the value, the loan-to-value ratio would be 7:10.

Simple Interest

Interest calculations use the formula:

loan balance × rate of interest = annual interest

1. A loan of $15,000 is repaid in full, one year after the loan is made. If the interest rate on the loan is 12.5%, what amount of interest is owed?

Solution: loan   ×   rate   =   annual interest
                  $15,000 × 0.125 = _____
                  product missing: multiply

Answer: $1,875 interest

Principal and Interest

2. On October 1, a mortgagor makes a $300 payment on her mortgage, which is at the rate of 10%. Of the $300 total payment for principal and interest, the mortgagee allocates $200 to the payment of interest. What is the principal balance due on the mortgage on the date of the payment?

   Solution: $200   × 12 mo = $2,400 annual interest income
                     principal × rate = annual interest
                     _____ × 10% = $2,400
                     factor missing: divide
                     $2,400 ÷ 0.10 = _____

   Answer: $24,000 mortgage balance on date of payment

3. If an outstanding mortgage balance is $16,363.64 on the payment date and the amount of the payment applied to interest is $150, what is the rate of interest charged on the loan?

   Solution: $150   ×   12 mo   = $1,800 annual interest
                     principal ×   rate   = annual interest
                     16,363.64 × _____ = $1,800
                     factor missing: divide and convert to percentage
                     $1,800 ÷ $16,363.64 = _____

   Answer: 11% interest rate (rounded)

Debt Service

4. The monthly amortized car payment Mr. Goldberg owes is $275. What is his annual debt service on this loan?

   Solution: debt service is monthly payment × 12
                     $275 × 12 = _____

   Answer: $3,300 annual debt service

5. A mortgage loan of $50,000 at 11% interest requires monthly payments of principal and interest of $516.10 to fully amortize the loan for a term of 20 years. If the loan is paid over the 20-year term, how much interest does the borrower pay?

   Solution: 20 years × 12 mo payments = 240 payments
                     240   × $516.10   = $123,864 total amount paid
                     total amount paid − principal borrowed = interest
                     $123,864   − $50,000   = _____

   Answer: $73,864 interest paid

Fees and Points

The typical fees for real estate mortgages are loan origination fee, points, discount points, interest escrows, and tax escrows. The amount of the fees and escrows often depends upon the loan amount or assessed annual taxes. The formula for calculating the dollar amount owed in points on a loan is:

loan × number of points (percentage) = dollars in points

6. A house sells for $60,000. The buyer obtains an 80% loan. If the bank charges 3 points at closing, how much in points must the buyer pay?

   Solution: loan   × number of points (%) = dollars paid

   ($60,000 × 0.80) ×   0.03   = _____

   $48,000   ×   0.03   = _____

   product missing: multiply

   Answer: $1,440 points payment

7. Mr. and Mrs. Schmidt borrow $64,000. If they pay $4,480 for points at closing, how many points are charged?

   Solution: loan   × number of points (%) = dollars paid

   $64,000 ×   _____   = $4,480

   factor missing: divide

   Answer: 7 points

8. Mr. and Mrs. Ortega borrow $55,000 at 11% interest for 30 years. The bank requires 2 months' interest to be placed in escrow and a 1% loan origination fee to be paid at closing. What is the amount of interest to be escrowed? What is the amount charged for the loan origination fee?

   Step 1:   Interest escrow

   Solution: $55,000 × 0.11 = $6,050 annual interest

   $6,050 ÷ 12 = $504.17 monthly interest

   $504.17 × 2 = _____

   Answer: $1,008.34 interest escrow

   Step 2:   Loan origination fee

   Solution: $55,000 × 0.01 = _____

   Answer: $550 loan origination fee

Loan-to-Value Ratios

9. In problem 8 above, the appraised value of the home purchased is $68,750. What is the loan-to-value ratio?

   Solution: loan   ÷   value   =   ratio

   $55,000 ÷ $68,750 = 0.80

   0.80   =   80:100

   Answer: 80% loan-to-value ratio

10. The Blacks apply for a loan. The purchase price of the home is $80,000. The bank authorizes a loan-to-value ratio of 90%. What is the amount of loan authorized?

    Solution: $80,000 × 90% = loan

    Answer: $72,000 loan

Yields

Loans issued by banks are repaid with interest. The interest the borrower pays is the profit the bank makes. The percentage of profit, however, may be greater than the interest rate charged. The percentage of profit is called the *yield* of the loan. Yields on loans are increased by points paid at closing. The points paid at closing reduce the amount of money the bank actually must fund. The bank can use the money paid in points to help fund the loan. Each point charged has the effect of raising the interest rate ⅛ percent.

11. The First Bank lends $100,000 to the borrower and charges 3 points at closing. The interest rate on the loan is 12% for 25 years. What is the bank's effective yield on the loan?

    Solution: $\frac{\text{actual annual interest}}{\text{amount funded}}$ = yield

    actual annual interest = $100,000 × .12 = $12,000
    amount funded = $100,000 − $3,000 = $97,000
    $\frac{\$12,000}{\$97,000}$ = _____

    Answer: 12.37% effective yield

Qualifying for a Loan

Typically, for a borrower to qualify for a loan, the ratios of the borrower's housing and total debts to income must meet the lender's requirements. The typical housing debt-to-income ratio for conventional loans is 25–28%. The typical total debt-to-income ratio for conventional loans is 33–36%. The 25–28% means that for the borrower to qualify, PITI (principal, interest, taxes, insurance) must not be more than 25–28% of the borrower's monthly gross income. The 33–36% means that for the borrower to qualify, the total monthly expenses (including housing expense) must not be more than 33–36% of the borrower's monthly gross income.

12. Mr. and Mrs. Jones have a combined total monthly income of $2,500. If the lender requires a debt-to-income ratio of 25:33 for housing and total expenses, what is the maximum house payment the Joneses will qualify for? What is the maximum total monthly expenses besides PITI that will be allowed?

    Solution:

    Step 1:   housing: $2,500 × 0.25 = $625

    Step 2:   total expenses: $2,500 × 0.33 = $825
               $825 − $625 = _____

    Answer: $200 other than PITI

APPRAISAL CALCULATIONS

Typical appraisal calculations deal with depreciation of improvements on property being appraised or estimation of the value of a property based upon a desired capitalization rate and the present annual net income of the property. (See Chapter 10 for a complete discussion of appraisal.)

Capitalization

As illustrated in Chapter 10, under the income approach, the estimate of value is arrived at by capitalizing the annual net income. The solution to these problems is based on the following formula:

value × capitalization rate = annual net income

1. An apartment building produces a net income of $4,320 per annum. The investor paid $36,000 for the apartment building. What is the owner's rate of return (cap rate) on the investment?

    Solution: value   ×   rate   = annual net income
    $36,000 × _____ = $4,320
    factor missing: divide and convert to percentage

    Answer: 12% annual rate of return on investment

2. An investor is considering the purchase of an office building for $125,000. The investor insists upon a 14% return on investment. What must be the amount of the annual net income from this investment to return a profit to the owner at a rate of 14%?

    Solution: value × rate = annual net income
    $125,000 × .14 = _____
    product missing: multiply

    Answer: $17,500 annual net income needed

3. In appraising a shopping center, the appraiser establishes that the center produces an annual net income of $97,500. The appraiser determines the capitalization rate to be 13%. What should be the appraiser's estimate of market value for this shopping center?

    Solution: investment ×   rate   = annual net income or value
    _____ × 13% = 97,500
    factor missing: divide
    $97,500 ÷ .13 = _____

    Answer: $750,000 market value

Depreciation

Depreciation is a loss in value from any cause. The two examples of depreciation that follow represent the types of depreciation problems a real estate student or practitioner may encounter. In the first problem, the present value of a building is given and the requirement is to calculate the original value. The second problem provides the original value to be used in arriving at the present depreciated value. Depreciation problems use the formula:

original value × % of value NOT lost = present value

4. The value of a 6-year old building is estimated to be $45,900. What was the value when new if the building depreciated 2% per year?

    Solution: 6 yrs × 2% = 12% depreciation
    100% (new value) − 12% = 88% of value not lost
    original value × % not lost = present value
    _____ × 88% = 45,900
    factor missing: divide
    $45,900 ÷ .88 = _____

Answer: $52,159.09 value when new (rounded)

5. A 14-year-old building has a total economic life of 40 years. If the original value of the building was $75,000, what is the present depreciated value?

Solution:
```
100%              ÷   40 yrs       = yearly depreciation rate
1.00              ÷   40           = .025, or 2.5% year depreciation
14 yrs            ×   2.5%         = 35% depreciation to date
100%              −   35%          = 65% not lost
original cost     ×   % not lost   = remaining dollar value
$75,000           ×   .65          = _____
Product missing: multiply
$75,000           ×   .65          = _____
```

Answer: $48,750 present depreciated value

INCOME TAX CALCULATIONS

Chapter 15 is devoted to a complete discussion of real estate taxation.

Deductions

1. Mr. Romero has owned his home for 12 years. His annual real property taxes are $360, annual homeowner's insurance is $270, annual principal payment on his mortgage is $13,000, and annual interest payment on his mortgage is $15,500. What is the total deduction allowed against his income for income tax purposes?

    Solution: Only mortgage interest and property taxes are deductible when dealing with the principal residence. Total deductions are the sum of mortgage interest and taxes.

    Answer: $15,860 total deduction

2. Ms. Jones and Ms. Lin are partners in a business. Total yearly expenses for the business are:

taxes	$450
insurance	$567
utilities	$890
wages	$13,333
postage	$275
advertising	$875

    Total income from the business is $75,880. What amount of income from the business is reportable for tax purposes?

    Solution: In a business, all reasonable and necessary business expenses are deductible against income.

    Answer: $59,490 reportable

Basis

3. Mr. and Mrs. Swift purchased their home 15 years ago for $32,500. During their ownership, they made capital improvements totaling $19,400. They sold the home for $72,900. What amount of gain did they make on the sale?

Solution: purchase price + improvements = basis
$32,500 + $19,400 = $51,900 basis
sales price − basis = gain
$72,900 − $51,900 =

Answer: $21,000 gain

4. In problem 3, above, if the Swifts were over age 55 and had never used the one-time exemption, how much gain would be taxable?

   Solution: The one-time exemption for persons over age 55 allows the exemption of $125,000.

   Answer: all $21,000 of gain is exempt; thus, none is taxable

5. In problem 3, above, if the Swifts purchase another home costing $90,000 and choose to defer reporting the gain, what is the basis in the new home?

   Solution: purchase price − any deferred gain = basis
   $90,000 − 21,000 = _____

   Answer: $69,000 basis in new home

Miscellaneous Calculations

1. A subdivision contains 400 lots. If a broker has sold 25% of the lots and his sales staff has sold 50% of the remaining lots, how many lots are still unsold?

   Solution:
   .25 × 400 = 100 sold by broker
   400 − 100 = 300
   300 × ½ = 150 sold by sales force
   400 − 250 sold = 150 unsold

   Answer: 150 lots still unsold

2. An owner purchases his home at 8% below market value. He then sells the property for the full market value. What is the rate of profit?

   Solution:
   market value = 100%
   100% − 8% = 92% purchase price
   8% ÷ 92% = rate of profit
   .08 ÷ .92 = _____

   Answer: 8.7% profit

REVIEW PROBLEMS

1. A sale is closed on February 12. The buyer is assuming the seller's mortgage, which has an outstanding balance of $28,000 as of the closing date. The last mortgage payment was made February 1. The annual interest rate is 7¾%, and interest is paid in arrears. What interest proration appears in the buyer's closing statement?

   a. $72.36 credit
   b. $77.52 credit
   c. $180.83 debit
   d. $253.19 credit

2. A real estate broker earns a commission of $4,900 at a rate of 7%. What is the selling price of the property?

   a. $24,000
   b. $44,400
   c. $65,000
   d. $70,000

3. A property is sold at market value. If the assessed value is 100% of market value, the tax rate is $1.50, and the annual tax is $540, what is the selling price of the property?

   a. $24,000
   b. $27,700
   c. $36,000
   d. $81,000

4. What is the annual rent if a lease specifies the rent to be 2½% of gross sales per annum, with a minimum annual rent of $4,800, if the lessee's gross sales are $192,000?

   a. $4,800
   b. $7,680
   c. $12,000
   d. $16,000

5. A rectangular lot measures 40 yards deep and has a frontage of 80 feet. How many acres does the lot contain?

   a. .07
   b. .21
   c. .22
   d. .70

6. A real estate salesperson earns $24,000 per year. If she receives 60% of the 7% commissions paid to her firm on her sales, what is her monthly dollar volume of sales?

   a. $33,333.33
   b. $45,000.00
   c. $47,619.08
   d. $90,000.00

7. A parking lot containing 2 acres nets $12,000 per year. The owner wishes to retire and sell his parking lot for an amount that will net him $12,000 per year by investing the proceeds of the sale at 8½% per annum. What must the selling price be to accomplish the owner's objective?

   a. $96,000
   b. $102,000
   c. $120,000
   d. $141,176

8. A group of investors purchases two tracts of land. They pay $48,000 for the first tract. The first tract costs 80% of the cost of the second tract. What is the cost of the second tract?

   a. $9,600
   b. $28,800
   c. $60,000
   d. $125,000

9. An office building produces a gross income of $12,600 per year. The vacancy factor is 5%, and annual expenses are $3,600. What is the market value if the capitalization rate is 12%?

   a. $15,120
   b. $69,750
   c. $99,750
   d. $105,000

10. If the monthly interest payment due on a mortgage on December 1 is $570 and the annual interest rate is 9%, what is the outstanding mortgage balance?

    a. $61,560.00
    b. $63,333.33
    c. $76,000.00
    d. $131,158.00

11. A building has a total economic life of 50 years. The building is now 5 years old and has a depreciated value of $810,000. What was the value of the building when it was new?
    a. $891,000
    b. $900,000
    c. $972,000
    d. $1,234,568

12. If the assessed value is 100% of the market value and the market value is $63,250, what are the annual taxes if the rate is $2.10 per $100?
    a. $132.83
    b. $1,328.25
    c. $3,011.90
    d. $3,320.16

13. If Mr. Jackson buys three parcels of land for $4,000 each and sells them as four separate parcels for $4,500 each, what percent profit does he make?
    a. 33%
    b. 50%
    c. 60%
    d. 150%

14. The current value of a 12-year-old house is $56,000. If this house has an economic life of 40 years, what was its value when new?
    a. $79,550.00
    b. $80,000.00
    c. $80,500.00
    d. $82,436.86

15. The outside dimensions of a rectangular house are 35 feet by 26.5 feet. If the walls are all 9 inches thick, what is the square footage of the interior?
    a. 827.5 sq ft
    b. 837.5 sq ft
    c. 927.5 sq ft
    d. 947.7 sq ft

16. A buyer is to assume a seller's existing loan with an outstanding balance of $20,000 as of the date of closing. The interest rate is 9%, and payments are made in arrears. Closing is set for October 10. What will be the entry in the seller's closing statement?
    a. $50 credit
    b. $50 debit
    c. $150 credit
    d. $150 debit

17. A house is listed for $40,000. An offer is made and accepted for $38,500, if the seller agrees to pay 5½% discount points on a VA loan of $33,000. The broker's fee is at a rate of 6%. How much will the seller net from the sale?
    a. $34,375.00
    b. $35,875.00
    c. $36,382.50
    d. $38,500.00

18. A house and lot were assessed for 60% of market value and taxed at a rate of $3.75 per $100 of assessed value. Five years later the same tax rate and assessment rate still exist, but annual taxes have increased by $750. How much has the dollar value of the property increased?
    a. $8,752.75
    b. $20,000.00
    c. $33,333.33
    d. $38,385.82

19. What is the sales price of an apartment complex having an annual rental of $80,000 with expenses of $8,000 annually if the purchaser receives an 8% return?
    a. $66,240
    b. $800,000
    c. $864,000
    d. $900,000

20. A lease specifies a minimum monthly rental of $700 plus 3% of all business over $185,000. If the lessee does annual gross business of $220,000, how much rent is paid that year?
    a. $6,000
    b. $9,450
    c. $11,550
    d. $12,600

21. An apartment building contains 20 units. Each unit rents for $480 per month. The vacancy rate is 5%. Annual expenses are $13,500 for maintenance, $2,400 insurance, $2,500 taxes, $2,900 utilities, and 10% of the gross effective income for management fee. What is the investor's net rate of return for the first year if she paid $195,000 for the property?
    a. 7.61%
    b. 8.62%
    c. 22.05%
    d. 39.59%

22. A house has a market value of $35,000, and the lot has a market value of $7,000. The property is assessed at 80% of market value at a rate of $2.12 per $100. If the assessed valuation is to be increased by 18%, what is the amount of taxes to be paid on the property?
    a. $712.32
    b. $840.54
    c. $890.40
    d. $1,050.67

23. An owner lists a property for sale with a broker. At what price must the property be sold to net the owner $7,000 after paying a 7% commission and satisfying the existing $48,000 mortgage?
    a. $49,354
    b. $56,750
    c. $57,750
    d. $59,140

24. A tract of land is divided as follows: one-half of the total area for single-family dwellings, one-fourth of the area for shopping, and one-eighth of the area for streets and parking. The remaining seven acres are to be used for parks. What is the total acreage of the tract?
    a. 28 acres
    b. 49 acres
    c. 56 acres
    d. 70 acres

25. The value of a seven-year-old building is estimated to be $63,000. What was the value when new if the building depreciated 2½% per year?
    a. $67,725
    b. $74,025
    c. $76,363
    d. $114,975

26. An investor builds an office building at a cost of $320,000 on land costing $40,000. Other site improvements total $20,000. What must be the annual net income from the property to return a profit to the owner at an annual rate of 12%?
    a. $31,666
    b. $38,400
    c. $43,200
    d. $45,600

27. A real estate sale closes on February 20. The real property taxes have not been paid. Market value of the property is $67,500, and the assessed value is 80% of market value. Tax rate is $1.50 per $100 of assessed value. What is the proper entry on the seller's settlement statement regarding real property taxes?
    a. $112.50 credit
    b. $112.50 debit
    c. $697.50 credit
    d. $697.50 debit

28. A triangular lot measures 350 feet along the street and 425 feet deep on the side perpendicular to the street. If a broker sells the lot for $.75 (cents) per square foot and his commission rate is 9%, what is the amount of commission earned?
    a. $5,020.31
    b. $6,693.75
    c. $10,040.63
    d. $14,875.00

29. A property owner is having a concrete patio poured at the rear of the house. The patio is to be rectangular and will be 4 yards by 8 yards. The patio is to be 6 inches thick. The labor cost for the project is $3.50 per square yard, and the material cost is $1.50 per cubic foot. What will be the total cost of the patio?
    a. $112
    b. $198
    c. $328
    d. $552

30. A broker's commission is 8% of the first $75,000 of the sales price of a house and 6% of the amount over $75,000. What is the total selling price of the property if the broker receives a total commission of $9,000?
    a. $79,500
    b. $93,000
    c. $105,000
    d. $125,000

31. A buyer pays $45,000 for a home. Five years later she puts it on the market for 20% more than she originally paid. The house eventually sells for 10% less than the asking price. At what price is the house sold?
    a. $44,100
    b. $48,600
    c. $49,500
    d. $54,000

32. The owner of a rectangular unimproved parcel of land measuring 600 feet wide (front) by 145.2 feet long is offered $15 per front foot or $4,000 per acre. What is the amount of the higher offer?
    a. $2,187
    b. $7,680
    c. $8,000
    d. $9,000

33. A city with rent-control guidelines says a landlord may increase the rent on apartments by 2.25% of the cost of improvements made to the property. The landlord spends $1,200 per unit for improvements, then raises the rent from $380 to $415. By how much has the owner exceeded the guidelines?
    a. $8
    b. $15
    c. $26
    d. $35

34. $150 is 2½% of what amount?
    a. $375
    b. $600
    c. $1,666
    d. $6,000

35. After purchasing a home containing 2,300 square feet on a rectangular lot 150 feet by 210 feet, the owner adds a two-car garage with interior dimensions of 23 feet by 22 feet. The house is valued at $26 per square foot, the lot at 25 cents per square foot, and the garage at $12 per square foot. What is the percentage of increase in value of the property resulting from the addition of the garage?
    a. 8.23%
    b. 8.97%
    c. 10.15%
    d. 11.15%

36. A broker negotiates the sale of the northeast ¼ of the northeast ¼ of the northeast ¼; section 25, township 2 south; range 1 east, for $700 per acre. The listing agreement with the owner specifies a 12% commission. How much does the broker earn?
    a. $480
    b. $840
    c. $3,360
    d. $8,400

37. A tract of land containing 560 square rods is sold for 12 cents per square foot. What is the total selling price?
    a. $6,720
    b. $11,088
    c. $18,295
    d. $20,160

38. A property owner plans to fence his land, which is rectangular in shape and measures 300 feet by 150 feet. How many fence posts will be required if there is to be a post every 15 feet?
    a. 45
    b. 60
    c. 61
    d. 450

39. A triangular tract is 4,000 feet long and has 900 feet of highway frontage, which is perpendicular to the 4,000-foot boundary. How many square yards does the tract contain?
    a. 200,000
    b. 300,000
    c. 400,000
    d. 1,800,000

40. The owner of an apartment building earns a net income of $10,200 per year. The annual operating cost is $3,400. The owner is realizing a net return of 14% on investment. What price was paid for the building?
    a. $48,572
    b. $72,857
    c. $97,143
    d. $142,800

41. A percentage lease stipulates a minimum rent of $1,200 per month and 3% of the lessee's annual gross sales over $260,000. The total rent paid by the end of the year is $16,600. What is the lessee's gross business income for the year?
    a. $73,333.33
    b. $260,000.00
    c. $333,333.33
    d. $553,333.33

42. A building now 14 years old has a total economic life of 40 years. If the replacement cost of the building is $150,000, what is the present depreciated value?
    a. $52,500
    b. $60,000
    c. $97,500
    d. $202,500

43. On February 1 a mortgagor makes a $638 payment on her mortgage, at the rate of 10%. The mortgagee allocates $500 to payment of interest. What is the principal balance due on the mortgage on February 1?
   a. $38,400
   b. $60,000
   c. $79,750
   d. $95,700

44. Plans for a house under construction include a rectangular basement 30 feet wide and 90 feet long that is to be excavated to a uniform depth of 14 feet. A subcontractor receives 50 cents per cubic yard for the excavating work. How much does the subcontractor receive?
   a. $315
   b. $700
   c. $1,050
   d. $1,400

45. A house valued at $60,000 is insured for 85% of value. The annual premium is 60 cents per $100 of the face amount of the policy. The homeowner pays a three-year premium on February 28. On April 30 of the following year, she closes the sale of the home. The buyer is having this policy endorsed to him. What will be the buyer's cost?
   a. $306
   b. $357
   c. $510
   d. $561

46. The scale of a map is 1 inch equals 2½ miles. What distance is represented by 4½ inches on the map?
   a. 7 miles
   b. 11¼ miles
   c. 18 miles
   d. 180 miles

47. In planning the development of a tract of land, the developer allocates one-half of the total area to single-family dwellings, one-third to multi-family dwellings, and 20 acres for roads and recreation areas. What is the total number of acres in the tract?
   a. 36.67
   b. 56.67
   c. 120
   d. 320

48. A developer pays $900 per acre for a 125-acre tract. His costs for grading, paving, and surveying total $1,300,000. He constructs 200 houses at an average cost of $115,000 each. What is the average sales price per house if the developer realizes a net return of 14% on his total investment?
   a. $64,267.00
   b. $121,906.25
   c. $139,151.25
   d. $154,062.52

49. A lender allows a loan-to-value ratio of 85% on a home loan for a buyer. If the purchase price is $96,000 and the appraisal is $97,500, what is the buyer's required down payment?
   a. $14,400
   b. $15,000
   c. $81,600
   d. $82,875

50. A builder has 26 acres of land with 1,320 feet of depth off the road. What is the value if the local prices are $1,500 per front foot?
   a. $1,132,560
   b. $1,181,818
   c. $1,287,000
   d. $1,980,000

SOLUTIONS TO REVIEW PROBLEMS

The letter of the correct answer choice appears next to the question number.

1. $28,000 × .0775 = $2,170/yr
   $2,170 ÷ 12 mos = $180.83/mo
   $180.83 ÷ 30 days = $6.03/day
   $6.03 × 12 days = $72.36 used portion
   As payments are made in arrears, this amount is a credit to buyer and a debit to seller

2. Sales price × rate = total commission
   _____ × 7% = 4,900
   Factor missing: divide
   $4,900 ÷ .07 = $70,000

3. Assessed value × tax rate = annual tax
   _____ × 1.50/100 = $540
   Factor missing: divide
   540 ÷ .0150 = $36,000

4. Rent is 2½% of gross sales
   2½% × gross sales = Rent
   .025 × $192,000 = _____
   Product missing: multiply
   .025 × $192,000 = $4,800

5. 40 yds × 3 ft/yd = 120 ft
   120 ft × 80 ft = 9600 sq ft
   9600 sq ft ÷ 43,560 sq ft = .22 acres

6. 24,000 is 60% of total commission
   60% × total commission = 24,000
   Factor missing: divide
   24,000 ÷ .60 = $40,000
   Sales price × rate of comm. = total comm.
   _____ × 7% = $40,000
   Factor missing: divide
   40,000 ÷ .07 = 571,429 per year in sales
   Divide by 12 to get monthly volume of sales
   $571,429 ÷ 12 = $47,619.08

7. Investment × rate of return = annual net income
   _____ × 8½% = 12,000
   Factor missing: divide
   $12,000 ÷ .085 = $141,176 (rounded)

8. 80% of second tract = first tract
   .8 × ? (2nd tract) = $48,000
   2nd tract = $48,000 ÷ .8
   2nd tract = $60,000

9. Market value (investment) × cap rate = annual net income
   12,600 − vacancy factor − expenses = Annual net income
   Vacancy factor = 12,600 × .05 = $630
   $12,600 − $630 − $3,600 = $8,370 annual net income
   _____ × 12% = 8,370
   Factor missing: divide
   $8,370 ÷ .12 = $69,750

10. Loan balance × rate of interest = annual interest
    _____ × 9% = (570 × 12)
    Factor missing: divide
    6,840 ÷ .09 = $76,000

11. Original value × % not lost = present value
    1 ÷ 50 = 2% lost each year
    _____ × (100% − 10%) = 810,000
    _____ × 90% = 810,000
    Factor missing: divide
    810,000 ÷ .90 = $900,000

12. Assessed value × tax rate = annual taxes
    63,250 × .0210 = _____
    Product missing: multiply
    Annual taxes $1,328.25

13. 4,000 × 3 = 12,000 invested
    4,500 × 4 = 18,000 sales price
    18,000 − 12,000 = 6,000 profit
    Investment × % of profit = dollars in profit
    12,000 × _____ = $6,000
    Factor missing: divide; convert to percentage
    6,000 ÷ 12,000 = 50%

14. 40 years − 12 = 28 remaining
    28 ÷ 40 = .70 = 70% not lost
    Original value × % not lost = present value
    _____ × 70% = 56,000
    Factor missing: divide
    $56,000 ÷ .70 = $80,000

15. 9 inches thick on each of two ends = 1.5 ft
    35 ft − 1.5 ft = 33.5 ft
    26.5 ft − 1.5 ft = 25 ft
    33.5 ft × 25 ft = 837.5 sq ft

16. Loan balance × rate of interest = annual interest
    $20,000 × .09 = _____
    Product missing: multiply
    Annual interest = $1,800
    1,800 ÷ 12 months = 150 per month
    150 ÷ 30 = $5 per day
    10 × 5 = $50 debit to seller

17. Expenses of sale and closing are points and commission.
    Points:
    Loan × number of points as percentage = dollars in points
    $33,000 × .055 = _____
    Product missing: multiply
    Dollars in points are $1,815
    Commission:
    Sales price × rate of commission = total commission
    38,500 × .06 = _____
    Product missing: multiply
    Total commission = $2,310
    2,310 + 1,815 = total expenses
    $38,500 − 4,125 = $34,375 net to seller

18. $750 incr. ÷ $3.75 = 200 ($100 units)
    200 ($100 units) × $100/unit = $20,000 tax value
    $20,000 ÷ .60 = $33,333.33

19. Investment of value × rate of return = annual net income
    _____ × 8% = 72,000
    Factor missing: divide
    $72,000 ÷ .08 = $900,000

20. $700/mo × 12 mo = $8,400/year base rent
    $220,000 − $185,000 = $35,000 (earnings over $185,000)
    $35,000 × .03 = $1,050
    $8,400 + $1,050 = $9,450

21. 20 units × $480/mo × 12 mos = $115,200 gross rent
    $115,200 − $5,760 (vacancy @ 5%) = $109,440 gross effective income
    $109,440 − 32,244 (expenses) = $77,196 net income
    Value × rate of return = annual net income
    195,000 × _____ = $77,196
    Factor missing: divide and convert to percentage
    $77,196 ÷ $195,000 = 39.59% (rounded)

22. 35,000 + 7,000 = 42,000 total assessed value
    42,000 × 1.18 = 49,560 increased valuation
    49,560 × .80 = 39,648 new tax basis
    Assessed value × tax rate = annual taxes
    39,648 × 2.12/100 = _____
    Product missing: multiply
    $39,648 × .0212 = $840.54 (rounded)

23. $7,000 + $48,000 = $55,000
    100% − 7% commission = 93%
    $55,000 divided by .93 = $59,140 (rounded)

24. ½ + ¼ + ⅛ = unknown area
    ⁴⁄₈ + ²⁄₈ + ⅛ = ⅞
    ⁸⁄₈ − ⅞ = ⅛ remaining
    Area = 7 acres = ⅛
    ⅛ of total = 7 acres
    Total = 7 acres × ⁸⁄₁ = 56 acres

25. 7 yrs × 2.5 = 17.5% depreciation to date
    100% − 17.5% = 82.5% remaining value
    Original value × % not lost = present value
    _____ × 82.5% = 63,000
    Factor missing: divide
    $63,000 ÷ .825 = $76,363 (rounded)

26. Investment × rate = annual net income
    380,000 × .12 = _____
    Product missing: multiply
    $380,000 × .12 = $45,600

27. Seller owes for 30 + 20 days = 50 days
    67,500 × .80 = 54,000 tax value
    Tax value × rate = annual taxes
    54,000 × .0150 = $810
    810 ÷ 12 = 67.50/month
    67.50 ÷ 30 = 2.25/day
    2.25 × 50 = $112.50 debit to seller

28. Area of a triangle = ½ × base × height
    ½ × 350 ft × 425 ft = 74,375 sq ft
    74,375 sq ft × .75/sq ft = $55,781.25 sales price
    $55,781.25 × .09 = $5,020.31

29. 4 yds × 8 yds = 32 sq yds
    32 sq yds × $3.50/sq yd = $112 labor costs
    ½ ft × 12 ft × 24 ft = 144 cubic feet
    144 cu ft × $1.50 = $216 material costs
    $112 + $216 = $328

30. $75,000 × .08 = $6,000 commission on first $75,000
    $9,000 − $6,000 = $3,000 commission on price over $75,000
    sales price × rate = commission
    _____ × 6% = 3,000
    Factor missing: divide
    $3,000 ÷ .06 = $50,000 sales over $75,000
    $75,000 + $50,000 = $125,000

31. $45,000 × 1.20 (120%) = $54,000 asking price
    $54,000 × .90 = $48,600 sold price

32. 600 ft × 145.2 ft = 87,120 sq ft
    87,120 sq ft ÷ 43,560 sq ft/acre = 2 acres
    2 acres × $4,000 = $8,000 acreage basis
    $15 × 600 ft = $9,000 front-foot basis

33. 1,200 × .0225 = $27 maximum allowable increase
    $415 − $380 = $35 increase
    $35 − $27 = $8

34. 2½% × _____ = 150
    Factor missing: divide
    $150 ÷ .025 = $6,000

35. 2,300 sq ft × $26 = $59,800 house value
    150 ft × 210 ft = 31,500 sq ft lot area
    31,500 sq ft × $.25 = $7,875 lot value
    $59,800 + $7,875 = $67,675 value of house and lot
    23 ft × 22 ft = 506 sq ft interior of garage
    506 sq ft × $12 = $6,072 garage value
    Value increase ÷ original value = percentage of increase
    $6,072 ÷ $67,675 = .0897, or 8.97%

36. ¼ × ¼ × ¼ × 640 acres = total acres sold
    .25 × .25 × .25 × 640 = 10 acres sold
    10 acres × 700 = $7,000 sales price
    Sales price × rate = commission
    7000 × .12 = _____
    Product missing: multiply
    $7000 × .12 = $840

37. 160 square rods = 1 acre (43,560 sq ft)
    560 sq rods ÷ 160 sq rods/acre = 3.5
    3.5 acres × 43,560 sq ft/acre = 152,460 sq ft
    152,460 sq ft × $.12 = $18,295

38. (2 × 300 ft) + (2 × 150 ft) = 900 feet
    900 ft ÷ 15 ft/post = 60 posts

39. ½ × base × height = area of a right triangle
    ½ × 900 ft × 4000 ft = 1,800,000 sq ft
    1,800,000 sq ft ÷ 9 sq ft/sq yd = 200,000 sq yd

40. Investment × rate = annual net income
    _____ × 14% = 10,200
    Factor missing: divide
    $10,200 ÷ .14 = $72,857

41. 12 mos × 1,200 = $14,400 minimum annual rent
    $16,600 − 14,400 = $2,200 above minimum
    $2,200 is 3% of what amount?
    3% × _____ = $2,200
    Factor missing: divide
    $2,200 ÷ .03 = $73,333.33 over $260,000
    $260,000 + $73,333.33 = $333,333.33 total sales

42. 1 ÷ 40 years = 2½% per year depreciation
    14 years × 2.5%/yr = 35% depreciation to date
    100% − 35% = 65% remaining value
    Replacement cost × % not lost = current value
    $150,000 × .65 = $97,500

43. $500 × 12 mos = $6,000 annual interest
    Loan balance × rate = annual interest
    _____ × 10% = 6,000
    Factor missing: divide
    $6,000 ÷ .10 = $60,000

44. Length × width × depth = cubic measure
    90 ft × 30 ft × 14 ft = 37,800 cu ft
    37,800 ÷ 27 cu ft/cu yd = 1400 cu yds
    1400 cu yd × $.50 = $700

45. $60,000 × .85 = $51,000 face amount
    $51,000 ÷ 100 = 510 units
    $.60 × 510 units = $306 annual premium
    $306 × 3 years = $918 premium for 3 years
    $918 ÷ 36 months = $25.50 per month
    $25.50 × 14 months = $357 used up
    $918 − $357 = $561

46. 4½" × 2½ = ?
    $\frac{9}{2} \times \frac{5}{2} = \frac{45}{4}$ = 11¼ miles

47. ½ + ⅓ = unknown area
    3/6 + 2/6 = 5/6
    6/6 (entire area) − 5/6 = 1/6
    Remainder = 20 acres
    1/6 = 20 acres
    Entire tract = 20 × 6 = 120 acres

48. 125 acres × $900 = $112,500
    200 houses × $115,000 = $23,000,000
    Other costs = $1,300,000
    $112,500 + $23,000,000 + $1,300,000 = $24,412,500 invested
    1.14 (114%) × $24,412,500 = $27,830,250 gross sales
    $27,830,250 ÷ 200 houses = $139,151.25 per house

49. The lender will lend based on the lower of appraised value or sale price
    85% × $96,000 = maximum loan
    .85 × $96,000 = $81,600
    $96,000 price − $81,600 loan = $14,400 down payment

50. 26 acres × 43,560 square feet per acre = 1,132,560 square feet
    1,132,560 square feet ÷ 1,320 feet deep = 858 feet of frontage
    858 front feet × $1,500 = $1,287,000 total value

APPENDIX A

Basic House Construction

The purpose of this appendix is to provide an elementary understanding of the principles, terminology, and methods of residential construction. The material is confined to wood-frame construction, which is the most typical construction method for houses.

ARCHITECTURAL TYPES AND STYLES

A popular style of home is the one-story or ranch style. With all the living space on the ground floor, there is ease of access that proves attractive to many persons, especially the elderly and handicapped. The ranch home tends to be of modest size and affordability, which contributes to its popularity. A one-and-a-half-story home typically provides expansion space on the upper level, such as for an additional bedroom.

Young families often prefer the two-story home, which provides the extra bedrooms and space that a growing family needs. There are many styles of the two story including the traditional, Colonial American, Tudor, and French Provincial. Each has its own distinctive styling and provides maximum space per construction dollar.

Many contemporary styles have appeared in recent years. One of the most popular is the split level. Typically, these homes take advantage of the terrain by having the lower level partially below the ground surface, similar to a basement. One disadvantage of this style is that stairs are involved to get to either level unless a hillside terrain provides access at both levels. In some cases, a trilevel may even provide ground level access at all three levels in steep terrain.

Many modern styles have emerged that take advantage of high and open ceilings and lofts or balconies. A wide variety of styles exists in this category to suit modern tastes. A recent trend is that of new construction in Victorian styling, including all of the distinctive exterior styling of that period.

In any style, the design of a floor plan that provides functional utility is of prime importance. Good design increases the comfort of the home. This includes adequate closets and storage space, an entrance hall to protect the living room from the immediate front door area, and the proper placing and size of windows to provide sufficient light and ventilation for all the rooms. The grouping of the bedroom and bathroom areas in one area or wing of the house so as to provide privacy is important. The kitchen should be designed to provide an efficient as well as attractive work area, and it should be located near a rear or side (garage) entrance for access to the outside. Rooms should be of a reasonably good size and should be sized proportionately to one another.

Modern design typically includes an attached two-car garage, wood decks, and a family room off the kitchen. The traditional living room seems to have decreased in functional significance in favor of the family room or den for the active family.

FOUNDATIONS

Location on Site

The location of the house on the building site is an important consideration. The proper location can have a significant effect on value. Land use regulations specify a required setback from the street, side, and rear property lines. A location that makes the most advantage of available views, privacy, and ease of access adds to the value and enjoyment of the home.

Footings

Building lines are usually laid out with batter boards, temporary wood members on posts forming an L-shape outside the corners of the foundation. Strings are run from the batter boards to line up the placement of the foundation. Trenches are then dug for the footings, which are normally made of poured concrete. The concrete must be placed on soil that has not been disturbed and that is below the frost line. The width of the footing is twice the width of the foundation wall. The depth of the footing is usually eight inches (more for masonry homes). The purpose of the footings is to support the foundation wall and, subsequently, the entire weight load of the structure. The footings must provide an adequate base for the structure to prevent settling of the house.

The foundation system must provide for proper drainage of ground water away from the structure.

Foundation Walls

Foundation walls are often constructed of 8-inch cinder blocks. The exposed portion of the blocks is then faced with a smooth mortar finish known as parging. The parged walls are painted to improve the appearance of the exposed foundation. A foundation wall system used less frequently in the state is that of poured concrete.

In level terrain, the foundation may be a concrete slab instead of a foundation wall. The concrete slab is poured directly on the ground and there is no excavation or crawl space. The slab provides the floor of the dwelling and the support for the exterior and interior walls. The concrete slab method is less expensive than the foundation wall construction.

Moisture control is a serious problem that must be addressed in any foundation system. First, grading of the soil must assure that surface water is directed away from the foundation and that proper drainage is provided. A porous drainage pipe is installed on a base of loose gravel at the footing to remove water from this area. The foundation walls must contain adequate ventilation to the crawl space underneath the house. This ventilation is provided by vents in the upper part of the foundation wall around the perimeter of the house. A waterproof vapor barrier, such as a plastic sheet, is placed over exposed soil underneath a home with a crawl space and no basement. In the case of a concrete basement floor or monolithic (slab) construction, both termite treatment and the vapor barrier are applied before the concrete is poured.

FRAMING

Framing refers to the wooden skeleton of the home. Framing members are lumber with a nominal dimension of two-inches thick, known as two bys. For example, these are 2×4 studs for walls, 2×10 joists for floors, and traditionally, 2×8 joists for roofs. The use of truss systems has largely replaced the method of framing the roof with individual wood 2×8 members.

Flooring

The top of the foundation wall is finished off with a course of solid concrete block masonry, or concrete. On top of this course of solid block rests the foundation sill. The sill is usually made with 2×6 lumber. This wooden sill is bonded to the foundation wall by anchor bolts imbedded in the wall. It is the first wooden member of the house and is used as nailing surface for the rest of the framework.

The box sill rests on the sill plate, and is usually 2×8 lumber. The box sill runs around the top of the foundation wall attached to the sill plate.

The floor joists span the distance between the foundation walls to provide the support for the subfloor. These joists are often 2×10 lumber, placed 16 inches on center in the typical framing pattern. The 16-inch spacing of framing members depends primarily on strength considerations for the lumber sizing. Additionally, covering materials, such as plywood or wallboard, are made in four-foot widths. The 16-inch spacing, therefore, provides a uniform nailing pattern of four rows for each piece of covering material.

Depending on the area to be spanned, the joists are put in double or even triple to support the load. Steel columns or concrete blocks (pilasters) support the floor joists where there would otherwise be a span of too great a length. Bridging is a system of smaller boards nailed in an "X" pattern between the parallel joists to provide stiffening against later movement of the joists.

Some modern construction methods use wooden floor trusses in place of single floor joists. A truss is a support member created in the factory by nailing a number of smaller members (2×4) together in a number of triangular patterns to provide maximum strength.

A plywood subflooring rests directly on top of the joists. Finish flooring consists of various systems, such as an underlayment of particle board and hardwood finish floors in better construction. Less well-designed systems may apply carpeting directly to the subflooring with little other base.

Walls

The floor system usually serves as a stage or platform (platform framing) for the wall system. The walls are usually built of 2×4 studs, 16 inches on center, and, less frequently, 2×6 studs on 24-inch centers. A horizontal base plate stud serves as a foundation for the wall system. A double top plate is used to tie the walls together and provide additional support for the ceiling and roof system. Both exterior and interior walls are framed in as a rough carpentry skeleton. Openings in the wall for doors or windows must be reinforced to pick up the missing support for the vertical load. This is done typically with two 2×8s, known as headers, on end over the top of the opening.

An alternative to platform framing is that of balloon framing. In this method, a single system of wall studs run from the foundation through the first and second floor to the ceiling support. This method is rarely used in modern construction, which employs platform framing almost exclusively.

Contemporary building sometimes uses post and beam framing. These members are much larger than ordinary studs and may be 4- or 6-inches square. The larger posts can be placed several feet apart instead of the 16-inch centers of the traditional wall studs.

Plumbing and electrical systems are run through the walls before they are covered up. Inspections must be

FIGURE A.1
Roof styles.

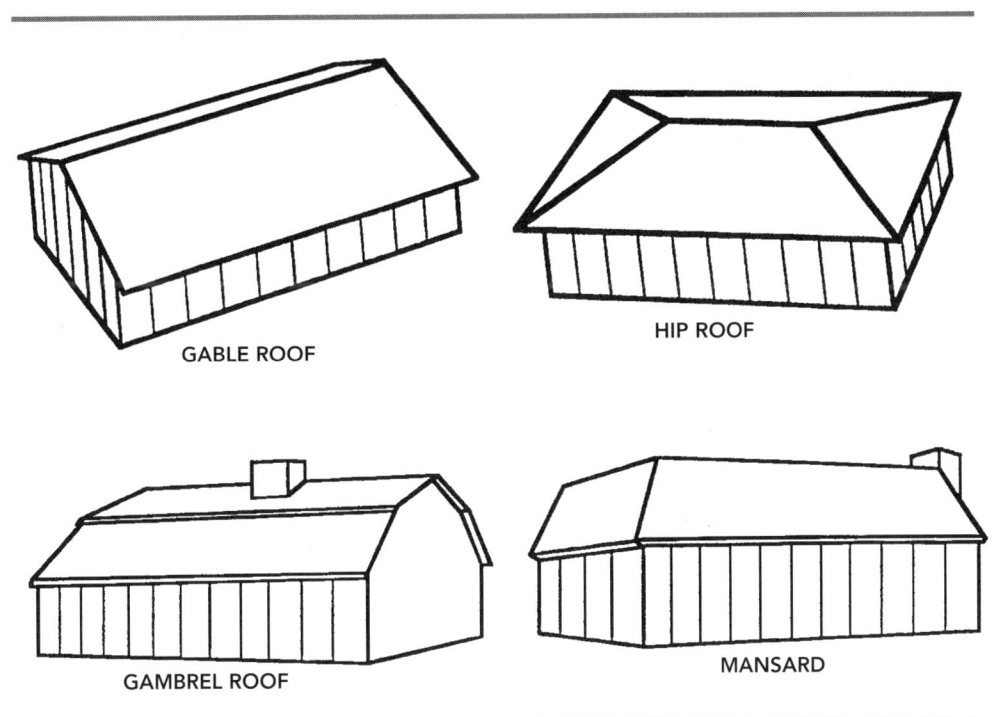

GABLE ROOF

HIP ROOF

GAMBREL ROOF

MANSARD

made before any of this utility framework (rough plumbing and electric) can be covered. Insulation is then placed between the studs and a plastic vapor barrier is applied to the warm (inside) wall. The vapor barrier is important in preventing the warm interior air from mixing with the cold exterior air and forming condensation within the wall.

Roof and Ceiling Framing

The ceiling joists rest on the top plate of the wall. These joists should be placed directly over the vertical stud for maximum-bearing strength. The joists span the structure between the outer walls. In traditional framing methods using 2 × 8 ceiling joists, the inner walls were important in helping to bear the load of the roof. This is different in the contemporary use of roof truss systems where the truss carries the load-bearing function to the outer walls. This feature provides freedom of placement of the inner walls. Since a roof truss is made up of a number of smaller 2 × 4 members (cords), the attic space is almost completely lost.

EXTERIOR WALLS

The exterior wall is covered with a sheathing material, traditionally a paper product of low insulating value. Modern systems use synthetic sheathing materials of high insulating value. Any sheathing material has little structural strength. To provide more strength and stiffening to the structure, plywood sheets are attached to the corners of the house. Only rarely would these plywood sheets be applied to the entire wall surface.

Various siding materials such as wood sheets or brick veneer (there is no such thing as a solid brick house) provide the finish exterior cover.

WINDOWS AND EXTERIOR DOORS

Windows fall into three general classes of sliding, swinging, and fixed.

Sliding Windows

Vertical Sliding (Double-Hung)

The most common type of windows are vertical sliding, known as double-hung windows. (See Figure A.2a.) These are two glass pane units (sashes) that slide by each other. In older construction, the weight of the heavy window unit was supported or balanced by a rope (sash cord) and pulley system in the wall. Lighter, modern systems are governed entirely by the friction of the unit sliding in its track.

The major parts of a window framework are labeled the same as the parts of a door opening; that is, the sill is the bottom or base part, the jamb is the side, and the header is the top of the rough opening.

The typical parts of a window include the sash, which is the glass panel unit that slides up and down. In the past, glass manufacturing was only able to make small glass panes for windows. These panes were held together with wood strips known as mullions. Today, many windows have nonfunctional mullions added as decorative strips to simulate a multiple pane appearance for decorative patterns. The stile is the side part of the sash and the top and bottom portions of the sash are known as rails.

Horizontal Sliding

Horizontal sliding windows are often found in modern ranch homes, sometimes as a ceiling unit in a bedroom.

These units often have two sashes that slide by each other horizontally. In the case of a three-sash unit, the central one is usually fixed, with only two sliding sashes.

Whereas older windows were a single pane of glass, most contemporary windows are of a thermal insulating design with a double-glass pane and small air space between the panes. This design provides excellent insulation and efficiency of heating and cooling, since windows make up a large portion of the wall surface area. Additionally, single-pane windows produce interior condensation in cold weather, which can damage interior woodwork.

These single-pane units require an exterior glass unit (storm window) to provide proper insulation in the winter.

Swinging Windows

Casement
The casement window has a sash hinged on one side, and it swings outward. (See Figure A.2b.) The swinging mechanism is usually a geared crank system with an operating handle on the interior sill. Latches are often used to close this type of window tight for a proper weather seal.

Jalousie
The jalousie is a series of horizontal glass slats. The slats are held together with a metal end that is attached to a gear mechanism. The slats open and close together similar to a venetian blind. When closed, the individual metal slats do not provide a very effective weather seal for most interior environments. Therefore they are generally limited to porches or patios in most climates.

Hopper
A hopper window has one unit hinged at the bottom so that the sash swings inward. This inward swing may have the disadvantage of interfering with interior living space.

Awning
The awning window is hinged at the top and swings outward. Care must be used in the placement of these windows so that they do not interfere with personal traffic outside the house, such as on porches or walkways. (See Figure A.2c.)

Fixed Windows

Fixed windows do not have any moveable sections. As air conditioning has become more popular and common, there is less need to have windows that open for ventilation.

The common types of fixed windows include the picture, bay, and bow window. In some window assemblies, a fixed window may just be a center section with some form of moveable window, such as vertical casement windows, on either side.

Doors

There is a major difference between interior and exterior doors. Interior doors are usually of a thin wood veneer and hollow interior core. Maximum insulation is desired in exterior doors, and therefore they are usually of a material such as solid wood. Modern construction employs steel doors with a high insulating interior core material.

It is essential that all doors and windows be tightly sealed to prevent leakage of air around them. Good workmanship finish carpentry is an important first step in this process. External caulking around windows helps complete the tight seal as does weatherstripping in the door frames. Consider the high surface area occupied by the doors and windows. If all of this space were leaking only a small amount of air, the total result would be similar to leaving a window open or having a large hole in the wall.

Common types of exterior doors include the flush door that is one smooth unit and the panel door that is composed of several decorative panels. The sliding glass door unit is very popular unit onto porches or decks. The glass door unit often has one fixed panel and one panel that slides on nylon rollers. French doors have become popular high-style decorative units that may open from a dining room onto a patio.

ROOFING

The roof construction consists of roof rafters, in older homes, normally 2×8 or 2×10 that rest upon the top plates of the exterior walls of the house. The rafters are joined at the peak of the roof and are fastened to the ridge board. Modern construction usually employs truss roof systems. The roof rafters are covered by boards or exterior plywood sheets. On top of this material, building paper or

FIGURE A.2
(a) Double-hung window (b) casement window (c) awning window.

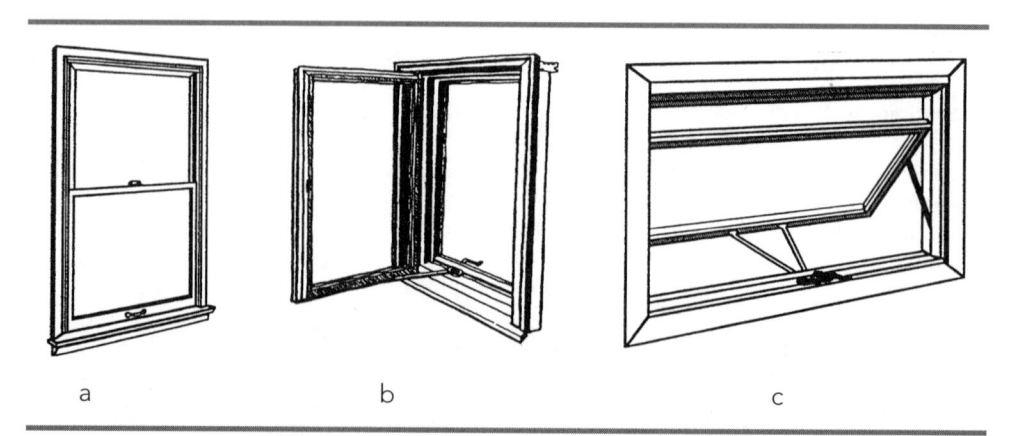

a   b   c

felt is nailed. The shingles are then put on top of the felt or building paper. To provide satisfactory roof drainage and to avoid the shingles being blown off by the wind, the pitch of the roof—that is the degree of slant of the roof—should not be less than 4 inches in every 12 feet.

The roof should extend at least 12 inches beyond the exterior walls of the structure. The larger this extension, or overhang, the more protection there is from sun and rain for the exterior walls as well as the windows. The area under the roof extension is called the soffit. The area of material facing the outer edge of the roof extension is called the fascia.

INSULATION

The primary purpose of insulation is that of resisting the flow of heat from one area to another. It provides the double benefit of preventing heat loss in the winter and protecting against heat load in the summer. Indeed, the addition of extra insulation to a poorly insulated home will give the impression of modest air conditioning the next summer. The ceiling is the most effective place to install insulation. Insulation is rated in an R factor, which stands for resistance to heat flow. The larger the R rating, the greater the degree of insulation. Homes built to superior energy efficient standards have R-19 floors and walls, and R-30 ceilings. Local electric power companies offer discount rates to homes meeting their energy efficient standards. Additionally, they often have low interest loan programs to help homeowners improve their insulation.

A common form of insulation is that of fiberglass in fifteen-and-a-half-inch wide rolls designed to fit in the space between framing members. A six-inch thickness provides an R-19 insulating factor. Unfaced rolls (without paper covering) can be added on top of existing attic insulation to improve the energy efficiency of existing homes.

Insulation also provides a measure of soundproofing between adjacent units of a condominium or apartment.

INTERIOR FINISHES

In most homes today the interior walls are finished by using a dry wall construction. This construction consists of panels of gypsum board (sheet-rock) material. The panels are essentially a core of gypsum covered with treated paper. The careful placement of these sheets and the finishing of seams requires a high degree of skill. Since this placement provides the interior finish and appearance of the home, it is usually done by a team of specialists other than the carpenter.

Wood paneling, either in sheets or individual boards, makes a very attractive interior finish. Often a home will contain a combination of sheetrock and wood paneling.

The most durable and satisfactory finish in bathrooms has been ceramic tile. This tile is used on the floors as well as a wainscot up to waist high or so around the bathroom wall and head high around the tub and shower area. The use of fiberglass tubs, showers, or tub and shower combinations has gained in popularity in recent years. The installation of these fiberglass units eliminates the necessity for ceramic tile around the tub or shower area.

A good deal of attention should be given to the finished carpentry on the interior of the house. The quality of the materials as well as the quality of the work that went into the construction of window frames, baseboards, door casings, and doors are strong indications of the quality of construction of the dwelling.

HEATING/AIR CONDITIONING SYSTEMS

HVAC is an acronym that stands for heating, ventilation, and air conditioning. A wide variety of heating and cooling systems is available for residential construction. Older structures relied on heating systems such as fireplaces and space heaters. In recent years there has been interest in fireplace inserts and various forms of freestanding wood stoves with high efficiencies. Although picturesque, a modern fireplace by itself is a terribly inefficient structure. It serves largely to exhaust air (and heat) from the house. If you inspect a historic or colonial home that had a functioning fireplace as the only source of heat, you will note that it was an extremely shallow structure designed for maximum radiation of heat to the room.

Despite America's love affair with wood stoves and the like, the only truly efficient heating system is a central unit either gas or electric. Older systems were gravity systems that expected warm and cool air to find their way around the house by convection currents resulting from the small difference in density of the heated air. This system required large ducts and vents to move the required volume of air.

Forced air systems added a central blower to distribute the treated air to various portions of the house. There needs to be an air duct to each room, and a return duct to the furnace.

Baseboard heating units are often found in new construction. Although these units offer moderate expense and ease of construction to the builder, electric units can be very expensive to operate. Correspondingly, a high degree of insulation is needed with any form of electric wire heating to minimize expense of operation.

Modern construction also uses a heating system of electric cable panels in the ceiling. This type of heating has the advantage of providing even heat as well as being clean. As previously stated, for this type of heat particular attention should be given to providing adequate insulation, a six-inch attic insulation being the minimum that is acceptable.

A recent innovation is the highly popular heat pump. The heat pump extracts heat from the outside, even in moderately cold weather, and transfers the heat into the home. The cycle is reversed in the summer to extract heat from the interior producing air conditioning. Since the system is not effective in the extremely cold temperatures of winter, they are commonly supplemented with auxiliary electric wire systems for these occasions.

Solar Heat

With the recent increase in the cost of heating, much attention has been given to solar heating systems. The concept of solar heat is not exactly new. Socrates advocated building homes with high southern exposure to capture the effect of the sun and low northern exposure to shield against winter winds. Accelerated interest in solar heating was seen with the experimental house built by the Massachusetts Institute of Technology in 1939.

Today we recognize two main types of solar heating. Passive solar heating simply takes advantage of exposure to the sun. Direct exposure just heats a given area during the day. Indirect exposure involves heating water units or a masonry wall to give up heat to the home during the night.

Active solar heating involves a more sophisticated method of collecting, storing, and distributing heat. The system starts with a collection panel of a glass front, water tubing, and black flat plates. Glass is very useful in allowing the solar energy to enter but preventing its escape. The black plates absorb the heat energy for transmission to the water tubing. The heated water is pumped to a storage tank for later distribution to the home. A heat exchange system in the living area provides for distribution of the heat from the circulated water.

Since solar systems often cannot provide more than fifty to sixty percent of the total heating needs, an auxiliary heating source, such as an oil furnace, is included in the system.

ELECTRICAL SYSTEMS

Care should be taken to ascertain whether or not the electrical system is adequate, because the great number of electrically operated appliances used these days makes adequate wiring of extreme importance. Modern construction requires a 110/220 volt wiring system that has a capacity of 150–200 amps. The system is fitted with circuit breakers. There should be sufficient electrical wall receptacles for the use of the household. They should be spaced at regular intervals in every room.

PLUMBING

The adequacy and quality of the plumbing system is another important facet in the quality of construction. Copper piping is quite superior to galvanized piping. Each bathroom should be vented to the exterior by the use of a metal pipe through the roof's surface. The venting of the trap in the kitchen sink is also necessary. All water fixtures should have separate cutoffs, so that a repair could be effected without shutting down the entire system.

GOVERNMENT REGULATION

Residential Building Codes

A building code is designed to ensure the safety and sanitation of structures. The primary focus of the code is on structure and electrical and plumbing systems. Each local government, county, or city has a building inspections department that enforces the local adaptations of the building code. Before any construction can begin, the builder must submit appropriate construction information in order to obtain a building permit. The inspection officer then must approve each stage of the construction before the next stage is allowed to begin. At the satisfactory completion of the construction and inspection process, a Certificate of Occupancy (CO) is issued. Typically, one cannot obtain permanent power or plumbing service to the home until the CO is issued.

HUD Minimum Standards

Homes to be built with any program of federal financing, such as an FHA or VA loan, must be approved in advance and inspected by the appropriate agency as construction proceeds. If this approval is not obtained in advance, the home must be at least one-year-old to obtain approval for these loan programs.

SUMMARY

Real estate agents should learn to distinguish those features in a dwelling that show quality construction as well as those things that indicate construction of inferior quality. As a suggestion, those not familiar with construction techniques might well spend some time looking at homes in various stages of construction in their areas. In doing so, a knowledge of the construction process and the various qualities of workmanship and materials can be gained.

Figures A.3 and A.4 illustrate a typical wall section of a single-family dwelling. Notice that on this drawing the various components of the wall section are identified and the dimensions of the materials are shown.

Construction Terminology

bridging—Short wooden pieces placed between timbers to help hold them in place.

column—A vertical shaft used to support the frame not supported by a foundation wall.

concrete slab—A foundation of poured concrete.

fascia—The wood covering attached to the end of the roof rafters at the outer end.

floating slab—A slab and footings poured in separate forms.

footing—A concrete base below the frost line used to support a foundation wall.

foundation wall—Bearing wall, set on footings, that supports the structure of a house.

gable roof—One consisting of two inclined planes joined over the center line of a house and resting on the two opposite roof plates on top of the studs. The triangular end walls are called gables.

gambrel roof—Similar to a gable roof except that each of two sides consists of two inclined planes. The upper planes are relatively flat and the lower planes are quite steep.

header—Timber used to support the free ends of joists, studs, or rafters over openings in the frame.

hip roof—One consisting of four inclined planes joined to form a rectangle.

joists—Horizontal timbers to support a floor or ceiling.

mansard roof—One like a gambrel roof except that there are two planes on each of four sides.

monolithic slab—A concrete slab poured in one piece to form an entire foundation.

pilasters—Rectangular concrete or concrete block columns attached to a foundation wall to provide additional support to the frame.

plates—Timbers placed horizontally on top of studs in a wall framework.

sill—Wood member of the frame attached to the foundation wall.

soffit—The covering, usually plywood, on the under side of a roof overhang.

stud—A vertical 2 × 4 or 2 × 6 timber used in the framework of a wall.

sub-flooring—Material on which the finished flooring is laid.

truss—A triangular framework nailed in W-shaped patterns to provide support over a long span as in roof construction.

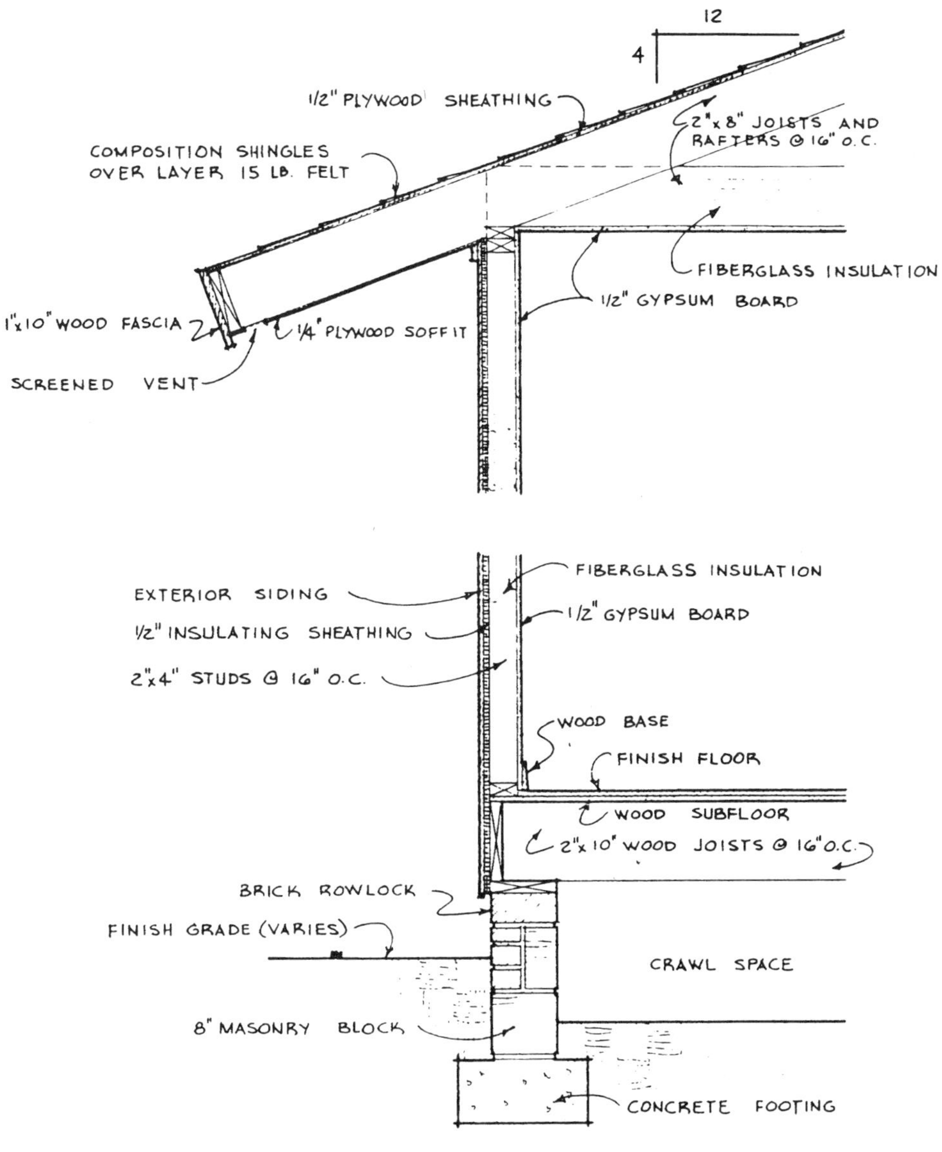

FIGURE A.3
Typical wall section.

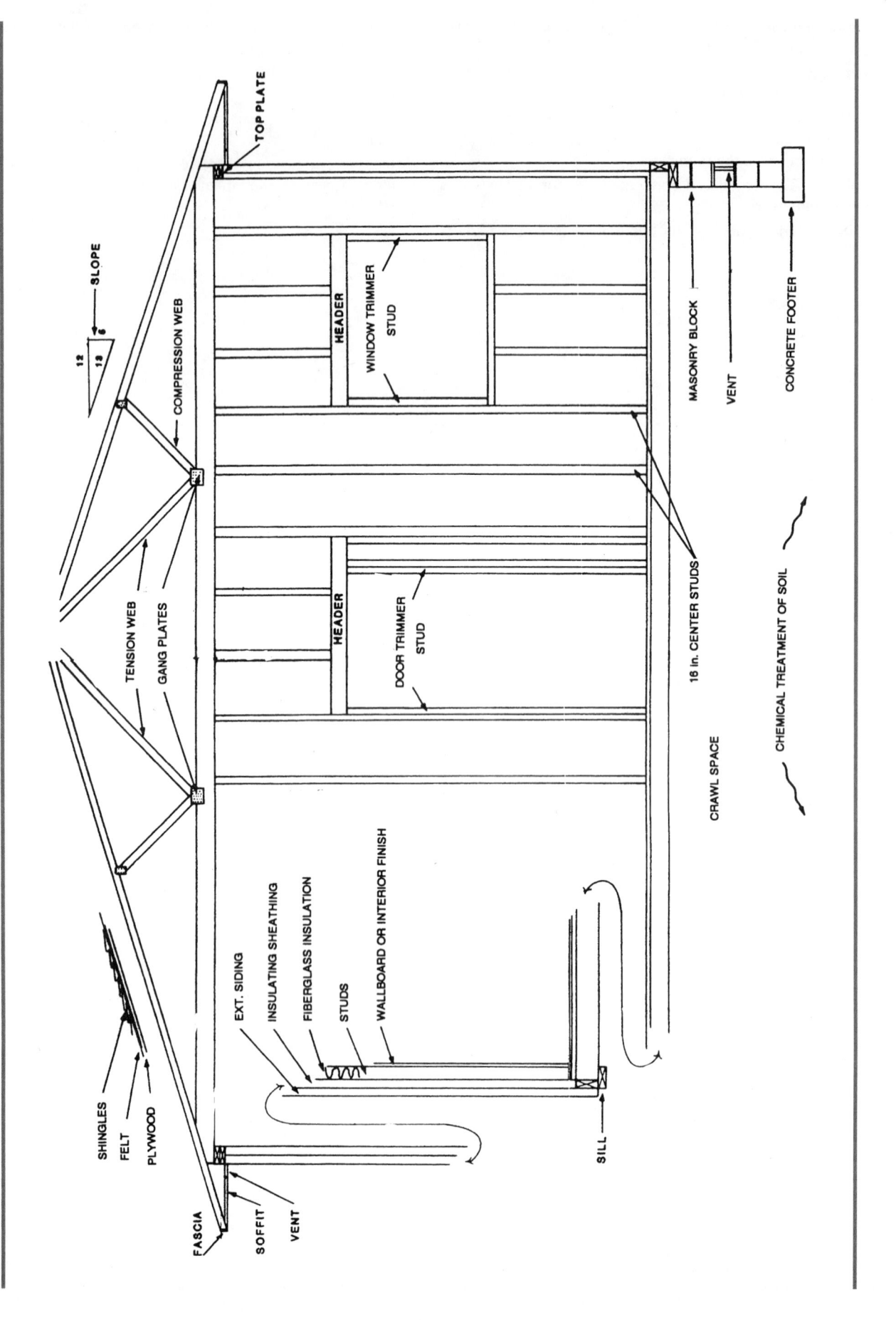

FIGURE A.4 Roof section using truss system.

APPENDIX B

A Guide to Common Real Estate Environmental Hazards*

INTRODUCTION

Does this home fit my needs and those of my family? Is this a safe, secure home, free from potential hazards? Is this home a good investment and will it retain and increase its value in the years ahead?

These are among the hundreds of questions that home buyers ask themselves as part of the home-buying thought process. It is a good policy, this questioning, a means of gathering hard facts that can be used to balance the emotional feelings that are so much a part of buying a home.

In ever-increasing numbers, home buyers today find it necessary to add new kinds of questions to their quest for information. Environmental concerns are becoming an element of the home-buying thought process.

Although it is unrealistic to expect that any home will be free of all forms of environmental influences, most homes (and the areas surrounding most homes) in the United States generally do not contain materials and substances that pose a health threat. However, in recent years, new concerns have been raised as our understanding of the natural environment has increased. Substances, such as radon gas and asbestos, have provoked new questions about how and where we build homes and manage their upkeep.

HOME-BUYING CONSIDERATIONS

For the majority of Americans, the purchase of a home is the single greatest investment of a lifetime. Will the presence of an undetected environmental hazard have a long-term negative impact on that investment? Does the presence of a hazard have the potential to affect the health of the occupants? If hazards can be safely removed or mitigated, will the process alter the homeowner's lifestyle? These questions—and others like them—are, and should be, part of the home buyer's thought process today.

As our knowledge of the natural environment evolves, the body of law governing potentially harmful environmental hazards and their effect on real estate transactions also is evolving. The rights and responsibilities of buyers and sellers are determined by state and local laws or terms negotiated into the sales contract between the buyer and seller.

Thus, before buying a home, prudent home buyers may want to obtain information about the potential impact of environmental hazards. Local, county, or state health or environmental departments are sources of such information. And while builders, real estate appraisers, real estate sales licensees, and lenders are not experts about the environment, these individuals may be of assistance in locating additional sources of information regarding environmental matters. Private home inspectors also may be useful in detecting the existence of potentially hazardous conditions if the sales contract provides for such an inspection.

The pages that follow provide general information about some of the environmental hazards that have the potential to affect the home environment. While this information is believed to be accurate, it is not meant to be comprehensive or authoritative. This publication provides introductory information to help home buyers understand the possible risk of exposure to potentially harmful environmental hazards in and around the home.

The agencies and individuals contributing to or assisting in the preparation of this booklet—or any individual

---

*Compiled by: National Council of Savings Institutions; Office of Thrift Supervision; Society of Real Estate Appraisers; The Appraisal Foundation; U.S. Environmental Protection Agency; U.S. League of Savings Institutions. This document is in the public domain.

acting on behalf of any of these parties—do not make any warranty, guarantee, or representation (express or implied) with respect to the usefulness or effectiveness of any information, method, or process disclosed in this material or assume any liability for the use of (or for damages arising from the use of) any information, method, or process disclosed in this material.

RADON

What is radon and where is it found?

Radon is a colorless, odorless, tasteless gas that occurs worldwide in the environment as a byproduct of the natural decay of uranium present in the earth. Radon is present in varying quantities in the atmosphere and in soils around the world.

How does radon enter a home?

Radon that is present in surrounding soil or in well water can be a source of radon in a home. Radon from surrounding soil enters a home through small spaces and openings, such as cracks in concrete, floor drains, sump pump openings, wall/floor joints in basements, and the pores in hollow block walls. It also can seep into ground water and remain entrapped there. Therefore, if a home is supplied with water taken from a ground water source (such as a well), there is greater potential for a radon problem. The likelihood of radon in the water supply is greatly reduced for homes supplied with water from a municipal water supply.

Is radon found throughout a home, or just in certain rooms or areas?

Radon generally concentrates most efficiently in the areas of a home closest to the ground. Radon levels generally decrease as one moves higher up in the structure.

How can I tell if a home has a radon problem?

The only way to know whether or not a home has a radon problem is to test it. Radon levels vary from house to house depending on the construction of the house and the soil surrounding it. There are several ways to make a preliminary screening test for radon. Preliminary screening test kits can be bought over-the-counter in many hardware, grocery, and convenience stores. Tests that measure the amount of radon in water normally require you to send a sample of tap water to a laboratory for analysis. State agencies should be consulted if the home water supply is suspected as a source of radon.

When purchasing a radon detection kit, you should examine the package for indications that the kit has been approved by federal or state health, environmental protection, or consumer protection agencies. Directions should be followed carefully when using a radon detection kit to assure that proper measurements are obtained. Short-term testing (ranging from a few days to several months) is one way to determine if a potential problem exists. Long-term testing (lasting for up to one year) is a more accurate way to determine if radon is present. Both short- and long-term testing devices are easy to use and relatively inexpensive.

Why is radon harmful?

Radon gas breaks down into radioactive particles (called decay products) that remain in the air. As you breathe these particles, they can become trapped in your lungs. As these particles continue to break down, they release bursts of energy (radiation) that can damage lung tissue. This damage can cause lung cancer. When radon gas and its decay products enter your home, they remain in circulation in the enclosed air. Out of doors, radon is not a problem for human beings because the surrounding air allows the gas to diffuse in the atmosphere.

What health risks are associated with radon?

The health risk associated with prolonged inhalation of radon decay products is an increased risk of developing lung cancer. There are indications that risk increases as the level of radon concentration and duration of exposure increase. The U.S. Environmental Protection Agency (EPA) has determined that short-term exposure to a high concentration of radon is not as severe a risk as long-term exposure to a lower level of the gas.

What is an acceptable level of indoor radon?

The concentration of radon in air is measured in units of picocuries per liter of air (pCi/L). Estimates suggest that most homes will contain from one to two picocuries of radon per liter of air. If preliminary tests indicate radon levels greater than four picocuries per liter of air in livable areas of the home, the EPA recommends that a follow-up test be conducted. No level of radon is considered safe; there are risks even at very low levels. To put this into perspective, the EPA estimates that the risk of dying from lung cancer as the result of an annual radon level of four picocuries is equivalent to the risk from smoking ten cigarettes a day or having 200 chest x-rays a year. A picocurie level of 40 equates to smoking two packs of cigarettes a day, while a level of 100 equates to 2,000 chest x-rays a year.

How are radon risk levels calculated?

The EPA's risk assessments assume an individual is exposed to a given concentration of radon over a lifetime of roughly 70 years and spends 75 percent of his or her time in the home.

Can the level of radon in a home be reduced?

Yes, there are many effective and relatively inexpensive methods of reducing radon levels in a home. The method used will vary from house to house and from region to region. The techniques used will depend on the source of the gas, the ways in which it enters the home, and the kind of construction used in the home. If radon is present in water supplies, it can be removed altogether or reduced by the installation of special filter systems.

What will it cost to reduce the level of radon in a home?

The costs for radon reduction will depend on the number of sources, the amount of radon in the surrounding land or in the water supply, and the kind of construction used in the home. Normally, the costs of installing radon reduction equipment range from several hundred dollars to several thousand dollars. If the system chosen involves fans, pumps, or other appliances, operating costs for these devices may cause increases in monthly utility bills.

Is radon removal a "do it yourself project"?

Not usually. In some cases, homeowners should be able to treat the problem themselves; however, it is not always possible for homeowners to diagnose the source of radon or to install systems that will reduce the level. Radon source diagnosis and mitigation normally require skills, experience, and tools not available to the average homeowner; therefore, it is always prudent to consider the use of trained personnel. When seeking a contractor to assist with a radon problem, you should first consult local, county, or state government agencies for recommendations of qualified radon-reduction contractors.

What is the government doing about radon?

The federal government has undertaken an extensive public outreach effort to encourage individuals to test their homes. This effort includes a national hotline, 1-800-SOS-RADON, for obtaining further information on radon testing. EPA also is working closely with state and local governments and the private sector to research and demonstrate cost-effective methods for reducing indoor radon levels and with builders to develop radon-resistant new construction techniques.

You also may contact your state's radon office at the telephone number listed below.

State Radon Office

Illinois   (217) 786-6384

The following resources and publications can provide additional information about radon.

Brochures

- *A Citizen's Guide to Radon*
- *Radon Reduction Methods (A Homeowner's Guide)*
- *Removal of Radon from Household Water*
- *The Inside Story—A Guide to Indoor Air Quality*

The above are available from:

U.S. Environmental Protection Agency
Public Information Center
401 M Street, SW
Washington, DC 20460
(202) 260-7751

ASBESTOS

What is asbestos and where is it found?

Asbestos is a fibrous mineral found in rocks and soil throughout the world. Asbestos has been used in architectural and construction applications because it is strong, durable, fire retardant, and an efficient insulator. Alone or in combination with other materials, asbestos can be fashioned into a variety of products that have numerous applications within the building industry—such as flooring, walls, ceiling tiles, exterior housing shingles, insulation or fire retardant for heating and electrical systems, etc.

Is asbestos dangerous?

Asbestos has been identified as a carcinogen. Once ingested, asbestos fibers lodge in the lungs. Because the material is durable, it persists in tissue and concentrates as repeated exposures occur over time. It can cause cancer of the lungs and stomach among workers and others who have experienced prolonged work-related exposure to it. The health effects of lower exposures in the home are less certain; however, experts are unable to provide assurance that any level of exposure to asbestos fibers is completely safe.

Under what circumstances do asbestos-containing products in the home become a health risk?

Home health risks arise when age, accidental damage, or normal cleaning, construction, or remodeling activities cause the asbestos-containing materials to crumble, flake, or deteriorate. When this happens, minute asbestos fibers are released into the air and can be inhaled through the nose and mouth. The fibers can cling to clothing, tools, and exposed flesh; cleanup operations can then dislodge the fibers and free them to circulate in the air.

Can I expect to find asbestos in newer homes, and where in the home should I look for asbestos?

According to the EPA, many homes constructed in the United States during the past 20 years probably do not contain asbestos products. Places where asbestos sometimes can be found in the home include: around pipes and furnaces in older homes as insulating jackets and sheathing; in some vinyl flooring materials; in ceiling tiles; in exterior roofing, shingles, and siding; in some wallboards; mixed with other materials and troweled or sprayed around pipes, ducts, and beams; in patching compounds or textured paints; and in door gaskets on stoves, furnaces, and ovens.

How can I identify asbestos in the home?

You may hire a qualified professional who is trained and experienced in working with asbestos to survey the home. A professional knows where to look for asbestos, how to take samples properly, and what corrective actions will be the most effective. EPA regional asbestos coordinators can provide information on qualified asbestos contractors and laboratories. In addition, the manufacturer of a product may be able to tell you, based on the model number and age of the product, whether or not the product contains asbestos.

What should I do if I think there is asbestos in a home I have purchased?

Generally, if the material is in good condition and is in an area where it is not likely to be disturbed, leave the asbestos-containing material in place. Extreme care should be exercised in handling, cleaning, or working with material suspected of containing asbestos. If the material is likely to be banged, rubbed, handled, or taken apart—especially during remodeling—you should hire a trained contractor and reduce your exposure as much as possible. Common construction and remodeling operations can release varying amounts of asbestos fibers if the material being worked on contains asbestos. These operations include hammering, drilling, sawing, sanding, cutting, and otherwise shaping or molding the material. Routine cleaning operations (such as brushing, dusting, vacuum cleaning, scraping, and scrubbing) can also release hazardous fibers from asbestos-containing materials. Vinyl flooring products that contain asbestos can be cleaned in a conventional manner, but these products can release some asbestos fibers if they are vigorously sanded, ground, drilled, filed, or scraped.

The repair or removal of asbestos-containing products from a home is generally a complicated process. It depends on the amount of these products present, the percentage of asbestos they contain, and the manner in which asbestos is incorporated into the product. Total removal of even small amounts of asbestos-containing material is usually the last alternative. You should contact local, state, or federal health or consumer product agencies before deciding on a course of action. To assure safety and elimination of health hazards, asbestos repair or removal should be performed only by properly trained contractors.

Many home repair or remodeling contractors do not yet have the requisite tools, training, experience, or equipment to work safely with asbestos or to remove it from a home. Furthermore, asbestos removal workers are protected under federal regulations that specify special training, protective clothing, and special respirators for these workers.

Are exterior asbestos shingles a health risk?

When properly installed on the exterior of a home, asbestos-containing products present little risk to human health. However, if siding is worn or damaged, spray painting it will help seal-in the fibers.

What is being done about the potential problem of exposure to asbestos in the home?

Over the years, the U.S. Environmental Protection Agency (EPA) and the Consumer Product Safety Commission (CPSC) have taken several steps to reduce the consumer's exposure to asbestos. Most recently these steps include requiring labeling of products containing asbestos and announcing a phased-in ban of most asbestos products by 1996.

The following sources and publications can provide additional information about asbestos in the home.

BROCHURES

- *Asbestos (Environmental Backgrounder)*
- *The Inside Story—a Guide to Indoor Air Quality*

The above are available from:

U.S. Environmental Protection Agency
Public Information Center
401 M Street, SW
Washington, DC 20460
(202) 260-7751

- *Asbestos in the Home*

Available from:

U.S. Environmental Protection Agency
TSCA Assistance Information Service
401 M Street, SW
Washington, DC 20460

Hotline

- *The Toxic Substances Control Act (TSCA) Assistance Information Service Hotline*

This Hotline provides both general and technical information and publications about toxic substances (including asbestos) and offers services to help businesses comply with TSCA laws (including regulatory advice and aid, publications, and audiovisual materials). The Hotline operates Monday through Friday from 8:30 a.m. to 5:00 p.m., eastern time. (202) 554-1404

LEAD

What is lead, and why is it hazardous to our health?

Lead is a metallic element found worldwide in rocks and soils. The toxic effects of lead have been known since ancient times. Recent research has shown that lead represents a greater hazard at lower levels of concentration than had been thought. Airborne lead enters the body when an individual breathes lead particles or swallows lead dust. Until recently, the most important source of airborne dust was automobile exhaust.

When ingested, lead accumulates in the blood, bones, and soft tissue of the body. High concentrations of lead in the body can cause death or permanent damage to the central nervous system, the brain, the kidneys, and red blood cells. Even low levels of lead may increase high blood pressure in adults.

Infants, children, pregnant women, and fetuses are more vulnerable to lead exposure than others because the lead is more easily absorbed into growing bodies and their tissues are more sensitive to the damaging effects of the lead. Because of a child's smaller body weight, an equal concentration of lead is more damaging to a child than it would be to an adult.

What are the sources of lead in and around the home?

Lead can be present in drinking water, in paint used to decorate the interior or exterior of a home, in the dust within a home, and in soil around the home.

Lead in Drinking Water

Are there acceptable levels of lead in drinking water?

The EPA Office of Drinking Water has proposed regulations under the Safe Drinking Water Act (SDWA) that establish a maximum contaminant level for lead in drinking water of five micrograms per liter and a maximum contaminant level goal of zero. [Note: One microgram per liter is equal to one part per billion (ppb).] These levels or goals are set by EPA to control contamination that may have an adverse effect on human health. Nonenforceable health-based goals are intended to protect against known or anticipated adverse health effects with an adequate margin of safety. Both the current maximum contamination level and goal are 50 micrograms per liter. Although the Public Health Service first set these levels in the 1960s before much of the current knowledge about the harmful effects of lead at low levels was gained, the EPA included them unchanged in the Safe Drinking Water Act of 1985. EPA, however, is now revising these standards to reflect its increased concern.

I have heard that materials containing lead have been banned from use in public water supplies. If this is true, how does lead enter drinking water in the home?

In 1986, amendments to the Safe Drinking Water Act banned any further use of materials containing lead in public water supplies and in residences connected to public water supplies. In 1988, the U.S. Congress banned the use of lead-based solder in plumbing applications within homes and buildings. However, many homes built prior to 1988 contain plumbing systems that use lead-based solder in pipe connections. In such systems, lead can enter drinking water as a corrosion byproduct when plumbing fixtures, pipes, and solder are corroded by drinking water. In these instances, lead levels in water at the kitchen tap can be far higher than those found in water at treatment plants.

The combination of copper pipes connected with lead-based solder is found in many homes and can result in high levels of lead in water. In these circumstances, galvanic corrosion between the two metals releases relatively large amounts of lead into the water. The amount of lead in this kind of home water system will be higher when water has been at rest in the pipes for a period of time.

The EPA has determined that newly installed solder is most easily dissolved. As the home ages, mineral deposits build up on the inner walls of water pipes and act as an insulating barrier between the water and the solder. Data compiled by the EPA indicates that during the first five years following home construction, water in the home may have high levels of lead, with the highest levels recorded during the first 24 months.

Can I tell by looking at pipes and plumbing fixtures whether or not water in the home will contain harmful levels of lead?

No. Visual inspection of pipe joints and solder lines is not an accurate means of determining whether or not decaying solder is a source of lead.

A simple chemical test can determine whether the solder used in a home is lead-containing or not. Many jurisdictions make use of this test as a regular procedure in plumbing inspections. And while many newer homes rely on non-metallic plumbing lines, the majority of faucets and plumbing fixtures used today can contribute some lead to home water supplies. However, these contributions can be eliminated effectively by running the faucet for 15 seconds before drawing drinking water.

How can I tell if a home has a problem with lead in the water?

The only way to determine lead levels in water is to test a sample of the water. Should you suspect that lead is present in drinking water, or if you wish to have water tested, contact local, county, or state health or environmental departments for information about qualified testing laboratories.

Is lead in water a concern in newly renovated older homes?

If the renovation included replacement of aging water pipes with copper or other metal piping, you should check with the renovating contractor to ensure that lead solder was not used in pipe joints. Further, some old homes contain water systems made of pipes that can contain high levels of lead. If the original water lines remain in the house, you should question the renovating contractor regarding his or her knowledge of pipe composition.

Lead-Based Paint

How prevalent is lead-based paint?

According to the EPA, it is estimated that lead-based paint was applied to approximately two-thirds of the houses built in the U.S. before 1940; one-third of the houses built from 1940 to 1960; and to an indeterminate (but smaller) portion of U.S. houses since 1960.

How can I tell whether the paint in a home contains lead?

The only accurate way to determine if paint in a home contains lead is to remove a sample of the paint and have it tested in a qualified laboratory. Should you suspect that lead is present in paint, or if you wish to have paint tested, contact local, county, or state health or environmental departments for information about qualified testing laboratories.

I have heard about problems when children eat chips of lead-based paint, but are there any other ways that lead-based paint can be harmful?

While the health hazards to children from eating lead-based paint chips have been known for some time, other sources of exposure to lead in household air and dust have been documented only recently.

Lead can enter the air within a home when surfaces covered with lead-based paint are scraped, sanded, or heated with an open flame in paint-stripping procedures. Once released into the home atmosphere, lead particles circulate in the air and can be inhaled or ingested through the mouth and nose. Lead particles freed in fine dust or vapors settle into carpet fibers and fabric and can be recirculated in the air by normal household cleaning (such as sweeping and dusting) and through the normal hand-to-mouth behavior of young children, which results in the ingestion of potentially harmful amounts of any lead present in household dust. Fine lead particles penetrate the filter systems of home vacuum cleaners and are recirculated in the exhaust air streams of such appliances. Lead also can enter household air from outdoor sources (such as contaminated soil) and from recreational activities that require the use of solder or materials containing lead.

How can I get rid of lead-based paint safely?

It is best to leave lead-based paint undisturbed if it is in good condition and there is little possibility that it will be eaten by children. Other procedures include covering the paint with wallpaper or some other building material, or completely replacing the painted surface. Pregnant women and women who plan to become pregnant should not do this work. Professional paint removal is costly, time-consuming, and requires everyone not involved in the procedure to leave the premises during removal and subsequent clean-up operations. In addition, if the house was built prior to 1950, there is a good chance that lead from exterior surface paint has accumulated in surrounding soils. Keep the yard well vegetated to minimize the likelihood of children being exposed to contaminated dust. Clean the floors, window-sills, and other surfaces regularly, preferably with wet rags and mops. Practice good hygiene with your children, especially frequent hand washing.

In 1992, Congress passed the Residential Lead-Based Paint Hazard Reduction Act. Regulations for this act were not formulated until 1996. See Chapter 5 for lead-based paint disclosure requirements.

The following publications provide additional information about lead in the home.

Brochures

- *Is Your Drinking Water Safe?*
- *Lead and Your Drinking Water*
- *The Inside Story—a Guide to Indoor Air Quality*

The above are available from:
U.S. Environmental Protection Agency
Public Information Center
401 M Street, SW
Washington, DC 20460
(202) 260-7751

Hotline

For additional information about lead in drinking water, contact EPA's Safe Drinking Water Hotline: (800) 426-4791; (202) 382-5533 (in the Washington, DC area)

HAZARDOUS WASTES

What are hazardous wastes?

Hazardous wastes are those waste products that could pose short- or long-term danger to personal health or the environment if they are not properly disposed of or managed. These wastes can be produced by large business and industries (such as chemical and manufacturing plants), by some small businesses (such as drycleaners and printing plants), and by individuals who improperly apply, store, or dispose of compounds that contain potentially toxic ingredients (which can be found in chemical fertilizers, pesticides, and household products).

Concentrations of hazardous wastes occur in the environment when these wastes are handled, managed, or disposed of in a careless or unregulated manner. For many decades, hazardous industrial wastes were improperly disposed of on land, and their toxic components remained in the earth or seeped into ground water and drinking water supplies. The widespread use of pesticides and other agricultural chemicals also has resulted in the seepage and run-off of toxic compounds into land and water supplies. In addition, EPA estimates that as many as two million of the more than five million underground storage tanks in the United States may be leaking—discharging gasoline, petroleum products, and other hazardous liquids into the soil and, potentially, into ground water sources.

What is being done to locate and clean up hazardous waste sites?

During the past 20 years, the U.S. Congress has enacted a body of interlocking laws and regulatory procedures aimed at the abatement of environmental hazards. The Superfund Act was enacted in 1980 (and amended in 1986) to provide more than $10 billion for the detection and cleanup of sites where hazardous waste is a problem.

The revenue for Superfund is raised through taxes on petrochemical companies and other manufacturers. Under the law, the EPA, other federal agencies, and individual states may draw the necessary funds to allow them to react in hazardous waste emergency situations and to conduct long-term, permanent cleanups of hazardous waste sites.

How can I determine if a home is affected by a hazardous waste site?

Generally, testing for hazardous waste involves skills and technology not available to the average homeowner or home remodeling contractor.

The EPA has identified more than 30,000 potentially contaminated waste sites nationwide and has completed a preliminary assessment of more than 27,000 of these sites. The Agency publishes a National Priorities List of sites that will require action through the Superfund. Sites suspected of containing hazardous wastes are mapped at the time of the EPA preliminary assessment and communities likely to be affected by the site are notified. Thus, the nearest regional office of the EPA should have information on the location and status of local hazardous waste sites. The addresses and telephone numbers of these regional offices are listed in the back of this publication.

Furthermore, local and state governments maintain offices and agencies for locating and managing hazardous waste sites. These offices often are good sources for current information about the location and possible effects of these sites.

What are the primary health hazards associated with hazardous wastes?

The specific health hazards in homes contaminated by hazardous wastes are determined by the kinds and amounts of toxic substances present. Some hazardous wastes can cause death even when ingested in small amounts. Other hazardous wastes have been linked to elevated risks of cancer, permanent damage to internal body organs, respiratory difficulties, skin rashes, birth defects, and diseases that attack the central nervous system.

Can hazardous waste concentrations be removed from my property or reduced to non-hazardous levels?

The ability to remove or mitigate hazardous wastes will depend on the kinds, amounts, and sources of the wastes that are present. Generally, the removal of hazardous wastes from a property is beyond the capability of an individual homeowner.

The following sources and publications provide additional information about hazardous wastes.

Brochures

- *A Consumer's Guide to Safer Pesticide Use*
- *Citizen's Guide to Pesticides*
- *Hazardous Wastes (Environmental Backgrounder)*

The above are available from:
U.S. Environmental Protection Agency
Public Information Center
401 M Street, SW
Washington, DC 20460
(202) 260-7751

Hotlines

- *National Poison Control Center Hotline*

    This Hotline provides information on accidental ingestion of chemicals, poisons, or drugs. The Hotline is operated by Georgetown University Hospital in Washington, DC. (202) 625-3333

- *RCRA (Superfund) Hotline*

    This Hotline responds to questions from the public and regulated community on the Resource Conservation and Recovery Act and the Comprehensive Environmental Response, Compensation and Liability Act (Superfund). The Hotline operates Monday through Friday from 8:30 a.m. to 7:30 p.m., eastern time. (800) 424-9346; (202) 382-3000 (in the Washington, DC area)

- *Emergency Planning and Community Right-to-Know Information Hotline*

    This Hotline complements the RCRA (Superfund) Hotline and provides communities and individuals with help in preparing for accidental releases of toxic chemicals. The Hotline operates Monday through Friday from 8:30 a.m. to 7:30 p.m., eastern time. (800) 535-0202; (202) 479-2449 (in the Washington, DC area)

GROUND WATER CONTAMINATION

What causes ground water contamination?

Ground water contamination occurs when hazardous chemical wastes, pesticides, or other agricultural chemicals (such as fertilizer) seep down through the soil into underground water supplies. Faulty private septic systems, improperly managed municipal sewer systems, and leaking industrial injection wells can also contribute to ground water contamination. In recent years, leaking underground storage tanks also have posed a threat to ground water. Half of all Americans and 95 percent of rural Americans use ground water for drinking water.

Is ground water contamination harmful?

The U.S. Center for Disease Control reports an average of approximately 7,500 cases of illness linked to drinking water in the United States each year. This estimate generally is thought to be considerably lower than the actual figures because drinking water contaminants are not always considered in the diagnoses of illnesses.

How can I tell if the water in a home is contaminated?

The only way to know whether or not the water in a home is contaminated is to test it. Since 1977, federal law has required water suppliers to periodically sample and test the water supplied to homes. If tests reveal that a national drinking water standard has been violated, the supplier must move to correct the situation and must also notify the appropriate state agency of the violation. Customers must be notified also, usually by a notice in a newspaper, an announcement on radio or television, or a letter from the health department that supervises the water supplier. If the home is supplied with water from its own private well, laboratory testing of a water sample is the only way to determine if the water supply is contaminated. Should you suspect that water is contaminated, or if you wish to have water tested, contact local, county, or state health or environmental departments for information about qualified testing laboratories.

What can be done to decontaminate a home water supply?

If the home is supplied by an outside water supply source, federal law requires the provider to correct any contamination problems. When homes are supplied by private wells, analysis and treatment of the contaminated water may solve the problem.

What will it cost to decontaminate a home water supply?

Normally, consumers bear no direct financial responsibility for eliminating contamination from water supplied by an outside source (if the water was contaminated when it was delivered); the supplier bears the primary responsibility for correcting contamination problems. In the case of contaminated water supplied from a private well (or water from an outside source that becomes contaminated after it is received from the supplier), the cost of decontamination will depend on the kinds and amounts of contaminants present.

In the majority of cases, decontamination of a private water source involves technology and knowledge beyond the scope of the average homeowner. State and local environmental and water quality officials may be able to provide additional information and assistance for decontamination of private water sources.

What is being done about ground water contamination?

The U.S. Environmental Protection Agency has the lead responsibility for assuring the quality and safety of the nation's ground water supply. The EPA's approach is focused in two areas: minimizing the contamination of ground water and surface waters needed for human consumption and monitoring and treating drinking water before it is consumed.

In 1986, the U.S. Congress passed a set of amendments that expanded the protection provided by the Safe Drinking Water Act of 1974. These amendments streamlined the EPA's regulation of contaminants, banned all future use of lead pipe and lead solder in public drinking water systems, mandated greater protection of ground water sources, and authorized EPA to file civil suits or issue administrative orders against public water systems that are in violation of the Act.

Working with the states, EPA has set national standards for minimum levels of a number of contaminants and is mandated to set such standards for additional contaminants by 1991. In addition, EPA and the states are working to devise a national strategy for the monitoring and management of ground water supplies.

The following sources and publications provide additional information on ground water contamination.

Brochure

- *Is Your Drinking Water Safe?*

Available from:
U.S. Environmental Protection Agency
Public Information Center
401 M Street, SW
Washington, DC 20460
(202) 260-7751

Hotline

- *Safe Drinking Water Hotline*

  This Hotline provides information and publications to help the public and the regulated community understand EPA's drinking water regulations and programs. The Hotline operates Monday through Friday, 8:30 a.m. to 4:30 p.m., eastern time. (800) 426-4791; (202) 382-5533 (in the Washington, DC area)

FORMALDEHYDE

What is formaldehyde?

Formaldehyde is a colorless, gaseous chemical compound that is generally present at low, variable concentrations in both indoor and outdoor air. It is emitted by many construction materials and consumer products that contain formaldehyde-based glues, resins, preservatives, and bonding agents. Formaldehyde also is an ingredient in foam that was used for home insulating until the early 1980s.

Where is formaldehyde found in the home?

Sources of formaldehyde in the home include smoke, household products, and unvented fuel-burning appliances (like gas stoves or kerosene space heaters). Formaldehyde, by itself or in combination with other chemicals, serves a number of purposes in manufactured products. For example, it is used to add permanent-press qualities to clothing and draperies, as a component of glues and adhesives, and as a preservative in some paints and coating products.

In homes, the most significant sources of formaldehyde are likely to be in the adhesives used to bond pressed wood building materials and in plywood used for interior or exterior construction. Urea-formaldehyde (UF) resins are found in wood products that are intended for indoor use. Phenol-formaldehyde (PF) resins are used in products intended for exterior uses. UF resins emit significantly more formaldehyde gas than PF resins.

Certain foam insulating materials once widely used in housing construction (urea-formaldehyde foam or UFFI) also contain large amounts of formaldehyde. While contractors have voluntarily stopped using UFFI foam insulation, the material is present in many homes that were originally insulated with UFFI.

What health risks are associated with formaldehyde?

Formaldehyde has been shown to cause cancer in animals, but there is no definitive evidence linking the chemical to cancer in humans. Higher-than-normal levels of formaldehyde in the home atmosphere can trigger asthma attacks in individuals who have this condition. Other health hazards attributed to formaldehyde include skin rashes; watery eyes; burning sensations in the eyes, throat, and nasal passages; and breathing difficulties. Most persons will first react to formaldehyde when the levels are in the range of 0.1 to 1.1 parts per million. Some individuals acquire a reduced tolerance to formaldehyde following their initial exposure to the gas. In these instances, subsequent exposures to even small amounts of formaldehyde will cause reactions.

Do some kinds of homes carry a greater formaldehyde health risk than others?

Yes, materials containing formaldehyde were used extensively in the construction of certain prefabricated and manufactured homes. Since 1985, the federal government, through the U.S. Department of Housing and Urban Development, has enforced regulations that sharply curtail the use of materials containing formaldehyde in these types of housing to the lower-emitting products. However, use of formaldehyde compounds is still widespread in the manufacture of furniture, cabinets, and other building materials.

What can be done to reduce formaldehyde levels in a home?

Reducing formaldehyde levels in the home can be a simple or complex task depending on the source of the gas. Initial procedures often include steps to increase ventilation and improve circulation of outside air through the home. If new furniture, drapery, or other sources are contributing to higher-than-normal levels of formaldehyde, removal of these items (or limiting the number of new items introduced into the home) may be all that is needed.

In some instances, home subflooring or walls may be the source of formaldehyde, or foam insulation between inner and outer walls may be emitting the gas. If increased ventilation does not produce acceptable results in these instances, homeowners may be required to remove the formaldehyde-bearing material. Such procedures will be costly, time-consuming, and temporarily disruptive of life in the home.

How can I tell if the home I wish to buy contains formaldehyde-bearing materials?

In the case of a new home, you should consult with the builder before you purchase the house if you suspect the presence of materials that emit high levels of formaldehyde. Most builders will be able to tell you if construction materials contain urea-formaldehyde or they may direct you to manufacturers who can provide information about specific products. In the case of an older home, formaldehyde-emitting materials may not be visually evident and the current owners may not have specific product information. Because formaldehyde emissions from building materials decrease as the materials age (particularly over the first two or three years), older urea-formaldehyde building materials most probably will not be a significant source of formaldehyde emissions.

If you suspect the presence of formaldehyde, you may wish to hire a qualified building inspector to examine the home for the presence of formaldehyde-emitting materials. In addition, home monitoring kits are currently available for testing formaldehyde levels in the home. Be sure that the testing device will monitor for a minimum of 24 hours to ensure that the sampling period is truly representative.

The following sources and publications provide additional information about formaldehyde in the home.

Brochures

- *The Inside Story—A Guide to Indoor Air Quality*

Available from:
U.S. Environmental Protection Agency
Public Information Center
401 M Street, SW
Washington, DC 20460
(202) 260-7751

- *Air Pollution in Your Home*
- *Home Indoor Air Quality Checklist*

Available from:
Local chapters of the American Lung Association.

- *Formaldehyde: Everything You Wanted to Know But Were Afraid to Ask*

Send a self-addressed, stamped envelope to:
Consumer Federation of America
1424 Sixteenth Street, NW
Washington, DC 20036

SOURCES OF ADDITIONAL INFORMATION

The EPA operates a variety of telephone hotlines to provide the public with easy access to EPA's programs, capabilities, and services. In addition to the hotlines, EPA has a variety of clearinghouses, libraries, and dockets that may provide information about a broad range of environmental issues. Information related to all of these sources is published in the *Guide to EPA Hotlines, Clearinghouses, Libraries, and Dockets*, which is available from EPA's Public Information Center (401 M Street, SW, Washington, DC 20460).

The regional offices of the U.S. Environmental Protection Agency are perhaps the best sources of additional information about environmental hazards in specific states and local areas. Each EPA regional office has information on states and areas within a single geographic area.

EPA Region 5
230 South Dearborn Street
Chicago, IL 60604
(800) 621-8431

Areas served: Illinois, Indiana, Michigan, Minnesota, Ohio, and Wisconsin

APPENDIX C

Preparing for the Illinois Real Estate Exam

ASI/REAL PROGRAM	397
GENERAL CONTENT OUTLINE FOR EXAM	399
ILLINOIS CONTENT OUTLINE FOR EXAM (with text page references)	401
PRACTICE QUESTIONS FOR ILLINOIS PORTION OF EXAM	402

ASI/REAL Program

The staff of Assessment Systems, Inc. (ASI) has developed a Real Estate Assessment of Licensure (REAL) program for various states, including Illinois. The ASI program uses standard objective multiple-choice questions with four options. With its pool of national exam questions on general principles of real estate, this program constructs exams specifically designed to the practices and statutes of the subscribing state.

There are two examinations, one for broker license applicants and one for salesperson license applicants. The tests are continually revised so the questions reflect current real estate laws and practices. A content outline of a typical ASI Illinois test is given in Figure C.1.

The state portion of the test is based specifically on the license law and rules and regulations of the state of Illinois. The state portion of the test consists of 50 questions.

The uniform portion of the test, consists of 80 questions and covers a variety of subjects that are standard, or uniform, in all jurisdictions. The questions, and to some extent the subject areas, are different on the exams for salespersons and for brokers. To be successful, the applicant must pass both the state test and the uniform test. In case of failure, the applicant must retake only the failed section of the examination. An applicant who fails the exam three times must take a 15-hour refresher course or its equivalent in order to be eligible to retest.

The candidate will be graded on 130 questions (80 uniform and 50 Illinois specific), but will be required to answer 12 additional pretest questions. The pretest questions are interspersed throughout the test and are not identified as pretest questions. Candidates answering these questions correctly will not receive any credit and candidates answering incorrectly will not lose any credit. The pretest questions are on the test to evaluate the question itself making sure there are no problems with the questions. If statistical data indicates there could be a problem with a particular question, the question will be rewritten and tested again. Since other test takers have pretested the candidate's questions, the candidate can be assured of clear concise questions. There should be 7 uniform pretest questions and 5 Illinois pretest questions.

The examination must be completed within four hours. If the applicant is adequately prepared and does not waste time, the amount of time allowed is sufficient to complete the examination successfully.

A candidate handbook is available from the OBRE and from approved schools. You may make a reservation to take the exam by calling (800) 274-0404. (More information on reservations is provided in Chapter 16 of this text.)

Scores

The passing score required for the examination is established by the state of Illinois at 70 percent in both the uniform and state specific portion of the test. Testing is by electronic pad, and score reports are provided immediately at the test site. If an applicant is successful, the score report reads PASS, with no score given. If the applicant is not successful, the report states FAIL, gives the percentage correct, and also gives the results by subject area. Students passing one portion of the test (uniform or state specific) are required to retake only the portion failed. Results on the test subject areas are reported on a bar graph. This method of reporting the results enables the applicant to determine the subject area(s) on which to concentrate in preparing to retake the examination. Neither ASI nor licensing agencies provide for a review of test results with applicants.

How to Prepare for the Illinois Test

The ultimate goal of most students is to successfully complete the state licensing test. Preparation for the licensing test goes beyond the classroom study. To mentally prepare for the test, plan for and be aware of the test setting.

- Visit the test site a day in advance to locate parking, bathrooms, and vending machines.
- Visit the test site to determine the lighting and seating in the room; heat and air conditioning.
- Assemble, the night before, all test-related items—calculator (no solar or paper-printing calculators allowed), confirmation number, photo identification, watch, and cashier's check or money order.
- Arrive at the test site early.

How to Take the Test

The following are suggestions that should be beneficial in taking the exam:

1. During the test, budget your time. Take a break to avoid fatigue.
2. Carefully mark answers on the electronic pad.
3. Do not change answers unless you are absolutely sure you made an error. The first answer is usually best.
4. Read all choices before answering.
5. Read carefully; watch for words that may point to an answer.
6. Do not leave any answers blank. You have a chance of choosing the correct answer even if you guess, but there is no chance of that if you leave the question blank.

If you have been prepared for the class as a whole, have memorized the vocabulary, read the text, and self-tested, your results should be favorable.

FIGURE C.1 Content outline for Illinois ASI real estate examination.

**GENERAL CONTENT OUTLINE
SALESPERSON AND BROKER**

The general examination contains 80 test questions for salesperson and broker candidates that will be used to determine the candidate's score. The general test also contains pretest questions mixed in throughout the examination.

Approximately twenty percent (20%) of the questions involve arithmetical calculations. These questions are distributed throughout the test.

Salesperson 22%, Broker 20%
  I. **Real Property**
      A. Definitions and Components
          1. Elements of Real Property
          2. Methods of Legal Description
          3. Estates in Real Property
          4. Forms of Ownership
      B. Transfer/Alienation of Real Property
          1. Voluntary
          2. Involuntary
          3. Deeds
              a. Types
              b. Characteristics/elements
              c. Warranties
      C. Assurance of Title
      D. Land Use Controls
          1. Public
          2. Private/Covenants, Conditions and Restrictions (CC & R's)
      E. Encumbrances
          1. Types and Priority of Liens
          2. Easements
          3. Encroachments

Salesperson 9%, Broker 14%
  II. **Government Controls and Law Affecting Real Estate**
      A. Real Property Tax Computations
      B. Income Tax Considerations and Computations
          1. Owner-occupied property
          2. Investment property
          3. Other income tax considerations (refinance, capital gains on sale)
      C. Federal Fair Housing
      D. Americans With Disabilities Act

Salesperson 13%, Broker 13%
  III. **Valuation and Appraisal**
      A. Types of Value
      B. Principles of Value
      C. Influences on Value
      D. Approaches to Value
      E. Appraisal Process

(continued)

FIGURE C.1 Continued.

Salesperson 20%, Broker 15%

IV. **Real Estate Finance**
    A. Finance Components
        1. Sources
            a. Primary mortgage market
            b. Secondary mortgage market
        2. Elements/Provisions
        3. Loan Types
        4. Instruments
            a. Notes
            b. Mortgages
            c. Contract for deed (land contract)
            d. Deeds of trust
    B. Lender Requirements
    C. Truth in Lending (Regulation Z)
    D. Other Financing Issues

Salesperson 10%, Broker 12%

V. **Settlement/Closing**
    A. Settlement Procedures
    B. Documents
    C. Real Estate Settlement & Procedures Act-RESPA
    D. Closing Costs/Prorations

Salesperson 26%, Broker 26%

VI. **Contracts/Agency**
    A. Types/Characteristics
    B. Elements/Requirements
    C. Listing Contracts
        1. Types
        2. Rights and Obligations of the Parties
        3. Specific Property Data
        4. Termination/Expiration
    D. Purchase/Sales Contracts
    E. Property Management Contracts
        1. Management Contracts
        2. Leases/Rental Agreements
    F. Agency Relationships and Responsibilities
    G. Disclosures
        1. Property
        2. Agency
        3. Environmental
        4. Federal Fair Housing

Practice Questions for Illinois Portion of Exam

Practice Questions for Illinois Portion of Exam

1. After passing the Illinois real estate licensing exam, the candidate will have:
   a. 1 month to get a real estate license
   b. 6 months to get a real estate license
   c. 1 year to get a real estate license
   d. 5 years to get a real estate license

2. When unlicensed persons engage in the practice of real estate they may:
   a. have a cease and desist action filed against them
   b. be disciplined by the board
   c. continue until a member of the public is harmed by their action
   d. be found guilty of a felony for a first offense

3. Salesperson Victor was found guilty of a violation of section 18 of the Illinois Real Estate License Act. Victor faces a civil penalty of as much as:
   a. $100
   b. $1,000
   c. $10,000
   d. $25,000

4. All of the following persons are exempt from licensing EXCEPT:
   a. a private owner selling or renting her own property
   b. a person acting under a court order
   c. a not-for-profit multiple listing service
   d. a person negotiating a sale for another person for a fee

5. A sponsor card may be issued to a person who:
   a. has taken and passed the real estate course
   b. has a license that has lapsed for over five years
   c. has a valid, inoperative license
   d. has a suspended license

6. All of the following are requirements for license renewal EXCEPT:
   a. completion of 30-hour licensing course
   b. payment of the proper fees
   c. proof of 12 hours of continuing education
   d. a license that has not been inoperative for more than five years

7. Which of the following statements is true about the Real Estate Recovery Fund?
   a. five dollars from each renewal fee is deposited in the Real Estate Recovery Fund
   b. licensees may seek recovery of a commission from the Recovery Fund
   c. fines and penalties are deposited in the Recovery Fund
   d. one dollar of each ten deposited goes toward a minority scholarship

8. Broker Susan is offering a $50 savings bond to sellers who list with her brokerage firm within the next 30 days. Which of the following is true?
   a. Susan cannot advertise an offer of inducement of any kind under any circumstances
   b. Susan may advertise the offer but must disclose in the advertisement the condition to be met
   c. Susan will have to give a $50 savings bond to all her sellers
   d. Susan can offer a trip or other item as an inducement, but money in any form cannot be offered

9. All of the following relationships are true regarding a broker and his salespersons EXCEPT:
   a. he cannot have agents representing both buyers and sellers in the same office
   b. he must have a written employment contract with each salesperson
   c. he is responsible for the actions of his salespersons
   d. he can give his salespersons permission to advertise their own listings

10. Salesperson Tom of Booker Realty was the designated agent of Buyer Frieda. Tom shared with Broker Ling of Winning Realty a commission paid by Seller Terry. Which of the following is true of Tom receiving part of the commission?
    a. it was proper if disclosure of such payment was made to Frieda
    b. it was proper if Tom was paid directly by Broker Ling
    c. it was improper because Frieda is required to pay her designated agent
    d. designated agents cannot share commissions

11. The Olins want an agent from Fair Share Realty to help them negotiate an offer on a property listed by First Star Real Estate. What is Broker Maria from Fair Share Realty most likely to do?
    a. refer the Olins to an office that offers buyer's brokerage only
    b. designate an agent in her office as the Olin's legal representative
    c. work with the Olins on a customer basis
    d. send the Olins to an agent in First Star Real Estate

12. Mr. and Mrs. Price told their designated agent, Anna, that they would be willing to sell their property below the list price. In seeking the assistance of her broker, Anna shared this information with him. Which of the following is true?
    a. Anna was guilty of sharing confidential information without the permission of the Prices
    b. Anna was guilty of sharing confidential information with her broker
    c. license law allows agents to share confidential information with their brokers
    d. license law allows agents to share confidential information with anyone

13. An agency relationship can be created or established by all of the following EXCEPT:
    a. written agreement
    b. oral agreement
    c. action of the parties
    d. payment of a commission

14. Confidential information:
    a. can be shared between designated agents and their brokers
    b. should be obtained by agents from customers
    c. can never be shared by licensees under any circumstances
    d. may always be disclosed in writing to customers

15. Broker Barstow offers dual agency at his brokerage. Which of the following is true?
    a. he is always acting as a dual agent in all transactions
    b. he can never offer single agency in his brokerage firm
    c. he can designate an agent to represent both the buyer and seller in the same transaction
    d. he will always collect a commission from both the buyer and the seller

16. A person who is being represented by a licensee is:
    a. a client
    b. a customer
    c. an agent
    d. a broker

17. A designated agent is one who:
    a. only represents sellers
    b. only represents buyers
    c. should not be given confidential information
    d. is the legal agent of a client

18. Which of the following is NOT a ministerial act?
    a. answering questions at an open house
    b. describing the condition of a property
    c. referring a customer to another broker
    d. providing a customer with confidential information

19. At the time a consumer enters into a brokerage agreement, a broker offering dual agency is required to advise the consumer of all the following EXCEPT:
    a. the designated agency relationship
    b. any other types of agency relationship available
    c. need for consent for a dual agency
    d. the amount of compensation the agent will be receiving

20. Which of the following statements is NOT true?
    a. customers should be advised before or at the time of the preparation of an offer that the agent is not working on their behalf
    b. consumers should be advised at the time of entering into a brokerage agreement of the name(s) of their designated agent(s)
    c. clients should be made aware of the designated agency relationship and other agency relationships that the broker offers
    d. brokers are considered dual agents if one of their designated agents is representing both the buyer and seller in the same transaction

21. Stigmatized properties are those properties that have been:
    a. on the market for longer than a year
    b. the site of a criminal activity
    c. found to have material defects
    d. resold within a six-month time period

22. The Quinlan and Tyson decision concerned the issue of:
    a. prohibiting brokers from practicing law by the drafting of contracts
    b. designating agents in a brokerage as the legal agent of either the buyer or the seller
    c. sharing a commission with a broker from another brokerage firm
    d. negotiating on behalf of buyers

23. Illinois recognizes all of the following forms of real property ownership EXCEPT:
    a. joint tenancy
    b. tenancy by the entirety
    c. community property
    d. condominium

24. A benefit of placing title to land in a trust is:
    a. concealment of the name of the beneficiary
    b. protection from building ordinance violations
    c. elimination of taxation on income from the property in the land trust
    d. reduction in property taxes

25. When a property's delinquent taxes are sold at a tax sale:
    a. the owner loses title to the property at the sale of the taxes
    b. the buyer gains title to the property immediately
    c. the buyer gains the right to collect interest on the unpaid taxes
    d. the owner cannot redeem the property after the sale of the taxes

26. One-half of the income the state receives from the title transfer tax is allotted to the:
    a. Illinois Affordable Housing program
    b. Responsible Property Transfer Act
    c. Minority Scholarship program
    d. Real EstateRecovery Fund

27. Persons wishing to sell timeshares in Illinois must:
    a. hold an Illinois broker's license
    b. reside in Illinois
    c. register with the Illinois Secretary of State
    d. provide a public offering statement

28. In an intermediate theory state such as Illinois:
    a. the title is transferred via a deed of trust to a trustee
    b. the owner holds legal title, subject to the lien created by the mortgage
    c. the loan simply creates a lien against the property used as security for the debt
    d. the lender is the holder of the title to the mortgaged property

29. In Illinois, when the mortgagor defaults on a mortgage, the mortgagee has the right to:
    a. take title to the mortgaged property at the time of the default
    b. bring a lawsuit against the borrower and obtain a judgment for the amount of the debt
    c. advertise and sell the property and retain the proceeds of the sale as repayment of the debt
    d. evict persons in possession of the property, rent the property, and retain proceeds

30. The Residential Real Property Disclosure Act requires that all sellers of residential property must provide prospective buyers with:
    a. proof of a recent property inspection
    b. a warranty regarding the property's major systems, such as plumbing and heating
    c. written disclosure regarding certain aspects of the property
    d. receipts for all major purchases and appliances

31. The Washingtons, prospective buyers of the Olivers' residential property, did not receive written notice of the fact that the furnace was in need of repair until after the acceptance of their offer to purchase. The Washingtons:
    a. may not terminate the contract, because their offer to purchase has been accepted
    b. may terminate the contract, if they do so within three business days of receiving the notice
    c. must terminate the contract because they received written notice of a material defect
    d. may terminate the contract now or at any time up to one week after the property is conveyed to them by the sellers

32. Broker Simpson, owner of a small real estate firm, does not maintain a special account for the escrow funds he receives but places these funds in his operating account. Which of the following is true?

   a. Simpson is guilty of commingling
   b. Simpson is guilty of conversion
   c. Simpson may use the operating account for escrow funds if he has the written consent of all parties
   d. Because Simpson's real estate firm is small, he does not need to maintain a special account

33. Withdrawals for special accounts take place at the direction of:

   a. the broker
   b. all parties to the transaction
   c. the designated agent
   d. the buyer

34. A resident manager is:

   a. required by the license law to hold a real estate license
   b. employed by the owner or managing broker and lives on the premises
   c. the actual owner of the property being managed
   d. a certified property manager

35. Broker Anthony moved his real estate business into an office where an insurance company was doing business. Which is true concerning the Office of Banks and Real Estate?

   a. Anthony was required to notify the OBRE before moving his office
   b. Anthony was guilty of a moving violation of the Illinois Real Estate License Act if he did not notify the OBRE
   c. The OBRE will allow a real estate office to operate in an insurance office if the two businesses are distinctly separate
   d. The OBRE will not allow a real estate office to operate in an insurance office under any circumstances

36. Janice, an owner of real property, died without preparing a valid will. Janice was a single adult without any children or siblings. How will her property be disposed of?

   a. Janice's surviving parents will each receive one part
   b. Janice's property will escheat to the state
   c. Janice's property will be shared equally by her parents and their siblings
   d. Janice's property will be sold at auction

37. The preparation of a valid will in Illinois requires all of the following EXCEPT:

   a. the will must be witnessed by two or more persons
   b. the will must by signed by the maker of the will
   c. the maker must be of sound mind and at least 18 years of age
   d. the will must be recorded to be valid

38. Seller Swenson refused to sell his home, listed with Broker Anderson, to a woman because she was single. Seller Swenson's refusal to sell on that basis is:

   a. a violation of the Federal Fair Housing Act
   b. a violation of the Illinois Human Rights Act
   c. not a violation of either the federal or state act
   d. a violation of both the federal and state fair housing laws

39. The Illinois homestead exemption:

   a. does not apply to unmarried persons
   b. protects a limited amount from all creditors
   c. will not exist unless applied for each year
   d. can be waived in writing with the signature of an individual or both spouses

40. Which of the following statements is true regarding continuing education for license renewal?

   a. all licensees must show proof of successful completion of 12 hours of continuing education
   b. broker licensees must show proof of successful completion of 12 hours of mandatory continuing education courses
   c. the only licensees who are exempt from continuing education for license renewal are attorneys who have been admitted to practice law before the Illinois Supreme Court
   d. licensees who are not exempt must show proof of successful completion of 12 hours of continuing education courses

APPENDIX D

Practice Exam 1

1. A salesperson associated with Lighthouse Realty effects a sale of property listed in the MLS with a universal offer of subagency by Point Hazard Realty. In this transaction the salesperson is a subagent of which of the following?

    a. seller
    b. Lighthouse Realty
    c. buyer
    d. seller and buyer

2. All of the following statements about agency are correct EXCEPT:

    a. the principal is responsible for acts of his agent while engaged in activities concerning the agency
    b. the agent is in a fiduciary relationship to her principal
    c. the agent in a real estate listing is usually the seller
    d. the principal has a duty to cooperate with the agent

3. If a salesperson lists and sells a property for $90,000 and receives 60% of the 7% commission paid to her employing broker, how much does the salesperson receive?

    a. $2,520
    b. $3,780
    c. $5,400
    d. $6,300

4. Sara Seller is satisfied with all of the terms of an offer to purchase her property from Bill Buyer except the date of possession, which she changes from April 9 to April 10. Which of the following is correct?

    a. Sara's acceptance creates a valid contract
    b. Sara cannot make a counteroffer
    c. Sara can always accept Bill Buyer's original offer if the April 10th date is not accepted
    d. Sara has rejected Bill Buyer's offer

5. A salesperson sold one-quarter of the southeast quarter of section 12 for $1,800 per acre. If the salesperson's commission was 60% of the 10% commission her broker received, how much did the salesperson earn?

    a. $2,880
    b. $4,320
    c. $11,520
    d. $17,280

6. At the time of listing a property, the owner specifies that he wishes to net $65,000 after satisfying a mortgage of $25,000 and paying a 7% brokerage fee. For what price should the property be listed?

    a. $90,000
    b. $94,550
    c. $96,300
    d. $96,774

407

7. When an option is exercised, it becomes which of the following?
   a. lease
   b. offer
   c. multiple listing
   d. contract of sale

8. An agreement that is a financing instrument and a contract of sale is called a(n):
   a. option
   b. lease
   c. contract for deed
   d. exclusive agency

9. A real estate broker sells a tract of land (described in the figure below) for $1,600 per acre and earns a 9% commission. How much does the broker receive? (answers rounded)
   a. $661
   b. $952
   c. $992
   d. $1,983

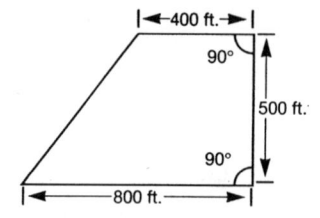

10. A lease agreement in which the landlord accepts another tenant and relieves the vacating tenant of any liability is:
    a. novation
    b. assignment
    c. accord and satisfaction
    d. carryover contract

11. Which of the following is a key word used to determine whether a real estate broker is or is not legally entitled to a commission?
    a. acceptance
    b. accountability
    c. assignment
    d. assumption

12. Buyer Berta makes an offer to purchase seller Steve's land if she also decides to buy another tract that adjoins his land. Which of the following describes Berta's offer?
    a. indefinite
    b. illusory
    c. unilateral
    d. fraudulent

13. Failure to comply with the terms of an offer as to the manner of communicating acceptance will result in which of the following?
    a. termination of the offer
    b. extension of the offer
    c. acceptance of the offer
    d. duress

14. The party who assigns a contract interest to another is the:
    a. grantor
    b. assignee
    c. assignor
    d. grantee

15. From the standpoint of both the agent and the seller, the best type of listing contract is:
    a. open
    b. exclusive agency
    c. net
    d. exclusive right to sell

16. In making an FHA-insured loan of $45,000, a lending institution charges sufficient discount points to increase the yield on the loan from 9% to 9¾%. The cost of the points is:
    a. $1,350
    b. $1,800
    c. $2,700
    d. $5,400

17. If the monthly payment on a $60,000 fully amortizing mortgage loan at 12% APR for a 20-year term is $660.65, how much is the principal reduced by the first monthly payment?
    a. $60.65
    b. $72.00
    c. $600.00
    d. $612.20

18. Hypothecate most nearly means:
    a. selling real estate
    b. pledging real estate as collateral for a loan
    c. leasing real estate
    d. giving an easement

19. The monthly payment of principal and interest on a 30-year mortgage at 10% for $40,000 is $351.03. How much interest will the borrower pay over the 30-year term?
    a. $40,000
    b. $86,371
    c. $126,371
    d. $160,000

20. Which of the following most accurately describes the major purpose of a mortgage or a deed of trust?
    a. to secure the payment of a note
    b. to convey a title to the trustee
    c. to provide for equity of redemption
    d. to prevent assumption

21. The acceleration clause provides for which of the following?
    a. equity of redemption
    b. prepayment penalty
    c. right of lender to require immediate payment of principal balance when borrower is in default
    d. alienation by borrower

22. Which of the following liens takes priority over mortgage foreclosure sale proceeds?
    a. mortgage lien
    b. income tax lien
    c. real property tax lien
    d. mechanic's lien

23. An alienation clause makes a mortgage:
    a. defeasible
    b. unassumable
    c. incontestable
    d. adjustable

24. A lending institution's sharing in the appreciation in value of property and sharing in the equity of property is called:
    a. shared appreciation mortgage
    b. amortization
    c. liquidation
    d. hypothecation

25. All of the following may be required prepaid items by the mortgagee EXCEPT:
    a. real property taxes
    b. hazard insurance
    c. property owner's assessment
    d. broker's commission

26. FHA requires which of the following documents to be signed by borrowers purchasing a home built before 1978?
    a. commission disclosure form
    b. lead-based paint test results disclosure
    c. lead-based paint information disclosure
    d. Fair Housing Disclosure form

27. Which of the following is a way in which a veteran borrower can have eligibility fully restored?
    a. sell the property on contract
    b. sell the property to a nonveteran who assumes the VA-guaranteed loan
    c. dispose of the property and pay off the VA-guaranteed loan
    d. lease the property with an option to buy

28. The financing arrangement in which the borrower and lender hold equitable title to the real estate and a disinterested third party holds legal title is:
    a. deed of trust
    b. note
    c. junior mortgage
    d. contract for deed

29. Nonjudicial foreclosure occurs in:
    a. friendly foreclosure
    b. foreclosure by action
    c. strict foreclosure
    d. foreclosure under power of sale

30. Minor changes to a signed accepted offer to purchase require each amendment or change to be initialed by:
    a. all parties
    b. buyer only
    c. broker and seller
    d. seller only

31. A blanket mortgage usually contains which of the following?
    a. closed-end clause
    b. release clauses
    c. good faith estimate
    d. due-on-sale clause

32. Which is the true statement regarding FHA loan assumptions?
    a. buyers must always qualify
    b. the need for buyer qualification depends on date of original loan origination
    c. FHA loans are not assumable
    d. buyers need not qualify

33. Which of the following regulates the advertisement of credit terms available for a house offered for sale?
    a. RESPA
    b. Fannie Mae
    c. Equal Credit Opportunity Act
    d. Regulation Z

34. Which of the following is limited to purchasing FHA-insured and VA-guaranteed mortgages?
    a. Fannie Mae
    b. Freddie Mac
    c. Maggie Mae
    d. Ginnie Mae

35. If a lease specifies the rent to be 2% of the gross sales per annum, with a minimum annual rent of $8,000, what is the annual rent if gross sales are $1,200,000?
    a. $8,000
    b. $12,000
    c. $24,000
    d. $28,000

36. Which of the following provides the grantee with the greatest assurance of title?
    a. special warranty deed
    b. deed of gift
    c. general warranty deed
    d. grant deed

37. Which of the following is a benefit of recording a deed?
    a. it prevents any liens from being filed against the property
    b. it protects the grantee against the grantee's creditors
    c. it protects the grantee against future conveyances by the grantor
    d. it makes a mortgage lien subordinate

38. Which of the following requires the grantor to execute a deed of confirmation if needed?
    a. covenant of seisin
    b. covenant for further assurances
    c. covenant against encumbrances
    d. covenant of right to convey

39. Which of the following statements about the rollover rule is correct?
    a. it is mandatory if the transaction qualifies
    b. it may be used only once in a lifetime
    c. it allows exemption of the gain from tax
    d. it applies only if the real estate was a principal residence five of the last eight years

40. All of the following are rights of a life tenant EXCEPT:
    a. encumber
    b. use
    c. alienate
    d. waste

41. Which of the following statements is correct?
    a. an easement provides right of possession
    b. an easement in gross has no servient tenement
    c. an easement is a fixture to real estate
    d. an appurtenant easement can be obtained by necessity

42. If the market value of a property is $90,000, the tax rate is 90 mills, and the assessment is 70%, what is the amount of the annual tax bill?
    a. $567
    b. $5,670
    c. $7,000
    d. $8,100

43. The owner(s) of real property may hold title in all of the following ways EXCEPT:
    a. tenants in common
    b. lessees
    c. severalty
    d. joint tenants

44. A claim, lien, charge, or liability attached to and binding upon real property is a(n):
    a. encumbrance
    b. community property
    c. license
    d. syndication

45. An owner of a condominium office:
   a. has a proprietary lease
   b. is assessed by the property owners association for maintenance to his office unit
   c. may pledge his property as security for a mortgage loan
   d. owns a share of stock in the corporation that owns the real estate

46. Timesharing is commonly associated with which of the following?
   a. cooperatives
   b. profits
   c. joint ventures
   d. condominiums

47. Which of the following clauses in an accepted offer to purchase protects the buyer from losing her earnest money in the event financing is not obtained?
   a. habendum
   b. contingency
   c. defeasance
   d. subordination

48. The Fair Housing Act of 1968 prohibits discrimination in the rental of all of the following EXCEPT:
   a. offices
   b. apartments
   c. houses
   d. residential lots

49. The Fair Housing Act of 1968 prohibits all of the following EXCEPT:
   a. discriminatory advertising
   b. use of brokerage services
   c. steering
   d. redlining

50. Inducing an owner to list property by telling the owner that people of a certain national origin are moving into the neighborhood is called:
   a. steering
   b. redlining
   c. blockbusting
   d. profiteering

51. Exemptions to the Fair Housing Act of 1988 are lost by all of the following EXCEPT:
   a. use of discriminatory advertising
   b. use of a broker
   c. use of a sign that states "Room for Rent"
   d. use of a REALTOR®

52. A property manager's fee usually consists of a base fee plus:
   a. a percentage of the rental income received
   b. a percentage of the gross potential income
   c. a percentage of the net income
   d. a percentage of the stabilized budget

53. When a lessee installs trade fixtures, these are:
   a. a permanent part of the real estate
   b. owned by the lessor
   c. the personal property of the lessee
   d. real property

54. A person living on the managed premises as a salaried employee engaged to manage and lease apartments is called a(n):
   a. property manager
   b. rental agent
   c. employee manager
   d. resident manager

55. The monthly accounting by the property manager is called a:
   a. stabilized budget
   b. property management report
   c. management budget
   d. financial report

56. All of the following are required of property managers EXCEPT:
   a. showing and leasing property
   b. deciding owner's objectives
   c. collecting rent
   d. providing for the protection of tenants

57. A buyer assumes a seller's existing 11%, $80,000 first deed of trust on the settlement date of June 12. The seller makes the monthly payment on June 1 with interest in advance. Which of the following is a correct settlement statement entry for the interest?
   a. $293.28 buyer's credit
   b. $439.92 seller's credit
   c. $293.28 seller's debit
   d. $439.92 seller's debit

58. Which of the following types of listing contracts gives the broker commission entitlement if anyone sells the listed property during the listing term?
   a. net
   b. open
   c. exclusive agency
   d. exclusive right to sell

59. A real estate salesperson advises a prospective buyer that the property the buyer is considering is scheduled for annexation into the city limits. This disclosure constitutes which of the following?
   a. disloyalty to principal
   b. misrepresentation
   c. required disclosure to buyer
   d. violation of disclosure of information by salesperson

60. After inspecting a property, the prospective buyer tells the salesperson that she likes the property but will not pay the listed price of $75,000. Knowing that the owner is anxious to sell, the salesperson suggests that the prospective buyer make an offer of $70,000. Which of the following statements about this situation is correct?
   a. the salesperson is violating his obligation as a special agent
   b. because the salesperson knows the owner is anxious to sell, he is acting correctly
   c. the salesperson is violating his obligations as a universal agent
   d. the prospective buyer can be found guilty of conversion

61. A salesperson receives two offers for a listed property within a 10-minute period. One offer is 2% less than the listed price, and the other is 6% less than the listed price. The salesperson should present to the seller:
   a. neither offer
   b. both offers
   c. the highest offer
   d. the first offer

62. Closing on a commercial property is April 18. The seller had paid real property taxes in the amount of $5,760 for the tax year that began June 1 of the previous year. Which of the following is the correct closing statement entry for taxes?
   a. $672 buyer's credit
   b. $5,088 buyer's credit
   c. $672 seller's credit
   d. $5,088 seller's credit

63. The amount of a purchase money mortgage appears in the closing statement as:
   a. seller's credit only
   b. buyer's debit only
   c. seller's debit; buyer's credit
   d. seller's credit; buyer's debit

64. A seller paid an annual hazard insurance premium of $540 for a policy effective February 12. At settlement on April 16 of the same year, the buyer purchased the policy from the seller. This transaction is correctly entered on the settlement statements as:
   a. $96 buyer's credit
   b. $444 buyer's credit
   c. $96 seller's credit
   d. $444 seller's credit

65. The amount of earnest money appears on closing statements as a:
   a. credit to buyer
   b. debit to seller
   c. credit to seller
   d. debit to buyer

66. When listing real property for sale, a real estate broker:
   a. does a competitive market analysis
   b. makes an appraisal to estimate market value
   c. estimates residual income
   d. correlates reproduction cost

67. An apartment building produces an annual net income of $10,800 after deducting $72 per month for expenses. What price for the property would provide a buyer with a net return of 12%?
   a. $90,000
   b. $97,200
   c. $116,641
   d. $129,600

68. An apartment building contains 30 units. Each unit rents for $200 per month. The vacancy rate is 4%. Annual expenses are $3,000 for maintenance, $1,100 insurance, $1,600 taxes, $1,200 utilities, and 15% of the gross effective income for management fee. What is the investor's net rate of return for the first year if he paid $260,000 for the property?
    a. 6.69%
    b. 11.64%
    c. 14.94%
    d. 19.94%

69. If a rental property provides the owner with an 11% return on her investment of $780,000, what is the net annual income from the property?
    a. $70,512
    b. $70,909
    c. $85,800
    d. $141,025

70. Which of the following methods is used to estimate the value of the land only, on which an apartment building is to be located the next year?
    a. cost approach
    b. income approach
    c. market data approach
    d. replacement cost

71. Gross rent multipliers are used in connection with which of the following?
    a. condominiums
    b. schools
    c. vacant land
    d. income property

72. Adherence to which of the following has the effect of maximizing land value?
    a. principle of contribution
    b. principle of change
    c. principle of anticipation
    d. principle of highest and best use

73. Which of the following statements about zoning is correct?
    a. in exclusive-use zoning, property may be used only for the uses specified for that specific zoned area
    b. if a nonconforming structure is destroyed, it may be replaced by another nonconforming structure
    c. all nonconforming uses are illegal
    d. a preexisting nonconforming use requires a variance

74. Restrictive covenants are:
    a. conditions
    b. encumbrances
    c. public land use controls
    d. zoning classifications

75. When land is torn away by the violent action of a river it is called:
    a. erosion
    b. avulsion
    c. reliction
    d. alluvion

76. The characteristic of land that has the greatest effect on land value is:
    a. nonhomogeneity
    b. location
    c. indestructibility
    d. immobility

77. All of the following are examples of public land use controls EXCEPT:
    a. deed restrictions
    b. building codes
    c. zoning
    d. environmental control laws

78. An estate created for the life of a person other than the life tenant is called a life estate:
    a. in remainder
    b. pur autre vie
    c. by dower
    d. in reversion

79. Freehold estates that are not inheritable are called:
    a. defeasible estates
    b. leasehold estates
    c. life estates
    d. fee simple estates

80. Which of the following is a right in the land of another by the owner of adjoining land?
    a. profit
    b. easement appurtenant
    c. license
    d. easement in gross

81. A trespass on the land of another as a result of an intrusion by some structure or other object is an:
    a. encroachment
    b. easement
    c. estate
    d. emblement

82. Easements may be created in all of the following ways EXCEPT:
    a. prescription
    b. condemnation
    c. lis pendens
    d. dedication

83. An owner lists her property with three brokerage firms. In each case she retains the right to sell the property herself without being obligated to pay a commission to any of the brokers. The type of listing contract given to each broker is called:
    a. exclusive right to sell
    b. open
    c. multiple
    d. net

84. As a result of a salesperson's negligence in filling in the provisions in a contract of sale, the seller incurs a financial loss. Liability for this loss may be imposed on:
    a. both the salesperson and the employing broker
    b. the salesperson's employing broker only
    c. the salesperson only
    d. neither party

85. A contract for deed or installment land contract is a(n):
    a. contingent proposition
    b. offer to purchase
    c. form of financing instrument and contract for sale
    d. option to purchase

86. All of the following are remedies available to a party to a contract upon breach of the contract EXCEPT:
    a. specific performance
    b. liquidated damages
    c. estoppel
    d. compensatory damages

87. A gift of real property at death is a(n):
    a. devise
    b. bequest
    c. escheat
    d. demise

88. Of the following types of deeds, which provides the grantee with the LEAST assurance of title?
    a. bargain and sale
    b. quitclaim
    c. grant
    d. special warranty

89. Recording protects which of the following parties?
    a. grantor
    b. seller
    c. vendor
    d. grantee

90. All of the following are rights of a mortgagor EXCEPT:
    a. defeasance
    b. foreclosure
    c. equity of redemption
    d. possession

91. Which of the following gives the mortgagee the right to declare the entire principal balance immediately due and payable if the mortgagor is in default?
    a. acceleration clause
    b. alienation clause
    c. statutory foreclosure clause
    d. assignment clause

92. Using the amortization schedule on page 168, determine which of the following is the monthly payment of principal and interest required to fully amortize a $50,000, twenty-year mortgage loan at 9.5% interest:
    a. $357.14
    b. $466.07
    c. $512.18
    d. $592.50

93. Which of the following provides the highest loan-to-value ratio?
    a. conventional
    b. FHA 245
    c. 95% insured conventional
    d. FHA 203B

94. On June 16, a seller closes on the sale of her home. Annual taxes of $861 for the current year were paid in full by the seller prior to the sale. If these payments are prorated, which amount will be returned to the seller?
    a. $357
    b. $397
    c. $430
    d. $464

95. If the GIM is 7.5 and the annual gross income is $250,000, what is the estimated property value?
    a. $1,875,000
    b. $2,500,000
    c. $3,000,000
    d. $3,333,000

96. Restrictive covenants are:
    a. private land use controls
    b. public land use controls
    c. variances
    d. statements of record

97. A right granted to a lessee to purchase a property if the owner decides to sell, where no price is established and no specific sum is paid for the right, is a(n):
    a. option
    b. right to the obligor
    c. defeasance clause
    d. right of first refusal

98. All of the following statements about the age-55-and-over exclusion are correct EXCEPT:
    a. it may be taken only once in a lifetime
    b. it is available to co-owners
    c. it is up to $125,000
    d. it is available on commercial property

99. In a tax-deferred exchange, which of the following is taxable in the year of sale?
    a. like-kind property
    b. boot
    c. exchange property
    d. salvage value

100. A salesperson licensee may receive commissions from which of the following?
    a. cooperating broker
    b. buyer
    c. seller
    d. employing broker

APPENDIX E

Practice Exam 2

1. Mary Seaver, a salesperson associated with Leisure Homes Realty, advised a seller that his property would sell for at least $150,000. Relying on this price quotation, the seller listed the property at a price of $150,000. Comparable sales and listings of competitive properties at the time were in the range of $105,000 to $110,000. The seller refused several offers between $106,000 and $112,000 during the 120-day term of the listing contract. The seller eventually sold his property for $98,000 because of depressed economic conditions since expiration of the listing with Leisure Homes. Which of the following statements about these events is true?

   a. Mary has done nothing wrong and thus is not liable for any damage
   b. because Mary is an agent of Leisure Homes Realty, Leisure Homes is the only party that may be held liable for the seller's damages
   c. Mary committed an act of misrepresentation and may be liable for the resulting financial loss the seller incurred
   d. because the seller did not sell the property during the listing period, Mary is entitled to a commission

2. While a broker was inspecting a property for listing, the property owner told the broker that the house contains 2,400 square feet of heated living area. Without verifying this information, the broker listed the property and represented it to prospective buyers as containing 2,400 square feet. After purchasing the property, the buyer accurately determined that the house has only 1,850 square feet and sued for damages for the difference in value between 2,400 square feet and 1,850 square feet. Which of the following is correct?

   a. the broker is not liable because he relied on the seller's positive statement as to the square footage
   b. the seller is not liable because the broker, not the seller, represented the property to the buyer as containing 2,400 square feet
   c. the theory of caveat emptor applies; thus, neither the seller nor the broker is liable to the buyer
   d. both the broker and the seller are liable to the buyer

3. The sales associates of Executive Realty, Ltd., obtained several excellent listings in Exclusive Estates by advising homeowners that a number of Chinese families were moving into Exclusive Estates and therefore their property values would be substantially depressed. This activity is most accurately described as:

   a. steering
   b. blockbusting
   c. soliciting
   d. redlining

417

4. A real estate salesperson earned $48,000 in commissions in one year. If she received 60% of the 6% her broker received, what was her average monthly sales volume?
   a. $66,666
   b. $80,000
   c. $111,111
   d. $133,333

5. The type of listing contract that is most beneficial to the broker and the seller is:
   a. exclusive right to sell
   b. net
   c. open
   d. exclusive agency

6. A real estate broker is responsible for all of the following EXCEPT:
   a. acts of sales associates while engaged in brokerage activities
   b. appropriate handling of funds in trust, or escrow, accounts
   c. adhering to commission schedule recommended by the local board of REALTORS®
   d. representing property honestly, fairly, and accurately to prospective buyers

7. A triangular tract of land is 8,000 feet long and has highway frontage of 4,000 yards. If Ajax Realty Company lists this property at 9% commission and sells it for $1,600 per acre, what amount of commission does Ajax receive?
   a. $105,785
   b. $158,678
   c. $218,160
   d. $317,355

8. When listing a home for sale, the broker advises the seller that because he owns only one house, the listing is exempt from prohibitions of the Fair Housing Act of 1968. Which of the following statements about the broker's advice is true?
   a. the broker is acting correctly in advising the seller about the exemption
   b. the broker always should give good legal advice to sellers and buyers
   c. the broker is in error because the exemption is from the Civil Rights Act of 1866
   d. the broker is acting incorrectly in that the property is not exempt because the seller is using a broker

9. A broker deposited a buyer's check for earnest money in the amount of $6,000 in her escrow account. Prior to the closing and at the seller's request, the broker took $1,200 from the escrow account to pay for the cost of damage repairs caused by termites in the house. This expense was necessary so the seller could provide the required termite certificate to the buyer at the closing. Which of the following statements about this transaction is correct?
   a. because the $1,200 disbursement from the broker's escrow account was made at the seller's request and benefitted both buyer and seller, the broker acted properly
   b. the broker's action constituted an act of commingling and, as such, was improper
   c. the broker's action was not proper and constituted collusion
   d. the broker's action was not proper without the buyer's agreement

10. A salesperson associated with Metro Realty, Inc., obtained an offer for a property listed by Preferred Real Estate Company, which she gave to Sam Slicker, the listing agent with Preferred, for presentation to the property owner. Realizing that the amount of the offer was such that it probably would not be accepted, Sam increased the amount by $3,000 prior to presentation. Which of the following statements correctly characterizes Sam's action?
   a. to make the change a proper and appropriate act, Sam should have obtained the approval of Metro Realty before changing the offer
   b. Sam's action was in violation of his fiduciary obligations and was completely improper
   c. Sam's action would have been appropriate with the seller's consent
   d. Metro Realty, Inc., will be entitled to the entire commission because of Sam's actions

11. In the process of preparing an offer for commercial property, a broker was asked by two potential purchasers to recommend the most beneficial way for them to take title to the property. Which of the following should the broker recommend?
    a. tenants in common
    b. in severalty
    c. ask an attorney
    d. ask the listing broker

12. Upon the broker's recommendation, a seller accepted an offer that was 8% below the listed price. The broker did not disclose to the listing seller that the buyer was the broker's brother-in-law. Which of the following is correct?

   a. the broker violated his obligations as agent of the seller
   b. the fact that the buyer is related to the broker is not required to be divulged to the seller
   c. the broker has done nothing wrong as long as he doesn't take any commission
   d. the broker has done nothing wrong if the appraised value of the home matches the offered price

13. Due to the curvature of the earth, under the rectangular survey method, adjustments must be made to the north and south baseline of every fourth township. These adjustments are called:

   a. curvature lines
   b. correction lines
   c. rectangular line adjustments
   d. base line adjustments

14. All of the following usually appear only in the seller's closing statement EXCEPT:

   a. broker's fee
   b. deed preparation
   c. prepayment penalty
   d. earnest money

15. If the closing date is November 10 and the seller had paid the real property taxes of $2,880 for the current tax year of January 1 through December 31, which of the following is the correct closing statement entry for taxes?

   a. seller's credit of $400
   b. seller's debit of $2,480
   c. buyer's credit of $400
   d. buyer's debit of $2,480

16. RESPA requires lending institutions to provide borrowers with which of the following at the time of or within three days after application for a mortgage loan for housing?

   a. good faith estimate
   b. HUD Form No. 1
   c. disclosure statement
   d. nonrecourse note

17. The buyer assumes a 9% loan with a balance of $74,000 mortgage at closing on July 12. The seller has already made the July 1 payment; the next payment of $638.69, including principal and interest for July, will be due on August 1. Which of the following is the correct closing statement entry for interest?

   a. buyer's debit of $222.00
   b. buyer's credit of $638.69
   c. seller's debit of $222.00
   d. seller's credit of $638.69

18. A sales contract provided that the buyer was to pay $65,000 for a seller's property by giving a purchase money mortgage for $30,000 and the balance in cash at closing. The buyer made a good faith deposit of $6,500 when he made the offer. The seller's share of the real property taxes credited to the buyer was $850. The buyer's other closing costs totaled $900. What amount must the buyer pay at closing?

   a. $27,650
   b. $27,700
   c. $28,550
   d. $35,050

19. Which of the following individuals usually brings the earnest money to the final settlement?

   a. broker
   b. buyer
   c. lender
   d. seller

20. Which of the following is most likely to have been prepared by a broker?

   a. deed
   b. closing statement
   c. certificate of occupancy
   d. lien waivers

21. A property manager's responsibilities include all of the following EXCEPT:

   a. maintenance
   b. collecting rents
   c. commingling
   d. negotiating leases

22. Which of the following is one of the basic responsibilities of a property manager?
    a. appraising the property annually
    b. evicting all minority tenants to provide for a more stable complex
    c. producing the best possible net operating income for the owner
    d. preparing the annual tax returns and attending audits with the IRS

23. What net annual operating income must a property manager produce from a property to provide an 8% return to the owner, who paid $763,000 for the property?
    a. $9,538
    b. $61,040
    c. $95,375
    d. $104,849

24. Which of the following most accurately describes a property manager?
    a. fiduciary
    b. trustee
    c. escrow agent
    d. resident manager

25. When all parties agree to the terms and conditions of a real estate contract, there is said to be:
    a. mutual satisfaction
    b. *sui juris*
    c. meeting of the minds
    d. equitable consent

26. A roofline extending without permission onto an adjoining property is an example of:
    a. easement appurtenant
    b. encroachment
    c. license
    d. easement in gross

27. John owns an apartment building in a large city. After discussing the matter with his legal advisers, he decides to alter the type of occupancy in the building from rental to condominium status. This procedure is known as:
    a. conversion
    b. partition
    c. deportment
    d. amendment

28. In the preceding question, after checking the applicable laws, John discovers that he must offer to sell each unit to the current tenant. If the tenant does not accept the offer, he then may offer the unit for sale to the general public. This requirement to offer the property to the present tenant is known as:
    a. contingent restriction
    b. conditional sales option
    c. covenant of present possession
    d. right of first refusal

29. An owner's office building is producing a net annual operating income of $140,000. If the owner paid $1,166,666 for the property, what rate of return is she receiving on her investment?
    a. 8.3%
    b. 12%
    c. 14%
    d. 16.3%

30. All of the following statements about options are correct EXCEPT:
    a. they must be in writing to be enforceable
    b. they are binding upon optionor and optionee
    c. when exercised, they become contracts of sale
    d. optionor and optionee must be competent

31. Which of the following is both a contract of sale and a financing instrument?
    a. installment land contract
    b. sale and leaseback
    c. lease with option to purchase
    d. executed contract

32. A lease providing for rental changes based on changes in the Consumer Price Index is which of the following?
    a. escalated
    b. graduated
    c. percentage
    d. index

33. Deed restrictions enforced by a suit for damages or by an injunction are:
    a. conditions
    b. conveyances
    c. covenants
    d. considerations

34. Public land use controls in the form of subdivision ordinances are an exercise of:
   a. power of eminent domain
   b. general plan for development
   c. police power of the government
   d. Interstate Land Sales Full Disclosure Act

35. A property owner in a recently zoned area is permitted to continue to use his property in a manner that does not comply with the zoning requirements. This use is described as:
   a. exclusive-use zoning
   b. deviation
   c. nonconforming use
   d. private control of land use

36. The covenant for further assurances may require the grantor to execute a(n):
   a. deed of confirmation
   b. executor's deed
   c. certificate of title opinion
   d. deed of devise

37. A life tenant may convey her life estate by executing which of the following?
   a. quitclaim deed
   b. deed of confirmation
   c. judicial deed
   d. certificate of title registration

38. A deed is made eligible for recording on the public record by which of the following?
   a. abstract
   b. avoidance
   c. alienation
   d. acknowledgment

39. A real estate broker may do all of the following EXCEPT:
   a. have a buyer's deed recorded
   b. make a title examination
   c. act as agent of the grantee to accept deed delivery
   d. execute a certificate of title opinion

40. Which of the following provides the exclusive right of possession and control of real property?
   a. easement
   b. leasehold
   c. license
   d. encumbrance

41. A co-owner of real property automatically received a deceased co-owner's share of ownership. This is called:
   a. intestate succession
   b. inheritance by devise
   c. right of survivorship
   d. inheritance by descent

42. Four brothers received title to a large tract of land from their grandfather, who gave each brother a one-fourth undivided interest with equal rights to possession of the land. All four received their title on their grandfather's seventieth birthday. The brothers most likely hold title in which of the following ways?
   a. in severalty
   b. as tenants in common
   c. as tenants by the entirety
   d. as remaindermen

43. John and his wife, Mary, live in a community property state. Mary inherits a large shopping mall in the city where they live. Which of the following statements about Mary's ownership of the mall is correct?
   a. Mary and John hold the property as tenants by the entirety
   b. Mary may encumber or convey the title only with John's participation in a mortgage or deed
   c. Mary holds title as separate property
   d. the property is considered community property because of the marriage status at the time of inheritance

44. Which of the following statements about the creation of a condominium is FALSE?
   a. a Declaration, Articles of Association, and Association Bylaws must be recorded in the public record in the county where the property is located
   b. a parking garage with rental spaces can be converted to condominium ownership
   c. an apartment complex can be converted to condominiums only with a majority vote of the tenants
   d. a shopping center can be converted to condominium ownership

45. All of the following are correct EXCEPT:
    a. owners of condominium apartments are assessed for their share of the cost of operating and maintaining the common areas
    b. stockholders occupying apartments under a lease pay fees as specified in the lease for maintenance and operation of the common areas of a cooperative
    c. owners of condominium apartments are assessed a prorated share of the real estate taxes on the entire complex
    d. stockholders in a cooperative do not receive an abstract, title insurance, or deed on the leased unit

46. The state took a part of an owner's property for construction of a building. Which of the following statements about this event is correct?
    a. the property owner must be compensated for the difference in market value of the property before and after the partial condemnation
    b. the building to be constructed may be used for the sole use and benefit of a private corporation
    c. the property owner has no recourse to challenge taking his property
    d. the value established is the average of the owner's desired value, the state's desired purchase price, and an independent appraisal

47. An easement that exists across adjoining land is a(n):
    a. easement in gross
    b. dedicated easement
    c. prescriptive easement
    d. appurtenant easement

48. A property with a market value of $80,000 is assessed at 75%. What is the tax rate per $100 if the tax bill is $900?
    a. $1.125
    b. $1.50
    c. $11.25
    d. $15.00

49. An encroachment is which of the following?
    a. lien
    b. party wall
    c. trespass
    d. fixture

50. In estimating the value of an office building containing 22,400 square feet, an appraiser established the annual rental income to be $400,000. The appraiser also learned that monthly expenses averaged $16,700. If the average investor in this type of property was realizing a net return of 13.5%, what would be the appraiser's estimate of the value of the property?
    a. $1,478,518
    b. $1,484,444
    c. $2,962,962
    d. $2,964,600

51. A competitive market analysis is performed when:
    a. assessing property
    b. pricing property
    c. appraising property
    d. condemning property

52. For which of the following types of property would the market data approach be the most relevant appraisal method?
    a. vacant industrial land
    b. library
    c. condominium office
    d. farm land with a large hog operation

53. The principle providing that the highest value of a property has a tendency to be established by the cost of purchasing or constructing a building of equal utility and desirability is the principle of:
    a. highest and best use
    b. competition
    c. supply and demand
    d. substitution

54. Dick and Jane's property has no road frontage. A property adjoining theirs that has road frontage was offered for sale. The value of the available property to Dick and Jane is most accurately described as:
    a. market value
    b. objective value
    c. appraised value
    d. subjective value

55. All of the following are included in a competitive or comparative market analysis EXCEPT:
    a. properties that have sold recently
    b. properties currently on the market
    c. properties sold at foreclosure
    d. properties sold by the owner without a REALTOR®

56. An appraiser who is estimating the value of a four-story government building determines that each floor measures 90 feet by 80 feet with a replacement cost of $60 per square foot. She also observes that the building has depreciated 25% as the result of physical and functional obsolescence. Other site improvements are estimated to have depreciated 20% from a new value of $160,000. The appraiser also estimates the land associated with the building to be worth $362,000. What is the correct estimate of the property value by the cost approach?

    a. $814,000
    b. $846,000
    c. $1,786,000
    d. $1,818,000

57. A building now 21 years old has a total economic life of 40 years. If the replacement cost of the building is $1,200,000, what is the value?

    a. $228,571
    b. $252,631
    c. $570,000
    d. $630,000

58. Which of the following is the most likely result of the homogeneous development of a residential subdivision?

    a. overinflated values
    b. maximized values
    c. stabilized values
    d. depressed values

59. Which of the following approaches to value is the most appropriate for estimating the value of a condominium apartment?

    a. cost approach
    b. income approach
    c. comparable approach
    d. gross rent multiplier

60. In the sale of a capital asset held for 12 months, the seller realizes a gain of $242,000. The amount of taxable gain is:

    a. $96,800
    b. $145,200
    c. $193,600
    d. $242,000

61. If a property producing an annual gross income of $290,000 sells for $2,465,000, what is the GRM?

    a. 7.2
    b. 8.0
    c. 8.5
    d. 11.8

62. The monthly payment necessary to fully amortize a 15-year mortgage loan of $100,000 at 8.5% APR is $984.74. How much interest will the mortgagor pay over the 15-year term?

    a. $77,253.20
    b. $127,500.00
    c. $176,892.41
    d. $276,892.41

63. In the preceding question, how much of the borrower's first monthly payment is applied to reducing principal?

    a. $57.32
    b. $276.41
    c. $458.33
    d. $568.50

64. A lender charges a 2% loan origination fee and three discount points to make a 95% conventional insured mortgage loan in the amount of $47,500. What is the cost of these charges to the borrower?

    a. $922
    b. $1,188
    c. $1,425
    d. $2,375

65. All of the following statements about promissory notes are correct EXCEPT:

    a. they are executed only by the borrower
    b. they provide evidence that a valid debt exists
    c. they provide security for a valid debt
    d. they are considered a negotiable instrument

66. Which of the following enables the mortgagor to avoid a record of foreclosure after default and prior to a foreclosure sale?

    a. statutory redemption
    b. deed in lieu of foreclosure
    c. deed of trust
    d. foreclosure by action

67. All of the following are ways in which a seller may finance the sale of her property for a buyer EXCEPT:

   a. wraparound purchase money mortgage
   b. contract for deed
   c. FHA-insured mortgage
   d. purchase money first mortgage

68. Bill and Betty Brown execute and deliver a $50,000 mortgage to Ajax Financial Associates at 10:30 A.M. on April 1. At 11:30 A.M. on the same day, they give a $10,000 mortgage pledging the same property to Fidelity Finance, Inc. Fidelity's mortgage is recorded at 1:10 P.M. that day, and the mortgage to Ajax is recorded at 1:42 P.M. on April 1. Which of the following statements about these mortgages is correct?

   a. because the mortgage to Ajax was executed and delivered first, Ajax holds the first mortgage
   b. Fidelity has the second mortgage because it was executed and delivered after the mortgage given to Ajax
   c. Ajax and Fidelity will be co-first mortgage holders because both mortgages were signed on the same day
   d. because the mortgage to Fidelity was recorded first, Fidelity holds the first mortgage

69. When a buyer signs a purchase contract and the seller accepts, the buyer acquires an immediate interest in the property known as:

   a. legal title
   b. statutory title
   c. equitable title
   d. defeasible title

70. Regulation Z specifies that the only specific credit term that may appear in an advertisement of a house for sale without the requirement of a full disclosure is which of the following?

   a. SAM
   b. APR
   c. ECOA
   d. RESPA

71. In the sale of their home, Van and Vera Vendor were required to satisfy their existing first mortgage of $40,000 so the buyers could obtain a first mortgage to finance their purchase. The Vendors' closing statement contained a debit in the amount of $800 because the Vendors paid off their loan prior to the full term. From this information, it can be determined that the Vendors' mortgage contained a(n):

   a. acceleration clause
   b. alienation clause
   c. prepayment clause
   d. defeasance clause

72. A developer gave the seller a $385,000 purchase money first mortgage to secure payment of part of the purchase price for a tract of land. The developer was able to convey unencumbered titles to the first six lot purchasers by paying only $8,000 on the purchase money mortgage because the mortgage contained:

   a. release clauses
   b. due-on-sale clauses
   c. prepayment clauses
   d. mortgaging clauses

73. In the purchase of an office building, the buyer gave the seller a mortgage for $200,000 more than the seller's first mortgage and took title to the property subject to the first mortgage. The purchase money mortgage required payments of interest only for the first five years, at which time the principal has to be paid and a new purchase money mortgage created. All of the following statements about these financial arrangements are correct EXCEPT:

   a. the purchase money mortgage is a wraparound term mortgage
   b. for this arrangement to work satisfactorily, the seller's first mortgage must not contain an alienation clause
   c. this arrangement must be approved by Fannie Mae
   d. the purchase money mortgage has a balloon payment

74. When Mr. Black bought real estate for investment purposes, he realized there would be certain expenditures for repair or replacement, maintenance, and management; however, the appraiser advised him to be aware of the point beyond which capital outlays would not result in increased returns. The appraiser was referring to which appraisal principle?
    a. supply and demand
    b. diminishing returns
    c. capitalization
    d. economic depletion

75. The definition of personal property is:
    a. any building permanently attached to real estate
    b. any tree or bush growing on real estate
    c. anything that is not real property
    d. the right to use the air above real estate

76. The real estate market is:
    a. quick to react to changes in supply and demand
    b. not subject to economic cycles
    c. subject to economic cycles
    d. not affected by supply and demand

77. The private ownership of land is known as:
    a. feudal ownership
    b. government ownership
    c. allodial ownership
    d. eminent domain

78. All of the following are powers of government EXCEPT:
    a. police power
    b. escheat
    c. taxation
    d. estovers

79. All of the following are specific liens EXCEPT:
    a. mortgage lien
    b. mechanic's lien
    c. judgment lien
    d. real property tax lien

80. A listing contract creates an agency relationship in which:
    a. the broker is a general agent
    b. the seller is the principal
    c. the seller is a general agent
    d. the broker is the principal

81. When a real estate broker or seller conceals a known defect, this is an example of:
    a. mutual mistake
    b. unintentional misrepresentation
    c. fraud
    d. mistake of law

82. An action or inaction by the lessor resulting in the property being unusable is:
    a. actual eviction
    b. assignment
    c. sandwich lease
    d. constructive eviction

83. A lease is all of the following EXCEPT:
    a. contract
    b. nonfreehold estate
    c. freehold estate
    d. binding obligation on the parties

84. All of the following are required to effect voluntary alienation of title during life EXCEPT:
    a. recordation of the deed
    b. acceptance of delivery by grantee
    c. delivery of a valid deed to grantee
    d. legal capacity of grantor

85. The statement made by a grantor to a qualified public official that the signing of a deed was done by her and was a voluntary act is called a(n):
    a. abstract
    b. acknowledgment
    c. covenant
    d. conveyance

86. A property description reading "¼ of the northeast ¼ of section 22" describes how many acres?
    a. 20
    b. 40
    c. 160
    d. 240

87. Which of the following enables the mortgagee to sell the mortgage in the secondary mortgage market?
    a. assignment clause
    b. due-on-sale clause
    c. mortgaging clause
    d. power-of-sale clause

88. Friendly foreclosure is also called:
    a. beneficial foreclosure
    b. statutory foreclosure
    c. strict foreclosure
    d. deed in lieu of foreclosure

89. Brantley Buyer obtained an FHA-insured loan to purchase a home. The difference between the purchase price and the loan amount was $3,100. Which of the following statements about the $3,100 is correct?
    a. Brantley must pay this amount from his existing assets, borrow on the security of another asset such as his stocks, or acquire it as a bona fide gift from a close relative or friend
    b. Brantley may satisfy this amount by giving the seller a purchase money second mortgage
    c. Brantley may borrow the $3,100 from a relative at 6% interest
    d. Brantley may obtain the money by giving a lending institution a second mortgage

90. When a buyer purchases a home using a VA-guaranteed loan, he is allowed to:
    a. pay a loan origination fee
    b. pay discount points
    c. purchase the property to be used as a rental
    d. both a and b

91. On April 1, Chuck and Sara Vollaro make the mortgage payment of principal and interest for March on their home, in the amount of $402.50. On April 20, the Vollaros close on the sale of their home to the Hudsons. The Hudsons assume the Vollaro's mortgage with a principal balance of $42,000 and an interest rate of 9%. Which of the following is the correct closing statement entry for interest?
    a. buyer's debit of $105
    b. buyer's credit of $105
    c. seller's debit of $210
    d. seller's credit of $210

92. The type of demand that affects market value is called:
    a. urgent
    b. unlimited
    c. effective
    d. restrictive

93. An owner whose property is condemned is entitled to be compensated for:
    a. book value
    b. assessed value
    c. market value
    d. mortgage value

94. Deed restrictions that provide for a reversion of title are called:
    a. certificates
    b. covenants
    c. clusters
    d. conditions

95. The Interstate Land Sales Full Disclosure Act requires which of the following?
    a. property report
    b. enabling act
    c. zoning
    d. cumulative use

96. Redlining applies to which of the following?
    a. brokers
    b. developers
    c. lenders
    d. landlords

97. A lease is a contract that is:
    a. bilateral
    b. unilateral
    c. collateral
    d. trilateral

98. Which of the following is a deductible expense for homeowners?
    a. real property taxes
    b. maintenance
    c. mortgage principal payments
    d. energy usage

99. Which of the following reduces the basis of a new residence?
    a. depreciation
    b. energy credits
    c. gain on which tax is postponed
    d. installment sale

100. All of the following may lead to the revocation or suspension of a license EXCEPT:
    a. failing to submit all written offers to the listing seller
    b. advising a prospective buyer that the seller will take a certain price for a property that is less than the listed price
    c. failing to obtain an accepted offer during the term of the listing
    d. failing to account for all funds belonging to other persons that come into the licensee's hands

Answer Key

ANSWER KEY TO CHAPTER-END REVIEW QUESTIONS

CHAPTER 1 BASIC REAL ESTATE CONCEPTS

1. c
2. b
3. a
4. d
5. d
6. c
7. b
8. d
9. b
10. c
11. b
12. a
13. c
14. c
15. a
16. b
17. a
18. d
19. a
20. a

CHAPTER 2 PROPERTY OWNERSHIP AND INTERESTS

1. c
2. a
3. b
4. d
5. d
6. b
7. b
8. a
9. a
10. d
11. b
12. b
13. a
14. c
15. c
16. c
17. b
18. c
19. a
20. c
21. b
22. c
23. c
24. d
25. c
26. c
27. a
28. c
29. c
30. d

CHAPTER 3 ENCUMBRANCES AND GOVERNMENT RESTRICTIONS

1. c
2. d
3. d
4. d
5. b
6. a
7. b
8. d
9. c
10. a
11. d
12. d
13. c
14. c
15. b
16. a
17. b
18. a
19. a
20. b
21. c
22. b
23. c
24. a
25. c

CHAPTER 4 BROKERAGE AND AGENCY

1. d
2. a
3. d
4. b
5. a
6. c
7. c
8. d
9. c
10. d
11. c
12. c
13. c
14. b
15. a
16. c
17. b
18. a
19. a
20. c

CHAPTER 5 REAL ESTATE CONTRACTS

1. c
2. c
3. d
4. d
5. c
6. a
7. d
8. b
9. b
10. c
11. c
12. b
13. a
14. c
15. b
16. c
17. d
18. c
19. b
20. d
21. c
22. d
23. c
24. d
25. c

CHAPTER 6 TRANSFER OF TITLE TO REAL PROPERTY

1. b
2. c
3. a
4. c
5. d
6. d
7. b
8. a
9. d
10. c
11. c
12. a
13. a
14. b
15. b
16. c
17. d
18. b
19. a
20. a
21. a
22. b
23. a
24. c
25. a

CHAPTER 7 REAL ESTATE FINANCE PRINCIPLES

1. d
2. d
3. d
4. b
5. a
6. b
7. a
8. d
9. a
10. c
11. d
12. d
13. b
14. c
15. c

CHAPTER 8 REAL ESTATE FINANCE PRACTICES

1. d
2. d
3. d
4. d
5. b
6. b
7. d
8. a
9. d
10. b
11. c
12. b
13. b
14. d
15. a
16. c
17. a
18. a
19. b
20. d

CHAPTER 9 CLOSING REAL ESTATE TRANSACTIONS

1. a
2. d
3. c
4. a
5. a
6. a
7. a
8. b
9. a
10. b

CHAPTER 10 PROPERTY VALUATION

1. d
2. b
3. c
4. c
5. d
6. c
7. a
8. a
9. c
10. a
11. b
12. b
13. b
14. d
15. c
16. d
17. b
18. b
19. b
20. d

CHAPTER 11 LAND USE CONTROLS

1. d
2. a
3. b
4. d
5. b
6. b
7. d
8. b
9. a
10. c
11. a
12. b
13. c
14. c
15. d
16. d
17. d
18. d
19. d
20. d

CHAPTER 12 FAIR HOUSING

1. b
2. c
3. a
4. d
5. b
6. d
7. c
8. a
9. b
10. d
11. d
12. a
13. d
14. d
15. b
16. b
17. d
18. d
19. c
20. c

CHAPTER 13 LANDLORD AND TENANT (LEASEHOLD ESTATES)

1. a
2. b
3. c
4. c
5. b
6. a
7. b
8. a
9. d
10. d
11. c
12. b
13. c
14. a
15. b
16. c
17. d
18. a
19. a
20. a
21. a
22. c
23. a
24. c
25. d

CHAPTER 14 PROPERTY MANAGEMENT AND INSURANCE

1. c
2. a
3. a
4. b
5. c
6. a
7. b
8. b
9. c
10. b

CHAPTER 15 FEDERAL INCOME TAXATION OF REAL ESTATE

1. c
2. b
3. b
4. a
5. a
6. b
7. c
8. b
9. c
10. b
11. c
12. c
13. c
14. c
15. a

CHAPTER 16 ILLINOIS REAL ESTATE LICENSE LAW

1. d
2. d
3. b
4. d
5. b
6. b
7. d
8. d
9. c
10. b
11. b
12. b
13. b
14. d
15. a
16. d
17. c
18. d
19. c
20. d
21. b
22. c
23. a
24. a
25. c

CHAPTER 17 REAL ESTATE MATH

1. a
2. d
3. c
4. a
5. c
6. c
7. d
8. c
9. b
10. b
11. b
12. b
13. b
14. b
15. b
16. b
17. a
18. c
19. d
20. b
21. d
22. b
23. d
24. c
25. c
26. d
27. b
28. a
29. c
30. d
31. b
32. d
33. a
34. d
35. b
36. b
37. c
38. b
39. a
40. b
41. c
42. c
43. b
44. b
45. d
46. b
47. c
48. c
49. a
50. c

SOLUTIONS TO THE REVIEW PROBLEMS FOUND AT THE END OF CHAPTER 17 APPEAR AT THE END OF THAT CHAPTER.

ANSWER KEY TO ILLINOIS PRACTICE QUESTIONS (APPENDIX C)

1. c
2. a
3. c
4. d
5. c
6. a
7. c
8. b
9. a
10. a
11. b
12. c
13. d
14. a
15. c
16. a
17. d
18. d
19. d
20. d
21. b
22. a
23. c
24. a
25. c
26. a
27. d
28. b
29. b
30. c
31. b
32. a
33. b
34. b
35. c
36. a
37. d
38. b
39. d
40. d

ANSWER KEY TO PRACTICE EXAM 1 (APPENDIX D)

1. a	26. c	51. c	76. b
2. c	27. c	52. a	77. a
3. b	28. a	53. c	78. b
4. d	29. d	54. d	79. c
5. b	30. a	55. b	80. b
6. d	31. b	56. b	81. a
7. d	32. b	57. b	82. c
8. c	33. d	58. d	83. b
9. c	34. d	59. c	84. a
10. a	35. c	60. a	85. c
11. a	36. c	61. b	86. c
12. b	37. c	62. c	87. a
13. a	38. b	63. c	88. b
14. c	39. a	64. d	89. d
15. d	40. d	65. a	90. b
16. c	41. d	66. a	91. a
17. a	42. b	67. a	92. b
18. b	43. b	68. d	93. d
19. b	44. a	69. c	94. d
20. a	45. c	70. c	95. a
21. c	46. d	71. d	96. a
22. c	47. b	72. d	97. d
23. b	48. a	73. a	98. d
24. a	49. b	74. b	99. b
25. d	50. c	75. b	100. d

ANSWER KEY TO PRACTICE EXAM 2 (APPENDIX E)

1. c	26. b	51. b	76. c
2. d	27. a	52. a	77. c
3. b	28. d	53. d	78. d
4. c	29. b	54. d	79. c
5. a	30. b	55. c	80. b
6. c	31. a	56. c	81. c
7. b	32. d	57. c	82. d
8. d	33. c	58. b	83. c
9. d	34. c	59. c	84. a
10. b	35. c	60. d	85. b
11. c	36. a	61. c	86. b
12. a	37. a	62. a	87. a
13. b	38. d	63. b	88. d
14. d	39. d	64. d	89. a
15. a	40. b	65. c	90. b
16. a	41. c	66. b	91. c
17. c	42. b	67. c	92. c
18. c	43. c	68. d	93. c
19. a	44. c	69. c	94. d
20. b	45. c	70. b	95. a
21. c	46. a	71. c	96. c
22. c	47. d	72. a	97. a
23. b	48. b	73. c	98. a
24. a	49. c	74. b	99. c
25. c	50. a	75. c	100. c

Glossary

The Language of Real Estate

This glossary presents definitions of real estate terms appearing in the text. Also included here are definitions of some terms that are not specifically discussed in this text but possibly may be of use to practitioners.

abandonment The surrender or release of a right, claim, or interest in real property.

abstract continuation An update of an abstract of title by a memorandum of a new transfer of title.

abstract of title A history of a title and the current status of a title based on a title examination.

accelerated depreciation A method of calculating depreciation under the tax code that is faster than the straight-line method.

acceleration clause A provision in a mortgage or deed of trust that permits the lender to declare the entire principal balance of the debt immediately due and payable if the borrower is in default.

acceptance Voluntary expression by the person receiving the offer to be bound by the exact terms of the offer; must be unequivocal and unconditional.

access The right to go onto and leave a property.

accidental agency An agency relationship created when the buyer is led to believe by the agent's actions and representations that the buyer is being represented by that agent; also known as unintended agency.

accord and satisfaction A new agreement by contracting parties that is satisfied by full performance, thereby terminating the prior contract as well.

accretion The gradual building up of land in a watercourse by deposits of silt, sand, and gravel over time.

accrued Accumulated.

accrued depreciation (a) The loss in value in a structure measured by the cost of a new replacement. (b) The amount of depreciation taken, as of a given date, for tax purposes.

accrued expenses Costs the seller owes on the day of closing and the buyer will eventually have to pay. On a closing statement these items are indicated as a debit to the seller and a credit to the buyer.

acknowledgment A formal statement before an authorized official (e.g., notary public) by a person who executed a deed, contract, or other document, that it was a free act.

acquisition The act of acquiring a property.

acquisition cost The basis used by the FHA to calculate the loan amount.

acquisition debt Debt secured by a primary residence or a second home that derives from the purchasing, building, or improving of a home.

acre A land area containing 43,560 square feet.

actual age Chronological age.

actual notice The knowledge a person has of a fact.

adjoining lands Lands sharing a common boundary line.

adjustable rate mortgage (ARM) One in which the interest rate changes according to changes in a predetermined index.

adjusted basis Value of property used to determine the amount of gain or loss realized by owner upon sale of the property; equals acquisition cost plus capital improvements minus depreciation taken.

adjusted sales price The amount realized minus fix-up expenses.

adjustments Additions or subtractions of dollar amounts to equalize comparables to subject property in the market data approach to estimating value.

administrative law judge An employee of HUD that may hear and rule on discrimination complaints. The ALJ can award injunctive relief, actual damages, and penalties up to $50,000.

administrator A man appointed by a court to administer the estate of a person who has died intestate.

administrator's deed One executed by an administrator to convey title to estate property.

administratrix A woman appointed by a court to administer the estate of a person who has died intestate.

ad valorem Latin meaning "according to value"; real property is taxed on an ad valorem basis.

adverse possession A method of acquiring title to real property by conforming to statutory requirement; a form of involuntary alienation of title.

aesthetic zoning Requires that buildings in the zone adhere to a certain style of architecture.

affirmative easement A legal requirement that a servient owner permit a right of use in the servient land by the dominant owner.

age-55-and-over exclusion A tax exemption available to sellers of a principal residence who are age 55 or older.

agency A relationship in which a real estate broker or licensee, whether directly or through an affiliated licensee, represents a consumer by the consumer's consent, whether express or implied, in a real estate transaction.

agent A real estate broker or licensee who, whether directly or through an affiliated licensee, represents a consumer by the consumer's consent, whether express or implied, in a real estate transaction.

agreement A contract requiring mutual assent between two or more parties.

air rights Rights in the air space above the surface of land.

alienation Transfer of title to real property.

alienation clause A statement in a mortgage or deed of trust entitling the lender to declare the entire principal balance of the debt immediately due and payable if the borrower sells the property during the mortgage term. Also known as due-on-sale clause.

allodial system The type of land ownership existing in the United States whereby individuals may hold title to real property absolutely.

alluvion Increased soil, gravel, or sand on a stream bank resulting from flow or current of the water.

amenities Benefits resulting from the ownership of a specific property.

Americans with Disabilities Act (ADA) A 1992 federal law intended to eliminate discrimination against the disabled and to provide access to jobs, government services, transportation, and public accommodations.

amortization schedule Designation of periodic payments of principal and interest over a specific term to satisfy a mortgage loan.

amortizing mortgage One in which uniform installment payments include payment of both principal and interest.

anchor store A well-known commercial retail business, such as a national chain store or regional department store, placed in a shopping center to generate the most customers for all stores in the shopping center.

annexation Addition of an area into a city.

annual Yearly.

annual percentage rate (APR) The actual effective rate of interest charged on a loan expressed on a yearly basis; not the same as simple interest rate.

annual tax sale The annual sale run by the county in which properties with unpaid taxes are sold.

anticipation The principle that property value is based on expectations or hopes of the future benefits of ownership.

appraisal An estimate of value of particular property, at a particular time for a specified purpose.

Appraisal Administration Fund An Illinois fund funded by fees for appraisal applications and renewals.

appraisal process An organized and systematic program for estimating real property value.

appraisal report A report containing an estimate of property value and the data on which the estimate is based.

appreciation An increase in property value.

approaches to value Methods of estimating real property value: market data, income, and cost.

appurtenance A right or a privilege that passes with and belongs to the land, but is not necessarily part of the land. Includes tangible and intangible items such as condominium parking stalls, storage lockers, water rights, and certain easements.

appurtenant easement *See* easement appurtenant.

arm's length transaction The standard under which two unrelated parties, each acting in his or her own best interest, would carry out a particular transaction.

arrears (a) Delinquency in meeting an obligation. (b) Paid at the end of a period (e.g., at the end of the month) for the previous period; payments in arrears include interest for using the money during the previous period.

Article 4 *See* brokerage relationship.

artificial person A corporation or other legally recognized entity.

asking price The price of a property specified in a listing contract.

assemblage The combining of smaller lots into one large parcel.

assessed value The dollar amount of worth to which a local tax rate is applied to calculate the amount of real property tax.

assessment A levy against property.

assessor An official of local government who has the responsibility for establishing the value of property for tax purposes.

assignee One to whom contractual rights are transferred.

assignment Transfer of legal rights and obligations by one party to another.

assignment of lease Transfer by a lessee of the entire remaining term of a lease without any reversion of interest to the lessee.

assignor The person transferring contractual rights to another.

Association of Real Estate License Law Officials (ARELLO) Founded in 1929, a group of real estate license law officials that regulates more than two million real estate licensees.

assumable mortgage One that does not contain an alienation clause.

attestation Witnessing of a document.

attorney-at-law A person licensed by a state to practice law.

attorney-in-fact A person appointed by someone to legally represent them in a particular transaction or circumstance.

auction A form of property sale in which people bid against each other.

avulsion Sudden loss or gain of land as a result of water or shift in a bed of a river that has been used as a boundary.

bail bond A bond given by a defendant under criminal charges to obtain release from custody.

balance The principle that states that a property is affected by the balance of the four agents of production: labor, capital, management, and land.

balloon mortgage One in which the scheduled payment will not fully amortize the loan over the mortgage term; therefore, to fully satisfy the debt, it requires a final payment called a balloon payment, larger than the uniform payments.

bargain-and-sale deed A form of deed with or without covenants of title.

baseline East-west line in the rectangular method of property description.

base rent The fixed or minimum rent portion in a percentage lease.

basis The value of property for income tax purposes; consists of original cost plus capital improvements less accrued depreciation.

benchmark Secondary reference point for vertical measurement.

beneficial title Equitable title to real property retained by a mortgagor or trustor conveying legal title to secure a mortgage debt.

beneficiary (a) Recipient of a gift of personal property by will. (b) Lender in a deed of trust. (c) The actual owner of a property held in trust, as opposed to the legal owner of a property held in trust. The trustee is the legal owner of the property, while the beneficiaries have all of the benefits of ownership but are not holders of legal title.

bequest A gift of personal property by will.

bilateral contract An agreement based on mutual promises that provide the consideration.

bill of sale An instrument transferring ownership of personal property.

blanket mortgage One in which two or more parcels of real property are pledged to secure payment of the note.

block A parcel of land consisting of numerous contiguous lots in the subdivision, lot, block, and tract method of land description.

blockbusting To induce or attempt to induce any person to sell or rent any dwelling by representations regarding the entry or prospective entry into the neighborhood of a person or persons of a particular race, color, religion, sex, or national origin.

blue sky laws A collective term for state security laws usually administered by the secretary of state's office.

bona fide purchaser One who purchases a property in good faith, relying on the records.

book value Dollar worth as it appears on the owner's books, usually for tax purposes; also known as historic value.

boot Cash received in a tax-free exchange.

breach of contract Failure, without legal excuse, to perform any promise that forms the whole or part of a contract.

broker A person or an organization acting as agent for others in negotiating the purchase and sale of real property or other commodities for a fee.

brokerage The business of bringing buyers and sellers together and assisting in negotiations for the terms of sale of real estate.

brokerage agreement A written or oral agreement for brokerage services to be provided to a consumer in return for compensation or the right to receive compensation from another.

Brokerage Relationship in Real Estate Transaction Law (Article 4) The law creating designated agency in Illinois.

budget A plan for systematic spending and receiving of income.

building codes Public controls regulating construction.

bulk zoning Collective term for setback, side-lot, rear-lot, green area, and minimum lot and yard requirements.

bundle of rights The rights of an owner of a freehold estate to possession, enjoyment, control, and disposition of real property.

buyer brokerage An agency relationship between the buyer and broker, wherein the buyer hires the broker to represent her. The buyer is the principal and the broker is the agent.

capital gain The taxable profit made from the sale of an asset.

capital improvement An item that adds value to the property, adapts the property to new uses, or prolongs the life of property; maintenance is *not* a capital improvement.

capitalization The process of converting future income into an indication of the present value of a property by applying a capitalization rate to net annual income, commonly used in the income approach for appraisal.

capitalization formula Investment or value of real estate times the capitalization rate equals the annual net income of the real estate.

capitalization (cap) rate The rate of interest appropriate to the investment risk as a return on the investment.

capital reserve budget Projected budget over the economic life of improvements on the property for repairs, decorating, remodeling, and capital improvements.

carryover clause A statement in a listing contract protecting the broker's commission entitlement for a specified period of time after the contract expires; also called extender or safety clause.

cash flow Income produced by an investment property after deducting operating expenses and debt service.

caveat emptor Latin meaning "let the buyer beware." The buyer has a legal obligation to inspect, examine, judge, and test the property.

certificate of eligibility A statement provided to veterans of military service setting forth the amount of loan guarantee to which they are entitled at that time.

certificate of occupancy A document issued by a local government agency, after a satisfactory inspection of a structure, authorizing that the structure can be occupied.

certificate of reasonable value A document setting forth the value of a property as the basis for the loan guarantee by the Department of Veteran Affairs to the lender.

certificate of title opinion A report, based on a title examination, setting forth the examiner's opinion of the quality of a title to real property.

chain In land measurement, a distance of 66 feet.

chain of title Successive conveyances of title to a specific parcel of land.

change The principle that change is continually affecting land use and therefore continually altering value.

chattel Personal property.

chattel mortgage One in which personal property is pledged to secure payment of a debt.

chattel real Nonfreehold interests in real property; also includes fixtures.

Chief of Real Estate Investigations Person in charge of the investigators and auditors of the Real Estate Unit of the Office of Banks and Real Estate.

chronological age Actual age of an item.

civil action A lawsuit between private parties.

Civil Rights Act of 1866 A federal law that prohibits all discrimination on the basis of race.

Civil Rights Act of 1968 Title VIII of the Civil Rights Act is also known as the Federal Fair Housing Act. The act prohibits discrimination on the basis of race, color, religion, national origin, sex, mental or physical handicap, and familial status.

client A person being represented by a licensee; the principal in an agency relationship.

closed-end mortgage One that cannot be refinanced.

closing The consummation of a real estate contract; also called settlement.

closing costs Expenses incurred in the purchase and sale of real property paid at the time of settlement or closing.

closing (settlement) statement An accounting of the funds received and disbursed in a real estate transaction.

cloud on a title A claim against a title to real property.

cluster zoning A form of zoning providing for several different types of land use within a zoned area.

Code of Ethics and Standards of Practice A standard of conduct required by license laws and the National Association of REALTORS®.

codicil A separate written amendment to a will.

coinsurance clause A requirement of hazard insurance policies that property be insured for a certain percentage of value to obtain the full amount of loss.

collateral Property pledged as security for payment of a debt.

color of title Deceptive appearance of claim to a title.

commercial property Property producing rental income or used in business.

Commercial Real Estate Broker Lien Act This allows lien rights to brokers who are entitled to commission on the sale or lease of commercial property.

commingling An agent's mixing money or property of others with the agent's personal or business funds or other property.

commission A fee paid for the performance of services, such as a broker's commission.

commissioner's deed A form of judicial deed executed by a commissioner.

commitment A promise, such as a promise by a lending institution to make a certain mortgage loan.

common areas Property to which co-owners hold title as a result of ownership of a condominium unit.

common law Law by judicial precedent or tradition as contrasted with a written statute.

common law agency Traditional agency regulated by the laws of agency as defined in law, custom, judicial theory, and juristic decisions.

community-based planning A form of land use control originating in the grassroots of a community.

community planning A plan for the orderly growth of a city or county to result in the greatest social and economic benefits to the people.

community property A form of co-ownership limited to husband and wife; does not include the right of survivorship.

comparable A property recently sold that is similar to a property being appraised by the market data approach.

comparison approach *See* market data method.

compensatory damages In the case of breach of contract, the court will award the damaged party the amount of monetary damage due to the breach.

competence Legal qualification to manage one's own affairs, including entering into contracts.

competition The principle that when the net profit a property generates is excessive, strong competition will result.

complete performance A method of terminating a contract whereby all parties fully perform all terms.

condemnation Exercise of the power of eminent domain; taking private property for public use.

condemnation value Market value of condemned property.

condition Any fact or event which, if it occurs or fails to occur, automatically creates or extinguishes a legal obligation.

condominium A form of ownership of real property consisting of individual ownership of some aspects and co-ownership of other aspects of the property.

condominium declaration *See* declaration of condominium.

confidential information Information obtained by a licensee from a client during the term of a brokerage agreement made confidential by the written request or instruction of the client; any information dealing with the negotiating position of the client or information the disclosure of which could materially harm the client.

conformity Homogeneous use of land within a given area, which results in maximizing land value.

consideration Anything of value, as recognized by law, offered as an inducement to contract.

construction loan A short-term loan, secured by a mortgage, to construct an improvement on land.

construction mortgage A temporary mortgage to borrow money to construct an improvement on land.

constructive eviction Results from some action or inaction by the landlord that renders the premises unsuitable for the use agreed to in a lease or other rental contract.

constructive notice One in which all affected parties are bound by the knowledge of a fact even though they have not been actually notified of such fact.

consumer One who seeks or receives the services of a real estate brokerage firm; a buyer or seller.

consumer price index (CPI) An index of the change in prices of various commodities and services, providing a measure of the rate of inflation.

contingency A condition in a contract relieving a party of liability if a specified event occurs or fails to occur.

continuing education requirement Licensing requirement for people holding an Illinois salesperson or broker license. They have to successfully complete 12 hours of continuing education. Some licensees are exempt from this requirement.

contour map Illustration of the elevation or topography of a site.

contract An agreement between competent parties upon legal consideration to do, or abstain from doing, some legal act.

contract buyer's policy Protects the contract buyer from defects in the contract seller's title prior to the contract.

contract for deed *See* installment agreement.

contract rent The amount of rent agreed to in a lease.

contribution The principle that for any given part of a property, its value is the result of the contribution that part makes to the total value by being present, or the amount that it subtracts from total value as a result of its absence; used in comparative market analysis (CMA).

conventional life estate One created by intentional act of the parties.

conventional mortgage loan One in which the federal government does not insure or guarantee payment to the lender.

conversion Change in a form of ownership, such as changing rental apartments to condominium ownership.

convey Pass to another.

conveyance Transfer of title to real property.

cooling-off period Period of time set by specific contract or by state law providing for a recision period in which the buyer can withdraw from a transaction without penalty.

cooperating broker One who participates in the sale of a property through the listing broker.

cooperative A form of ownership in which stockholders in a corporation occupy property owned by the corporation under a lease.

co-ownership Title to real property held by two or more persons at the same time; also called concurrent ownership.

corporation An organization that exists as an entity.

corporeal Tangible.

corrective maintenance Repairs of a nonfunctioning item.

correlation A step in appraisal in which the appraiser weighs the appraisal approaches to reach a rational conclusion as to the value of the subject property; also known as reconciliation.

cost approach An appraisal method whereby the cost of constructing a substitute structure is calculated, depreciation is deducted, and land value is added.

counteroffer A new offer made by an offeror rejecting an offer.

covenant A promise in writing.

covenant against encumbrances A promise in a deed that the title causes no encumbrances except those set forth in the deed.

covenant for further assurances A promise in a deed that the grantor will execute further assurances that may be reasonable or necessary to perfect the title in the grantee.

covenant of quiet enjoyment A promise in a deed (or lease) that the grantee (or lessee) will not be disturbed in his or her use of the property because of a defect in the grantor's (or lessor's) title.

covenant of right to convey A promise in a deed that the grantor has the legal capacity to convey the title.

covenant of seisin A promise in a deed assuring the grantee that the grantor has the title being conveyed.

covenant of warranty A promise in a deed that the grantor will guarantee and defend the title against lawful claimants.

credit In a closing statement, money to be received or credit given for money or an obligation given.

creditor One to whom a debt is owed.

cubic foot method The method of estimating the current new construction cost of a building in which the cost new is determined by multiplying the total cubic feet in the building by the cost per cubic foot.

cul-de-sac A lot located at the end of a street that dead ends in the shape of a circle. The lot will be irregular in shape and be much larger in the rear than in the front.

cumulative zoning Allowing a use of higher priority in an area zoned as a lower priority.

curable depreciation A condition of property that exists when correction is physically possible and the cost of correction is less than the value increase.

curtesy A husband's interest in the real property of his wife; not recognized in Illinois.

customer A consumer who is not being represented by a licensee but for whom the licensee is performing ministerial acts.

damages The amount of financial loss incurred as a result of another's action.

datum Primary reference point for vertical measurement.

debit In a closing statement, an expense or money received against a credit.

debt service Principal and interest payments on a debt.

decedent A dead person.

declaration of condominium The master deed that contains a legal description of a condominium facility.

declaration of restrictions The instrument used to record restrictive covenants on the public record.

decree A court order.

dedication An appropriation of land or an easement therein by the owner to the public.

deductible expenses Expenses that reduce the amount of taxable income such as mortgage interest, real property taxes, and insurance.

deed A written instrument transferring an interest in real property when delivered to the grantee.

deed in lieu of foreclosure Conveyance of title to the mortgagee by a mortgagor in default to avoid a record of foreclosure. Also called friendly foreclosure.

deed in trust A deed transferring title to a trustee in a land trust.

deed of bargain and sale A deed with or without warranties except an implied covenant that the grantor has title and possession.

deed of confirmation A deed executed to correct an error in a prior deed; also called a deed of correction.

deed of gift A warranty or quitclaim deed conveying title as a gift to the grantee.

deed of release A deed executed by a mortgage lender to release a title from the lien of a mortgage when the debt has been satisfied; also used to release a dower right.

deed of surrender A deed executed by a life tenant to convey his or her estate to the remainder or reversionary interest.

deed of trust A form of mortgage wherein there is a third party, who is called a trustee.

deed restriction Limitation on land use appearing in deeds.

default Failure to perform an obligation.

defeasance clause A statement in a mortgage or deed of trust giving the borrower the right to redeem the title and have the mortgage lien released at any time prior to default by paying the debt in full.

defeasible Subject to being defeated or lost.

defeasible fee A title subject to being lost if certain conditions occur.

deficiency judgment A court judgment obtained by a mortgagee for the amount of money a foreclosure sale proceeds were deficient in fully satisfying the mortgage debt.

delivery and acceptance To effect a transfer of title by deed, a grantor must deliver a valid deed accepted by the grantee.

demise To convey an estate for years; synonymous with lease or let.

density Number of persons or structures per acre.

Department of Housing and Urban Development (HUD) Federal agency involved with housing.

depreciable asset Property, other than land, held as an investment or for use in a business.

depreciated value The original basis of a property less the amount of depreciation.

depreciation Loss in value from any cause.

descent The distribution of property to legally qualified heirs of one who has died intestate.

designated agency A contractual relationship between a broker and a client in which one or more licensees affiliated with the broker are designated as agent(s) of the client.

designated agent A licensee named by a broker as the legal agent of a client.

devise A gift of real property by will.

devisee Recipient of a gift of real property by will.

directive zoning Follows the municipality's urban growth plan, which uses different zoning classifications to control the amount and the orderly growth of residential, commercial, and industrial properties.

disability Defined under the ADA, a disability is a mental or physical disability that impairs any life function.

disclosure of information Prompt and total communication to the principal by the agent of any information that is material to the transaction for which agency was created.

disclosure statement An accounting of all financial aspects of a mortgage loan required of lenders to borrowers in residential mortgage loans by Regulation Z of the Federal Reserve Board.

discount points A percentage of the loan amount the lender requires for making a mortgage loan.

discriminatory advertising Any advertising that states or indicates a preference, limitation, or discrimination on the basis of race, color, religion, sex, national origin, disability, or familial status in offering housing for sale or rent.

disintermediation The loss of funds available to lending institutions for making mortgage loans, caused by depositors' withdrawal of funds for making investments that provide greater yields.

dominant tenement Land benefiting from an easement appurtenant.

dower A wife's interest in her husband's real property; not recognized in Illinois.

dual agency The agency relationship created when a real estate firm attempts to represent both the buyer and the seller in the same transaction. Both buyer and seller must agree in writing to the dual relationship.

due-on-sale clause *See* alienation clause.

duress The inability of a party to exercise his or her free will because of fear of another party.

duty of disclosure The principal's common law duty to reveal to any third parties all information that affects the agency agreement.

earnest money A deposit a buyer makes at the time of submitting an offer, to demonstrate the true intent to purchase; also called binder, good faith deposit, escrow deposit. Also includes rental deposits.

easement A nonpossessory right of use in the land of another.

easement appurtenant A right of use in the adjoining land of another that transfers with the title to the property benefiting from the easement.

easement by condemnation Created by exercise of the government's right of eminent domain.

easement by grant Created by the express written agreement of the landowners, usually in a deed.

easement by implication Arising by implication from the conduct of the parties.

easement by necessity Exists when a landowner has no access to roads and is landlocked.

easement by prescription Obtained by use of the land of another for the legally prescribed length of time (20 years in Illinois).

easement in gross A personal right of use in the land of another without the requirement that the holder of the right own adjoining land.

economic depreciation Results from physical deterioration of property caused by normal use, damage caused by natural or other hazards, and failure to adequately maintain the property.

economic life The period of time during which a property is financially beneficial to the owner.

economic obsolescence Loss in value caused by things such as changes in surrounding land use patterns and failure to adhere to the principle of highest and best use; considered incurable.

economic rent The amount of rent established by the market value of a property.

effective age The age of a property based on modernization, maintenance, etc.

effective demand A desire for property accompanied by financial ability to purchase the property.

effective interest rate Actual rate of interest being paid.

egress The right to leave a parcel of land entered (ingress) by law.

ejectment Legal action to evict a tenant from property.

emblements Personal property growing in the soil, requiring planting and cultivation; annual crops.

eminent domain The power of government to take private property for public use.

enabling acts Laws passed by state legislatures authorizing cities and counties to regulate land use within their jurisdictions.

encroachment Trespass on the land of another as a result of intrusion by some structure or other object.

encumbrance A claim, lien, charge, or liability attached to and binding upon real property.

endorsement Additional coverage on an insurance policy to include a specific risk.

enforceable A contract in which the parties may legally be required to perform.

environmental impact statement A requirement of the National Environmental Policy Act prior to initiating or changing a land use that may have an adverse effect on the environment.

Environmental Policy Act Federal law passed in 1969 requiring a developer to file an environmental impact statement with the Environmental Protection Agency (EPA) before starting any development. The act regulates air, noise, and water pollution and chemical and solid waste disposal.

Environmental Protection Agency (EPA) A federal agency created to consolidate environmental activities of the government under one agency.

Equal Credit Opportunity Act (ECOA) A federal law prohibiting discrimination in consumer loans.

equalization factor A factor applied by the state to the assessed value of properties.

equitable title An interest of sufficient worth in real estate for court protection of that interest.

equity of redemption The borrower's right to redeem the title pledged or conveyed in a mortgage or deed of trust after default and prior to a foreclosure sale by paying the debt in full, the accrued interest, and the lender's costs.

escalated lease One in which the rental amount changes in proportion to the lessor's costs of ownership and operation of the property.

escalation clause A statement in a lease permitting the lessor to increase the rent.

escheat The power of government to take title to property left by a person who has died without leaving a valid will (intestate) or qualified heirs.

escrow The deposit of funds or documents with a neutral third party, who is instructed to carry out the provisions of an agreement.

escrow account (a) An account maintained by a real estate broker in an insured bank for the deposit of other people's money; also called trust account. (b) An account maintained by the borrower with the lender in certain mortgage loans to accumulate the funds to pay an annual insurance premium, a real property tax, or a homeowner's association assessment.

escrow agent A neutral third party named to carry out the provisions of an escrow agreement.

escrow instructions Written directions to the escrow agent setting forth terms for the escrow closing.

estate at sufferance A leasehold estate in which a tenant continues to occupy property after lawful authorization has expired.

estate at will A leasehold estate that may be terminated at the desire of either party.

estate for years A leasehold estate of definite duration.

estate from year-to-year A leasehold estate that automatically renews itself for consecutive periods until terminated by notice by either party; also called estate from period-to-period or periodic tenancy.

estate in fee An estate in fee simple absolute.

estate in real property An interest sufficient to provide the right to use, possession, and control of land; establishes the degree and duration of ownership.

estate tax A tax on all property the heirs inherit.

estoppel Preventing a person from making a statement contrary to a previous statement.

estoppel certificate A document executed by a mortgagor or mortgagee setting forth the principal amount; executing parties are bound by the amount specified.

estovers The right of a life tenant or lessee to cut timber on the property for fuel or for making repairs.

et al. Latin for "and others."

et ux. Latin for "and wife."

evaluation A study of the utility of a property without reference to the specific estimate of value.

eviction A landlord's action that interferes with the tenant's use or possession of the property. Eviction may be actual or constructive.

exclusive agency listing A listing given to one broker only (exclusive), who is entitled to the commission if the broker or any agent of the listing broker effects a sale, but imposes no commission obligation if the owner sells the property to a person who was not interested in the property by efforts of the listing broker or an agent of the listing broker.

exclusive right-to-sell listing A listing given to one broker only, who is entitled to the commission if anyone sells the property during the term of the listing contract.

exclusive-use zoning Property that may be used only for the use specified in the zoning classifications.

executed contract An agreement that has been fully performed.

execution Signing a contract or other legal document.

execution of judgment Judicial proceeding in which property of a debtor is seized (attached) and sold to satisfy a judgment lien.

executor A man appointed in a will to see that the terms of the will are carried out.

executory contract An agreement that has not been fully performed.

executrix A woman appointed in a will to see that the terms of the will are carried out.

exempt Relieved of liability.

exercise of option Purchase of optioned property by the optionee.

express contract One created verbally or in writing by the parties.

expressed agency An agency relationship created by an oral or written agreement between the principal and the agent.

extended coverage An insurance term referring to the extension of a standard fire insurance policy to cover damages resulting from wind, rain, and other perils.

extender clause *See* carryover clause.

face amount Amount of insurance coverage shown on the declaration page.

face-to-face closing Closing in which the buyer, seller, and closing agent meet for execution of documents and disbursement of funds.

Fair Housing Act of 1968 Federal prohibition on discrimination in sale, rental, or financing of housing on the basis of race, color, religion, sex, or national origin.

Fair Housing Amendments Act of 1988 Federal prohibition on discrimination in sale, rental, financing, or appraisal of housing on the basis of race, color, religion, sex, national origin, disability, or familial status.

fair market value An amount determined by dividing the assessed value on one's tax bill by the percentage used to determine the assessed value.

familial status Defined under the ADA as an adult with children under the age of 18, a person who is pregnant, one who has the legal custody of a child, or one who is in the process of obtaining such custody.

Fannie Mae The shortened name for the Federal National Mortgage Association.

Federal Home Loan Bank System The U.S. agency that regulates federally chartered savings and loan associations.

Federal Home Loan Mortgage Corporation (Freddie Mac) A corporation wholly owned by the Federal Home Loan Bank System that purchases FHA, VA, and conventional mortgages.

Federal Housing Administration (FHA) The U.S. agency that insures mortgage loans to protect lending institutions.

Federal National Mortgage Association (Fannie Mae) A privately owned corporation that purchases FHA, VA, and conventional mortgages.

Federal Reserve System A network of 12 central banks created to act as agents in maintaining member bank reserves, issuing bank notes, lending money to banks, and supervising banks. Most national banks and many state chartered banks are members of the Federal Reserve System.

fee simple absolute An inheritable estate in land providing the greatest interest of any form of title.

fee simple determinable A defeasible fee (title), recognizable by words "as long as."

fee simple subject to a condition subsequent A defeasible fee (title), recognizable by words "but if."

feudal system A type of land ownership common in medieval Europe, whereby only the king could hold absolute title to real property.

FHA-insured loan A mortgage loan in which payments are insured by the Federal Housing Administration.

fiduciary relationship A position of trust in relation to the person for whose benefit the relationship is created.

final settlement Consummation of a contract to buy and sell real property.

finance charge An amount imposed on the borrower in a mortgage loan, consisting of origination fee, service charges, discount points, interest, credit report fees, and finders' fees.

Financial Institutions Reform, Recovery and Enforcement Act (FIRREA) The savings and loan bailout bill signed into law by President Bush in 1989.

fire insurance policy *See* homeowner's policy.

first mortgage One that is superior to later recorded mortgages.

fixed expenses Expenditures such as property taxes, license fees, and property insurance; subtracted from effective gross income to determine net operating income.

fixed lease One in which the rental amount remains the same for the entire lease term; also called flat, straight, or gross lease.

fixed-rate mortgage One in which the interest rate does not change.

fixture Personal property that has become real property by having been permanently attached to real property.

fix-up expenses Costs incurred by the seller in preparing a principal residence for sale.

flat lease One in which the rental amount does not change during the lease term.

flood hazard area Area identified by the Federal Emergency Management Agency as being in danger of flooding from excess water from rain or melting snow.

foreclosure The legal procedure of enforcing payment of a debt secured by a mortgage or any other lien.

forfeiture clause A statement in a contract for deed providing for giving up all payments by a buyer in default.

four agents of production Labor, capital, management, and land; part of the principle of balance.

fraud An intentional false statement of a material fact.

Freddie Mac The short name for Federal Home Loan Mortgage Corporation.

freehold estate A right of title to land.

free market An economic condition in which buyer and seller have ample time to negotiate a beneficial purchase and sale without undue pressure or urgency.

friendly foreclosure An absolute conveyance of title to the lender by the mortgagor in default to avoid a record of foreclosure. Also called deed in lieu of foreclosure.

front foot A linear foot of property frontage on a street or highway.

fruits of industry Items on real estate that are not part of real estate but instead are personal property, such as crops.

fruits of nature Items on real estate that are part of real estate, such as trees and shrubs.

fully amortizing mortgage One in which the scheduled uniform payments will pay off the loan completely over the mortgage term.

function of appraisal The use the appraisal is to be put to, such as for a property settlement in a divorce, for an appeal of assessed value, or for pledging property as collateral for a loan.

functional obsolescence Loss in value resulting from things such as faulty design, inadequacies, overadequacies, and equipment being out of date.

future interest The rights of an owner of an estate who will vest at some future date.

gain realized The excess of the amount realized over the adjusted basis.

general agent One who is authorized to act on behalf of the principal in all matters relating to a particular transaction or enterprise.

general lien One that attaches to all of the property of a person within the court's jurisdiction.

general plan See master plan.

general warranty deed A deed denoting an unlimited guarantee of title.

gentrification The upgrading of a neighborhood to a more affluent one by remodeling and upgrading the housing stock.

good faith estimate Lender's estimate of borrower's settlement costs, required by RESPA to be furnished to borrower at time of loan application.

Government National Mortgage Association (Ginnie Mae) A U.S. government agency that purchases FHA and VA mortgages.

government survey system See rectangular survey.

graduated lease One in which the rental amount changes in specified amounts over the lease term.

graduated payment mortgage (GPM) A loan in which the monthly payments are lower in the early years of the mortgage term and increase at specified intervals until the payment amount is sufficient to amortize the loan over the remaining term.

grant A transfer of title to real property by deed.

grant, bargain, and sale deed In Illinois, conveys a fee simple title and warrants that the title is free from encumbrances made by the grantor.

grant deed A statutory form of deed in which the warranties are implied from the statute rather than being spelled out in the deed.

grantee One who receives title to real property by deed.

granting clause The statement in a deed containing words of conveyance.

grantor One who conveys title to real property by deed.

gross effective income Total potential income less deductions for vacancy and credit losses plus other income.

gross income Income received without subtracting expenses.

gross lease One in which the lessor pays all costs of operating and maintaining the property and real property taxes.

gross operating income Gross scheduled rental income minus losses from vacancies and credit losses.

gross potential income The amount of rental income that would be received if all units were rented 100 percent of the time and there were no credit losses.

gross rent multiplier (GRM) A method of estimating the value of income property; also called gross income multiplier.

ground lease A lease of unimproved land.

ground rent Lessee's payment under a ground lease.

growing equity mortgage (GEM) Mortgage loan for which the monthly payments increase annually, with the increased amount applied directly to the loan's principal, thus shortening the term of the loan.

habendum clause The statement in a deed beginning with the words "to have and to hold" and describing the estate granted.

habitable Suitable for the intended occupancy.

heirs Persons legally eligible to receive property of a decedent.

hereditament Any property capable of being inherited, be it real, personal, corporeal, or incorporeal.

heterogeneous A variety of dissimilar uses of property; nonhomogeneous.

highest and best use The legally permissible, physically possible use that gives a property its highest value. Highest and best use is typically determined as if the land was vacant. In some instances, highest and best use "as improved" may need to be considered.

historical cost index The method of estimating the current new construction cost of a building in which the building's original cost is multiplied by a current cost factor.

holdover tenant A tenant who remains in possession of property after a lease terminates.

holding period The length of time a property is owned.

holographic will One handwritten by the testator.

Home Buyer's Guide A booklet explaining aspects of loan settlement required by RESPA.

home-equity debt Debt secured by a primary or second home that is borrowed for reasons other than the purchase, building, or improving of a home.

homeowners' association Organization of owners with responsibility to provide for operation and maintenance of common areas of a condominium or residential subdivision; also called property owners association.

homeowner's policy An insurance policy protecting against a variety of hazards.

homeowner's warranty (HOW) An insurance policy protecting against loss caused by structural and other defects in a dwelling.

home rule Gives municipalities unlimited authority to exercise police powers and pass laws governing the use of land.

homestead The land and dwelling of a homeowner.

homestead exemption An exemption of a specified amount of value of a homestead from the claims of creditors; provided by state statute.

homogeneous Similar and compatible.

Horizontal Property Act The title of condominium statutes in some states.

Housing and Urban Development (HUD) An agency of the federal government concerned with housing programs and laws.

HUD Form No. 1 A standard settlement form required by RESPA.

hypothecate To pledge property as security for the payment of a debt without giving up possession.

Illinois Affordable Housing Act Assists low-income families with affordable housing.

Illinois Environmental Protection Act Created the Illinois Pollution Control Board and the Illinois Environmental Protection Agency.

Illinois Human Rights Act Prohibits discrimination against a person because of his or her race, color, religion, national origin, ancestry, age, sex, marital status, handicap, or unfavorable military discharge.

Illinois Mortgage Foreclosure Law Regulates mortgage foreclosures in Illinois. Included is the foreclosure of trust deeds and long-term land contracts.

Illinois Plat Act Requires that a survey of each parcel and a plat of subdivision be recorded whenever an owner divides a parcel of land into two or more parts, any of which is five acres or smaller.

Illinois Real Estate Solicitation Statute Prohibits real estate solicitations and inducements to sell or purchase by reason of race, color, religion, national origin, ancestry, creed, disability, or sex. It also prohibits the solicitation of homeowners who have given notice not to be solicited.

Illinois Security Deposit Return Act Provides that persons leasing residential property with five or more units cannot withhold any part of a security deposit for compensation for property damage unless an itemized statement of the damage along with the estimated or actual cost of repairs is provided to the lessee.

illusory offer One that does not obligate the offeror.

immobility Incapable of being moved, fixed in location; an important physical characteristic of land.

implied agency Agency that exists as a result of actions of the parties.

implied contract One created by deduction from the conduct of the parties rather than from the direct words of the parties; opposite of an express contract.

implied warranty One presumed by law to exist in a deed, though not expressly stated.

impound account Another term for escrow account.

improved land Land on which structures or roads exist.

improvements Changes or additions made to a property, such as walls or roads, and so on. These typically increase the value of a property, except in some cases of overimprovement.

imputed knowledge Information that is binding upon the principal(s); in a disclosed dual agency relationship, the licensee is not allowed to possess imputed knowledge regarding any party in the transaction.

inchoate In suspension or pending, possibly occurring at some future time.

income approach The primary method for estimating the value of properties that produce rental income; also called appraisal by capitalization.

income property One that produces rental income.

income shelter Deductible allowances from net income of property to obtain a taxable income. Tax losses allowed to offset passive and active income.

incompetent In law, a person who is not capable of managing his or her own affairs.

incorporeal Intangible things such as rights.

increasing and decreasing returns This appraisal principal acknowledges that the first improvements to a property will contribute in value an amount greater than their costs, but as the property is further improved, less and less of a return (value vs. cost) will be achieved.

incurable depreciation That which is not physically correctable or not economically practical to correct.

indemnification Reimbursement or compensation paid to someone for a loss already suffered.

index lease One in which the rental amount changes in proportion to changes in the Consumer Price Index.

ingress The right to enter a parcel of land; usually used as "ingress and egress" (both entering and leaving).

inheritance basis The tax basis for heirs, which is the market value of the property on the date of the decedent's death.

injunction A court instruction to discontinue a specified activity.

inoperative licensee A status of licensure in which the licensee holds a current license but is prohibited from engaging in licensed activities. This occurs when the licensee is unsponsored or when the broker with whom the licensee is associated or with whom he is employed holds a license that is currently expired, revoked, or suspended.

inside lot A lot located in the interior of a block; not a corner lot.

installment agreement A contract of sale and a financing instrument wherein the seller agrees to convey title when the buyer completes the purchase price installment payments; also called contract for deed, land contract, and conditional sales contract.

installment sale A transaction in which the seller receives the sale price in more than one tax year.

instrument A written legal document such as a contract, note, mortgage.

insurable interest The degree of interest qualifying for insurance.

insurance value The cost of replacing a structure completely destroyed by an insured hazard.

insured conventional loan One in which the loan payment is insured by private mortgage insurance to protect the lender.

interest (a) Money paid for the use of money. (b) An ownership or right.

interim financing A short-term or temporary loan such as a construction loan.

intermediate theory Basis for the legal practice followed in some states in which the title pledged in a mortgage is conveyed if the mortgagor is in default.

Interstate Land Sales Full Disclosure Act A federal law regulating the sale across state lines of subdivided land under certain conditions.

interval ownership Co-ownership based upon intervals of time.

intestate The condition of death without leaving a valid will.

intestate succession Distribution of property by descent as provided by statute.

invalid Not legally enforceable.

investment The outlay of money for income or profit.

investment syndicate A joint venture typically controlled by one or two persons hoping for a return for all investors.

investment value The value of a property to a specific purchaser.

involuntary alienation Involuntary transfer of property as a result of a foreclosure sale, bankruptcy, eminent domain, or adverse possession.

irrevocable That which cannot be changed or cancelled.

joint tenancy A form of co-ownership that includes the right of survivorship.

joint venture Participation by two or more parties in a single undertaking.

judgment A court determination of the rights and obligations of parties to a lawsuit.

judgment lien A general lien resulting from a court decree.

judicial deed One executed by an official with court authorization.

judicial foreclosure A court proceeding to require that property be sold to satisfy a mortgage lien.

junior mortgage One that is subordinate to a prior mortgage.

jurisdiction The extent of authority of a court.

key lot The least desirable lot in a subdivision.

laches Loss of legal rights because of failure to assert them on a timely basis.

land The surface of the earth, the area above and below the surface, and everything permanently attached thereto.

land capacity The degree to which land can sustain improvements created to make the land productive.

land contract *See* installment agreement.

land grant Conveyance of land as a gift for the benefit of the public.

landlocked Describes property with no access to a public road.

land trust Type of trust in which title to land is transferred to a trustee who holds the title for the benefit of the beneficiaries.

Land Trust Recordation and Transfer Tax Act This act provides for payment of transfer taxes on the transfer of a beneficial interest in a land trust.

land use controls Governmental restrictions on land use (e.g., zoning laws and building codes).

lawful Legal, not prohibited by law.

lease A contract wherein a landlord gives a tenant the right of use and possession of property for a limited period of time in return for rent.

leased fee Lessor's interest in leased property.

leasehold estate Nonfreehold estate; of limited duration, providing the right of possession and control but not title; a tenant's interest in property.

leasehold mortgage One in which a leasehold (nonfreehold) estate is pledged to secure payment of the note.

leasehold policy A title insurance policy insuring a lessee against defects in the lessor's title.

leasing agent license In Illinois, a limited scope real estate license that would allow the licensee to lease and collect rentals on residential properties.

legal capacity The ability to contract.

legal description A description of land recognized by law.

legal entity A person or organization with legal capacity.

legality of object Legal purpose.

legal life estate One created by exercise of the right of dower, curtesy, or a statutory substitute.

legal rate of interest The maximum rate permitted by law.

lessee A tenant under a lease.

lessor A landlord under a lease.

less-than-freehold estate *See* nonfreehold estate.

leverage The use of borrowed funds; the larger the percentage of borrowed money, the greater the leverage.

levy Imposition of a tax, executing a lien.

license A personal privilege to do a particular act or series of acts on the land of another.

lien Claim by one person against the property of another for some debt or charge, entitling the lienholder to have the claim satisfied from the property of the debtor.

lienee One whose property is subject to a lien.

lien foreclosure sale A legally forced sale of a property to satisfy a debt.

lienor The one holding a lien against another.

lien theory The legal tenet holding that a mortgage creates a lien against the real property pledged in the mortgage to secure payment of a debt.

life estate A freehold estate created for the duration of the life or lives of certain named persons; a noninheritable estate.

life estate in remainder A form of life estate in which certain persons, called remaindermen, are designated to receive the title upon termination of the life tenancy.

life estate in reversion A form of life estate that goes back to the creator of the estate in fee simple upon termination.

life estate pur autre vie *See* pur autre vie.

life tenant One holding a life estate.

like-kind property Real or personal property that qualifies for tax treatment as a tax-free exchange.

limited common element In a condominium, a part of the common elements that only a particular unit owner has the right to use, such as an assigned parking space, a balcony, or a storage locker.

limited liability company A company that has the liability protection of a corporation but is taxed as a partnership.

limited partnership An organization consisting of one or more general partners and several partners with lesser roles.

liquidated damages Money to be paid and received as compensation for a breach of contract.

liquidation value The price an owner is compelled to accept if the property is unable to be adequately exposed within the marketplace.

liquidity The attribute of an asset's being readily convertible to cash.

lis pendens Latin meaning "a lawsuit pending."

listing contract A contract whereby a property owner employs a real estate broker to market the property described in the contract.

litigation A lawsuit.

littoral rights Rights belonging to owner of land that borders a lake, ocean, or sea.

loan commitment Obligation of a lending institution to make a certain mortgage loan.

loan origination fee An upfront fee charged by a lender to raise the lender's yield on the loan.

loan-to-value ratio The relationship between the amount of a mortgage loan and the lender's opinion of the value of the property pledged to secure payment of the loan.

location (situs) An economic characteristic of land having the greatest effect on value in comparison to any other characteristic.

L.S. Signifies *locus sigilli*, a Latin term meaning "place of the seal."

management agreement A contract wherein an owner employs a property manager.

management plan A long-range program prepared by a property manager indicating to the owner how he or she will manage a property.

management proposal A program for operating a property submitted to the owner by a property manager.

margin A mark-up (expressed as a percentage) over an index such as the 30-year treasury bill or cost of funds index to which an adjustable rate mortgage is tied.

marketable title One that is free from reasonable doubt and that a court would require a purchaser to accept.

market data method The primary method of estimating the value of vacant land and single-family, owner-occupied dwellings. Also called comparison approach.

market value A property's worth in terms of price agreed upon by a willing buyer and seller when neither is under any undue pressure and each is knowledgeable of market conditions at the time.

master deed The instrument that legally establishes a condominium; also called condominium declaration.

master plan A town's long-range (5–20 years) plan for the orderly growth of a community enforced through the town's zoning ordinance.

material fact Important information that may affect a person's judgment.

materialman's lien *See* mechanic's lien.

mechanic's lien A statutory lien available to persons supplying labor (mechanics) or material (materialmen) to the construction of an improvement on land if they are not paid.

meeting of the minds A condition that must exist for creation of a contract.

menace The threat of force.

merger The absorption of one thing into another.

metes and bounds A system of land description by distances and directions.

mill One-tenth of a cent.

mineral lease A nonfreehold (leasehold) estate in the area below the surface of land.

mineral rights A landowner's ability to take minerals from the earth or to sell or lease this right to others.

ministerial acts Services provided for a customer that are informative in nature but do not involve active representation on behalf of a consumer.

minor A person who has not attained the statutory age of majority.

misrepresentation A false statement of a material fact.

modification by improvement An economic characteristic of land: The economic supply of land is increased by improvements made to the land and on the land.

mortgage A written instrument used to pledge a title to real property to secure payment of a promissory note.

mortgage assumption The transfer of mortgage obligations to a purchaser of the mortgaged property.

mortgage banker An organization that makes and services mortgage loans.

mortgage broker One who arranges a mortgage loan between a lender and a borrower for a fee.

mortgagee The lender in a mortgage loan, who receives a mortgage from the borrower (mortgagor).

mortgagee's policy A title insurance policy that insures a mortgagee against defects in a title pledged by a mortgagor to secure payment of a mortgage loan.

mortgage insurance premium (MIP) The cost of the insurance paid by the borrower on an FHA loan.

mortgage loan value The value sufficient to secure payment of a mortgage loan.

mortgage satisfaction Full payment of a mortgage loan.

mortgaging clause The statement in a mortgage or deed of trust that demonstrates the mortgagor's intention to mortgage the property to the mortgagee.

mortgagor The borrower in a mortgage loan who executes and delivers a mortgage to the lender.

multiple exchange A transaction in which more than two like-kind properties are exchanged.

multiple listing service (MLS) An organized method of sharing or pooling listings by member brokers.

mutual assent The voluntary agreement of all parties to a contract as evidenced by an offer and acceptance.

mutual mistake A mistake of material fact by both parties; may nullify a contract.

mutual rescission The agreement of all parties to an executory contract to release each other.

mutual savings banks Similar to the savings and loan associations; an institution that provides a substantial source of financing for housing.

narrative appraisal report A statement of an opinion of value containing the element of judgment as well as the data used in arriving at the value estimate.

National Association of Real Estate Brokers (NAREB) An organization predominantly of African American real estate brokers, chartered in 1947. Members are called Realtists®. NAREB is the largest minority real estate organization.

National Association of REALTORS® (NAR) The largest and most prominent trade organization of real estate licensees.

National Association of Securities Dealers (NASD) An organization of stockbrokers empowered to regulate the over-the-counter securities market and with authority to expel members guilty of fraudulent or unethical practices.

National Flood Insurance Program Instituted to reduce flood losses through flood plain management and to provide insurance to property owners already located in flood plains.

negative amortization A loan in which the payments are not large enough to cover the interest on the loan, causing the loan balance to grow larger during the term of the loan, rather than smaller.

negative covenant *See* restrictive covenant.

negative easement A right in the land of another prohibiting the servient owner from doing something on the servient land because it will affect the dominant land.

negligence The failure to use the amount of care a reasonable person would under a particular circumstance.

net income Gross income less operating expenses; also called net operating income.

net lease One in which the lessee pays a fixed amount of rent plus the costs of operation of the property.

net listing Not a type of listing but a method of establishing the listing broker's commission as all money above a specified net amount to the seller.

net operating income Gross operating income minus operating expenses.

net salvage value *See* salvage value.

nonconforming use Utilization of land that does not conform to the use permitted by a zoning ordinance for the area; may be lawful or unlawful.

nonfreehold estate Leaseholds; estates with a length determined by agreement or statute; establishes possession of land as opposed to ownership in fee.

nonhomogeneity A physical characteristic of land describing that land as a unique commodity.

nonjudicial foreclosure A form of foreclosure that does not require court action to conduct a foreclosure sale; also called foreclosure under power of sale.

nonrecourse note A note in which the borrower has no personal liability for payment.

notary public A person authorized by a state to take oaths and acknowledgments.

notice of lis pendens A statement on the public record warning all persons that a title to real property is the subject of a lawsuit and any lien resulting from the suit will attach to the title held by a purchaser from the defendant.

novation Substitution of a new contract for a prior contract.

null and void Invalid; without legal force or effect.

obligee One to whom an obligation is owed.

obligor One who owes an obligation to another.

obsolescence Loss in property value caused by economic or functional factors.

occupancy Physical possession of property.

offer A promise made to another conditional upon acceptance by a promise or act made in return.

offer and acceptance Necessary elements for the creation of a contract.

offeree One to whom an offer is made.

offeror One making an offer.

Office of Banks and Real Estate The licensing and disciplinary authority for Illinois real estate brokers, salespersons, and appraisers. Also regulates state banks, savings and loans, and trust companies.

open-ended listing contract One without a termination date.

open-end mortgage One that may be refinanced without rewriting the mortgage.

open listing A listing given to one or more brokers wherein the broker procuring a sale is entitled to the commission but with no commission obligation on the owner if the property is sold by someone other than one of the listing brokers.

operating budget A yearly budget of income and expense for a specific property, prepared by a property manager.

operating expenses Costs of operating a property held as an investment.

operating statement A report of receipts and disbursements resulting in net income of rental property.

operation of law The manner in which rights and liabilities of parties may be changed by application of law without the act or cooperation of the parties.

operative license A broker, salesperson, or leasing agent currently licensed to practice real estate.

opinion of title *See* certificate of title opinion.

option A contract whereby a property owner sells a right to purchase his or her property to a prospective buyer. Also called option to purchase.

optionee One who receives an option.

optionor One who gives an option.

option to purchase A unilateral contract whereby a property owner sells a right to purchase his or her property at an established price to a prospective buyer.

option to renew A clause in a lease giving the lessee the right to renew the lease. The right to renew usually provides for an increase in rent.

ordinance A law enacted by a local government.

origination fee A service charge by a lending institution for making a mortgage loan.

ostensible agency *See* implied agency.

overimprovement An improvement to land that results in the land not being able to obtain its highest and best use.

ownership The right to use, control, possess, and dispose of property.

ownership in severalty Title to real property held in the name of one person only.

owner's policy A title insurance policy insuring an owner of real property against financial loss resulting from a title defect.

package mortgage One in which personal as well as real property is pledged to secure payment of the note.

package policy Insurance coverage for property damage and liability loss all within one premium.

parol An oral statement.

parol evidence rule Oral explanations can support the written words of a contract but cannot contradict them.

partially amortizing mortgage One in which the schedule of uniform payments will not completely satisfy the debt over the mortgage term and therefore will require a final payment larger than the uniform payments to completely satisfy the debt; the final payment is called a balloon payment.

participation mortgage (a) One in which two or more lenders share in making the loan. (b) One in which a lender shares in the profit produced by an income property pledged to secure the loan payment in addition to receiving interest and principal payments.

partition A legal proceeding dividing property of co-owners so each will hold title in severalty.

partnership A form of business organization in which the business is owned by two or more persons, called partners.

party wall A common wall used by two adjoining structures.

percentage lease One in which the rental amount is a combination of a fixed amount plus a percentage of the lessee's gross sales.

perch A surveyor's measure 16.5 feet in length.

perc test A test of soil to determine if it is sufficiently porous for installation of a septic tank.

periodic lease A lease that automatically renews for successive periods unless terminated by either party; also called an estate from year-to-year.

permanence A physical characteristic of land. Land as a permanent commodity cannot be destroyed.

permanent index numbers Used by county assessors to delineate parcels of land from each other; also known as PIN numbers.

personal property All property that is not land and is not permanently attached to land; everything that is movable; chattel.

physical deterioration Loss in value caused by unrepaired damage or inadequate maintenance.

PITI Acronym denoting that a mortgage payment includes principal, interest, taxes, and insurance.

placed in service For tax purposes, the date when an asset is ready and available for a particular use.

planned unit development (PUD) (a) Generally a mixed-use development that does not meet a municipality's standard zoning classifications. Usually will allow for a higher unit density. (b) A form of co-ownership in which the owner owns a unit and the land under the unit, while the ownership of the common areas are vested in a corporation (association). Association by-laws govern the use of the common areas.

planning A program for the development of a city or county designed to provide for orderly growth.

plat A property map, recorded on the public record in plat books.

pledge To provide property as security for payment of a debt or for performance of a promise.

plottage The increase in value derived from the assemblage (combining) of lots.

POB Point of beginning in a metes and bounds description.

pocket card Card issued by the Office of Banks and Real Estate to signify that the person named on card is currently licensed under the act.

points *See* discount points.

police power The power of government to regulate the use of real property for the benefit of the public.

population density The number of people within a given land area.

positive misrepresentation A person's actual statement that is false and known to be false.

potential income *See* gross potential income.

power of attorney An instrument appointing an attorney-in-fact; creates a universal agency.

prepaid expenses Costs the seller pays in advance, but for which she has not received full benefit. These items are shown as a credit to the seller and a debit to the buyer.

prepaid items Funds paid at closing to start an escrow account, as required in certain mortgage loans; also called prepaids.

prepayment penalty A financial charge imposed on a borrower for paying a mortgage prior to expiration of the full mortgage term.

prescription A method of acquiring an easement by continuous and uninterrupted use without permission.

prescriptive easement One obtained by prescription.

preventive maintenance Program of regularly scheduled checks on equipment to assure proper functioning.

prima facie Latin meaning "on the face of it"; presumed to be true unless disproved by contrary evidence.

prima facie case A suit that is sufficiently strong that it can be defeated only by contrary evidence.

primary financing The loan with highest priority.

primary mortgage market The activity of lenders' making mortgage loans to individual borrowers.

prime rate The interest rate a lender charges to the most creditworthy customers.

principal (a) In the law of agency, one who appoints an agent to represent him or her. (b) Amount of money on which interest is paid or received.

principal meridian The north/south line in the government (rectangular) survey system used to number ranges.

principal residence The home the owner or renter occupies most of the time.

priority lien A lien that receives preferential treatment over other liens.

private land use control Regulations for land use by individuals or nongovernment organizations in the form of deed restrictions and restrictive covenants.

private mortgage insurance (PMI) A form of insurance coverage required in high loan-to-value ratio conventional loans to protect the lender in case the borrower defaults in loan payment.

private property That which is not owned by government.

privity of contract Mutual or successive interests in a contractual relationship such as buyer/seller or lessor/lessee.

probate The procedure for proving a will.

procuring cause The basis for a direct action that results in successfully completing an objective.

profit a prendre The right to participate in profits of another's land.

progression The economic principle that states that the value of a less expensive property in an area is drawn up to the value of the more expensive properties in an area.

promissory note A written promise to pay a debt as set forth in the writing.

promulgate To put in effect by public announcement.

property management An area of specialization in real estate that consists of the managing, record keeping, marketing, and maintenance of properties. The property manager is charged with maximizing the owner's investment.

property management report A periodic financial report prepared for the owner by a property manager.

property manager One who manages properties for an owner as the owner's agent.

property report Disclosure required under Interstate Land Sales Disclosure Act.

proprietary lease A lease in a cooperative apartment.

proration Division of certain settlement costs between buyer and seller.

public land use control Regulation of land use by government organizations in the form of zoning laws, building codes, subdivision ordinances, and environmental protection laws.

public offering statement The disclosure concerning the developer and the project that is required by the Illinois Real Estate Time-Share Act to be filed with the Office of Banks and Real Estate and provided to prospective purchasers.

public property That which is owned by government.

public record Constructive notice, for all to see, of real property conveyances and other matters.

punitive damages Monetary award in the case of extremely bad behavior by a party, awarded to punish the party; typically not allowed in breach of contract.

pur autre vie Latin meaning "for the life of another"; a life estate measured by the life of someone other than the life tenant.

purchase money mortgage A mortgage given by a buyer to a seller to secure payment of all or part of the purchase price.

purpose of appraisal To estimate some type of value such as market value, investment value, or liquidation value.

quantity survey method The detailed determination of the exact quantity of each type of material to be used in construction and the necessary material and labor costs applicable to each.

quarter section One-fourth of a section, containing 160 acres.

quiet enjoyment Use or possession of property that is undisturbed by an enforceable claim of superior title.

quiet title A lawsuit to clear a title to real property.

quiet title action A lawsuit to remove a cloud on a title.

quitclaim To relinquish or release a claim to real property.

quitclaim deed A deed of release that contains no warranty of title; used to remove a cloud on a title.

radius Distance from the center of a circle to the perimeter; part of a metes and bounds description.

range An area of land defined by the rectangular survey system of land description.

range lines Imaginary lines located every six miles east and west of the principal meridian in the rectangular survey system.

rate of return Percentage of net income produced by a property or other investment.

ratify To reaffirm a previous action.

ready, willing, and able Describes a buyer who is ready to buy, willing to buy, and financially able to pay the asking price.

real estate Land and everything permanently attached to land.

Real Estate Administration and Disciplinary Board Nine-person board appointed by the governor and charged with the review of disciplinary cases brought by the Office of Banks and Real Estate.

Real Estate Appraisal Committee A committee of 10 members, appointed by the governor, which conducts hearings on charges against state-certified or -licensed appraisers; makes recommendations on rules and regulations to be followed by state-certified or -licensed appraisers; recommends standards of professional conduct, discipline, precertification, and continuing education; and submits renewal procedures and examination requirements.

real estate broker *See* broker.

real estate commission A state agency charged with enforcing real estate license laws.

Real Estate Division The division of the Office of Banks and Real Estate that regulates Illinois real estate licensees.

Real Estate Education Advisory Council Committee that makes recommendations to the board on rules and regulations relating to pre-license and continuing education.

real estate investment trust (REIT) A form of business trust owned by the shareholders (beneficiaries) of the trust. REITs investing in mortgages are referred to as mortgage REITs, and REITs investing in property are called equity REITs.

Real Estate License Administration Fund A fund used for the operating expenses of the OBRE and the Real Estate Administration and Disciplinary Board in administering the Illinois Real Estate License Act.

real estate market A local activity in which real property is sold, exchanged, leased, and rented at prices set by competing forces.

Real Estate Recovery Fund The fund used to reimburse aggrieved persons who suffer loss from a real estate licensee's violation of the act.

Real Estate Research and Education Fund The fund used to offset the expenses of the Office of Real Estate Research at the University of Illinois.

real estate salesperson *See* salesperson.

Real Estate Settlement Procedures Act (RESPA) A federal law regulating activities of lending institutions in making mortgage loans for housing.

real estate sponsor card A card issued by a real estate broker certifying that the real estate broker, real estate salesperson, or leasing agent named on the sponsor card is employed by the issuing broker.

reality of consent Mutual agreement between the parties to a contract; meeting of the minds; to exist and be free of duress, fraud, undue influence, and misrepresentation.

realized gain Actual profit resulting from a sale.

real property Land and everything permanently attached to land and the aggregate of rights, powers, and privileges conveyed with ownership.

Realtist® A member of the National Association of Real Estate Brokers.

REALTOR® A registered trademark of the National Association of REALTORS®; its use is limited to members only.

realty Land and everything permanently attached to land.

reappraisal lease One in which changes in rental amount are based on changes in property value, as demonstrated by periodic reappraisals of the property.

reciprocity Mutual agreement by states to extend licensing privileges to licensees in each state.

recognized gain The amount of profit that is taxable.

reconciliation (a) The process of checking the accounting of settlement statement. (b) In appraisal, often referred to as correlation, the process of evaluating the results of the different approaches to value to arrive at a final estimate for the subject property.

recordation Registering a document on the public record.

rectangular survey A type of land description utilizing townships and sections. Also known as government survey system.

redemption *See* equity of redemption.

redlining The refusal of lending institutions to make loans for the purchase, construction, or repair of a dwelling because the area in which the dwelling is located is integrated or populated by minorities.

reentry The owner's right to regain possession of real property.

referral fee A percentage of a broker's commission paid to another broker for sending a buyer or seller to him or her.

refinancing Obtaining a new mortgage loan to pay and replace an existing mortgage.

regression The economic principle that states that the value of a more expensive property in an area is drawn to the value of the less expensive properties in an area.

Regulation Z Requirements issued by the Federal Reserve Board in implementing the Truth-in-Lending Law, which is a part of the Federal Consumer Credit Protection Act.

reject To refuse to accept an offer.

release clause A provision in a mortgage to release certain properties from the mortgage lien when the principal is reduced by a specified amount.

release of liability A release sometimes provided by a lender and sought by a borrower that has allowed a purchaser to assume his loan.

remainder A future interest in a life estate.

remainderman One having a future interest in a life estate.

remise To release or give up.

replacement cost The amount of money required to replace a structure with another structure of comparable utility.

replacement reserve A fund to replace assets when they wear out.

repossession Regaining possession of property as a result of a breach of contract by another.

reproduction cost The amount of money required to build an exact duplicate of a structure.

rescission Cancellation of a contract when another party is in default.

Residential Real Property Disclosure Act Legislation whose purpose is to ensure that all prospective buyers of residential property (one to four units, condominiums, and cooperatives) are made aware of known material defects regarding that property.

resident manager A person living on the premises who is a salaried employee of the owner or the managing broker.

residual income Income allocated to the land under the principle of highest and best use.

restrictive covenant Restriction placed on a private owner's use of land by a nongovernmental entity or individual.

Revenue Reconciliation Act (RRA) The Revenue Reconciliation Act of 1993 combined federal tax increases and spending cuts intended to help reduce the federal deficit over the following 5 years.

reverse annuity mortgage (RAM) Mortgage allowing elderly homeowners to borrow against the equity in their homes to help meet living expenses.

reversion Return of title to the holder of a future interest, such as the grantor in a life estate not in remainder.

reversionary interest A future estate in real property created by operation of law such as the interest in a property held by a lessor or held by the grantor of a life estate.

revocation Withdrawal of an offer.

right of assignment Allows lender to sell mortgage at any time and obtain money invested rather than wait for completion of loan term.

right of first refusal Provides for a lessee or an association to have the first opportunity to purchase the property before it is offered to anyone else.

right of inheritance The right for property to descend to the heirs of the owner as set out by will or by intestate succession.

right of survivorship The right of an owner to receive the title to a co-owner's share upon death of the co-owner, as in the case of joint tenancy and tenancy by the entirety.

right to emblements The right of former owners or former tenants to reenter property to cultivate and harvest annual crops planted by them.

riparian rights The rights of an owner of property adjoining a watercourse such as a river, including access to, and use of, the water.

risk management Controlling and limiting risk in property ownership.

rollover rule A mandatory provision in the tax law providing that tax on any gain realized in the sale of a principal residence must be postponed if the sale and purchase qualifies.

run with the land Rights moving from grantor to grantee along with a title.

sale and leaseback A transaction whereby an owner sells a property to an investor who immediately leases the property to the seller as agreed in the sales contract.

sales contract An agreement between buyer and seller on the price and other terms and conditions of the sale of property.

salesperson A person performing any of the acts included in the definition of real estate broker but while associated with and supervised by a broker.

salvage value The amount estimated by an owner that will be realized from the sale of an asset at the end of the useful life of the asset; net salvage value is less the cost of removal.

savings and loan associations A major source of funds for financing residential real estate.

scarcity An economic characteristic of land denoting that land is a commodity with a fixed supply base.

scarcity In short supply in comparison to demand.

scavenger sale A sale in which properties with taxes delinquent for more than two years and not purchased at the annual tax sale are sold.

"S" corporation Corporate formation whereby corporate income and expenses flow through to shareholders as if a partnership.

secondary mortgage market The market in which lenders sell mortgages.

second mortgage One that is first in priority after a first mortgage.

Securities and Exchange Commission (SEC) The federal agency charged with regulating the sale and issuance of securities.

section A one-mile square area of land described by the rectangular survey system, consisting of 640 acres.

security deposit Deposit given to the lessor by the lessee for the purpose of providing money to be forfeited if the lessee defaults or damages the property.

seisin (seizin) Possession of a freehold estate in land.

self-help The removal of a tenant by the landlord because the tenant breached a condition of a lease or other rental contract. Also known as actual eviction.

separate property Property owned in severalty by one's spouse.

servient tenement Land encumbered by an easement.

setback The distance from a front or interior property line to the point where a structure can be located.

settlement Consummation of a real estate contract; also called closing.

settlement costs Expenses paid by buyers and sellers at the time they consummate a real estate sales contract; also called closing costs.

severalty Ownership by only one person.

shared appreciation mortgage (SAM) One in which the lender shares in the appreciation in property value in return for making the loan at a fixed rate lower than the rate in effect at the time the loan is made.

sheriff's deed A judicial deed transferring the title to property sold to satisfy a debt.

situs Location of land.

sole proprietorship A business owned by one individual.

special agent Agent with limited authority to act on behalf of the principal, such as created by a listing.

special assessment A levy by a local government against real property for part of the cost of making an improvement to the property, such as street paving, installing water lines, or putting in sidewalks.

special warranty deed A deed containing a limited warranty of title.

specific lien One that attaches to one particular property only.

specific performance A court instruction requiring a defaulting party to a contract to specifically perform his or her obligations under the contract.

spot zoning Rezoning of a certain property in a zoned area to permit a different type of use than that authorized for the area.

square-foot method A technique used to estimate the total cost of construction, in which the total number of square feet to be constructed is multiplied by a cost per square foot figure to derive total cost.

stabilized budget A forecast of income and expense as may be reasonably projected over several years, prepared by a property manager.

Starker exchange Exchange of like-kind property in which the exchange property is not identified at the time of exchange (Internal Revenue Code 1031).

Starker Trust Trust account in which money from Starker exchange is placed until exchange property can be identified.

Statute of Frauds A law in effect in all states requiring certain contracts to be in writing to be valid.

statute of limitations State laws establishing the time period within which certain lawsuits may be brought.

statutory foreclosure A foreclosure proceeding that allows a statutory time period after a foreclosure sale during which the borrower may redeem the title.

statutory redemption period The period of time set by state law in which a borrower may redeem property after a tax or foreclosure sale.

steering The practice of directing prospective purchasers toward or away from certain neighborhoods to avoid changing the racial/ethnic makeup of neighborhoods.

stigmatized property Property whose appeal to buyers may be compromised by factors relating to the property (such as acts of violence on the property or a previous occupant with HIV) that do not affect the environment or physical condition of the property.

straight-line depreciation A depreciation method whereby the property is depreciated in equal annual installments.

strict foreclosure A proceeding in which a court gives a mortgagor in default a specified time period in which to satisfy the debt and thereby prevent transfer to the lender of the title to the mortgaged property.

strip center Four or more stores (usually adjacent to each other) that are easily accessible by automobiles and have ample parking.

subagent A person appointed by an agent to assist in performing some or all of the tasks of the agency.

subdivision, lot, block, and tract Method of land description defining a parcel of land by reference to where it can be found in a tract block.

subdivision regulation (ordinance) Public control of the development of residential subdivisions.

sublease The transfer of only part of a lease term with reversion to the lessee.

subordinate Lower in priority.

subordination clause Clause in a mortgage subordinating a first lender's lien interest to that of a second lender's (a junior lien holder). The second lender is usually a construction lender.

subrogation of rights A substitution of one person in place of another with reference to a lawful claim. The substitute has the same rights as the person substituted.

substitution The principle providing that the highest value of a property has a tendency to be established by the cost of purchasing or constructing another property of equal utility and desirability provided that the substitution can be made without unusual delay.

substitution of entitlement The exchange of entitlements that takes place when a veteran assumes another veteran's VA loan.

subsurface rights Rights to the area below the earth's surface, also called mineral rights.

supply and demand The principle stating that the greater the supply of any commodity in comparison to demand, the lower the value; conversely, the smaller the supply and the greater the demand, the higher the value.

surplus productivity The amount left over after labor, capital, and management have been satisfied. This amount is attributable to the land and illustrates the axiom that the value of the land is residual.

survivorship The right of the surviving co-owner to automatically receive the title of a deceased co-owner immediately without probate.

tacking The summing of successive interests in a property to reach the required number of years for claiming title by adverse possession.

take-out loan Long-term permanent financing that usually replaces (takes out) the construction loan.

taking title subject to a mortgage Accepting a title pledged to secure a mortgage and with no personal liability for payment of the note.

taxable gain The amount of profit subject to tax.

taxation One of the four powers of government, to tax, among other things, real property.

tax basis *See* basis.

tax credit Amount of money that may be deducted from a tax bill to arrive at the net amount of tax due.

tax-deductible expense Amount of money that may be deducted from gross income in arriving at net taxable income before depreciation, if any.

tax-deferred exchange Trading of like-kind properties held as an investment or for use in business.

tax depreciation Tax deduction allowed for the effects of wear and tear and obsolescence on business assets.

tax shelter A method of tax avoidance such as protecting income from taxation by allowable depreciation.

tenancy by the entirety Co-ownership with the right of survivorship, limited to husband and wife.

tenancy in common Co-ownership that does not include the right of survivorship.

tenements Right of ownership of real estate held by a person.

term mortgage One that requires the mortgagor to pay interest only during the mortgage term, with the principal due at the end of the term.

testate To have died leaving a valid will.

testator A man who has died and left a valid will.

testatrix A woman who has died and left a valid will.

timesharing Ownership in which the purchaser owns the property for a certain specified time interval.

title Evidence of the right to possess property.

title examination A search of the public record to determine the quality of a title to real property.

title insurance An insurance policy protecting the insured from a financial loss caused by a defect in a title to real property.

title theory The legal theory followed in some states, holding that a mortgage conveys a title to real property to secure payment of a debt.

title transfer tax A tax imposed on the conveyance of title to real property by deed.

T-lot A lot that is at the end of a T-intersection, often called the key lot.

Torrens system A system of title recordation used by some states.

township A township is a unit in the government (rectangular) survey system. A township is 6 miles by 6 miles and contains 36 sections.

township line A line in the government survey system running east and west that is used as a reference line for numbering townships.

tract An area of land.

trade fixtures Items that are installed by a commercial tenant and are removable upon termination of the tenancy.

transferability The ability to transfer property ownership from seller to buyer.

trapezoid An area with two parallel sides and two nonparallel sides.

trespasser One who enters the land of another unlawfully.

trust A legal relationship under which title to property is transferred to a person known as trustee.

trust deed *See* deed of trust.

trustee One who holds title to property for the benefit of another called a beneficiary.

trustor One who conveys title to a trustee.

Truth-in-Lending Simplification and Reform Act *See* Regulation Z.

underimprovement Use of land that is not its highest and best use and thus does not generate the maximum income.

underwriting Evaluation of the risk associated with making a loan. The underwriter will analyze the borrower's ability to pay, and the condition and value of the collateral.

undisclosed principal A principal whose identity may not be disclosed by an agent.

undivided interest Ownership of fractional parts not physically divided.

undue influence Any improper or wrongful influence by one party over another whereby the will of a person is overpowered so that he or she is induced to act or prevented from acting according to free will.

unencumbered property Property free of any lien.

unenforceable contract A contract that appears to meet the requirements for validity but is not enforceable in court.

Uniform Commercial Code (UCC) A standardized and comprehensive set of commercial laws regulating security interests in personal property.

Uniform Standards of Professional Appraisal Practice (USPAP) A set of standards created by the Appraisal Foundation that appraisers and their appraisals must meet in federally related financial transactions.

Uniform Vendor and Purchaser Risk Act Under this act, if the property suffers destruction, the seller bears the risk once the contract has been signed but before title has passed or possession has taken place. The contract cannot be enforced and the seller must give back any earnest money. Once title has transferred or the buyer has taken possession, the contract is valid and enforceable. The full purchase price must be paid even if the property has been partially or totally destroyed.

unilateral contract An agreement wherein there is a promise in return for a specific action, which together supply the consideration.

uninsured conventional loan One in which the loan payment is not insured to protect the lender.

unintended agency *See* accidental agency.

unintentional misrepresentation An innocent false statement of a material fact.

unities Time, title, interest, and possession.

unit-in-place method Technique used in appraising real estate under the cost approach, in which the cost of replacement or reproduction is grouped by stages of construction.

universal agent Agent that has complete authority over any activity of principal; for example, an attorney in fact.

unlike-kind property Non-qualifying property in a tax-deferred exchange. Property that is not similar in nature and character to property being exchanged.

useful life The period of time that a property is expected to be economically useful.

usury Charging a rate of interest higher than the rate allowed by law.

utility Capable of serving a useful purpose.

vacancy rate A projected rate of the percentage of rental units that will be vacant in a given year.

VA-guaranteed loan A mortgage loan in which the loan payment is guaranteed to the lender by the Department of Veteran Affairs.

valid contract An agreement that is legally binding and enforceable.

valuable consideration Anything of value agreed upon by parties to a contract.

valuation Establishes an opinion of value utilizing an objective approach based on facts related to the property, such as age, square footage, location, cost to replace, and so on.

value The amount of one commodity that can be exchanged for another commodity.

value in exchange The amount of money a property may command for its exchange; market value.

value in use The value to an owner based on the productivity derived from the property.

variance A permitted deviation from specific requirements of a zoning ordinance because of the special hardship to a property owner.

vendee Purchaser.

vendor Seller.

vendor's affidavit Document signed under oath by vendor stating that vendor has not encumbered title to real estate without full disclosure to vendee.

vicarious liability A principal is responsible for the actions of his or her agent.

voidable contract An agreement that may be voided by the parties without legal consequences.

void contract An agreement that has no legal force or effect.

voluntary alienation The transfer of title freely by the owner.

waste A violation of the right of estovers.

with reserve An auction sale with a minimum opening bid.

words of conveyance Wording in a deed demonstrating the definite intention to convey a specific title to real property to a named grantee.

wraparound mortgage A junior mortgage in an amount exceeding a first mortgage against the property.

writ of attachment A court order preventing any transfer of the attached property during litigation.

yield The return on an investment.

zoning A public law regulating land use.

zoning map Map showing a community and the community's respective zoning classifications.

zoning ordinance Sets forth the uses permitted under each zoning classification and specific requirements for compliance.

INDEX

Abandonment, 22, 50, 61, 294
Abstract:
   continuation, 134
   of title, 34–35, 120, 134, 154, 209, 226, 322
Accelerated depreciation, 314, 316
Acceleration clause, 146, 150
Acceptance:
   and delivery, 126
   of offer, 11, 89–90, 100
Access, 281, 282
Accession rights, 20, 41
Accidental agency, 66, 71
Accord and satisfaction, 84, 95
Account:
   escrow, 69, 164, 184, 199, 202–203, 215–216, 221, 223–224, 226, 307, 339, 341
   impound, 164, 184
Accretion, 16, 20, 41
Accrued expenses, 206, 211
Acknowledgment, 95, 120, 124, 126, 143, 150–151
Acquisition cost, 175–178
Acre, 5, 140, 357, 376–377
Action to quiet title, 123
Actual:
   age, 240
   eviction, 293
   notice, 135, 290
ADA, 281–283
Adjustable rate mortgage (ARM), 164, 169
Adjusted basis, 314, 319–321
Administrative law judge (ALJ), 272, 275, 278, 282
Administrator, 120–122, 129, 131, 342–343
Administratrix, 120–121
Ad valorem tax, 53, 56, 61, 352, 359
Adverse possession, 61, 120, 123, 134, 136, 143
Advertising, discriminatory, 272, 276, 278, 282
Affirmative easement, 48–49
Age:
   actual, 240
   chronological, 230, 240
   effective, 107, 230, 240, 245

55-and-over exclusion, 314, 320, 328
Agency, 67–76
Agent:
   general 66–67, 79, 305
   responsibility to principals, 69, 70, 71, 73
   responsibility to third parties, 70, 73
   special, 66–68, 79, 100, 115, 197
   sub, 66–68, 70–72, 75–77, 79
   universal, 66–67, 79
Air rights, 16–18, 33, 35, 41
Alienation:
   clause, 120, 146, 150, 173, 185
   voluntary/involuntary, 121–123
Allodial system, 2, 23, 41, 59
Alluvion, 16, 20, 41
Americans with Disabilities Act (ADA), see ADA
Amortization:
   chart, 167–168, 170
   negative, 164, 169, 171, 175
Amortizing mortgage, 160, 166–168
Anchor store, 302, 304
Annual percentage rate (APR), 157, 164, 167, 196–197
Anticipation, 7, 230, 238, 253
Appraisal:
   approaches, 234, 240–241, 244, 246, 249, 252–254
   correlation, 252
   methodology, 240–241, 244, 252–254
   principles, 236–240
   reconciliation, 252
   report, 190, 241–242, 252–254, 343
Appreciation, 165–166, 172, 202, 240, 324
Approaches to value, 241
Appurtenance, 48
Appurtenant easement 18, 46, 48
Area computation, 190, 356
ARELLO, 9, 333
Arrears, 146, 148, 211, 221, 223, 288, 362, 374
Artificial person, 38, 125

Assessed value, 53–55, 61, 104, 232–233, 253, 357, 359–360, 374–375
Assessment, 46, 53, 78, 151, 153, 223
Assessor, 53–55, 106, 136, 141, 241, 359
Assignee, 84, 94, 97, 291
Assignment:
   of a lease, 97, 211, 288, 291
   right of, 146, 152
Assignor, 84, 97, 291
Association of Real Estate License Law Officials, 9, 333
Assumption:
   formal, 154
   mortgage, 154
Assurance, title, 11, 133
Attachment, writ of, 46, 52, 58
Attorney:
   at law, 335
   in fact, 335
Auction:
   sales, 99
   with reserve, 100
Availability, 3–4, 6
Avulsion, 16, 20, 41

Bail bond 52–53
Balance 24, 239
Balloon mortgage, 164, 168
Baseline, 120, 138–139
Base rent, 297, 375
Basis:
   adjusted, 314, 319–321
   inheritance, 314, 322
   tax, 314, 317–318, 321–322, 328, 375
Benchmark, 120, 142
Beneficiary, 40, 42, 94, 120, 122, 149–150
Bequest, 120, 122
Bilateral contract, 84, 86, 90, 102
Bill of sale, 16, 20, 210
Blanket mortgage, 131, 164, 166, 173
Blockbusting, 276
Bona fide purchaser, 120–121, 135
Book value, 230, 233–234, 253

457

Index

Boot, 314, 326, 328
Breach of contract, 98, 99
Broker
    buyer's, 70, 72
    seller's, 70, 72
Brokerage, 72, 76
    buyer, 66, 70, 72, 78, 100
Budget:
    account, 69, 164, 184, 199, 202–203, 215–216, 221, 223–224, 226, 307, 339, 341
    capital reserve, 302, 306–307
    operating, 302, 306–308
    stabilized, 302, 306–307
Building code, 110
Bundle of rights, 16–18, 23, 26, 47, 60, 235, 294
Buyer:
    agency, 70
    brokerage, 66, 70, 72, 78, 100
    representation, 70, 72, 73
Buyer brokerage, 66, 70, 72, 78, 100

Capital:
    computation of, 318, 320
    gain, 314–315, 319
    reserve budget, 302, 306–307
Capitalization:
    formula, 244, 246, 248, 352, 366
    rate, 230, 246, 248, 254, 352, 366
Carryover clause, 340
Cash:
    flow, 247
    sale, 147, 154, 213–216, 218–219
CERCLA, 264
Certificate:
    of eligibility, 345
    of occupancy, 210, 256, 261
    of reasonable value, 164, 180, 184, 202
    of title opinion, 120, 134
Chain of title, 120, 133–134
Change, principle of, 240
Chattel, 16, 20–22
Civil Rights Act:
    of 1866, 272–273, 282
    of 1968, 272–273, 282, 293
    1988 amendments to, 264, 272–274
Closing:
    costs, 209–214
    escrow, 206–208, 213, 215, 221, 223
    face-to-face, 207
    funds, 184, 192, 207–208, 213, 219
    prorations at, 211, 215, 361
    statement, 213–222
Cloud on a title, 129
Code of Ethics, 2, 8, 77, 79
Codicil, 120, 122

Coinsurance clause, 302, 310, 312
Collateral, 11, 51, 94, 148, 185, 191, 199, 202, 232, 264
Color of title, 123, 143
Commercial:
    bank, 155–156, 159–160, 292
    property, 304
Commingling, 307, 336
Commission:
    computation of, 77, 78, 354, 355
    entitlement, 100
    flat fee, 77–78
    percentage of final sale, 77
    splits, 77–78, 354
Common:
    areas, 33–35, 42, 48, 50, 304
    tenancy in, 16, 29–32, 35, 41
Community:
    based planning, 6, 260
    property, 16, 28–29, 32–33, 41, 129
Comparables, 105–107, 241, 244, 246, 249
Comparison approach, 230, 241, 253
Compensatory damages, 84, 98–99, 115
Competence, 84, 91
Competent parties, 114–115, 160
Competition, 56, 78, 106, 230, 234, 239, 253
Competitive market analysis (CMA), 105–107, 234, 281
Complete performance, 84, 87–88, 95
Comprehensive Environmental Response, Compensation, and Liability Act (CERCLA), 264
Concurrent ownership, 29, 33, 41
Condemnation:
    easement by, 46
    value, 233, 253
Conditional sales contract, 115
Conditions, 265
Condominium declaration, 33
Confidentiality, 70
Conforming loan, 146, 150, 160
Conformity, 230, 237–238, 253
Consideration, 90
Construction, 379–386
    mortgage, 151, 156, 164, 173
Constructive:
    eviction, 292, 294, 298
    notice, 22, 61, 110, 120, 135, 151, 290
Contour map, 141
Contract:
    bilateral, 84, 86, 90, 102, 106, 110
    breach of, 4, 84, 98–99, 110, 115
    buyer's policy, 120, 134–135

    for deed, 34, 53, 84, 96, 98, 110–111, 115, 135, 157, 174, 210, 214, 310, 323
    discharge of, 95–96, 108
    essential elements of, 87–89, 93, 97, 287
    executed, 84, 87, 95, 114, 135
    execution of, 20, 124, 126, 129, 131, 207, 216, 262
    executory, 84, 87, 95, 110, 114
    express, 84–86, 102, 106, 110, 112, 114
    implied, 84, 86, 114
    land, 34, 53, 84, 96, 98, 110–111, 115, 135, 157, 174, 210, 214, 310, 323
    listing, 101–104
    performance of, 4, 84, 86–88, 95, 98, 108, 114
    privity of, 286–287
    release of, 95, 98, 110
    remedies, 98, 115
    termination, 71, 91, 94–95, 98, 108, 112, 339–340
    unenforceable, 84, 87, 91, 96, 114
    unilateral, 84, 86–87, 90, 112, 114
    valid, 84, 87–93, 96, 106, 124, 149
    void, 84, 88, 92, 114, 263
    voidable, 84, 88, 91–92, 110, 114–115
Contribution, 230, 238–239, 241, 253
Conventional:
    life estates, 27
    mortgage loan, 156, 164–167, 170, 202
Convey, 23, 24, 121–124
Cooling-off period, 164, 196
Cooperative, 16, 35, 42, 309
Cooperating broker, 70–71, 78
Co-ownership, 16, 28–30, 32–33, 36, 41
Corporation, 38, 39
Corporeal, 16, 22
Corrective maintenance, 302, 308
Correlation, 230, 252–254
Cost approach to valuation:
    replacement, 250
    reproduction, 230, 249–251
Costs, closing, 12, 89, 154, 168, 175–179, 184, 192, 195, 209, 318, 320–321
Counteroffer, 84, 89–90
Covenant:
    against encumbrances, 120, 128
    deed, 120, 128, 150, 256, 265
    declaration of restrictions, 256, 266, 268
    enforcement of, 59, 257, 265–268

Index

for further assurances, 120, 128–129
of quiet enjoyment, 120, 128–129
restrictive, 7, 58, 59
of right to convey, 120, 128
of seisin, 120, 128
termination, 267
of warranty, 120, 128–129
Credit:
report, 11
unions, 156–157, 166, 191
Cubic-foot method, 230, 250
Cul-de-sac, 138, 141–142
Cumulative-use zoning, 258
Curable depreciation, 252
Curtesy, 24, 27–28, 32

Damages:
compensatory, 84, 98–99, 115
liquidated, 84, 98–99, 106, 115, 290
mitigating, 294
punitive, 84, 99, 279
Data sheet, 104–105
Debit, 211–212, 215–221, 223–227, 362, 374–375
Debt service, 35, 247, 325, 351–352, 362–363
Dedication, 46, 50
Deductible expenses, 314, 323, 325, 328
Deed, 124–131
administrator's, 131
bargain and sale, 120, 130–131
commissioner's 131
of confirmation, 120, 131
general warranty, 54, 108, 110, 120, 125–129, 131, 143
of gift, 120, 131
grant, 120, 131
judicial, 94, 131
in lieu of foreclosure, 94, 146, 153
master, 16, 33, 42
quitclaim, 120, 123, 125, 129–131, 143
of release, 120, 129, 131, 143, 149
restrictions 7, 58–59
sheriff's, 120, 131, 152
of surrender, 120, 131
of trust, 148–151
types of, 131
Default, 98
Defeasance clause, 146, 149–151, 160
Defeasible, 16, 24–25, 235, 265
fee, 16, 24–25, 265
Deficiency judgment, 146, 153–154
Delivery and acceptance, 120, 124, 126, 143

Department of Housing and Urban Development (HUD), 174–179
Depreciation:
accelerated, 314, 316
economic, 230, 314, 323
straight line, 234, 314, 316, 352
tax, 247, 314, 323–324, 328, 352
Depreciable asset, 324, 328
Descent, 28, 41, 60, 120–122, 143
Description by reference, 138
Devise/devisee, 120, 122
Diminishing returns, 239
Disability, 55, 104, 181, 272, 275–279, 281–283, 338
Disclosure:
of information, 69, 73–75, 263
statement, 94, 105, 118, 164, 196, 210, 263
Discount points, 164, 194–196, 203, 214, 227, 318–319, 364
Discriminatory advertising, 272, 276, 278, 282
Disintermediation, 146, 158, 161
Dissolution, 32, 38, 94
Dominant tenement, 46, 48–50
Dower, 24, 27–28, 32, 131
Dual agency, 66, 71, 74–75, 79, 86, 104, 108
Due-on-sale clause, 110, 146, 150
Duress, 84, 88, 91–92, 115, 253
Duty of disclosure, 69

Earnest money, 84, 90, 106
Easement, 18, 23–24, 46–51, 59, 61, 126
affirmative, 48–49
appurtenant, 18, 46, 48–49
condemnation, 46, 50, 60
creation, 47, 49–51, 60
by grant, 24, 46, 50
in gross, 46–48
by implication, 46, 50
by necessity, 46, 50, 60
negative, 48–49
by prescription, 46, 50, 59, 61
termination, 50
Economic:
demand, 235
depreciation, 230, 314, 323
obsolescence, 4, 230, 250–253
Effective:
age, 107, 230, 240, 245
demand, 234–235, 253
Egress, 47, 50, 134
Emblements, 16, 20, 41
Eminent domain, 46, 50, 59–61, 94, 108, 123–124, 143, 233, 320
Enabling acts, 256, 258, 260
Encroachment, 46, 59, 61
Encumbrance, 30, 41, 46–47, 60, 128, 279

covenant against, 120, 128
Endorsement, 302, 308, 311–312
Enforceable, 84, 87
Environmental:
guide to common hazards, 387–395
impact statement 190, 264
Policy Act 256, 264
Protection Agency (EPA) 256, 262, 264, 268
Equal Credit Opportunity Act (ECOA), 164, 202–203, 277
Equal housing, 273–274, 280
Equitable title, 84, 90, 108, 110, 115
Equity of redemption, 146, 151–152
Escheat, 26, 46, 59–61, 121–123, 143
Escrow:
account, 69, 164, 184, 199, 202–203, 215–216, 221, 223–224, 226, 307, 339, 341
closing, 206–208, 213, 215, 221, 223
instructions, 206, 208
Estate:
in fee, 23–25
pur autre vie, 25
at sufferance, 24, 295–296
at will, 24, 295–296
for years, 24, 35, 174, 294–296
from year to year, 24
Estoppel, 66, 68, 210
Estovers, 16, 27
Evaluation, 232
Eviction:
actual, 293
constructive, 292, 294, 298
remedies, 293
Exclusive:
agency listing, 84, 101–102
right-to-sell listing, 84, 101–102
use zoning, 256, 258
Executed contract, 84, 87, 114
Execution:
of deed, 126, 131
of judgment, 46, 57, 61
Executor, 120–122, 129, 131
Executory contract, 84, 87, 95, 110, 114
Executrix, 120, 122
Exercise of option, 112, 118, 210
Expenses:
accrued, 206, 211
deductible, 314, 319, 323–325, 328
fixed, 230, 246–247
fix-up, 239, 314, 319
operating, 230, 246–247, 296–297, 314, 325, 328, 341, 352
Express:
agency, 68

contract, 84–86, 102, 106, 110, 112, 114
Extended coverage, 34, 302, 308, 312

Face amount, 134–135, 302, 310, 312, 376
Face-to-face closing, 207
Fair market value, 46, 53–54, 59, 124, 135, 233
Fair Housing Act of 1968, 273–279
   1988 amendments to, 272–274
   enforcement of, 278
   exemptions to, 273, 278
   prohibited acts, 273, 277
Fair housing, state laws, 307
False promise, 336
Familial status, 275
Fannie Mae, 146, 158–161, 177, 231
Federal Fair Housing Act of 1968 273–279
Federal Home Loan Mortgage Corporation (Freddie Mac), 146, 158–159, 161, 177, 231
Federal Housing Administration (FHA). See FHA
Federal National Mortgage Association (Fannie Mae), 146, 158–161, 177, 231
Federal Reserve Board, 196, 202
Fee simple estate, 23, 25, 41
   absolute, 16, 23–25, 41, 126
   defeasible, 16, 24
   determinable, 23–25
   subject to a condition subsequent, 24–25
Feudal, 2, 7, 23
FHA, 273–279
   insured loan program, 273–279
   mortgage insurance premium (MIP), 164, 174, 176, 184, 192, 202
Fiduciary, 40, 66, 68, 70–72, 76, 79, 94, 129, 303, 305
Fifty-five-and-over exclusion, 314, 320, 328
Finance charge, 196
Financing statement, 22
Fire insurance policy, 302, 308, 312
First mortgage, 151
Fixed:
   expenses, 230, 246–247
   lease, 286, 297–298
   rate mortgage, 148, 197
Fix-up expenses, 239, 314, 319
Fixture, 16, 21–22, 41, 226
   trade, 16, 22
Flood hazard area, 190, 256, 264
Foreclosure, 152, 153
   friendly, 153
   judicial, 94, 146, 149, 152

   statutory, 152
   strict, 146, 153
Forfeiture clause, 99
Four agents of production, 230, 239
Fraud, 9, 72, 84, 88, 91–92, 115, 133, 136, 327
Freddie Mac, 146, 159, 161, 177, 231
Freehold estates, 16, 23–24, 28, 41
   fee simple, 23, 25, 41
   life, 16, 23–30, 41, 126, 131
Free market, 2, 11
Fruits:
   of industry, 16, 20
   of nature, 16, 20
Fully amortizing mortgage, 160, 166–168
Functional obsolescence, 230, 250–253

Gain realized, 317–318, 320–321
General:
   agent, 66–67
   lien, 46, 51–52, 57–58, 61, 123, 153
   plan, 256, 266–267
   warranty deed, 120, 127–129, 131, 143
Gentrification, 230, 240
Ginnie Mae, 146, 159, 161, 231
Good faith estimate, 164, 197–198
Government National Mortgage Association (Ginnie Mae), 146, 158–159, 161, 231
Government survey system, 23, 120, 137
Graduated:
   lease, 286, 296, 298
   payment mortgage (GPM), 164, 169, 171 174
   payment adjustable mortgage, 164, 171
Grandfathered in, 259
Grantee, 125
Granting clause, 120, 124–126, 128–129
Grantor, 124
Gross:
   effective income, 230, 246–247, 375
   income multiplier (GIM), 248–249
   lease, 286, 296–298
   operating income, 314, 325
   potential income, 246
   rent multiplier (GRM), 230, 248–249, 254
Ground lease, 286, 297–298
Growing equity mortgage (GEM), 164, 172, 202

Habendum clause, 120, 126, 143
Habitable, 290, 298
Handicap, 273, 275
Heirs, 28
Hereditaments, 16, 22
Highest and best use, 2, 6–8, 230, 232, 236–237, 251, 253
Historical cost index, 230, 250
Holdover tenant, 286, 293
Homeowner's:
   association, 176, 181, 304
   policy, 309
   warranty (HOW), 177
Homebuyer's Guide to Settlement Costs, 199
Horizontal Property Act, 33
Housing and Urban Development (HUD), 273–279
HUD Form No. 1, 199–200, 210
Hypothecating, 148

Illinois Real Estate Solicitation Statute, 272, 281, 283
Illusory offer, 89
Immobility, 2–5, 11–12
Implied:
   agency, 66, 68
   contract, 84, 86, 114
Impossibility of performance, 95
Impound accounts, 164, 184, 199, 206, 221
Income:
   approach to property valuation, 176, 230, 234, 238, 246, 248–249, 252–253, 366
   gross operating, 314, 325
   net operating, 230, 247–248, 306, 312, 314, 325
   property, 40, 248–249, 296, 304, 306, 308, 312, 316, 324–325, 352, 366
   shelter, 314, 324–325
Incompetent, 91, 125, 143
Incorporeal, 16, 22
Increasing returns, 239
Incurable depreciation, 252
Indestructibility, 3–4
Index lease, 286, 297–298
Ingress and egress, 47, 50, 134
Inheritance basis, 314, 322
Injunction, 59, 258, 265–266, 268, 273, 279
Installment:
   land contract, 84, 110
   sale, 110, 314, 323, 328
Insurable interest, 135, 302, 309–310, 312
Insurance:
   calculation, 310
   coinsurance, 302, 310, 312
   types of, 165, 308, 309, 311

value, 233, 253
Insured conventional loan, 165
Interest, 147, 148
Interim financing, 173
Intermediate theory, 146, 148, 160
Interstate Land Sales Full Disclosure Act, 256, 263, 268
Intestate:
   defined, 46, 60
   succession, 16, 28, 94, 121
Investment:
   property, 8, 196, 237, 304, 306, 314–315, 318, 323, 325–326, 328
   syndicate, 314, 327
Involuntary alienation, 120–121, 123, 143

Joint:
   tenancy, 16, 29–33, 41–42
   venture, 36, 40, 327
Judgment:
   deficiency, 146, 153–154
   execution of, 46, 57, 61
   lien, 46, 57–58
Judicial:
   deed, 94, 131
   foreclosure, 94, 146, 149, 152
Junior mortgage, 164, 166, 174

Land:
   contract, 34, 53, 84, 96, 98, 110–111, 115, 135, 157, 174, 210, 214, 310, 323
   landlocked, 50–51
   trust, 16, 40, 42, 94, 110, 120, 133
   use controls, 2, 7, 12, 47, 257–259, 261, 263, 265–269, 271
Landlord obligations, 290
Lease:
   application, 288–289
   elements of, 287
   escalated, 286, 297–298
   proprietary, 35, 42
   types of, 296–298
Leasehold:
   estate, 16, 23–24, 28, 35, 174, 294–296
   mortgage, 164, 174
   policy, 120, 134–135
Legal:
   capacity, 89, 91, 115, 125, 128, 287
   description 137–142
   life estates, 27–28, 41
Legality of object, 89, 92, 115
Lessee/lessor 287–290
   obligations 290
Liability:
   insurance, 309–310

release of, 154, 164, 179, 182, 185
License, 51, 60
Licensee, inoperative, 340
Licensing:
   broker, 337
   salesperson, 337
Lien:
   bail bond, 53
   definition of, 51
   estate, 53, 58, 66, 78–79, 216
   foreclosure sale, 53, 120, 123, 143
   general, 46, 52, 57–58, 61, 123, 153
   income tax, 58
   judgment, 46, 57–58
   materialmen's, 46, 51–52, 61, 133, 151
   mechanics', 34, 46, 51–52, 61, 129, 133, 151, 153
   mortgage, 61, 126, 151, 173
   priority, 46, 51–53, 57–58, 61, 151, 153
   real property tax, 52–53, 153
   specific, 46, 52–53, 56, 60–61, 123, 216
   theory, 146, 148, 160
   vendee, 53
   vendor, 53
Life estate, 16, 24–30, 41, 126, 131
   conventional, 27
   in remainder, 24, 26
   in reversion, 24, 26
   pur autre vie, 16, 25, 41
   statutory, 27–28, 41
   tenant, 16, 25–27
Like-kind property, 314, 323, 326–328
Limited common element, 33
Limited liability company, 16, 39, 42
Limited partnership, 37
Liquidated damages, 84, 98–99, 106, 115, 290
Liquidity, 146, 152, 157–159, 161
Lis pendens, 46, 57–58, 61, 133
Listing:
   contract, 101–104
   data sheet, 104–105
   definition, 101
   exclusive right-to-sell, 84, 101–102
   open, 74, 78, 84, 101–102
   termination, 71, 105, 108, 340
   types of, 77–78, 101–102
Littoral rights, 16, 20, 41
Loan:
   conforming, 146, 150, 160
   conventional, 164–165, 167, 172, 192, 195, 319
   FHA-insured, 154, 156, 159, 164–165, 174, 177, 179, 184, 202

origination fee, 164, 195–196, 214, 222, 319, 364
processing, 179, 190–191
to-value ratio, 164, 167, 174, 176–178, 195, 351–352, 362, 364–365
underwriting, 11, 164, 191–192
VA-guaranteed, 154, 156, 159, 164–165, 180–181, 202
Location (situs), 4–6
Locus sigilli (LS), 155, 160
Lot:
   inside, 141, 142
   key, 141, 142
   T-, 141, 142

Maintenance:
   corrective, 302, 308
   preventive, 302, 308
Management:
   agreement, 302, 305, 312
   duties, 305, 344
   fee, 306, 325
   proposal, 302, 305
   report, 302, 308, 312
Margin, 169
Market data method, 230, 241, 244
Marketable title, 34, 106, 110, 129, 133, 150, 208–209, 216
Master deed, 16, 33, 42
Master plan, 260
Material fact, 92
Materialmen's lien, 46, 51–52, 61, 133, 151
Mechanics' lien, 34, 46, 51–52, 61, 129, 153
Menace, 84, 88, 92, 115
Merchantable title, 120, 133
Merger, 46, 50, 61
Metes and bounds, 120, 137–138, 141–142, 144
Mill, 53, 357, 359–360
Mineral:
   lease, 19
   rights, 3, 16–17, 19, 50
Minor, 91, 202
Misrepresentation, unintentional, 92
Modification by improvement, 4–6
Mortgage:
   adjustable rate (ARM), 164, 169, 171, 193
   amortizing, 160, 166–168
   assumption, 97, 133, 146, 154, 214, 220–221, 224, 226
   balloon, 164, 168
   banker, 146, 156
   blanket, 131, 164, 166, 173
   broker, 146, 156
   clauses, 150
   construction, 151, 156, 164, 173

conventional, 154, 156, 164–167, 170, 202
elements of, 87, 89, 97, 124, 238, 253, 287
fifteen year, 168
graduated payment (GPM), 164, 169, 171, 174
growing equity (GEM), 164, 172, 202
insurance premium, 164, 174, 176, 184, 192, 202
junior, 164, 166, 174
open-end, 164, 168
package, 164, 173
participation, 164, 172
principal, 247
purchase money, 164, 173–174, 214, 217–219
shared appreciation (SAM), 164, 172, 202
subject to, 24, 149, 154, 160, 172–173, 361
term, 164, 166–167
wraparound, 164, 172–173
Mortgagee, 148
Mortgagee's title insurance policy, 120, 134–135, 209
Mortgagor, 148
Multiple:
exchange, 314, 326
listing service (MLS), 8, 10, 66, 75–79, 101, 106, 241, 277–278, 340
Mutual:
assent, 84, 89, 91
mistake, 84, 88, 91–92, 115
savings banks, 155, 159–160

Narrative appraisal report, 253
National Association of REAL-TORS® (NAR), 2, 8–10, 12, 77, 79, 102, 281, 303, 333
National Association of Real Estate Brokers (NAREB), 2, 9, 12
National Association of Securities Dealers Regulatory (NASDR), 16, 39
National Flood Insurance Program, 256, 264
Negative:
amortization, 164, 169, 171, 175
easement, 48–49
Negligence, 69, 286, 291–292, 309, 343
Net:
lease, 286, 296–298
listing, 77
operating income, 230, 247–248, 306, 312, 314, 325
Nonconforming use, 256, 259, 267
pre-existing, 259

Nonfreehold estate, 16, 23–24, 28
Nonhomogeneity, 2–4, 12
Nonrecourse note, 146, 153
Notary public, 126
Notice:
constructive, 22, 61, 110, 120, 135, 151, 290
of lis pendens, 46, 57–58, 61, 133
Novation, 84, 95, 97, 150
Null and void, 53, 88

Obsolescence:
economic, 4, 230, 250–253
functional, 230, 250–253
physical, 250–253, 323
Offer and acceptance, 10, 84, 89, 115, 208
Offer to purchase, 340
Offeree/offeror, 89–90, 99–100, 106, 115, 266, 276
Office of Banks and Real Estate (OBRE), 36, 38, 42, 262, 267, 280, 332–334, 336–345
Oil and gas lease, 297–298
Open:
-end mortgage, 164, 168
listing, 74, 78, 84, 101–102
mortgage, 164, 168
Operating budget, 302, 306–308
expenses, 230, 246–247, 296–297, 314, 325, 328, 341, 352
statement, 230, 246–247, 325
Operation of law, 27, 31, 38, 41, 71, 84, 88, 93, 95–96, 123
Opinion of title, 120, 134
Option:
to purchase, 73, 87, 112–114, 118
to renew, 286, 288
Optionee, 87, 112, 118
Optionor, 87, 112, 114, 118
Ordinance, 23, 40, 59, 190, 210, 233, 256, 258–261, 265, 267
Overimprovement, 237, 251
Ownership:
by business organizations, 36
combination forms of, 33
of estates in real property, 23–28, 294–296
partnerships, 28, 37, 39, 42, 91
of personal property, 18, 20–21
in severalty, 29, 41
sole proprietorship, 16, 36–37
Owner's title insurance policy, 120, 134, 214, 218

Package:
mortgage, 164, 173
policy, 302, 309
Parol evidence rule, 84, 93
Participation mortgage, 164, 172

Partition, 31, 123, 131
Partnership, 16, 29, 31, 36–40, 42, 76, 125, 334–335, 342
Passive income, 316
Percentage:
computation of, 353
lease, 286, 297–298
Perc test, 206, 210, 214
Periodic estate/lease/tenancy, 24, 286, 294–296
Permanent index numbers, 120, 141
Personal property, 20, 21
Physical deterioration, 250–253, 323
Planned unit development (PUD), 256, 258, 305
Planning urban and regional, 7, 260
Plat, 33, 50, 120, 137–138, 141–142, 256, 261, 265–267
Pledge, 24, 27, 30–32, 148, 184, 202, 281
POB, 120, 137
Points, discount, 164, 194–196, 203, 214, 227, 318–319, 364
Police power, 46, 59–61, 258, 260, 267, 333
Possibility to complete, 89, 93, 115
Power:
of escheat, 59–60
police, 46, 59–61, 258, 260, 267, 333
of taxation, 59–60
Practice exams, 402–427
Preexisting nonconforming use, 259
Prepaid:
expenses, 206, 211
items, 164, 178, 184, 192, 211–212
Prepayment penalty, 146, 150, 160, 164, 185, 202, 319
Prescription, easements by, 50, 134
Preventative maintenance, 308
Primary mortgage market, 157, 161
Principal:
agent, 66–69, 71–72, 76, 79
duties to agents, 68, 69, 73
duties to third persons, 70, 73
meridian, 120, 139
mortgage, 247
Private land-use control, 58
Private mortgage insurance (PMI), 164–165, 167, 192, 202, 225
Privity of contract, 286–287
Probate, 27–28, 94, 120, 122, 235
Productivity, surplus, 239
Progression, 230, 238, 240
Promissory note, 146–147, 160
Property description, 33, 125, 131, 136, 143–144, 160, 288
metes and bounds, 120, 137–138, 141–142, 144

rectangular survey, 23, 137, 139, 141–142, 144
    by reference, 136, 138
Property disclosure form, 93
Property management, 303–308
    fees, 247, 306, 325
    proposal, 302, 305
    report (Full Disclosure Act), 302, 308, 312
Property manager, 9, 67, 247, 302–308, 312, 354
Proration, 106, 108, 206–207, 211–212, 218, 352, 361–362
Proprietary lease, 35, 42
Public land-use control, 7, 257–258, 260, 266, 268
    building codes, 6–7, 60–61, 236, 256, 258, 260, 268
    subdivision regulations for, 261
    zoning, 257
Public offering statement, 16, 36, 42
Punitive damages, 84, 99, 279
Pur autre vie, 16, 25, 41
Purchase money mortgage, 164, 173–174, 214, 217–219

Quantity survey, 230, 250
Quiet:
    enjoyment, 17, 24, 120, 128–129, 131, 143, 286–288, 290
    title action, 123

Ranges, 138–139
Rate of return, 352, 366, 374–375
Ready, willing, and able, 84, 100–101
Real estate, 1
Real Estate Investment Trust (REIT), 36, 40, 42, 157
Real Estate Settlement Procedures Act (RESPA), 164, 197, 200, 203, 213
Real property, 1, 18
Reality of consent, 84, 89, 91, 115
Realtist®, 2, 9, 12
REALTOR®, 8, 9
Realty, 2–4
Reappraisal lease, 286, 297–298
Reconciliation, 252
Recordation, 120, 133, 135–136, 151, 154, 288, 290
    of leases, 133, 290
    of mortgage, 151
Rectangular survey system, 23, 137, 139, 141–142, 144
Redlining, 272, 277
Reentry, 25
Referral fee, 75, 78
Regional planning, 7, 260
Regression, 230, 238
Regulation Z, 164, 196–197, 202–203

REIT, 36, 40, 42, 157
Release:
    of contract, 95, 98, 110
    of liability, 154, 164, 179, 182, 185
Remainder, 26
Remainderman, 26–27
Rent:
    schedule, 247, 306
    withholding, 292
Replacement:
    cost, 34, 230, 233, 249–251, 309, 376
    reserve, 230, 246–247
Reproduction cost, 230, 249–251
Rescission, 84, 98, 115, 196
Reserve account, 221
Resident manager, 302–303
RESPA, 164, 197, 200, 203, 213
Restrictive covenants, 7, 58, 59
    enforcement of, 257, 265–268
    termination of, 267
Revenue Reconciliation Act, 314–315
Reversion, 16, 24, 26, 41, 265, 291, 294, 298
Reversionary interest, 26–27, 131, 286–287
Revocation, 90, 104–105, 281, 335
Right:
    of assignment, 146, 152
    to emblements, 20
    of first refusal, 16, 34–35, 84, 114, 288
    of inheritance, 16, 29–30
    of survivorship, 16, 29–32, 42
    of way, 47
Riparian water rights, 19
Risk:
    factor, 248
    management, 302, 308
Rollover rule, 314, 317, 319–323, 326, 328
Roof styles, 381
Running with the land, 46, 48

Sale and leaseback, 286, 298
Sales contract, 89–93, 340
SARA, 264
Savings and loan associations (S&Ls), 155
Scarcity, 2–6, 12, 234–235, 253
Second mortgage, 157, 166, 172, 224, 226
Secondary mortgage market, 157–158
Section, 139–140
Security:
    agreement, 22
    deposit, 276, 286, 292, 298

Securities and Exchange Commission (SEC), 16, 39, 138, 281, 327–328
Seisin, covenant of, 120, 128
Separate property, 16, 29, 31–33, 41
Servient tenement, 46, 48–50
Setback, 256
Settlement:
    costs, 195, 197–199
    statement, 211–223
Severalty, 16, 28–29, 31–33, 35, 41–42, 104, 129, 320
Shared appreciation mortgage (SAM), 164, 172, 202
Sherman Antitrust Act, 77–78
Situs, 2, 4–6
Sole proprietorship, 16, 36–37
Special:
    agent, 66, 68, 100, 115
    assessment, 46, 56, 151
    warranty deed, 120, 127, 129
Specific:
    lien, 46, 52–53, 56, 60–61, 123, 216
    performance, 4, 84, 94, 98, 108, 115
Spot zoning, 256, 260, 267
Square-foot method, 230, 250
Stabilized budget, 302, 306–307
Standard fire policy, 308
Standards of Practice, 2, 8
Starker:
    exchange, 314, 327
    trust, 314, 327
Statute of Frauds, 84, 93, 108, 110, 112, 114, 124, 149, 288
Statute of limitations, 96
Statutory foreclosure, 152
Statutory redemption period, 46, 56
Steering, 272, 275–276
Straight-line depreciation, 234, 314, 316, 352
Strict foreclosure, 146, 153
Strip center, 302, 304
Subagent, 66, 68, 70–72, 75, 79
Subdivision, lot, block, and tract, 120, 137, 141–142
Subdivision regulation (ordinance), 256, 261
Sublease, 286, 291
Subordination, 151
Subrogation of rights, 120, 134
Substitution:
    of entitlement, 164, 182
    principle of, 237
Subsurface rights, 16, 18–20, 41
Superfund Amendments and Reauthorization Act (SARA), 264
Supply and demand, 2, 4, 11–12, 230, 232, 237, 253, 306
Survivorship, 16, 29–32, 42

Syndications, 39, 42

Tacking, 120, 123
Take-out loan, 164, 173
Taking title subject to a mortgage, 154
Tax:
    basis, 314, 317–318, 321–322, 328, 375
    computation, 132, 143
    deductible expense, 314, 317, 322–323, 325, 328
    depreciation, 247, 314, 323–324, 328, 352
    inheritance basis, 322
    Reform Act of 1986, 324
    shelter, 314, 324, 328
    title transfer, 120, 132
Taxable gain, 318, 320–321, 324, 328
Taxation, 53–55, 60, 315–328
Tenancy:
    by the entirety, 29, 31–32, 41–42
    in common, 16, 29–33, 35, 41
Tenement, 16, 22
    dominant, 46, 48–50
    servient, 46, 48–50
Term mortgage, 164, 166–167
Testate, 46, 60, 94, 121
Testator, 26, 120–121
Testatrix, 120–121
Timesharing, 9, 16, 36, 41–42
TILSRA, 164, 195–196
Title:
    assurance, 11, 133
    chain of, 120, 133–134
    examination, 11, 120, 133, 136, 143, 195–196, 209
    insurance, 134, 135
    legal, 40, 110
    recordation, 135
    registration, 135–136, 266
    theory, 146, 148–149, 160
    transfer tax, 360
Torrens system, 120, 123, 136, 144
Township, 120, 138–140, 357

Trade fixture, 16, 22
Transferability, 230, 234–235, 253
Trespasser, 46, 59, 296, 298
Trust, real estate investment (REIT), 36, 40, 42, 157
Trustee/trustor, 40, 148, 149
Truth-in-Lending Simplification & Reform Act (TILSRA) 164, 179, 195–196

Unauthorized practice of law, 340
Underimprovement, 237, 251
Underwriting, 11, 164, 191–192
Undivided interest, 30, 159
Undue influence, 84, 88, 91–92, 115
Unenforceable contract, 84, 87
Uniform Commercial Code (UCC), 22, 293
Uniform Residential Appraisal Report (URAR) 242, 243
Uniform Standards of Professional Appraisal Practice (USPAP), 230–232, 341
Unilateral contract, 84, 86–87, 90, 112, 114
Uninsured conventional loan, 165
Unintentional misrepresentation, 92
Unities, 16, 29–32, 42
Unit-in-place, 230, 250
Universal agent, 66–67
Unlike-kind property, 314, 326, 328
Urban planning, 260
Usury, 194
Utility, 235

VA-guaranteed loan, 180–184
    eligibility for, 182
    qualifying for, 34, 181–182
    worksheet, 182
Vacancy rate, 230, 246
Vacation homes, 36, 322–323
Valid contract, 84, 87, 89–93, 124, 149
Valuable consideration, 88, 90
Valuation, 231, 232

Value:
    approaches to, 232, 238, 241, 249–253, 366
    assessed, 53–55, 61, 104, 232–233, 253, 357, 359–360, 374–375
    book, 230, 233–234, 253
    condemnation, 233, 253
    in exchange, 172
    in use, 7, 233, 253, 366
    factors affecting, 235–236, 252
    insurance, 233, 253, 310
    investment, 230, 232–233, 253, 306, 312, 352, 366, 374–375
    liquidation, 232–233, 253
    market, 232
    mortgage, 150, 164, 172–173, 194
Variance, 256, 260, 267
Vendee/vendor 53, 96, 110
    affidavit, 209
Void contract, 84, 88
Voidable contract, 84, 88, 114
Voluntary alienation, 120–122, 143

Waste, 27, 210, 262, 264, 291
Water rights, 17, 19, 48
Weighted average, 244
With reserve, 84, 99
Words of conveyance, 124–125, 143
Wraparound mortgage, 164, 172–173
Writ of attachment, 46, 52, 58

Zoning, 257–260
    aesthetic, 256, 259
    bulk, 256, 259
    cluster, 256, 258
    cumulative, 256, 259
    directive, 256, 259
    map, 256, 258
    nonconforming use, 259, 267
    ordinance, 190, 256, 258–260, 265, 267
    spot, 256, 260, 267
    variance for, 256